ARCHITECTURE AND SUBURBIA

The publication of this book was assisted by a bequest from Josiah H. Chase to honor his parents, Ellen Rankin Chase and Josiah Hook Chase, Minnesota territorial pioneers.

ARCHITECTURE AND SUBURBIA

From English Villa to American Dream House, 1690–2000

John Archer

University of Minnesota Press / Minneapolis • London

See pages 443–45 for information on previously copyrighted material reprinted in this book.

Every effort was made to obtain permission to reproduce material used in this book. If any proper acknowledgment has not been made, we encourage copyright holders to notify us.

Published by the University of Minnesota Press
111 Third Avenue South, Suite 290
Minneapolis, MN 55401-2520
http://www.upress.umn.edu

Library of Congress Cataloging-in-Publication Data

Archer, John.
   Architecture and suburbia: From English villa to American dream house, 1690–2000 / John Archer.
      p. cm.
   Includes bibliographical references and index.
   ISBN: 978-0-8166-4304-2 (pbk: alk. paper)   ISBN–10: 0-8166-4304-0 (pbk: alk. paper)
   1. Suburban homes—United States. 2. Suburban homes—England. 3. Architecture, Domestic—
United States. 4. Architecture, Domestic—England. 5. Architecture and society—United States.
6. Architecture and society—England. I. Title.
   NA7571.A58 2005
   728'.0973'091733—dc22

                              2004025706

Printed in the United States of America on acid-free paper

The University of Minnesota is an equal-opportunity educator and employer.

16 15 14 13 12 11 10 09 08   10 9 8 7 6 5 4 3 2 1

For Richard

Contents

PART III. TWENTIETH-CENTURY AMERICA: THE DREAM HOUSE IDEAL AND THE SUBURBAN LANDSCAPE

Illustrations

Acknowledgments

For a book whose historical scope spans four centuries, it may be fitting that the labor put into it has spanned two or more decades. Less fitting, perhaps, is that the list of acknowledgments remains so short, partly because time has inevitably erased traces of many who contributed (and herewith I offer my apologies), and partly because listing everyone who influenced this project would be a Sisyphean feat. The material in the following pages is a consequence of decades of interaction with colleagues and students in many disciplines, in many fields, in various institutions, classrooms, and conferences. Much of the pleasure of this project has been in the exchange of information, ideas, and critiques, and I hope to return that in the book that follows.

Perhaps Richard Guy Wilson put this book in motion, even though I did not know it at the time, when he invited me to make a presentation on the American villa and pastoralism in 1989, thereby preventing my complete escape into other fields and topics. Two colleagues in my own graduate program, Comparative Studies in Discourse and Society at the University of Minnesota, Richard Leppert and Bruce Lincoln, have been an ongoing source of intellectual stimulation and strength; while both have added to the book in very specific ways, their intangible contributions have gone far beyond. I also owe a debt of gratitude to many of the highly talented graduate students with whom I have worked, especially Craig Wilkins: thank you for challenging my thinking and leading me in new directions.

My colleague Katherine Solomonson has been an inveterate advocate, critic, and interlocutor, and perhaps more than anyone helped to see this project through to fruition. Her advice has been keen and insightful, both with respect to the conceptualization of the entire book and in regard to specifics of theory and history; I can only hope the book repays expectations. Her contributions would be far too numerous to acknowledge individually or in the notes. I have benefited as well from many profitable exchanges with Robert Fishman and Mary Corbin Sies, not to mention their numerous publications. During the years William Morrish was director of the Design Center for American Urban Landscape at the University of Minnesota I profited from considerable time spent with him and his staff, not least during the 1999 conference "Reframing the 1945–1965 Suburb" organized by the Design Center, Katherine Solomonson, and myself. I am grateful to the Design Center (now called the Metropolitan Design Center) for welcoming me then and making me its first faculty fellow under the current director, Ann Forsyth.

For remarkably effective research assistance, including many suggestions for new avenues to pursue and connections I never would have recognized, I am indebted to Tiffany Johnson Bidler, Jennifer Horne, Betty Joseph, David Monteyne, and especially Holley Wlodarczyk. Timothy Mennel also provided challenging insights and information.

At Sudbrook I was kindly hosted by Mr. R. Wilkins and Mrs. Margaret Woodcock of the Richmond Golf Club. For their assistance in Dublin and in obtaining materials relating to the Casino at Marino, I am grateful to Andrew Kincaid, Constance Kincaid, and Peter McAuley. For generous help with the history of St. Margaret's, Twickenham, and a tour of the estate, I am indebted to the late Arthur E. Calvert-Smith. Susan Grieve was very generous with materials relating to the history of Short Hills, New Jersey. I was especially fortunate to have Andrew Wiese as a guide to some of the African American suburbs in the vicinity of Miami.

My work has been funded generously by grants from a number of sources, including the Guggenheim Foundation, the National Endowment for the Humanities, and the Getty Center for the History of Art and the Humanities. At the University of Minnesota, I am grateful for support from the McKnight Arts and Humanities Endowment, the Graduate School, the Office of International Education, and the College of Liberal Arts. I am particularly fortunate that my own Department of Cultural Studies and Comparative Literature has been eager to support my research in whatever ways it could. The intrepid librarians of Interlibrary Loan and Lumina to U at the University of Minnesota also have been a treasured resource.

Jane Hancock was unfailingly supportive of my work throughout its early stages, and remains so. Richard Archer may have had little other vision of his father than as terminally engaged with writing this book, but with any luck there may have been glimpses of a different persona, too. Joyce Schonhardt unstintingly put up with me and the book until the end, and I look forward to sharing the result.

Labor Day, 2004

Prologue: Self, House, and Suburb

The world of the "dream house" is all about us. People save up to buy their dream houses, and then to buy better ones; magazines are full of advertisements for dream houses and things to furnish them with; stores are replete with products for equipping dream houses; and real estate developments are full of dream houses of many styles and sizes. In the suburbs of many major cities, annual and semiannual trademarked real estate shows such as "Street of Dreams"® and "The Parade of Homes, Where Dream Homes Come True"℠ constantly maintain the propensity to think of one's current or future dwelling as a "dream house." The drumbeat often is so strong that moving to a house in suburbia is perceived as tantamount to achieving the American dream. More often than not there is no specific definition behind these terms, dream house or American dream, but rather a general understanding that there are opportunities to be realized or goals to be fulfilled. As explored throughout this book, those opportunities and goals commonly are personal and private—oriented around the individual self. Indeed the twentieth-century (and now the twenty-first-century) American dream house has been recognized for a considerable part of its history as a highly specialized instrument for realizing many aspects of bourgeois selfhood.

Dwellings always have provided shelter, and by their given configuration always affect the personal activities, feelings, and social relations of those who live in them. But to serve as a "dream house," and specifically as an instrument of bourgeois self-fulfillment, is to perform a cultural function confined (until recently) largely to Western society, and Anglo-American society in particular. Early chapters of this book analyze the origins of this function in terms of responses to challenges brought upon the nascent bourgeoisie by philosophical, economic, and political circumstances beginning in late seventeenth-century England. That response, I argue, was directly articulated in the early eighteenth-century production of a new architectural type, the compact bourgeois villa, and a new settlement pattern, the modern suburb as we know it.

One of the fundamental premises of this study is that there is a necessary connection between the belief system (or ideology) of a culture and the material apparatus in which people conduct their daily lives. It need not necessarily be a one-to-one correspondence, or an immediate correspondence, but there are always relations, reactions, and consequences established between how people think of themselves and the physical configurations of their daily environments. In many respects this book is a study of how architecture, as a material apparatus of daily life, engaged challenges posed by shifting political and economic ideologies and afforded people affected by those challenges the means to new life courses, sustained by new ideologies. In this way the early eighteenth-century invention and evolution of the compact single-family house on its own parcel of private property may well be seen as a response to challenges posed by new notions of selfhood, individuality, and property crystallized in the late seventeenth-century writings of John Locke—an evolution hastened by the pressures and opportunities of advancing capitalism and the possibilities afforded by membership in the bourgeoisie.

One of the most attractive possibilities open to the middle and upper echelons of the bourgeoisie, well refined by the middle of the eighteenth century, was the culture of "retirement," often centered on compact villas isolated in the rural (and eventually suburban) landscape. Generally involving a nonproductive landscape available solely for the private leisure pursuits of the owner, and set in clear contradistinction to the culture, commerce, and society of the city, the culture of retirement was instrumental in establishing the suburban ideological paradigm for centuries to come. Translated to America in the nineteenth century, this engagement between ideology and architecture evolved to embrace a broader culture of pastoralism, one of the central themes taken up in part II.

In America the head of the family, often the owner of a detached dwelling, commonly subscribed to the ideology of the "self-made man." This figure, realized in the form of a private entrepreneur or farmer, may have had a smaller economic stake than his English bourgeois counterpart, but he likely had a greater ideological investment in (as Tocqueville put it) his own individualism. A pastoral ideology suited these American bourgeois well, even when they took city jobs and suburban residences, as those residences still could incorporate and sustain certain beliefs about household domesticity (gender roles and household upkeep), morality (rural values), and identity (as formed in part through spatial practice). These same beliefs translated well into the layout of suburban developments, as countless architectural manuals, literary essays, and promotional materials soon made clear. And the enduring popularity of those nineteenth-century suburban prototypes suggests that America continues to be engaged with the ideological concerns that led to their invention.

Part III of the book focuses more closely on just one theme, the trope of the

American dream, and how in the early twentieth century it became synonymous with the notion of the dream house—partly as a deliberate consequence of government policy, partly as a consequence of ways in which consumerist practices afforded new opportunities for dwellings to engage the ideological imperatives of selfhood. In the ensuing decades the dream house ideal has sustained critique from many sides (as commodity, as pretext for sterile homogeneity, as something just plain facile), and yet its popularity persists. In the concluding chapter of the book, I return to some of the original ideological premises underlying the single-nuclear-family house and suburb in order to frame a discussion of this debate from a wider perspective, and then to engage certain specific concerns that surround suburbia today. In the end I propose some possibilities for a different mode of critique, one that forgoes condemnation of suburbia and those who live there in favor of greater hybridity in design, leading to more opportunity for the articulation of connections and differences across the social and political spectrum.

Three centuries ago the foundations of our modern Western ways of thinking about self and society originated in a philosophical movement now known as the Enlightenment. The roots of this movement extended further back into the seventeenth century, it held sway well into the nineteenth, and many of its conventions and principles still form the basis of Western values, ideals, politics, and notions of self. But along with these new conventions and principles, and especially notions of self, came new challenges. For example, since Enlightenment philosophy now promised that people could enjoy the freedom to determine their own selfhood, just how should anybody go about doing that? Philosophers provided few answers, but they did offer some hints. They suggested that the material world around us should have a new primacy in defining self and anchoring consciousness. This laid important groundwork for architects, landscape designers, and eventually planners to provide new terms in which to formulate some material solutions to the existential challenges of Enlightenment selfhood.

A primary goal of this book is to explore efforts to respond to this challenge, concentrating on England and America, in the three centuries since its appearance. It has spawned, among other things, the bourgeois single-family dwelling and the residential suburb, both of which in turn embraced new ideas of privacy, property, and selfhood in Enlightenment philosophy. In taking such a long view, my purpose is to bring the history of domestic architecture and suburbia into better connection with the more enduring ideological and historical circumstances surrounding their production.

A broader aim in writing this book is to establish useful foundations for an approach to present-day discussions about housing, neighborhoods, difference, sprawl, gated communities, and other contentious issues in order to improve knowledge of the conditions under which present circumstances have come to be as they are. In many respects our current ways of thinking and living remain embedded in past

Anglo-American culture and practice. Ostensibly obsolete ideologies of past centuries still find strong echoes in the present, if not in what we say or do, then in where and how we live.

To begin this process of framing the present, I have provided a brief introduction that addresses from a theoretical and methodological standpoint some of the issues relating to architecture and identity that become relevant in the context of this study, particularly in Anglo-American culture following the work of John Locke, especially his *Essay Concerning Human Understanding* and *Two Treatises of Government,* both formally published in 1690. The seven central chapters of the book then undertake a historical exploration of the role of the single-family dwelling, both as a monadic unit and clustered together in suburbs, in Anglo-American culture from the early stages of the Enlightenment to the end of the millennium. I have focused on Anglo-American culture because the single-family house took on a special prominence in England and America, flourishing both earlier and more widely there than anywhere else. This occurred for several reasons, ranging from the early rise of a mercantile economy in England, along with the rise of a prosperous bourgeoisie, to the genesis in English political philosophy of highly refined notions of self and property—notions elaborated even more in America as it evolved its own form of statehood in the nineteenth and twentieth centuries. For this reason chapter 1 is devoted to an examination of the relevant work of John Locke, the late-seventeenth-century philosopher whose writings had widespread and lasting influence on the course of Anglo-American politics, epistemology, education, property relations, and many other fields of social relations. In particular, his work more than that of comparable figures such as Descartes set out the basic premises of Enlightenment selfhood for Anglo-American culture, premises that incorporated crucial implications for the course of architecture as the nascent bourgeoisie sought means for defining that selfhood within (and against) the larger frameworks of society.

Locke in effect set a challenge: once he articulated the notion of a politically free self who was able to appropriate property for private purposes, there lay an opportunity in architecturally elaborating that property, especially what was regarded as one's most private property, the home, to articulate a person's individuality and selfhood. Prior to Locke single families, large and small, of diverse classes, including the emerging bourgeoisie, had certainly been sheltered in a variety of suitable dwellings. But a type of dwelling particularly suited to the bourgeoisie and adaptable to the articulation of individual bourgeois types had yet to be conceived or constructed.[1] This afforded a second opportunity: not only might someone make use of an architectural instrument to articulate selfhood, but an architectural *type,* the single-family detached dwelling, might be generated to suit an emerging *class,* the bourgeoisie, the ascendant political and economic forces in England and America in the centuries following Locke. Third, and finally, a locale in which the bourgeoisie as a collective group, or class, might effectively sustain and reinforce common aspects of its identity had yet to appear at the time Locke wrote, but within two decades the first beginnings of what we now know as suburbia were apparent along the banks of the Thames near Twickenham west of London. Suburbia has since remained the bourgeois locale par excellence. Chapters 2 and 3 are devoted to an examination of the eighteenth-century response to these challenges and opportunities, and specifically to the genesis of the bourgeois suburban villa in England and of early suburbia in the vicinity of London.

In chapters 4 and 5 the focus turns primarily to America. Following the Revolutionary War the implementation of a republican form of government, with its attendant ideologies of private virtue, public morality, and "self-made men," presented bourgeois American men—the land- and homeowners—both the obligation and the opportunity to engage in more intensive opportunities for self-identification through various forms of architectural house plans, stylistic rhetoric, and furnishings. Able to choose from a wide range of styles, plans, furniture, and ornament, owners used their dwellings not only to demonstrate their social status and virtuous stature for all to see but also as an instrument to sustain and regenerate that status and stature from year to year and generation to generation. As improvements in transportation technology, increasing wealth, and the growth in numbers of professionals, managers, and even clerks made increased suburbanization of bourgeois families possible, the aesthetic conventions and physical planning techniques invented and adopted in nineteenth-century suburbia served to advance, often with ill-disguised irony, bourgeois ideals of privacy, property, selfhood, family, and a quasi-pastoral lifestyle.

Chapters 6 and 7 continue the examination of dwelling and suburb in the twentieth century, concentrating now on a single theme that is carried through both chapters: the American dream house. Originally the "American dream" was associated with Horatio Alger novels and immigrant success stories, although the term itself seems not to have come into use until the 1930s. But already in the 1920s the notion of the American dream became melded with a very different ideal, that of the single-family house. The latter had been promoted by the U.S. government as a patriotic goal since the beginning of the decade, and in 1926 this ideal was united with the term *American dream* in the first of what became a long history of romantic "dream house" songs. Chapter 6 explores the political and cultural origins of these merged dreams, and chapter 7 traces the course of the now-merged dream as it has become increasingly complex, controversial, and no less influential in American culture from World War II until the present day.

Building on the historical analysis laid out in the preceding seven chapters, the conclusion offers a more theorized approach to specific concerns that animate (and agitate) the discussion of single-family housing and suburbia today. These include such questions as whether suburbia is such a bad place after all, given the fact that many of its residents prefer to live there; whether better planning techniques, such as design codes, can produce better communities and neighborhoods; whether close attention to design affords or erases subjectivity; and how to provide for and sustain difference in modern housing and communities, especially given the notable disjunction between "individuality," a core feature of much of the original and ongoing discussion of bourgeois identity, and the sameness that some say has pervaded so much tract housing for the past half to three-quarters of a century. These and many comparable questions that now face architects, planners, policy makers, clients, and citizens were each partly implied in the challenge that Locke posed in 1690; while there is no way to simply "solve" that challenge, this book is an effort to render its presence in our culture more evident and to frame it in ways that may lead to a more diverse range of outcomes.

Introduction: Built Spaces and Identity

The internal Parts [of a building] may be made to suit the Temper, Genius, and Convenience of the Inhabitant, by enlarging, or reducing the Scale.
> —Thomas Rawlins, *Familiar Architecture,* 1768

I would have, then, our ordinary dwelling-houses built to last, and built to be lovely; as rich and full of pleasantness as may be, within and without; with what degree of likeness to each other in style and manner, I will say presently, under another head; but, at all events, with such differences as might suit and express each man's character and occupation, and partly his history. This right over the house, I conceive, belongs to its first builder, and is to be respected by his children; and it would be well that blank stones should be left in places, to be inscribed with a summary of his life and of its experience, raising thus the habitation into a kind of monument . . .
> —John Ruskin, *The Seven Lamps of Architecture,* 1849

A House Should Suit Its Inhabitant

A house should suit its inhabitant: both John Ruskin, whose writings stood at the forefront of British architectural theory for half a century, and the lesser-known eighteenth-century practitioner Thomas Rawlins advanced this architectural principle as an exemplary goal of domestic design. As a formal principle it is simply enough stated, but in the analysis and execution it can become considerably more problematic. It is a goal that in many respects pervades almost the entire history of architecture, both temporally and geographically, but since the advent of modern Enlightenment concerns about identity, it has proved to be an increasingly urgent, sometimes vexing, matter for designers of dwellings, developments, and their clients. The stories of how English, and later American, architects and planners responded over the course of three centuries to the challenges that Enlightenment notions of property, privacy, labor, and selfhood posed for the understanding of identity anchor much of the discussion in this book. Many of these challenges resulted in profound changes in the history of architecture and planning: the invention of the single-family bourgeois dwelling as a building type, and the residential suburb as a bourgeois locale. However, before turning to the historical account, some discussion is appropriate of the problems that will be addressed and the approaches that may be used in both historical and present-day analysis.

I have framed the general problem, particularly for the eighteenth century, in terms of a challenge and a response: given new terms in which Enlightenment political, legal, and economic theory construed the human being, as an individual charged with the constitution and fulfillment of his or her selfhood, how did architects and designers proactively address the challenge by offering new types of apparatus for articulating the individual in those new terms? Too often architecture has been held up as a "mirror" of society, a mere "reflection" of something that "really" happens somewhere else. My argument is an effort to counter that approach: given new uncertainties and anxieties about selfhood, how in fact have architecture and housing been instrumental parts of the very process of evolving Enlightenment norms and forms of identity?

Crucial to architects' efforts to address the challenge of constructing selfhood was the proposition that a house should suit its inhabitant. To introduce this concept, two short passages have been cited as epigraphs to this part of the book. Just these two disclose some of the principal ways in which responses to the challenge have remained consistent, as well as evolved and changed, over time. One axis on which Rawlins and Ruskin clearly converged, for example, was the selection of *personal* criteria according to which an inhabitant would be identified, characteristics that would be emphasized in the design process. Previously, from the Renaissance to the eighteenth century, such criteria generally had been derived according to the principle of "decorum," which required that design and decoration of a building suit an owner's *position* within certain established social hierarchies such as rank, status, wealth, and ancestry. The criteria to be suited, in other words, were less a matter of qualities inherent to the particular individual than attributes accorded to social position. With Rawlins and Ruskin, the criteria now shifted to qualities that were considerably more individualistic: temper and genius, as specified by Rawlins, to which Ruskin added character, occupation, and history. Dwellings now could be construed as instruments whose design could articulate, even legitimate, the dimensions of the owner's personal identity—dimensions that could be regarded as self-chosen and self-realized, and might even register the degree to which the individual was differentiated from the social nexus.

But Ruskin, writing a century after Rawlins, also introduced another respect in which the design of a dwelling ought to accord with the identity of its owner. Noting that a house should age with its owner, becoming a material record of "his life and experience," Ruskin added the expectation that the owner of each house should be a unique person whose individuality the house would serve to document as it evolved over time. And there was a further implication: that unless the resident capitalized on this potent capacity, his life might not be consummated to the fullest potential possible. In other words, by the mid-nineteenth century the dwelling had become more than an instrument of self-articulation. Clearly embracing the challenge laid out for post-Enlightenment individuals, the dwelling had become necessary to self-fulfillment.

For most of the nineteenth century American architectural writing and practice had remained dependent on knowledge of English treatises, handbooks, and practices, and as chapter 4 shows, Ruskin could have spoken for many Americans throughout that period. But during the late nineteenth and early twentieth centuries American architectural education began to incorporate a broader range of perspectives and approaches. One in particular, phenomenology, has not only remained of lasting influence but has also introduced a complementary perspective on the relation between dwelling and self. Gaston Bachelard, perhaps the chief exponent of dwelling as a critical medium for articulation of the self, argued that the house actually takes an active role in articulating the individual resident's life practices. In so doing he inverted the orientation of the relationship between dwelling and resident that Ruskin had proposed. Instead of the house simply representing the character of the inhabitant, or progressively embodying that character over time, now the inhabitant is transformed by certain capacities endemic to the house. The house, or dwelling, becomes the instrument by which the activity of "dwelling"—which fellow phenomenologist Martin Heidegger had directly equated with living, with being a human being—is ingrained in the self.[1]

By the end of the twentieth century the understanding of domestic architecture as instrumental to self-realization had thus become an article of faith in much American architectural writing and practice. As Christopher Alexander, a standard figure in the curricula of most American architectural schools, has written of the potential in domestic design:

> Each family has a house which fits them perfectly: it has their wishes, their dreams, their ideas of life; it has to do with their children, their ways of cooking, their ways of gardening, their ways of sleeping. It is a place which they can love, because through it, and in it, they have constructed their world.[2]

The notion of the dwelling as necessary and instrumental to self-fulfillment had also become pervasive in American popular culture, a theme examined closely in chapters 6 and 7. One illustration of the widespread recognition of that notion is a *Life* magazine feature article presenting "The 1999 *Life* Dream House," a dwelling broadly suited to upper-middle-class Americans. The design, by Sarah Susanka of the firm of Mulfinger, Susanka, Mahady and Partners, can be varied and adapted to a variety of personal interests and needs. It includes elements such as nooks, private alcoves, and flexible spaces that can be modified and changed, in almost Ruskinian fashion, as family members grow and age, elements that are meant to suit the inhabitants' varied, and changing, identities. As the closing lines in the accompanying article affirm:

Look at the pictures of the early prairie families standing in front of their homes. They were careful not to block the view of the house. It's almost as if the house was another member of the family. The home in our country is a part of our identity.[3]

Architecture as an Instrument of Identity

As detailed in the next chapter, the evolution of Anglo-American political and economic thought since the late seventeenth century has increasingly cast the self as obligated to establish its own place in the social and economic nexus, and free to succeed or fail in that quest. Likewise in progressively reconceiving the self as more independent and autonomous, with a capacity to liberate itself from inflexible regimes of status, privilege, and sometimes even gender,[4] there has been a corresponding shift toward understanding the self as fundamentally an *individual*. Or, to state the shift another way, the challenge came to be understood as an obligation to fashion one's individual identity.[5]

Given such a challenge and opportunity, architects, theorists, and clients soon joined in a process, slow at first, more rapid by the nineteenth and twentieth centuries, that transformed the private dwelling into one of the most effective media for (literally) constructing that individuality, the goal sketched briefly above. This was accomplished through a variety of typological and design innovations, not least of which included isolation of the single-family house from others, separation of the dwelling from its economic, social, and political contexts, typological differentiation (e.g., the ranch house), and stylistic distinction (e.g., Greek Revival). Perhaps the clearest beneficiaries of these shifts were members of the emerging bourgeoisie, with whom these sorts of typological and stylistic architectural distinctions became associated. Indeed most such individualizing techniques introduced over the past three centuries have been for the benefit of the middle classes. Still, the focus of innovation has for the most part been narrower than that, confined largely to articulating the identity of the male head of the household in a culture that has remained largely patriarchal. Nevertheless such is the process by which over the past three centuries the dwelling has commonly, perhaps even necessarily, become recognized as instrumental to, or even part of, identity.

Before exploring the complex course of that historical trajectory, the brief outlines of a related, methodological concern have to be addressed: how to account for the means by which architecture—or for that matter all of "built space," which also includes landscape, planning, and other modes of design—may function as an essential constituent of personal identity. In general, there are two complementary arguments. The first concerns the manner in which any given person's spatial surroundings are configured and used, and how they serve from birth as an anchor of cognition. The specific spatial elements that are present or absent in those surroundings—body, climate, geographic scale, to name some of the most basic—establish the very categories, axes, and dimensions in which one's place and role in the world will be understood.[6]

The second argument turns from cognition to practice. Built spaces serve everywhere as a necessary and selective medium of human practice. They establish and facilitate favored activities and relations while limiting and even erasing knowledge of others. Built spaces are three-dimensional apparatuses that people intentionally lay out for explicit purposes ranging from survival and satisfying basic needs to ordering society, enabling economic activity, producing knowledge, advancing spirituality, affording pleasures, and so on. Given that nearly all human experience occurs in spaces that already have been humanly fashioned, it follows that the terms in which spaces are configured and the uses to which those configurations are put serve as apparatuses for inculcating highly particularized systems of social relations and of one's role within them.[7] As such, space articulates many of the parameters according to which personal identity is established. Put another way, because built spaces shape what people do and how they live in highly specific ways, they also necessarily shape who those people are.

In terms of cognition and practice, built space thus plays an instrumental role in shaping categories of external relations by which people relate to each other, such as status and gender. From apartheid regulations and gated suburban enclaves to matters of caste and purdah, space delimits the categories of one's being. Of course that does not preclude various modes of resistance to such categorization,[8] or conceiving of other categories, but it does materially assert the hegemony of those categories.[9] In addition, built space plays an equally crucial role in shaping internal states of being and awareness—things such as feelings, sentiment, and affect.[10] From the decor of one's bedroom or study to geomancy and many forms of religious architecture, the articulation of space is expected in considerable measure to sustain a certain affect or even transform one's outlook.

Nor was the relation between architecture and affect a new concern. As early as 1485 the influential Italian theorist Leon Battista Alberti approached the analysis of architecture in terms of such an affective capacity. In his treatise *De re aedificatoria* he boasted of the material ways in which architecture facilitated personal and social activities, such as by fashioning places for exercise and bathing, and by providing tabernacles, churches, fortresses, and other structures for collective activity. In addition to praising architects for such skills in enriching society he also commended their ability to excite feelings or to enhance certain emotional states. Exhibiting little modesty, Alberti trumpeted architecture's capacity to extend or enhance personal consciousness: "we are exceedingly obliged to the Architect; to whom, in time of Leisure, we are indebted for Tranquility, Pleasure and health, in time of Business for Assistance and profit; and in both, for Security and Dignity."[11] In foregrounding such notions as tranquility, pleasure, and dignity, in addition to considerations of a more material aspect (profit, security), Alberti outlined a contributory role for architecture in shaping human self-consciousness, albeit not yet a necessary role in articulating individual identity.

As an architectural theoretician and practitioner Alberti's focus lay with the potential of architecture to affect the mind far more than with the structure of the mind per se. But others before and after Alberti who did concern themselves with the mind brought another dimension of analysis to the relation between architecture and the self. From before Alberti's time to the Enlightenment, it had become something of a commonplace to regard the mind and the way that it retains and structures knowledge as if it were an architectural composition.[12] Frequently the metaphor of a "closet" or "cabinet" was used, alluding to the private domestic chambers and elaborate articles of furniture that aristocrat-intellectuals used in their efforts to harness knowledge and extend its dimensions (Figure I.1).[13]

Even John Locke, whose sweeping critique of epistemology in *An Essay Concerning Human Understanding* (1690) was a foundational moment of the European Enlightenment, still conceptualized the mind in this customary way. Despite his radical analysis of thought processes, recasting them in terms of rational abstractions, Locke still characterized the mind itself in terms—cabinet and closet—that metaphorically anchored those processes within the structured confines of a private domestic chamber. Such were the terms in which he characterized a newborn infant's mental apparatus, which in other respects Locke characterized as entirely blank (a tabula rasa). Discussing the process by which this blank slate first came to be provided with raw data from the five senses, he noted the emptiness and lack of furnishings but implied no lack of structure:

> The Senses at first let in particular *Ideas,* and furnish the yet empty Cabinet: And the Mind by degrees growing familiar with some of them, they are lodged in the Memory, and Names got to them. . . .
>
> External and internal sensation, are the only passages that I can find, of Knowledge, to the Understanding. These alone, as far as I can discover, are the Windows by which light is let into this *dark Room.* For, methinks, the *Understanding* is not much unlike a Closet wholly shut from light, with only some little openings left, to let in external visible Resemblances, or *Ideas* of things without; would the Pictures coming into such a dark Room but stay there, and lie so orderly as to be found upon occasion, it would very much resemble the Understanding of a Man, in reference to all Objects of sight, and the *Ideas* of them.[14]

What Locke envisioned was at best a simplified and generic apparatus within the mind, cast in the form of a single-room cabinet, in which individuals produced consciousness from sense data according to a standard set of logical, rational principles. But by casting that apparatus as a cabinet, a type of room proprietary to the private self, he advanced substantially a conceptual approach to the architecturalization of personal identity.

Neither Locke's *Essay* nor his equally seminal *Two Treatises of Government* (1690) interrogated architecture per se any further, forgoing inquiries into ways in which

Figure I.1. Agostino Ramelli, design for a machine for a person who takes pleasure in study, illustrated in the context of a Renaissance private "closet" or "cabinet." Plate 188 in *Le Diverse et Artificiose Machine,* 1588.

architecture, for example, might be instrumental in the articulation of human consciousness or selfhood. Nevertheless by exploring the production of knowledge as a solitary process, centered in the individual, and by recognizing the mind itself as an architecturally framed apparatus for the apprehension of information, Locke articulated an intimate relationship between architecture, self, and knowledge. Here, as well as in discussions of property and self, to be examined in following chapters, Locke laid the groundwork for eighteenth-century and later architects to articulate the instrumentality of architecture in the individualization of identity.

The trajectory on which designers embarked was to incorporate into dwelling design a strategy of *identification*. As a field for the shaping of cognition and practice, to be experienced by visitors as well as lived by residents, the dwelling afforded designers an apparatus that could be doubly instrumental. On the one hand, it could articulate a public identity for the inhabitant qua individual. Many nineteenth-century architects, for example, were fond of utilizing the variety of available stylistic vocabularies such as Doric, Tuscan, Gothic, and Tudor to this end. On the other hand, the dwelling also could help shape the very architecture of the resident's consciousness. It could do so, for example, by inculcating a disposition to virtuous behavior, a particular concern of many nineteenth-century authors, through an apt configuration of the house plan or a properly aestheticized interior.

Given the diverse imperatives in England and America to individualize the bourgeois self in political, social, legal, and economic terms, architects and clients readily recognized dwellings, particularly detached, single-household structures, as capable of both displaying and shaping the inhabitant's identity. Their efforts to achieve these goals across the often rapidly shifting circumstances and conditions of three centuries are the focus of the ensuing chapters.

Constituting Identity

Two hundred years after Locke's *Essay* and his *Treatise,* his proposition—that the individual, beginning as a tabula rasa, is obligated to fulfill its selfhood—was in one sense long outmoded: modern theories of psychology, biology, education, and politics had rendered much of what he had written obsolete. But on another level the fundamental challenge remained. Atomized as a political and economic monad within advancing industrial capitalist society, the individual had recourse to few resources other than the dwelling (transformed as it may have been by a consumerist culture) for purposes of articulating many dimensions of identity. Since the middle of the nineteenth century, this isolation of the person within modern industrial society has commonly been recognized, and critiqued very productively, from several perspectives outside of Anglo-American culture. But rather than survey the many avenues that major critiques of modern selfhood and Enlightenment identity have pursued (e.g., Marxism, psychoanalysis), I want to trace the strands of just a few theoretical approaches to relations between the built environment and identity as they have unfolded over the course of the twentieth century. These approaches, coming largely from outside of Anglo-American culture, not only help to set in some relief the historical production of dwellings and suburbs in England and America between 1690 and 2000, as examined in chapters 2 through 7, but also in the closing chapter suggest bases for embarking on a more productive critique.

Two social scientific disciplines of growing importance at the beginning of the twentieth century were functionalist sociology and structural anthropology, and by then serious investigation of the role of architecture in the production of human identity had largely moved beyond the realm of architectural writers and practitioners and into the hands of these newcomers. The subject was particularly germane to their analyses of human belief and behavior in relation to physical settings. Perhaps ironically these analyses were little concerned with individual subjectivity—a blindness that, in a world increasingly devoted to the pursuit of individualism, eventually limited the currency of such approaches. But in establishing the instrumentality of built space in constituting positions and roles within society, as well as in instantiating larger frameworks of cosmic and social relations, these approaches laid important foundations for theorizing and analyzing the architectural and spatial constitution of the individual self.

In some respects such a functionalist approach had long roots. As early as the middle of the eighteenth century, Baron Montesquieu's seminal *Spirit of the Laws* (1748) had analyzed the effect of varying geographical contexts on different cultures. Focusing in particular on variations in climate, Montesquieu sought to explain not only the corresponding differences in the physical constitution of diverse peoples but also their different intellectual and political orientations in terms of the physical and environmental forces that shaped them. But as important as Montesquieu's contributions may have been for disciplines of geography and anthropology, his analysis extended only to the influence of natural contexts—not building—on human behaviors and cultures.

Only at the beginning of the twentieth century did Émile Durkheim examine the spatial arrangement of dwellings and entire settlements in relation to social structures and belief systems, in his structuralist analysis of Australian, Native American, and other "primitive" cultures.[15] By documenting homologies among the physical spaces that a people inhabited, the clans and other apparatuses by which they organized their collective interests, and the cosmic spaces of their belief systems, Durkheim analytically examined the instrumentality of built space in the production of consciousness. Laying groundwork for much structuralist social theory in decades to follow, Durkheim established the importance of the material environment, and buildings in particular, in the formation of human consciousness. What he did not do was suggest the possibility that individuals might choose, or even be aware of choices, among different identities.

A more recent approach developed by Pierre Bourdieu is more sympathetic to choice, or at least sympathetic to opportunities for voluntary shifts of identity.

Bourdieu, a philosopher who retrained himself in the field of ethnology, undertook fieldwork in north Africa in 1962. In his subsequent prolific writing he was in part concerned to refocus the discipline away from inelastic systems of social relations and more on problems of personal subjectivity. In his *Outline of a Theory of Practice* (1972), substantially revised as *The Logic of Practice* (1980), Bourdieu not only offered ethnographic analysis of correspondences between built space and social practices and beliefs, but also introduced a theoretical account of the mental apparatus through which individuals come to recognize themselves in specific positions in a given culture and become accustomed to performing specific roles.[16] In brief, he offered an account of cognitive and practical means by which, from birth, each individual articulates an identity that is particular to his or her specific gender, religious beliefs, economy, dwelling architecture and decoration, and other cultural considerations. It is an approach that ultimately helps us to establish a sophisticated basis for understanding (among other things) the complex ways in which built space intersects with the production of personal identity.

Bourdieu's approach hinged on his identification of a particular dimension of human consciousness, the *habitus*. Simply defined, the habitus is the set of personally held *dispositions* around which any person's thought and activities are structured. In the case of most everyday occurrences (e.g., greeting an acquaintance or using cutlery), the individual human being does not completely think out a rationale for action every time a choice has to be made or some activity performed. Instead, each person operates almost automatically, without much thought, according to a set of dispositions that already embody, among other things, that person's understood status, value system, and experience of "what works" in terms of sustaining and advancing understood interests. Adults may find themselves automatically speaking in stilted language to strangers while using baby talk with infants; one's disposition to perform in a certain way in a given circumstance is commonly acted upon without deliberate reflection. Considerations that may factor into any given person's disposition to act in a particular way include professional status, gender, wealth, class, caste, religion, age, and so forth.[17] The habitus can be understood, then, as a set of principled structures embedded in each person's consciousness, structures that in turn structure the person's responses to, engagement with, and understanding of the world at large.[18] Put another way, the habitus is a system of both *cognitive* and *motivating* structures. It is the dispositions according to which the individual fashions knowledge and according to which the individual initiates activity. Still, a crucial point for Bourdieu was that the habitus is not a limitation on agency.[19] Given changes in conditions, circumstances, or other factors, the individual is as free to change those dispositions as a bourgeois client of the popular nineteenth-century American architect Andrew Jackson Downing was to choose the decorative style of his villa.

Though not central to Bourdieu's argument at every point, a critical feature of the habitus is that it is spatially anchored with respect to cognition, motivation, and agency.[20] Built space is a critical element of the reference system within which knowledge is produced and applied, and the physical forms according to which people establish and discipline their lives are correspondingly instruments for shaping social relations. This was documented in Bourdieu's examination of the settlements and dwellings of the Kabyle people of northern Africa, where he examined relations between the dwelling as a material apparatus for living and the complex of relations and beliefs that the built structure subtended. In his analysis, the specific manner in which all components of the built environment were fashioned was central to the process of maintaining the larger framework of social relations, and the house took center stage:

> Inhabited space—starting with the house—is the privileged site of the objectification of the generative schemes [of social organization], and, through the divisions and hierarchies it establishes between things, between people and between practices, this materialized system of classification inculcates and constantly reinforces the principles of the classification which constitutes the arbitrariness of a[ny given] culture.[21]

As such the house was considerably more than a simple representation of an extrinsically situated system of social organization. It was, rather, both a cognitive apparatus by which social relations were directly embodied in its residents and a practical instrument by which the maintenance of that system was continuously prompted and performed. Among the Kabyle, for example, Bourdieu showed that such aspects as directional orientation, placement of door openings, lighting, partitions, upper and lower levels, storage locations, and fireplace placement all established and sustained (through social practice) a number of fundamental cultural divisions, including male/female, cooked/raw, and fire/water, as well as distinctions between the house and other divisions of the universe, such as the male world, the fields, and the market. All the actions performed in such spaces immediately "function as so many structural exercises through which is built up practical mastery" of the taxonomic principles that organize the culture.[22]

To put Bourdieu's contribution in more general terms: as built forms structure the location, orientation, and attitude of the body in physical space, they not only "shape the dispositions constituting social identity" but also naturalize those dispositions within society.[23] For example, relations such as high (on a dais) and low ("below stairs"), facing and oblique, exposed (a dormitory) and enclosed (a private chamber) all establish social identities through bodily location and orientation. These identities come to be naturalized as people consistently and habitually conform their self-conception and their relations with others to the circumstances of the spatial apparatus.[24] A given habitus thus is linked inextricably to the characteristics of a particular spatial environment. And within that context, particularly if knowledge of alternative contexts was unavailable, Bourdieu suggested that the power of the habitus could approach hegemony: "the habitus engenders all the thoughts, all the perceptions, and all the actions consistent with those conditions, and no others."[25] Still, for literate and industrializing societies such as post-Enlightenment England and America, and particularly for the swelling ranks of their bourgeoisies, such ignorance of other possibilities would be unlikely. More to the point, the variety of *different* identities afforded by choices of lifestyle and consumer goods, as Bourdieu raised in his later work,[26] suggests many more dimensions and directions in which any given habitus may grow.

Comparable concerns with difference and identity have continued to engage poststructuralist theorists, and the role of architecture has been crucial for some. Michel Foucault's *Discipline and Punish* (1975), which remains one of the most important analyses of the architectural formation of identity and does account for the elaboration of certain kinds of difference, ultimately offers a much bleaker outlook than Bourdieu's. Foucault's approach focuses on the rise of nineteenth-century technologies such as measurement, classification, forensics, surveillance, recording, and cartography, and delineates the manner in which these could accord any given person an identity as unique as any point in a vast multidimensional matrix. But all those new degrees of difference were defined in terms that embodied the political and technological interests of the society at large. As Foucault might have put it, they were but a deployment of power.[27] And crucially for Foucault, it was clear that architecture was but the handmaiden of this system of power relations, rendering concrete the tiers, echelons, ranks, and positions through which power was deployed.[28] The self, in sum, was defined in terms of the overall system of social relations. Individuality became at best a matter of one's relative position within the social matrix.

Foucault himself remained little concerned with the analysis of dwellings per se, but an approach such as his would conclude that dwellings have as much a capacity for erasing selfhood as enhancing it. For example, one might point to the way dwelling units in large housing blocks resist individualization but nevertheless furnish a crucial component of modern-day identity: an address. Indeed those without an address, the homeless, are not only denied many of the credentials by which identity is commonly recognized, but when they need to rest or sleep, are also banished from nominally "public" spaces that ostensibly are open to all members of the society. Without a place in the socio-architectural matrix, one has no identity.

But the pessimism of a Foucauldian approach is not necessarily warranted. Without wholly rejecting the poststructuralist stance, several authors make clear that existing architectural and planning apparatuses also provide opportunities for differentiation and resistance. Allen Feldman, for example, in *Formations of Violence: The Narrative of the Body and Political Terror in Northern Ireland* (1991), demonstrates that even in the harsh regime of a maximum-security British prison in Northern Ireland, inmates' identities are not erased (nor their spirits broken) by their rigid architectural confines. Rather, through techniques of resistance that necessarily rely on the prisoners' mental and bodily endurance, such as refusing to wear clothing or fouling their cells, they not only subvert the deployment of state power against themselves but even turn the architectural apparatus against those who wield it. In the process they not only reassert their identities but also potently establish through spatial means their autonomy from the state.

Alternatively Michel de Certeau argues in *The Practice of Everyday Life* (1980) that articulation of identity in terms out of accord with the social order need not be an extraordinary act but rather can be an everyday occurrence. Outlining an approach to understanding architecture and cities that is the "reciprocal of Foucault's analysis of the structures of power," de Certeau has proposed a broad diversity of ways in which people can engage built space that he calls a host of "tricky and stubborn procedures" or, more specifically, "pedestrian speech acts" and "walking rhetorics." These are practices by which people can reappropriate space and thereby exercise the capacity to "structure the determining conditions of social life."[29] De Certeau argues, in other words, that individuals can and commonly do intervene in already-built spaces in a way that sustains agency, maintains social relations on terms partially of their own making, and in the process affords opportunities to explore, enact, and embody constantly shifting dimensions of identity. Again, the import of de Certeau's approach is not only that individuals have agency, but that to a certain degree they can make use of that agency by appropriating and deploying diverse elements of the built environment. In the process, selfhood becomes further defined and refined.

A third line of inquiry, originating in debates between Theodor Adorno and Walter Benjamin, expanded the analysis to address the rapid rise over the past two centuries of the culture of consumption. A crucial component of this shift has been the marketing of identity through mass-produced commodities, which now more than ever includes houses that can be fabricated in a full range of themed, regional, and historical styles (e.g., log-cabin, ranch, or colonial), as well as the furnishings for those dwellings, such as ornamental trim, draperies, carpets, cabinets, furniture, appliances, media, and media equipment. On the one hand this broad array of consumer choice, and the retail apparatus dedicated to its distribution, bespeaks a culture ever more enamored of individualism, conveniently supplied with a large number of different identities to choose from.[30] But on the other hand the consumer who has no say in determining the available choices, no matter how wide the array, may well despair at the impossibility of articulating a truly individualized identity. Such is the thrust of Adorno's critique of the tyranny of a mechanized, industrial-capitalist culture: identities selected from a field of marketing choices are no identity at all.

But Benjamin set out a more optimistic analysis. Focusing on architecture and cinema, Benjamin argued that modern subjects are as a matter of course "habituated" to the products of mechanized society.[31] As such, individuals are sufficiently accustomed to the demands and constraints of modern culture—sufficiently savvy, we might say—that they are also free to define and pursue their own projects, and so to appropriate products of the culture efficaciously to their own ends.[32] In other words consumer choice, not least with respect to dwellings, might well be far more an opportunity to exercise personal agency in the articulation of one's individuality than helpless subjection to precast roles and identities.

The pertinence of a Benjaminian approach to the question of dwelling and identity, to be revisited in this volume's conclusion, may be enhanced in light of anthropologist Daniel Miller's analysis of consumption, beginning with his observation that consumption has long been integral to processes of individuation. This is a point that holds true for numerous cultures around the globe and across time periods: people routinely appropriate objects of many sorts, often including mass-produced products, in order to "utilize them in the creation of their own image." By choosing from the array of available objects, the "specific nature" of the individual person "is confirmed in the particularity of the selection." Moreover, "the relation between [one selected] object and others provid[es] a dimension through which the particular social position of the intended individual is experienced."[33] In other words, consumption is an activity that functions in a dual fashion. On the one hand, by virtue of a culture's common recognition that the various items produced are of certain types and have a certain range of significances, consumption has an integral role in maintaining social cohesion and in establishing a normative order against which individuality can be asserted. On the other hand, the specific objects that a person selects to consume (or reject) are the particular means by which the terms and dimensions of that individuality are chosen. The choice of a particular type, style, decorative pattern, or other characteristic for one's home, therefore, could well be part of the process of upholding the social order. Making what would seem to be an arbitrary choice from a nineteenth-century catalog of house styles, or from a Home Depot shelf, might in fact be nothing more than finding the product that best accords with, and sustains, one's own habitus.[34]

PART I

EIGHTEENTH-CENTURY ENGLAND:
THE GENESIS OF THE BOURGEOIS DWELLING

1. Locating the Self in Space

To help frame one of the most significant challenges that has faced individuals in Western society for the past three centuries, this study opens with an examination of the writings of John Locke (1632–1704), the early Enlightenment philosopher whose work has remained fundamental to English and American politics, epistemology, and ideology of self. Locke was not an architect and made only the slightest of references to architectural subjects in his writings; nor was he the only influential philosopher in early Enlightenment England. But Locke did address certain issues—identity, property, space, privacy, and family—in significant, even radical ways that became crucial to the evolution of Anglo-American architecture. They did so because they contributed to a new and challenging notion of selfhood as proprietary to the individual person: in effect each person, not the state or other authority, possessed his own selfhood. This brought advantages such as greater political freedom and economic independence, which in turn allowed a nascent bourgeoisie to flourish, particularly in London and Britain's major cities. After 1700 a corresponding market for specifically bourgeois dwellings, and designers for those dwellings, began to develop. There also were potentially darker consequences to this new notion of selfhood, especially a potential for existential uncertainties. For example, since this new notion was largely incompatible with the traditional belief in a preordained order of being, whether spiritual or political, just how could anyone be sure of who he or she was any longer? The remedy for those uncertainties often was cast in terms of an obligation to define and sustain a new kind of selfhood through one's own private, material efforts.

This new approach particularly suited the emerging bourgeoisie, especially in their appropriation of architecture as an innovative medium in which to articulate selfhood in material form, to engage it daily in material practice, and thus to assure its continuity. Doing so provided a way of articulating the reality of the bourgeois self that was new and different from that established by previous ecclesiastical and political orders, not to mention the basis for considerable (revolutionary) change to those orders. In a reciprocal fashion interest in Lockean notions of selfhood also gave a new urgency, particularly among the bourgeoisie, to understanding the dwelling as an apparatus that was capable of defining and realizing characteristic attributes of a given individual. As the eighteenth and later centuries progressed, bourgeois individuals turned to the dwelling as a premier instrument by which to establish and fulfill selfhood, and the evolution of means for doing so is the central subject of this book. To understand the premise of the problem, however—the selfhood at stake—an examination of Locke and the context of his writings is appropriate first.

Identity Is Personal

From Subject to Individual

Three centuries of hindsight strongly suggest that one of the most problematic legacies of Enlightenment ideology has been the challenge to articulate personal identity. Interwoven with shifts in economic relations, property law, and land tenure, already visible in the rise of capitalism and enclosure in seventeenth-century England, the basic understanding of what it meant to be a human being, both individually and in society, had become subject to radical redefinition. In many ways the terms of that redefinition were crystallized in two seminal treatises by John Locke, *An Essay Concerning Human Understanding* and *Two Treatises of Government*, both in preparation for many years but formally published in 1690.[1] Among his most notable contributions in the *Essay* is his articulation of the human mind at birth as a tabula rasa, which set the stage for Enlightenment notions of equality and personal independence. Here, by casting the newborn as an organism awaiting the arrival of sensory data as the material necessary for the empirical construction of a complete person, Locke effectively discounted both the biological and the social complexities of the processes according to which consciousness, knowledge, and identity were formed. Not only did this suggest that the self was comparatively autonomous in relation to society but, as a corollary, it atomized people as *individuals*. This notion of each individual in possession of an autonomous consciousness was critical to much of the economic and political change that would follow in the next century, particularly in the rise of mercantile capitalism. In *An Inquiry into the Nature and Causes of the Wealth of Nations* (1776), the classic theorization of capitalism, Adam Smith relied even more narrowly on such a notion of the private autonomous individual as the entrepreneurial engine of economic activity, and thus the basis of both individual prosperity as well as social welfare in general.

Prior to the recognition of people as individuals, a person's relation to society most commonly would have been expressed in terms of hierarchical structures of subjection, mechanisms according to which one was enduringly subject to the authority of feudal rulers, authorized by belief in a system of immutable bonds and linkages such as the doctrine of divine right, or the Great Chain of Being. As late as 1734 Alexander Pope defended such a model of society in his *Essay on Man,* a tour de force of poetic rigor that mirrors the permanence and stability that Pope accorded to the Chain itself. To challenge the legitimacy of the Chain was, in his eyes, not simply a challenge to the immediate social order but rather a challenge to the order of all Creation. Suggestions that people might act as autonomous individuals in terms of how they acquired knowledge, owned property, or managed capital—actions that would allow people to choose and change their positions in society—were precisely the sorts of concerns that Pope sought to refute, in quite alarmist terms, in the *Essay.* Describing first the perfection and beauty of the Chain in its vast extent, he then warned of what might happen should anyone become dissatisfied with the position of his or her link and attempt to move up or down the Chain:

> See, thro' this air, this ocean, and this earth,
> All Matter quick, and bursting into birth
> Above, how high progressive life may go?
> Around how wide? how deep extend below?
> Vast Chain of Being! which from God began,
> Natures Ethereal, human, Angel, Man,
> Beast, bird, fish, insect; what no Eye can see,
> No Glass can reach: from Infinite to thee,
> From thee to Nothing!—On superior pow'rs
> Were we to press, inferior might on ours;
> Or in the full Creation leave a Void,
> Where, one step broken, the great Scale's destroy'd:
> From Nature's Chain whatever link you strike,
> Tenth or ten thousandth, breaks the chain alike.[2]

Hindsight of course shows that Pope's efforts amounted to a rearguard action. His Enlightenment contemporaries evolved an ideology that endowed individuals with inalienable rights, such that people had titular sovereignty over their own beings. The notion that the sovereign could exercise degrees of control over the various ranks under him was supplanted by a new presupposition that, in the words of the American Declaration of Independence, "all men are created equal."[3] Political equality afforded the freedom to occupy any of various spots, all of which formerly had been links on the Chain. The corollary was that the structure of the Chain itself was now gone, and one had to construct one's own position.

Defining Selfhood

The Lockean understanding of personal sovereignty required radically changed notions of personhood—a change the profundity of which is apparent in examining his ongoing struggles, a century before the Declaration, with defining "self" and related terms. Begun in the late 1670s, his *Two Treatises of Government* are largely concerned with proposals for a radical restructuring of political authority and social organization. But while immersed in these political questions, he found it necessary to probe a complex of closely related matters concerning human knowledge and identity. And in his ensuing treatise, *An Essay Concerning Human Understanding*, Locke took many of these matters up again, working to clarify intersecting notions of identity, self, person, and consciousness that were critical to notions of political autonomy and liberty that he sought to develop.

Crucial to Locke's overall argument was the high degree of abstraction with which he discussed epistemology and ontology—not simply conceptual abstraction but also abstraction of the individual from the social fabric of society and the physical fabric of the material world. Struggling with the political need to detach the self from existing political and ideological structures such as monarchy and absolutism, he chose to situate the autonomous self prior to society. The way that he did so was to define the *self* primarily as the presence of *consciousness*:

> For since consciousness always accompanies thinking, and 'tis that, that makes every one to be, what he calls *self*; and thereby distinguishes himself from all other thinking things, in this alone consists *personal Identity, i.e.* the sameness of a rational Being: And as far as this consciousness can be extended backwards to any past Action or Thought, so far reaches the Identity of that *Person;* it is the same *self* now it was then; and 'tis by the same *self* with this present one that now reflects on it, that that Action was done.[4]

To further prove the self's autonomy, Locke argued that far from being a product of material conditions, the self existed prior to them. As he put it, the self-as-consciousness had the capacity to "join it self" with a material presence:

> *Self* is that conscious thinking thing, (whatever Substance, made up of whether Spiritual, or Material, Simple, or Compounded, it matters not) which is sensible, or conscious of Pleasure and Pain, capable of Happiness or Misery, and so is concern'd for it *self*, as far as that consciousness extends. . . . That with which the *consciousness* of this present thinking thing can join it self, makes the same *Person*, and is one *self* with it, and with nothing else; and so attributes to it *self*, and owns all the Actions of that thing, as its own. . . .[5]

Self and Society

Notably absent from Locke's discussion of self is any reference to its ontological origins in society. For him, the human was not a product of the social realm. Rather, the self was constructed in terms of an abstract epistemological domain (of consciousness), which in turn was prior to society. This neatly superseded any political question of self in relation to society and replaced it with a *priority* of self over society.

The political and social consequences of this move would be profound, but it also implied substantial shifts in the understanding of personhood on the level of the individual. For a necessary condition of this Enlightenment "selfhood"—if it was indeed ontologically antecedent to society—was the implicit obligation of each individual to secure some means for the articulation of identity. Part of the seductive appeal of the Great Chain of Being had been that it ostensibly guaranteed every being a place not only in society but in the entire universal order. By casting the self as an individual prior to society, Locke in effect reversed the terms of membership in society. Now, at least in theory, each person actively had to negotiate a role and position. The mind was simply a tabula rasa at birth, and the location of the self in space would always be in the first instance a matter of abstract relations to arbitrary points. By means of these ideological shifts, Locke substantially undermined a fixed (and politically repressive) hierarchical apparatus of identity construction in favor of a framework in which persons were provided "liberty" to engage a more flexible but less stable process of identity construction. By replacing feudal relations of subjection with inalienable rights, and stipulating that all are created equal, then social identity became, at least ostensibly, a matter of relations freely negotiated between private selves and the body politic. Here one could expect a measure of exhilaration but also considerable trepidation. For (according to Locke) having forged both the terms and the extent of one's own identity, the individual also would have to establish terms in which to assure that it would be recognized, sustained, and protected.[6]

An Apparatus of Identity

And thus arose much of the urgency—and uncertainty—that underlay architects' and clients' opportunities to redefine domestic space during the eighteenth century and thereafter. In many respects the private dwelling—its elevation, plan, functions, furnishings, location, adjacent gardens, and landscape—had potential to be the perfect apparatus for defining and realizing characteristic attributes of a given individual.[7] More than every man's home being his castle, the dwelling might come to be an articulation of the dimensions and pursuits in which he would realize selfhood.

The stakes were remarkable: the promise was the opportunity to fully realize in material terms the newly privatized dimensions of one's own identity. There also were concerns. For example, unless one undertook this architectural effort to "join" oneself (in Locke's terminology) with the material realm in the most effective fashion—unless one made all the best possible choices in designing a house—one's identity might fail to reach its full potential, or perhaps remain fragmented, or worse. A poorly or foolishly designed house might only be damning.

Perhaps even more troubling were those who clearly needed housing, for example, those displaced by clearances, enclosures, or estate reorganizations. Unlike the newly emergent bourgeoisie, these people had neither the social standing nor the financial wherewithal nor the design expertise even to consider matters such as the privatization of identity. Nor was there any doubt during the eighteenth century that these strata of the British population lacked decent housing. Some effort to redress the problem is evident in books of model dwelling designs for farmers and rural laborers, published from the mid-eighteenth century onwards.[8] But the books themselves were a telling product of attitudes toward those whom they proposed to house. Paternalistic in approach, they often consisted of certain designs each prepared to suit a given type of farmer, in a certain region of the country, and as such differed little from Pope's allocation of certain lower links on the Chain of Being to those very same people.

In contrast a growing bourgeois clientele was increasingly able to afford a different class of books,[9] appearing in the last third of the century, elegantly depicting collections of dwelling designs from which to choose, in a variety of sizes and styles.[10] And while most readers would not have been likely to have such a dwelling built immediately or to the full specifications shown, these books did become popular for browsing and as the object of daydreams. Tailored as these books were in cost, size, and subject matter to a bourgeois market, at the very least they became prime instruments in prompting the discourse surrounding identity to focus on single-family dwellings.

One early example is *Familiar Architecture* (1768), a book whose title incorporates a delightful double entendre. The first word signifies both "pertaining to the family" and "closely acquainted, to the point of intimacy," and thus it articulates the notion of domesticity (the dwelling being the terrain of selfhood) in its fullest. The author was Thomas Rawlins, a Norwich stonemason and architect who clearly recognized that his opportunities lay with provincial clients riding the tides of regional prosperity, not London elites. Specifically addressing his work to a bourgeois clientele—gentlemen, tradesmen, parsons, and merchants—he framed the subject of designing a dwelling as a matter of defining and accommodating the specialized pursuits and individual needs of the male householder. In doing so he stressed the individualized nature of human identity:

> Every Man has some favourite Aim in view, be it Study, Business, or Pleasure. That which the Mind is most earnestly bent upon, we most closely pursue: That which is most closely pursued, will doubtless be brought nearest to Perfection: The Study which Nature directs us to, has unquestionably the strongest Prevalence on the Mind: For while we labour, we may be said to sport; and Toils are converted to Delight.[11]

Rawlins was quick to point out that there were many respects in which the dwelling designs that he provided, and the principles on which they were based, would be ideal instruments for advancing those individualized pursuits, accomplishments, and delights. For example, he encouraged flexibility in the use of proportion, the fixity or variability of which had long been a matter of contention among architects. For Rawlins, it was a matter of developing an architectural apparatus capable of

...t's individual characteristics: "the internal Parts [of a building] may be suiting tht the Temper, Genius, and Convenience of the Inhabitant, by enlarging, madcing the Scale."[12]

The notion that architecture should suit an individual's particular pursuits and personality marks a significant departure from the classical principle of "decorum" that had continued to inform the design of most building types well into the eighteenth century. For unlike that convention, according to which the design must suit the owner's position within certain established social hierarchies such as rank, gender, status, wealth, and ancestry, mid-eighteenth-century designers began to construe dwellings as instruments whose design might articulate, even legitimate, the ostensibly autonomous owner's self-chosen dimensions of personal identity. Nevertheless such opportunities were available only to a relatively limited (generally male) clientele: nouveaux riches, upwardly ambitious members of the bourgeoisie, and lesser members of the aristocracy, sufficiently well off to justify their ambitions.

Still left open is the question whether such an identity actually was realized. Certainly it might have been well enough represented through a variety of architectural techniques, such as style, plan, scale, or ornament, as subsequent chapters will explore. Indeed it can be argued that effective representation is tantamount to realization.[13] But representation also takes place in a material context, and a key aspect of appropriating that context to the self—in making that representation have material force—lay in recasting the material environment in a manner that allowed appropriation to individuals. This in turn engaged another challenge: a radical redefinition of property.

Property Makes the Man

Following the Glorious Revolution of 1688, as very large estate owners consolidated their control of the land, opportunities for political reform and economic growth and change in Britain diminished correspondingly. Landowning elites, unlike manufacturers, merchants, financiers, traders, and other members of the nascent bourgeoisie, had little grounds for transforming the way business was done. Neither did the antiquated legal and political apparatus that so poorly served Britain's growing indigenous economy and nascent global trading empire. Nevertheless against such established interests there were growing pressures for reform. These stemmed in part from the opportunities to be derived from the capitalization of agricultural land, turning it into an improvable, exchangeable, profit-taking resource.

Such was the situation that confronted Locke as he worked on completing his *Two Treatises of Government*. One key principle on which he proposed to proceed was to make property (land in particular) contingent on the *individual* for its existence qua property. It also was necessary to define new mechanisms for the outright ownership, parcelization, and disposability of land—in short, its commoditization. These were complex processes. As Locke showed, the principles necessary to sustain these new mechanisms extended into law, finance, political ideology, even epistemology.

But once finished, much of Locke's argument concerning property be~~~~
to Anglo-American jurisprudence, extending intact well into the present. Li~~ntral~~
corollary to Locke's privatization of property, his rationale for the clear differentiat~~
of public and private realms, remained of continuing significance in many dimensions of Anglo-American culture.[14] Both of the shifts that Locke helped theorize, privatization of property and differentiation of private and public realms, were crucial to the course of domestic architecture in the eighteenth century, and they will be taken up in the discussion that follows.

Converting Land to Property

The central role of property in Locke's argument derived from his initial concern with a political question: how to detach the political self from claims of existing political structures (such as monarchy and patriarchy) to perpetual and unassailable authority. His initial arguments were simple enough. He declared that the autonomous individual exists prior to society, just as he had declared that the mind is autonomous in its freedom from innate thoughts. But the political, intellectual, and spatial tabula rasa into which Locke then deployed this autonomous individual, prior to property and society, offered no inherent structure for *belonging*. His solution lay in positing two kinds of relations through which people could articulate attachments to each other and to space: family and property. Neither required prior social institutions. Instead, each was anchored to the individual—especially property, which as Locke construed it was the consequence of applying one's own labor to the land.

Briefly put, Locke argued that one could appropriate a given parcel of land through the application of one's personal labor, thus necessarily turning that parcel into *private* territory, the personal property of that one individual, distinct and detached from all other interests, including the public or collective interest. The right to appropriate land, to convert it to one's personal use, to retain possession of its produce, to bar others from it, and ultimately to alienate or dispose of it—in other words, to convert land to private property—all these rights derived from a single act, the application of one's own labor to the land.

> *As much Land* as a Man Tills, Plants, Improves, Cultivates, and can use the Product of, so much is his *Property*. He by his Labour does, as it were, inclose it from the Common. . . .
>
> God and his Reason commanded him to subdue the Earth, *i.e.* improve it for the benefit of Life, and therein lay out something upon it that was his own, his labour. He that in Obedience to this Command of God, subdued, tilled and sowed any part of it, thereby annexed to it something that was his *Property*, which another had not Title to, nor could without injury take from him. . . .
>
> So that God, by commanding to subdue, gave Authority so far to *appropriate*. And the Condition of Humane Life, which requires Labour and Materials to work on, necessarily introduces *Private Possessions*.[15]

Public Realm, Private Land, Bourgeois Identity, and Selfhood

Notwithstanding Locke's suggestion of biblical authority for his argument, he located rights of possession in the actions of individuals. He provided for collective ownership of some parcels of land in common by the community at large, but such tracts were "left common by Compact, *i.e.* by the Law of the Land," entered into voluntarily by the consent of all.[16] But apart from these specific instances, Locke construed land as a resource *intended* for alienation by private individuals. Individuals could make improvements in the form of labor or, later, in terms of capital investment, but the critical consequence of the Lockean position was this: land no longer was a societal resource, available (at least in theory) to meet the needs and demands of collective interests. Unlike Robert Filmer, Locke's adversary who maintained that public and private realms were one and the same, Locke articulated a material basis for the clear differentiation of the two realms: terrain that the individual personally appropriated necessarily became private territory, distinct and detached from the public realm.

This thoroughly privatized conception of property also implied consequences for the understanding of personal identity, particularly for members of the growing bourgeoisie who could afford to own, trade, and live on holdings of their own. The first consequence lay in opportunities for understanding personal autonomy in much fuller terms, especially with respect to the private domain, the body, and economic activity. Certainly prior to this time select elite individuals had appropriated land to their personal interests, acquiring it generally through purchase or through military, ecclesiastical, or political means, and passing it on through inheritance. But Locke's notion of appropriating territory to the self was radically different in grounding such appropriation ontologically in the application of personal labor, and thus nominally affording the possibility of ownership to a broad range of people. And once land was appropriated by a single person, it became a resource for the exclusive private consumption of the owner. In other words it was a domain appropriated to the self, a notion that would become increasingly important to the articulation of dwelling and landscape as the century progressed.[17]

As a complement to his notion of the political self as anterior to society, Locke also introduced the principle of property as applicable to understanding the human body: "every Man has a *Property* in his own *Person*. This no Body has any Right to but himself."[18] By thus construing individuals as autonomous actors possessed of rights prior to society, and casting this argument in terms of property rights, Locke furthered his objective of showing that ontologically the self is prior to any form of state control. But, no less important, it necessarily made the independence of that self contingent on the ongoing preservation of the institution of property. As Peter Laslett has put it, "property to Locke seems to symbolize rights in their concrete form."[19]

Although Locke's notions of property remained open to doubt in some quarters, crucial elements of his argument became central to writing in many others throughout the rest of the century. A generation before *Wealth of Nations,* David Hume already saw the necessity of Locke's position for Britain's economy. Even though Hume explicitly rejected Locke's notion that "joining" one's labor to anything conferred a right of property, arguing that "We cannot be said to join our labour to any thing but in a figurative sense," he in 1739 more than agreed with Locke in arguing for the necessity of property as an instrument of individual economic freedom and profit:

> property may be defin'd, [as] such a relation betwixt a person and an object as permits him, but forbids any other, the free use and possession of it, without violating the laws of justice and moral equity. If justice, therefore, be a virtue, which has a natural and original influence on the human mind, property may be look'd upon as a particular species of causation; whether we consider the liberty it gives the proprietor to operate as he please upon the object, or the advantages, which he reaps from it.[20]

For Hume as for Locke, the existence and purpose of property were anchored to the individual, and its instrumentality lay in serving to advance such bourgeois interests as the individual's autonomy and profit.[21]

If the first consequence of Locke's position was greater autonomy for the propertied bourgeois individual, the second consequence lay in his explicit recognition that the individual was the agent by which property became privatized. This necessarily implied a far greater degree of agency and autonomy for the individual than if property holding were instead at the pleasure of monarch, state, or church. And although the advance of capitalism was hardly Locke's primary goal,[22] one consequence of his position for modern capitalism was clear: land could be alienated as a private economic resource, that is, private capital. In some respects, privatizing land already was a frequent practice, notably through private Acts of Enclosure. Enumerations of benefits to be reaped by such means could be found in many contemporary treatises.[23] But ultimately what Locke proposed was a radical shift in the basis on which property was understood. Instead of land having to be privatizable at the will of the monarch or Parliament (e.g., through Acts of Enclosure) for the benefit of specific landowners, land would be recognized as a privatized commodity that already existed prior to the state, with ownership established through acts of personal labor or economic transactions, not state dispensation.[24]

A corollary to this argument, necessary to Locke's larger political agenda, was that fundamental aspects of the individual's political identity, such as liberty, equality, or agency, would be constituted in material actions, that is, by applying labor to land. Labor therefore became the initial means by which a person would articulate selfhood, in terms of autonomy, agency, and especially *propriety,* a word for which the *Oxford English Dictionary* gives the meaning, "the fact of being one's own,"[25] and also a word that Locke and his contemporaries commonly interchanged with "property." Thus one's labor served to perpetuate one's selfhood in space and over time by melding with the land to establish *property,* that is, the concrete evidence and vehicle of that selfhood.[26]

Property and Landscape

Locke's articulation of property relations, while hardly affording a populist sense of ownership in the land, ironically conformed to what beneficiaries of enclosure acts had sought all along: sundering from the land any sense of obligation to those who lived, worked, and depended on it. Once privatized, land proclaimed a very different social schema. By replacing a feudal system of mutual obligations (some would say paternalism) and community-based traditions, which had been evidenced in the array of copyholds around a given manor, a unitary enclosed tract signaled not only the private appropriation of resources but also the dissolution and abandonment of community. The consequences for understanding the nature of dwelling on such a tract were profound: the house became the axis of the privatized domain. As Tom Williamson and Liz Bellamy put it, "the medieval house is associated with activity and the community, and the estates of the eighteenth century with the exclusion of the everyday world of the mass of the population."[27] Again, the consequences for dwelling and landscape in general were clear. At least for a bourgeois clientele, architecture was to become a principal vehicle for privatization and cultivation of the self and family.

Property thus became crucial to the categorical differentiation of personal identity from society at large. Replicated again and again from one household to the next, summed across a rapidly expanding bourgeois population, that imperative to categorical differentiation also led to an incipient suburban imperative, as chapter 3 will explore in much greater detail. Here it is only necessary to point out that in gross terms such a categorical differentiation of identity could be accomplished most obviously by establishing one's residence, that is, one's site for establishing one's personal and private identity, in a locale that was both literally and rhetorically *contrapositional* to that most social and urbane of places, the city. The answer was the suburb.[28] In other words, the city came to be identified as the social or public domain against which personal identity necessarily was defined. Thus to articulate one's identity soon came to require a vocabulary of building forms and landscape types that had a dual voice: on the domestic scale, accentuating autonomy and privacy, while on the metropolitan or regional scale, proclaiming an antiurban position and stance.

The consequences of such a process were enormous and far-reaching. In the context of the present discussion, however, just one point needs emphasis: the ultimate privatization of the landscape at large. Thousands of longtime copyholds, many of which would have existed side by side for centuries, simply disappeared. Even whole villages were eradicated from the terrain.[29] But this privatization was not just a matter of changes in land tenure in the legal sense, or in the economic use to which the land was put. For the articulation of any given parcel of land as a capital resource afforded a further possibility: that its nature as capital might eventually be transformed again. On the one hand enclosed land, and land purchased in freehold, could serve as a capital instrument, affording many possibilities for the deployment and exploitation of resources, labor, and equipment. On the other hand any given parcel of land, if divested of all labor and capital improvement, by virtue of its setting in an evolving capitalist economy, could take on a very different aspect. If left in a self-consciously "natural" state, and/or embellished with garden structures and other features that articulated the owner's personal beliefs and affections, as did many an eighteenth-century landscape garden, the land itself would have been converted into not only an aesthetic resource for the exclusive private consumption of the owner but also an important instrument for articulating and extending further dimensions of the owner's identity.

What Locke and his successors laid out in ideological terms also was instrumental to the changing physical and economic landscape of Britain from the late seventeenth century onwards. It likewise became a crucial apparatus for the construction of bourgeois identity, especially with respect to notions of the autonomous and private nature of the self. On land appropriated as one's own, disengaged in many respects from the social, the dwelling now served as an instrument by which the possibility of a singular and autonomous identity could be explored and constructed in material terms—a considerable challenge that has occupied architects and clients over the ensuing three centuries.[30]

Geometrics of Selfhood

The Reassurance of Geometry

The shifts that Locke proposed arose from concerns over the structure of social relations within early modern society. The position against which Locke had argued was that societies were constituted according to an immutable order, such as the doctrine of divine right or the Great Chain of Being, which attributed a preordained and fixed essential identity to each individual. Locke's polemic likewise targeted doctrines extending such systems of universal order to the level of state and family, such as Robert Filmer's contention that the patriarchal organization of state and family was simply part of the nature and order of the universe.

But although the arguments of Locke's adversaries may have been regressive in denying human autonomy and social mobility, they also possessed the advantage of offering considerable certainty about any given person's place, position, and role in society, knowledge that often served well as a basis for personal contentedness (or complacency) and political stability.[31] The rigor and certainty of such intellectual schemata of course were acceptable to those who were thereby privileged, but in many respects the tranquility and reassurance afforded by a stable religious, political, and economic order would have been no less attractive to many others. An alternative approach, offering the possibility of order and stability for all, involved an appeal to the universal order of geometry to define space in a uniform and equitable manner, prior to political or other material considerations.

Abstract Space and the Mind-Body Split

The promise of Lockean epistemology, in tracing the mind to a tabula rasa at birth, was not that it simply allowed for human autonomy, but that it did so through arguments carefully anchored in abstract concepts and analytical rigor—again, all prior to the establishment of social institutions. In his analysis of space, a notion that others ordinarily thoroughly integrate into the discussion of architecture, another social institution, Locke was at his most abstract. Indeed the argument arrived at such an abstract result that it ended up begging such questions as whether abstraction (or reason) must be prior to space, and if abstraction (reason) was a human construct, then whence did space arise. Of perhaps greater import here, Locke also made a point of distinguishing (abstract) space from the material objects and beings that inhabited it. This was a particularly vexing problem because it left unresolved the tension between two disparate concepts that threatened to describe two different worlds: that of space per se, as something abstract, absolute, uniform, infinite, and transcendent; and that of the physical world, as a material, economic, and political resource, which nevertheless necessarily inhabited space somehow.

Still, as Locke wrestled with his larger political project, he found himself pressed to differentiate space—in all its abstract uniformity and geometric clarity—as clearly as possible from any properties of matter. These properties included not only "Body," but even the very notion of an object's dimension, or "Extension":

> the determined *Idea* of simple *Space* distinguishes it plainly, and sufficiently from *Body;* since its Parts are inseparable, immovable, and without resistance to the Motion of Body.
> . . . Extension is an *Idea* belonging to Body only; but *Space* may, as is evident, be considered without it. At least, I think it most intelligible, and the best way to avoid Confusion, if we use the Word *Extension* for an Affection of Matter, or the distance of the Extremities of particular solid Bodies; and *Space* in the more general Signification for distance, with or without solid Matter possessing it.[32]

There were advantages and disadvantages to this formulation of space. On the positive side was the benefit that all matter and beings, no matter how different and distinct they may be from each other, could now be recognized, analyzed, classified, and understood in a common, uniform, and ostensibly mappable universal field. As did Descartes, Locke in his own way laid out a fundamental structure for pursuing Enlightenment disciplines of knowledge and inquiry. More specifically, it was a universal field in which people lived, worked, played, built houses, and did many other things that shaped their personal and social existence. Giving each individual a fresh start in that universal field in which to build his own house—in effect a tabula rasa on which to raise a dwelling for the self—is the challenge that Locke afforded to Enlightenment individuals, responses to which the following chapters will trace.

On the negative side of Locke's proposition, space remained both distinct from and anterior to the actual facts of material existence. Although the difficulties of this position were considerable, it was necessary for purposes of his political and epistemological arguments. Wanting to establish the most rational basis possible for selfhood, Locke as much as possible eliminated any reliance on physical embodiment, which to Locke's skeptical mind would be unreliable as well as almost unnecessary. Instead he eventually reduced identity (and notably the self) to consciousness:

> For since consciousness always accompanies thinking, and 'tis that, that makes every one to be, what he calls *self;* and thereby distinguishes himself from all other thinking things, in this alone consists *personal Identity, i.e.* the sameness of a rational Being.[33]

Locke's penultimate word, "rational," signaled a particularly crucial aspect of his argument, his premise that rationality was requisite to identity. Giving primacy to reason surely satisfied some of Locke's most fundamental political concerns, but only at a price. A key advantage was the possibility that humankind was connected by a consistent, universal, even infallible, common characteristic. The drawback, however, was that this characteristic existed only in the abstract, leading him to arrive at only the most dematerialized notion of identity. This was a problem that may not have troubled Locke, but it entailed a mind-body split that has engaged Western culture ever since.[34]

Spaces Suited to Selfhood

Enlightenment arguments appealing to logic and reason nevertheless had considerable utility for those working to overcome the limitations of entrenched hierarchical political regimes, for they provided means to articulate a universal basis for human consciousness and liberty. In an almost parallel fashion British architects began to explore the possibilities of introducing the certainty of geometric logic into the articulation of human space, particularly as older Baroque modes of hierarchical form and affective expression became correspondingly suspect in the new epistemological framework of the Enlightenment (Figure 1.1).[35]

Nor was this shift in design ideology lost on partisans of the old order such as Alexander Pope, who pointedly cautioned one of the leading proponents of this neoclassical turn to architectural rigor, Lord Burlington, against adherence to totalizing systems of geometric order. For while such rational systems might be grand in their intellectual abstraction, Pope argued that they were hardly congenial to human habitation or other material needs. With thinly veiled reference to the cold geometry of the buildings designed by members of Burlington's circle (Figure 1.2), Pope assailed the human discomfort that ostensibly resulted from adherence to abstract systems of proportion:

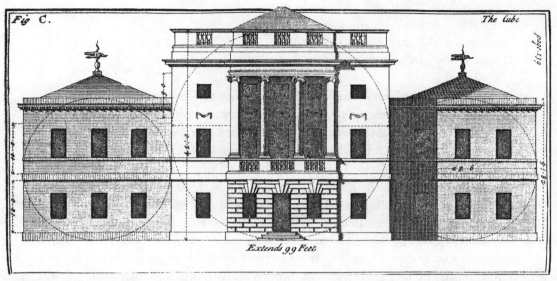

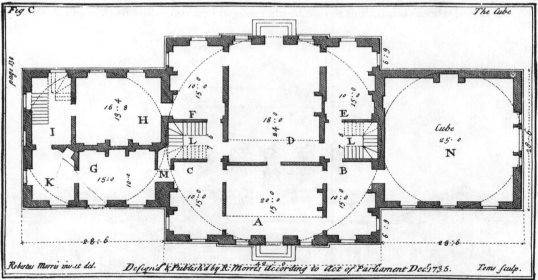

Figure 1.1. Robert Morris, design for a dwelling based on the cube (elevation and plan). Figure C in *Lectures on Architecture*, 1734–36. Morris used this and similar diagrams to demonstrate the incorporation of geometric logic into dwelling space, and to show how it could readily be apprehended by the viewer and user.

Just as they are, yet shall your noble Rules
Fill half the Land with *Imitating Fools,*
Who . . .
Shall call the Winds thro' long Arcades to roar,
Proud to catch cold at a *Venetian* door;
Conscious they act a true *Palladian* part,
And if they starve, they starve by Rules of Art.[36]

Significantly the "rules of art" that Pope condemned—rules of geometry, proportion, symmetry—were the very rules that had become necessary to manage autonomous existence in Enlightenment Cartesian-Lockean space. Just as three orthogonal axes defined the very dimensions in which Cartesian consciousness obtained, so Locke's definition of a person's location in space as a matter of geometrical relations to arbitrary points radically shifted the basis of knowledge on which one could determine who and where one was. The abstract basis of this new "kind of free-floating vision of the self" (as Jean Bethke Elshtain put it)[37] may have been more appealing than divine right or the Great Chain of Being because it was epistemologically simpler and cleaner, more democratic, and above all more amenable to principles of logic and reason. But it also had the capacity to disperse humans into separate private spheres (or cubes) whose connections to one another were at best recondite. As the eighteenth

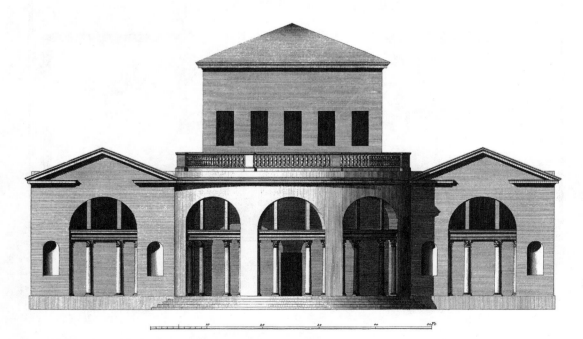

Figure 1.2. Richard Boyle, 3rd Earl of Burlington, The Assembly Rooms (elevation), York, 1731–32. Plate 79 in volume 1 of *Vitruvius Britannicus,* by John Woolfe and James Gandon, 1767–71. Alexander Pope disparaged this sort of cold geometric design.

century progressed the task of articulating those new private spheres in terms of the individual's newfound autonomy became a central challenge for both architects and clients while engaging the process of designing dwellings and other sorts of buildings. Moreover, this task became increasingly critical since architecture, as a medium of bricks and mortar in fixed locations, could very well replenish in the material realm some of the certainty that was either lost in the departure of old political and social hierarchies or wanting in the arrival of new epistemologies.

Uniformity and Differentiation

But within the domestic realm a further problem of differentiation remained. Although the liberatory aspects of Locke's arguments with respect to individual rights and freedoms have often been celebrated, in his ontology of identity the emphasis on uniformity among individuals actually outweighed the emphasis on differentiation. Alexander Pope, whose notion of the Great Chain of Being certainly was inimical to Locke's thinking, had provided for a wealth of difference in the *Essay on Man* by tying each person to a specific link on that chain, with each person in a location inherently higher or lower than any other link. Locke, by rendering his argument on an abstract plane, provided for equality among human beings, a notion of no small import in the decline of absolutism and the rise of democracy and capitalism, but leaving little room for the articulation of human difference.

The paradoxical nature of this concern may be seen when Locke's arguments about the abstract nature of space and the rational nature of consciousness were addressed in the material domain of architecture, particularly the private dwelling. Put briefly, the question concerns the terms in which identity may be lived and represented. On the one hand, the appeal to the abstract suggests a form of dwelling that affords self-realization on an ideal (abstract) plane, especially through such means as rarefied style, geometric proportion, and the representation of harmony (Figure 1.3).[38] Here the objective is a kind of ideal uniformity with the universal, to be defined and achieved in terms of principles of logic and abstraction.

But such appeals to the uniform or universal necessarily precluded articulation of the kinds of distinction among individuals that were the hallmarks of emerging bourgeois society in the early eighteenth century, and have remained so ever since. In many respects bourgeois society always has concerned itself with the distinction and differentiation of its members in material terms, not only in professional, artistic, and entrepreneurial pursuits, but also through the various material practices and representational techniques by which people secure relative advantages. Yet in those very respects bourgeois society exceeded the capacity of Lockean epistemology—the epistemology that legitimated its members' political and economic interests—to render its members as distinct and different individuals. At that point the challenge that Locke had set for architects and their clients no longer became one that they could answer in terms consistent with the questioner's own position—nor perhaps with the question itself.

Recasting Privacy

A Place to Call One's Own

Although the Enlightenment gravely sold short the problem of human difference, Locke as well as many other writers, artists, architects, and their clients remained keen to explore dimensions of individuality in their work.[39] One of the most successful ways this was explored in architecture was by developing ways to articulate specific aspects, or portions, of the dwelling as *private*.

In some senses the modern notion of privacy already was well established by the period of the Restoration, not only in the sense of a domain restricted from general or public access but also in the sense of a state of personal solitude and the locales where that could be sustained. To some extent this could be achieved through the dedication of specific places to solitude and study, including so-called cabinets adjacent to bedchambers and "secret houses" on the grounds of large estates.[40] Still, as the

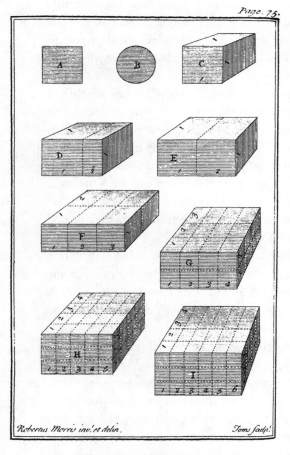

Page. 75.

ARCHITECTURE. 91

As I confider the Affinity between *Architecture* and *Mufick*, fo I have produc'd thofe Proportions from the fame Rules: In *Mufick* are only feven diftinct Notes, in *Architecture* likewife are only feven diftinct Proportions, which produce all the different Buildings in the Univerfe, *viz.*

THE Cube,——the Cube and half,—— the Double Cube,—— the Duplicates of 3, 2, and 1,——of 4, 3, and 2,——of 5, 4, and 3,——— and of 6, 4, and 3, produce all the Harmonick Proportions of Rooms.

LET me, for Example, propofe a Building whofe principal Floor is 12 Foot high, how to proportion thofe Rooms which are to be in the internal Part by the preceding Rules.

If

Robertus Morris inv.' et delin.   *Toms fculp.*

Figure 1.3. Robert Morris, diagrams of the harmonic proportions of rooms, demonstrating connections between architecture and music. Plate facing page 75 and text on page 91 in *Lectures on Architecture*, 1734–36.

terms suggest, these were well-demarcated spaces that were both small and remote, hardly suited to the expression of individuality and the individual in terms appropriate to emerging bourgeois culture.

But if Locke's challenge regarding individual identity had put architects and builders on the spot, and if cabinets and secret houses were no answer, Locke's discussion of property did offer a solution. For just as he argued on economic and political grounds for the privatization of property through appropriation of terrain to the self, architects soon recognized that dwellings could be appropriated as instruments for the cultivation of bourgeois identity. One consequence of Locke's argument had been to articulate individuals as political and economic agents apart from society at large. Soon the dwelling would become a domain in which individuals could be further differentiated from that public world of politics and commerce and brought to a more refined state of personhood. Defining distinct terms in which to articulate the *privacy* that would sustain that personhood quickly became a central challenge of domestic architecture.

Robert Castell was among the first to examine the subject of architectural privacy, in his lengthy and detailed examination of the Laurentian villa built by the Roman essayist Pliny the Younger (ca. 61–ca. 113 CE) near Rome, largely through an analysis of Pliny's letters, published in 1728 as *The Villas of the Ancients Illustrated* (Figure 1.4). This was hardly a manual for the emerging bourgeoisie: the oversize publication, measuring twenty by fourteen inches and commissioned by Lord Burlington, was intended for the likes of Burlington's circle, and the villa itself was well beyond the scale that any merchant would imagine undertaking. Nevertheless the implications of Castell's analysis did extend to a broad clientele, in particular those who soon would be building so-called villas on a far smaller scale than Pliny's grand opus throughout Britain and America for the next century and beyond.[41]

Focusing on criteria that were at least as much of his own time as of Pliny's, Castell examined in particular the qualities of solitude and independence that the villa was expected to sustain. He noted, for example, that despite the great size of Pliny's estate, this was neither "a magnificent Villa" nor "a Seat which he liv'd in at all Seasons," but "a Place rather proper for Study, and to retire to with a few select Friends"—in other words, a locale for intimate and isolated pursuits. Castell made it clear that this was a retreat "from the Business of the City," a site clearly oppositional to the realm of trade and public affairs.

Within the villa itself Castell also differentiated between public and private spaces. The Cryptoporticum between the Atrium and Cavaedium, for example, "was not esteem'd for private Use," nor was the Cavaedium itself. Among "Rooms for more private Use," on the other hand, there was a "Room for Day Sleep." Here Castell suggested that Pliny had specifically selected decor that conduced to more private, solitary pursuits. Pliny had chosen "the most simple and natural Manner of designing to adorn this Room; preferring here that Manner which only pleased the Eye by Colours, to that which moved the Passions, as History Pieces, which perhaps he thought more proper for larger and more publick Rooms."[42] Castell's concern with privacy, therefore, not only incorporated an inclination to characterize spaces as either private or public but also embraced more than the simple notion that privacy meant excluding the public. It also incorporated understandings of retreat, study, solitude, and decor that might offer release from the social and political dimensions of consciousness. As Castell's analysis may suggest, it was not difficult for his contemporaries in literature, painting, philosophy, and other endeavors to make comparable contributions to the notion that privacy per se was necessary to and constitutive of identity. Recent scholarly inquiries have focused on many dimensions in which this notion was developed in the eighteenth century, notably with respect to privacy as an aspect of family, domesticity, and especially intimacy. Numerous artistic and literary representations of the time also explored how relations of an intimate nature between individuals could be fashioned architecturally, especially through intimate and extensive knowledge of sequestered spaces such as dressing rooms and bedchambers.[43]

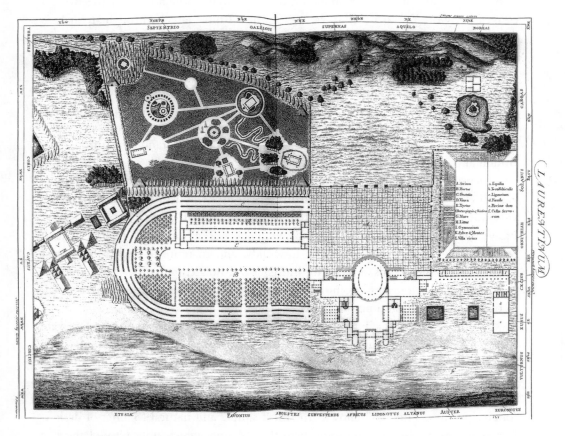

Figure 1.4. Robert Castell, reconstruction of Pliny's villa and estate at Laurentinum (plan). From *The Villas of the Ancients Illustrated*, 1728.

In a parallel fashion, as Jürgen Habermas has shown, as the individual and family distanced themselves spatially from work, commerce, and politics, the newly isolated domestic realm afforded perfect conditions for articulating a notion of private autonomy that, even though it was hardly genuine, "provided the bourgeois family with its consciousness of itself."[44] Even more crucial, perhaps, was the manner in which the house, now understood as a realm distinct from work and public, was instrumental in making the axis of domestic privacy a distinguishing feature of modern bourgeois society. As Karl Marx suggested more than a century later, well after the problem had become pandemic, the issue was not simply the performance of distinct life activities in separate places. It was, rather, the division of human subjectivity. "The worker," Marx wrote, "feels at home [zu Hause] when he is not working, and when he is working he does not feel at home."[45] The dwelling, by rendering in material form the terms of that division of subjectivity, became a principal instrument and symbol of modern alienation.

Active Privacy

Nevertheless, to return to Castell, there is one additional respect in which his discussion clearly set the tone for eighteenth-century domesticity, by encouraging an active privacy. In contrast to seventeenth-century estates, such as that described in Andrew Marvell's early-1650s poem "Upon Appleton House," which largely provided the resident a static catalog of already established characteristics and pursuits,[46] the eighteenth-century villa and its landscape often became a site of directed activity, offering the opportunity for articulating those characteristics and pursuits dynamically. As Stephen Switzer wrote in 1733, gentlemen who from time to time might retire to a rural location ought to equate leisure with productive interests, particularly through active engagement with the land. He specifically urged that they should "at all leisure times apply themselves to Husbandry and Planting."[47]

Castell offered a richer catalog of private but active pursuits. Even though the villas that Pliny owned were vast structures, particularly by eighteenth-century standards, Castell emphasized a range of functions and activities there that were predominantly personal, and frequently private, while seldom alluding to social functions or affairs that might take place. Thus we read that the dwelling was dedicated to retreat, exercise, reading, studying, eating, sleeping, bathing—a bodily activity much subdivided, into steaming, perspiring, washing, anointing—enjoying the pleasure garden, hunting, walking, and other forms of exercise. Clearly it was a site devoted to the culture of the individual body and mind, and Castell's account emphasized the dedication of the structure and its site to the private needs of a single man, not a large household or even a simple nuclear family. In proper neoclassical fashion Castell characterized his interest in history as being motivated by a desire to find rules. But his text made it apparent that his search for rules and his ensuing literary archaeology were marshaled in service of other ends: discovering principles for designing a country dwelling that instead of serving as an ancestral seat (a predominantly static articulation of status, wealth, and other such characteristics) could dispose the retired site to categorically different purposes: the pursuit of activities constitutive of the private individual.

Unlike most contemporary architectural treatises, which primarily concentrated on such matters as the orders, moldings, and designs for actual dwellings, Castell's book was an analysis of historical texts, augmented with plates depicting reconstructions of historical examples. Yet the import of his inquiry was far more than a matter of augmenting the historical record. In addressing the uses of particular rooms and spaces as much as their shape and decoration, Castell spearheaded a threefold change in thinking about domestic architecture. First, in focusing as much on practical matters of living as on design, Castell was shifting the terms in which people thought about domestic architecture away from long-standing principles of decorum, which prescribed a certain fit between the design of a residence and the status of its resident, toward notions of an instrument for sustaining specific personal activities and dimensions of consciousness. Second, in concentrating narrowly on the dwelling as the domain of a single individual, Castell pointedly stressed the status of the dwelling as an apparatus particular to the self. And third, in proceeding room by room through Pliny's account, concentrating on the activities occurring in those rooms, Castell stressed the degree to which particular activities might be differentiated according to specific rooms within the house, and the degree to which rooms might intentionally be designed to sustain very specific functions. In the second and third respects particularly, Castell's approach, like that of many of his contemporaries, was a radical shift from seventeenth-century practices, advancing a new emphasis on the dwelling as a domain of private pursuits.

Gentleman and Family

So far this chapter has focused on newly emerging understandings of identity, property, space, and privacy and on the implicit challenges these posed for the architectural articulation of modern bourgeois identity in the early eighteenth century. Of equal import are some of the shifting terms in which individuals related to each other as part of the evolving bourgeois social fabric of the eighteenth century. To some extent a history of these shifts would necessitate an entire history of the bourgeoisie. But with respect to dwelling design, two specific categorizations of people within the bourgeoisie require closest attention, the gentleman and the patriarchal family.

Gentleman: From Position to Performance

In a most obvious respect, the term *gentleman* is gendered, bespeaking the host of conventions according to which English society has been articulated according to gender categories throughout the history of the word's usage. Equally implicit in the term itself would have been knowledge of certain behavioral conventions. In the late seventeenth and early eighteenth centuries a "gentle" man was one who had learned to perform with both refinement and restraint. But these were not meanings according to which the word generally was used prior to that time. Rather, until then *gentleman* had been primarily a distinction of rank. Among the earliest and most basic connotations of the term was the notion of a person who was entitled to bear arms but did not rank among the nobility. Still, as early as the beginning of the seventeenth century, Thomas Dekker had begun to suggest that aspects of character that might also serve to define a gentleman: "A soft, meeke, patient, humble, tranquill spirit: The first true Gentleman that ever breath'd." And in 1636 Edward Dacres anticipated the eighteenth-century notion of bourgeois retirement—that is, being landed, resplendent in leisure, and unconcerned with labor—by defining the term *gentleman* in terms of wealth and leisure: "Those are call'd Gentlemen, that live in idlenesse yet deliciously of the profits of their estates, without having any care to cultivate their lands." Still, it remained for essayist Richard Steele in 1710 to make it explicit that the place of "gentleman" was attained through one's personal *performance*. "The Appellation of Gentleman is never to be affixed to a Man's Circumstances, but to his Behaviour in them," he wrote, implying a more flexible and fluid notion of bourgeois identity rather than one established by virtue of an inheritable or otherwise fixed (hierarchical) *position*.[48]

Edward Cave marked a defining moment in the rise of the bourgeois gentry when in February 1731, using the pseudonym "Sylvanus Urban," he issued the first number of the *Gentleman's Magazine; or, Trader's Monthly Intelligencer. . . . By Sylvanus Urban of Aldermanbury, Gent.* This periodical was soon to be one of the most prominent among many journals of politics, business, literature, and taste that flourished in the first half of the eighteenth century. Cave shrewdly pegged his audience as the emerging mercantile elite ("traders"), men with aspirations to a social status ("Gentleman") that had some cachet.[49] Apart from tellingly styling himself "Gent." on the title page, he also used a suggestive pseudonym, "Sylvanus Urban," suggesting that, perhaps through his work, he represented the union of two disparate realms, country (the sylvan, the pastoral) and city (the urban and urbane). But while this representation certainly bespoke a rising trend in British taste,[50] it nevertheless also betrayed a certain anxiety over an already apparent fragmentation of modern experience.

Writing only two years before the *Gentleman's Magazine* appeared, Daniel Defoe made it apparent that the question of how to define a "gentleman" already had become a matter of some contention, tellingly adumbrating the modern "nature versus nurture" debate concerning human ability and personality. In particular, he noted an ongoing controversy over whether birth or breeding alone could suffice to qualify one as a gentleman, or whether both might be required. On the one hand, he stated, ancestry and antiquity counted:

> the word gentlemen is understood to signify men of antient houses, dignify'd with hereditary titles and family honours, old mansion houses, . . . innumerable ancestors, names deriv'd from the lands and estates they possess, parks and forrests, . . . and such like marks of the antiquity of the race.

On the other hand, it was clear that those who came into new wealth could, with proper education and other efforts at self-improvement, attain genuine gentlemanly status within as little as one generation. Defoe declared that mere accumulation of wealth, as many had recently done in trade, war, navigation, finance, and the law, was insufficient grounds on which to claim that status de facto: "we can not call them gentlemen." Nevertheless he did not oppose attempts by such individuals to become gentlemen through efforts at education and self-improvement. One who succeeded would be, in Defoe's words, a "compleat gentleman," a man whose "conjugal life is all harmony and musick"; a man who was the best father, the best master, the best magistrate, and the best neighbor; a man who was a blessing to his family, his country, and himself; and one who was kind to all, was beloved by all, and had the prayers of all. The dimensions of a gentleman's existence, therefore, were understood not to derive simply from the accumulation of wealth or the inheritance of status. Rather, they were seen to engage the full range of social relations, as husband, father, master (of the household and its staff), judge, statesman, and benefactor.[51]

Not surprisingly, Defoe's treatise betokened an elaborate recasting of the terms in which the notion of "gentleman" was construed. Clearly Defoe did not want to devalue the attributes of status and prestige that accrued to a gentleman of elevated ancestry or landed wealth. But his concession that ancestry and land were not necessary is crucial, for therein lay the thrust of his polemic. Instead of accepting fixed genetic attributes as criteria for being a gentleman, Defoe recast those criteria flexibly as pedagogical and performative, to be understood in terms of a certain combination of roles, actions, and attitudes that a gentleman was expected to learn and then sustain. Defoe's understanding of gentlemanly status as something to be learned lay fully in accord with Lockean epistemology—the human as born with no innate ideas but rather capable of acquiring understanding of whatever sort through rational instruction. But given this accord, perhaps the most striking aspect of the set of roles that Defoe specified was that he kept them consistent with hierarchy and patriarchy. In each case, he articulated a role for the gentleman that was not only elevated but also tied by a reciprocal relation of obligation and authority to those in lesser roles and lower ranks.

Significantly Defoe noted that building a substantial dwelling had become a familiar means, especially in Essex and Kent, for would-be gentlemen such as "merchants and trades-men" to suggest the historical longevity of their family "houses" and to elevate their status. Defoe cited an estimate that less than a fifth of the "antient families" in Kent and Essex remained, while almost two hundred houses of new-monied tradesmen, merchants, soldiers, and seamen had sprung up recently. Among these were six "capital houses of the first rate," at least two of which were owned by members of the Palladian circle of Lord Burlington: Sir Richard Childs (for whom Colen Campbell designed Wanstead House) and Sir Robert Furnesse. The architectural merits of these houses notwithstanding, Defoe lamented the change from the old standard to the new:

what will be the consequence of all this but that the next age will acknowledge these all to be gentlemen, without enquiring into the length of time when their houses and lines began; nay, the present age does reciev them as such even allready.[52]

A notable aspect of his lament was a recognition of the utility of architecture in articulating status. He implicitly acknowledged the ability of architecture, through such means as style, scale, and grandeur, to represent everything from the antiquity of one's lineage to the qualities of one's character—as well as the increasing frequency, and widespread acceptance, of such claims to status on the part of the bourgeoisie.

Defining a Family Sphere

Simultaneously with shifts in Enlightenment epistemology and incipient undermining of existing social hierarchies of the sorts described above, entrenched patriarchal structures likewise came under pressure to change, both in the household realm and in the wider political arena. At the crux of the problem was a conflict between the ideological imperative toward individual freedom, and the need for a stable social framework in which to accumulate and enjoy benefits of this freedom. Put differently, the notion of personal autonomy was essential to Enlightenment goals of social, scientific, and economic progress. Yet it was still necessary to maintain a basis of political authority and order so that those goals could be achieved, on scales ranging from family to state. And here, at least for Locke and his contemporaries, patriarchy still remained the fundamental principle of political organization.

Locke's reliance on patriarchy as the anchor of the social order was not entirely regressive, since it hinged on a novel inversion of precedence: the basis of all authority lay not in the state, he argued, but in the family. Patriarchy, according to Locke, was a form of human relations that actually preceded society, and therefore remained basic to any form of human organization. And though he insisted on the autonomy of human consciousness, Locke simultaneously saw the clear danger of anarchy attendant on the rise of any corresponding *political* autonomy. Thus it was crucial for him to establish a workable basis for state authority, which he did by anchoring the origins of political power in "natural" relations that were antecedent to society, specifically domestic patriarchy. As he stated it, the roots of political authority lay in "the Power that every Husband hath to order the things of private Concernment in his Family."[53]

It had been convenient for Locke's predecessors, such as Robert Filmer and Richard Brathwait, to apply consistently a single trope—patriarchy—as the model for organization of all social relations, ranging from the family to the state to the biblical origins of the human race.[54] But Locke was able to reject this notion by establishing the patriarchal family as prior to society, and arguing instead in *Two Treatises of Government* for a contractual form of government.[55] Arguing against patriarchy as the basis of political relations, Locke also found it necessary to redefine its role within the family. He contended that it should be recast in terms befitting the scale of the family, specifically in terms of *paternal* and especially *parental* authority[56]—to be shared between both parents (albeit unequally) and exercised only temporarily, during the child's minority.

This in turn afforded a new formulation of the relation between family and society. Instead of endorsing the prevalent notion that biblical, civil, and family relations all were structured according to a common patriarchal paradigm, thereby granting that each would sustain and legitimate the other, Locke offered distinctly different paradigms: civil society organized according to a consensual but durable contract, and family organized according to an involuntary but temporary relation of duty and obligation. Two consequences were implicit. First, family was severed from its presumptive integration within a fixed social and religious hierarchy. And second, family now was understood to function according to principles and purposes quite different from those of civil society.

In both respects, there would be significant consequences for the spatialization of families. Instead of the implicit understanding that the household was the locale in which one's civil identity was grounded and produced,[57] the household would be distanced, literally as well as figuratively, from the state or commonwealth. Likewise the householders' participation in civil society now would be understood as a matter of consensual association rather than preordained fixed relations. As a result the stage was set for the evolution of the modern, bourgeois dwelling: a type that could, through a host of architectural and spatial techniques, begin to articulate such a distinction between itself and the larger society. The desideratum that emerged was a dwelling that physically, functionally, and rhetorically could separate itself as a discrete entity from the larger social and civic fabric, providing a site for the purposeful establishment of relations that were not only distinct and different from those of civic life but perhaps even an implicit challenge to civil patriarchy.[58] In other words, by virtue of the opposition he established between family and society, Locke helped to precipitate a reconceptualization of the place and purpose of the dwelling. In addition to (or instead of) its role in locating individuals and families *within* society, it might also define and articulate positions and relations *apart* from society.

Autonomy and Patriarchy

As Jean Bethke Elshtain has shown, in the patriarchal world of Robert Filmer that Locke sought to change, there were no such things as distinctly private or public spheres: family and state were part of the same political continuum.[59] But by disengaging both state and family from civil patriarchy, and by doing so in terms that differentiated each from the other, Locke destined each to be a site for a very distinct type of activity. Locke also argued that each realm operated according to distinct, different rules. And a notable consequence of this was that political liberty and equality, which he championed in the public realm, were denied in the domestic realm. For while the public realm, according to Locke, would operate according to processes of contract and consent, neither of these applied within the family. Instead the family would be governed according to rules that were grounded less in rational principle and more in religious, historical, and biological tradition:

> God, in this Text, gives not, that I see, any Authority to *Adam* over *Eve,* or to Men over their Wives, but only foretels what should be the Womans Lot, how by his Providence he would order it so, that she should be subject to her husband, as we see that generally the Laws of Mankind and customs of Nations have ordered it so; and there is, I grant, a Foundation in Nature for it.[60]

This primacy of very different rules for family clearly informed the organization of many individual households. The words of a colonial American, yet still very English, settler offer clear testimony of this patriarchal viewpoint. Like numerous contemporaries throughout the colonies as well as Britain itself, William Byrd II, entrepreneurial proprietor of an extensive estate at Westover in Virginia, indulged in the ideal of a politically autonomous, paternalistically ruled, as well as pastorally bountiful, domestic realm. Echoing Locke's strictures on domestic patriarchy as late as 1726, he cast this conspicuously overblown description of his provincial household in biblical terms:

> Like one of the Patriarchs, I have my Flocks and my Herds, my Bond-men and Bond-women and every sort of trade amongst my own servants, so that I live in a kind of independence on everyone but Providence.[61]

Arguments such as Locke's may have served to initiate debates over autonomy and patriarchy, or only exacerbate them. Perhaps most directly affected were the emergent bourgeoisie, who were constantly engaged in negotiating a role for the private self not only in relation to both the domestic and the public realms but also in a constantly shifting balance with entrenched systems of family, local, and state authority. And as the next chapters explore in detail, efforts to engage these tensions have been at the forefront of progressive (and sometimes regressive) designs for dwellings and their surrounding landscapes throughout the ensuing centuries.

2. Villa Suburbana, Terra Suburbana

The country model, and that of a suburb villa, are different. The former partakes of the nature of a court, as a lord of a manor doth of regality, and should, like the court, have great rooms to contein numbers, with fires suitable and other conveniences, according to his condition. A villa, is quasy a lodge, for the sake of a garden, to retire to injoy and sleep, without pretence of enterteinment of many persons; and yet in this age, the humour takes after that, and not the other.

—Roger North, *Of Building,* 1698

This chapter and the next explore the invention, beginning about the turn of the eighteenth century, of a new type of dwelling and a new type of locale whose features began to address many of the concerns that the emergent bourgeoisie faced over selfhood and identity. The new dwelling type, the bourgeois compact villa, drew from sources as distant as ancient Rome and the Italian Renaissance but shifted to a far more compact size and scale. The historical sources of this type, its formal and stylistic characteristics, and its ideological redefinition in the eighteenth century as a site of bourgeois selfhood, are discussed in this chapter. Chapter 3 examines specific functions and activities associated with bourgeois selfhood, and the interior spatial apparatus that evolved to sustain them. To complete the broader story of the historical context in which the compact villa evolved, this chapter concludes with a brief history of the genesis of a new kind of locale, the modern suburb, focusing especially on the Thames Valley west of London in the period after 1700.[1]

A Site for Self-Creation

Across the span of human building, dwellings always have served as anchors and instruments for the production of human identity, not only in personal terms but also in relation to family and society. As modern anthropologists are keenly aware, the terms in which one's daily routines and relations are formed, and in which one's larger relations with the culture and universe are established, become the terms of one's identity. These also are terms that the built spaces of dwellings serve to establish.[2] And beginning in the Italian Renaissance, then coming to fruition in England during the eighteenth century, architects explored in theoretical and practical dimensions just this problem: what role did dwellings play in shaping human consciousness and identity.

On a material level, the capacity of dwellings to abet ordinary states of physical well-being was self-evident to the prominent Italian architectural theorist Leon Battista Alberti, who wrote in the late fifteenth century that private houses in general "conduce to the repose, tranquillity or delicacy of life." Focusing on villas as a specific type, however—a type in which there would be heightened interest in eighteenth-century England—Alberti noted that they had more specific pointed purposes. These "pleasure-houses just without the town," he wrote, were intended for the use of businessmen or politicians who needed to be near town to conduct their affairs but who also, as "master of a family," wanted a nearby retreat that was "not wholly destitute of pure air." At such a conveniently sited retreat, Alberti indicated, the owner would be "at liberty to do just what he pleases." And although Alberti noted a host of private or semiprivate activities that the Roman poet Martial had described in ancient Roman villas, including eating, drinking, singing, playing, bathing, sleeping, eating again, reading, and luxuriating in the "train" of the Muses, Alberti devoted a considerable portion of his discussion instead to two larger concerns: how the exterior of the villa would present itself to visitors on arrival, and the sequence of spaces that visitors would encounter once inside. For Alberti, then, the villa was a family space, a social space, and a site of recreation, but not yet an especially private space.[3]

Andrea Palladio introduced a broader and more complex notion of a villa. In his *Four Books of Architecture* (1570), the second book of which was devoted to domestic architecture, he discussed villa establishments in terms of a tripartite purpose: agricultural production and improvement, affording exercise on foot and horseback to maintain the owner's health, and sustaining the owner in private, inwardly directed activities. With respect to this third function, the villa was a site "where the mind, fatigued by the agitations of the city, will be greatly restor'd and comforted, and be able quietly to attend the studies of letters, and contemplation," and where, unlike in "city houses," one "could easily attain to as much happiness as can be attained here below."[4]

Palladio's endorsement of such self-focused activities as psychological regeneration, study, and contemplation would have been eagerly appreciated by an eighteenth-century English audience. Still, for Palladio the villa in its sixteenth-century Italian context remained very much an economic enterprise first, a place of retreat and recreation second.[5] Eighteenth-century England eventually reversed these priorities, patently isolating the villa from the intercourse of economic life. This was possible due to the nascent bourgeoisie's financial, mercantile, and professional sources of income, which allowed them to live well away from their places of work. The effect was to afford opportunities for a more intensified pursuit of selfhood than anticipated in previous centuries. And among the leading early eighteenth-century intellectual foundations for such a rarefied focus on private self-realization were the neoplatonically inspired writings of landscape designer Stephen Switzer and architect Robert Morris.

In the third volume of his major treatise on landscape, *Ichnographia Rustica* (1718), Switzer argued in effect that country seats or villas became engaged in a dynamic binary relation with the owner. On the one hand, to build such a dwelling was an act of human "creation" that Switzer explicitly compared to the biblical act by which God created the earth. And on the other hand, once created, it served to sustain a state of "Harmony" in the dweller's mind.

> [Among] all the Works of the Creation, . . . a Country Seat distributed with Judgment, may well be accounted one of the greatest; in this every Person makes to himself a Kind of a new Creation, and when a Seat or *Villa,* is decently and frugally distributed, what a Harmony does it create in a virtuous Mind, besides, the many grosser Uses of it to the Body.[6]

It might be tempting to read this statement as having claimed for the individual the autonomy and individuality that an act of "Creation" implied, particularly in an intellectual climate recently invigorated by Locke's understanding of the mind as a tabula rasa at birth, ready to engage in the process of self-formation. But as part of that understanding Locke had stipulated the rule of logic, reason, and abstract systems of order, in disregard of which the individual proceeded at his or her peril. Thus for Locke self-formation was very much a process of harmonizing sense data acquired through life experience with overarching systems of intellectual order. Affording an opportunity to skirt certain long-entrenched systems of knowledge, Locke's epistemology did so by establishing a fundamentally autonomous process of knowing. Nevertheless any such effort could be valid only insofar as the individual organized that knowledge in concert with universal principles of logic and reason. Thus for Switzer, as for Locke, the ostensible autonomy of the act of "Creation," whether of self or knowledge, was belied by a necessary compliance with an overall legitimating system of order. Although Switzer only alluded to such a system in the above passage, it was still readily apparent in his reference to the "Harmony" afforded by a "decently and frugally distributed" dwelling—a reference, as will be seen, to the power of the plan in general, and a systematically proportioned plan in particular, to enhance substantially the mentality of the resident.[7]

It is necessary to differentiate Switzer from Locke on one important point: rather than remaining narrowly focused on questions of epistemology, that is, knowing, Switzer's discussion extended to an actual act of creation, and specifically to creation of an instrument with the capacity to shape the user's consciousness. This bears comparison to the third Earl of Shaftesbury's influential neoplatonic treatise *Characteristicks of Men, Manners, Opinions, Times* (1711), which six years earlier described a comparable dynamic process through which a dweller-to-be could transform a site, which then generated a reciprocal transformation in the consciousness of the dweller. A crucial point in Shaftesbury's discussion of such a process was that artistic design had the power to raise the imagination completely into a higher realm of consciousness: "There is a Power in Numbers, Harmony, and Proportion, and Beauty of every kind, which naturally captivates the Heart, and raises the Imagination to an Opinion or Conceit of something *majestick* or *divine.*" In the case of landscape, design should be able to lead the viewer to the site's inner, central quality, its "Sole Animating and Inspiring Power," which when perceived, would elevate the imagination to the realm of "Beauty and Virtue."[8] What Shaftesbury thus discussed in terms of landscape alone, Switzer, a landscape designer, sought to apply as well to the design of a dwelling. For him, dwelling and landscape both could be instruments that, through design, would conduce to that higher, ideal consciousness.

Switzer's own words notwithstanding, the kind of dwelling that he proposed was hardly one that "every Person" could hope to realize. Clearly he was talking only to an audience capable of affording the site, materials, and labor necessary to erect a country house or villa. But more than having land and wealth, his intended clients also had to be able to afford, and understand, leisure as a necessary component of their lives. Leisure both as a state of mind and as a surplus of time was practically a requisite for experiencing the dwelling or landscape as conducive to such a nonproductive, uneconomic state as "Harmony." Likewise the process of "Creation" required a concerted orchestration of the mind, senses, labor, and material surroundings toward the experience of this very singular, solitary goal. And yet despite the very individualistic nature of such a pursuit, Switzer argued that in the end personal gratification in such a manner would have a supreme benefit to society (or, as he termed it here, "Posterity"). In a retired country seat, he wrote,

> there is a happy Composition of every thing, that can possibly make Man's Life and Labour agreeable, and give an Innocent Gratification to all his Senses: The general View of his well dispos'd Seat gratifies the Sight, the numberless feather'd Choiristers that perching amongst his Woods, warble out their natural and melodious Strains the Hearing, the refreshing Breezes of Air the Feeling, and the Palate is gratify'd by an almost an [*sic*] innumerable Number of pleasant and nectareal Juices, and Fruits, and the Smell of Flowers, cheers the Organs of the Head in a wonderful manner. How sweetly glides the Blood thro' its several Offices, how exhilarated the Mind, and with what Flagrance and Joy (as our great Poet expresses it) does the Heart and the whole Frame of Nature overflow.
>
> [In this way] . . . the Business of Gardening, Planting, and Husbandry, affords both the Mind and Body all that is good or agreeable to our Natures, and gives us the Opportunity of being more beneficial to Posterity, than any other Study or Employ whatsoever.[9]

Switzer's discussion still focused as much on the realization of pleasure as on the attainment of harmony. In the eyes of many, however, the dedicated pursuit of harmony alone was by far the superior pursuit. The most eloquent exponent of dwellings as instruments of this kind for solitary "retirement," emphasizing retirement not simply as a state of withdrawal from society but as active pursuit of a "higher" state of mind, was another disciple of Shaftesbury, Robert Morris.[10] One of the earliest architects to publish designs for dwellings on a small scale appropriate for bourgeois clients,[11] Morris also addressed the nature of domestic architecture from a theoretical perspective in his *Lectures on Architecture* (1734–36). Among his leading concerns in the design of a dwelling he laid out three interdependent desiderata: a mode of retirement that would be both solitary and secluded, the private dwelling as a site for retirement, and the pursuit of an almost epiphanic state of personal intellectual enlightenment or "harmony" as the outcome of retirement.

The basis of that state of harmony, for Morris as for Switzer, was retirement, a condition of self-conscious withdrawal from society that became central to much eighteenth-century discussion of the ideology of the self.[12] Morris, who placed considerable emphasis on retirement, distinguished explicitly in his *Lectures* between opportunities available in a dwelling for "Pleasure" and in a dwelling for "Retirement." Clearly valuing the latter more highly, Morris portrayed retirement as a physically very private, and intellectually very rarefied, pursuit: as a "recluse from gay Fancies," the owner "might secrete himself" in such a structure, "to contemplate the important *Themes* of *Human Life*." After all, "in the silent Recesses of Life, are more *noble* and *felicitous* Ideas," which in such moments and locales can "more immediately concern our Attention."[13]

Presenting his design for a "double cube" dwelling (Figure 2.1), with its plan and elevation explicitly orchestrated according to elementary geometric ratios, Morris indicated that this was particularly suited to the needs of "a contemplative Genius" in "Retirement." More so than with Switzer, Morris found that both house and site were critical to this process. Thus he first discussed the necessary particulars of "a Situation capable of raising such elevated *Ideas*," a necessarily secluded and remote locale that would sustain his vision of "silent Retreats of Solitude." Such a site would be conducive to an especially rarefied privacy, where one could be *recluse* and *secreted*. The setting would be orchestrated as well to stimulate and facilitate contemplative activities. The kinds of activities that he envisioned were wholly private: sustaining the imagination, stimulating speculation and reflections, expanding ideas from one associative chain to another, and realizing the pleasures attendant on an undisturbed retirement.[14]

The dwelling itself provided a necessary and complementary dimension to this state of contemplative privacy: a perfect geometric balance that afforded the mind a state of harmonic awareness conducive to such "elevated" thoughts. Morris's trust in the affective power of harmonic proportion, as it already was understood to operate in music, and his efforts to translate that into architecture were explicit: as "Nature has taught Mankind in *Musick* certain Rules for Proportion of Sounds, so *Architecture* has its Rules dependant on those Proportions." And when experienced in material form, in a building isolated in a private setting free from all distraction, the effects of those proportions would be profound:

> Beauty, in all Objects, spring[s] from the same unerring Law in Nature, which, in *Architecture,* I would call Proportion. . . . When I consider Proportions, I am led into a Profundity of Thought. . . . If we immerse our Ideas into the infinite Tract of unbounded Space, and with the Imagination paint out the numberless Multitudes of Planets, or little Worlds, regularly revolving round their destin'd Orbs . . . we must feel Emanations of the Harmony of Nature diffus'd in us; and must immediately acknowledge the Necessity of Proportion in the Preservation of the whole Oeconomy of the Universe.[15]

In contrast to the Renaissance cabinet of curiosities, which had been a small apparatus of knowledge lodged in a remote recess in a large establishment, Morris inverted the paradigm. He produced designs for dwellings of comparatively modest size, of which the entire structure served as an instrument for attaining a heightened state of consciousness. And it did so with a very different sort of involvement by the resident: not through contemplation of objects in search of connections and correspondences

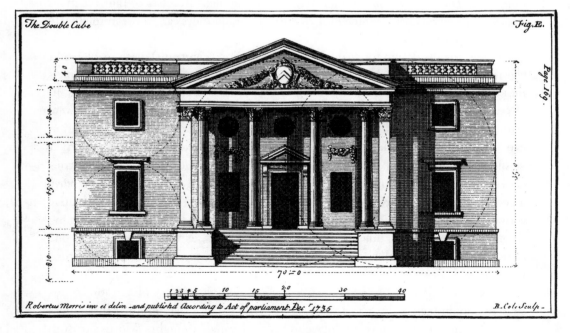

Figure 2.1. Robert Morris, design for a dwelling based on the double cube (elevation). Figure E in *Lectures on Architecture,* 1734–36. Explicitly orchestrated according to elementary geometric ratios, the dwelling was intended to serve the needs of "a contemplative Genius" in "Retirement."

but by undertaking contemplation in a setting so perfectly isolated and proportioned that one could glimpse a domain of ideal harmonies. The intended experience was a kind of Shaftesburean-neoplatonist excursion to the domain of harmonies that lay beyond the material realm, but which nevertheless could be accessible through a well-orchestrated configuration of natural and artificial elements.[16] It is notable that Morris chose to situate this configuration in the private, domestic, bourgeois realm (in contrast with very different locales designated for such transcendental experiences found in other cultures, or at other periods in European history). While Morris's goal was more Shaftesburean transcendence than Lockean appreciation of the abstract logic and rigor that ostensibly underlay the material world, his proposals still constituted designs on a bourgeois scale that offered reasoned alternatives to current stylistic and typological hierarchies. And although many of Morris's designs were presented as "Family" dwellings, it is clear that Morris's remarks were directed to the male head of the household, and that the goal of Morris's emphasis on privacy, seclusion, contemplation, and harmony was the self-constitution as individual of that primary resident. Ultimately the kind of "retired" activity that Morris championed here was necessarily a far more lonesome pursuit, and result, than might have been sought in the seventeenth-century cabinet of curiosities—clearly consistent with, and indicative of, the atomizing currents of Enlightenment culture.

Architectural treatises from the Italian Renaissance to England in the early eighteenth century provided new grounds on which to address many of the challenges and concerns raised by Enlightenment problematics of selfhood. To be sure, few bourgeois clients would have been capable of the scale of building that Alberti or Palladio described, or fully disposed to the neoplatonic approach embraced by Switzer and Morris, derived as it was from a philosophical school of waning influence. But in other respects these treatises did raise crucial considerations that allowed the eighteenth century to become a watershed in the evolution of Anglo-American domestic architecture. Among these were the notion of a bourgeois dwelling as a type unto itself; that it was a site of retreat, to a realm distinct and apart from the political and economic nexus of urban life; and especially that it could be a site built on a scale and according to a design that could afford personal self-definition and fulfillment. Ultimately a new genre of dwelling evolved, the bourgeois compact villa; the next section is an introduction to its typology.

The Bourgeois Compact Villa

The new genre of dwelling that originated in the eighteenth century may well be described in terms of its formal and stylistic characteristics—especially its diminutive or "compact" size compared to the models from which it was derived—and the "villa" nomenclature that it adopted, which is examined in the following section. Other considerations, such as geographic and social context, innovations in plan and use, and the relation of this type to broader ideological concerns, are taken up in later sections. The present section focuses on the formal and stylistic characteristics of a few select examples, which are discussed primarily as precursors and paradigms of the compact villa type, rather than as typical of bourgeois building practice thereafter. Such an approach runs a risk of skewing the analysis in favor of extant evidence, which tends to include dwellings of the most elite bourgeoisie and even a few of the more adventurous nobility. But it also recognizes the examples that the growing bourgeoisie would see published in architectural treatises and topographical view books for decades to come, and therefore held up as objects of emulation. Thus an account of several early examples, even if their owners were far from middling bourgeoisie, can help to explore the terms that architects and clients evolved in which to develop this type during the eighteenth century.

To examine those terms requires first outlining some of the features common to the beginning of the genre. Perhaps the principal characteristic of the type, as elegantly laid out by Sir John Summerson in 1959, is its elevation: two or three stories (a principal floor plus one more above, and optionally a basement or "rustic" floor below), with five windows orchestrated across the facade in groupings of 1—3—1, and frequently a portico framing the center group of windows (Figure 2.2).[17] Consistent with historical connotations of the term *villa,* some exemplars allowed a certain informality of plan that could evoke the character and atmosphere of a rural farming establishment. On the other hand, equally consistent with a modern suburban locale and the bourgeois status of the owner, the working and productive aspects of a farming establishment were always excised (or at very least concealed) in favor of what appeared to be a secluded, affectedly "natural" setting, not only detached from the nexus of Court and City but also deliberately differentiated from it, an enclave devoted instead to private retirement and personal regeneration. An *idea* of landed wealth and horticultural productivity, then, while not realized in fact, might be present in the name *villa* and in certain echoed design motifs. But the overall scale and distribution of rooms would conduce to activities of a very different sort, oriented toward the definition of self and self-improvement, harboring family, and safeguarding retreat from the mercantile and political nexus, in addition to facilitating leisure and social activities that could involve a larger circle of people as well.

Of the five examples chosen for discussion here, the first, James Gibbs's Sudbrook (1715–19) has been selected because it was the first example of an original design by an English architect to be completely erected, illustrated in a formal publication, and described there as a "villa." The second, Lord Burlington's own house at Chiswick, completed in the late 1720s, has by virtue of its perfect elevation long stood as exemplary of the compact villa type. The third example, Gibbs's Whitton (ca. 1725), was another design that he described as a "villa," and an early instance of deliberate efforts to deemphasize, or even hide, large service spaces in efforts to make the dwelling appear less grandiose. Fourth is Sir Robert Taylor's Asgill House (1761–64), one of several designs by Taylor for bourgeois clients that brought the compact villa down to a genuinely bourgeois scale. And finally the Casino at Marino, Dublin (1757), by Sir William Chambers, is included because it was such an elaborate exercise in cultivation of the self in a such a nominally minimalist, privatist fashion.

Sudbrook (James Gibbs, 1715–19)

The first original designs for residences specifically called "villas" to be published in an English treatise appeared in James Gibbs's *Book of Architecture* (1728). One, Sudbrook, was erected near Richmond between 1715 and 1719 for John Campbell, 2nd Duke of Argyll and Greenwich (Figure 2.3).[18] Gibbs designed the other, Whitton, for Argyll's

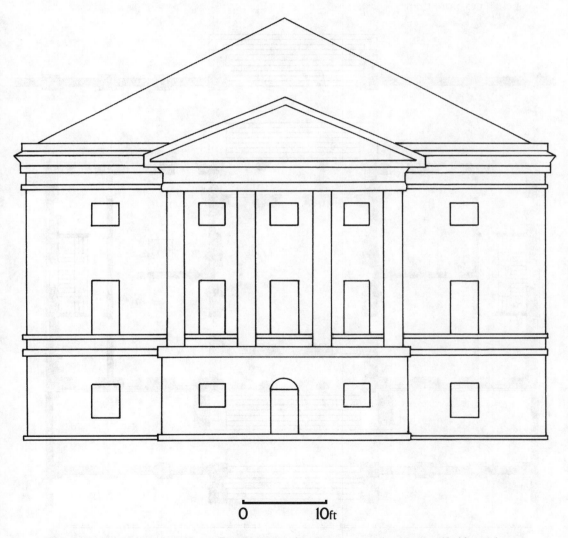

0   10ft

Figure 2.2. Diagram of the compact villa type. Typically this type of dwelling was two or three stories and had five windows across the facade grouped 1—3—1; frequently a pediment framed the center group of windows. Drawing by Holley Wlodarczyk.

brother Archibald Campbell, Earl of Ilay, about 1725. Although Gibbs's clients were hardly nouveaux bourgeoisie, and each design was two stories tall and over eighty feet wide, both designs were considerably smaller in scale than the rest of the residences that he published in his book, and they clearly were intended for purposes quite different from a standard town or country residence of the period, uses that approach a more modern notion of "suburban." Regarding the design for Sudbrook, for example, one manuscript associated with Gibbs alluded to the activities and purposes for which it was built, describing its site as "a plesent situation," and its intended function as a "retraite from bussiness . . . being but twelve miles from London,"[19] evoking immediately the general characteristics of Pliny's Laurentian villa.

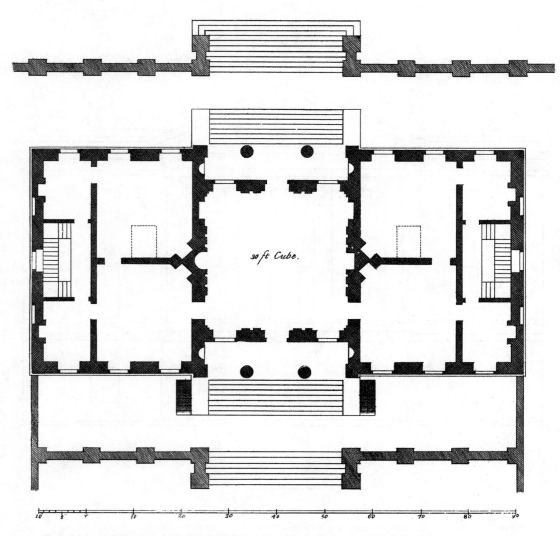

Figure 2.3. James Gibbs, design for Sudbrook (plan). Plate 40 in *A Book of Architecture*, 1728. Sudbrook was one of the first two designs published in an English treatise for a residence termed a "villa."

But examination of the plan also discloses nonstandard aspects with respect to any previous types of villa or dwelling—Roman, Italian, or British—that made this design a significant shift in the villa genre. Ordinarily a dwelling of this size would be laid out with two rooms, a hall and a saloon, on the central axis, the hall opening out onto the entrance facade and the saloon doing likewise on the garden facade. At Sudbrook the space between the two facades became a single two-story cube room thirty feet on a side, fronted by porticoes on both sides of the house. Gibbs specified no purpose for the room, but the fact that it communicates directly with the outdoors on both sides clearly indicates receptions and entertainments of a comparatively informal character.[20] Symmetrically flanking the cube room to the left and right are two private suites, or "Apartments," each consisting of an antechamber, a bedroom (with bed marked on the plan), two closets (rooms recessed into the farthest corners of the dwelling), and a staircase accessible only through one or other of the closets. The lack of a central or public staircase here is as striking as the absence of parlor and saloon. Taken together with Gibbs's comment that the upper floor consists of "Lodging Rooms," these features suggest that the principal function of this house, apart from social affairs in the central cube room, was to provide temporary overnight accommodation for guests. Therefore the informality of a retreat not only was facilitated by the house, it was guaranteed. Formal group activities such as banqueting, dancing, gaming, music making, and the like that normally were carried on by moving successively through a series of spaces dedicated to each are comparatively limited.[21] Add to that the direct entry from outdoors into the single "public" space, and there remains a considerably less formal ambience than in the standard country residence of the period. At Sudbrook one must imagine activities of a limited nature, such as receptions before and after the hunt, or comparatively informal entertainments for visitors coming "down" from London for the night or the weekend—a relatively informal and leisured endeavor compared to life either in London or on the country house circuit, and one in which activity is scaled down into one common space at the pleasure and in the presence of the owner.

Whitton (James Gibbs, ca. 1725)

The second of two designs that Gibbs described as a "villa" was produced for Archibald Campbell, Earl of Ilay, about 1725 (Figures 2.4, 2.5). Gibbs's two versions of the design, intended for Whitton near Hampton Court but never executed, drew heavily on prototypes in the work of Palladio, including his Villas Emo, Pisani, and Foscari.[22] In the first version the unusual Sudbrook plan is repeated, with a single central room flanked on each side by what Gibbs described as an "Apartment" consisting once again of antechamber, bedroom, closet, and staircase. Although there still is no central public staircase, circulation would have been a little less restricted, with semi-private back staircases apparently accessible from the outdoors (underneath the front portico) as well as from the private closets of the main-floor apartments. Presumably this would have allowed people assigned to upstairs lodgings to reach them without passing through the semiprivate apartments of others, although the inelegance of getting to one's room by this method still would have emphasized the informality of the situation. The alternate design, while slightly smaller, incorporates a somewhat more elaborate circulation system. Once again there is a single central room entered directly from either side of the house, but now neither entrance is recessed into the facade under a portico. Access to the apartments on the principal floor is from the central salon, as well as from corridors that extend laterally from the salon and provide direct access to staircases at the far ends of the house. Access to and from all chambers, therefore, is available via a corridor and without passing through the salon or another chamber.

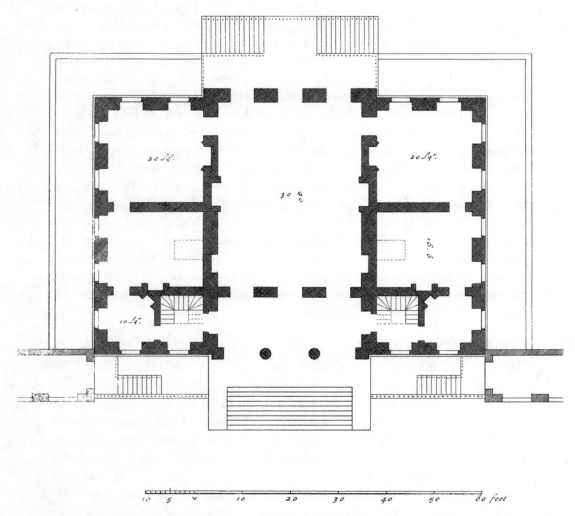

Figure 2.4. James Gibbs, design for Whitton (plan; one of two proposals). Plates 59 and 60 in *A Book of Architecture*, 1728. Whitton, along with Sudbrook, was one of the first two designs published in an English treatise for a residence termed a "villa."

In addition to the increased privacy afforded in this second design, it sharply differentiates between those staying "above stairs" and their activities, and those below. The design thus emphasizes the portion of the house occupied by the elite owners and their guests, while providing for but emphatically deemphasizing the requisite "offices" (kitchen, pantries, etc.) and quarters necessary to house staff and servants. Considering the full extent of the offices and servants' quarters, the design exhibits a clear willingness to diminish the mass of the whole, at the expense of some potential grandeur and prestige, in favor of making a clear distinction between quarters for the elite (aboveground, with tall windows, and elegant moldings) and territory for the servants (below grade, with unmolded windows that are almost entirely submerged,

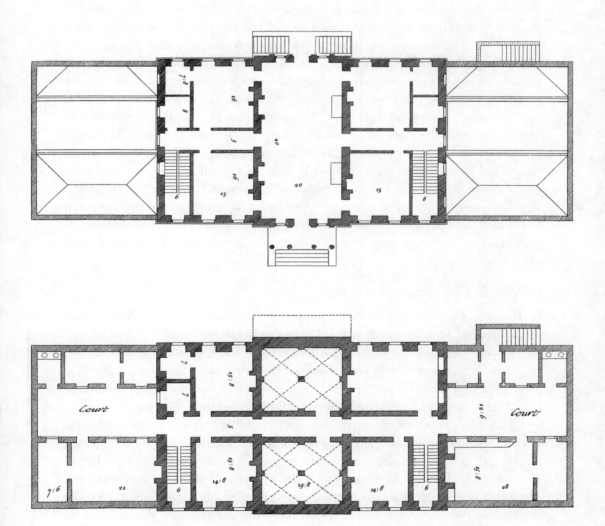

Figure 2.5. James Gibbs, design for Whitton (plan; one of two proposals). Plate 62 in *A Book of Architecture*, 1728.

and offices hidden in courtyard wings that are relegated to a severe anonymity behind plain windowless masonry walls). In fact the solution is not a very happy one, since the disparity between open and closed, rising and sunken, decorated and barren is at best uncomfortable and certainly begs the question as to what aspects of life are being concealed and why.

Certainly when compared to an early effort such as Whitton, a highly refined example such as Thomas Jefferson's Monticello, undertaken at the end of the century, is far cleaner and more decisive. He removed the offices totally from view, landscaping the house so that on approach the visitor would see only the roofs of the "dependencies," and then perceive them only as elevated promenades, not service quarters. Compared to Monticello, where the service areas are hidden from view and thus denied, the design for Whitton achieves a stark contrast, between two domains that are acknowledged and somewhat uncomfortably differentiated. The center of the house appears to rise, advance, and engage the eye with its three-dimensional articulation. The service wings physically recede and sink, and they disengage the viewer by virtue of their plain, flat surfaces. The viewer thus perceives that the service quarters are clearly subordinated to and distinctly smaller than the rest of the villa. Yet measurement of the plans shows that the area appropriated to servants' use exceeds that for owners and guests by a ratio of nine to eight. The visual subordination of servant spaces on the main facade was in and of itself not a new practice in domestic architecture at the beginning of the eighteenth century. Attics, parapets, service wings, and basements all were commonly used for this purpose at the time when Gibbs designed Whitton. But to deemphasize and almost bury over half the dwelling's floor space, leaving the viewer to apprehend a far less grandiose structure than might have been possible, was a radical turn. And it bespeaks some of the ideological priorities that were beginning to shift with respect to the purposes for which such villas were built.

Chiswick (Lord Burlington, ca. 1727–29)

By the end of the seventeenth century some of the greatest concentrations of substantial retreats for City merchants and their families were located in Chiswick and neighboring villages to the west such as Twickenham and Richmond. Richard Boyle, 3rd Earl of Burlington, already owned one seventeenth-century property in Chiswick, although that was not his principal residence. His family seat was at Londesborough in Yorkshire, and his London residence was at Burlington House. Nor was Burlington, a very wealthy person, in any respect bourgeois, but like Argyll at Sudbrook, he was in effect establishing a sub-urban situation for himself with his new villa at Chiswick (Figure 2.6), in the planning stages since 1719 but probably not constructed until 1727–29.[23] The fact that Burlington built the new villa at all would have been evidence that the extant house was in some measure unsuitable as configured. The villa implemented not only a new manner of living and entertaining, embodied in its distribution of rooms and stylistic configuration, but in its location and room layout also facilitated a specific relation to the city, enabling and encouraging more frequent stays at this suburban retreat.

As Kerry Downes has pointed out, Chiswick House was designed primarily not as a residence but rather as a house for the Muses. It was to be a repository for Burlington's library, collection of art and sculpture, and architectural drawings, and in many ways the architecture was able to showcase those collections to great effect.[24] Unlike what one might expect in a private residence, therefore, the ground-floor rooms were not devoted to service functions such as the kitchen or pantry. Rather, that floor was entirely Burlington's private space, featuring his library along the entire northwest side, with the rest possibly devoted to waiting areas for visitors, rooms for his draftsmen, and the like (Figure 2.7). On the upper floor, the main entrance of the villa led to the central tribunal or saloon, beyond which was the tripartite gallery; little is known about the decoration or use of these rooms in Burlington's time other than to presume that they would have shown off some of his art collection and served as elegant settings for entertainment on the comparatively intimate scale of this building compared to Burlington's other properties (Figure 2.8). The remaining rooms on this floor were standard apartment suites of the day, each leading through a bedchamber to a closet, presumably for overnight guests. And while such formal suites were if

Figure 2.6. Richard Boyle, 3rd Earl of Burlington, southeast facade of Chiswick House, Chiswick, 1727–29. Although Burlington was hardly a member of the bourgeoisie, the comparatively diminutive scale and rational layout of this house intended for entertainment and study contributed to the evolution of a new standard of bourgeois architectural design. Photograph by author.

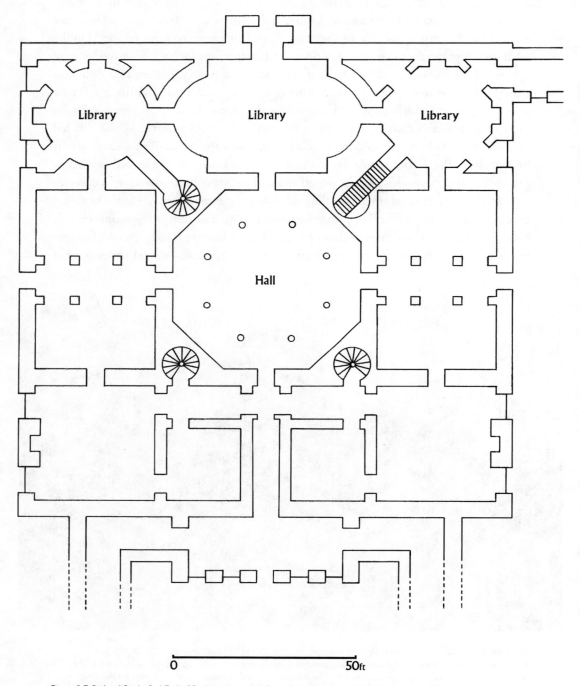

Library

Library

Library

Hall

0   50ft

Figure 2.7. Richard Boyle, 3rd Earl of Burlington, ground floor, Chiswick House (plan). Drawing by Holley Wlodarczyk.

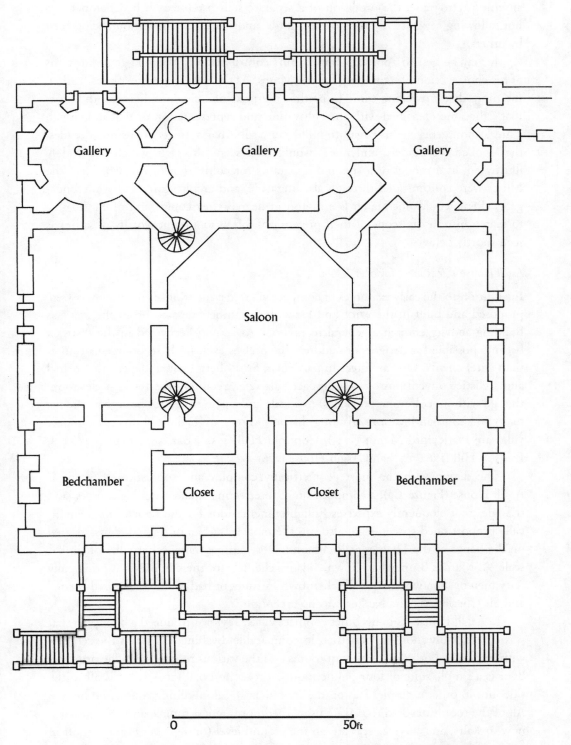

Gallery Gallery Gallery

Saloon

Bedchamber Closet Closet Bedchamber

0 50ft

Figure 2.8. Richard Boyle, 3rd Earl of Burlington, principal floor, Chiswick House (plan). Drawing by Holley Wlodarczyk.

anything retrograde, the provision of a separate staircase for each bedchamber was not, allowing servants to tend to their lords' and ladies' needs without being seen by others.

It may be best to approach Burlington's contribution to the villa genre in terms of his construction of a dwelling for the Muses. As the next chapter explores further, the more that a dwelling came to be the enterprise of a single individual, the more that it became identified with the cultivation and representation of that individual. Thus as bourgeois clients began to build more suburban retreats in ensuing decades, they looked for models, and many would have seen Chiswick, which was widely illustrated, as a model of a site and apparatus for cultivation of the self. Here the Muses were concentrated through art, literature, and architecture, and while bourgeois clients could not match Burlington in degree, they could (and often did) try to match him in the scope of their pretensions, often to a point worthy of satire, as seen shortly below.

Asgill House (Sir Robert Taylor, 1761–64)

In addition to the early examples of compact villas just mentioned, many others were proposed and built in the 1710s and 1720s, but numbers tapered off in the 1730s as building activity entered a general recession.[25] As activity recovered in the 1750s, it became possible for designers to address themselves exclusively to bourgeois (rather than elite) clients. One architect in particular, Sir Robert Taylor, adapted the formal and stylistic conventions of the compact villa (e.g., retaining the 1—3—1 elevation, though without columnar porticoes) to a scale and a plan suited for bourgeois clients, many in suburban locations. Among the best known of Taylor's bourgeois compact villas are Harleyford Manor (1755), Coptfold Hall (1755), Barlaston Hall (1756–57), Danson Hill (1762–67), and Asgill House (1761–64).

The design with the most geometrically complex and sophisticated facade is Asgill House (Figure 2.9), a composition of intersecting squares, double squares, and triangles that eloquently expresses Enlightenment ardor for the rigor of mathematically proportioned space. Asgill also was the most suburban of these designs, located on the banks of the Thames at Richmond, close among many other villas of similar scale. As Marcus Binney has shown, Taylor's clientele for these houses was principally "city men or men who had made their own fortunes or had recently acquired them," and Sir Charles Asgill, a banker, was no exception.[26]

In Asgill House, as in his other compact villas, Taylor introduced a floor plan that was considerably more modest than in comparable dwellings earlier in the century, with respect to both the number of rooms and the various room types. The principal floor is a simple suite of four public rooms: a reception hall (at Asgill it is off to the side, but in other examples it is on the central axis), salon, dining room, and library. All of the rooms devoted to private uses—bedrooms, guest rooms, and the like—are now upstairs, and service areas are on the ground level (or, in other examples, off in service wings). In this process, by virtue of the public/private separation between

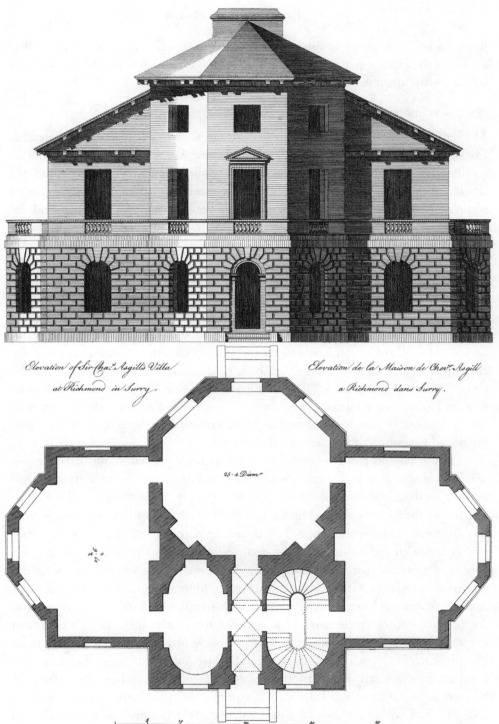

Elevation of Sir Cha.ᵗ Asgill's Villa at Richmond in Surry.

Elevation de la Maison de Chev.ʳ Asgill a Richmond dans Surry.

Figure 2.9. Sir Robert Taylor, Asgill House (elevation and plan), Richmond, 1761–64. Plate 74 in volume 1 of *Vitruvius Britannicus,* by John Woolfe and James Gandon, 1767–71. Typical of Taylor's designs for compact villas, the private rooms are located on the upper floor, service areas are on the ground level, and four public rooms (reception hall, salon, dining room, and library) that intersect in a simplified, continuous suite are on the principal floor, shown here. See also Figure 2.14.

floors and the enhanced intimacy of the condensed scale, Taylor's compact villas advanced the genre a step closer to the scale of modern nuclear-family dwellings, to becoming the apparatus of modern bourgeois domesticity.[27]

The Casino at Marino (Sir William Chambers, 1757 ff)

The reduction in size and scale of Sir Robert Taylor's compact villas, and the exclusive orientation of his work to a bourgeois clientele, betokened the broader shift in dwelling design and practice after midcentury toward the bourgeoisie. This did not signal a diminished inclination to follow elite models or to engage the challenges of Enlightenment ideology, the examination of which is continued below. And the incorporation of specifically bourgeois social and political interests in domestic design is considered in subsequent chapters. But one final example of the compact villa, in this case erected for an elite client, illustrates the full potential of the genre. For if the importance of concerns such as retreat, selfhood, and identity was epitomized in one eighteenth-century building, that was the Casino at Marino, a diminutive dwelling on the estate of James Caulfield, 4th Viscount and later 1st Earl Charlemont, on the outskirts of Dublin. Designed as early as 1757 by Sir William Chambers, though not completed until the 1770s, it was located less than two miles from the center of the city, close to the shores of Dublin Bay, on a modest estate originally surrounded by farms (Figures 2.10, 2.11, 2.12).[28] Charlemont used the much larger house on the estate, Marino House, as a suburban retreat from his town house a mile and a half away in central Dublin. But evidently he also required a retreat from his retreat, and so commissioned Chambers to produce this design.

The Casino—its name borrowed from Italian, signifying a diminutive dwelling—therefore existed at a double remove: removed once from the city with its attendant bustle, crowding, and distractions, and removed again from the main household headquarters of the Marino estate, which despite its suburban location, was a substantial establishment. This second removal produced, in effect, a rarer degree of domesticity: for although the Casino could be occupied comfortably by a family with a full retinue of servants, that is neither apparent from the scaling and features of its elevation nor consistent with its siting, which is appropriate more to a monument or a pavilion than a residence. Instead, all suggests a structure tailored to a single person. Such features as the single entrance portal, the apparently single interior cella, and the fact that Chambers's elevation, with the smoking urn on top, makes it look more like a mausoleum than a dwelling all suggest a singularity of purpose, function, and occupancy. In contrast to Marino House, this design clearly eschewed references to business or social activities. Instead, as a structure of such simple proportions,[29] it accorded well with such private aspects of country retirement as contemplation, study, and relaxation.

The fact is that the design is a masterwork of dissembling. The main floor includes a vestibule, a saloon, a study, and a bedroom. To either side of the entry, not immediately visible upon entering, are a staircase and closet. On the upper floor, virtually undetectable from outside, are a bedroom, dressing room, valet's room, and one extra room, lighted by windows hidden behind the exterior balustrades. And below the main floor is a cellar story that includes a kitchen, scullery, servants' hall, and various pantries and cellars. A half-mile tunnel connected the cellar to the main house, ensuring that servants would remain out of sight. Perhaps the most telling feature of Chambers's dissimulation is that the floor area of the cellar story is more than double that of the main floor, an indication of extraordinary expense having been made to hide, indeed deny, the presence of a house*hold* while suggesting instead a monument to individualism.

The nature of this house as a solitary monument perhaps may be better understood in light of Charlemont's politics. Having joined the Opposition in the House of Lords in the late 1750s, he determined to back up that oppositional stance by residing at a suitably oppositional distance, in Ireland: "it was my indispensable duty to live in Ireland . . . [I] determined by some means or other to attach myself to my native country. Ireland must be served in Ireland. The man who lives out of his

To the Lord Viscount Charlemont is humbly Inscribed by his Lordships

This Design of his Lordships Casine at Marino, most Obedient Servant, William Chambers.

Figure 2.10. Sir William Chambers, Casino at Marino (north elevation), Dublin, 1757 ff. Plate 1 in *A Treatise on Civil Architecture*, 1759. Giving the appearance of a monument or even a mausoleum, the Casino actually consisted of three stories, with sufficient living space and servants' quarters to sustain the household indefinitely, though permanent or sustained residence was never intended.

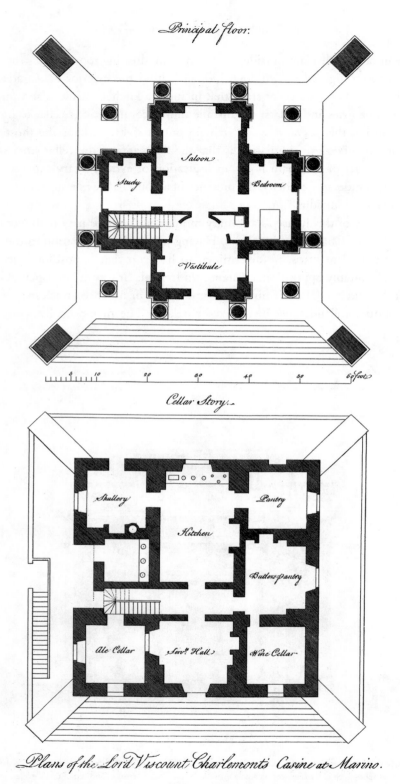

Principal floor.

Saloon

Study

Bedroom

Vestibule

Cellar Story.

Skullery

Pantry

Kitchen

Butlers Pantry

Ale Cellar

Serv.t Hall

Wine Cellar

Plans of the Lord Viscount Charlemonts Casine at Marino.

Figure 2.11. Sir William Chambers, principal floor and cellar, Casino at Marino (plans). Plate 2 in *A Treatise on Civil Architecture*, 1759.

country is guilty of a perpetual crime."[30] At the same time that he began to build the Casino, Charlemont also began complementary improvements to the surrounding estate that included hermitages, alcoves, a cane house, moss houses, and a Gothic-style Rosamund's Bower adjacent to the principal lake.[31] Together these suggest that the Casino perhaps served as something more than an affirmation of political independence, and moreover as part of a site for solitary reflection and self-improvement.[32]

In several respects Chambers's design pointedly addresses these problematics of self and identity. First, his scaling techniques, especially in the door and windows, suggest to the viewer that this is but a building for one. Likewise Chambers's use of proportions and detailing produce a supremely confident statement of grandeur and monumentality, effects that are heightened by use of stylistic and compositional allusions to mausoleums. The result is a design that served in an orchestrated fashion to monumentalize the self for whom the building was constructed. It is, notably, a very privatized self: specific allusions to politics, economy, society, geography, ancestry, and family all are lacking. The principal elements of the sculptural program are four

Figure 2.12. Sir William Chambers, Casino at Marino (south elevation). Photograph by author.

statues above the entablature, representing Bacchus, Ceres, Apollo, and Venus. Collectively these allude to dimensions of pleasure and beauty to which this building ostensibly afforded its owner access. Nevertheless the crucial point of the design rhetoric is the assertion that the building is devoted to dimensions of private consciousness. By disguising such a fully functional dwelling, with its entire apparatus of living and service spaces (including the servants themselves), in the semblance of a monument to or for an individual, and by secluding that edifice in a pastoral-Arcadian landscape setting, Chambers constructed a sophisticated apparatus for the isolation, articulation, and enrichment of private identity.[33]

Reconceiving a Type

James S. Ackerman, surveying the variety of buildings that have been termed "villas" since ancient Roman times, concludes in his book *The Villa* (1990) that a clear characteristic of life associated with the villa has long been "the pleasure factor":

> A villa is a building in the country designed for its owner's enjoyment and relaxation. Though it may also be the center of an agricultural enterprise, the pleasure factor is what essentially distinguishes the villa residence from the farmhouse and the villa estate from the farm.[34]

But as Ackerman also shows, there have been considerable shifts in understanding at various points in history—in particular, whether "villa" has denoted an entire estate, a single building, or a complex of buildings. At the beginning of the eighteenth century knowledge of historical examples was understandably limited, and it is from that limited basis that eighteenth-century domestic architecture borrowed certain characteristics, and transformed others, to address the purposes of the times.

What was known in early eighteenth-century Britain about ancient Roman and Renaissance villas, villa life, and villa ideology made the villa a potentially attractive paradigm for the emerging British bourgeoisie. Associated with retreat, leisure, and pastoralism, the villa could suit any social stratum with sufficient surplus time and wealth. To be appropriate for the bourgeoisie in particular, the British villa would evolve in three respects. First, although some writers continued using the term *villa* to describe an entire estate, including land and outlying buildings, well into the eighteenth century, that usage died out well before the end of the century. From the early eighteenth century onward, *villa* came to denote only the dwelling itself, and increasingly it denoted dwellings of a diminutive or compact scale quite different from ancient or Renaissance examples. Second, the understanding of villas as generally associated with pleasurable activities, away from centers of politics and commerce, now shifted to modes of leisure that included opportunities for defining, centering, and fulfilling the private individual self. And third, as villas progressively became more diminutive, suburban, and sized to a nuclear family, they shifted from being retreats for the wealthy and elite to being models for bourgeois domesticity. The first of these threads will be taken up below, while the second and third will be addressed more fully in the following two chapters.

In 1698 architect Roger North initiated the "downsizing" of the villa, at least on paper, by characterizing a lesser counterpart to the large country seat as a "suburb villa," a neologism by which he meant a place "to retire to and enjoy and sleep, without pretence of entertainment of many persons."[35] Two years later Timothy Nourse expanded on this vision of a diminutive retreat, specifically emphasizing the casual, private, nonaristocratic, unpretentious, even diversionary possibilities of a villa. He described it as a "little House of Pleasure and Retreat, where Gentleman and Citizens betake themselves in the Summer for their private Diversion, . . . sequestered from the Noise of a City, and the Embarras and Destraction of Business."[36] And in remarks composed about the same time, architect Henry Aldrich specifically rejected traditional Latin and Italian definitions of the term *villa* as a "farm" or "farm village" and characterized it instead as "a house built for rural retirement; in the size, situation, and structure of which the plan of a farm house is not to be lost sight of."[37] Close on the heels of the Enlightenment's intensifying regard for the private self, architects correspondingly had offered their readers a new range of possibilities: adaptation of an established building type to new conditions in form (now diminutive), locale (now suburban), and purpose (now private).

But even though architects' future livelihood might eventually lie in modest dwellings for the ascendant bourgeoisie, their interest in ancient Roman authors and archaeological sites only intensified. Much of this bespoke a search for principles that, in proper Enlightenment fashion, still could be applied to modern circumstances, and to domestic architecture in particular. A landmark treatise in both of these efforts was Robert Castell's *Villas of the Ancients Illustrated* (1728), an examination of the historical typology and uses of Roman villas completed under the patronage of one of the leaders of Britain's Palladian Revival, Lord Burlington, the builder of Chiswick House. Castell explained that the writings of the first-century BCE Roman architect Vitruvius treated villas only cursorily, so he had turned to a variety of other sources to determine "the Rules that were observed in the situating and disposing of the Roman Villas."[38] He incorporated several accounts of villas in Roman agricultural treatises, while making the detailed descriptions of first and second-century CE Roman essayist Pliny the Younger's Laurentian and Tuscan villas the central focus of his study.

Three of the characteristics that Castell identified in his analysis of Pliny's Laurentian villa had particular significance for the course of eighteenth-century English villas. First, he observed that this villa was "not a Mansion House, round which *Pliny* had a large Estate, and all manner of Conveniences for Life upon his own Ground." In fact Pliny's villa was in size and facilities at very least equivalent to what in Castell's time actually was considered a mansion, and either would have had a substantial surrounding estate as well. But by arguing explicitly that Pliny's residence was something other than a mansion, Castell afforded an opportunity for the authority of ancient Roman theory and practice to suggest a more bourgeois scale of lot size and building in eighteenth-century Britain.

Second, Castell observed that Pliny's villa was not "a Seat which he liv'd in at all Seasons, but where he spent only those Hours he had at leisure from the Business of the City." His point was well taken, but the terms in which he put it also afforded a decidedly modern understanding of the purpose for erecting a villa, as a place for spending a span of just a few "Hours" as a retreat from city affairs, and perhaps for little else. By highlighting these notions of temporary habitation and oppositionality to the city, Castell framed an understanding of the villa as a site for purposeful private recreation in terms suitable to the emerging bourgeoisie. Castell's inference that Pliny could easily retreat here for only a few hours may exaggerate Pliny's actual practice, but it does hint at the consequences of improved transportation facilities and compressed time frames multiplying the number of retreats in suburban locations as the eighteenth and subsequent centuries proceeded.

And third, despite the extent of the structure that Pliny described, Castell suggested that Pliny's life there was characterized by some austerity: "he possess'd nothing but the House and Gardens, nor diverted himself otherwise than by studying."[39] Again, this probably characterized Pliny's actual range of activities too narrowly, but it suggested that eighteenth-century architects and clients thought of the dwelling more narrowly—as a site focused on the culture of the individual, minimally encumbered by possessions (with their corresponding responsibilities), and able to devote full energies to a self-focused activity, for example, study.

Castell's examination of Roman writings also extended to a broader typological analysis of Roman villas, bringing to his English audience a system of categorization that would be useful in rethinking the purposes of the eighteenth-century villa. As explained by the agricultural writer Columella (via Castell), the Roman villa ordinarily consisted of three parts: the *villa urbana,* a dwelling set aside for the master's own use; the *villa rustica,* consisting of offices for animal husbandry and farming; and the *villa fructuaria,* containing storehouses for corn, wine, oil, and other products. But sometimes, as Castell noted in the case of Pliny's Laurentian villa, the establishment consisted of only the *villa urbana,* that is, "only a Country-House of Pleasure," built without any regard to the *villa rustica,* or anything relating to farming. Castell observed that the terminology was not consistent even in ancient times, and that Varro, for example, would not have agreed that a residence without an agricultural establishment could have been called a villa. Castell's discomfort with the notion of a villa simply as an isolated country house dedicated entirely to pleasure is evident in his devotion of nearly a fifth of his book to compiling what "other Authors on Agriculture esteem'd necessary to a compleat *Villa.*"[40] Nevertheless Castell's struggle with the notion, and his insistence on tying the villa to an agricultural base of production,[41] also suggests awareness of the economic and social challenges occupying his contemporaries as they confronted the spread of an increasingly capitalized landscape and commodified economy.[42]

Perhaps of greatest interest to Castell's English readers would have been information that Castell presented on location, siting, and orientation of a villa. The distance of the Laurentian villa from Rome, given by Castell as seventeen miles,[43] compares closely with the distance from London to the area of most concentrated villa building in Castell's time, Richmond and its vicinity: it was seventeen miles from the Tower to central Richmond via the Thames. Castell noted that it was possible for Pliny, "having finished the Business of the City," to arrive at his villa "with Ease and Safety by the Close of the Day." Along the way there was "a great Variety of Views"; from within the villa itself the importance of views was even greater, including ocean vistas as well as prospects of "several [other] beautiful *Villas.*" The coast was "adorn'd with a grateful Variety, by Prospects of *Villa's,* sometimes seemingly join'd together, and at other times farther asunder; which exceeds the Prospects of many Cities"—a description that also characterized the upper reaches of the Thames Valley between London and Richmond in Castell's time (Figure 2.13). Equally important to Pliny, and reemphasized by Castell, were the specific prospects that were framed by windows of individual rooms within the villa itself. In one room, for example, "from the Bed's Feet you have a Prospect of the Sea, from its back that of neighbouring *Villas,* and from the head you see the Woods, so many Windows affording so many Prospects." At the Laurentian villa, the vistas most frequently emphasized were of the sea and of other

Figure 2.13. A. Heckell, *A Perspective View of Twickenham,* engraving by Michael Rooker, 1749. From *A New Display of the Beauties of England,* 1776. A number of prominent villas, as well as a few clusters of row houses, can be seen flanking the Thames early in the eighteenth century.

villas along the coast. At the Tuscan villa, Castell praised Pliny's attention to views of both productive and unproductive land.[44] In sum, the villa was presented as an instrument for appropriation of the surrounding landscape—both its natural aesthetic beauty and the labor that transformed other parts of it into a productive landscape—for the benefit of the owner through carefully constructed siting and orientation.

Equally important for discussion of the villa, and domestic architecture in general, was Leon Battista Alberti's Renaissance treatise *De Re Aedificatoria*. First published in Florence in 1485, it was not translated into English until James Leoni's edition, issued just two years before Castell's treatise, in 1726.[45] Alberti did not devote a major portion of his ten-book treatise to a discussion of dwellings, but several points in chapters 14 and 15 of the fifth book became pertinent to the discussion of domestic architecture in eighteenth-century Britain. Among his remarks on "private houses," he observed that "a house is a little city," in that it needed to be healthy and well supplied. He also established as a primary consideration that it be "a useful and convenient abode" for the family. Much of its utility lay in maintaining specific hierarchical relationships within that family, relationships of a sort that still held some import for eighteenth-century readers' concerns with patriarchy and gender. As Mark Wigley has shown, Alberti's interest was not simply in housing nuclear or extended family groups but rather in articulating a distinctly domestic realm in which, through architectural form and spatial relations, explicitly gendered relationships were constructed. As Wigley puts it, Alberti literally understood the house "as a mechanism for the domestication of (delicately minded and pathologically embodied) women."[46] Given the tensions in Lockean political theory between patriarchy and equality, no matter how well Locke may have finessed them, such an understanding of the dwelling as an apparatus of autonomy and subjection would have been of considerable import to the generation following Locke. And Alberti's text enhanced both the appreciation of autonomy, in the sense of a little city unto itself with its own structures of authority, and of subjection, in that the woman, like the contents of the house, was under the man's control.

Focusing then on one specific class of dwellings termed *Ville*, which Leoni translated variously as "Country Houses" and "Villas," Alberti described a type that was suited to commuting, close enough to a primary residence in town that the family could easily and frequently travel back and forth:

> It will be also very convenient to have your way to it lie thro' a gate of the City that is not far from your Town house, but as near as it may be, that you may go backwards and forwards from Town to Country and from Country to Town with your wife and family, as often as you please.

Described by Alberti as "pleasure-houses just without the town," villas also were seen as sites of recreation, convenient sites for a man of "private business" or "public affairs," who had a family, to enjoy the "health" and "pure air" of the country. Here the man of the household could be "at liberty to do just what he pleases"—not an invitation to licentiousness but rather an opportunity to enjoy the pleasures of the countryside, such as "pleasant landskapes, flowery meads, open champians, shady groves, or limpid brooks, or clear streams and lakes for swimming."[47] Again, as did Pliny, Alberti presented the villa as a dwelling within commuting distance, suited to personal recreation, and well sited for appropriating the best air and views the countryside had to offer.

The first English designer to employ the term *villa* frequently in his text was the landscape architect Stephen Switzer, whose *Ichnographia Rustica: Or, the Nobleman, Gentleman, and Gardener's Recreation* appeared in 1715–18. But consistent with the sort of uncertainty that motivated Roger North to coin the term *suburb villa,* which led others to consult authorities such as Pliny and Alberti and in turn left Leoni uncertain how to translate Alberti's term *ville,* Switzer's usage of the term still was inconsistent and ambiguous. In his treatise he shifted among three usages of the word, using it to refer to a farm, an estate or manor, and a seat.[48] Yet it would be unfair to presume that Switzer's inconsistency was due to ignorance, carelessness, or the fact that this was still a foreign word. Rather, given the intended diversity of his audience (the "Nobleman, Gentleman, and Gardener") and their varying personal and social expectations during this period, it might be more appropriate to recognize the villa as a type that was not yet subject to modern rules and categories, and thus open to variation. Even in the 1730s, well after Castell and Leoni had published their work, Switzer renewed his use of the term *villa* as synonymous with a farm. He did so in an essay in which he explored the typology of the Roman villa, but he hewed more closely to Alberti's taxonomy than to Castell's, mentioning only two types of villa. One was a productive working farm, or "Villa Rustica." The other was a "Villa Urbana," which he notably characterized as part of a larger dwelling: "that part of the Manor-House only, wherein the Landlord himself lived, and which was generally furnished in as neat and elegant a Manner as his City-House." This was, he indicated, "that Place wherein the Roman Worthies passed all their leisure Hours in the greatest Solitude, Retirement and Pleasure."[49] Although Switzer characterized the villa unusually, but not uniquely for his time, as part of a larger establishment and not as an isolated unit unto itself, the purposes that he determined for it resonated with the needs and opportunities among the emerging bourgeoisie for defining, centering, and fulfilling the private self.

After midcentury, as the role of the villa became increasingly central to British architectural typology in the description, design, and critique of actual dwellings, its definition still remained applicable to a variety of dwelling types and locations. With somewhat more consistency villas were of modest scale and built for bourgeois clients in suburban or rural parts of the country. But the transition was slow, and examples that were recorded often were those for which there was an audience who could purchase the expensive illustrated volumes in which they appeared. In the Woolfe and

Gandon volumes of *Vitruvius Britannicus* (1767–71), for example, three dwellings were called villas. One, Asgill House (1761–64), was located in Richmond, by then perhaps the quintessential suburban locale in Britain (Figure 2.14). Like Danson Hill, also by Sir Robert Taylor, it was a perfect example of a compact villa for a bourgeois client. The two other dwellings also called villas were somewhat larger, and farther afield. One, Combe Bank, was well southeast of London, about five miles from Sevenoaks in Kent. The other, Thoresby Lodge, "the seat of his grace the duke of Kingston," about eighteen miles north of Nottingham, was described as "one of the most delightful spots in the kingdom."[50] Indeed at Thoresby the remote location may have been as much a consideration as anything else in choosing the term *villa*, perhaps in view of the esteem that Castell had accorded to Pliny's Tuscan villa, some 150 miles from Rome, and the scenery to be appreciated there and along the way.

An earlier sense of the term *villa* persisted in Samuel Richardson's novelistic *History of Sir Charles Grandison* (1753–54), where in usage similar to Switzer's it designated an outbuilding on an estate, employed on a temporary basis for entertaining and lodging guests:

W. Watts delin et sculp.

The Seat *of* Sir Charles Asgill *Bar.ᵗ near* Richmond *in* SURRY.

Published as the Act directs, Sep.ᵗ 1.ˢᵗ 1782 by W. Watts, Chelsea.

Figure 2.14. William Watts, Asgill House, Richmond. Plate 34 in *The Seats of the Nobility and Gentry*, 1779. Asgill was one of several prominent villas along the Thames in the vicinity of Twickenham and Richmond by the middle third of the eighteenth century.

On the south side of the river, on a natural and easy ascent, is a neat, but plain villa, in the rustic taste, erected by Sir Thomas; the flat roof of which presents a noble prospect. This villa contains convenient lodging-rooms; and one large room in which he used sometimes to entertain his friends.[51]

Something like what Richardson described may be found in a book of designs by Thomas Overton, *Original Designs of Temples* (1766), in which six designs described as "villas" clearly were intended as places for temporary entertainment or shelter in a landscape park or garden (Figure 2.15). Offered in a variety of styles, and even presented as objects of fantasy—the design in plates 37–38 has the "appearance of a fort," from which ordnance could be fired on "rejoicing days"—all but one are simply one room in plan and two stories high. The single one-story design for a three-room plan (plates 46–47) may have been meant for a lengthier period of personal retreat rather than for entertainment: the central room, fifteen feet square, is flanked by two rooms each ten feet by twelve feet. One is designated for a servant, and the other, containing a bed, is for "retirement."[52] In all these cases, but Overton's examples in particular, the focus is on private occupation, perhaps with a few personal guests, on a temporary basis, for purposes of recreation in the sense of restoration of self.

Nevertheless the structures described by Richardson and offered by Overton were affordable by only a very limited clientele. Meanwhile an interest in smaller but more permanent structures, in the form of private bourgeois dwellings, had begun to mushroom. Architectural authors likewise recognized that their audience was shifting: even such a massive architectural treatise as Isaac Ware's folio *Complete Body of Architecture* (1756), at 748 pages and 115 plates, was ostensibly no longer directed to the nobility but rather to an audience that consisted of "the gentleman" and "the practical builder," notwithstanding the likelihood that few in those categories could afford it. In the few text portions and illustrations that were specifically oriented to bourgeois clients, Ware nevertheless introduced advanced criteria for designing a bourgeois dwelling, specifically the possibility of articulating the design according to characteristics of the bourgeois client's business or profession. Thus he wrote of variations that might be required among dwellings for "a person in trade," compared to "a person of fashion," a "merchant's house," or "persons of distinction." One design that he illustrated, Wrotham Park (Figure 2.16), although it was located well beyond the suburban reaches of London at the time, conformed well to the standard bourgeois compact villa type, here with two one-story wings added. In this case Ware emphasized the nature of the bourgeois dwelling as an instrument of private regeneration by describing it as an instance where "a gentleman intends to retire from *London*."[53]

Yet because of the nature of the architectural treatise as a very expensive form of publication in the eighteenth century, and therefore limited in subject matter and clientele, it can only provide a partial perspective on the growing interest in villas as temporary or permanent retreats among the affluent bourgeoisie. In some cases critical and satirical attacks reveal more about their spread than any remaining theoretical

'C:Overton ,delin.

R:Pranker.Sculp.

Figure 2.15. Thomas Overton, design for a small villa of two stories (elevation). Plate 38 in *Original Designs of Temples*, 1766. This design, though called a "villa," is only one room in plan and two stories high; it clearly was intended as a place of temporary entertainment.

or visual documentation. One such example appeared shortly after midcentury, when accounts began to appear deriding bourgeois villas erected by city folk a few miles outside of town as hopelessly pretentious and insubstantial "boxes." A mocking poem appearing in *The Connoisseur* in 1756, ridiculing as wasteful and pretentious the growing tendency of the middle classes to suburbanize the outskirts of London, identified as the object of its scorn the "Villa" that many a "wealthy Cit" would erect barely beyond the outskirts of the city. Three to four miles, or an hour's ride, from the center of the city, these were places where according to the poem the owner could restore his health, engage in exercise, and enjoy the country air. But in addition to affording opportunities for retreat and relaxation, the villa, or "country box," also apparently served as a site for the articulation of personal taste and prestige—efforts that as far as this poet was concerned were laughable in their conformity to fad and fashion.

> Lo! a new heap of whims are bred,
> And wanton in my lady's head.
> "Well! to be sure, it must be own'd,
> It is a charming spot of ground:
> So sweet a distance for a ride,
> And all about so *countryfy'd!*
> 'Twould come but to a trifling price,
> To make it quite a paradise.
> I cannot bear those nasty rails,
> Those ugly, broken, mouldy pales:
> Suppose, my dear, instead of these,
> We build a railing all *Chinese*. . . ."
>
> No doubt, her arguments prevail;
> For Madam's Taste can never fail.
>
> Blest age! when all men may procure

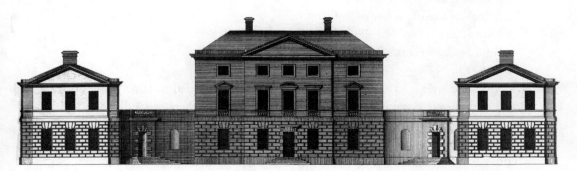

Figure 2.16. Isaac Ware, Wrotham Park, Middlesex (elevation). Plate 54/55 in *A Complete Body of Architecture*, 1756. A design for a dwelling for "a gentleman [who] intends to retire from *London*."

The title of a Connoisseur. . . .
    Now bricklayers, carpenters, and joiners,
With *Chinese* artists and designers,
Produce their schemes of alteration,
To work this wond'rous reformation.
The useful dome, which secret stood
Embosom'd in the yew-tree's wood,
The trav'ler with amazement sees
A temple, *Gothic* or *Chinese,*
With many a bell and tawdry rag on,
And crested with a sprawling dragon.

Twice the poem derides the fashion for a prototypically suburban front lawn: "In front a level lawn is seen, / Without a shrub upon the green." Clearly such villas were intended for use as weekend retreats, notably for entertaining guests at a Sunday meal. The overall tone of the poem, while recognizing their proliferation, is one of ridicule and condemnation, partly because of the unwarranted pretentiousness of the residents who had them built, but equally because these "boxes" were true to no established standards. They were houses appropriate neither to the city nor to the country, and their clientele were neither landed gentry and aristocracy nor part of the local social nexus. In many respects these villas were the means by which their inhabitants sought to selectively escape the various limitations of those categories. Those aspirations of course ultimately threatened a breakdown in the social and political order, and such worries probably lay at the base of the author's critique. On the other hand, that critique also recognized precisely the efforts of such suburban villa builders to articulate a middle-ground suburban space in which their individualistic pretensions could be gratified by very modern means—in particular the purchase and application of ready-designed decoration in a style of one's choice, as available in pattern books such as those by William and John Halfpenny (Figure 2.17):

A wooden arch is bent astride
A ditch of water four feet wide;
With angles, curves, and zigzag lines,
From *Halfpenny's* exact designs.[54]

A decade later a letter in the *London Magazine* continued to lament the breakdown in domestic typology, noting that "in former times" there was a distinct difference between "seats in the country" and "abodes in the town." The author observed that the former were surrounded by "a great property," while grousing that "modern country-houses have many of them scarce an inch of ground more than they can measure with a stone's throw, and which serves them as a cabbage-garden." Instead of the nobility's continuous and permanent "hospitality" to all around them, the new class of suburban dwellers was far narrower in its outlook: "Their hospitality consists perhaps in keeping open-house upon a Sunday for their own friends." The writer criticized the residents' indulgence in commoditized instant fashion, such as decorating the coach house "in the Gothic taste *entire new,* and as clean as red bricks and white paint can make them; or, if Madam should happen to fancy it, with zig-zaged railing and pailing round about the dunghill." Indeed the entire apparatus was to be censured for its ersatz character: "the only thing rural about the house is perhaps some leaden aloes painted green in white and gold pots of the same metal, placed in rows along the free-stone approach to the lacquered knocker." Instead of enjoying the opportunities and benefits of the country environment, such as a "cool refreshing walk, or other rural exercise and amusement," residents imported urban customs such as card playing, often crowding people together indoors "in as disagreeable a situation as the Black Hole at Calcutta." The author's complaint ultimately amounted, in large part, to discomfort with an increasingly bourgeois landscape on the outskirts of the city. Unlanded city people of comparatively modest means appropriated the country

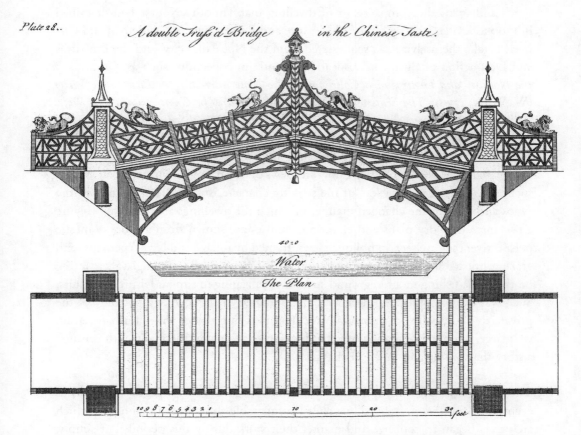

Figure 2.17. William and John Halfpenny, design for a double trussed bridge. Plate 28 in *Rural Architecture in the Chinese Taste,* 1755. According to some mid-eighteenth-century critics, this fashionable, all too easily copied kind of patterning ostensibly was incorporated far too wholeheartedly by suburban villa builders into their own inadequate yards and surroundings.

landscape for uses hitherto deemed inappropriate, but which suited well the needs and processes of bourgeois expansion and private consumption.[55]

Critics such as the letter writer to the *London Magazine* surely skewed the terms in which these new suburban villas created challenges to the established sociospatial order, focusing on ticky-tacky fences and less than wholesome pursuits in order to condemn shifts in the landscape of social relations as well as in the physical landscape. But the momentum and breadth of those shifts were undeniable. Comparable shifts occurred in the illustrated content of British architectural literature. Early in the century British architectural books had been characterized by large-format treatises such as James Gibbs's *Book of Architecture,* illustrating a range of major building types from churches to mansions. By the end of the century architects' published output was characterized instead by fancifully illustrated books of designs for bourgeois "villas" and "cottages."[56] Even in topographical and historical publications commit-ted to including the corpus of British architecture, the emphasis gradually shifted from presentations of vast estates and mansions, such as in the earlier volumes of *Vitruvius Britannicus,* to dwellings of more bourgeois scale and domestic demeanor. By the late 1770s and 1780s the compact sort of dwelling that Timothy Nourse had described in 1700 as a villa, a "little House of Pleasure and Retreat, where Gentleman and Cit-izens betake themselves, . . . sequestered from the Noise of a city, and the Embarras and Destraction of Business," appears frequently in collections such as *The Seats of the Nobility and Gentry, in a Collection of the Most Interesting & Picturesque Views* (W. Watts, 1779), *The Seats of the Nobility and Gentry, in Great Britain and Wales* (William Angus, 1787), and *Picturesque Views of the Principal Seats of the Nobility and Gentry in England and Wales* (Harrison & Co., [ca. 1789?]). Mixed in among views of older estates such as Burghley and Hatfield, and large-scale Palladian residences such as Holkham and Kedleston, there now are views of compact villas in suburban locales, such as Asgill and Chiswick. But the striking characteristic of these volumes of the 1770s and 1780s is the changed manner in which the dwellings are presented (Figure 2.18). Instead of dry plans and elevations, houses are shown from a more domestic perspective: they are seen in oblique views, framed by foliage and lawns, perhaps with grazing horses, sheep, or deer, and often with figures strolling along walks, sitting on the grass, fishing in a foreground stream, or engaging in similar leisurely pursuits. Such was the pastoral vision that became ingrained in the ideology not only of the private dwelling with its immediate surroundings but also of the suburban terrain writ large, a now-bourgeois vision that blossomed widely in the nineteenth century, a story that will be continued in chapter 5.

The social and spatial disruption in which the bourgeoisie was engaged, especially as exemplified in the cases above, paralleled comparable shifts in the manner in which architects began to conceive and market their work during this period. Put simply, the typology of residential architecture itself came under attack. At the beginning of the century, a simplified account of that typology would include a simple four-tier hierarchy of dwellings: palaces, mansions, villas, and cottages; apart from that, two marginal tiers, town houses and farmhouses, were discussed by some but not all authors.[57] But the rapidly growing number of middle-class entrepreneurs, tradesmen, merchants, and professionals who could afford to build according to their own needs and tastes led to pressures for significant variations and departures from that typology. Part of the traditional hierarchical system had been an implied understanding that the design of any dwelling should accord with the rank and status of the owner or resident.[58] But these categories did not correspond with the trades and businesses by which the bourgeoisie pursued their own livelihoods, or the modes of consumption by which status and identity increasingly were defined. Designers correspondingly began to seek more appropriate criteria for the articulation of dwellings, such as the resident's profession or occupation. In the mid-1730s, for example, Robert Morris distinguished in his *Lectures on Architecture* among the specific needs of merchants, wine merchants, cotton merchants, and courtiers. Isaac Ware allowed similar variations in his 1756 treatise, mentioned above.[59]

By the early nineteenth century the number of publications offering bourgeois villa designs pegged to specific occupations and professions had grown dramatically, all but eclipsing the genre of the classical architectural treatise.[60] And the fact that these designs for bourgeois dwellings normally were depicted in quasi-bucolic or quasi-pastoral settings was not unrelated to the growing popularity of suburban layouts of

Figure 2.18. View of Whitton Place, Middlesex. From Harrison & Co., *Picturesque Views of the Principal Seats of the Nobility and Gentry in England and Wales,* 1786. The dwelling had become a setting for a pastoral vision of leisure, with elegantly manicured lawns and quiet sedentary pursuits. See also Figure 3.33. Courtesy of Yale Center for British Art, Paul Mellon Collection.

a comparable sort. In both cases, dwelling and suburb, the bourgeoisie had begun to develop instruments for addressing the challenges posed by Enlightenment ideology: apparatuses that could be privatized as an individual's own domain and (to a gradually increasing extent) customized to an individual's needs. The consequent emergence of modern suburbia will be addressed in the following section, and the next chapter will turn to the privatization and individualization of the dwelling itself.

Terra Suburbana: The Thames Valley

The history of the bourgeois compact villa is interwoven with the history of modern suburbia in multiple respects, ranging from the appearance of Sudbrook and Chiswick in the immediate neighborhood of the earliest modern suburbs to the fact that both evolved as responses to the needs and desires of the emerging bourgeoisie. Thus to complement the preceding examination of the emergence of the compact villa as an architectural type, the following brief account of the rise of the modern suburb provides a sense of the larger context in which bourgeois clients were articulating responses to the challenges of self and society.

Pre–Eighteenth-Century Suburbs: A Diversity of Types

Historians of suburbs and cities commonly have accepted the notion that prior to the eighteenth century suburbs simply were places where activities of a foul and illicit nature took place, often taking their cue from the *Oxford English Dictionary*'s examples of pejorative usages of the term prior to the that time.[61] Certainly there are many solid accounts that bolster such a perspective. John Twyning's recent *London Dispossessed* (1997), for example, shows the enormous extent of prostitution and other "unofficial work" found in the suburbs of London. But he also argues against the notion that life there approached any sort of anarchy.[62]

By the late sixteenth century some members of the gentry began to establish residences outside of the city, and the consensus among observers seems to have been that at least some suburbs were quite agreeable places to live. As early as 1579 a courtesy book counseled the gentlemen of England on the question of where to "make most abode," in the country or in the city, and arrived at the following answer, in which "Subburbes" is quite evidently a nonpejorative designation for the outskirts of a city:

> The manner of the most Gentlemen and Noble men also, is to house them selues (if possible they may) in the Subburbes of the Cittie, because moste commonly, the ayre there beeinge somewhat at large, the place is healthy, and through the distaunce from the bodye of the Towne, the noyse not much: and so consequently quiet. Also for commoditie wee finde many lodginges, both spacious and roomethy, with Gardaines and Orchardes very delectable. So as with good gouernment, wee haue as litle cause to feare infection there, as in the verye Countrey.[63]

Middlesex already was just such a place, as described by John Norden in 1593, evidently well peppered with the temporary retreats of London's commercial gentry: "This shire is plentifullie stored, and as it seemeth beautified, with manie faire, and comely buildinges, especially of the Merchants of *London,* who haue planted their houses of recreation not in the meanest places: which also they haue cunningly contriued, curiously beautified, with diuers deuises, neatly decked with rare invencions."[64] By the beginning of the Restoration, Thomas Fuller's chapter in *The History of the Worthies of England* (1662) on Middlesex could open with the blunt statement that Middlesex "is in effect but the suburbs at large of London, replenished with the retiring houses of the gentry and citizens thereof, besides many palaces of nobelmen, and three (lately) royal mansions."[65]

Thus suburbs in general, and Middlesex in particular, were not necessarily places of disfavor and disrepute. As early as 1623 Henry Cockeram prepared an English dictionary in which he attempted to produce a more elevated language for the use of "Ladies and Gentlewomen"—a refined clientele—and one of the words he chose to coin defined a "Neighbourhood in the Subburbs" as a "Suburbannitie."[66] Given his elite audience, and presuming that Cockeram was searching for a term that they might commonly employ, it would be safe to presume that this was not a pejorative usage. To the contrary, it would have been an attempt to find a term that distinguished this recognized form of suburban environment inhabited by gentry from the areas chronicled in Twyning's *London Dispossessed. Suburbannitie* even may have been an effort to formulate a word that encompassed a range of meanings comparable to what *suburbia* signifies today. However, the greater point is that even in the sixteenth century the "suburbs" were regarded according to an emerging range of values, with vice and pollution at one end and the other embracing healthy and beautiful landscapes.

The Gentrification of London's Suburbs

By the beginning of the eighteenth century, as roads, bridges, and travel safety improved, the attractions of London's outlying regions far exceeded the growing pollution and congestion in the center, and those who could afford to maintain a residence as a part-time or permanent retreat increasingly did so. Thus during the early part of the century one commonly noted aspect of suburban life, not always met with approval, was the growing tendency of gentlemen and their families—sometimes old money, sometimes the new bourgeoisie—to "retire" to suburban areas in the vicinity of London for a season, a weekend, or even on the basis of a daily commute. Daniel Defoe commented on this in 1724 in his *Tour through England & Wales,* remarking on the increasing number of bourgeois residents ("gentlemen" and "citizens") in many of London's western and southwestern suburbs, and the purposes for which they would build and "retire" to these houses:

these fine houses and innumerable more, which cannot be spoken of here, are not, at least very few of them, the mansion houses of families, the antient residences of ancestors, the capital messuages of the estates; . . . these are all houses of retreat, like the Bastides of Marseilles, gentlemen's meer summer-houses, or citizen's country-houses; whither they retire from the hurries of business, and from getting money, to draw their breath in a clear air, and to divert themselves and families in the hot weather; . . . so that in short all this variety, this beauty, this glorious show of wealth and plenty, is really a view of the luxuriant age which we live in, and of the overflowing riches of the citizens. . . .[67]

From Defoe's description it appeared that Epsom, to the southwest, already exhibited many aspects of the modern commuter suburb, including a low-density, well-landscaped environment and a mercantile class of residents who commuted on a daily basis, at least in the summer, to London:

this place seems adapted wholly to pleasure, so the town is suited to it; 'tis all rural, the houses are built at large, not many together, with gardens and ground about them; that the people who come out of their confin'd dwellings in London, may have air and liberty, suited to the design of country lodgings. . . . The greatest part of the men, I mean of this grave sort, may be supposed to be men of business, who are at London upon business all the day, and thronging to their lodgings at night, make the families, generally speaking, rather provide suppers than dinners; for 'tis very frequent for the trading part of the company to place their families here, and take their horses every morning to London, to the Exchange, to the Alley, or to the warehouse, and be at Epsome again at night; and I know one citizen that practis'd it for several years together, and scarce ever lay a night in London during the whole season.[68]

Innovation in Seventeenth-Century Dwellings of the Suburban Gentry

Well before Defoe set about chronicling Epsom to the southwest of London, suburban development already had become better established in some of the towns and villages immediately west of London. These would become sites of what we recognize as the first modern-day suburbs in the sense in which we commonly understand the term, sites for detached, landscaped, comparatively modest, bourgeois dwellings in easy commuting distance of the city (Figure 2.19). Some of this development simply was due to the convenience of the Thames above London as a line of reliable daily transportation, in addition to the two main roads leading westward out of London past Kensington and Chelsea. Some of it was due as well to the attraction of several royal properties in this direction, including Hampton Court, Kensington Palace, Kew Gardens, and the onetime palace at Richmond. Although the palace that Henry VIII occupied at Richmond beginning in 1501 was demolished beginning in 1650, the cachet of the royal park and the presence of mineral springs were an incentive for London merchants to begin building terraced and semidetached houses there in the

1690s, both for personal occupation and as investments.[69] Throughout the eighteenth century those who built in Richmond remained in the upper echelons of the social scale, but they also commissioned some of the more advanced suburban designs. The Duke of Argyll's villa at Sudbrook, for example, was on the outskirts of Richmond, while banker Sir Charles Asgill's midcentury compact design by Sir Robert Taylor had a very prominent setting on the riverbank, along with Marble Hill House and other exemplary villas of the period.

The intermediate ground between London and Richmond may have taken on a proto-suburban character as early as the beginning of the seventeenth century when several large houses were built in present-day Kensington by men of great mercantile wealth with close court ties, who were eventually (but not yet) to be ennobled (Figure 2.20).[70] These included Holland House, a large Jacobean dwelling, which was built in 1606–7 by Sir Walter Cope, a gentleman of the Privy Chamber to James I, to which John Thorpe would make additions after Cope's death in 1614. Camden

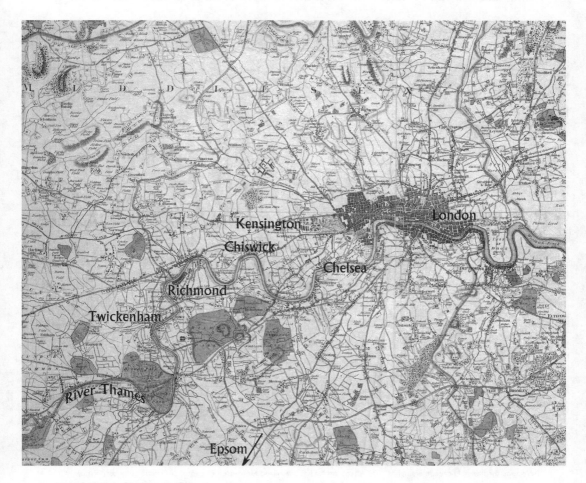

Figure 2.19. Map of London, ca. 1790.

House, also by Cope, may have been begun about 1612 and was sold in 1616 to Sir Baptist Hicks, a London financier who was reputed to know "how to amass money as a merchant and spend it as a prince." By the time Hicks died in 1629 he had been ennobled for a year as Viscount of Campden and had transformed his residence into an elegant Jacobean mansion. Shortly after 1605 Sir William Coppin, Clerk of the Crown to James I, began work on what later became known as Nottingham House, after the Earl of Nottingham purchased it in 1681. (Only in 1689 did it become a royal palace, when William III and Queen Mary, irritated by the "smoak of London," found it the only winter residence that suited their needs. Subsequently it became known as Kensington Palace.)[71]

As Nicholas Cooper has shown, and chapter 3 explores in more detail, Holland, Camden, and Nottingham Houses were revolutionary in part because of their interior plans.[72] These were gentry dwellings, and although the owners ultimately had high pretensions, the dwellings as built incorporated a significant advance in planning that helped to facilitate the invention and evolution of the bourgeois dwelling

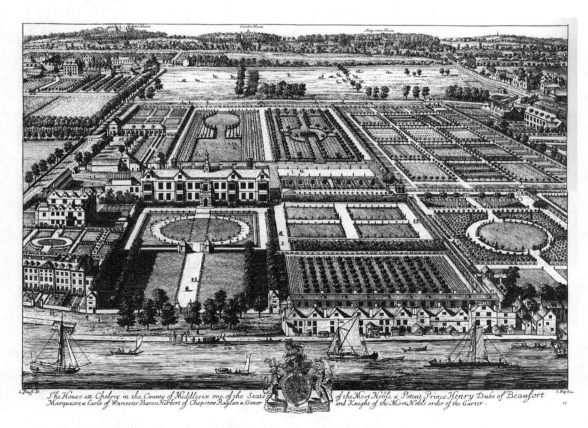

Figure 2.20. Leonard Knyff and Johannes Kip, *The House att Chelsey in the County of Middlesex.* Plate 13 in volume 1 of *Nouveau théâtre de la Grande Bretagne,* 1708. At top on far left is Holland House; left of center is Camden House; right of center is Kensington House.

of the later seventeenth and eighteenth centuries. As Cooper has detailed, these three houses made a pointed break with common practice in the layout of large dwellings by adopting nonhierarchical plans. Instead of the main hall establishing distinctions between higher and lower social strata and segregating them by directing their paths away from each other to different parts of the house, the plans of Holland, Camden, and Nottingham houses began to abandon such hierarchical screening functions. Put differently, these three dwellings suggested by example that, even at the very highest echelons of the gentry, the need for ceremonious distinctions would not need to be built into the dwellings of the bourgeoisie. Instead of the hall being a space for defining relations between upper and lower strata, it could become domesticated and privatized for much different purposes, as chapter 3 analyzes further.

But the reason that these three houses are so crucial to the present discussion is that they were a critical presence in the close-in part of Middlesex. They were not just gentry houses with innovative plans but just the sort of temporary retreat that many bourgeois merchants, traders, and the like would soon emulate on a much smaller scale as they "retired" to Middlesex or another suburban area on a regular basis. In fact by the start of the eighteenth century the direction in which suburbia would develop had already been set, to a great extent both architecturally and geographically, by the forays a century earlier of Cope, Hicks, and Coppin.

Twickenham: The Coalescence of Modern Suburbia

In many respects Defoe's account of Epsom, which may or may not have been a unique locale, affords a viable narrative of the invention of modern suburbia in the sense that he portrayed gentry who established residences in a common location on a seasonal or commuting basis. But examination of the historical development of towns in the Thames Valley west of London, particularly Twickenham, suggests that for reasons in addition to the innovations in house plans discussed above this was the region in which modern suburbia first coalesced.

By the end of the seventeenth century villages westward along the Thames between Chelsea and Richmond such as Chiswick and Twickenham had begun to prosper, taking advantage of the convenience of the river for transportation. By this time Chiswick in particular had many substantial Tudor houses used as summer retreats by city merchants and their families, while some of the more ordinary retreats of the gentry along the riverfront were in the form of terrace-style housing. This density of housing may have been due to land values, since Chiswick had such an elite cachet that acreage here commanded prices many multiples of what the cost would have been elsewhere on the periphery of London. Thus erecting a detached villa with its surrounding gardens and the like in Chiswick soon became an opportunity for only the wealthiest.[73]

Yet Chiswick was somewhat an anomaly, and the broad westward shift of the gentry past Kensington and along the Thames toward Richmond, sustained by England's rapid economic and mercantile growth, meant that this area west of London, and

Twickenham and Richmond in particular, was probably the earliest to be suburbanized anywhere. In some respects the Twickenham house of poet Alexander Pope may be considered emblematic of many characteristics of this bourgeois suburbanization. This is not because Pope set a particular paradigm, but because as a prolific literary and artistic figure of his time, his work allows us to understand his residence and the way he lived there in an especially illuminating fashion.[74]

Late in 1719 Pope moved to his riverfront dwelling at Twickenham, which although it was very modest in comparison to either of Pliny's villas, Pope described as "my Tusculum" (Figure 2.21).[75] Here Pope pointedly invoked the notion of a classical villa, albeit not employing its actual design or scale, almost a decade before Castell's publication of Pliny appeared. The house that Pope purchased, which he engaged James Gibbs to renovate the next year,[76] displayed the standard three-story, 1—3—1 elevation that characterized the compact bourgeois villa. Soon Pope undertook intensive improvements to the small private garden there, including an elaborate grotto (the entrance to which is the arch visible in the basement story, leading to a tunnel under the London road and then into the garden), transforming the whole into an apparatus of introspection and self-expression, a quintessentially active private space.[77] For despite its small size, the garden, which lay across the main road from his house and fronted the Thames, also managed to serve as a terrain of isolation and sanctuary from the religious and political persecution in London that he as Catholic and Tory partisan had suffered, in which he could self-consciously, almost heroically, constitute his own identity. The garden, in other words, served Pope less as *landscape*

Figure 2.21. View of Alexander Pope's villa, ca. 1748–49. From *A New Display of the Beauties of England*, 1776. Like those shown in Figure 2.13, this was one of the prominent villas along the Thames in the vicinity of Twickenham.

than as an enabling apparatus that allowed him to pursue his work, and through that his selfhood, in this very private way.[78]

If one were to seek the highest concentration of detached compact villas in the area surrounding London before the middle of the eighteenth century, the evidence clearly would point to Twickenham and its vicinity. By midcentury concentrations of compact villas figure prominently in John Rocque's map (Figure 2.22) and in an engraved view of Twickenham (Figure 2.13), clearly distinguishing it as a site already well identified with this manner of building. As with neighboring suburbs, some elites had been erecting houses in Twickenham since the early seventeenth century, but a majority of those building there had been people with no previous connection to the place.[79] Twickenham grew not because of indigenous forces, in other words, but because it attracted bourgeois residents from other parts of the region.

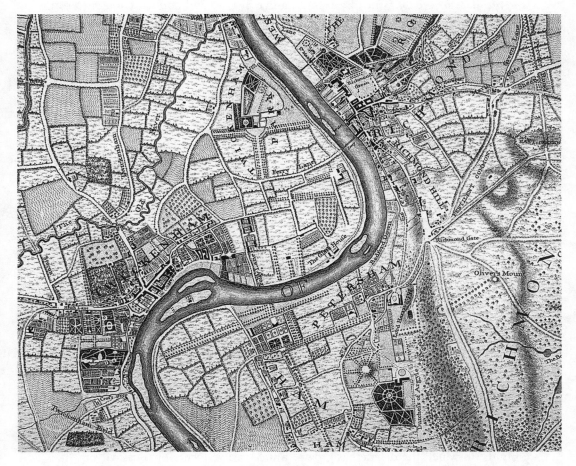

Figure 2.22. John Rocque, *A Plan of London ... with Improvements to 1769*, 1769. This detail shows Twickenham, Richmond, and vicinity. All along the banks of the Thames individual villas and their landscaped gardens are visible, some represented in great detail. Pope's garden can be seen here as a black area, cut through by thin avenues and oval-shaped clearings, just above the westernmost bend of the Thames at the left side of the image.

By midcentury Twickenham held a reputation as almost exemplary of suburbia. The opening stanza of a love poem published in 1751 suggests that Twickenham would be the perfect place for the writer and his beloved to settle down to a perfect bourgeois existence:

Give me, ye Gods, a calm retreat,
No splendid, yet a genteel seat,
    Near *Twick'nam's* velvet meads:
Let there be neither pomp nor state,
The plague and torment of the great,
    Yet all that pleasure needs.[80]

Less than a decade later, *A Short Account, of the Principal Seats and Gardens, in and about Twickenham,* issued by Henrietta Pye in 1760 and popular enough to run to three editions, offered the assessment that Twickenham had become an "earthly Elysium." And tellingly the means to that end seems to have been domestic architecture: "The genius of the inhabitants inclines not towards commerce; architecture seems their chief delight: in which, if any one doubts their excelling, let him sail up the river, and view their lovely villas beautifying its banks: lovers of true society, they despise ceremony; and no place can boast more examples of domestic happiness."[81] Although the text consists largely of descriptions of better-known dwellings such as Pope's villa, Marble Hill House, and Strawberry Hill, too much weight should not be laid on that point. The reputation of Twickenham as a whole, including many unmentioned, quite ordinary compact villas, was here confirmed as a highly desirable elite-bourgeois suburb.

Twickenham was neither the only locale in which bourgeois villas proliferated nor the only one where they coalesced to a notably early degree. Enclaves of bourgeois villas sprang up almost contemporaneously in other areas about London and around other large English towns. Even in America during the first half of the eighteenth century villa estates began to line the banks of the rivers outside of a few major towns such as Philadelphia, Williamsburg, and Boston.[82] In England and America few locales, if any, so rapidly attained the sort of architectural identity that Mrs. Pye discerned at Twickenham—a discrete locale of bourgeois retreats dedicated to domestic happiness. Nor does her definition necessarily cover all the modes of suburbanization that legitimately must be considered, including terrace housing, cottages, shacks and derelict buildings, merchandising, service, transportation, and the ongoing spread of vice and crime. Defoe clearly had a very different opinion of suburbanization from Mrs. Pye, as have many others over time, and subsequent chapters will examine the grounds on which the debate has grown. But Mrs. Pye in her own casual way, like theorists and designers before and after, expressed an ideal: that the local environment in which one lives might be an apparatus for making an "earthly Elysium." Not only did this form a partial response to the Enlightenment challenge to articulate selfhood, it did so in the exact terms that many nineteenth-century designers would use to describe their planned suburban communities, as chapter 5 explores further.

But the suburbanization of selfhood, if it may be called that, introduces a range of additional considerations. Many will be taken up in subsequent chapters, and only one will be introduced here, by way of conclusion: the role of land. As merchants, traders, and other bourgeois householders began building dwellings in the suburban outskirts of major towns and cities, they commonly surrounded their houses with sufficient land to sustain some measure of aesthetic pleasures and leisure pursuits— an amount of land presumably proportional to what they could afford. Increasingly authors of architectural treatises, cottage and villa design books, and landscape treatises emphasized the importance of providing the client with not simply a dwelling but also sufficient landscape resources to sustain those aesthetic pleasures and leisure pursuits. The reason, though often unstated, was that these had come to be understood as a necessary part of bourgeois selfhood.[83]

But if the suburban dwelling and its lot were perfect instruments to this end, it could *only* be achieved by what had amounted to a revolution in the entire land-holding system of Great Britain, the introduction of private property ownership. As chapter 1 describes, this was a system that shifts in British economic practice and jurisprudence had necessitated, and that Locke had theorized in his *Two Treatises*. But as it evolved thereafter in legal practice, it created specifically advantaged and disadvantaged strata in British society. As E. P. Thompson has shown, it divided the country into a world of property that had legal status and rights of its own versus propertyless people who had no standing at all.[84] The suburban locales that developed in the environs of London and elsewhere from the eighteenth century onwards depended on that division. Bourgeois householders there required what Thompson termed the institution of "absolute property ownership"—the privatization of property—as a necessary basis for the building, landscaping, and private self-defining activities that would be undertaken at any given homesite.

Suburbia: Looking Back and Ahead

Only at the very end of the eighteenth century was the first formal design for a speculative suburban development committed to paper, a design for semidetached villas laid out in geometric arrays on Eton College lands at St. John's Wood. Prior to this eighteenth-century suburbs were not laid out with forethought or according to comprehensive plans. Places that contemporary commentators identified as thriving suburbs had grown that way in a piecemeal fashion over time, and once a place attained a reputation as a good suburban destination (long before Defoe or Mrs. Pye would have noticed), it would have strengthened that reputation by attracting people at an increasing rate. But the layered and accretive nature of these early suburbs makes it difficult to define completely what made them notable "suburbs" at the time, or to extract characteristics that definitively mark a suburb such as Twickenham as the site where most aspects of modern suburbia first coalesced.

Still, several characteristics of early eighteenth-century suburbs do stand out in some relief in light of contemporary trends—the rise of capitalism, the corresponding growth of the bourgeoisie, the importance of ideologies of the economic and political self for the bourgeoisie, and the invention of the bourgeois compact villa—and it is appropriate to conclude this chapter with a brief enumeration of some of these characteristics of early suburbs. Part of the reason for their early growth was simply the growth of the bourgeoisie, and this put the stamp of this class of people on the places where they moved. As more people sought opportunities to retreat, at least temporarily, from the increasing pressure, corruption, congestion, and duplicity of city life and to withdraw from the competitive pressures of capitalist finance and trade, the destination of choice, explicitly recognized as such a haven, was the suburb. It provided a perfect basis for doing this by virtue of its many degrees of oppositionality to the city. As commentators had noted since the sixteenth century, the suburban environment was purer and healthier in many respects, and (as Pope and many others would testify) living there provided both a refuge and a moral stance against the city. The oppositionality of suburbia was enhanced by its capacity to facilitate many pursuits that were integral to the bourgeois ideology of self. These included such things as the study of literature and history, the appreciation of art and music, and venturing outdoors to study the arts of landscape design and appreciation. These all were considered leisure pursuits, and in a social and economic sense they were precisely that since they were nonproductive activities. With respect to suburbs at large, these pursuits also served to establish a double (oppositional) relation of leisure to the metropolis, the first by virtue of the wholly residential environment in which they took place, and the second by the uneconomic nature of the activities themselves. And finally, the ideal instrument for undertaking these pursuits was the detached dwelling, as it provided not only the opportunity for material articulation of the self as an individual, but also—to the extent that surrounding grounds could be extended and improved—for repeated engagement with many of the additional endeavors and pursuits deemed important to bourgeois selfhood.

3. The Apparatus of Selfhood

In 1624 Henry Wotton, author of *The Elements of Architecture,* outlined several ways in which a house might serve a man of some means in articulating the dimensions of his life. These included the hospitality that he could demonstrate for society at large as well as his own sense of self, comfort, and patrimony:

> Every Mans proper *Mansion* House and *Home,* being the *Theater* of his *Hospitality,* the *Seate* of *Selfe-fruition,* the *Comfortablest part* of his owne *Life,* the *Noblest* of his Sonnes *Inheritance,* a kinde of priuate *Princedome;* Nay, to the *Possessors* thereof, an *Epitomie* of the whole *World:* may well deserue by these *Attributes,* according to the degree of the *Master,* to be *decently* and *delightfully* adorned.[1]

In some respects Wotton pointed to the very same things that are at the center of this book: how architecture, and domestic architecture in particular, could be a highly versatile instrument for constituting the self in multiple respects, in multiple personal and social contexts. In contrast to Wotton, this chapter focuses on dwellings produced in the eighteenth century for bourgeois (no longer elite) clients. They were still trying to achieve a kind of "selfe-fruition" but under very different terms. The capitalist underpinnings of the bourgeoisie were markedly different from the landholdings of the aristocracy for whom Wotton wrote, so that even rhetorically the notion of a "private princedom" was no longer appropriate to the bourgeois dwelling, and the capital resources available to any one individual were far more limited. And as previous chapters have shown, the ideological notions of what constituted self and identity had changed markedly. To explore the response of the eighteenth-century compact villa to these changing circumstances, two broad, intertwining threads will anchor the discussion in this chapter: first, the increasing desire and opportunity to articulate spaces within a dwelling as private, and to reserve them for use by the individual; and second, the growing preference to define spaces according to specific uses and functions.

Private Pursuits

The challenge facing those establishing bourgeois households was, in some respects, comparable to the challenge laid out at birth to a mind born as a Lockean tabula rasa: how to define and maintain an identity. The Enlightenment ideology of Locke and his successors had cast that challenge in particularly difficult terms, posing identity as an individual personal characteristic, that is, as something ontologically prior to the social realm—prior to family, state, and everything else in between. Dwellings too, as the century progressed, came to be linked ever more literally to the personal identity of the householder, not only as an *indication* of selfhood but also as an *instrument* for the fullest articulation and realization of the self. But incorporating this sort of instrumentality into the dwelling also required narrowing some of the previous century's elaborate expectations, such as those indicated by Wotton, and concentrating instead on concerns such as privacy that would pertain more to the self.

Ultimately the evolution of the compact bourgeois villa resulted not only in the enhancement of personal privacy but also in a redefinition of what it meant to be "private."[2] The room layout of the Elizabethan household had hardly been an apparatus of private individuation. Rather it had been one of stratification and differentiation of status.[3] Then, as Nicholas Cooper has shown, in the mid-seventeenth century a few houses of the elite gentry on the outskirts of London made innovative leaps in developing two specific features of the plan that differentiated them from their predecessors. These features would become significant for the emergent bourgeoisie in the eighteenth century by establishing an apparatus for privatizing individual spaces within the dwelling. The first was a shift from a hierarchical to a nonhierarchical plan. Previously the hall had served as a central space that welcomed but also mediated among various social strata, distributing them to their appropriate stations, directing them to upper and lower ends of the building. The innovative nonhierarchical plans in the proto-suburban environs of London abolished those directions and distinctions. The hall at Holland, Camden, and Nottingham Houses became an entirely symmetrical space, without "high" and "low" ends, and thus a space without the complexities of rank orderings. The second shift was from the dwelling that consisted of a single range of rooms to a dwelling with a double range of rooms, the so-called double-pile house. The advantage of the double-pile, created by backing one range of rooms up against the other, was a much more compact plan, although it meant that light and air could be provided to only one side of a room instead of two. Still, the double-pile plan allowed for far better opportunities for circulation patterns within the building, economies of construction, and a more compact outline, all attractive features to the emerging bourgeoisie.[4] And at the turn of the eighteenth century both shifts, the nonhierarchical plan and the double-pile plan, offered considerable future potential to privatize space within the bourgeois dwelling.

At that time privacy still would have been experienced in terms of a scale of degrees or gradations: as one passed from one room to the next, hall to antechamber to chamber to cabinet, further into the confidence and respect of the owner, one arrived at places that were increasingly restricted but by modern standards never perfectly "private." Only toward the end of the seventeenth century was the architectural apparatus of staircases and corridors being developed that could provide the modern sense of comparatively absolute, inviolate privacy, such as a person now expects in one's "own" room. And the growing tendency during the eighteenth century to harden and limit the functions of many rooms within the dwelling, such as the library or dining room, was paralleled by practices of closing off and dedicating other rooms, such as the study and bedchamber, to more intimate, personal purposes. By these processes of narrowing and dedicating rooms to private purposes and specific functions, dwellings began to address the new challenges of identity formation in the burgeoning bourgeois culture of eighteenth-century Enlightenment England.

Apparatuses of Privacy

Well before the eighteenth century architects already were aware of notions of privacy in domestic architecture. In the fifteenth century, for example, Florentine architect and theorist Leon Battista Alberti discussed a "Country house for a Gentleman" in terms of gradations of privacy. He wrote that certain portions of the house "belong to the whole Family in general, others to a certain number in it, and others again only to one or more persons separately." The various parts included the courtyard, which he analogized to "a publick market-place to the whole House," to which husband, wife, children, relations, servants, and guests all would have access, as well as "Bed-Chambers, and lastly the private Rooms for the particular uses of each person in the family," although those uses went unspecified.[5] Of course Alberti was describing country houses of some magnitude, for elite clients, but his suggestion that "private Rooms" might be dedicated to "particular uses" would have struck a note of interest among eighteenth-century readers looking for an authoritative source on which to base architectural initiatives to produce private spaces for the articulation of selfhood.

As Orest Ranum has shown, the rise of intimate practices during the Renaissance was accompanied by a corresponding rise in kinds of spaces that would lend themselves to intimacy.[6] These would include private gardens, sites of love and courtship, as well as spaces inside the house such as closets and chambers that might afford similar kinds of semiprivate encounters. Still, unlike the private chambers of mid- and late-eighteenth-century households, these would be connected by multiple doors to several other rooms, and thus not yet fully isolated from other rooms and circulation patterns throughout the house.

By the mid-eighteenth century interest in matters of intimacy had grown to encompass architectural efforts not only to afford greater intimacy by securing greater privacy, as will be discussed shortly, but also to hide things that may have become too intimate, or private, for others to view. Much of that concern revolved around growing awareness of the body as an instrument by which the self was defined both in absolute terms (e.g., in terms of intellectual powers) and in respect to others (e.g., in terms of social graces). In this respect the privy, an obvious etymological cognate of "private," took on increasing status as an object of concern in dwelling design. Perhaps not so remarkably, an entire discourse on the subject of privies was prepared as late as 1751 for delivery to a society of antiquaries, introducing Greek and Roman authority and practice to bolster the principal arguments.

Tellingly the discourse was introduced in the form of a dialogue between two "Gentlemen" visiting the author's country house. While in this bucolic, domestic setting, they embarked on a discussion of matters "of *modesty,* or *decency,* or more properly *shame.*"[7] At stake here, albeit always couched in philosophical or medical terms, was a growing awareness that bourgeois culture depended on the assertion and assurance of modesty and decency,[8] and that domestic architecture could be a means to securing that end. Fully half of the book was devoted to "A Critical and Historical Dissertation on Places of Retirement for Necessary Occasions," such as Roman latrines and "public boghouses" as well as "closestools and other vessels made use of for the reception of human excrement." In other words, in anticipation of the private water closet—a feature that could not be widely and fully realized until the introduction of indoor plumbing in the nineteenth century—the eighteenth-century bourgeoisie was not only concerned with the spatial privatization of self and body in ways that individualized one from another, but also eager to architecturally reinforce practices that amplified such dimensions as class, status, character, and moral standing.

But the factor of greatest interest for eighteenth-century architects with respect to privacy, in addition to intimacy and modesty, was selfhood: how, by such measures as enhancing isolation and creating spaces conducive to sustained contemplation and reflection, they could provide clients suitable opportunities for articulating bourgeois subjectivity. A striking example of the shift in priorities that this implied is found in a design by Robert Morris that he discussed in his *Lectures on Architecture* (1734–36) (Figure 3.1). A thoroughly diminutive dwelling by elite standards, its size would have been quite respectable for a bourgeois gentleman, including family and servants. But Morris pointedly deemphasized the domestic possibilities of such a design in favor of the possibilities for selfhood. It could be suited to "a Family," he wrote, but he chose to emphasize its suitability to "a single Person, not over-fond of Company, one studious, and who prefer'd a contemplative, *rural Life,* with few Attendants, to one Generally esteem'd *fashionable* and gay." Not only that, it would be the owner's "chief Residence," not a simple rural or suburban retreat, thus emphasizing his isolation and privacy.[9] Designing such apparatuses of selfhood did not become common stock in trade for eighteenth-century architects, although the frequency of such designs for

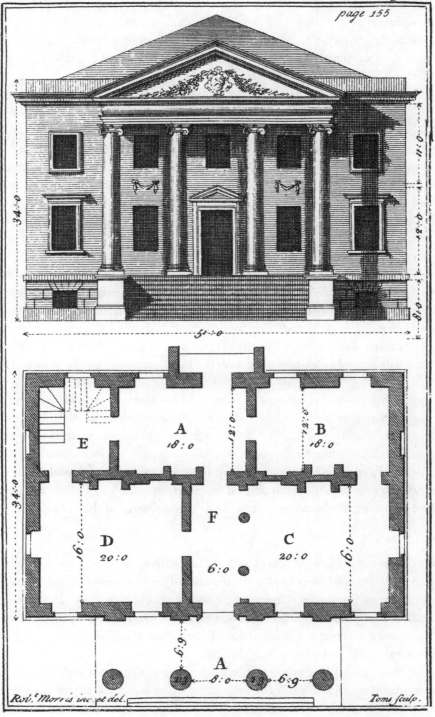

Figure 3.1. Robert Morris, design for a dwelling based on the double cube (elevation and plan). Figure D in *Lectures on Architecture*, 1734–36. Morris stressed the suitability of this design to a single individual, rather than a family, and preferably someone inclined to study and contemplation.

"contemplative" or "studious" or "retired" individuals did increase considerably toward the close of the century. The notable aspect of Morris's design was that a principal residence of such substantial size had been dedicated to the use of a single individual in his "studious," "contemplative" pursuit of bourgeois selfhood.

Morris's design also signaled a major shift in the manner of articulating an individual's subjectivity within a given dwelling. In the standard seventeenth-century household configuration there had been a graduated hierarchy of social relations. One experienced incremental gradations of status and intimacy as one passed from the most public to the most private areas. This linear sequence of an antechamber leading to a chamber followed by a closet or a cabinet at the farthest end, a series of semipublic to semiprivate rooms, was gradually superseded in the eighteenth century by the disuse of antechambers, the decline of closets and cabinets to vestigial status, and a more immediate communication of the chamber with a corridor or stair that allowed it to be rendered entirely private. This led to an increasing disjunction between social activities in public areas of the house, and intimate or solitary activities in private areas. Ensuing changes in later decades furthered this distinction, first by locating main-floor bedroom suites at greater distances from public areas such as halls and drawing rooms, and then by banishing bedrooms altogether to the next floor up. Private activities thus literally became stratified as a different class of activities, now demarcated as incompatible with the public activities on the principal floor.

The eighteenth-century dwelling did more than become an instrument for hardening new distinctions between self and society. It also helped to articulate specific dimensions of the private self.[10] It did so by a number of complementary means to be discussed next, including the introduction of new means of circulation (specifically staircases and corridors), arranging many rooms as end destinations instead of in suites, allotting specific rooms to defined purposes, and carefully segregating servants and service areas from both the "public" and "private" areas of the house.

Staircases

Two methods for privatizing spaces within the dwelling involved new modes of circulation: staircases and corridors. In the instance of staircases, they could be placed at new locations within the dwelling, or their number could be multiplied, in ways that could afford private access to specific rooms or wings. Or they could provide separate, hidden access for servants so that those of lower status would not be seen by any householders while performing their duties.

Precedents for such a manner of segregated access existed in early Tudor times, when staircases occasionally did not connect all floors directly. Early in the sixteenth century, for example, a staircase might bypass one or two floors to afford access from ground level to the roof, to afford privacy and security to the inhabitants of the intermediate floors. Or a staircase might just lead from private rooms of the household to a turret. The Duke of Buckingham had the reverse, a private staircase from the upper floor to his privy garden.[11] In all these cases, staircases had begun to evolve as instruments of *privacy*. More than just the necessary means of getting to and from the various parts of the dwelling, they also became a means of isolating portions of the residence for the exclusive use and safety of the owner.

At Coleshill House, begun in 1649 and completed in 1662, architect Roger Pratt switched from using such special-purpose staircases to providing back staircases, at the ends of corridors near bedchambers, to afford private means of access for servants away from public view (Figures 3.2, 3.3).[12] This doubly enhanced privacy within the household, since due to the corridors the chambers could remain fully private, and due to the back stairs only householders and guests would encounter each other in

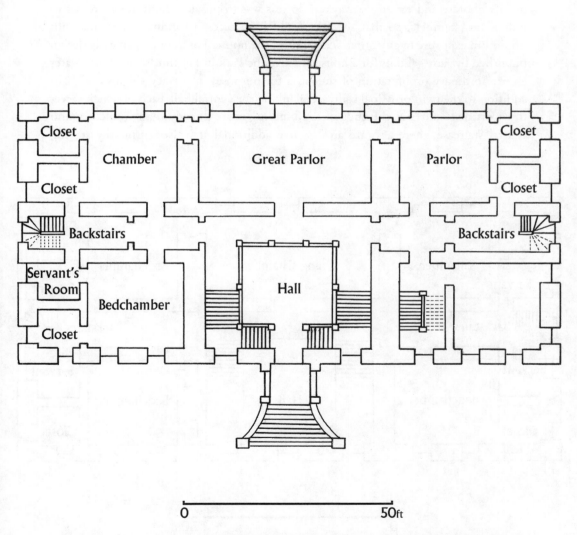

Figure 3.2. Roger Pratt, principal floor, Coleshill, 1649–62 (plan). Back stairs at each end of the main corridor allowed servants to tend to their duties while keeping out of public view. Drawing by Holley Wlodarczyk.

the corridors. Thus for each member of the household and their guests, the result was a fully isolated suite consisting of a bedchamber, closet, and servant's room. And although this was an unusually early instance of such planning mechanisms, it is significant that they occurred in a dwelling owned by member of the gentry, the architect's brother Sir George Pratt.

By the 1720s even comparatively modest establishments could be found with multiple staircases by which servants' access to chambers and suites could be facilitated with minimum exposure to any other occupants of the house. And the interest of many architects in providing privacy, particularly to bedchambers, had become so strong that they produced correspondingly complex designs for multiple, redundant, and hidden staircases in order to maximize the privacy of each room.[13] Among the more elaborate and expensive ways to do this was to provide duplicate staircases to individual chambers, so that servants could have access to individual rooms with minimum exposure to any other occupants of the house. For example, an early design published by James Gibbs for a house at Sacombe Park in Hertfordshire incorporates an extraordinary proliferation of staircases for purposes of privacy (Figure 3.4).[14] In addition to the twin principal staircases flanking the central hall, each of which serves the apartment suites at the ends of the building more directly than would a grand central staircase, there also are at least five additional staircases, primarily serving

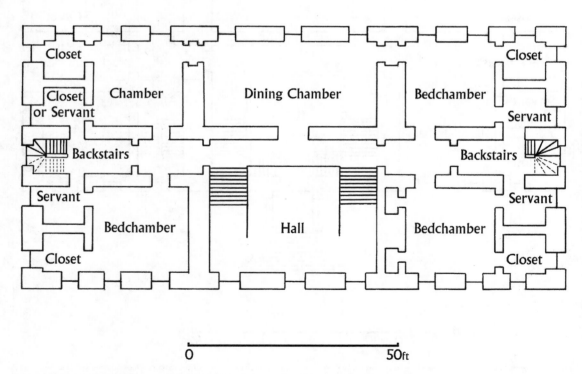

Figure 3.3. Roger Pratt, upper floor, Coleshill (plan). Drawing by Holley Wlodarczyk.

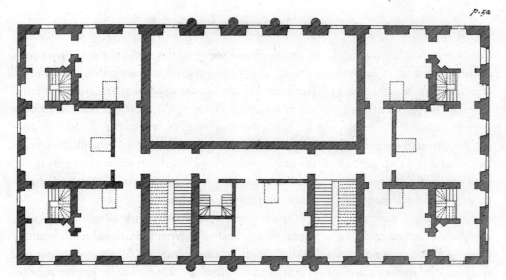

The one pair of Stairs

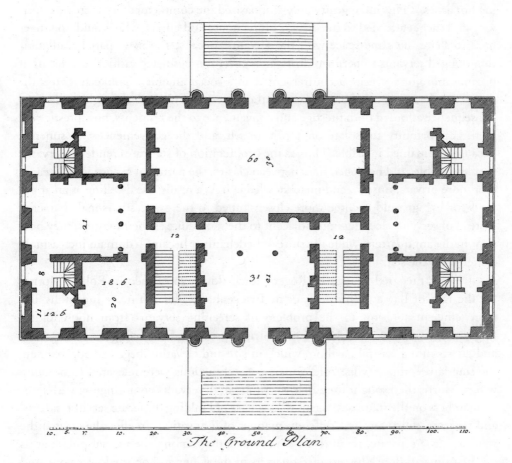

The Ground Plan

Figure 3.4. James Gibbs, ground floor and upper floor, Sacombe (plans). Plate 52 in *A Book of Architecture*, 1728. Gibbs introduced multiple private staircases as a means of further sequestering servants as they performed their duties.

bedchambers. Here overnight accommodation seems to be one of the principal functions of the house, as the two principal floors contain just four public rooms and
eleven apartment suites or bedchambers. Yet the screening of all guests from servants'
activities was evidently a paramount concern, as ten of the eleven private chambers
communicate directly with one of the service staircases. Access to the eleventh apparently is through a semipublic corridor and then to a staircase (above the ground-floor
hall) that quite impractically leads only upward, thus requiring servants to pass up at
least one flight before then descending down one of the other staircases to the basement. Still, the principal goal was accomplished: servants would not be seen.

The service staircases that Gibbs designed for Sacombe Park all were quite narrow with sharply angled steps, impractical at best and virtually impassable for women
wearing full eighteenth-century skirts. Such an inconvenience of passage, while bespeaking the menial status of servants and servants' work, was hardly appropriate to
the risk and difficulty of tasks servants were expected to perform on these stairs, such
as carrying away the contents of chamber pots, providing fuel for fireplaces, or removing hot ashes.[15] This incongruity only emphasized the complementary increase in privacy and cachet afforded to the owners of the house and guests, who would no longer
have to share the same space with the servants. Because the new spatial configuration obliged servants to perform duties in an ever more isolated fashion, service itself
became more of a private accoutrement than a social amenity. Unlike seventeenth-
century and earlier households, in which the presence of servants throughout the spatial sequence afforded both prestige and convenience to the residents, now prestige lay
in the opportunity to isolate one's private self, and the convenience was superior
because it remained invisible. Thus as the proliferation of staircases rendered servants
ever less visible, and hardened lines between classes, the nature of service itself became
ever more private, unseen, and unacknowledged. As a result, the dwelling as an apparatus for living could become more closely tuned to the owner's personal character.
Instead of servants sleeping in or adjacent to the same suite as their masters, they now
slept in distant quarters, while the suite or bedchamber became a domain increasingly
centered on the self.

Designs prepared in 1727 by Roger Morris (kinsman of theorist Robert Morris)
for the Earl of Ilay at Whitton Park in Twickenham offered a more ingenious and
more efficient solution to the problem of screening servants from householders
(Figures 3.5, 3.6, 3.7). To begin with, Morris consolidated the living areas for family
and guests into a central pavilion, which in size and elevation began to approximate
the standard compact villa. Additional service functions were relegated to outlying
wings. Morris then sought to resolve the problem of servants commingling with family members on the staircases, versus the expense of building duplicate sets of residents'
and servants' staircases, by a different manner of innovation. In effect he created the
staircases as a separate, semiprivate zone, mediating among the formal public areas
on the principal floor, the servants' quarters in the wings and on the lower floor, and
the residents' and guests' sleeping areas upstairs in the central bloc. In other words,

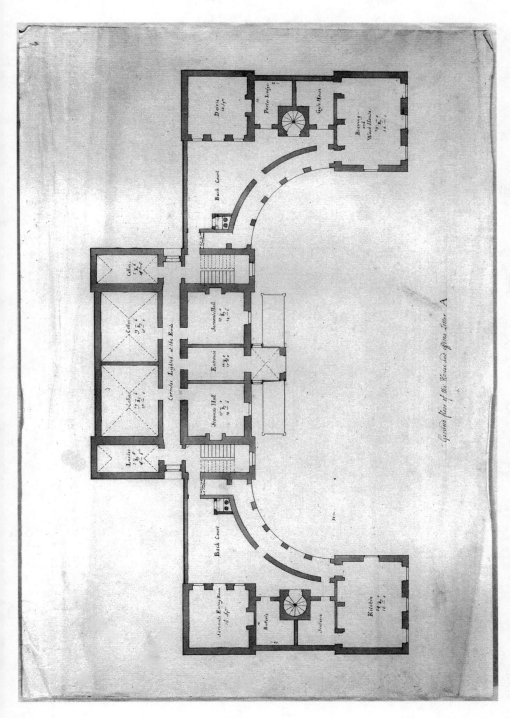

Figure 3.5. Roger Morris, ground floor, Whitton House, Middlesex, 1727 (plan). In this design, Morris abandoned the grand staircase in favor of dual staircases, each semisequestered to function as a transitional zone between public and private, between family and service. B1977.14.1142, pen and black ink, grey wash, over graphite on laid paper, 12⅜ × 18¼ inches (31.4 × 46.4 cm). Courtesy of Yale Center for British Art, Paul Mellon Collection.

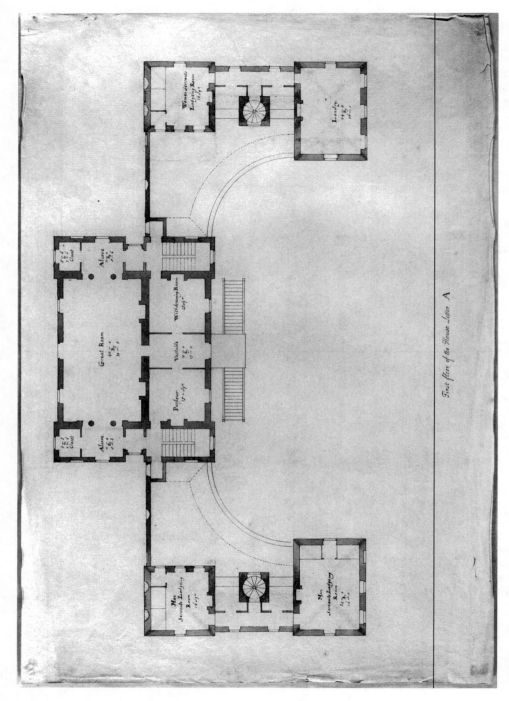

Figure 3.6. Roger Morris, first floor, Whitton House (plan). B1977.14.1144, pen and black ink, grey wash, over graphite on laid paper, 12½ × 18½ inches (31.8 × 47.0 cm). Courtesy of Yale Center for British Art, Paul Mellon Collection.

The first Front towards the Court. Letter A

Figure 3.7. Roger Morris, design for Whitton House (elevation), B1977.14.1137, pen and black ink, grey wash, over graphite on laid paper, 12¼ × 18⅜ inches (31.1 × 46.7 cm). Courtesy of Yale Center for British Art, Paul Mellon Collection.

staircases in this design are transitional zones between public and private, and between family and service. The plain rectangular envelope in which each is housed and the location of each at the ends of a bloc indicate that the staircase is not a ceremonious place, although its size and presence in the main bloc still befit the status of the principal figures in the house. Perhaps most striking of all aspects is the staircases' comparative seclusion. Visitors entering the house in the normal manner on the principal floor could only reach one of the staircases by passing through the vestibule and then through the parlor, or through the drawing room, or by an even longer route via the great room, thus contributing to a greatly heightened sense of privacy for the rest of the house.[16]

As the bourgeois villa became a more common building type, architects developed more techniques for utilizing staircases as an apparatus of privacy. The compact villas of Sir Robert Taylor were exemplary, as he developed something of a formula for locating staircases at the center, and having all of the main rooms open onto either the entrance hall or the staircase (Figure 2.9).[17] By doing so Taylor made a virtue out of the small size of house, something not possible in a larger dwelling with more bedrooms. Each room became a single terminus, a single nodal point radiating off of the central circulation core, and thus a privatizable space.

But for many the preferred solution, when affordable, remained an array of multiple staircases, duplicating access for residents and servants. On the first folio of *Some Designs for Buildings both Public and Private* (1726), James Leoni noted proudly that his design for Thomas Scawen at Carshalton House incorporated a hierarchy of staircases, with larger stairs ascending to the upper apartments, and smaller stairs descending to the "subterraneous" offices or ascending to the mezzanine levels, where the servants' quarters were. Perhaps the most distinctive element of Leoni's design was the pride he took in isolating individual rooms (and thus individuals) by rather expensive means, individual staircases: "I have taken care to place the stairs in the most convenient parts of the House, and at hand for the Master's service, that is to say, not far from the Bed-chambers."[18]

But the allure of a grand open staircase did not die easily. In Robert Mylne's design for a certain Mr. Prescot, drawn perhaps half a century later, a "Great Stairs" measuring fifteen by twenty feet reappears directly adjacent to the grand entrance hall (Figure 3.8). The only apparent concession to the service staff for such a large dwelling is a seven-foot-square winding staircase inserted awkwardly within an interior wall, from the top of which five large bedrooms on the floor above had to be cared for. Or, as one visitor to Nostell Priory in 1750 observed, as he viewed the recently completed work of architects James Moyser and James Paine, dual grand staircases remained much in fashion, and a single back stairs for servants was quite suitable:

> I went four miles to Wrexby, near which is an old monastery call'd Nostal, turned into a mansion house now belonging to Sr Rowland Wynne, but almost destroyed, as he has built a large new house near it, which is the most convenient I have seen;

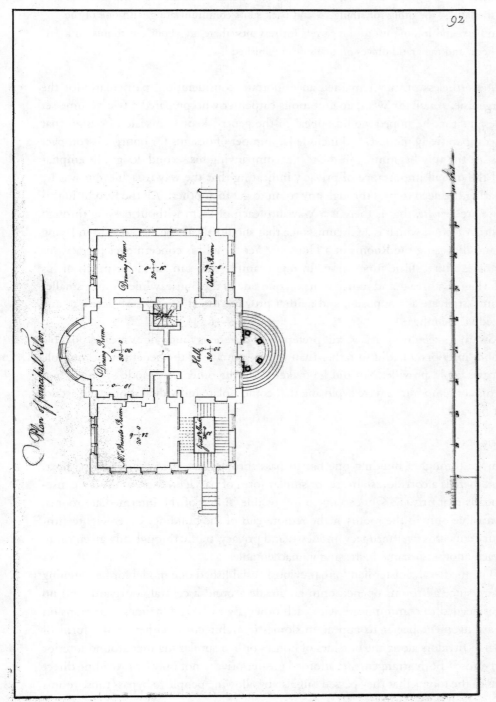

Plan of Principal Floor

Drawing Room
20-0

Dining Room
30-06
10-0

China &c Room
6-0

Hall
20-0
30-0

Mr. Prescot's Room
20-0
6-0

Great Stairs
2

in Feet

Figure 3.8. Robert Mylne, principal floor. "Design for Mr. Prescot" (plan), undated. The contrast between the spacious "Great Stairs" and the cramped and awkwardly located service staircase illustrates how in many cases show still took precedence over servants. Courtesy of Research Library, Getty Research Institute, Los Angeles (850939), sheet 92.

there are two grand staircases, one leading to the apartments in the attick story for the family, the other for strangers, and back stairs communicating with one of the others, and leading up to the garrets for servants; there are about ten rooms on a floor, and the grand offices on one side are finished.[19]

Nevertheless privacy remained an important consideration, particularly for the bourgeoisie. Abraham Swan, an ambitious carpenter who prepared a two-volume set of designs that he hoped would appeal to the gentry, kept to a scale of design that was comparatively modest, and included a number of designs for bourgeois compact villas. At the very beginning, in the text accompanying his second design, he emphasized the overall importance of privacy, indicating that the way to achieve it was by obviating the need to pass through any room to get to another: "All the Rooms in this House are *private,* that is there is a Way into each of them without passing through any other Room; which is a Circumstance that should always be attended to in laying out and disposing the Rooms of a House."[20] Yet for all his concern over privacy, his designs exhibited little innovation. In one example that can stand for much of his work (Figure 3.9), a grand staircase sits on one side of the house, while a much smaller servants' staircase sits opposite, and neither provides direct or exclusive access to any individual chamber.

Swan, so keen on privacy, still preferred to devote as much floor area as possible to room interiors. He did so rather than take advantage of the benefits that multiple staircases could provide. Nor did he make use of the other new mode of circulation that his contemporaries were exploring that could isolate individual rooms and secure their privacy.

Corridors

To move through a building one has to pass through one room to reach the next, unless there is a corridor, staircase, or similar form of passageway around. The consequence is that privacy is uncertain to impossible in any of the intermediate rooms, and feasible only in the rooms at the remote end of the building. Given eighteenth-century concerns over intimacy, modesty, and privacy, traffic through any given room to reach another became increasingly unacceptable.

The medieval cloister had long previously established one model for heightening privacy, since all rooms opened onto an arcade around a central courtyard, and no longer needed to communicate with each other. By early Tudor times, variations on this arrangement began to appear in domestic architecture, either in the form of external corridors along the outsides of houses or in a similar manner around interior courtyards.[21] Both arrangements afforded greater privacy not only by providing direct access to the rooms that they passed but also by allowing people to bypass those rooms on their way to any other.

The innovation of the double-pile house at Coleshill allowed the formalization of the internal corridor as a means of primary access to the rooms on both sides

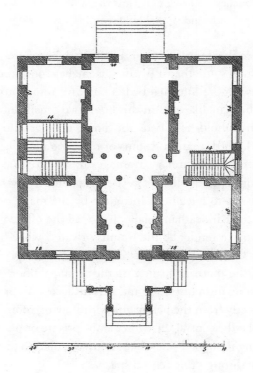

Figure 3.9. Abraham Swan, *A Design for a House of Six Rooms upon a Floor* (plan). Plate 3 in volume 2 of *A Collection of Designs in Architecture*, 1757. Typical of Swan's proposed dwellings for bourgeois clients, this design incorporates a main staircase and a servants' staircase off the central axis. Notwithstanding Swan's stated interest in personal privacy, neither staircase apparently affords access to any individual chamber.

(Figures 3.2, 3.3). Although this was costly in terms of the floor area of the house that it consumed, entry into any one room no longer required passing through any other. Bedrooms and private suites could now remain private for their intended occupants.

By the beginning of the eighteenth century, architect and playwright Sir John Vanbrugh strongly recommended the use of corridors to one of his clients specifically because they afforded advantages of greater privacy. In a letter concerning a design for a country house, he urged that the advantages of privacy, among other things, outweighed the cost in space:

> Some People may Object, that there is too much Space allow'd to the Corridors or Passages; But there is so Vast[?] a Convenience by them by making every Room private, and Quiet, and safe from fire; and so much Beauty and State in them, when rightly and regularly Dispos'd that they well deserve the small increase of Expence they Occasion. I say the small increase, because they Occasion no more Windows or Chimneys than wou'd be without them, require no fine finishing within, nor no more ornaments without, than else would be, nor stand in need of any Furniture more than a few Couches, and Mapps against the Wall; which wou'd in the two end Corridors, be very properly and agreeably Dispos'd.

Vanbrugh also spoke to the question of privacy in one's bedchamber, concluding that privacy might be of such value that it justified a smaller room (because of space lost to corridors) and thus a more informal bed. Thus with respect to rooms for lodging guests, he argued: "There are likewise on this floor, two Small Rooms, Private, Quiet, & Warm; big enough to hold field Beds for Single People, who may probably like much better to be so Lodg'd, than in Rooms of more Parade."[22]

James Gibbs incorporated similar advantages in his proposal for Sacombe Park: the corridors on the upper floor afford direct access and privacy to the bedchambers (Figure 3.4). Gibbs seems to have been intrigued by the many possibilities of corridors; in his proposal for Kirkleatham Hall, circa 1728, he offered "a convenient Passage of Communication to render all the Rooms private," while his far more modest proposal "made for a Gentleman" in 1720 (Figure 3.10) incorporates an experiment in variable privacy for the apartment suites on the principal floor.[23] Here the four corner suites enjoy a combination of public and private access. Each is accessible from a corridor as well as directly from the hall or the withdrawing room. And, as Gibbs put it, it is possible to make the central Octagon Salon "private or publick at pleasure" by means of passages along its angled sides that permit circulation from any room to any other without passing through this central space.

Still, as Isaac Ware attested in 1756, the former practice of configuring rooms in suites without intervening corridors had by no means disappeared. At that late date he still felt compelled to berate such configurations as a great "inconvenience . . . , from the necessity of passing through one [room] to go to another."[24] And of course that inconvenience was threefold. It meant inexpedient detours to get to one's destination,

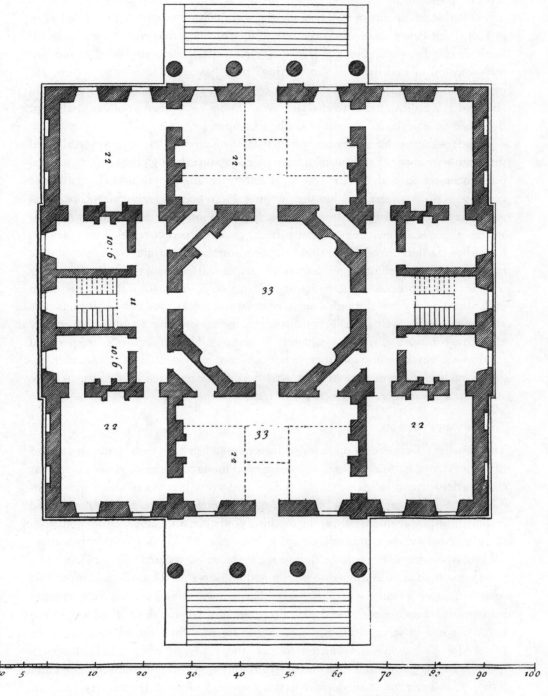

Figure 3.10. James Gibbs, design for Kirkleatham Hall (plan). Plate 44 in *A Book of Architecture*, 1728. The various passageways and doorways controlling access to the four corner rooms and the central octagon allow each room to be made "private or public at pleasure."

it meant passers-through would need to disrupt activities of those along the way, and it meant that occupants of rooms along the way could not enjoy a proper degree of privacy. John Payne emphasized the importance of that privacy the next year in his book *Twelve Designs of Country-Houses* (1757), in which he complained of the "inconvenience" of bedchambers "interfering" with passage to any other rooms. He suggested that any space accessible only by passing through a bedchamber should "be used as a Study, or else divided into two Closets"—in other words, restricted for the private use of the inhabitant of the bedchamber.[25]

Thus as the eighteenth century progressed, the increasing use of corridors allowed the chamber suite to be transformed from part of a route through the house to a nodal point opening onto a corridor system, thereby effecting a profound change in the character of internal space within the dwelling. From being a hierarchical concatenation of connected spaces, the house gradually turned into a series of monadically privatizable spaces. Likewise circulation patterns changed: people traveled via corridors instead of via suites. And as the suite changed from being a route through the house to a terminal point along a corridor system, social and personal relations changed as well. Instead of people and activities being tied to each other (or differentiated from each other) by degrees, through a nexus of serial and hierarchical connections, people and their activities were spatially constituted as discrete, singular termini, each equally accessible (or isolable) from a circulatory armature.[26] The consequences for personal relations within the household then were clear. Each individual, each gender, each age group, each relation, each guest, each activity could be rendered more distinct, more autonomous, and more sequestered with respect to the whole.

The Servant Problem

The ongoing efforts of ever more individuals to establish bourgeois status, or pretend to higher status, naturally meant a growing need for apparatuses of various sorts that could articulate and validate that status. Building a dwelling of one's own was one of the best ways of doing this, but bricks and mortar were expensive, and the costs could literally multiply geometrically as the dwelling got larger. Still, labor in the eighteenth century remained comparatively cheap, so bourgeois dwellings, particularly accommodations for servants, could be quite large by today's standards. Nor was the bourgeois household at all equipped to be run without servants. Thus the fullest possible complement of servants was desirable, which in turn sometimes led to apparently incongruous consequences: for those who could afford to build, the floor area of the house devoted to servants often exceeded that reserved for residents and guests. In Roger Morris's drawings for Whitton, for example, 52 percent of the household spaces (even excluding garrets and interior courtyards) are devoted to servants' lodgings and activities, and 48 percent are devoted to the residents and guests (Figures 3.5, 3.6, 3.7). The proportions are the same in Robert Mylne's drawings for a house for Mr. Prescot, 52 percent for servants (not including garrets and upper floors to the wing pavilions), and 48 percent for residents and guests (Figure 3.8).[27]

The attendant difficulty lay in establishing one's privacy—maintaining one's bourgeois individuality—in proximity to those who were required to serve and tend one's needs. In *Villas of the Ancients* Robert Castell readily faulted Pliny for having failed to discuss "Rooms peculiar to the Servants." Robert Morris put it more bluntly in his *Lectures on Architecture,* stating that the householder could only enjoy the "Pleasure of Retirement" if the servants were unable to observe.[28] Even in the second half of the seventeenth century, architects clearly had become aware of this problem and were beginning to develop solutions. As several of the above examples show, a definite segregation of servants to certain floors or wings, where residents would seldom need to venture except to maintain supervision, was one means of achieving the required separation. Such a gathering of servant activities all on one floor was suggested as early as 1660 by Sir Roger Pratt, who recommended that

> the kitchen and all its offices [would do best] to lie together, and the butter and cellar with theirs, etc. and all these to be disposed of in a half ground storey, with their backcourts, convenient to them; in that no dirty servants may be seen passing to and from by those who are above, no noises heard, nor ill scents smelt.[29]

Pratt likewise laid prime importance on rendering servants and their work invisible by means of a back-stairs circulation system:

> Let the whole be so contrived so that each [upstairs] room lieth to other with the best convenience, and let it be so furnished with back stairs and passages to them, that the ordinary servants may never publicly appear in passing to and fro for their occasions there; let the little parlour have 2 closets there, the one for the man the other for his wife, and each of the bed-chambers a closet to it, and a chamber for a servant, which has a door as out of his master's chamber, so another landing him upon some other passage near the back stairs, so that he need not foul the great ones and whatsoever is of use may be brought up or carried down the back way.[30]

Coleshill, which Pratt designed, was something of a watershed. Because of its multiple hidden staircases, servants could conduct their duties out of sight of the family and guests, thus contributing to the nascent fiction that the dwelling space was self-sustaining.

By the mid-eighteenth century Sir William Chambers had produced a quintessential design for the visual segregation of servants in the Casino at Marino (1757) (Figures 2.10, 2.11, 2.12), with absolutely no visual clue as to their presence, but many other designs of the same decade demonstrate much the same goal. Sir Robert Taylor's splendidly compact bourgeois villas, for example, achieve part of their understated jewel-like perfection by concealing as many of the service spaces as possible below grade. A visitor to Harleyford, Buckinghamshire, (ca. 1755) observed in 1767 that "the whole of the offices are so contained in a pit as to be perfectly invisible."[31] A view of

Coptfold Hall, Essex, (begun 1755) suggests that no portion of the building lay below grade, but an 1828 sale catalog actually described two levels underground, including "housekeeper's room, large servants' hall and knife room adjoining, a butler's pantry, a very capital kitchen and scullery and two larders." Vaulted rooms underneath incorporated the larder, dairy, scullery, and an icehouse.[32]

In many respects all these devices for segregating servants and clarifying the boundaries between spaces allotted to residents, guests, and servants—devices such as corridors, multiple staircases, private wings, service wings, and floors that physically and visually isolated servants unto their own world—were devices invented to facilitate a new bourgeois social order in which all seemed to willingly participate as if by a Lockean social contract. As Harriet Grandison so optimistically but so tellingly attempts to legitimate it in *The History of Sir Charles Grandison* (1753–54):

> The very servants live in paradise. There is room for every thing to be in order: Every-thing *is* in order. The Offices so distinct, yet so conveniently communicating—Charmingly contrived!—The low servants, men and women, have Laws, which at their own request, were drawn up, by Mrs. Curzon, for the observance of the minutest of their respective duties; with little mulcts, that at first *only* there was occasion to exact. It is a house of harmony, to my hand. Dear madam! What do good people leave to good people to do? Nothing! Every one knowing and doing his or her duty; and having, by means of their own diligence, time for themselves.[33]

Family

In addition to segregating self and servants, eighteenth-century architects also developed ways to separate the family into its own distinct zone, quadrant, or level of the dwelling. In some cases the means could be as simple as a bilateral left-right separation or an upstairs-downstairs division. Examples of the former included Harewood, Doddington, and Hagley (1754) (Figure 3.11). At Hagley the family areas—dressing rooms, bedrooms, and library—were clustered on one side, while areas for public entertainment such as the dining room, drawing room, and gallery were on the other side of the axially centered hall and saloon.[34]

But eighteenth-century architects also explored opportunities for a more dramatic manner of segregation, enhanced by the rigor of neoclassical symmetry and geometric proportion, by designing clearly separate wings or pavilions, each of which would sustain a certain subgroup or function within the household. An early instance of this approach appeared at Ragley Hall, begun in 1677, the general configuration of which has been traced to French prototypes and thence to the work of Sebastiano Serlio (Figures 3.12, 3.13).[35] Here four private apartment wings now were separated from the central public area, each with its own antechamber, bedchamber, closet, servant's room, and private back stairs.

This new approach spread slowly at first, no doubt because it was a highly expensive solution to the problem. Peter Leach has documented several houses in the vicinity of Ragley that adopted a similar configuration of pavilions in the years immediately spanning 1700.[36] Perhaps the most dramatic instance was the design for Holkham Hall, which, albeit an elite household by any standard, ironically showed that larger dwelling types also had begun to imitate the compact villa genre. William Kent, a protégé of Lord Burlington, undertook the design in 1734 (Figure 3.14), and the indebtedness of the Holkham mansion to Burlington's much smaller Chiswick villa has long been noted.[37] However, this inverted genealogy was not the only unusual feature of Holkham. So was the parcelization of the household and its functions into separate wings. One wing in effect provided a smaller-scale house (on the

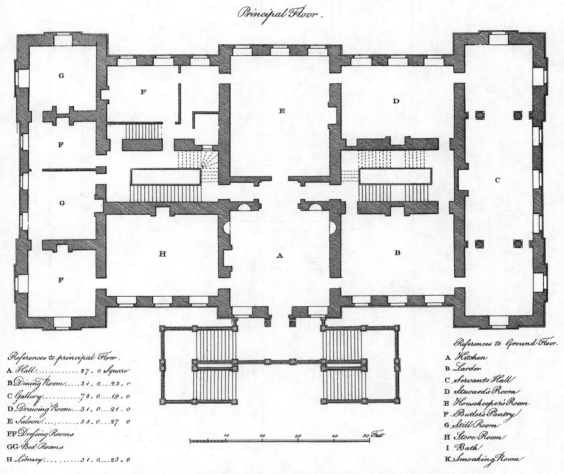

Principal Floor.

References to principal Floor.
A Hall............27. 0. Square
B Dining Room.....31. 0...23. 0
C Gallery..........78. 0...19. 0
D Drawing Room...31. 0...21. 0
E Saloon...........35. 0...27. 0
FF Dressing Rooms
GG Bed Rooms
H Library.........31. 0...23. 0

References to Ground Floor.
A Kitchen
B Larder
C Servants Hall
D Steward's Room
E Housekeeper's Room
F Butler's Pantry
G Still Room
H Store Room
I Bath
K Smoaking Room

Figure 3.11. Sanderson Miller, principal floor, Hagley Hall, Worcestershire, 1754–60 (plan). Plate 14 in volume 2 of *Vitruvius Britannicus*, by John Woolfe and James Gandon, 1767–71. Here the family areas, including the dressing rooms, bedrooms, and library (labeled F, G, and H), are clustered on the left; areas for public entertainment, such as the dining room, gallery, and drawing room (labeled B, C, and D), are clustered on the right.

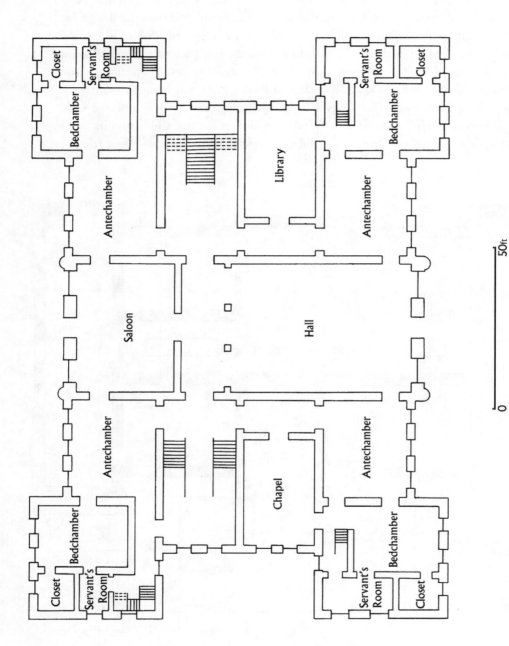

Figure 3.12. Robert Hooke, principal floor, Ragley Hall, Warwickshire, 1679–83 (plan). Four private apartment wings, each with bedchamber, servant's room, and closet, are arrayed at the four exterior corners of the plan. Drawing by Holley Wlodarczyk.

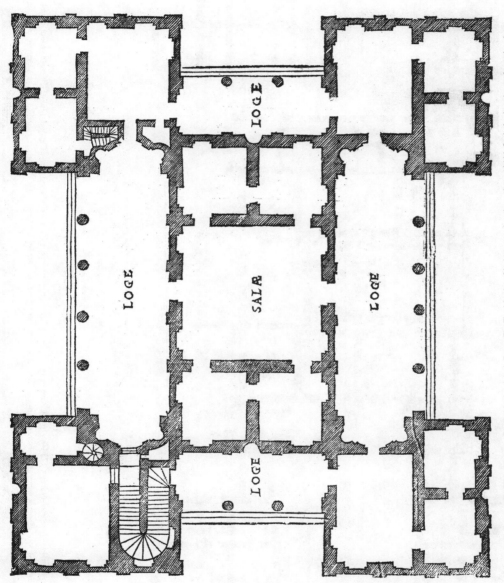

Figure 3.13. Sebastiano Serlio, Poggio Reale, Naples (plan). From *The Third Booke of Architecture*, London edition, 1611. Serlio's plan shows four chamber suites disposed at the corners of the building.

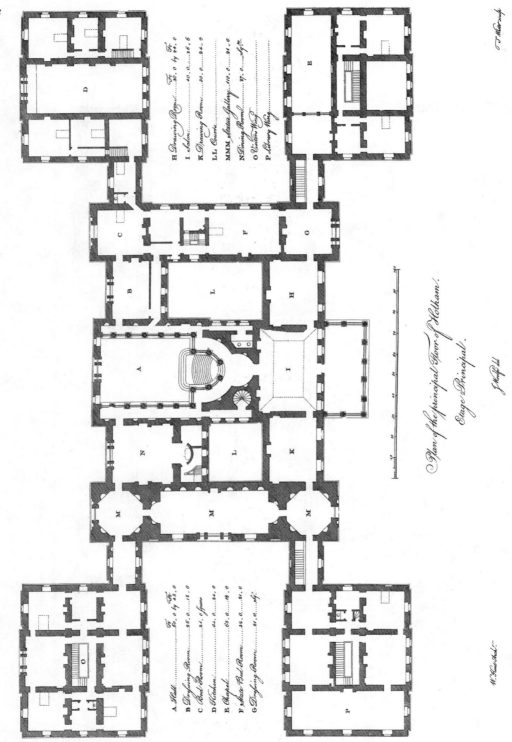

W. Kent Arch.t

J. Woolfe del.

T. Miller sculp.

Plan of the principal Floor of Holkham.
Etage Principal.

A Hall .... Ft. 0 by Ft. 0
B Drawing Room .... 26..0....18..0
C Bed Room .... 24..0 square
D Kitchen .... 24..0....24..0
E Chapel .... 65..0....48..0
F State Bed Room .... 30..0....24..0
G Drawing Room .... 24..0..27½

H Drawing Room .... Ft. 0 by Ft. 0
I Salon .... 40..0....26..6
K Drawing Room .... 30..0....24..0
L L Courts
MMM State Gallery .... 110..0....24..0
N Dining Room .... 27..0....24..0
O Victoria Wing .... 27..0....27½
P Library Wing

Figure 3.14. William Kent, Holkham Hall, Norfolk, 1734–65 (plan). Plate 65 in volume 2 of *Vitruvius Britannicus*, by John Woolfe and James Gandon, 1767–71. Instead of four chamber suites at the corners of the main bloc, now four separate wings are detached from that bloc. One consists of living quarters for the family, while the others contain a chapel, a kitchen, and guest accommodations.

order of a bourgeois villa) for the family itself. Three other wings were given over to a chapel, a kitchen, and guest accommodations. The central body of the house was reserved for the grand entrance hall, the display of art, the state suite, and rooms for entertaining. Thus the grandeur of a country mansion suitable for a state visit was retained, but the privacy of the family was now physically and visibly articulated in a manner heretofore unprecedented.

By midcentury several prominent architects had executed designs of the same type, prominently separating family spaces from public, guest, and service areas. James Paine's 1757 plan for Kedleston Hall (Figure 3.15) was perhaps the quintessential design of this type, segregating the family quarters in one of four physically and visually distinct wings, with the other three devoted to a music gallery, a greenhouse and chapel, and a kitchen and laundry. The central bloc of the house remained dedicated to entertainment and state functions. Isaac Ware's 1754 design for a comparatively modest client, Admiral George Byng, at Wrotham Park (Figure 3.16), well north of London, provided even greater separation. Not only did the central facade take on the look of a bourgeois compact villa but now, with the service areas suppressed below grade, separate wings could be attached, one on either side, forming dual private pavilions. That on one side incorporated a bedchamber and dressing room. That on the other side was a library, a place of private retreat and study, and of quiet retreat for family.

The impracticalities of segregating family rooms and private activities in separate wings or pavilions would be too great for most bourgeois clients. The building expense, on top of the ongoing maintenance costs of such an extended structure, would simply be beyond reach. Still, a nearly equivalent sort of separation could be accomplished within a standard unitary bloc, as architects sought ways to regularize family relations during the eighteenth century. As discussed above, this could be accomplished by devoting one side of the principal floor to rooms for private activities, the other side to public activities. More commonly by the end of the century, the division would be an upstairs-downstairs division, with private activities on the upper floor, as in the work of Sir Robert Taylor.

But more than just separating family from other spheres of life, the dwelling also served to articulate specific aspects of family relations, not least the bourgeois companionate marriage. Samuel Richardson's *History of Sir Charles Grandison* (1753–54) provides a rich illustration of a dwelling transformed into such an instrument. Toward the end of the novel, after Grandison Hall has undergone a series of extensive "alterations," the narrative shows that one of the principal tasks of the house has become the validation of Grandison's own ancestry. The gallery is "adorned with a long line of ancestors," portraits of whom almost serve to constitute the story of the family and legitimate the family's present claim to status and influence. In a comparable way the trees that these ancestors planted in the garden ostensibly sustain the same claim.[38] But Sir Charles also is eager to articulate a place in that family for his bride, Harriet, through architectural means. For instance, her first visit to the newly renovated house

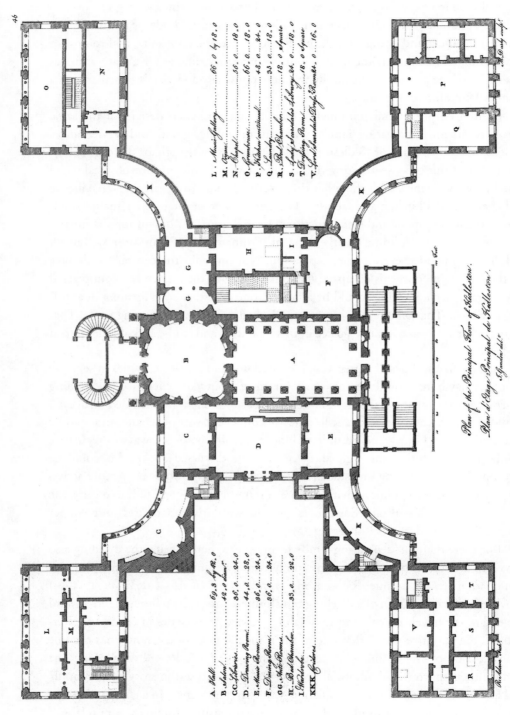

46

Plan of the Principal Floor of Kedleston.
Plan d'l'Etage Principal de Kedleston.

A. Hall .... 69. 3. by 42. 0
B. Salon .... 42. 0. diam.ʳ
CC. Libraries .... 36. 0 ... 24. 0
D. Drawing Room .... 44. 0 ... 28. 0
E. Music Room .... 36. 0 ... 24. 0
F. Dining Room .... 36. 0 ... 24. 0
GG. Anti Rooms ....
H. Bed Chamber .... 33. 0 ... 22. 0
I. Wardrobe ....
KKK. Gitchens ....

L. Music Gallery .... 66. 0 by 18. 0
M. Organ .... 42. 0 diam.ʳ
N. Chapel .... 36. 0 ... 18. 0
O. Greenhouse .... 66. 0 ... 18. 0
P. Kitchen continued .... 42. 0 ... 24. 0
Q. Laundry .... 33. 0 ... 18. 0
R. Bed Chamber .... 18. 0 square
S. Lady Scarsdale's Library 24. 0 ... 18. 0
T. Dressing Room .... 18. 0 square
V. Lord Scarsdale's Dress Room 0 ... 16. 0

Figure 3.15. James Paine, Kedleston Hall, Derbyshire, 1759–60 (plan). Plate 46 in volume I of *Vitruvius Britannicus*, by John Woolfe and James Gandon, 1767–71. Perhaps the finest example of a house with four separate wings: one wing contains family quarters while the other three include a music gallery, a greenhouse and chapel, and the kitchen and laundry.

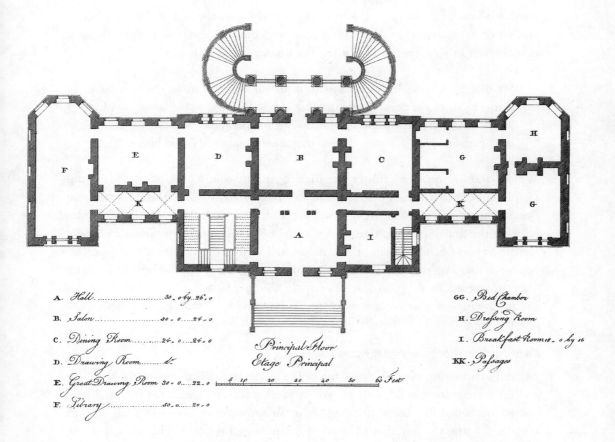

A. *Hall* .... 30. 0 by 26. 0	GG. *Bed Chamber*
B. *Salon* .... 30. 0 .. 24. 0	H. *Dressing Room*
C. *Dining Room* .... 24. 0 .. 24. 0	I. *Breakfast Room* 18. 0 by 16
D. *Drawing Room* .... d.º	KK. *Passages*
E. *Great Drawing Room* 30. 0 .. 22. 0	
F. *Library* .... 30. 0 .. 20. 0	

Principal Floor
Etage Principal

5 10 20 30 40 50 60 Feet

Principal Front of Wrotham Park in Middlesex the Seat of George Byng Esq.ʳ
Elevation Principal de Wrotham Park dans Middlesex Maison de George Byng Ecu.ʳ

Isaac Ware Arch.ᵗ

J. Woolfe delin.

T. White Sculp.ᵗ

5 10 20 30 40 50 60 Feet

Figure 3.16. Isaac Ware, Wrotham Park, Middlesex, 1754 (plan and elevation). Plates 45 and 46 in volume 2 of *Vitruvius Britannicus*, by John Woolfe and James Gandon, 1767–71. The pavilion on the left (F) is the library; that on the right (G and H) contains the dressing room and bedchamber.

features a visit to a room that is hers alone, her new closet, which is destined to contain all of her books after she finishes "classing" them.[39] She is also explicitly given domain over other physical portions of the house. As she puts it:

> My dear Sir Charles led me, followed by all our rejoicing friends, thro' a noble dining-room to the drawing-room, called The Lady's: The whole house, my dear, said he, and every person and thing belonging to it, is yours: But this apartment is more particularly so. Let what is amiss in it, be altered as you would have it.[40]

Within another quarter century the drawing room would be understood as uniformly under the woman's purview, and this passage in *Grandison* adumbrated that. But as of this point at midcentury, it was not under Harriet's purview simply by virtue of being the drawing room. Rather, it was to be "The Lady's" room in its own right, serving as part of the domain openly negotiated in the companionate marriage. The bourgeois dwelling thus was not entirely a matter of framing the identity of the gentleman proprietor. To a degree that still remained limited—indeed at the discretion of the proprietor—it also became a terrain within which members of a family might develop a status of quasi-independence vis-à-vis each other.

Codifying Uses: Rooms with Dedicated Purposes

Beyond articulating new methods for isolating the individual within the dwelling, and for segregating public from private from servants, eighteenth-century architects also strengthened the role of the dwelling as an apparatus of the private self by clarifying and fixing the function of most of the principal rooms.[41] This shift is readily apparent from changing conventions in architects' plans and drawings over the course of the century. Early in the century rooms would be unlabeled, or described simply as "room." Later, architects accorded specific functions to individual rooms. James Gibbs's *Book of Architecture* (1728) is an example of the former type, simply repeating the term "Room" for numerous spaces throughout the dwelling in one design after another (Figure 3.17). The initial volumes of the major eighteenth-century architectural publication *Vitruvius Britannicus* (1715–25) similarly include very few plans with specific indications of room uses, other than dashed outlines of beds to indicate bedchambers. The advantage of such a nonspecific approach was flexibility: depending on different owners' interests or different activities at different times of day, the use of a given room could be changed. Robert Morris, for example, was happy to refrain from indicating any uses for the rooms in a dwelling he had designed: "As to the present Design, (to which I have added a Plan of the Offices with the great Apartment) I shall leave the Names and Uses of the Rooms to the Judgment of others, to employ each in his own way of thinking." Likewise, a more explicit passage from his *Lectures:*

> The applying *Rooms* to proper Uses, is best done by those who consider the Wants for which Families require them, according to the Number or Quality of the Inhabitants;

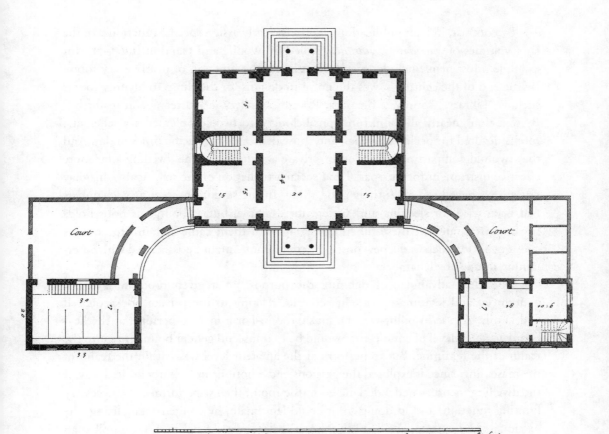

PLATE LXIII.

A Houſe of 58 by 44 feet, containing ſix Rooms on a Floor, with
two Stair-caſes. The Kitchin is on one ſide of the Court, and the
Stables on the other, with Rooms over them, and are join'd to the
Houſe by circular Arcades. The Rooms on the principal Floor are
12 feet high. The Front is plain, with Architraves round the Windows. The Deſign was made for a Gentleman in *Yorkſhire*.

Figure 3.17. James Gibbs, design for a house (plan). Plate 63 and text from *A Book of Architecture*, 1728.

therefore I shall shew only the Form, and Magnitude, and Manner of compleating those Rooms, leaving their Uses to those who best can apply them according to the Necessities which are most requisite.[42]

By contrast, in later publications captions clearly assign specific functions. In the later volumes of *Vitruvius Britannicus* issued by Woolfe and Gandon (1767–71), for example, most plans include legends identifying the function of nearly every room. By the end of the century it was the norm in designs for dwellings to identify rooms such as "Library," "Study," "Breakfast Room," "Gallery," "Nursery," and so forth.[43] By that time, nearly all room functions belonged to two complementary schemata: rooms devoted to specific activities, and those dedicated to specific times of day. And that twofold compartmentalization of private activity made the dwelling a far more effective instrument for the spatial and social articulation of the self. Again, this may not always have been an entirely good thing. In the seventeenth century, chambers had been used for sleeping and sitting, for example, but as bourgeois households began to separate out these functions, along with them came certain expectations about behavior, such as the new possibility that shame might be associated with entertaining in one's bedchamber.

One clear advantage of defining the purpose of a given room was that it announced and legitimated certain activities relating to the private bourgeois self and family. A case in point was the music room. For a man to perform at the keyboard at a high level of competence would be to transcend gender boundaries into the realm of the feminine. But to perform at the amateur level was within the realm of the masculine, since it explored the passions and emotions in a clearly limited way. If the dwelling incorporated a designated music room, then it performed the necessary limiting function, and in doing so, it could legitimate, by compartmentalizing, the passionate and emotional side of the owner's selfhood.[44] To perform also implied an audience, including family and guests, and the room thus provided a locale for active engagement of all concerned, both as listeners and participants, anchoring the owner both in the culture of sensibility and at the center of an affectionate family.[45]

As an apparatus for defining aspects of personal identity and family relations, the music room was available only to comparatively well-to-do members of the bourgeoisie. It was an additional, nonessential space that required extra, expensive furnishings. By contrast dining rooms were a feature of every bourgeois household, and their evolution also helped to define aspects of personal identity. Two early predecessors of the dining room were the "dining chamber," an early incidence of which Nicholas Cooper has dated to 1525, and the "dynynge parler," as found at Holcroft in Lancashire in 1559. By the second half of the seventeenth century both these terms largely had been superseded by the term "dining room," although its use and location still were not consistent with later times. As Mark Girouard has pointed out, the shifting usages among these terms reflected changes in the spatial segregation of servants. Formerly, all members of the household ate in the "great chamber," but once a smaller "dining chamber" on the ground floor was introduced for the servants' meals, then a proper "dining room" could be located on the principal floor for use of family and guests. This in turn meant that as the eighteenth century progressed, other rooms on the principal floor could be dedicated to other specific purposes: saloons, for example, could be used for dancing and formal entertainment instead of serving multiple purposes that also included dining.[46]

Only when there was a dedicated, formal space for dining could dining, in turn, become a formal activity. Prior to the middle of the eighteenth century it had been necessary to set up meals at several smaller tables, pulled out and set up expressly for each meal, in the saloon or in early dining rooms. Only in the last quarter of the century did it become very common to have a single, large, central dining table as a regular feature of the dining room, and only then was the function of the dining room thereby fundamentally fixed. Along with this spatial resolution, certain social perceptions and rituals also became fixed, including the notion that after dinner the dining room became an exclusively male space, for brandy, cigars, talk of politics and coarser subjects, while women correspondingly withdrew to the drawing room for tea and polite talk.[47] Adumbrations of these changes came as early as midcentury, in a letter dated 1752 from Lord Lyttelton regarding Sanderson Miller's plans for Hagley: "Lady Lyttelton insists about [i.e., on eliminating] dark closets and back stairs. She wishes for a room of separation between the eating room and the drawing room, to hinder the ladies from the noise and talk of the men when left to their bottle, which must sometimes happen even at Hagley. . . ."[48] A quarter century later, the authoritative statements of Robert and James Adam left little doubt that these changes had taken hold. Noting that dining rooms were reserved after dinner for male conversation about politics and other matters, and with the unspoken recognition that cigar smoking was part of the ritual, they indicated that the style of decoration was, at least in part, determined by the desire not to have materials that would retain smells.[49]

Room for Intimacy: Chamber, Dressing Room, Closet

But if public spaces such as the music room and dining room were helpful in defining many aspects of personal identity, private rooms such as chambers, closets, and other personal spaces were crucial for the articulation of the individual self because they could be designated as the domain of a single person. Staircases and corridors did much to articulate the boundaries of such rooms, but to articulate them as private domains assignable to private individuals also involved two further ideological considerations: these rooms constituted an always available space for private activity, and they legitimated that activity by being designated as private spaces belonging to given individuals (e.g., the "master," the "mistress") within the dwelling's design.

Today the room most commonly associated with the private individual is the bedroom, but the history of this room, formerly termed "bedchamber" or just "chamber," entailed a profound shift in the formulation of private space for the individual. In the seventeenth century the word *chamber*, at least in a dwelling larger than a farmer's or laborer's house, generally signified a room whose furnishings may well have included a bed but in many other respects differed substantially from the modern notion of a bedroom.[50] The chamber, for instance, was not a private retreat. Rather, it was a place where visitors would be received. In larger households, visitors' status could be measured by how far through the house they were allowed to proceed toward the chamber. Only those of highest status or, alternatively, greatest intimacy were permitted through the sequence of audience rooms and antechambers to the actual chamber itself. Such a concatenation of spaces spatially established a graduated hierarchy of social relations. Incremental degrees of importance were acquired and acknowledged as one passed from the most public to the most intimate areas.

This kind of chamber was hardly "private" in the modern sense of being isolated from general household circulation, reserved for the exclusive habitation of one or two household residents. To the contrary, servants often would be present performing their duties or reporting for instruction. Often the servants' quarters might be part of the bedroom suite. Even as late as the 1770s Robert and James Adam published a design that showed an intersol over the closet and powdering-room adjacent to the chamber that provided a "servant's sleeping-room."[51] Likewise the chamber itself often was situated only partway along a sequence of rooms that culminated in a "cabinet" or "closet," rooms that were smaller than the chamber, employed for purposes ranging from private study to confidential discussions but seldom for sleeping. These rooms could be approached only by passing through the chamber itself (Figure 3.18). And finally, the chamber was not restricted to activities related to sleeping and dressing. Business transactions, estate management, discussions with servants, conversations with friends, letter writing, reading, perusing merchants' samples of prints, fabrics, clothing, and the like—all these were activities commonly undertaken in one's chamber.

By the mid-eighteenth century the graduated social hierarchy that had centered on the bedchamber was well on its way to being replaced by a clear division between public and private realms within the dwelling, as earlier discussion has made clear. Necessary to this process, and to the concomitant hardening of the function of bedrooms as isolated private spaces, were further changes in the overall house plan. Perhaps most important was the elimination of the sequence of semiprivate antechambers that had separated the bedchamber from less restricted areas of the dwelling. On the one hand, this meant that the opportunity to progress through a series of graduated stages toward a more elevated or more intimate position was now lost. For the owner as well as visitors, this meant a consequent loss in the degree to which architecture could render the complex distinctions of social hierarchies in material, spatial terms. On the other hand, this change afforded a harder, firmer distinction—even disjunction—between comparatively common or "public" areas of the house in which a broad range of social activities took place, and secluded or "private" areas to which people retreated for intimate or solitary activities. Other changes in domestic planning could aid this distinction, when possible, such as by locating main-floor bedrooms at greater distances from public spaces such as the hall or saloon, either to one side of the house or in separate wings; and, later, by banishing bedrooms altogether to the next floor up.[52] Thus "private" activities eventually were made physically and literally incompatible with the "public" activities on the principal floor.

At the beginning of the eighteenth century two room types commonly located adjacent to bedrooms were the dressing room and the closet, both of which initially had quite varied functions but which during the course of the eighteenth century began the long decline toward their comparatively vestigial roles today. In the seventeenth century the dressing room might well have been considered a site of greater intimacy than the bedroom, since it was located on the far side of the bedroom from the more public areas of the house.[53] To receive a visitor there would be to accord greater respect and friendship than meeting in the bedroom. But as the bedroom became an ever more private space during the eighteenth century, the dressing room was not yet moribund. Rather it became a site for facilitating interpersonal, sometimes illicit, relations. In *The History of Sir Charles Grandison,* for example, it became a place of intimate assignations, serious family conversations, as well as tête-à-têtes between two women.[54] At the same time Isaac Ware's encyclopedic *Complete Body of*

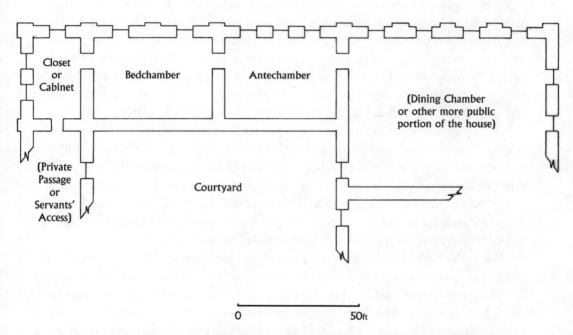

Figure 3.18. Diagram of a typical apartment sequence. A visitor seeking to meet with the owner of the house would first have to be granted access to the house itself, then would proceed through its public areas, where, if the visitor were lowly enough, the owner might choose to hold the meeting. If not, the visitor would be invited into the antechamber, where the owner might choose to grant an audience. If the visitor were particularly favored, he or she might be invited beyond the antechamber into the bedchamber. Especially close associates could be granted one further degree of access to the private closet or cabinet. It was common to discuss business and political affairs in any of the rooms in the apartment sequence, including the bedchamber (unlike today). Drawing by Holley Wlodarczyk.

Architecture (1756) indicated that a dressing room (evidently from a male perspective) could be "a room of consequence, not only for its natural use in being the place of dressing, but for the several persons who are seen there." Ware also indicated that it was a room that many chose for "dispatching business," requiring servants to appear there in the morning to await orders while the proprietor was dressing.[55]

In the seventeenth century closets (or cabinets, often a synonym[56]) generally had functions that were quite distinct from those of dressing rooms. Even in the Middle Ages they had been used for diverse purposes such as prayer, study, and business.[57] By the seventeenth century the closet increasingly became identified with private needs; in some cases, it would be reserved for bodily functions such as use of the close-stool. More commonly it would store and display collections of rare, scientific, and otherwise curious objects that the owner had collected and then carefully arranged. Nor was this simply for show. Using the room in this manner also had an important role in constituting the elite owner's subjectivity. As Francis Bacon noted late in the sixteenth century, the cabinet was essential to a person's quest for wisdom. Like a well-designed garden, where "you may have in small compass a model of the universal nature made private," so a cabinet would be furnished with "whatsoever the Hand of Man, by exquisite Art or Engine, hath made rare in Stuff, Form, or Motion, whatsoever Singularity, Chance and the Shuffle of things hath produced, whatsoever Nature hath wrought in things that want Life, and may be kept." The goal of such a collection, like that of the garden, was to arrange material objects "in such a way as to represent or recall either an entire or a partial world-picture."[58] As such, the cabinet offered the opportunity for its elite owner to establish a highly articulated form of premodern subjectivity, by affording a direct relation to a set of objects that structured and synthesized as much as possible of the world that could be known.

After the turn of the eighteenth century closets, like dressing rooms, also served as spaces for social encounters, particularly for entertaining a guest of some standing in a rich and congenial setting. By midcentury the closet was perhaps the most intimate social space in the entire dwelling. As Richardson made clear in *The History of Sir Charles Grandison,* the closet had become a place of personal "retirement," even spiritual introspection, where the proprietor might sit immersed in his or her collection of books, and others might feel some trepidation at entering.[59]

But if the closet had long been a place of personal retreat, that status was primarily a consequence of its traditional location at the end of a suite of rooms, where its intimacy was largely achieved by requiring the visitor to gain access progressively through that sequence of spaces. Likewise the bedchamber, just one step closer to the public portions of the house, was part of a progressive continuum that fully embraced the gamut from public to private. Then with the eighteenth-century separation of public and private spaces came a corresponding hardening in the understanding of the bedchamber's function, a shift that went hand in hand with changes in ways the bourgeois body itself was understood. As Norbert Elias has shown, early in the seventeenth century a person might not be ashamed to appear partially or wholly naked before some people, such as servants, but quite ashamed before others, or in public. But as Enlightenment society sought to enhance its respect for the political, juridical, and economic integrity of the body, it also found it necessary to make harder distinctions between certain types of bodily functions and activities. Thus urinating, defecating, farting, and having sex all became activities that increasingly were viewed as restricted to "private" or "secret" occasions.[60] Along with this restriction came the understanding that the places where these activities took place, the privy and the bedchamber, increasingly should be off limits to any but their primary occupants. Therefore servants, other household members, and friends eventually became disinclined to enter bedchambers, particularly when occupied by the person "whose room" it was, because of the notion that there existed certain functions in life (such as sex) that must be kept private and secret.[61] For this and related reasons, such as shifts in the understanding of identity, the bedchamber increasingly became the private domain of the self or the (patriarchally dominated) married couple.

In sum, the typology of domestic spaces simultaneously became more limited and more extreme. Instead of being able to position oneself within a gradational continuum where the many parts remained connected, individuals increasingly faced a reduced set of just two choices—public or private—which came to be understood as antithetically opposed to each other. This shift, from the seventeenth-century practice of linking rooms in suites to the eighteenth-century practice of privatization, also effected a critical change from a dynamic understanding of space, according to which one was always part of a sequence or series, to a more static understanding: in the eighteenth-century chamber, one was located within spatial bounds, and isolated there. The chamber thus became an instrument for hardening distinctions between the private self and society in an increasingly absolute fashion, ever more clearly separating private consciousness from the social domain.

William Halfpenny published a design in 1749 that took the possibilities for individual privacy almost to a point of literal extremes (Figures 3.19, 3.20).[62] Ordinarily the two wings in a dwelling design such as this would have been given over to service areas as a way of keeping odors and noise from upsetting the elegance and pleasures of the central pavilion. Instead Halfpenny chose to devote the upper story of each wing to use as a private room, one for the master (marked "Q") and the other for the mistress of the household (marked "R"). Not only is each of these rooms clearly separated from the main body of the house, and access to each room quite restricted,[63] but each is placed at maximum distance from the other, quite clearly emphasizing the role of each occupant as an individual private self apart from the other, from the collective family, and from the social functions of the central pavilion. The literal extremity of Halfpenny's design is unusual, and its awkwardness and impracticalities no doubt did not recommend it as a prototype for future bourgeois villas. But the ingenuity with which Halfpenny articulated an isolated domain for two private selves within a single dwelling was a clear response to Enlightenment demands for spatialization of the private self. And in many respects Halfpenny's design also prefigured another consummate celebration of the isolated individual two centuries later in Frank Gehry's Norton House (Venice, California, 1982–84), where the writer's solitary study, detached from the house, is elevated in open space overlooking the beach and ocean (Figure 3.21).

Solitary Improvement: Study and Library

In addition to the bedchamber and closet, another space commonly reserved for private pursuits in eighteenth-century dwellings was the library or study. As Nicholas Cooper has shown, rooms devoted to this kind of purpose date to the sixteenth century, accommodating the gradual rise of literacy, an increasing predilection for private Protestant devotions, and a preference for transacting business affairs within one's own domicile, particularly among elites.[64] The sort of private intellectual expansion that a study could offer was richly described by Thomas Elyot early in that century:

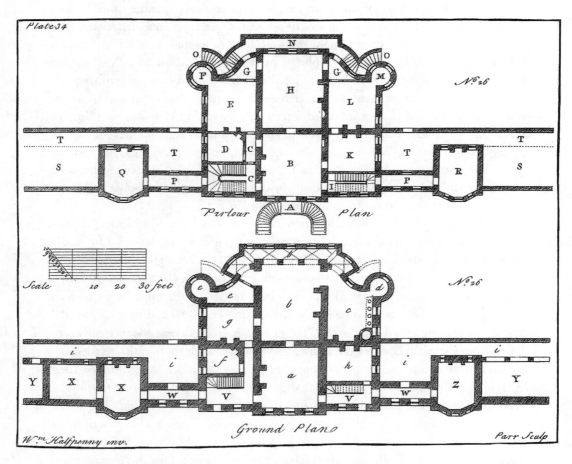

Figure 3.19. William Halfpenny, parlor floor and ground floor, design for "a house and wings which extends 156 feet" (plans). Plate 34 in *A New and Compleat System of Architecture*, 1749. In the parlor floor plan, the room at the far left (labeled Q) is the master's room, and the room at the far right (labeled R) is the mistress's room.

For what pleasure is it, in one houre to beholde those realmes, cities, sees and moun-taynes, that uneth in an olde mannes life can nat be journaide? What incredible delite is taken in beholding the diversities of people, beastis, foules, fisshes, trees, frutes, and herbes? to know the sondry manners and conditions of people, and the varietie of their natures, and that in a warme studie or perler, without perill of the see, or daunger of longe and paynfull journayes? I can nat tell, what more pleasure shulde happen to a gentil witte, than to beholde his owne house every thynge that with in all the world is contained.[65]

In this respect the purpose of the study seems to have differed little from that of the closet as Francis Bacon had described it. In fact the terms *study* and *closet* remained interchangeable for much of the seventeenth century.[66] But by the end of that century the nomenclature was changing. A space that would have been familiar to Elyot or

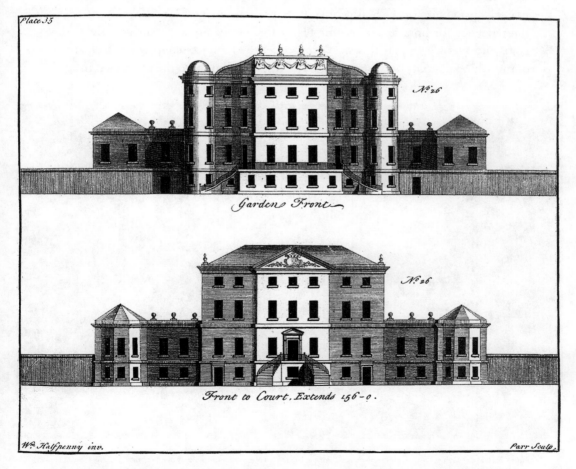

Figure 3.20. William Halfpenny, garden front and court front, design for "a house and wings which extends 156 feet" (elevations). Plate 35 in *A New and Compleat System of Architecture*, 1749.

Bacon as a study or closet was now the "library" of Samuel Pepys's house in London. An often reproduced view, circa 1693, depicted a sparsely furnished room with a bare floor, bookcases covering portions of two walls, portraits hanging above the bookcases, a large map on one wall, and a carpet-covered desk covered with a reading desk on top of that.[67]

But if the terms *study, closet,* and *library* might have been interchangeable at various points prior to the early eighteenth century, that did not last. The closet, as discussed above, had begun a slow decline toward a more vestigial role in the bourgeois household, while the study and library each began to take on quite separate functions. Mark Girouard has found that by the end of the seventeenth century, libraries had become more common in country houses of the elite, in part due to the need to separate burgeoning collections of books from collections of everything else, which remained in the closet or cabinet.[68] Thus even before the eighteenth century a certain separation of functions had been established, with libraries identified as rooms reserved for holding books, although given the expense of books at that date, it was not yet a paradigm for the bourgeoisie. Perhaps of more significance for the latter was the tendency for libraries to become places for socializing, apparent as early as the 1730s and 1740s.[69] In part this was a consequence of a new, semipermanent manner of furnishing that displaced the storage and display of books to the perimeter. Instead

Figure 3.21. Frank Gehry, Norton House, Venice, California, 1983. A quintessential example of the celebration of the individual self in contemporary architecture: the writer's solitary study, detached from all other parts of the house, in an elevated and isolated position overlooking the landscape. Photograph by author.

of freestanding bookcases, as in previous decades and centuries, bookshelves increasingly were built into the walls as part of the overall design,[70] no doubt partly for show but also to allow greater flexibility for the central space within the room. This permitted the introduction of furniture that facilitated comfortable conversation within the center.

Mid-eighteenth-century accounts show that the library no longer was used for the sort of intensive inquiry that had been undertaken in studies and closets. Instead reading was a more casual and leisurely activity, although still observed with some rigor as part of one's daily routine. For just such reasons a library often was incorporated in architects' designs for bourgeois compact villas. Robert Morris addressed the subject in his *Lectures on Architecture,* recommending that the library should be situated on the east side of house because of the ability of the morning sun to "enliven" nature.[71] Thus the householder could benefit doubly—first by making reading a regular part of the morning routine, and then by enjoying the play of sun both inside and outside the room.

Letters written in the 1740s by Marchioness Grey of Wrest Park confirm that the daily routine was orchestrated around both the study and the library, although not quite in the same way in which Morris prescribed. Mornings she would withdraw to her closet for private study, perhaps reading a few chapters of Locke, until breakfast. Evenings, she and her husband, Philip Yorke, would sit in the library, reading by candlelight in front of a fire.[72] In a position to afford her own private study, she could make use of that as a private space for a more concentrated form of inquiry in the mornings, while the library that she and her husband used in the evening functioned much like the family gathering place that most libraries would become in subsequent decades.

Meanwhile Ware's remarks in his voluminous *Complete Body of Architecture* paralleled Morris's, suggesting that a study should be oriented toward the east, "for the morning is the time for resorting thither"—in effect arguing that by having the study facing east it would encourage and facilitate the user's pursuit of literary and other erudite activities at the beginning of the day. The importance of such a room was evident even in one of Ware's smallest designs, suitable for "a small family," where he indicated that the ground floor should include just two parlors, a staircase leading to "lodging rooms" above, a kitchen and wash-house, and adjacent to one of the parlors a study nearly the same size as the parlors.[73]

The Modern Builder's Assistant (1757), a collection of designs by William and John Halfpenny, Robert Morris, and Timothy Lightoler, was considerably more oriented to the bourgeoisie and included designs for a number of modest houses that incorporated a study. The comparative importance of the study and its expected role in the life of the householder can be seen from the plans: even some of the smaller designs devote a considerable portion of the space on the principal floor to a study (Figure 3.22).[74] Another publication, Thomas Rawlins's *Familiar Architecture* (1768), includes thirty-two designs for dwellings directed entirely at bourgeois clients, plans for fifteen

Plate 30

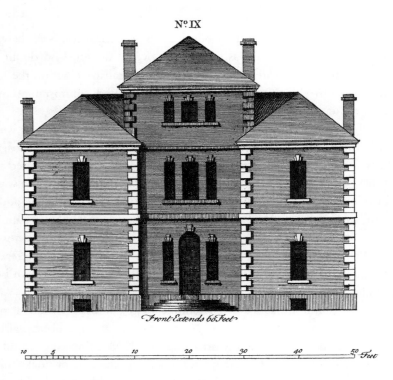

N.º IX

Front Extends 66 Feet

10 5   10   20   30   40   50 *Feet*

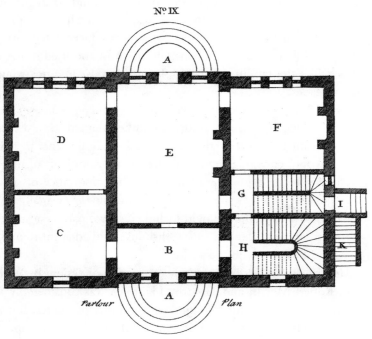

N.º IX

Parlour   *Plan*

Will.ᵐ Halfpenny Inv.ᵗ   R. Benning Sculp.ᵗ

Figure 3.22. William Halfpenny, design no. IX, for "a Country Seat, suitable for a small Family" (elevation and parlor floor plan). From *The Modern Builder's Assistant,* by William Halfpenny, John Halfpenny, Robert Morris, and Timothy Lightoler, 1757. The principal rooms include hall (B), front parlor (C), back parlor (D), withdrawing room (E), and study (F).

of which specify a study. Often in Rawlins's designs, as in those of many contemporaries, the study is found at the far end of a wing or in a corner. In some cases access appears to have been deliberately restricted, emphasizing the room's isolation. In Rawlins's plate 28, for example, although the study is directly adjacent to the "Little Parlour," access is possible only through a passage at the rear of this parlor, then down a short flight of stairs, then along another short passage, and then into the study. The isolation of the study clearly is meant to provide the individual a site for undisturbed inquiry and reflection.[75]

For the eighteenth-century bourgeoisie the study, as successor to the cabinet or closet, developed into a room intended for the private use of a single individual. With the library, on the other hand, the situation could be more ambiguous. In general, it grew to become a place for family and social gatherings on a smaller scale and in a less formal manner than would be appropriate for the main hall or saloon. But in at least a few cases, libraries were intended for separate individuals, possibly for use as a personal reception space as well as for a place for reading and study. Two such examples appear in the book of designs published by John Crunden in 1767, each a single dwelling offering dual his-and-her libraries that are differentiated according to the user's gender (Figures 3.27, 3.28).[76]

Still, as a place for informal socializing, particularly among family and close friends, the library remained part of the private or domestic zone within the dwelling.[77] And whether devoted to the private self or to informal gatherings centered on the family, the library facilitated a strategic seclusion of the bourgeois householders from the comparatively "public" domain of formal entertainment and society. Here books of history, topography, drama, philosophy, science, politics, fiction, etiquette, and such, instruments of private study by which the eighteenth-century bourgeois individual aspired to become a finished "virtuoso," were literally the material in which personal and family space was framed, as well as elements from which personal knowledge and consciousness would be shaped.[78] This incorporation of books into the private domain, indeed the furnishing of the private domain in books, became a significant part of the process of forming the self as a private locus of knowledge and learning apart from society in general.

The instrumentality of study and library in the constitution of the bourgeois self may be seen and compared quite dramatically in Richardson's *History of Sir Charles Grandison*. At the newly completed Grandison Hall the study, continuing the tradition of many a seventeenth-century closet, is both a place of private self-edification and a place for intimacy with close associates. It also is among the portions of the house increasingly instrumental in gender segregation. Sir Charles, greeting three visitors—one woman and two gentlemen, who are preparing to make unfriendly demands—asks the men to come into his study, while the woman is asked to remain behind. Once in the study, the authority of Sir Charles's learning is clearly represented in the objects on display, while the mere pretensions of the visitors are similarly revealed in their responses to the same objects: "They entered; and, as if they would have me think them connoisseurs, began to admire the globes, the orrery, the pictures, and busts."[79] Here is a place for heightening the proprietor's personal presence, in which Sir Charles chooses to confront his visitors and ultimately dismisses his male challengers on his own terms, using his superior knowledge of his own collections. In contrast, the library is a room whose furnishings are hardly specified at all. Instead, it is a relatively neutral environment in which it is possible to have a more friendly and personal discussion with a female guest concerning the amorous interests of other parties. As such it is tied less to his personal learning and authority than is his study, and so it offers a more open terrain for exchanges of personal feelings and intimate knowledge that still would not be acceptable in a more public locale.[80]

Domestic Geometry

William Halfpenny offered a considerably more radical technique for the parcelization of domestic space into isolated domains in a design published in 1749 (Figures 3.23, 3.24).[81] Instead of the broad planar facade that customarily would front a

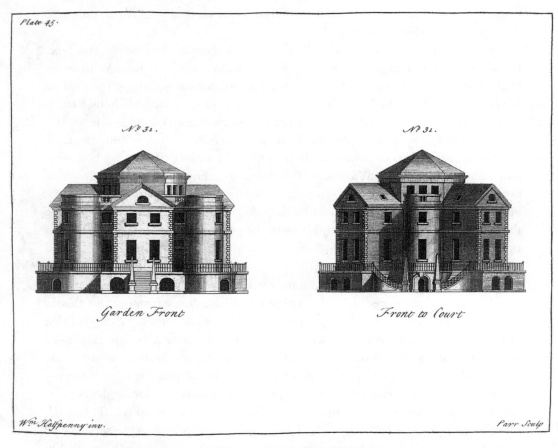

Figure 3.23. William Halfpenny, garden front and court front, design for "a building form'd by an equelateral triangle" (elevations). Plate 45 in *A New and Compleat System of Architecture*, 1749.

dwelling of this size and scale,[82] the exterior of this design is a three-dimensional array of geometric solids. A hexagonal prism forms the core, and the six projecting wings are either cylinders or rectangular prisms with square faces topped by triangular pediments. Circles, rectangles, and a hexagon are even more apparent in the plan, as is an equilateral triangle the sides and points of which connect all parts.[83] Such a rationalization of architectural form into geometric figures often has been analyzed in the context of artistic concern for neoclassical composition, philosophic interest in ideal harmonies, or humanistic concern for ideal principles.[84] All these considerations were material to this design, but discussion to date has tended to emphasize the formal geometric qualities of the composition, while neglecting the manner in which such a design served to articulate the functions and activities of the household. Architectural form, indeed, facilitates specific practices. It articulates and shapes human conduct. Not only were geometric forms introduced to ennoble or rationalize human presence, but for

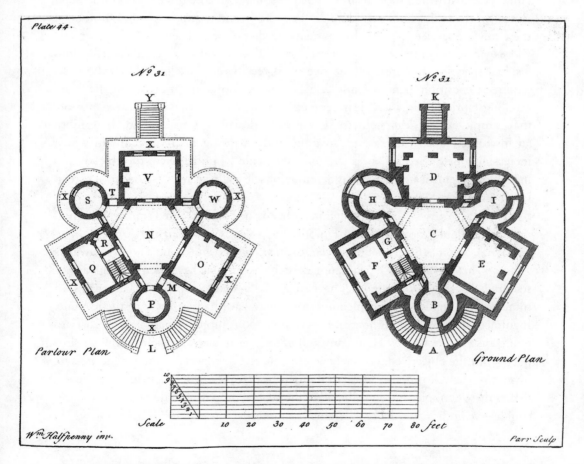

Figure 3.24. William Halfpenny, parlor floor and ground floor, design for "a building form'd by an equelateral triangle" (plans). Plate 44 in *A New and Compleat System of Architecture*, 1749. On the parlor floor, the principal rooms include the hexagon hall (N), parlor (O), study (Q), and dining room (V). R, S, and W are closets. Rooms on the ground floor include the servants' hexagon hall (C), kitchen (D), housekeeper's room (E), and cellar (F).

Halfpenny they also articulated the relations, balance, and distinctions among different realms of human conduct in a radical manner. Perhaps most salient is the perfect triangular balance of the three principal rooms on the parlor floor, the dining room, parlor, and study. Each extends centrifugally from the central hexagonal hall, which in turn serves as an anchor, as a social gathering place, and as the access route from any room to any other room on the same level. The other peripheral rooms are devoted to less consequential and more intimate activities: a housekeeper's room, kitchen, cellar, pantry, and larder on the servants' level, and four closets on the upper level.

Returning to the three principal rooms on the parlor floor—the dining room, parlor, and study—here, crystallized in tension with each other, are three constituent activities of household life: eating, conversation, and study, counterbalanced by the no less private pursuits or conversations that would be conducted in the adjacent small closets. The geometric clarity of this demonstration must have been important, because it would have been obtained at some cost. The three ten-foot-diameter closets on the parlor floor would no doubt be novel and intimate spaces. But none of these nor the service rooms below actually needed to be isolated in such a dramatic and expensive manner in a cylindrical turret. They could have been squeezed into residual spaces in a more cost-effective plain rectangular envelope. The extra costs required to position them in nearly detached turrets, not to mention having the entire dwelling fabricated in such clear geometric elements, betrayed an interest in more than simple neoclassical geometry. It was an endeavor to transform the house into an instrument for demarcating, isolating, and balancing discrete realms in which increasingly privatized activities and pursuits would be undertaken, thereby advancing a more sophisticated apparatus defining for self and private consciousness, here in ideal, geometrical terms.

By midcentury several other architects had issued and executed similarly geometric designs. Publications included Timothy Lightoler's *Gentleman and Farmer's Architect* (1762), Thomas Overton's *Original Designs of Temples* (1766), and Thomas Rawlins's *Familiar Architecture* (1768).[85] Still, not all such designs may have been developed with such radical purposes in mind as I have suggested in connection with Halfpenny's. In some cases a highly geometric composition may have had a purely aesthetic value. Lightoler's designs for farmhouses, for example, do exhibit a superficial similarity to bourgeois villa designs by Halfpenny and others, particularly in their geometric simplicity, but the objective most likely was to enhance "prospects" on the owner's estate by means of a well-proportioned farmhouse-object somewhere in the distance. Nevertheless these examples still contributed to the general proposition: that ideal geometries could serve both internally and externally to improve the domestic environment.

A Museum for the Self

As the previous discussion suggests, rooms such as studies and libraries would have become increasingly important to bourgeois efforts toward self-definition and self-articulation, particularly as these became closely intertwined with rising bourgeois literacy and the proliferation of literature specifically for bourgeois audiences, both fiction and nonfiction. Bourgeois dwellings likewise afforded spaces for comparable activities such as performing music, drawing, and art connoisseurship. In effect, one might describe the entire dwelling as an apparatus increasingly devoted to the culture of the self. More dramatically, the dwelling might be reduced to a single concerted instrument for self-cultivation. One such example is the Casino at Marino (1757), discussed in the previous chapter, a private retreat articulated to resemble a large personal monument. An earlier, and more extraordinary, example appears in a book titled *Harmonic Architecture* by J. Shortess, a follower of Robert Morris (Figure 3.25).[86] Published in 1741, this small collection of plates illustrates Shortess's design for a single-room "museum," to be set "in a retired situation of a park or garden." The term *museum* was at the time not yet associated primarily with the modern notion of a structure housing objects for public display. Rather, combined with the isolated siting of the structure, the term signaled Shortess's interest in a structure dedicated to the private culture of the individual. The word's etymology, rooted in the Greek *museion*, or "seat of the Muses," suggests a site where one might go to draw inspiration from the gods and goddesses of poetry, music, and the other arts.[87] Perhaps more important, the book's title, *Harmonic Architecture*, clearly echoes Morris's lengthy discussion of the "*Principle* of the *Harmonick* Proportions," indicating an understood correspondence between architectural proportion and musical harmony, and the expectation that both could elevate one's consciousness according to a rarefied system of abstract ratios.

During the eighteenth century the word *museum* would gradually progress toward its modern meaning, first to signify a locale for thinking or learning, such as a study or library, and then a disciplinary institution that undertakes to ordain systems of knowledge.[88] In contrast Shortess's museum, antecedent to and functionally unlike the modern, remained a domain intended for the elevation of private consciousness. The actual design, a simple cube "octagonized" inside, together with the specified "retired situation" in which it should stand, effectively crystallized the notion of private contemplation, as both solitary and secluded. By virtue of its remote location, solitary space, and exclusive function, it effaced almost any connection to social or family relations, economic pressures, political conventions, or other concerns outside the nominal domain of the individual. And the design of the building itself, with its ideal proportion and spare articulation, oriented the individual to the ideal plane of contemplation. With its perfect cubical proportions, the building was an isolated, perfected unity unto itself, both anticipating and catalyzing the simple uncorrupted perfection of the contemplative relation to be established.

Much later in the century, across the Atlantic, Thomas Jefferson produced a very different realization of a comparable ideal in his villa at Monticello (Figure 3.26). Establishing himself (at least to begin with) as a secluded man of letters, he erected his villa secure in its retired location high atop a hill, remote from the domain of public affairs, well provided with multiple apparatuses of literary, philosophical, and scientific inquiry, ranging from books to agricultural plantations. In light of his commitment to such a range of intellectual pursuits, one of the most celebrated architectural features of his house also is one of the most telling: the position of his bed in between his bedroom and his study (which, with the later expansion of the house, connected to the library), so that he could step out of bed equally easily into either domain. The bed, by positioning Jefferson physically at the juncture of the two rooms, also served to unite both realms in the single body: the realm of the private and personal joined with the realm of knowledge and learning. Jefferson's villa thus became a quintessential architectural apparatus for facilitating the terms in which the production of knowledge became concentrated in the solitary, retired individual.[89]

Figure 3.25. J. Shortess, design for a "museum" (elevation). Plate 1 in *Harmonic Architecture,* 1741. This single-room structure was to be set "in a retired situation of a park or garden," presumably to assist its occupant in drawing inspiration from the gods and goddesses of poetry, music, and the other arts. Courtesy of Yale Center for British Art, Paul Mellon Collection.

Identifying Gender

The Enlightenment privatization of the self, however much it may have afforded individuals some sense of economic, intellectual, or political autonomy, also entailed a host of consequences in everyday life, especially in domestic relations, that were at best inconsistent with full autonomy. In part this was due to the Enlightenment's ambivalent relationship with patriarchy. On the one hand, private autonomy was essential to Enlightenment goals of social, scientific, and economic progress. But on the other hand, patriarchy still remained a cardinal principle of eighteenth-century politics. As shown in chapter 1, Locke had foreseen the danger in doing away with patriarchy altogether. His solution was to anchor the roots of society in the family, and of the family in patriarchy. As he put it, the roots of political authority lay in

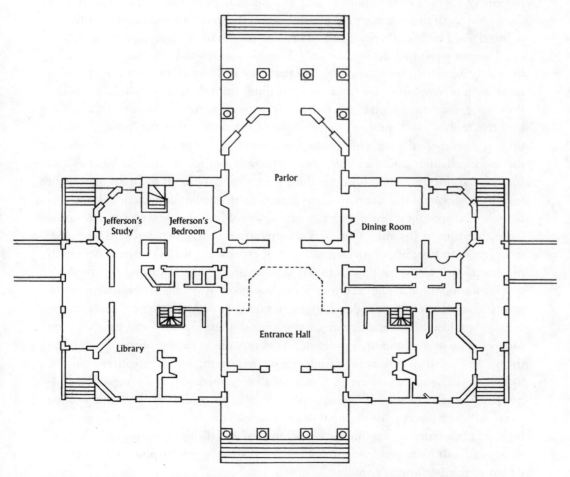

Figure 3.26. Thomas Jefferson, Monticello, Charlottesville, Virginia, 1768–1809 (plan). With Jefferson's bed straddling the opening between his bedroom and his study, that entire side of the villa became a highly orchestrated instrument for the production of the cultivated private individual. Drawing by Holley Wlodarczyk.

"the Power that every Husband hath to order the things of private Concernment in his Family."[90]

There remained, then, a persistent conflict between autonomy and patriarchy. Limited by no means to the realm of ideology and political discourse, this conflict was of particular consequence to the emergent bourgeoisie in their homes: the nominal autonomy of the private self, in both the domestic and the public realms, was subject to entrenched systems of patriarchal authority. The old, seventeenth-century practice of linking rooms in concatenated suites had facilitated several layered systems of hierarchical relations, including rank, age, seniority, gender, and even occupation or pursuit. Yet such a system of complex ties was incompatible not only with the notion of a privatized, isolated, monadic individual but also with the hardening bonds and boundaries of patriarchy. And so, just as Locke and others sought to balance some of the risks of personal autonomy by enhancing the political legitimacy of patriarchy, the task of the domestic architect became more complex: how to provide the spatial apparatus necessary for self-realization without undermining the system of political and family authority that had become central to bourgeois culture.

Designs published during the early Enlightenment show that architects clearly were struggling with such concerns, and that they involved more than simply differentiating a private bourgeois realm (the dwelling) from the public. Modern scholarship has greatly overemphasized the importance of a division during this period between "public" and "private" spheres, and of the notion that the "private" sphere became essentially the woman's domain, a discussion that is taken up more fully at the end of chapter 4. Rather, given the proliferation of rooms such as libraries and studies, and the safe assumption that these were meant at least as often for men as for women, it is evident that the patriarchal presence remained quite evident in bourgeois households throughout the eighteenth century. And in only a few exceptional cases, those that proved the rule, there was a countertrend, in which separate but equal spaces seem to have been provided as a sort of experiment for the discrete definition of gender. Two variations on this theme are discussed in the following paragraphs.[91]

Most designs for eighteenth-century bourgeois dwelling incorporated some spaces that were clearly gendered. A man would have his study, for instance, or women would retire to the drawing room after dinner. Libraries and galleries were somewhat more ambiguously gendered. The library might be appropriated to serve as the owner's personal preserve for study and conversation, while the gallery could be used to collect and display art in a manner that defined him as an authority, connoisseur, benefactor, *man* of letters, and the like. In either case the furnishing of the room followed the taste of the man of the house.[92] But because the library increasingly was construed as a room for family and for socializing, it also may have been recognized as a more gender-neutral space (or perhaps a gender-plural space) in the design of the dwelling as a whole.

In light of this fluid situation some imaginative architects experimented with proposals that made use of not one library per dwelling but two, one for each person of the couple. Instead of a single shared library, individuated spaces could be provided for each, distinctly labeled according to gender. One of the designs issued by John Crunden in 1767, for example, includes a "lady's library" among the bedrooms on a chamber floor, apparently serving to complement the "library," understood as the gentleman's, on the lower floor (Figure 3.27). In another, grander, design Crunden provided not only a "principal library"—perhaps a place for quiet family social gatherings—but also a flanking pair of smaller, more individuated, libraries, described as the "lady's library" and "gentleman's library" (Figure 3.28).[93]

Crunden's designs were a telling response to the dilemma of autonomy versus patriarchy. On the one hand, the explicit gendering of space established a distinct spatial domain for each adult that nominally omitted the other, thereby affording the opportunity for heightening private autonomy. But on the other hand, that spatial gendering also reinforced patriarchal paradigms, particularly in the case where the two libraries are on different floors. Compared to the "library" on the lower floor that is presumably the domain of the gentleman, the upper-floor "lady's library" is sequestered at a much greater remove from the front-door boundary between the interior (domestic) and exterior (public) realms, thus asserting and preserving the male's patriarchal primacy and prerogative. Likewise in Crunden's other design, with gendered subsidiary libraries flanking the "principal library," it is evident that there could be no challenge to patriarchy per se. Instead he offered little more than a regime of separate-but-equal spaces—to be sure, better than no "lady's" space at all but also a stark representation of at least one Enlightenment perspective on gender, as a system of categorization still beholden to a larger patriarchal apparatus.

William Halfpenny's 1749 design for a dwelling with dual his-and-her rooms at extreme ends of the two wings is a similar case in point (Figures 3.19, 3.20).[94] Of eight substantial rooms on the principal-floor level, Halfpenny provided for two to be situated, quite isolated, at opposite ends of the building's two partially detached wings, each designated for the exclusive use of a single individual. Autonomy literally is taken to extremes here, not only in terms of distance but even in terms of restricted access. The approach to each room is neither conspicuous nor elegant. It is afforded by a single narrow passage, at the end of which lies only the single private room. The passage can be entered only via a doorway at the landing of an enclosed staircase: the principal staircase (for the master's room) or the service staircase (for the mistress's room).[95] Notwithstanding the comparative subordination of the mistress's room because of the need to pass through the service staircase, the most striking aspect of such restricted access is the double degree of isolation afforded to both individuals: not just from the public or "outside" realm but even from the household or domestic realm itself, from which the room is cut off by an isolating corridor and by a staircase.

By clearly separating each of these rooms from the main body of the house as well as placing them at the maximum distance from each other, Halfpenny not only emphasized the isolation of each individual from the other and their detachment from the collective family and social functions of the central pavilion, but also introduced

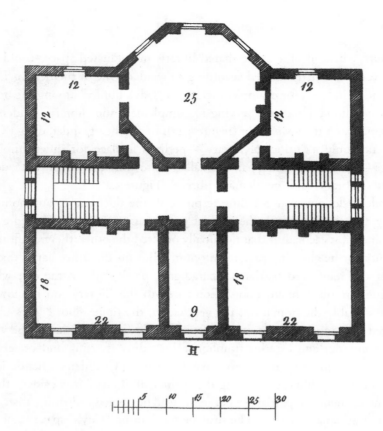

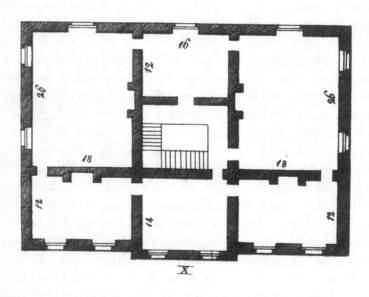

Figure 3.27. John Crunden, design for a country house. Plate 42 in *Convenient and Ornamental Architecture*, 1767. On the chamber floor plan (marked X), one of the rooms (unspecified) was to be "a lady's library." The others (also unspecified) include three bedrooms and two dressing rooms.

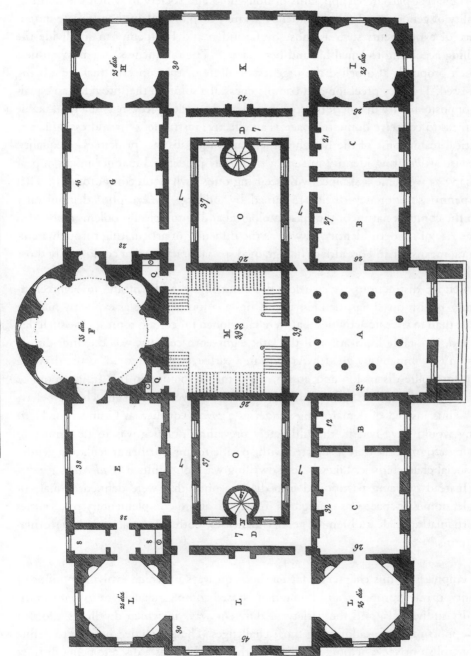

Figure 3.28. John Crunden, design for a country house. Plate 52/53 in *Convenient and Ornamental Architecture*, 1767. The plan includes the "gentleman's library" (H), "lady's library" (I), and "principal library" (K), all aligned along the far right side.

an exceptional degree of gender polarity. The dilemma that accompanied such efforts was the persistent conflict between gender, proffered as a dimension of autonomy, and the larger patriarchal apparatus of household and society to which the nominal equality of gender remained beholden. This may help to explain the ultimate untenability of experiments such as those by Crunden and Halfpenny to subdivide the dwelling according to equal his-and-her spaces.[96] The uniqueness and awkwardness of such proposals also belied the urgency or allure of the concerns that were being addressed. The very precision and completeness of a solution that provided an equal-but-opposite binary distinction between male and female spaces suggest a remarkable eagerness to conceive domestic space as an effective instrument for addressing in the practical realm some of the Enlightenment appeal to abstract principles of equality. Likewise articulating identity in such a rigorously predefined manner might appear to many as welcome assistance with securing one's own bourgeois autonomy. That Halfpenny's solution nevertheless remained, by and large, the exception demonstrates both the complex nature of the epistemological and ontological problems embedded in the rise of modern identity, as well as the difficulty of articulating through architectural means the full breadth of fine-grained spatial practices that could satisfy those challenges.[97]

Gender distinctions nevertheless did flourish by other means in eighteenth-century British dwellings, tied less to any designation of spaces as explicitly male or female than to specific activities that were sanctioned for certain rooms. One such distinction, a notable innovation of the later eighteenth century, was the after-dinner division of company by gender. As indicated earlier, women retired to the drawing room for polite discussion and gossip, while men remained in the dining room to discuss politics and, not infrequently, indulge themselves in lewd speech and behavior.[98] Thus instead of demarcating gender as a *private* quality, as Crunden or Halfpenny would have had it, the ultimately prevailing practice was to tie gender to certain *activities* that were associated with specific rooms, further articulating gender as a social characteristic. Likewise the dwelling was not so much *gendered* as *gendering*. Instead of being partitioned into discrete units that were defined as male or female, domestic space was configured in ways to afford complementary possibilities for articulating male and female gender identities, both in spatial and in performative terms.[99]

The emphasis of this chapter so far has been on ways in which evolving notions of identity, privacy, property, and domesticity posed complex challenges to eighteenth-century individuals, and the variety of different ways in which dwellings afforded new opportunities for addressing those challenges. These included helping to define and establish privacy; helping to articulate the individual as a discrete being distinct from others and from society; institutionalizing specific activities, conventions, and practices that helped to define certain dimensions of identity; and articulating certain gender distinctions. In the remainder of the chapter, I turn to a complementary set of ideological considerations and practices, embraced in the eighteenth-century usage of the term *retirement,* which characterized the relation of life in and around the bourgeois villa to that in the city, politics, business, and other more populated venues of society.

Dimensions of Retirement

In addition to efforts to advance self-definition and self-fulfillment through architectural improvements to the dwelling, eighteenth-century bourgeois individuals increasingly engaged in the practice of separating themselves from the city, from the world of affairs, work, corruption, intrigue, and many other factors seen as threatening or limiting personal fulfillment. This practice of distancing the self from the center of society, business, politics, and culture was called *retirement.*

The term *retirement,* which describes a practice dating to Roman times, originally meant a withdrawal, generally from politics, civic affairs, business, and urban life for a period, perhaps brief or perhaps lengthy, devoted to contemplation and regeneration. By Renaissance times in England the term denoted a frequent practice among elites of withdrawing from the world of society and affairs into seclusion and privacy, generally at a country estate, for more than a nominal period of time.[100] By the early eighteenth century, however, "retirement" began to acquire different connotations as it became an activity increasingly common among the growing bourgeoisie, as they built dwellings for temporary and permanent habitation in the semirural outskirts of London and other urban centers. Embedded in previous practice had been a notion that withdrawal from public affairs and society was, in large measure, an opportunity to indulge oneself in a state of temporary innocence and self-sufficiency. Less than an *oppositional* state to public affairs, the state of retirement offered a *complementary* position of regeneration and inner strengthening.[101] With the eighteenth century the notion of retirement increasingly came to imply a domain that, as distinguished from and ultimately oppositional to public life, was quintessentially *private.*[102]

The eighteenth-century domestic landscape, including the garden as well as the dwelling, was not simply a preserve for isolation of the self. As noted above, it became a site for specific practices that served to define and individualize that self. Views and descriptions of eighteenth-century people at home in their dwellings indicate a wide range of domestic activities in which they and their guests could engage. Indoors, these included eating, dancing, conversation, art appreciation, drawing, painting, reading, music making, private contemplation, and of course sleeping. Outdoors, the immediate landscape was often the site of strolling, botanical study, and contemplation of nature; hunting extended into the surrounding countryside. Distinctly absent were activities that had to do with manufacturing or trade, although husbandry occupied an ambiguous place, sometimes featured as part of an explicitly pastoral prospect, and sometimes screened off as incompatible with states of solitude and abstract contemplation.[103]

Eighteenth-century English bourgeois retirement, which incorporated activities of all the sorts mentioned above, was neither a state of idleness nor a simple state of mind. It was, rather, an effort that engaged body and mind in a quest for personal fulfillment. This might be realized in terms of a self-conscious form of leisure that distanced the individual from the city, politics and commerce, and the labors of husbandry, while encouraging sport, entertainment, and other forms of consumption, as well as genteel artistic and literary pursuits such as collecting works of art, reading and writing essays, and performing or listening to music. All of these activities were directed toward construction and gratification of the bourgeois self as a sentient and intelligent being.

Urban dwellings, in their inability to sustain these sorts of activities, obviously were unfit for retirement. Older country estates, which traditionally had served as power bases balanced against the strength of the court and had been capable of supporting a large number of residents and staff in a now-archaic layout, likewise were unfit models for privacy or isolation from the world of commerce and politics. The innovations particular to the compact bourgeois villa, on the other hand, afforded opportunities for a host of "retired" practices that came to be understood as critical to realization of a bourgeois individual's personal identity. Indoors, the emphasis on privacy, self-definition, and self-improvement could produce an almost absolute preserve of the self. As early as 1728 Robert Morris provided a design for a three-story dwelling in which half the upper story was devoted to "retirement and study."[104] Outdoors, the natural environment of a bourgeois villa also could be orchestrated to enhance privacy, affording opportunities for personal growth and recreation, while landscaping techniques could conceal any connection with provincial society, the rural economy, or the world of urban politics, commerce, and trade.

Consistent with these techniques of privacy and isolation, eighteenth-century bourgeois retirement flourished in connection with the apparent absence of economically productive activity. This did not imply sloth. Rather, it entailed industrious leisure, including such pursuits as art, poetry, literary or scientific study, or even certain kinds of entertainment such as banqueting and visiting—activities all of which maintained a clear differentiation from politics, trade, or production. The retired individual might well engage quite self-consciously in activities that were patently *un*economic, such as transforming arable land into a pleasure garden. To do so would strike an attitude of independence from the nexus of production, trade, and finance. Still, as the century progressed, such distancing became increasingly symbolic, as merchants, financiers, and even tradesmen sought country retreats where they could "retire" for a weekend or a week, retreats that in reality could only be reached at the expense of a commute no more pleasant than is found around any major city today, and which certainly offered no real independence from their commercial and industrial sources of income. By the middle of the century the situation had become ripe for ridicule, as in this poetic jibe published in 1754:

A little country box you boast
So neat, 'tis cover'd all with dust;
And nought about it to be seen,
Except a nettle-bed, that's green;
Your Villa! rural but the name in,
So desart, it would breed a famine.[105]

But such ridicule only bespoke the extent to which the practice of bourgeois retirement had begun to pervade all strata of merchants and tradesmen, with a corresponding spread of bourgeois country retreats throughout the metropolitan peripheries of London and, eventually, the major Midlands industrial centers. And while attempts to effect a bourgeois manner of retirement in such places frequently miscarried, as suggested in the poetic critique above, few if any in the eighteenth century actually questioned the objective of retirement per se. To escape the pressures of the city for the tranquility of an ostensibly antiurban, private retreat was considered an essential complement to a political, mercantile, or entrepreneurial career. The underlying and unquestioned assumption was that pressures of politics and commerce not only required some sort of counterbalance in terms of relief and release, but also that one's individuality could be defined only in a realm well differentiated from those public pursuits.

Solitude, Retreat, Isolation

By the early eighteenth century the importance of retirement to the pursuit of human happiness already had been well established, in terms ranging from the existential to the artistic, psychological, and social.[106] Discussion over the ensuing decades centered not on the need for retirement, which was a given, but rather on ways of pursuing it in different media and dimensions. In the approaches of architects and architectural critics to retirement, three such dimensions became crucial to eighteenth-century practices of retirement: solitude, retreat, and isolation. Their role in the definition and articulation of bourgeois domestic space is explored in the following pages.

Solitude

Solitude has a long and honored position in Western culture, not least in the form of the medieval Christian hermit, who in turn afforded endless opportunities for the articulation of architectural spaces devoted to solitude—hermitages with all their appurtenances of isolation, contemplation, and mental expansion. By the period of the English Renaissance a distinct shift in the apparatus of solitude was noticeable, away from the ostensible selflessness of the medieval monk in a remote cell or grotto and toward an emphasis on the private self. As early as 1603 the notion of architecturally defining a secular space for private contemplation entered English literature via the Florio translation of Montaigne:

> We should reserve a store-house for our selves, what need soever chance; altogether ours, and wholy free, wherein we may hoard up and establish our true libertie, and principall retreit and solitariness, wherein we must go alone to ourselves, take our ordinarie entertainment, and so privately, that no acquaintance or communication of any strange thing may therein find place.[107]

Exactly what Montaigne had in mind by a "store-house" is open to interpretation, but in England by then examples of private solitary retreats on the grounds of aristocratic estates already had become quite elaborate.[108]

In 1711 essayist Joseph Addison, writing quite specifically for an English bourgeois audience, argued that true happiness could only be had in a retired situation. Since retirement was fundamentally a pursuit of the self, solitude therefore was the most effective state in which to conduct that pursuit:

> True happiness is of a retired nature, and an enemy to pomp and noise; it arises, in the first place, from the enjoyment of one's self; and in the next, from the friendship and conversation of a few select companions; it loves shade and solitude, and naturally haunts groves and fountains, fields and meadows: in short, it feels every thing it wants within itself, and receives no addition from multitudes of witnesses and spectators.[109]

The importance of solitude to self-fulfillment was more richly developed four years later in a gentleman's conduct book, *The Gentleman's Library, Containing Rules for Conduct in All Parts of Life* (1715), which in devoting an entire chapter to the subject of retirement confirmed its growing importance to a bourgeois readership. From the beginning, retirement was understood as a state of idyllic privacy:

> Retirement is a sort of Sleep to wearied Nature; when we have run thro' the Tumults and Fatigues of Life, when we are harrass'd out with Business and Hurry, we are glad to take Shelter in a calm Privacy, and put in as to a safe Harbour out of a troubled Ocean.

But the author was quick to insist that retirement should not be an opportunity for indolent leisure, citing the dangers of unstructured retirement, without purpose or goal:

> It may still be argued in Discountenance of Solitude and Retirement, that Men's natural Parts, lying unemploy'd for lack of Acquaintance with the World, contract a kind of Filth or Rust and Craziness thereby. For sottish ease and a Life wholly Sedentary, and given up to Idleness, spoils, and debilitates not only the Body but the Soul too.[110]

Nor was solitude in and of itself necessarily a perfect state for humankind. The existential consequences of being completely solitary were perilous. God, this author argued, saw that Adam was "imperfect, and that 'twas *not good for him to be alone*. If . . . Solitude, strictly taken, wo'n't do in Paradise, 'tis in vain to expect from it elsewhere. . . . Solitude gives too much Leisure for Reflexion, opens an unacceptable Scene, and shews a Man the Poverty of his own Nature." Yet this did not deter the author's emphatic enthusiasm for solitude overall. On balance it was not only desirable, it was a duty, for it helped to clarify and confirm one's place as an individual in the larger cosmic order. Drawing a biblical analogy, he extolled retirement to the country as akin to retreating to the state of Eden: "the Country is the Scene which supplies us with the most lovely Images. This State was that wherein God placed *Adam* when in Paradise. . . . A Gentleman in a Country Life enjoys Paradise with a Temper fit for it; [likewise he] who understands the Station in which Heaven and Nature have plac'd him" has a greater capacity for benevolence to those beneath him.

Here was a spiritual ontology that attempted to supersede oppositional relations between country and city: one retreated into the country to apprehend that a person was placed on earth *as an individual;* any social, economic, and political relations implicitly were understood to be subsequent and subordinate. As the author explained, embracing such a vision readily afforded a differential advantage to the book's intended "gentleman" readers. In effect it rationalized as virtuous, rather than selfish, the practice of retirement into the country, for doing so ostensibly enhanced their capacity to improve the lot of those of lower "Station" through benevolence.

Retirement, then, required both solitude and some sort of retreat, but the destination was not so much an alternate, oppositional space to society at large as a place of refuge and protection from various sinister forces and intrusions, possibly much like a hermitage. As the author of the conduct book put it, "Your Philosophical Cell is a safe shelter from Tumults, from Vices, from Discontentments. . . . You sit as on a high Rock above the Waters." In such an elevated locale, solitude afforded the possibility for a near ecstasy of the soul:

> Solitude hath certainly more Pleasures in it, than any publick Employment, for it drives us into Contemplation, which is so charming, that it may rather be said to ravish than please, committing so open a Rapture upon our Souls, that it puts them almost into a State of Separation. . . . [I]f we are engag'd in more refin'd and intellectual Entertainments, we shall be something more than ourselves, that is, than this narrow Circumference of Earth speaks us, the Soul being always like the Object of its Delight and Converse.[111]

The state of solitude in retirement did not necessarily entail unprotected exposure to nature. Instead, several eighteenth-century architects and landscape designers found ways that architecture could be harnessed to facilitate a state of protected solitude. One, William Wrighte, published a book of designs for hermitages and other retreats in 1767 that was reissued in at least five subsequent editions (Figure 3.29).[112] Typically his designs—for huts, retreats, hermitages, and the like—were composed with a clear concern for principles of geometric proportion, being based on circles, squares, and other regular figures, but the facades consisted of rootwork, shells, thatch, tree branches, and other materials that gave them an overall "rustic" quality consistent with making the occupant be and feel immersed in nature.

More important than connecting with nature was the need to be, or at least feel, removed from contact with others. As early as the beginning of the century, essayist Timothy Nourse had envisioned the construction of a diminutive retreat perfectly suited for retirement, specifically emphasizing its "sequestered" character and specifying the principal activity there as "private Diversion" in the company of only "a Friend or two."[113] Though not yet a prescription for complete isolation, Nourse's commentary nevertheless suggested a retreat from community. Not simply describing an escape from the vices of business and politics, Nourse mentioned only one or two friends, suggesting a structure that could not hold more. It became an instrument for the proprietor himself—male, alone, or in the company of a friend or two when it suited him—to employ as a retreat for his private and personal regeneration.[114]

Matthew Prior, who in 1719 acquired the Down estate in Essex, engaged James Gibbs to prepare two designs for rebuilding the residence there as a compact villa, one of which was published in Gibbs's *Book of Architecture* (1728) (Figure 3.30).[115] Through explicit references to notable Roman villas, asserting that he loved Down "more than Tully did his Tusculum, or Horace his Sabine field,"[116] Prior expressed his aspirations to a "retired existence." But given the extensive scale of Roman villas compared to the diminutive size of Gibbs's design, a modest expansion of the compact villa formula, bearing an elevation that shared much with Whitton (Figures 2.4, 2.5), Prior also may have expressed a desire for a more low-key, or at least suburban, retirement.

Still, the need for a site for personal reflection and meditation weighed heavily on Prior as it did on many of his Enlightenment contemporaries. Anxious after reading Jacques Robbe's *Methode pour apprendre facilement la geographie* over the enormity of space he would have covered in his life without ever having found a "Foot of Earth my own," an anxiety over the vastness of Enlightenment global space and knowledge contrasted with the need to anchor his own personal life, Prior made a poetic appeal to the Greek goddess Rhea, Mother of the Gods, for a humble site of retreat and personal consolidation:

GREAT MOTHER, let Me Once be able
To have a Garden, House, and Stable;
That I may Read, and Ride, and Plant,
Superior to Desire, or Want;
And as Health fails, and Years increase,
Sit down, and think, and die in Peace.[117]

Gothic Grotto.

Pl. 10.

5 f.ᵗ Sqʳ.

10 f.ᵗ Sqʳ.

5   10   20 f.ᵗ

Figure 3.29. William Wrighte, design for a Gothic grotto (elevation and plan). Plate 10 in *Grotesque Architecture, or, Rural Amusement,* 1767. Wrighte obviously was loath to let the appeal of the rustic overwhelm the authority of geometry; the result is an awkward tension between reason and appeals to the sublime that nevertheless resonated with his audience. The book saw at least five subsequent editions.

In the face of expanding dimensions of Enlightenment consciousness, from epistemology to cartography, Prior articulated a complementary need to fashion his own life in a carefully bounded private realm. His expressed desire for little more than the opportunity to "Sit down, and think, and die in Peace" anticipated the growing popularity, as the century progressed, of hermitages and hermit literature.[118] The mental and physical experience of such an isolated site was both parallel and conducive to a private, personal journey to the least encumbered, most elementary, and

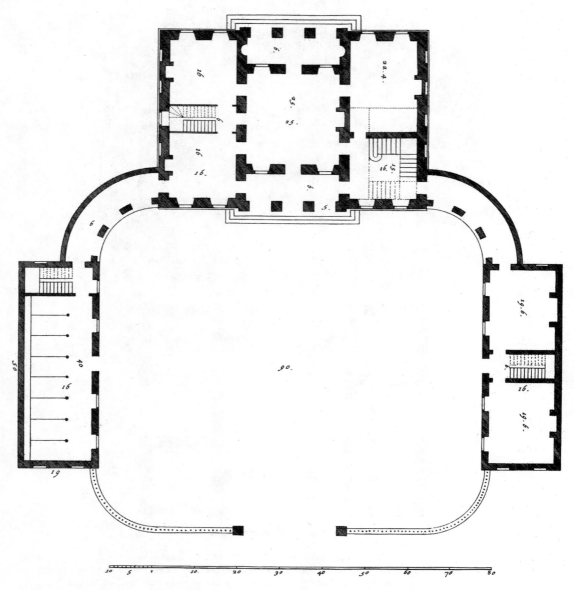

Figure 3.30. James Gibbs, design for Down Hall, Essex (plan). Plate 55 in *A Book of Architecture*, 1728.

most germinal, regions of the self and back. A retreat, whether one's own chamber or study, or a purpose-built hermitage or villa, that afforded the possibility of spatial retreat and personal solitude was the architectural instrument by which that journey could be undertaken.

Country as a Site of Retreat and Isolation

One crucial factor in defining retired locales was being able to articulate notions of "country" as oppositional to "city." In part this was an extension of the Roman distinction between "otium" as the ideal of country life—the opportunity for seclusion, serenity, and leisure pursuits, often associated with pastoral settings—and "negotium," the urban nexus of commerce and public affairs.[119] But the antiurban orientation of eighteenth-century retirement also was the product of tensions peculiar to the late Stuart and early Georgian era, when political tensions and economic shifts invested the terms *city* and *country* with a more complex range of meanings.[120] Apart from the political rivalry between court and country parties, which sometimes was conveniently articulated in city/country terms, attributes of morality, status, and prestige often were articulated in terms of a country or city ethos. Attacks on the City (i.e., the City of London, the capital of finance) portrayed it as the seat of corruption and moral decline. Industrialization and population growth led to demographic shifts that turned the metropolis into an instrument of class stratification, as the bourgeoisie sought terrain such as the suburbs west of London in which to spatialize their own ideals of self and family.

The greater consequence was a dichotomizing approach to the accelerating pace and scale of social change, differentiating the individual, as capable of pursuing moral and intellectual ideals, from the social nexus, as incapable in its own right of sustaining a collective virtue or morality—an approach that the country/city debate seemed only to reinforce.[121] Sanction for this manner of oppositional thinking that privileged country over city could be found in the poetic discourse of Horace, Virgil, and their contemporaries, who in their own time had eagerly contrasted the pastoral and georgic with the urban. For even though the social and political circumstances of ancient Rome and modern Britain were hardly similar, classical poetics provided a ready paradigm for modern critics who would differentiate the ostensible virtue of a private "retired" existence from the duplicity and putatively amoral domain of court politics and mercantile capitalism.

Nevertheless there were unmistakable differences. Classical poetry tended to be concerned with commodious villas on sizable estates, the produce of which would be used to sustain the household, against which the eighteenth-century English villa represented a considerable shift in scale. Typically it was a far smaller dwelling, with fewer facilities, suited to a smaller household, on a much smaller and largely unproductive tract of land, though it remained at about the same distance from the city as its classical counterpart. The preference for bourgeois scale was already apparent early in the century, for example, in the work of Ambrose Philips, who in the preface to his pastoral poems (1708) contrasted the pretensions of stately urban architecture unfavorably with a diminutive dwelling associated with retirement:

> To see a stately, well-built Palace strikes us, indeed, with Admiration, and swells the Soul, as it were, with Notions of Grandeur. But when I view a little Country Dwelling, advantageously situated amidst a beautiful Variety of Fields, Woods and Rivers; I feel an unspeakable kind of Satisfaction, and cannot forbear wishing, that my good Fortune would place me in so sweet a Retirement.[122]

A remote or secluded country location was considered an essential attribute of retirement not simply because it was pretty and pleasant, as Philips's statement suggested, but also because it was instrumental to the mentality of retirement. As Philips put it, using a poetic analogy, "*Pastoral* gives a sweet and gentle Composure to the Mind; whereas the *Epick* and *Tragick* Poem put the Spirits in too great a Ferment by the Vehemence of their Motions."[123]

Robert Morris, the leading architectural theorist of the first half of the eighteenth century, who was introduced above, also undertook a pointed inquiry into the effects of architecture and landscape on the mind. In his *Lectures,* delivered beginning in 1730 and published in 1734–36, Morris addressed the practice of country retirement—to grand "seats" as well as modest villas—in terms of detachment from the city, opportunity for transcendent contemplation, and the authority that Roman example provided for such practices:

> Noblemens Seats, besides Grandeur, are erected for a Retirement, or as a Retreat from Publick Cares, perhaps in some silent unfrequented Glade, where Nature seems to be lull'd into a kind of pleasing Repose, and conspires to soften Mankind into solid and awful Contemplations, especially a curious and speculative Genius, who in such distant and remote Recesses, are [*sic*] free from the Noise and Interruptions of Visitors or Business, or the Tumult of the Populace, which are continually diverting the Ideas into different Channels. . . .[124]

The kind of retirement that Morris proposed was predicated on both physical and psychological isolation. Recognizing that "Pleasures are attendant upon a *Calm* undisturb'd Retirement," he prescribed "silent Retreats of Solitude" in which one "might secrete himself." Here the private individual could enter the "silent Recesses of Life," discovering "what *Tranquillity* and *Sereneness* of Temper he may possess" and so affording the expansion of "his *Ideas* from one *Chain* of Thought to another."[125]

A crucial feature of Morris's theorization of retirement was his emphasis on the instrumentality of the actual site. Instead of a busy and economically productive landscape, such as might have been seen at a Roman villa, or even surroundings of pastoral plenty such as Roman poets extolled, he described as essential to retirement a site that was not only unimproved but preferably even untouched. Morris offered two grounds for this argument. First, such a site would guarantee the solitary character of the experience, eliminating interruptions due to noise, visitors, or business. Second, the opportunity for sustained concentration, together with the uncomplicated character of the site, would greatly facilitate imaginative expansion. In other words, the site itself was instrumental to achieving a heightened state of consciousness. And to afford the imaginative expansion necessary to this end, the site must be pristine both in its isolation from civilization and in being free of improvements.

Superficially this may appear to be equivalent to the country/city opposition found in Roman pastoral poetry, but it is not. Roman writers in fact recognized city and country as two complementary types of locale that, although different, were both positive components of human culture that did not categorically impair each other. However, in Morris's case they were clearly *antithetical* locales: presence of the city or its influence would undermine the capacity of the country locale to sustain pursuits of retirement. In addition Morris, along with many of his Georgian contemporaries, was engaged in a fundamental redefinition of the Roman notion of *otium,* or leisure, one that was crucial to architecture and dwelling in the eighteenth century but has too commonly been overlooked. For Romans such as Pliny the Younger, *otium* was not leisure in the sense of inactivity. Rather, it still required work but of a different sort, such as study, writing, stimulating conversation, art, and music. Likewise for Morris and his contemporaries, leisure and retirement both required work, but increasingly they were definable in bourgeois terms, both in terms of the kind of activity that was involved, that is, contemplation, and the sorts of locales such as compact villas where they might be undertaken.[126] The key for Morris was that the sort of work required, intellectual work, was thoroughly consistent with the rising cult of "genius" in eighteenth-century aesthetics.[127] For the educated bourgeoisie, not only could the economic value of manual labor be replaced by a more highly valued labor, that of the mind, but this could be sanctioned as part of the process of living in one's own dwelling, exploring the dimensions of selfhood.

In sum, Morris proposed dwellings that would be erected for narrowly limited purposes, retreat and retirement. And since he provided for such narrowly circumscribed activity, the dwelling effectively cast the resident as divorced from the realms of labor, politics, commerce, and production, with access instead (for better or worse) to the domain of intellectual engagement. This process of differentiation occurred in three ways simultaneously. First, since the activity of retirement, for Morris, was largely ideational, the corresponding static nature of existence in retirement would contrast sharply with the active and dynamic nature of work and relations in the world beyond. Second, the isolation of the locale would likewise contrast with the complex economic and political nexus elsewhere. And finally, the purpose of retirement, at least according to Morris, was transcendent: to "feel Emanations of the Harmony of Nature diffus'd in us."[128]

Such ideals, popular as they became during the eighteenth and later centuries, were not without their ironies and contradictions. One particular problem that consistently occupied aestheticians, architects, and landscape designers was the question whether nature should be understood as a realm of absolute and abstract perfection or as an unfettered domain free of human control, and whether in turn those two notions were at all compatible. In some respects both of these positions were Enlightenment abstractions. Part of the impetus for this situation stemmed from Locke's epistemological stipulation of a realm of abstract spatial relations prior to human consciousness, as well as from his origin myth of a "State of Nature" prior to political organization. To understand political power at all, he said,

> The *State of Nature* has a Law of Nature to govern it, which obliges every one: And Reason, which is that Law, teaches all Mankind, who will but consult it, that being all equal and independent, no one ought to harm another in his Life, Health, Liberty, or Possessions.[129]

Following such a premise, Enlightenment philosophers had little trouble articulating "Nature" as a realm of general perfection both morally above and ontologically prior to the corruptions and vices of human society. This was a realm that many individuals sought to approach via retirement. Personally and privately the individual could aspire to that realm of perfection, even if human society produced its antithesis. Only uncorrupted nature could be a medium of approach to such a realm. Thus Stephen Switzer deplored the corruption of nature in landscape gardens by geometric patterns: "If we would therefore arrive at any greater Perfection, than we are [at] in Gardening, we must cashiere that Mathematical Stiffness in our Gardens, and imitate Nature more . . . ." Instead, he extolled the "natural Gardener," whose "Wood is entirely for walking in; it lyes high, and he is not observ'd to have cut down any noble Trees; . . . neither has he shewn himself fond of any Mathematical Figure, but has made his Design submit to Nature, and not Nature to his Design."[130]

Still, many architects were uncomfortable if they were unable to rely on systems of proportion, and some argued that the rules of proportion were in fact defined in Nature. As Isaac Ware wrote at midcentury in his encyclopedic *Complete Body of Architecture:*

> When we can see how any thing in architecture is deduced from nature, there is a rule for judging of its propriety by refering to that standard. . . . Accordingly we see that architects never depart much from the proportion established by nature, and if they should we should censure them accordingly.[131]

More to the point of the "retired" villa, if the design of such a dwelling could be realized according to the laws of Nature, according to whatever authority one used to define them, and likewise isolated in an uncorrupted natural setting such as Morris proposed, both architecture and landscape could unite to become a site for the perfect consummation of the private self. Naturally the seclusion of the contemplative individual in an environment thus sanitized of other human traces only accentuated the peculiarly isolated, solitary nature of eighteenth-century retirement, especially in the form that eighteenth-century poets idealized and eighteenth-century architects would render. Private retreats such as they would portray accommodated both existential and transcendental purposes, facilitating the periodic physical, social, and intellectual disengagement of individuals from society in favor of a private existence focused on the recognition and cultivation of the unencumbered self.

By midcentury it was a commonplace of architectural theory that a dwelling in a locale beyond the city could be devoted to the pursuit of retirement, and architectural treatises increasingly discussed the issue and included designs for just such structures, for both temporary and permanent habitation. Among many current fashions that William and John Halfpenny sought to encompass in their 1752 collection of summer-houses and garden seats, *Rural Architecture in the Gothick Taste,* two were designs for "a Lodge, or House of Retirement" (Figure 3.31).[132] The plans for these structures show that they were intended neither as casual destinations for an afternoon's outing nor as permanent residences. Instead, they were apparently intended for brief overnight stays, perhaps as much as several days. The plans also suggest a fairly solitary regime. There is room for the owner to spend the night and to receive an occasional guest or two, but not to lodge guests overnight. The design in plate 11, for example, consists of a parlor (D) and a dining room (E), both of which would be appropriate for entertaining visitors, as well as three separate rooms dedicated to the owner's private activities: a closet (G), a study (H), and a bedchamber (above E). Servants would be housed in a room over F and G. Significantly this room is not apparent in the facade, in order not to betray the image of an establishment dedicated to privacy and solitude.

Isaac Ware's far more substantial and authoritative *Complete Body of Architecture* (1756) offered no designs intended explicitly for purposes of retirement, but his text unambiguously recognized the practice as central to the bourgeois audience that he addressed: "Retirement is what we seek in the country." Like the anonymous author of *The Gentleman's Library* (1715), Ware was concerned that too much solitude could itself bring on "fatigue" and "melancholy"—thus the need to make provision for visitors—but that did not change the basic desire and need for retirement. Ware explicitly blamed the ills of urban life for that need, but he also went further, indicating that it was the very oppositionality of the retired locale and the activities undertaken there that rendered it worthwhile. To lose one's awareness of that oppositionality while in retirement would rob the exercise of its significance and value:

> When we first think of leaving a populous city, the charms of a retreat appear double, because of the opposition to that noise and hurry; but when the comparison is forgot we grow weary of the sameness of the scene.[133]

Self-described "Stone Mason" Thomas Rawlins issued a collection of designs titled *Familiar Architecture* in 1768, the title of which played on the various senses of

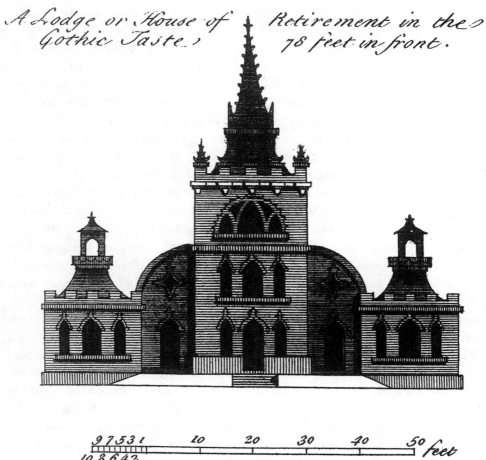

Pl. 11.

A Lodge or House of   Retirement in the
Gothic Taste.   78 feet in front.

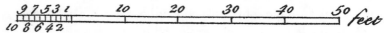

9 7 5 3 1   10   20   30   40   50 *feet*
10 8 6 4 2

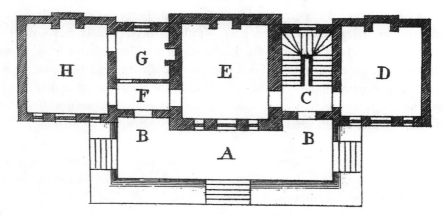

Figure 3.31. William and John Halfpenny, design for a lodge or house of retirement (elevation and plan). Plate 11 in *Rural Architecture in the Gothick Taste,* 1752. The plan consists of a parlor (D), dining room (E), closet (G), study (H), bedchamber (above E), and servants' quarters (above F and G).

the word *familiar* pertaining to self, family, and household. Rawlins also intended the wording of his title to evoke the ordinary and the plain, as opposed to the "lofty Views" and "too extensive" plans issued by more prominent architects, who according to Rawlins ignored "the Uses required in the Country." These intentions bespoke the most distinctive aspect of the book, its explicit appeal to a bourgeois clientele. Both on the title page and in descriptions of individual designs he specified gentlemen, merchants, parsons, and tradesmen as his audience. Stressing the individuality of every client, he suggested that each had his own personal goal or vocation, vested in him by "Nature," the pursuit of which to perfection would be the basis of lasting pleasure:

> Every Man has some favourite Aim in view, be it Study, Business, or Pleasure. That which the Mind is most earnestly bent upon, we most closely pursue: That which is most closely pursued, will doubtless be brought nearest to Perfection: The Study which Nature directs us to, has unquestionably the strongest Prevalence on the Mind: For while we labour, we may be said to sport; and Toils are converted into Delight.

Thus in the array of designs for villas and retreats that he offered, expressly tailored for a "Gentleman," a "Merchant," a "Tradesman," a "Wine-Merchant," and the like, the dwelling was presented as an instrument for the personal fulfillment of the individual inhabitant: "commanding," for example, "some extensive Prospects which may exhilarate and add fresh Vigour to the Mind of the wealthy and industrious Inhabitant."[134]

Some of Rawlins's designs were large enough to accommodate a small household, but others clearly were intended simply to accommodate leisure pursuits. One "Retreat" on a "pleasant airy" site, for example, was designed for use by a merchant who, thus "divested of the cares of Business," might "enjoy the Converse of a few select Friends" (Figure 3.32). The plan of the ground floor would sustain genteel, intimate entertainment and retreat. It has two parlors, a closet attached to one parlor, a dining parlor, a drawing room, and a study that, significantly, is located in the center of the garden facade, with direct access out through the main door and down three steps into the garden.

For Rawlins as for his contemporaries, theorists and practitioners alike, domestic architecture had become an effective instrument for taking on the challenges posed by new dimensions of Enlightenment autonomy. As an apparatus of retirement, it provided a structured setting of retreat and isolation that afforded the necessary solitude in which to undertake the new work that came along with bourgeois selfhood.

Land, Pastoral, and Profit

Unlike the mercantile and professional bourgeoisie who might erect villas on very small landholdings, those who owned estates of substantial size could not afford to forgo income from their land. With the increasing capitalization of agriculture during

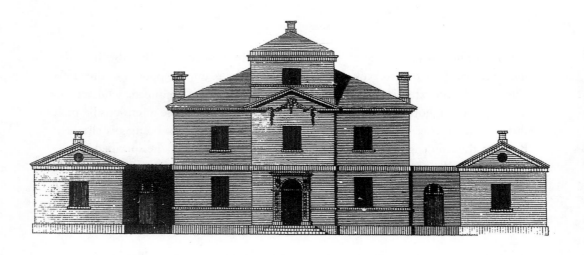

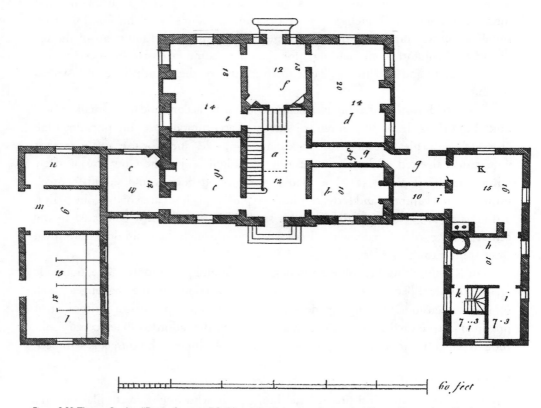

Figure 3.32. Thomas Rawlins, "Design for a small Building to be situate in a pleasant airy Villa, as a Retreat for a Merchant, &c., where divested of the cares of Business he may enjoy the Converse of a few select Friends" (elevation and plan). Plate 24 in *Familiar Architecture*, 1768.

this period, estate owners were pressed to regard their land less as a source of provisions for the estate and more as an economic resource from which to maximize income.[135] Particularly in the case of smaller and newer estate owners, cumulating profits from landholdings were increasingly important both as a source of wealth and as a claim to social position. Thus architects' treatises insistently reassured their readers that improvements to house and landscape alike could be a source of both pleasure and profit.

Stephen Switzer, arguing against the rigid formality of Continentally inspired landscapes, argued that it would be acceptable in the name of profit to replace geometric parterres and other formal designs, at least partly, with productive fields. His goal was a mode of design that could acknowledge both the nascent capitalist agricultural economy as well the interests of an increasingly privatized self. The result would subsidize as well as complement the practice of retirement. He wanted:

> to mix the profitable Part of a Country Seat with the pleasurable, that one may pay the Expence of the other.
>
> To accomplish which nothing (in my slender Opinion) can conduce more than this rural and extensive Way of Gardening I am here proposing, where a whole Estate will appear as one great Garden, and the *Utile* harmoniously wove with the *Dulci;* and I believe, I am not singular in my Opinion, if I affirm, that an even decent Walk carry'd thro' a Corn Field or Pasture, thro' little natural Thickets and Hedge Rows, is as pleasing, as the most finish'd Partarre [*sic*] that some Moderns have been so fond of.

Along similar lines, he argued that planting a wood would have patriotic value, in expanding the resources of the nation. And he provided a host of economic reasons for the practice of enclosing an estate: doing so would increase fertility, permit lasting capital improvements, increase yields, provide employment for the poor, sustain a growing population, diminish the opportunity for damage, for example, by stray cattle, and increase the owner's profits.[136]

Yet by 1734 Robert Morris, with a more bourgeois clientele in mind, appeared far more equivocal, even duplicitous, on the subject of productivity. Of chief importance was securing "a Rural Situation," which in his view meant the lack of any "Impediments . . . to Proportion and Convenience," that is, impediments to the pristine geometrical perfection that he espoused in architecture. Following that, Morris also nodded briefly to the concerns of the "Gentleman who delights in mixing Profit with his Pleasures, . . . and making the most Advantage of the Produce of his Ground." But within a few pages he refocused his discussion exclusively on "Seats built only for Pleasure or Retirement," that is, unproductive landscapes, where the owners "partake the Pleasure without mixing with it the Labour." The most that Morris might permit to be visible from such a villa was a combination of two types of landscape: cultivated fields, presumably on somebody else's estate, and land that was "*wild* and *woody.*"

Together these would comprise a vista that encompassed in a single gaze a harmonious juxtaposition of production (so long as it was not one's own) and leisure.[137]

Still, woven throughout the literature of retirement, including many architectural treatises, there was a growing preoccupation with the pastoral: a fascination with and desire to attain a life of simultaneous plenty and ease, where the bounties of nature were so plentiful that their consumption was effectively a leisurely and virtuous activity.[138] It would not be hard to argue that in all the genres of artistic expression in eighteenth-century England, encompassing media from poetry and landscape gardening to painting and even music, pastoral may have been the most characteristic mode. Ranging from Alexander Pope's imitations of Horace to Richard Wilson's paintings and Capability Brown's landscapes, pastoral depiction of the comfortable and secure individual enjoying leisure, ease, and plenty offered a potent paradigm for English culture throughout the century. Even if the paradigm was in most cases a fiction, it stood as a construct according to which (or against which) the positions and roles of many people and institutions were articulated.[139]

In this respect two aspects of English eighteenth-century pastoral are relevant to the further discussion of domestic bourgeois retirement. First, the standard pastoral notion of a plentiful landscape, an economy of abundance, was soon hyperbolized into representations of abundance without economy. The standard pastoral myth of land as spontaneously fruitful served, when convenient, to occlude and contradict any understanding of land either as a productive capital instrument or as a resource that could be rendered productive only through labor. And second, eighteenth-century pastoral afforded a correspondingly mythical vision of labor. Labor such as it was represented was commonly performed by workers who individually seemed prosperous and content in a naive and rustic simplicity, or who collectively appeared to be part of a spontaneously happy community, or (perhaps most often) simply were absent.[140] Thus unlike the respected seventeenth-century genre of country-house poetry, which tended to present dwellings either as show-houses or as working estates, and unlike the empiric topographic detail of early eighteenth-century estate views, eighteenth-century architects, painters, landscape designers, poets, and even topographers increasingly gave architecture and landscape a very different cast: as simultaneously bountiful and beautiful, often in a self-consciously unimproved manner. And this transformation was all the more notable because of its inverse relation to the increasingly enclosed, capitalized landscape and dispossessed labor force that Britain in fact was becoming.

Timothy Nourse sounded a keynote to this shift in his 1700 essay *Campania Foelix,* even the Latin title of which alluded to pastoral prosperity. In the text he noted that "The Poets of Ancient and Modern Times" had described "the true Felicity of Man" through accounts of "the Pastoral Life." From this he extrapolated that "Pastoral Methods" likewise might be considered as a basis for modern political organization. More practically, he saw pastoral as a medium for pursuing one's personal and spiritual identity, and notably included dwellings as part of that pastoral apparatus.

He presented both "Country Houses" as well as their smaller counterparts "Villas" as "Places of Pleasure and Retreat" that, he suggested, not only had a mental and physical recuperative function but also aided the individual in regaining a lost earthly position of spiritual bliss and innocence:

> The True design then of such Places of Pleasure and Retreat is to sweeten the Fatigues both of the Body and of the Mind, and to recover us to our former Bent of Duty, which is but in some measure to restore Man to his lost Station: For God doubtless would never have placed him in a Paradise, had not a Garden of Pleasure been Consistent with Innocence.[141]

A generation later the poem "Dawley Farm" (1731) celebrated several ways in which just such a villa provided Lord Bolingbroke with a ready-made pastoral existence on his return from political exile in 1725. Uneconomically he turned four hundred acres into pasture and orchard to provide a pastoral air with which to surround his villa—which in turn he painted "with trophies of rakes, spades, prongs, &c. and other ornaments merely to countenance his calling the place a farm."[142] As the poem elaborated:

> See! Emblem of himself, his Villa stand!
> Politely finish'd, regularly Grand!
> Frugal of Ornament; but that the best,
> And all with curious Negligence express'd.
> No gaudy Colours stain the Rural Hall,
> . . .
> Here the proud Trophies, and the Spoils of War
> Yield to the Scythe, the Harrow and the Car;
> . . .
> Whilst Noble St. J—— in his sweet Recess,
> (By those made greater who would make him less)
> Sees, on the figur'd Wall, the Stacks of Corn
> With Beauty more than theirs the Room adorn,
> Young winged Cupids smiling guide the Plough,
> And Peasants elegantly reap and sow.
> . . .
> While Thou, ingrate, infatuate, as thou art,
> Of thy mad Conduct long shalt feel the Smart,
> Long mourn the Folly which thy Weal destroys,
> And rue the blest Retirement he enjoys.[143]

Decorative schemes associated with grand seats such as gaudy colors and trophies here were replaced by images of the simple implements of husbandry. Other ornaments and illustrations depicted the bounty of nature as well as cupids who assisted happy peasants to render their labors as effortless as possible. Isolated from political strife and economic cares, Bolingbroke was "blest" in this pastoral retirement. As the ostensible "Emblem" of Bolingbroke, the villa also served as the *instrument* of his personal fulfillment.[144]

At Dawley, the villa itself also became exemplary of the pastoral as ideological paradigm. Compared to architectural examples from the previous century such as Appleton House, as celebrated in Andrew Marvell's poem of the mid-1650s, Dawley afforded (even required) a highly pastoralized vision of the owner's position. Bolingbroke's villa articulated the dimensions of his retirement as a pastoral realm antithetical to his previous political career. By contrast Appleton, like many other dwellings of its era, shone almost as a stage apparatus serving to complement, even augment, the military career of its proprietor. The eighteenth-century villa as a realm of retreat thus meant more intense isolation, greater separation from court and commerce, and more refined opportunities for introspective solitude.

Six or seven miles from Pope's villa at Twickenham, Dawley was visited frequently by Alexander Pope, who, like Bolingbroke, keenly felt his ostracism from court society and sought to make his villa an instrument for articulating that state of quasi-exile in a positive fashion. Nevertheless there were times when the effects of exile were all too poignant even for Bolingbroke, despite his status (albeit diminished) and wealth. Often he was quoted as having described his existence at Dawley as being "in a hermitage, where no man came but for the sake of the hermit; for here he found that the insects which used to hum and buzz about him in the sunshine fled to men of more prosperous fortune, and forsook him when in the shade."[145]

Ironically georgic might have been more appropriate than pastoral as the leading paradigm for design and representation of the British domestic landscape. As a notion that extolled the virtues and rewards of productive labor, georgic was better suited to those who could afford a "retired" lodging, since in fact they generally were dependent on the managed productivity of land somewhere to sustain such leisure pursuits.[146] In this light the popularity, and at times preponderance, of pastoral topoi in eighteenth-century literature, painting, and landscaping is telling. The more the wealth of the nation increased, and the more the ranks of the wealthy bourgeoisie grew, the more the labor and resources necessary to sustain leisure and consumption were screened from view and in many cases negated or denied.[147]

To put it another way, the pastoral vision of plenty and tranquility, like the retired domain of self, family, and domesticity, was purposely detached from the economic and material world in two ways. First, residential buildings were preferably dissociated from land that was in production or that even showed evidence of its economic capacity.[148] And second, the fruits of the land, as well as riches accumulated in production and trade, were understood as best enjoyed and consumed in a rarefied environment defined according to idealized notions of a benign, benevolent, and tranquil nature.

Concern over the problematic nature of such expectations—particularly the contradictions inherent in overlaying a pastoral ideal on productive individuals, society, and landscape—was evident throughout the eighteenth century. But resolution of that concern remained elusive. Some, such as Switzer, sought a middle ground where labor and leisure might be united. Others sought grounds on which the comparative merits of pastoral might outweigh those of georgic. Before Switzer even published his call to unite "utile" with "dulci" in an estate dually dedicated to profit and pleasure, the arguments in favor of pastoral over georgic had begun to prevail. A 1713 essay in the *Guardian,* for example, argued distinct epistemological justifications for pastoral. It argued that educated men were distinguished in their thinking by their ability to abstract:

> Men, who by long Study and Experience have reduced their Ideas to certain Classes, and consider the general Nature of things abstracted from Particulars, express their Thoughts after a more concise, lively, surprising Manner. Those who have little Experience, or cannot abstract, deliver their Sentiments in plain Descriptions, by Circumstances, and those Observations, which either Strike upon the Senses, or are the first Motions of the Mind.

The essay then contrasted educated men with shepherds, figures long associated with pastoral landscape, arguing that shepherds were not only "rude and uncultivated" but constitutionally incapable of elevated thinking. And it was due to this contrast, as John Barrell has shown, that eighteenth-century intellectuals would have achieved such pleasure from contemplating, or even occupying, pastoral landscapes.[149] Not only was the bourgeois superior in his capacity to abstract, but through the power of abstraction the bourgeois could bound, aestheticize, and possess the terrain in which the shepherd lived. Indeed, pastoral in all its respects—poetic, landscape, ideological—may well have appeared the best medium, the best context, in which to address the challenges of Enlightenment thought. Certainly the trope of the prosperous hermit (such as Bolingbroke and others much less wealthy than he), isolated but therefore more readily liberated from the constraints of material concerns, and able to explore the higher realms of abstract thought, appealed to many an elite and bourgeois estate owner throughout the eighteenth century. In a certain way the same trope also informed the emerging suburban ideal, in the sense that the bourgeois villa could be a place of pastoral retreat for the purposes of more elevated pursuits.

Yet at the very heart of the pastoral ideal there always remained a fundamental contradiction. This lay in the presumption that viewer and viewed—poet and shepherd, artist and laborer, owner and tenant, landed and landless, subject and object—existed on entirely different planes of consciousness. The plane on which a landowner understood his lands and the people who lived and worked there was a plane that could encompass and "abstract" the labor of those people into a broader matrix of sophisticated relations. In contrast those who worked there, such as shepherds and tenant farmers, could encompass little more than their immediate needs and surroundings with their "plain" manner of thinking. As such they represented no challenge to the superior mental capacities of educated individuals. Understood in such terms, the working inhabitants of pastoral domains as well as the land itself could easily be appropriated into the consciousness of landowners as adjuncts to such complex and overarching concepts as "Nature" or the autonomous (landowning) self.[150]

This distinct epistemological and ontological synthesis held a strong attraction not only for the landowner but also for the bourgeois consumer of novels, illustrated books, and single prints offering vicarious possession of the eighteenth-century pastoral landscape. This was notably apparent in several collections of views of houses and country seats, published in the last quarter of the century in formats affordable by bourgeois customers. Bearing titles such as *The Seats of the Nobility and Gentry, in a Collection of the Most Interesting & Picturesque Views* (1779), and *The Seats of the Nobility and Gentry, in Great Britain and Wales in a Collection of Select Views* (1787), these volumes included scores of plates showing off the domestic architectural heritage of Britain from previous centuries through to the present, ranging from grand castles to modest villas. While the different architectural styles of these houses may have been emphasized as a way of underscoring their historical connections to different ages, almost every dwelling represented in these volumes was depicted in an exquisitely pastoral setting of lawns or meadows replete with grazing deer, horses, or livestock, accented perhaps by a figure fishing in a stream, or by a man playing music on a flute to his lover seated on the grass (Figure 3.33).[151] The attraction of the pastoral, in other words, was seen as almost universalizing. It bespoke simplicity and even innocence, just as it was delightful to contemplate as a realm in which to escape the complexities of civilization and to indulge the pleasures of a sophisticated and superior intellect.

And yet, perhaps ironically, the pastoral figure also could be an object of considerable longing, particularly on the part of those who might be tied to city politics or trade. Almost by definition the pastoral figure lived in close harmony with nature. Likewise by virtue of his or her innocence of intellectual, political, and financial corruption, the pastoral figure was incapable of existing beyond the unspoiled realm of plenty and tranquility. And so, for the retired (or suburban) gentleman the shepherd-in-the-pastoral-landscape in many respects became the model for articulating precisely the dimensions of withdrawal and private existence that he sought. The result was many highwayside "little boxes," of the sort satirized in *The Connoisseur* in 1756, by William Cowper in 1782, and even by Malvina Reynolds in 1963—imperfect efforts, because many of them were attempts to achieve an ideal with either insufficient resources or an imperfect understanding of what that ideal entailed. Nevertheless the fact that many such bourgeois efforts did fail is not in itself fair grounds for condemnation of those who tried, as in the satirical critiques just mentioned. Rather, fault, blame, and concern, if any needed to be assigned, lay in the confluence of much larger economic, political, and ideological pressures and expectations that confronted the bourgeoisie, as this and previous chapters have shown. Despite the host of architectural and spatial innovations introduced in the eighteenth century, the nature of the process was that economic and other material resources regularly available to the bourgeoisie commonly failed to meet the constantly rising expectations generated by the broader culture surrounding them. Again and again this dilemma has bedeviled the modern middle classes through to the present day, a matter to which later chapters, and especially the conclusion, will return.

A Place to Perform the Self

Enlightenment challenges of self-definition and self-realization also brought with them a corresponding imperative to establish locales that could sustain the kind of work that was necessary to respond. The gradual privatization and individualization of the domestic realm during the eighteenth century were principal ways that this occurred. Dwellings shifted from being sites for the maintenance of social hierarchies and the articulation of social linkages to instruments of isolation and alienation, not only by articulating autonomous selfhood for the owner but also by a complementary

Figure 3.33. William Angus, *Fonthill House in Wiltshire*. Plate 50 in *The Seats of the Nobility and Gentry, in Great Britain and Wales*, 1787. By the last quarter of the eighteenth century, it became commonplace to depict dwellings in settings full of pastoral references such as grazing livestock, human figures playing music, lush but well-manicured vegetation, and an overall compositional framework reminiscent of the French landscapist Claude Lorrain.

distancing of other individuals and spheres from that self. In contrast to the public realm—the domain of the public, of collective interest, of political and business affairs—the dwelling came to be recognized, in contradistinction, as the domain of the self. Strategies for articulating the self correspondingly came to be rooted in the apparatus of that domestic realm. Viable possibilities ranged from articulating the dwelling and its particular landscape as a field of opportunities, or an array of instruments, for engaging in activities the *performance* of which established the dimensions of one's identity, to fashioning the dwelling and its associated landscape into an array of *representations,* a field of images, as it were, proffering a favored portrayal or narrative for consumption by the resident or visitor. And in both cases the function of the apparatus was much more than to gratify personal desires (e.g., for delight). In a much richer way, it helped to fashion many aspects of the owner's selfhood.

Both modes already were in use at the beginning of the eighteenth century, but as the century progressed a clear trend toward greater active engagement of the owner was evident.[152] From a seventeenth-century paradigm according to which the house served in great measure as a static emblem of certain characteristics of status and position, the bourgeois villa instead became an instrument by which the owner might articulate his identity. This was an endeavor to be freely undertaken, according to Locke, and in the bourgeois villa it could be pursued through self-directed activity in any of several purpose-built spaces, as well as by distancing oneself physically from city, labor, production, or even the sight of other people and dwellings. The dwelling, in other words, had become a crucial apparatus for the material implementation of Enlightenment notions of privacy and autonomous personhood, and for their naturalization into a belief system that persists as "normal" to the present day.

PART II

NINETEENTH-CENTURY AMERICA:
REPUBLICAN HOMES IN ARCADIAN SUBURBS

4. Republican Pastoral:
Toward a Bourgeois Arcadia

The Individual, the Republic, and the Public

The remarkable variety of architectural and spatial innovations in eighteenth-century English dwellings was more than a set of instruments for the comfort and well-being of the rising bourgeoisie. As discussed in part 1, this metamorphosis in housing also addressed broader challenges embedded in new Enlightenment ideologies of self, individuality, autonomy, equality, property, and capitalism. Among the material innovations introduced to meet these challenges was a new dwelling type (the compact bourgeois villa), the tendency to articulate explicitly private spaces, the dedication of rooms to specific purposes, and the genesis of suburbia as we know it today. Eighteenth-century England thus set the stage for the widespread proliferation of single-family dwellings, and the suburbs that would house them, in centuries to come.

Toward the end of the eighteenth and early nineteenth centuries, the American bourgeoisie took a progressively greater stake in this process. In the United States a different set of political, economic, and historical circumstances (more republican, more individualistic than in England) rendered this newly invented nation the terrain where the single-family house and suburbanization increasingly became defining elements of the social and physical landscape—in effect, paradigmatic. In part 2 I therefore shift the focus to America, first exploring its political and economic history, then examining ways in which the bourgeois dwelling and suburb became central to American aesthetic discourse and material practice.

As opportunities increased for the bourgeoisie (and the would-be bourgeoisie) to engage in mercantile or professional roles in the expanding American economy over the late eighteenth and early nineteenth centuries, there were corresponding opportunities to build dwellings that recognized their new status. The grand fortunes that early- and mid-eighteenth-century English entrepreneurs had amassed became more difficult to achieve later in the century and in the United States, but the breadth of the bourgeoisie correspondingly increased as many smaller entrepreneurs succeeded. For builders and architects to enter this market, therefore, the challenge was to produce more affordable dwellings, less elaborate and on a scale more diminutive than in the past, perhaps suitable to families who could afford smaller numbers of servants, or had less land, or wanted fewer rooms or less showy ornament.

For some nouveaux bourgeois, dwellings also had to be affordable to build without the services of an architect. Changes in the architectural profession, in the nature of book manufacturing, and in the book trade made this possible after 1785. One outcome was a proliferation of modest publications showing designs for dwellings, most of them appropriate for a bourgeois clientele. These books were no longer cast as authoritative architectural treatises, but rather they eagerly addressed their readers as potential customers.[1] An eventual consequence was the commodification of the dwelling, both as a design and as a product to be purchased from a builder or developer.

The shifts in book publication originated in England, making England a principal site for the genesis of new bourgeois dwellings and suburban planning types well into the nineteenth century.[2] But following the American Revolution, the particular emphasis in the United States on a republican form of government, sustained by a population keyed to the ideal of "self-made men," produced a political and economic climate in which the isolated single-family dwelling, tied to the identity of the householder, became a popular ideal that garnered ever expanding ideological importance. Thus this chapter shifts focus to America, with occasional looks back to England to acknowledge important sources or parallels for American designers' ideas, in order to examine the advancing role of architecture in constituting bourgeois domesticity and selfhood. In particular this chapter explores the different modes in which housing became a critical dimension of American privatist and individualist political ideologies of the nineteenth century.[3]

Self-Made Men

With the formation of the new American state, its constitutional apparatus based solidly in Enlightenment principles of identity and property ownership, the political infrastructure soon permitted expanded opportunities (compared to England) for exploring the Lockean ideal of self-realization. Still, as with Locke and as in England, such opportunities were limited almost exclusively to men. Not only did men alone hold the franchise, but during the nineteenth century the man increasingly was seen as the family member whose fulfillment other members were there to support. Nevertheless this heightened emphasis on the role of the man in the household afforded fertile new possibilities for the integration of domestic architecture into the economic and political agenda of the new republic. This was especially the case in connection with one key American ideological tenet of the nineteenth century, the "self-made man," a notion that became essential to understanding the dwelling as an instrument for definition, articulation, and nurture of the owner—the self.

From a nineteenth-century point of view, the "self" was something to be treated with considerable suspicion and kept under careful control. As Anthony Rotundo has shown, the self did not achieve its present status as the locus of identity and personal worth until the twentieth century. Predominant nineteenth-century concerns focused instead on ways of shaping and molding the self, through such means as self-improvement, self-control, and self-advancement.[4]

But underlying all such concerns was a fundamental recognition that full and proper articulation of the self was requisite to the fulfillment of the bourgeois individual. In many respects the detached dwelling would become the instrument for accomplishing these tasks, articulating values that evolved along with the course of American republican capitalism,[5] while the essential task remained for each individual, at very least each individual male, to "make something of himself."

That clearly was the sentiment embodied in the expression "self-made man," apparently coined by Henry Clay in a speech on the floor of the U.S. Senate in 1832 defending the "American System" of trade protectionism. He argued on two grounds against claims that high tariffs would foster a new aristocracy. First, he said, the joint stock companies that flourished under tariffs actually were owned by hundreds of people of small means. And second, tariffs provided protection for small entrepreneurs: "In Kentucky, almost every manufactory known to me, is in the hands of enterprising and self-made men, who have acquired whatever wealth they possess by patient and diligent labor."[6] In other words, America was a terrain in which individuals could pursue their own self-interest free from the marketplace distortions that often resulted from other countries' similar protectionist policies. Underlying Clay's position was an apparent ready familiarity and acceptance of the term *self-made men* among his senatorial colleagues, as embodying a principle central to the understanding of free white manhood in America.

As historians such as David Leverenz and Michael Kimmel have shown, the paradigm prior to the self-made man was the "artisan" figure, nominally self-sufficient, typically the yeoman farmer or the shopkeeper in a patriarchal village.[7] Unlike the artisan, Clay's self-made man was no longer immune to external economic conditions, as Clay's defense of protectionist barriers made clear. Still, Clay strongly supported capitalist entrepreneurship within those barriers, and his vision might best be understood as a shift from a nation of artisans to a nation of bourgeois entrepreneurs. That his vision was widely shared is evident from the proliferation of the term and its use in such titles as John Frost's *Self Made Men of America* (1848), and Charles Seymore's *Self-Made Men* (1858).[8]

How the detached dwelling became instrumental in this process of self-fabrication, particularly in America, will be the focus of much of the rest of this chapter. In many instances the dwelling served a purpose exactly parallel to what Clay described. Building a house was an effort to establish a material and rhetorical apparatus that could sustain and advance the economically and politically more liberated self in a world of competitive individualism. It did so by means of the way it facilitated family relations within the house, with the sort of values it communicated in its exterior design and landscaping, and in the way it related spatially to other dwellings in the neighborhood and vicinity. This is not to say that the relations and values articulated were always appropriate. A considerable portion of nineteenth-century domestic design was more concerned with a nostalgic recreation of an image of the "genteel patriarchy"[9] of past decades and centuries, generally by building houses on a scale, or in a stylistic vocabulary, unsuited to their present circumstances. But the greater point is that the values each householder displayed were chosen in part as a measure of personal expression.

The notion of "making" the self, whether economically, politically, or architecturally, continued to grow throughout the nineteenth century, to the point where early in the twentieth century the notion could easily be rendered through an architectural metaphor such as *Building the Young Man,* the title of a book issued by Kenneth H. Wayne in 1912. A remarkably lonesome self-help manual, it placed responsibility for making something of oneself squarely on the individual alone: "In what way influences and environments affect him is determined by the young man himself. Every man builds himself."[10] And yet in many ways that is exactly what many nineteenth-century designers had prescribed in architectural terms: single-family dwellings isolated on multiacre lots, screened visually and aurally from contact with any others so that the individual (male) householder and his family could flourish to their fullest potential. Some even likened this mode of self-fulfillment to America's national destiny. Bruce Price, known for his work at Tuxedo Park, New York, one of America's earliest, wealthiest, and most exclusive gated suburbs (1886), wrote that because suburban housing afforded the possibility for a man "to assert his individuality and independence by owning a home which is the outgrowth of his special taste and needs," it was in effect the apotheosis of American nationalism.[11]

Individualism

A complementary facet of American nineteenth-century bourgeois selfhood was its strong investment in the exercise of individualism, in domestic and social life as well as in economic enterprise. While individualistic endeavor might be expected according to the principles of a comparatively unregulated laissez-faire capitalist economy such as that of early nineteenth-century America, the specific manner in which Americans embraced individualism at home took at least some major observers by surprise. Perhaps most famously Alexis de Tocqueville, the French author of *Democracy in America* (1835–40), reported that he was particularly troubled by a distinction that he could make between the English and American peoples: the one he characterized by "individuality," the other by "individualism."

"Individuality," Tocqueville observed in another publication of 1835, was the basis of the English character.[12] In this he drew on the Enlightenment heritage of the French term *individualité,* which connoted personal liberty and equality. Here Tocqueville was in accord with James Mill, who had written as early as 1824 that English middle-class philosophy depended directly on what he had termed "individualism," referring to the reigning laissez-faire ideal according to which individual competition maximized opportunities for economic success.[13] And both Mill and Tocqueville concurred that in working to establish advantages for themselves, individuals also eagerly formed "associations" to further their interests in business, politics, science, and pleasure.[14]

Having chosen *individualité* as the basis of the English character, Tocqueville adopted a different term to describe the American character, *individualism*—confusingly, the same term that Mill had used in his 1824 essay to describe the British character. But by making the distinction, Tocqueville was able to signify a predisposition of each member of the American community to sever himself or herself from the mass of others and to associate closely with just family and friends.[15] Tocqueville suggested that this predisposition was a consequence of democracy, since that form of society tended to sever the links of obligation that formerly existed between classes and to give individuals the sense that they owed nothing to anyone and could expect nothing from anyone.[16]

But while Tocqueville was accurate in identifying a strong current of individualism in America, he was mistaken in attributing it wholly to democracy. For American individualism also was indebted to the heritage of German idealism and American Unitarianism, which focused on the pursuit of human perfection through individuality, liberty, and self-government. William Ellery Channing was a powerful exponent of this intellectual movement,[17] and it is a foundation of much of Emerson's writing as well, including his seminal transcendentalist essay on "Nature" (1836).[18] This intellectual heritage informed the desire of many Americans to live isolated in the countryside or in quasi-rural suburbs. Here would be ideal sites for the soul to pursue unsullied communion with nature, isolated from contact with other human beings and thus free, like Emerson's "transparent eyeball," to come alive in transcendental Nature.

Whatever were the dimensions in which American individualism originated, it would be fair to tie its rise closely to the state of American capitalism at the time. As David Leverenz observed in an analysis of the northeastern United States from the 1820s through the 1850s, there was a "battle for dominance between the old mercantile and landowning elite and the new middle class of entrepreneurial businessmen. The new middle class won, and its ideology of manhood as competitive individualism still pervades American life." That ideology was the same that Tocqueville observed, and the same that can be found in the design, selling, and lives of those inhabiting nineteenth-century single-family bourgeois dwellings.

One indication of the degree to which individualism became a core consideration in domestic design is evident in the writings of Andrew Jackson Downing, a prolific and very popular American writer on architecture. In 1850 he stated blatantly and directly that the quintessential American residence should manifest individualism above all else. To achieve this goal, the dwelling "should say something of the character of the family within—as much as possible of their life and history, their tastes and associations, should mould and fashion themselves upon its walls."[19] In other words, the dwelling should become at very least a material portrait of the family living within, and by extension an apparatus for sustaining the unique character of that family in the context of a fundamentally competitive economy and society. Thus Downing intended his own designs to accommodate the specific circumstances and needs of the family, in effect calling for an even more individualized architecture. And in a complementary fashion he stressed opportunities for architectural style and expression to strengthen the morality and character of the inhabitants as they faced the challenges of the larger competitive environment.

During the next decade it was clear that individualism had become a topic of widespread interest among American architects. For example, Zephaniah Baker observed in 1856 that Americans preferred houses over apartments, a statement not inconsistent with Baker's own self-interest in building detached dwellings. But the reason he chose to promote such buildings was telling: the dwelling sustained an individualism that was necessary to selfhood and manhood. As he put it, houses were more popular in America than in Europe, "perhaps, on account of the *individualism* of our people, each man desiring to be a man in and of himself." In fact, living in a home was necessary to achieve that state of individualism, which in turn was necessary (as a natural right) to achieve the greatest fulfillment of manhood:

> No man can be fully a man, and enjoy the blessings and privileges of life, who is destitute of a HOME; and . . . it is on the broadest ground we assume man's right to a *home* of some kind, and with the highest appreciation of his powers, that this home shall be as neat, and convenient, and beautiful as Nature herself.[20]

Some notion of what the individualist paradigm may have looked like on a larger scale may be found in an 1850 essay by Downing in which he published a description of an ideal "rural village—newly planned in the suburbs of a great city." (The adjective *rural* often served among Downing and his contemporaries to denote the epitome of a suburban bourgeois dwelling environment, not a genuinely rustic environment or one economically dependent on agricultural production.)[21] The village that Downing delineated incorporated "a large open space, common, or park, situated in the middle," extending over twenty to fifty acres and covered with lawn and trees (Figure 4.1). "This park would be the nucleus or heart of the village, and would give it an essentially rural character." The "best cottages and residences" would front on the park. Wide streets bordered with elms or maples would lead to other parts of the village, in which the minimum lot frontage would be 100 feet. Thus all parts of the village would have "space, view, circulation of air, and broad, well-planted avenues of shade-trees." In addition the park would serve as a center for social gatherings and musical performances.[22]

That there was a designated space for social gatherings and other community events was certainly an acknowledgement that some sort of community activities needed to take place, activities that were badly underrepresented or absent in Downing's major publications. But as a whole the plan was a statement of private, individual isolation, prefiguring so many suburban developments in its low density and elevated clientele, each dwelling at a sufficient distance from the next to ensure visual and aural seclusion, particularly so if an appropriate regime of landscape gardening were introduced. The result would be an entire community of concentrated individualism, perhaps a contradiction in terms for modern observers, although not so from Downing's perspective, since it was the self-made man who was the foundation of the community in the first place.

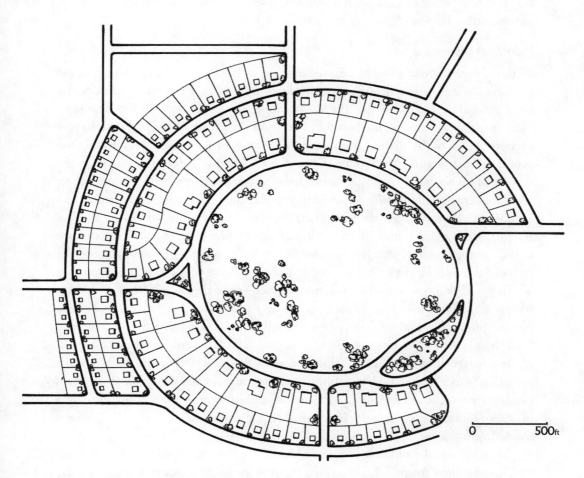

Figure 4.1. Conjectural layout of Andrew Jackson Downing's ideal "rural village," originally proposed in 1850 to have "an essentially rural character," with a large central common or park of twenty to fifty acres and minimum lot frontages of 100 feet. Drawing by Holley Wlodarczyk.

But later in the decade Josiah Holland, author of a popular advice manual, did bemoan the unfortunate consequences resulting from the architectural proliferation of individualism: "Neighborhood should mean something more than a collection of dark and selfishly-closed hearts and houses. A community should be something better than an aggregation of individuals and homes governed by the same laws, and sustaining equal civil burdens." The basis of this critique has conspicuously persisted ever since, if anything growing stronger, as it increasingly targets suburbia, the locus of so much isolated private housing, as the site of individualism's worst consequences. Such a perceived lack of community in suburbia actually formed the basis of an early twentieth-century critic's highly ironic embrace of her suburban environment precisely because it satisfied her disposition toward individualism: "It is an opportunity for individualism. In a Suburb you can be as unneighborly as you wish. . . . In a suburb, every man obeys the injunction of Voltaire, to cultivate his own garden." Appearances, in other words, could often be deceiving, and whether a suburb appeared to be a community did not necessarily make it one.[23]

Republican Domesticity

With the separation of the American colonies from Britain and the fashioning of the new state as republican democracy, a work in progress that extended over decades both preceding and following the Revolution, the American political apparatus became markedly more focused on the interests of the private individual than its predecessor. Much of this derived from a sharp concern for protecting the interests of the people against tyranny of the state. For example, Thomas Jefferson, long before he developed his now well-recognized views favoring a democracy of agrarian gentry, was more concerned with a politics of resistance to decadence and corruption.[24] And one of the best ways to stabilize the interests of the people against the state was not a class system, as in England, but the institution of private property. Thus the importance of the agrarian enterprise to Jefferson lay not so much in its production of goods or its social noblesse but in its self-interest in resisting the state. A much later extension of this principle came with the homestead movement of the 1840s and 1850s, culminating in the Homestead Act of 1862, as property ownership gave families not only a new economic freedom but also a political stake in the expansion of the American West. Much the same happened on the emerging suburban front in the early decades of the nineteenth century, as individuals began to purchase land on the peripheries of towns and cities and started to form an extraurban constituency there. In all these cases, the principle underlying the private ownership of property was not entirely a matter of economic opportunity but perhaps equally or more so a matter of political checks and balances.

Yet while the distribution of private property across the population was in itself perhaps sufficient for protection against tyranny, it was hardly a guarantee that the society would flourish. For that to happen, republican theory held that individuals needed to possess a strong sense of *virtue*. In fact virtue would have to become a

cardinal aspect of all households—both morally and physically, as detailed below—
since that would provide a common basis of agreement on which the country's political decisions could be made.[25] In addition, each individual had to have a strong and
sound *character,* in order to sustain republican virtues, family values, and more. Nor
would it be a coincidence that many of the qualities that a man of virtue and sound
character possessed, such as integrity and frugality, were identical or closely analogous
to qualities that architects extolled as primary principles of design during this period.

The connection among virtue, character, and architecture was by no means
fortuitous. In efforts to secure a stable and continuous government, the framers of
America's constitution were loath to give full reign to democracy but rather placed
limits on the franchise and direct election to such offices as the presidency. The presumption was that those possessed of property, and who therefore tended to be
enfranchised, would be those with greatest virtue.[26] Correspondingly as early as the
1720s American political writers began to develop notions of an engineered government, one with checks and balances, and separation of powers, to counteract the
potential for tyranny that a monarchy posed.[27] The Constitution of 1787 was in its
own time an elegant example of just such an engineered government, and in an era
when architecture was deemed to have the capacity to influence human feeling and
behavior,[28] the notion that a house might be designed to engineer, or at very least
sustain, a republican individual was not far behind. Authoritative grounds for tying
together design and morality could soon be found in many Victorian architectural
tracts. For example, in an 1842 collection of designs, James Cunningham added
remarks on the problems associated with dilapidated dwellings, calling them a major
source of "grossness" and "immorality." Quoting from a recent study of pauperism in
Berwickshire, he implied that buildings profoundly shaped character, virtues, morality, even class: "the better the class of cottages designed for the labouring population,
the higher will be the class of persons who will occupy them, and the less likely to
contain among them the seeds of pauperism."[29]

Andrew Jackson Downing, as a strong partisan of American republican democracy, was one of many designers, clerics, and advice givers who during the nineteenth
century found it appropriate to represent dwellings as sites of virtue and character formation. In an 1848 essay titled "Moral Influence of Good Houses," Downing stated
that "we have firm faith in the *moral* effects of the fine arts. We believe in the better-
ing influence of beautiful cottages and country houses." The provision of a good house
for oneself also would have a moral benefit for the public at large:

> The first motive which leads men to build good houses is, no doubt, that of in-
> creasing largely their own comfort and happiness. But it is easy to see that, in this
> country, where so many are able to achieve a home for themselves, he who gives to
> the public a more beautiful and tasteful model of a habitation than his neighbors, is
> a benefactor to the cause of morality, good order, and the improvement of society
> where he lives.

In another essay of the same year, titled "Hints to Rural Improvers," Downing all but presented the suburban residence as the ideal republican dwelling. Comparing American versus European dwelling design, he wrote that

> a really successful example at home is based upon republican modes of life, enjoyment, and expenditure,—which are almost the reverse of those of an aristocratic government. . . . Hence, smaller suburban residences, like those in the neighborhood of Boston, are perhaps, better models, or studies for the public generally, than our grander and more extensive seats; mainly because they are more expressive of the means and character of the majority of those of our countrymen whose intelligence and refinement lead them to find their happiness in country life.[30]

A few years later, after Downing's unfortunate early death, his lesser known contemporary John Bullock offered his own analysis of the reciprocal relation between domestic architecture and the character of the inhabitants: "Perhaps nothing is more indicative of the character of its occupants than the external appearance of a country dwelling." And reciprocally those same houses had a moral influence on their indwellers: "Were our country residences more generally decked with simplicity and taste, we imagine that the number of our young men who wander from the patrimonial estate, and precipitate themselves into the dissipated and vitiated follies of a city life, would be very materially lessened."[31]

Perhaps the most explicit discussion of the moral affectivity of architecture and its role in the cultivation of virtue appeared in *Villas and Farm Cottages* (1856) by Henry W. Cleaveland, William Backus, and Samuel D. Backus. From the very beginning they stressed that "the dwellings of men often exert a powerful influence on their habits and character." The authors counseled that a man should try to make his house "a teacher and promoter of virtue, by its evident regard for order, neatness, truth, and beauty."[32] Inside and outside, in every element of design, from exterior style to floor plan and interior furnishings, the implication was that each decision would have a profound effect on the character and lives of those who lived there.

Well beyond midcentury, the understanding remained that the dwelling functioned as a primary teacher of republican values. As John J. Thomas wrote in 1865 in the *Illustrated Annual Register of Rural Affairs:*

> A house is always a teacher; it may become an agent of civilization. While builders minister to deceit and vanity, those vices will prevail; when their works embody fitness, truth and dignified simplicity, these republican virtues will be firmly rooted in the nation. Few are aware how strong an influence is exerted by the dwelling on its inhabitants.[33]

Many of the same arguments could be marshaled with respect to the arrangement of communities at large. In her 1848 *History of Architecture,* for example, Louisa

Tuthill drew lessons from towns and villages in certain parts of the country that she held up as exemplary for all. In particular she admired towns of the Connecticut River valley, which she presented in words penned by Timothy Dwight a quarter century earlier:

> They are not, like those along the Hudson, mere collections of houses and stores, clustered around a landing. . . . The settling in them is not merely to acquire property, but to sustain the relations, perform the duties, and contribute to the enjoyments of life. Equally, and, to my eye, happily, do they differ from most European villages. The villages on the other side of the Atlantic are exhibited as being generally clusters of houses, standing contiguously on the street. . . .
>
> [In contrast,] New England villages, and, in a peculiar degree, those of the Connecticut Valley, are built in the following manner. . . .
>
> The town-plot is originally distributed into lots, containing from *two to ten acres,* (not twenty by fifty feet!)[.] In a convenient spot, on each of these, a house is erected at the bottom of the court-yard, often neatly enclosed, and is furnished universally with a barn and other convenient out-buildings. Near the house there is always a garden, replenished with culinary vegetables, flowers, and fruits, and very often also, prettily enclosed. The lot on which the house stands, universally styled the home-lot, is almost, of course, a meadow, richly cultivated, and containing generally a thrifty orchard.

To such an exemplary model Tuthill proposed adding little more than "a public garden and promenade, open and free to all." She promised that the influence and benefits of this kind of planning would readily be apparent in improving "the purity of morals, the simplicity and sobriety of the citizens of the United States."[34] Or as Eugene C. Gardner succinctly put it four decades later, "the well ordered home" could be understood simply as "a tremendous missionary society."[35]

A Simulacrum of the Self

During the nineteenth century the American single-family detached dwelling became an ever more refined instrument for fashioning the self. As the preceding pages suggest, America was particularly fertile ground in this process for several reasons. One was the growth of the bourgeois economy, permitting a rise in numbers of people who could afford to own such a house, as well as those who had the time and types of jobs that permitted them to commute back and forth. No less important was the rise of national ideologies of individualism and republican virtue, as discussed above. Other factors ranged from the rise of mass transportation commuter systems such as ferryboats and railroads to changes in household customs and technologies that made single-family living more efficient.

Once the means were available, prospective homeowners could consider residences as apparatuses for fashioning the self in terms of three available frameworks, material, moral, and rhetorical. In material terms, the detached dwelling afforded the obvious benefits of privacy, independence, at least a semblance of self-sufficiency, and the opportunity for the head of the household to determine its look, layout, and operation according to his own preferences. In moral terms, the interior furnishings of the dwelling could afford family members outright instruction in matters of morality, making the dwelling an excellent fount of republican virtue, and it would simultaneously display the owner's virtue to visitors. And finally in rhetorical terms, nineteenth-century designers—often misunderstood as having "no style of their own" and therefore clumsily borrowing styles from the past—made extensive use of the wide range of styles available from the past as a complex rhetorical apparatus that could display aspects of the owner's character and sensibility on the exterior of the dwelling for all to see. In practice all three of these frameworks intersected each other in multiple ways, in different stages of designing the house and in different elements of its design and fabric. To explore the variety of new and sometimes extraordinary ways in which nineteenth-century designers articulated these frameworks, the following discussion turns first to a brief analysis of some of the important design principles that were imported from England, and then to an examination of specific components of the design in which aspects of selfhood were realized: type, style, plan, and interior furnishings.

Principles from England

By far the most widely recognized compilation of domestic architectural design principles in the first half of the nineteenth century in England was John Claudius Loudon's truly encyclopedic *Encyclopaedia of Cottage, Farm, and Villa Architecture* (1833), originally consisting of 1,138 pages and eventually expanding to 1,317 pages. Achieving at least fourteen editions over approximately forty years, passing through two major editorial revisions and several minor ones, Loudon's book had a sufficiently broad market, at least among its bourgeois readers, that it aided considerably in the popularization of architectural taste on both sides of the Atlantic. Even Andrew Jackson Downing, the most influential writer on architecture in America at mid-century, drew heavily on Loudon at the beginning of his career.

Early in the *Encyclopaedia* Loudon set out three principles of architectural design, in descending order of importance: fitness, or making sure the building would have the material strength to suit its purpose; expression of purpose, for example, designing a church to look like a church; and style, or producing a "characteristic effect." In Downing's first major publication on architecture, *Cottage Residences,* he presented this triad almost verbatim as his own three principles of design: "FITNESS or *usefulness*," "*Expression of* PURPOSE," "*Expression of Style*."[36] Elaborating on these points to his American audience, he explained that "fitness" meant an appropriate adaptation of the design to suit the particular circumstances and needs of each individual family. For instance, a family with "a literary taste" might use a given room space as a library, while others would use it for a bedroom. "Expression" in turn was largely a matter of association. A church, for example, should have a spire; in a dwelling features such as chimneys, windows, a porch, a verandah, a piazza, an entrance door, and oriel windows could heighten the appreciation of such things as "ideas of comfort" or "elegant enjoyments which belong to the habitation of man in a cultivated and refined state of society."[37]

For both authors style became a more complex matter. At some points Loudon suggested that style was little more than a veneer applied to the exterior of the house, something that came in many varieties (such as Castellated, Greek, and Gothic) that could be applied as an option once the requirements of fitness and expression were fulfilled. But on a more sophisticated plane Loudon also indicated that architectural style could be orchestrated with the surrounding scenery in ways that could affect the imagination, especially to raise emotions of grandeur and beauty.[38]

In *Cottage Residences* (1842), perhaps with his American audience in mind, Downing took a more pointed interest in the potential of architectural style, although his presentation of the subject was hardly rigorous. Early in the discussion, for example, he equated style with "language," a fairly sophisticated connection that would evolve later in the century. But for the time being Downing was content to reduce that language to a fairly simple set of aesthetic concordances, suggesting that the features of the Rural Gothic and Italian styles, including pointed gables and projecting roofs, were most appropriate for American country dwellings because "their outlines are picturesque and harmonious with nature." In fact the notion that the dwelling should harmonize with its surrounding scenery had been a common tenet of eighteenth-century English picturesque aesthetics, and it appeared in the American literature well before Downing. As early as 1818, for example, John Haviland recommended that the style of a dwelling "be adapted to, or regulated by, the nature of the place."[39] And as late as 1898 Samuel Reed suggested that a cottage replete with pointed-arch windows, bargeboarding, and vertical board-and-batten cladding was still a fashionable design, "homelike, tasteful, and picturesque" in its appearance, on the aesthetic grounds that these stylistic features were particularly suited to a suburban or country location.[40]

But Downing also made some concession to the possibility that a given style might be in accord with, or reveal something of, the owner of the dwelling. Rural Gothic and Italian, for example, were "highly expressive of the refined and unostentatious enjoyments of the country," while "the Italian mode is capable of displaying a rich domestic character in its balconies, verandas, ornamental porches, terraces, etc." (Figure 4.2). Unlike the Greek Revival, which Downing said was suited to a temple, the "modern Italian" style was "in unison with the variety of wants, occupations, and pleasures which compose the routine of domestic life."[41] By the end of the decade such correspondences, and better yet such opportunities for expressing the qualities of those living within any given dwelling, would become the stock in trade of American architectural publications and their clientele, the self-made men of the flourishing republic. And more generally, the principles that Downing chose to emphasize in

DESIGN VI.
A Villa in the Italian Style, Bracketed.

Fig. 48.

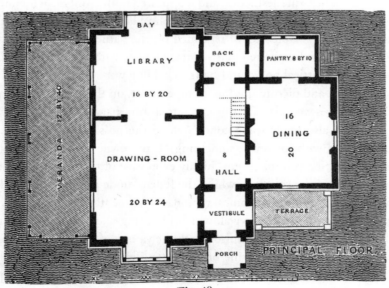

Fig. 49.

Figure 4.2. Andrew Jackson Downing, "A Villa in the Italian Style, Bracketed." Figures 48 and 49 in *Cottage Residences*, 1842. Downing found this style particularly suited to "displaying a rich domestic character."

his texts set the tone for nineteenth-century suburban architecture by removing dwellings from the economy of capital and incorporating them instead into the economy of distinction, emphasizing such aspects as prestige, stature, and individualism.

Type

Before the nineteenth century there had always been a clear hierarchy of types within European domestic architecture, a hierarchy that in many respects remained unchallenged well into the century. Palaces were at the apex of prestige and importance, followed by mansions and then villas. Cottages, when their status as architecture became recognized in the eighteenth century, assumed the lowest rung on the scale. This hierarchy was necessarily wedded to the social hierarchy of time and place, however, and with the rise of the bourgeoisie there came challenges to both the social and architectural hierarchies: the increasing wealth, political power, and landholdings of the bourgeoisie challenged the entrenched interests of the aristocracy, and the transformation of the villa from an elite into a bourgeois housing type likewise disrupted a system that had been entrenched for centuries.

But if the disruption and challenge to an established order were largely initiated in the eighteenth century, the nineteenth century introduced an awareness of a new potential encompassed within the villa type. Previously it would have been difficult, if not impossible, to find any explicit statement of what the villa as a *type* said about its inhabitant. A given villa might have a decorative apparatus that would suit its occupant's tastes, tell his history, or proclaim his politics, such as with Bolingbroke at Dawley Farm, but the notion that the type itself had some import for the identity of the occupant was not yet recognized. Nevertheless such a notion did evolve in America, most notably in the work of Downing.

At midcentury Downing issued his consummate design book, *The Architecture of Country Houses* (1850), which achieved ten editions by 1921, long after Downing's premature death in 1852. For an American audience, he had little need to address the European hierarchy of palaces and mansions, while he did need to present designs for dwellings at the lower end of the scale. He thus devoted most of his 484 pages to cottages, then farmhouses, and finally villas. That he presented these three types in a nonhierarchical order was perhaps a gesture to democracy, but it also allowed him to begin and end his discussion on topics about which he had the most to say; he simply appeared least interested in farmhouses, at the lowest end of the scale. As one critic already had noted sourly, Downing's previous works contained designs for farmers and mechanics, but unfortunately they seemed best suited to "what are termed gentlemen farmers, and mechanics who work, if at all, in gloves."[42]

The first of Downing's three dwelling types was the cottage. Originally a laborer's dwelling, by the mid-nineteenth century it had become synonymous with the middle-class country or suburban dwelling. Because of its history of working-class associations, the type was less pretentious than a villa, and so it could be accorded more freedom in terms of innovation and style. For Downing, however, the matter of identifying the building type with the occupants was a critical concern. In the case of cottages:

> What we mean by a cottage, in this country, is a dwelling of small size. . . . The majority of such cottages in this country are occupied . . . by industrious and intelligent mechanics and working men . . . who own the ground upon which they stand, build them for their own use, and arrange them to satisfy their own peculiar wants and gratify their own tastes.[43]

In other words, the cottage was the perfect residence of the petit bourgeois republican small landholder.

Downing's second type, to which he devoted only one brief chapter, was the farmhouse. Here the text even more patently delineated the expected congruity between the type and the farmer occupant: "His dwelling ought to suggest simplicity, honesty of purpose, frankness, a hearty, genuine spirit of good-will, and a homely and modest, though manly and independent, bearing in his outward deportment."[44] Two years later Lewis F. Allen's book *Rural Architecture* focused primarily on farm dwellings and made explicit the arguments that Downing passed over in haste: that a family comfortably and tidily, though humbly lodged in a rural dwelling "have usually a corresponding character in their personal relations," and that therefore "the farm house is the chief nursery on which our broad country must rely for that healthy infusion of stamina and spirit into those men who, under our institutions, guide its destiny and direct its councils."[45]

But Downing was most interested in villas. He devoted more space to designs for villas than to either of the other two types and waxed far more enthusiastic in describing the potential in villas for advances in domestic design. And with respect to typology, Downing had a well-fixed notion of just what the villa indicated about its occupant. After noting some geographic and historical variations in the use of the term, he stated that "a villa, in the United States, is the country house of a person of competence or wealth sufficient to build and maintain it with some taste and elegance," or as he put it one page later, "the home of its [America's] most leisurely and educated class of citizens."[46] It might not be too much of a simplification to say that a villa denoted its owner as one of America's bourgeois republican elite.

To some extent Downing still had drawn on Loudon for his definition of the villa, but Loudon had been less direct, saying that to possess a villa the owner needed wealth and taste, or at least enough good sense to get assistance in taste from others.[47] Downing's belief in the potential of the villa clearly went much further: "The villa—the country house—should, above all things, manifest individuality. It should say something of the character of the family within—as much as possible of their life and history, their tastes and associations, should mould and fashion themselves upon its walls." Here Downing echoed the early writings of Ruskin, which Downing may have read in Loudon's *Architectural Magazine,* or in *The Seven Lamps of Architecture,* in which Ruskin proposed that the house should almost be a living and lasting monument of the owner's character.[48] But Downing had also in mind the much greater potential that he and his fellow architects invested in architectural *style* to engage actively in the articulation of the individual householder.

Style

Nineteenth-century American architects generally understood architectural style in terms of two aspects that, as constituent elements of an entire design, they found most effective in articulating selfhood in the bourgeois dwelling. One was the capacity of style for *expression,* that is, its ability to serve as a representation of some aspect of the owner's character, aspirations, persona, status, or other dimension of distinction. The other capacity of style was its *affectivity,* its ability to impart virtue and serve as a moral regulator. Both of these aspects of style would play crucial roles in architects' efforts to fashion the single-family dwelling as the site of republican bourgeois individuation and fulfillment.

As an apparatus of expression, style long had been understood as an instrument for the articulation of certain qualities associated with personal character. At the beginning of the eighteenth century, the principle of decorum still demanded that a building's style be in keeping primarily with the *status* of the inhabitant. Toward the end of the century, architects began to explore style as an apparatus for the expression of specific traits of the inhabitant's personal *character.*[49] In this respect style became an opportunity for the articulation of different axes and degrees of distinction among inhabitants. Or to put it another way, the long-term shift onto the bourgeois individual of the responsibility for self-definition had required some apparatus of distinction, and architectural style became one part of that apparatus. As Pierre Bourdieu has shown, the cult of personal distinction has become a quintessential hallmark of bourgeois culture,[50] and nineteenth-century architects explored and expanded the dimensions of distinction by continually extending the parameters of stylistic expression. The panoply of styles and historical associations, of furnishings and their moral referents, was the expanding material culture in which individuals were encouraged to define and fashion the new republican bourgeois self.

The other aspect of style that recommended itself to the nineteenth-century architect was its potential instrumentality in another dimension of republican identity, imparting and maintaining virtue. Early in the nineteenth century it had been a cardinal principle of French theorist Claude-Nicolas Ledoux that architectural design was able to inspire and instruct the observer on many levels, ranging from banishing ignorance and expanding knowledge to "dashing into barbarism those ungrateful or heedless people who ignore its favors." More specifically, in a manner that later would be dubbed "architecture parlante," the particular characteristics of a given building could be orchestrated to provide moral instruction for visitors and occupants.[51] Awareness of Ledoux's writings among Downing or his contemporaries is uncertain, but the notion that architecture could serve as moral instructor did suit perfectly the needs of the American bourgeois republic. To the extent that a given design could serve as a reminder of, or instruction in, a certain aspect of moral behavior—for the benefit of the republican householder, husband or wife, parent, and so on—that design would be understood as an asset to the owner of the dwelling. In other words, the stylistic articulation of the exterior was not only a self-presentation, or an expression of one's desired persona; it was also a constant reminder and admonition to maintain the moral standards that the stylistic apparatus represented.

In many ways Downing set the tone and the pace for the discussion of style in America, just as his intended audience, republican bourgeois householders, became the most fertile terrain for the sort of dwellings and range of stylistic expressions that he proposed. A prolific writer on horticulture as well as architecture, Downing was America's best-known architectural author by midcentury, having published *A Treatise on the Theory and Practice of Landscape Gardening* (1841), *Cottage Residences* (1842), and *The Architecture of Country Houses* (1850). *Rural Essays,* published posthumously in 1857, collected many pieces on architectural, horticultural, and other topics.

At an early point Downing already had embraced the notion of identifying each house with an individual self, as a passage in the 1841 *Treatise* made clear. The ardent wish of every man, he wrote, was "to have a 'local habitation,'—a permanent dwelling, that we can give the impress of our own mind, and identify with our own existence."[52] To render that habitation "local" evidently became less a matter of geographic locality and more a matter of personal distinction, not only as his emphasis on "the impress of our own mind" makes clear, but also because of his interest in the capacity of style to express distinctive aspects of the self. His essays repeatedly emphasized that point when discussing expression. For example:

> In Domestic Architecture, though the range of expression may at first seem limited, it is not so in fact, for when complete, it ought to be significant of the whole private life of man—his intelligence, his feelings, and his enjoyments.

As examples of what might be expressed, Downing included designs in numerous styles that he tied to specific bourgeois qualities and traits. In the following passage, for instance, he addressed qualities that Greek, Roman, Renaissance ("Italian"), castellated, Tudor, and cottage styles might express:

> . . . the classical scholar and gentleman may, from association and the love of antiquity, prefer a villa in the Grecian or Roman style. He who has a passionate love of pictures and especially fine landscapes, will perhaps, very naturally, prefer the modern Italian style for a country residence. The wealthy proprietor, either from the romantic and chivalrous associations connected with the baronial castle, or from desire to display his own resources, may indulge his fancy in erecting a castellated dwelling. The gentleman who wishes to realize the *beau ideal* of a genuine old English country residence . . . may establish himself in a Tudor villa or mansion; and

the lover of nature and rural life . . . will very naturally make the choice of the rural cottage style.[53]

But having a house in any particular style did not necessarily differentiate the owner entirely from other bourgeois individuals. In the case of one design in the Rural Gothic Style, for example (Figure 4.3), "We have designed this villa to express the life of a family of refined and cultivated taste, full of home feeling, love for the country, and enjoyment of the rural and beautiful in nature."[54] Although Downing felt the Italian style was less suited to the country landscape, he nevertheless stated that it too was "remarkable for expressing the elegant culture and variety of accomplishment of the retired citizen or man of the world."[55] Yet between the two styles, which architecturally and historically were quite distinct, there also was room for some overlap with respect to what they expressed about the resident. The former style expressed a "cultivated taste," while the latter expressed "elegant culture"—a distinction that was largely without a substantive difference.

DESIGN XXIX
RURAL GOTHIC VILLA

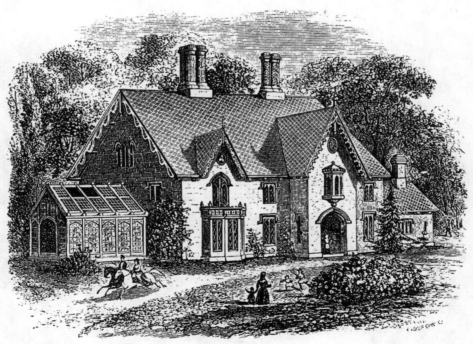

Fig. 148

Figure 4.3. Andrew Jackson Downing, a "Rural Gothic Villa." Figure 148 in *The Architecture of Country Houses*, 1850. This design expressed "the life of a family of refined and cultivated taste, full of home feeling, love for the country, and enjoyment of the rural and beautiful in nature."

Some precedent for understanding style in this manner had been established in England more than a decade before Downing's publications, and further examples appeared contemporary with his work, although the English examples tended to be more simplistic. For example, James Thomson published a collection of designs titled *Retreats* in 1827, in which he produced designs in Gothic, Doric, Ionic, Corinthian, and other styles that he tied with various degrees of success to different expressive possibilities. The Gothic Villa, for example, was suited to "persons fond of retirement and study." Yet it was clear that Thomson, along with his contemporaries, was more concerned with the use of style as a manner of maintaining existing social categories, while Downing and other Americans grew more attuned to articulating varied opportunities for self-made men. Thus Thomson's Corinthian, which he indicated was associated with such qualities as elegance and refinement, was appropriate to the "residence of a nobleman," a dwelling that "should possess an elevation of character corresponding to the rank of its inhabitant." At the other end of the scale, the Doric, as the earliest of the orders, offered associations of permanence and longevity, associations implicit in Thomson's description of the house (Figure 4.4):

> Surely, to persons of extensive landed property, there is not a more laudable or advantageous exercise of its revenue than the erection of a stately mansion commensurate

Figure 4.4. James Thomson, design for a Doric villa. Plate 26 in *Retreats*, 1827. Thomson intended his design to communicate the owner's permanence, prestige, and privilege.

with it. It enables the possessor to live with becoming dignity; and he has the gratification which none but the wealthy can fully enjoy, of giving aid to national industry and talent, in the various branches that engage the artist and the artisan; while
to his posterity he leaves a useful and honourable bequest, to remain for ages—a
monument of parental regard and patriotic munificence.[56]

Nor was the import of this stylistic apparatus only a matter of portraying the status, dignity, and reputation of the owner. Thomson's prose left little doubt that it was
at least as much about maintaining the place, prestige, and privilege of landed property. A contemporary author of more than half a dozen books of designs for dwellings
and associated buildings, Peter Frederick Robinson, also included a varied repertory
of styles, although with greater leanings toward Tudor and Elizabethan than Thomson.
And even more than Thomson, Robinson made clear the role that style played was
not to signal personal character but rather to embrace Britain's historical social hierarchy. Use of the Castellated style, for instance, would "lead the mind back to the days
of our feudal system, and in wandering among the neighbouring hills we almost
expect to see the ancient Baron, surrounded by his followers, ascending the valley."[57]

The contrast with American perspectives on style thus was striking. Louisa Tuthill,
who published the first American history of Western architecture in 1848, included
several chapters on the present state of architecture in America. Here she found that
the Doric should be used only rarely in a dwelling because as a style it was grave and
majestic, while the house should instead be cheerful. Nevertheless, she conceded, "if
it be true, as has been asserted, 'that the character of a family, will generally be found
to have some resemblance to the house in which they live,' some grave and sober citizens will, here and there, rear a majestic front of granite, with Doric columns. . . ."[58]
In other words, whether one chose Doric because it was grave and sober, or because
its absence allowed for cheerfulness, the principal concern was the manner in which
the style represented the character of the family within.

James Hammond, who published *The Farmer's and Mechanic's Practical Architect*
in the same year, was not so concerned as his contemporaries with which particular
historical style a householder might choose. His discussion centered instead on the
degree to which the style as rendered could situate the owner within America's republican democracy:

The style of the dwelling-house in this country in particular, should be marked by
plainness and simplicity. We are all politically equal, and are more remarkable than
the people of any other nation for our jealousy of a superior. Although we exceed
other people in the ostentatious style of our private dwellings, we ought, more than
any other people in the world, to adapt the style of our houses to the republican
simplicity of our institutions. Let the decorations of a house be made as pleasing as
they can be made to the eye, without extraneous ornaments, that it may seem to be
the abode of a sensible and humble minded republican. . . .[59]

By the mid-1850s the regard for dwellings as possible windows into the character of their inhabitants had escalated. Fredrika Bremer, a foreigner who was greeted on arrival by Downing and hosted by him for much of her visit, observed interests that went much beyond what Downing had described in his own writings: "The desire is now that the habitation should be symbolic of the soul within."[60] Such a notion was much more in line with the thinking of two other figures who rose to prominence in the decade after Downing's death, Orson Fowler and Henry Ward Beecher. Fowler, the architect of octagon houses and author of *A Home for All* (1848) (Figure 4.5), also was the principal proponent of the popular pseudoscience of phrenology, by which a person's character traits could be assessed by measuring the contours of the cranium. This positivist understanding of the mind carried over into Fowler's approach to architecture. People's dwellings, he found, could bear a close resemblance to their respective characters. Intellect, ambition, fancy, and mentality all could be embodied in domestic design. Unfortunately he cast his argument largely on a Darwinist foundation, arguing that since "the domiciles of all animals bear a close resemblance to their respective characters. . . ," the same must be true for humans. He then continued to analogize, arguing that "primitive" people build crude hovels, while those of high talents and aspirations build elegant and refined structures. Thus "other things being equal, the better a man's mentality, the better mansion will he construct, and the characteristics of the house will be as those of its builder or occupant."[61]

RESIDENCE OF JOHN J. BROWN, WILLIAMSBURGH, N. Y.

Figure 4.5. Orson Fowler, "The Octagon Cottage." Figure 20 in *A Home for All*, 1848.

Henry Ward Beecher, himself a devotee of phrenology and a friend of Fowler, also was a popular and influential Protestant minister, whose sermons were attended by thousands and whose publications were read by countless more. In "Building a House," published in 1855, he focused closely on the potential that a dwelling held for expression of the self. For him, building a dwelling was a creative act of the highest intellectual caliber: "A house is the shape which a man's thoughts take when he imagines how he should like to live. Its interior is the measure of his social and domestic nature; its exterior, of his esthetic and artistic nature. It interprets, in material forms, his ideas of home, of friendship, and of comfort." Nevertheless Beecher acknowledged that this was an ideal: "one's dwelling is not always to be taken as the fair index of his mind" since there were always mitigating considerations such as finances, material needs, climate, and so forth.[62] Still, the notion remained that the house and its stylistic expression were fundamentally contingent on, and a cardinal expression of, the self living within.

Architects writing at the same period offered formulations of this notion in less idealistic terms, geared as one might expect more to securing clients and selling designs. For instance, Samuel Sloan offered a design in *Homestead Architecture* (1861) that would "sustain the idea that the proprietor, if not in possession of an unlimited store of wealth, has been touched by the spirit of elevated taste."[63] Henry Cleaveland and the brothers Backus, in their collection of designs for *Villas and Farm Cottages* (1856), proposed that it should be an explicit requirement of domestic design that the dwelling accord with the character of the resident:

> The aspect of a dwelling-house naturally suggests to us some idea in regard to the character and condition of its occupants. There may be, and there ought to be, in the expression of a house something that shall aid us in this matter. It is not a mere fancy, that the spirit and character of the inmates may be made in some measure to appear in the outward expression of the structure.[64]

Through the end of the century, although many other trends and principles in American architecture had undergone considerable change, this particular notion still remained commonplace. In 1878 Henry Hudson Holly wrote about the possibilities of expressing in one's dwelling such "delicate" qualities of human character as literary taste, fondness for society, and generous hospitality.[65] Two decades later Charles Rich, describing the building of a suburban residence, again repeated what had become a common formula: "since every man has what may be called his own distinct character, so it seems to us that his home should reflect somewhat of this character."[66] S. B. Reed, whose *House-Plans for Everybody* appeared in at least eight editions between 1878 and 1898, wrote plainly that "one's dwelling is an index of one's character. Any effort at building expresses the owner's ability, taste, and purpose."[67] And in 1909 Gustav Stickley, well known as a major figure in the Craftsman movement, left no doubt about the expressive capacity that was expected of domestic architecture: "a house expresses character quite as vividly as does dress and the more intimate personal belongings." To this he added a statement of undiminished confidence in the reciprocal notion that style and design could shape the inhabitant: "the influence of the home is of the first importance in the shaping of character."[68]

Plans and Interiors

Although most nineteenth-century American authors concentrated on designs for exteriors, some recognized the possibility that configuring the plan and furnishing the interior could have as much a role in articulating the self as the style of the facade. Indeed the statements of the final two authors mentioned above, Rich and Stickley, were at least as much concerned with plan and furnishings as they were with the exterior in their concern for ways in which design could shape the resident's character.

In Britain concerns for the effect of interior space on the character of residents dated at least to the last half of the eighteenth century, when the "model farms" movement among large estate owners began to address the living conditions of those who worked there. Likewise the efforts of reformers such as Robert Owen at New Lanark during the 1810s had been focused in considerable measure on providing salubrious housing for mill workers. In 1842 Robert Dunn recognized a more gender-specific need: he argued in an essay on cottage design that a private upstairs bedroom was necessary, even among laboring classes, since it would provide a "sacred asylum" for women that would help develop their character and virtues.[69]

From an American perspective, the interior of the house soon would be understood as a far more complex instrument for shaping the identities of those who lived there. As Clarence Cook wrote some years later in *The House Beautiful* (1881), long after this way of understanding the dwelling had matured, specific rooms took crucial roles in articulating specific aspects of the lives of those who used them. Among the most important for Cook was the living room, which he tellingly characterized in the role of an instructional "agent":

> I look upon this living-room as an important agent in the education of life; it will make a great difference to the children who grow up in it, and to all whose experience is associated with it, whether it be a beautiful and cheerful room, or a homely and bare one, or a merely formal and conventional one. . . . For it has a serious relation to education, and plays an important part in life.

Here the choice of furniture was important. Depending on which period style was chosen, it could do much toward inculcating good taste and refined manners. But Cook found the dining room to be a very different kind of terrain, considering its effect on the inhabitants as something unresolved. In his words, it was a site of conflict "between our two lives, the domestic one and the social one," where formality and ostentatiousness in the pursuit of social interests ultimately suppressed opportunities to develop a better family life.[70]

In more general terms, the nineteenth-century American dwelling in both theory and practice became a series of specialized precincts each of which contributed to the articulation of self in its distinct way. For example, on the main floor the parlor (its name deriving from the French word for "speak") was the room for polite discourse, and its furnishings played an important role in shaping the "social demeanor" of the participants, as Katherine Grier has put it. Just as the exterior of the house had become in many ways a portrait of the character of the resident, so the parlor and its furnishings served to portray and shape the taste, morals, and character of the family within. But in contrast to the extent of social intercourse that was expected on the main floor, it was understood that upstairs rooms were dedicated to the culture of individuals. The study, boudoir, and bedroom all were sites for reading, prayer, meditation, writing, and other private activities. In some instances the main floor became explicitly gendered, particularly when a library or office was included. Ordinarily regarded as masculine spaces, such rooms often were situated toward one of the rear corners of the house, in some respects offsetting the feminine space of the kitchen toward the other rear corner. Still, the fact that kitchens were well isolated from the rest of the house by corridors and pantries, and libraries generally were connected by communicating doors or at least closer to the parlor and other fashionable rooms, bespeaks a far greater importance accorded to masculine space (as well as acknowledgment of the fire risk still associated with kitchens). Perhaps more to the point, given that the woman took on the task of furnishing the parlor, the library or office became for the man his gendered complement to that space, its status apart from feminine influence frequently confirmed by the presence of a separate doorway directly from the library, office, or an adjacent corridor to the outdoors. And in all these cases, the former center of household activity and family relations, the kitchen, had been bypassed, no longer a matter for architects' interest and no longer the central feature of the American house that it had been throughout the eighteenth century.[71]

There were only one or two exceptions to this general disregard for kitchens and the necessary labor that took place in them, and not surprisingly they occurred in nineteenth-century feminist writings on women in their relations to the household and larger society. The best known of these writers was Catharine Beecher, sister of the author of *Uncle Tom's Cabin,* Harriet Beecher Stowe, and of the minister Henry Ward Beecher mentioned above. Already in 1841 she had recognized the political dilemma in which women found themselves in the American republic. Disenfranchised and relegated to the domestic realm, they were expected to serve as adjuncts to the articulation of the male self. But their contemporaries also had said much about the importance of morality and virtue to the constitution of the male character and thus to the success of the republic. And in this Beecher saw a corresponding necessity for the role of women in securing the future of America's political institutions:

> The success of democratic institutions, as is conceded by all, depends upon the intellectual and moral character of the mass of the people. If they are intelligent and

virtuous, democracy is a blessing. . . . It is equally conceded, that the formation of the moral and intellectual character of the young is committed mainly to the female hand. The mother writes the character of the future man; the sister bends the fibres that hereafter are the forest tree; the wife sways the heart, whose energies may turn for good or for evil the destinies of a nation.[72]

Much of Beecher's concern lay in the amount of labor demanded of women house-holders, a situation made worse by room plans that made concessions to what Cook would call "social lives" at the expense of increased and inefficient labor. For example, kitchens often were placed behind the house or in the basement, while the nursery was on the upper floor, necessitating repeatedly climbing stairs, carrying children back and forth or leaving them unsupervised, and other inefficiencies. Worse, many house plans were designed with the presumption that a certain number of servants would be available to take care of all the work, when in fact few if any were available, or those who could be found were minimally competent. Thus in her *Treatise on Domestic Economy* (1841) Beecher supplied an initial house plan that began to address the problem of minimizing household labor.[73] Some years later another female voice attended to the issue of woman's labor, and it is evident that she had read Beecher. In 1853 Mrs. L. G. Abell noted how important it was that men recognize the amount of labor necessary to maintain a family; she correspondingly emphasized the importance of the kitchen layout to the health of the women and the functioning of the household.[74]

Beecher later returned to the issue, well after the Civil War, when she published a plan that was designed specifically to minimize female labor in all respects (Figure 4.6). This she did by placing the kitchen in the center of the house and orchestrating a variety of bins and counter surfaces for the best efficiency of operation. That her audience was the families of the new republican bourgeoisie—those perhaps unaccustomed to having many servants or unable to afford them—is apparent not only from the small size of the kitchen and the direct role a single person might have to take in household operations. It also is indicated by the fact that Beecher addressed a suburban commuter audience, referring to those living in "suburban vicinities" and to the "special blessing" that railroads accorded to those who made the daily journey back and forth.[75]

Like her contemporaries, Beecher found that the dwelling had a great capacity for moral affectivity, in multiple respects. On the one hand, despite her interest in consolidating and minimizing labor, she was not averse to labor. Rather, as her chapters such as "Early Rising" make apparent, she endorsed it. And unlike Downing, who simply articulated the household plan in terms of spaces of leisure (for the bourgeois man of leisure), Beecher pointedly put the kitchen at the very center of the dwelling plan. On the other hand, Beecher also discussed "the aesthetic element" of the design, to which she accorded great importance because it could wield great power over younger members of the household, as well as contribute to the education of all in "refinement, intellectual development, and moral responsibility."[76]

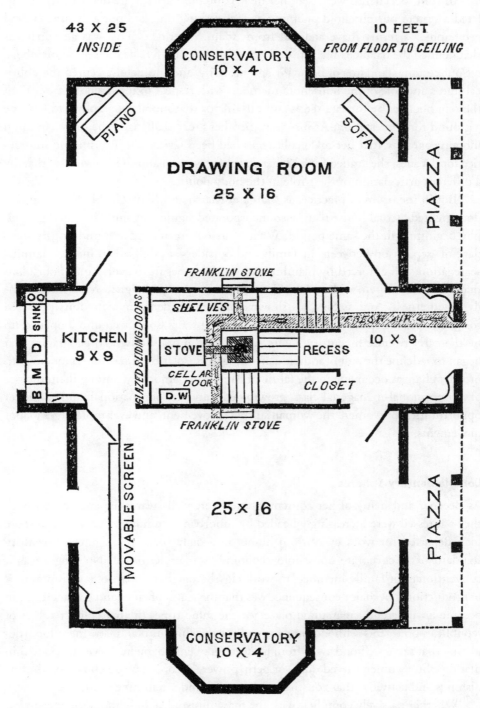

Figure 4.6. Catharine Beecher, "A Christian House" (plan). Figure 1 in *The American Woman's Home*, 1869. A labor-saving design intended in part for the women of the new republican bourgeoisie, left to manage their homes alone by husbands commuting to work elsewhere.

In sum, Beecher as well as all her male contemporaries quite deliberately articulated a system of household planning and furnishing that laid out a definite "moral geography," a term I have adapted from Adam Sweeting.[77] This was an apparatus that defined the balance of leisure and labor for male and female household members, set out certain standards of behavior and morality, and ultimately secured the political status and role of the household members with respect to the larger framework of the republic. Yet by the late 1860s and early 1870s that moral geography had become a ground for contestation. As just seen, Beecher's text challenged the more common moral geography that her male colleagues had been laying out in print and in practice for decades; she argued for a higher status for women and their labor, and thereby a different articulation of their role in the body politic.

But in the realm of practice, as Margaret Marsh and Mary Corbin Sies have well documented, actual house plans also incorporated significant shifts in moral geography beginning in the same period. What Marsh characterized as a midcentury standard of "separation between the family and outsiders" as well as "an internal familial segregation," all enforced by planning conventions, began to evolve into floor plans that were more open, with greater flows between spaces, designed to facilitate family togetherness. And as Sies has shown, inglenooks, dens, and boudoirs provided sometime private spaces, but even the plans of upstairs floors were more opened up by the early twentieth century.[78] The result was a moral household geography that began to redefine the cult of individuality in far less isolationist terms, in tandem with broader changes occurring in the fabric of American democracy, among them the rise of a professional-managerial class, growing educational, occupational, and volunteer opportunities for women, the woman suffrage movement, and ever more urgent labor movements.

Complementary Spheres

As Beecher and many of her contemporaries were well aware, the audiences whom they addressed were increasingly headed by suburban commuters. As more and more men departed for work away from home on a daily basis, the eighteenth-century standard of a "corporate household economy" was undermined. No longer was it conventional for family members to work closely together as part of a common unit of production.[79] A major consequence was that the realm of cities and commerce soon became an inherently masculine place. At the same time, the masculinist values of republican bourgeois selfhood transformed the dwelling into an instrument for articulating that same selfhood away from its domain of employment. Nevertheless within that dwelling women carved out—or perhaps were accorded by default—certain furnishings and activities that constituted a domain under feminine influence.

Whether passively complicit with the masculinist ideal of selfhood or engaging it more actively in a manner such as Beecher did, women's influence remained confined to the interior of the dwelling for most of the nineteenth century. Even Beecher failed to discuss exteriors. Nineteenth-century authors addressed this spatial separation of influence by referring to the notion of "woman's sphere" or the "domestic sphere." Lydia Sigourney did so as early as 1835 in *Letters to Young Ladies,* noting that "the sexes are manifestly intended for different spheres," those of women being what she called "eminently practical" in connection with her discussion of the science of house-keeping.[80] However it was termed, the notion of the woman's sphere incorporated on its surface an understanding of the female as the one who physically maintained the household. Along with that ordinarily came an implicit recognition that the woman was obligated to be the moral stronghold of the family. Few recognized that placing the female as keeper of the domestic realm was, as Anthony Rotundo has shown, a political necessity: in order to maintain the public virtue of men everywhere, it became a civic need for women to undertake these domestic responsibilities.[81]

References such as those by Sigourney to a "woman's sphere" or "domestic sphere" have given rise over the past several decades to a large and controversial literature on the subject of so-called separate spheres in English and American society of the eighteenth and nineteenth centuries,[82] but the question remains just how separate those spheres were. Catherine Hall has argued strenuously that "the separation of spheres was one of the fundamental organising characteristics of middle-class society in late eighteenth and early nineteenth-century England."[83] But Amanda Vickery has convincingly challenged this connection and Hall's conclusions, and Dror Wahrman likewise has shown that Leonore Davidoff and Hall present a flawed picture of the role of separate spheres in the rise of the middle class.[84] Regarding America in the nineteenth century, a considerable body of criticism has explored the degree to which those spheres may have been separate, and what may have been the implications of any separation.[85]

In this light, but also given the linked roles of men and women within the home as part of the larger national political framework, it may make better sense to regard the different spheres as intersecting and complementary rather than in any funda-mental respect separate. Certainly the dwelling itself was not the sphere of either party, man or woman. The exterior, for example, often served to represent the beliefs and aspirations of the man, while the kitchen and nursery were domains in which the woman was the principal and sometimes sole presence. Male and female each had complementary interests within the whole. And within certain specific spaces, such as the parlor, both had complementary interests, intersecting in multiple ways. For instance, it was the purview of the woman to exercise her taste in decorating the parlor in order to sustain the virtue of the head of the household. At the same time, the parlor served as a domain of leisure for both the man and the woman, involving reading and polite conversation, while for the woman it also involved the labor of cleaning and upkeep.

Certainly complementarity did not mean equality. Examples of a genuine balance between masculine and feminine interests in the nineteenth-century household would be hard to document, although some nineteenth-century authors attempted to frame their arguments as if such conditions existed.[86] The usual strategy was to essentialize men and women as "naturally" having dispositions toward certain different kinds of behavior, and then declaring that the nineteenth-century household allowed these natural characteristics to flourish to their fullest. But even if the dwelling did not provide for equality, neither did it prescribe separation. Rather, it provided for the intersection of different complementary "spheres" that were recognized as active in the articulation of male and female bourgeois selfhood.

5. Suburbanizing the Self

Privatizing Arcadia

The nineteenth-century bourgeois dwelling was in many ways a highly complex instrument for fashioning personal identity: not only did it presume a certain economic and transportation system that permitted the bourgeois man to commute between home and work, it also was part of a framework of a nationalist politics that equated self-made men with the strength of a republican state. To facilitate that politics meant facilitating that housing, specifically housing of a suburban character: detached dwellings in which individual men and their families lived separately on their own plots of land, able to articulate identity by means of dwelling type, style, plan, interior furnishings, and even gender relations. As Downing and other nineteenth-century authors made clear, suburban dwellings were premiere instruments for self-articulation and, in America, for fashioning republican domesticity. To ensure the best possible functioning of the dwelling for the self and for the state, a proper environment was in order. The answer was a suburb, whether a formally developed and enclosed development, or the outskirts of a town built up piecemeal over time, a site preferably given over to single-family detached houses.[1] Overt and widespread government support of suburban housing such as this did not occur until the twentieth century, but from the beginning suburbia implicitly supported the American republican form of polity. Indeed the growth of the nineteenth-century bourgeoisie almost rendered it an imperative that a form of environment such as the modern suburb come to fruition, in which the bourgeois dwelling could maximize the potential of the nineteenth-century individual for self-fulfillment.

To address these issues, this chapter focuses primarily on political, ideological, and literary considerations as a way of exploring the genesis of "suburbia" as a place apart from city and country, a distinct type of locale in its own right, to be reckoned with (or against) as a site for the production of a distinct new segment of the population. Doing so necessarily tends toward accounts of suburbs in the middle and upper end of the social scale, since these were the suburbs that set the terms of the discussion and the debate. But while these accounts may offer an unbalanced picture of suburbia at the time—for there already were many suburban areas housing blue-collar and minority families—to describe suburbia is not the principal goal of the ensuing discussion. Rather, the purpose is to examine the leading paradigms, principles, and tropes according to which suburbia evolved in the nineteenth century as a way of understanding how it became integral both to the fulfillment of the private self and to American society in general.[2]

Early Suburbanization in America

During the course of America's early suburbanization even the notion of what constituted a "suburb" varied considerably from time to time and place to place. Often what was a suburb was as much a matter of what lay in the eye (or mind) of a contemporary observer as it was a matter of any distinct boundaries, particular building types, densities, definable land uses, or other considerations that a modern historian might choose. Kenneth Jackson designated Brooklyn as the first commuter suburb with the introduction of steamboat commuter service there in 1814, followed by an influx of fashionable merchants, shopkeepers, and even some laborers. (In fact commuters appear to have been using steamboat service there since the 1790s.) Dolores Hayden has dated the rise of American suburbia to 1820.[3] Eighteenth-century accounts of the vicinity of Boston, however, make parts of it seem quite suburban. Architect William Strickland, approaching from the west in 1794, characterized "the last 12 or 14 miles into Boston" as unsurpassed "by any equal space in any country I have been in. Many of the scenes it [this area] affords are truly romantic, others rich as population and a multitude of elegant villas belonging to the inhabitants of Boston can make it; the whole is a continued street, crouded with houses, almost like the vicinity of London." Sometimes a suburb was neither detached from the city nor an exclusive site for bourgeois commuters. An 1832 essay in the *Rural Repository* recounted an early morning walk "through the suburbs of our city," and although it noted no formal boundaries between city and suburbs, it did find the "suburbs" to be a distinct locale where there was a constant contrast between "cheerless hovels" and "splendid edifices." In one miserable tenement the rafters were exposed and the windows were gone, so the snow had blown in, and "Poverty had written his presence in intelligible characters."[4] In her 1852 novel *Clovernook* Alice Cary likewise described development around some of the young cities along the Ohio River as "suburbs," and again the scenes were mixed. Sometimes she waxed romantic over their idyllic qualities such as smooth lawns and prim houses, while at other times she complained of industrial chimneys spewing forth dense smoke, decrepit multistoried and multifamily housing, and filth and sewage in the streets. Nevertheless four years earlier a contributor to the *Horticulturist* (1848) praised the extent to which people of all classes apparently were enjoying the advantages of the Cincinnati suburbs:

> The lawyer lays aside his green bag, and for a season, at least, forgoes the rich pockets of his clients, and delves the pregnant earth in the home of luscious rewards hereafter. The merchant tarries longer at his villa; and even the grocer and the soap-boiler rid themselves of the cares of the shop, by spending their time upon their snug suburban grass plats; inhaling, for a portion of the year, the balmy breezes of the country. It has become quite a mania, of late, to possess a country residence; and the fruits of their well directed taste are being seen all around us, on the hill-tops and in the valleys.[5]

Authors of architectural books and landscape publications, on the other hand, gave a very different impression of suburbia, especially considering some of the designs that they published, which were specifically labeled as intended for suburban locales. Since these various publications generally were oriented to a bourgeois clientele, the type of surrounding neighborhood or landscape that might be illustrated, or that the text might suggest, would be equally bourgeois, or even tend to be more elite. The very first design in Downing's *Cottage Residences* (1842), for example, is "A Suburban Cottage." In plan it is formally situated in a tightly laid out lot measuring 75 by 100 feet (Figure 5.1), suitable for subdivisions on the outskirts of many cities and towns of that time, but in one view it is incongruously set in a grove of trees near the banks of a small river, on a site far more elaborate than the small lot shown. Similarly the *Horticulturist,* a monthly journal for which Downing served as editor and contributor, includes layouts specifically for suburban gardens, and these designs also suggest that suburbs were upper-bourgeois locales. Generally the design for each garden shows a dwelling encompassed by drives, formal and informal plantings, plus a kitchen garden, all incorporated into a rectangular plot of approximately a quarter acre to a full acre or more.[6]

Both landscapes and dwellings remained important in the evolution of suburbia, and from an early date designers especially sought ways to develop designs for dwellings that could be marketed specifically for suburbs. Architects had begun to prepare explicitly "suburban" dwelling designs by the 1830s, if not earlier. In 1837 William Bailey Lang built a number of what he termed "suburban residences" in Roxbury, south of Boston, which he later published as a collection of designs in 1845.[7] Four years after that S. B. Gookins, writing in the *Horticulturist,* offered no designs but nevertheless provided a remarkably crystallized ideology of the suburban dwelling type. Equating the American bourgeois goal of financial success with owning a suburban dream house, he wrote: "Every cit has his day-dream of a country seat or suburban villa, where the retired merchant, artist or professional man, relieved from the bustle of business, is to enjoy his eventide in the calmness and quietude of rural life."[8]

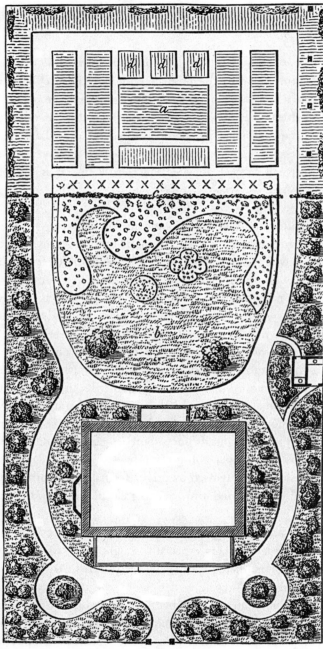

[Fig. 8.]

Figure 5.1. Andrew Jackson Downing, "A Suburban Cottage for a Small Family" (plan and layout of grounds). Figure 8 in *Cottage Residences*, 1842. Putting this nominally suburban design at the front of his book, Downing (like many other authors) signaled his interest in appealing to America's rising bourgeoisie. This design suggests a standard lot size of 75 by 100 feet, generally too expensive for the city but too small to produce the goods needed by a rural household, and therefore best suited to commuters.

By midcentury a flood of designs for explicitly "suburban" dwellings began to appear in print. Nine appeared in Downing's *Architecture of Country Houses* (1850), Calvert Vaux included half a dozen in *Villas and Cottages* (1857), at least one appeared in the *Horticulturist* for 1849, and an 1855 article in *Ballou's Pictorial* titled "Suburban Residences" showed vignettes of bourgeois dwellings in Roxbury and Brookline.[9]

But as architects such as Downing and his contemporaries took a greater interest in the shaping and selling of suburbia to their bourgeois audience, suburbia also became the focus of a now long-standing struggle surrounding issues of planning and aesthetics. Simply put, the concerns were twofold: whether the suburb should be considered as an aesthetic entity, and if so, to what degree the talents of an architect would be necessary for its satisfactory design. In favor of both propositions was the possibility that a properly trained designer could use the environment to effect the sorts of bourgeois ends that Gookins had incorporated into the ideal of a suburban dream villa. But the counterargument faulted this approach for its profoundly undemocratic character, allowing the taste of a few to prescribe for all. Something of both approaches can be seen in the remarks of William Ranlett, a prominent mid-century architect, depending on whether one reads with or against the grain. He began with a broad indictment of suburbia: "The suburbs of our cities are, generally, like a shabby frame to a fine picture." The cause, he said, was that "they are put up in a hurry by careless speculators, and very little regard is paid to their externals."[10] Some would have said that the "careless speculators" were actually developers doing a service by making inexpensive housing for those who needed it. Ranlett's implicit solution lay in the intervention of aesthetics. The redeemers of suburbia would be people professionally trained in architecture and landscape arts, either designing suburbs in the first place, or remediating them through proper design techniques. In many respects Ranlett's proposition has remained part of the debate over suburbia ever since, as the conclusion to this volume explores further. Within his own time, arguments such as Ranlett's set the stage for the apotheosis of suburbia as the physical paradigm of the bourgeoisie.

A Model of National Taste

Aesthetic concerns were not the only interests built into the design of suburbia. Certainly in America, as in England, the desire for Horatian-style "retirement" remained strong. As one American essayist wrote in 1833, for example, for many Americans it was the object of their prayers "to acquire possession of the *suburban rus* for which they have panted so long."[11]

But in the ensuing decades a number of essayists also strongly associated America's suburbs with a spirit of nationalism and patriotism. Suburbs, at least the elite ones, were becoming a type of terrain increasingly associated with the bourgeois self-made individualist who epitomized the American republican form of polity. As such, those suburbs called out for cultivation and enhancement. Essays frequently emphasized the variety of benefits—moral, social, economic, political—that could accrue in suburban life from close daily contact with the soil. One essay of 1845 made it an article of patriotism that it was best to view all of one's relations to government from the perspective of a horticulturist. No longer a Jeffersonian yeoman farmer, the ideal householder seemed to be more a gentleman suburbanite whose political status derived from gardening: "Give a man a few roods of soil; let him cultivate it and adorn it; let him plant his home in the midst of it; let him pass his life there, viewing all his relations to the government from that fixed locality. . . ." The essay continued: "Gardening and architecture are arts that promote a genuine patriotism."[12]

An essay printed three years later on "The Morale of Rural Life" opened and closed with a discussion of patriotism and centered on the need for an intermediate agricultural zone, a zone between the city and savage wilds, to defend against encroachment on one by the other. But while the author characterized this zone in terms of a Jeffersonian agrarian model, in reality its "patriotic" value was less its capacity to sustain a republican-agrarian society than to sustain a republican-bourgeois society.[13] A few years later the editor of *Harper's* expressed a like-minded concern for "our new and unformed national character," and had no trouble locating its most promising future in that intermediate zone. He wrote that there was "a strong republican element seated in the life of our American nation," manifested particularly "in the multiplication of the out-of-town houses for working-men which are springing up in every direction." Suggesting that proper attention to design considerations could make these "new suburban towns" the appropriate apparatus to shape the national character in a distinctly American manner, he urged many planning techniques that would take full advantage of the natural landscape, such as winding roads, multiple views, irregularly shaped lots, and odd nooks and corners.[14] Here again the introduction of aesthetic techniques was recommended, in this case as a means for enhancing and strengthening the republican fabric of the nation.

But as essayists sought to recommend ways of planning that could reinforce certain nationalist ideals, it also was clear that they did not envision all Americans sharing in those ideals. On the very first page of *The Architecture of Country Houses* Downing proclaimed the importance of cultivating "the national taste," and that any real progress a people makes is dependent on advancing that taste. Nevertheless further into the book, in the discussion of villas, Downing made it evident that the nation as he imagined it was racially and ethnically limited to those "largely descended from this Anglo-Saxon stock." Bourgeois and republican though it may have been, the ideal of nationhood held by many at midcentury still conformed narrowly to the notion of an English heritage, automatically excluding those who did not fit, such as those of Continental European heritage, African Americans, and Native Americans.[15]

Rhetorics of Rus in Urbe: Appropriating the Best of Both Worlds

As seen in previous chapters, a great deal of eighteenth-century English suburban development was cast in terms of a desire to reconcile two seemingly disparate realms of human practice and experience—the urbane and the natural, the city and the country, the urban and the rural. The implicit need to address those same binary opposites remained a central consideration in theoretical analysis and practical design of suburbia throughout the nineteenth and well into the twentieth century, in printed discussions as well as built examples, on both sides of the Atlantic. Much of this literature and many of these sites became increasingly well known to American readers and visitors,[16] and the associated notion of *rus in urbe* established much of the theoretical framework for the design and discussion of the nineteenth-century American suburb. This may be clarified by following the genealogy of the notion from its introduction into eighteenth-century English town planning to its maturation in various forms during the nineteenth century on both sides of the Atlantic. Indeed by the middle of the nineteenth century the phrase *rus in urbe*—confidently announcing a marriage of country and city—already was commonly used as descriptive rhetoric for announcing new subdivisions in the United States.

The literary keynote may have been sounded in 1731 with the appearance of the first issue of the *Gentleman's Magazine,* edited by the pseudonymous Sylvanus Urban, whose very name paralleled the dualistic efforts of many a bourgeois householder to give his "country box" an air of simultaneous rusticity and sophistication.[17] But as early as 1717 the Earl of Carnarvon may have had an actual building project under way on the edge of the West End of London to effect something of a similar end, beginning with two wings of a projected mansion on the north side of Cavendish Square (Figure 5.2). From there south, the area had been developed according to a pattern of blocks and squares, while to the north, Carnarvon retained a large enough parcel of open land that his mansion, had it been completed, would have faced city life on one side and pastoral fields on the other. By midcentury there was an attempt to better integrate the two separate blocs, by introducing a lawn, some plantings, and grazing sheep into the center of the square. But such efforts were seen as little more than folly and pretentiousness, at least so close to ever-expanding London. As James Stuart, the presumed author of *Critical Observations on the Buildings and Improvements of London,* wrote in 1771, "the *rus in urbe* is a preposterous idea at best; . . . and he that wishes to have a row of trees before his door in town, betrays almost as false a taste as he that would build a row of houses for an avenue to his seat in the country."[18] He managed to show his contempt for the Cavendish Square proposal, grazing sheep and all, by a more than unflattering view of a statue recently added to the square (Figure 5.3). *Rus in urbe,* in other words, was not something readily achieved simply by an antiurbanistic gesture.

In contrast, contemporary examples of larger-scale designs that engaged the rural with the urban were proving highly successful. This was particularly apparent in the fashionable resort town of Bath, known for its rigorously formal and inward-looking geometric spaces such as Queen Square (1729) and The Circus (1754). By the late 1760s and early 1770s a very different sort of structure was under way: the Royal Crescent, in the shape of a modified half ellipse, open on one side and looking out across a valley to a range of hills in the distance (Figure 5.4). The architectural vocabulary incorporated an elegant colossal Ionic order, as formal and dignified as one might want in a town residence, but the structure now turned its back on the town, facing instead the distant horizon and bringing the landscape into direct visual contact with the dwelling complex itself.

Still, the Royal Crescent was more of a visual pairing of *rus* with *urbs* than a successful integration of the two. For the latter to happen, dwelling had to occur not just in sight of a rural landscape but within a setting whose rural characteristics would complement the urbane character of the dwelling itself and especially the inhabitant. For this to happen, the monolithic terrace was far less suitable than the single detached dwelling of the sort that had been populating bourgeois suburbs of London for most of the eighteenth century. What was new in the nineteenth century was the radically enlarged scale of suburban entrepreneurship, where a whole tract could be laid out in multiple units by a single owner or developer, often accompanied by promotional rhetoric explicitly featuring the union of country and city as a principal merchandising feature.

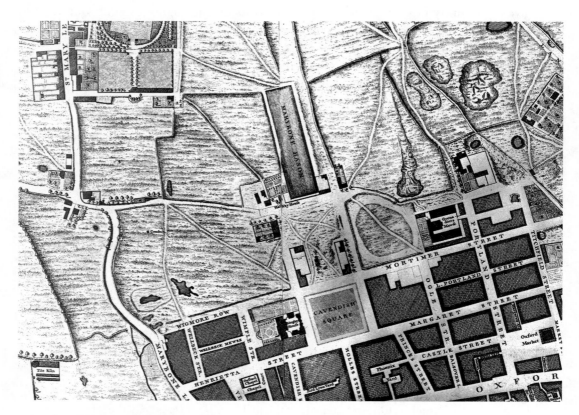

Figure 5.2. John Rocque, detail of Cavendish Square and vicinity, from *A Plan of the Cities of London and Westminster*, 1746. Immediately across from the open end of Cavendish Square are the two wings of the mansion begun by the Earl of Carnarvon.

CRITICAL OBSERVATIONS

ON THE

BUILDINGS

AND

IMPROVEMENTS

OF

LONDON.

—————— Nil fuit unquam

Sic impar.   Hor.

LONDON:

Printed for J. DODSLEY, in Pall-Mall,
MDCCLXXI.

Figure 5.3. [James Stuart?], title page of *Critical Observations on the Buildings and Improvements of London,* 1771. The two wings of the mansion begun by the Earl of Carnarvon are visible to either side of the statue, but Stuart's contempt for Carnarvon's attempt at *rus in urbe* may be seen in his unflattering view of the statue in conjunction with the mansion.

One such tract was the comparatively vast area of Regent's Park in the north-western part of London, developed between 1811 and 1832 by John Nash for the Crown Estate. Hailed by critics as a success on all fronts, a "farm-like appendage to our metropolis,"[19] it was a hybrid design of terraces and villas, composed primarily of large terraces much more grandiose and imposing than the Royal Crescent, the only advances being that there were now multiple terraces, they faced inwards toward common park land, the external perimeter was enclosed and gated, the landscaping was more elaborate, and a small number of detached villas were deployed throughout the interior parkland (Figure 5.5). But for all the picturesque qualities of Regent's Park, it is unlikely that Nash undertook this extension of a fundamentally urban landscape as a project to combine city and country. Certainly nothing in his own writings has come to light suggesting this, and only in the 1820s, as the phrase *rus in urbe* found currency in connection with somewhat less elite housing estate developments, did Regent's Park also seem to be recognized as a prototype. Not until 1828, for example, was it described as "combining, to a certain extent, the characteristics of both town and country."[20]

In contrast certain detached, privately developed enclaves of detached and semi-detached villas on the outskirts of resort towns, begun in the mid- and late 1820s, were promoted almost from the beginning as specifically fulfilling the ideal of *rus in urbe*. Pittville, for example, was an estate laid out beginning in 1824 on the fringe of the

Figure 5.4. John Britton, *The Royal Crescent, Bath.* From *Bath and Bristol,* 1829. Unlike previous major urban spaces in London or Bath, which were tightly enclosed geometric figures, the Crescent opened outward to the surrounding landscape and embraced nature.

resort town of Cheltenham (Figure 5.6). Its design consisted of detached and semi-detached villas and short terrace blocks forming a self-contained community separated by half a mile from the center of town, far enough away to avoid the bustle of urban life but close enough to ensure access to markets and services. The center of Pittville's social life was its own "Spa," or pump room, at the farthest end of the estate from town (Figure 5.7). Pittville's villas and terraces, all suited to middle-class occupants, were surrounded by a series of rides and walks that focused on the pump room. Thus in 1826 town historian and booster S. Y. Griffith could boast with pride that Cheltenham was "the happy union of town and country" and that the Pittville environs were true "*rus in urbe.*"[21]

Perhaps the most effectively executed marriage of country and city, at least in the first half of the nineteenth century, occurred in another resort town, Tunbridge Wells.

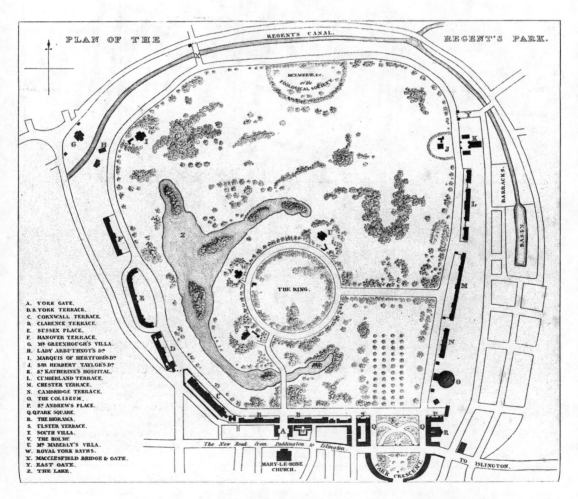

Figure 5.5. Thomas Shepherd and James Elmes, *Plan of the Regent's Park*. From *Metropolitan Improvements*, 1827. John Nash's plan incorporated extensive peripheral terraces and a small number of villas among the landscaped interior parklands.

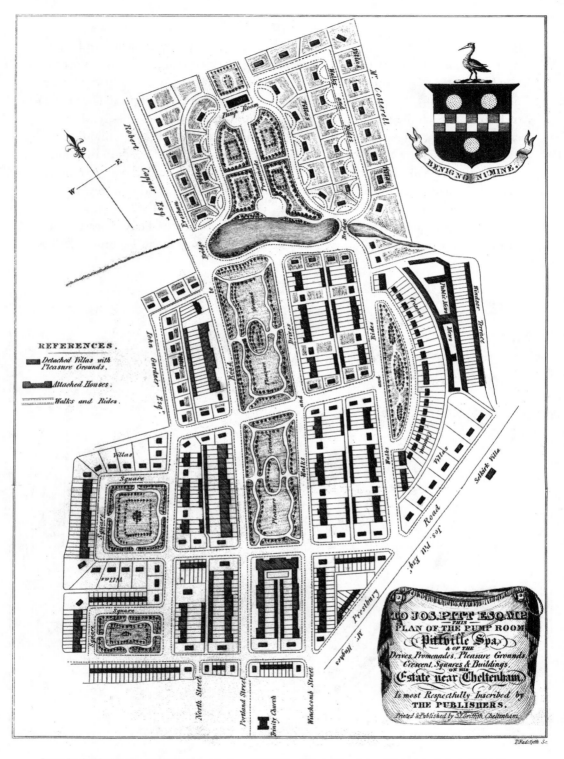

Figure 5.6. S.Y. Griffith, plan of the Pittville estate. From *Griffith's New Historical Description of Cheltenham,* 2nd ed., 1826. Laid out beginning in 1824 and soon touted as having achieved true *rus in urbe,* Pittville consisted of detached and semidetached villas and short terrace blocks.

Since the early years of the century, Tunbridge Wells had catered increasingly to residential, rather than transient, patrons. As early as 1810 one writer had noted that the patrons "seek rather the pleasures of retirement and the comforts of moderate society, than of dissipation."[22] The emphasis on retirement, here as at Cheltenham, led to a preference for secluded, detached villas in relatively isolated and segregated private estates. The geography of the town, consisting of three hills and the valleys in between, helped to facilitate this isolation. Along the crest and side of one of the hills lay the Calverley estate, owned by John Ward, and at his behest laid out as a single, comprehensive villa estate by Decimus Burton in 1827–28 (Figure 5.8). The center-piece was an open parklike space, lined on one side by detached and semidetached villas, all middle class in character (Figure 5.9). Trees and hedgerows between the houses gave each a feeling of isolation in nature, while open space in front accommodated pleasure walks and commanded views of the distant hills. A. B. Granville, author of a voluminous study of English resorts in 1841, could not restrain his praise for Calverley Park, calling it "a magnificent and deep dell." John Britton called it "a fashionable hamlet so rural." And other writers specifically referred to the successful combination here of *rus* and *urbs*.[23]

But despite the evident appeal of the notion of *rus in urbe* for purposes of marketing real estate, abetting civic boosterism, or suggesting retired fulfillment, the uses of this trope also disclosed a more complex side of nineteenth-century bourgeois

Figure 5.7. S. Y. Griffith, *Landscape View of Pittville Spa, Cheltenham*. From *Griffith's History of Cheltenham*, 1838. The center of Pittville's social life was its own "Spa," or pump room, at the farthest end of the estate from town.

suburban design. For the various examples above also show that in the nineteenth-century suburban context *rus in urbe* began to imply repudiation at least as much as inclusion. In simple terms, the phrase means "country in the city," or a union of rural and urban. But from the very beginning much of the attraction of a suburban locale was its antithetical character with respect to the city. Pope lived at Twickenham because it afforded him the status of proud outcast from court society; William and Mary moved to Kensington because of the irritating smoke of London; Defoe reported that families moved to Epsom because it provided them "air and liberty."[24] The same near-antithetical relation held true with respect to country: whether at Regent's Park, Cheltenham, or Tunbridge Wells, there was precious little there to connect any such locale with the country at large, or pastoral living in particular. Any dwelling would have been surrounded with lawns and profuse plantings, some even in a highly "natural" style, but hardly anything that could have been mistaken for

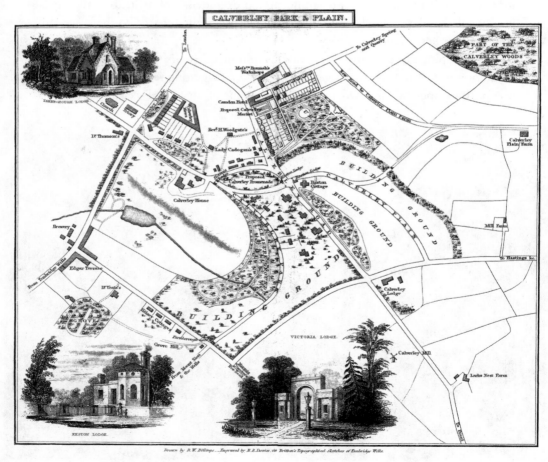

Figure 5.8. John Britton, *Calverley Park & Plain*. From *Descriptive Sketches of Tunbridge Wells*, 1832. Housing, recreation, market, and stable areas all were carefully segregated from each other in this estate plan, and the whole was gated off at all entrances from the rest of Tunbridge Wells.

actual rural living. Any sheep to be seen would have been obtained primarily for orna-mental reasons, as in Cavendish Square. Larger estates might have had kitchen gar-dens, but the productive value of the land was not a primary consideration in laying out any suburban plot. Instead it would be fair to say that the rhetoric of *rus in urbe* seriously belied nineteenth-century suburbia's stance vis-à-vis much of the city as well as the country, a stance that might best be described as neither-nor.

In other respects *rus in urbe* suggested great potential for the private dwelling as a positive apparatus for appropriating the best of both worlds. The dwelling was the focal point where the private individual could accumulate the resources necessary to take advantage of both simultaneously. Yet each of those worlds still remained an artificial construct. The appreciation of "country" was at best a relation to nature cast in aesthetic terms, and for the bourgeois suburbanite, to be "urban" or "urbane" might well be as much a matter of education, profession, and commuter access to the city as actually maintaining an urban lifestyle.

Instances of this two-faced perspective, simultaneously joining the objects that were ostensibly repudiated, flourished on both sides of the Atlantic by the 1850s.[25] Two in particular stand out as remarkably well-designed and executed examples, one at St. Margaret's in Twickenham and the other at Llewellyn Park in West Orange, New Jersey.[26]

Figure 5.9. John Britton, *Villas in Calverley Park*. From *Descriptive Sketches of Tunbridge Wells*, 1832. The centerpiece of the Calverley Park estate was a row of detached and semidetached villas, below which lay an open parklike space sloping down toward the town proper.

Judged on an aesthetic basis, the St. Margaret's Estate in Twickenham may be the best example of *rus in urbe* in a suburban subdivision in Britain. A project of the Conservative Land Society, the layout and proposed design for the estate were published in 1854, incorporating the richest balance possible between dwellings and a quasi-pastoral setting in the suburban reaches of London (Figure 5.10). Located at the intersection of a major railway route and the Thames, and a very short walk or ride across the river to Richmond Green, central Richmond, and Richmond station (it was less than a mile from the station to the nearest corner of the estate), St. Margaret's was in prime suburban territory. Perhaps the most remarkable aspect of this design is its incorporation of a richly embellished swath of landscape, interwoven back and forth among the houses; it remains separate from the public streets and footpaths, yet it allows the houses to engage it directly as a place of leisure and retirement. Although from an aerial view or a map the various portions of this "ornamental garden or pleasure ground," as it first was called, appear to be distinct, separated from each other by houses and roadways, they are all linked by the sorts of grade-separated passages that already had been introduced early in the previous decade at Prince's Park in Liverpool and in Birkenhead Park, and soon would be incorporated by Frederick Law Olmsted into the plan for Central Park in New York (Figure 5.11).

Figure 5.10. Conservative Land Society, *Saint Margaret's, Near Richmond,* promotional plan, 1854. Richmond Green and rail station are just beyond the frame of the image to the left; the train shown about to cross the river is heading in the direction of London. To travel toward London via the Thames, one would have proceeded toward the bottom of the image.

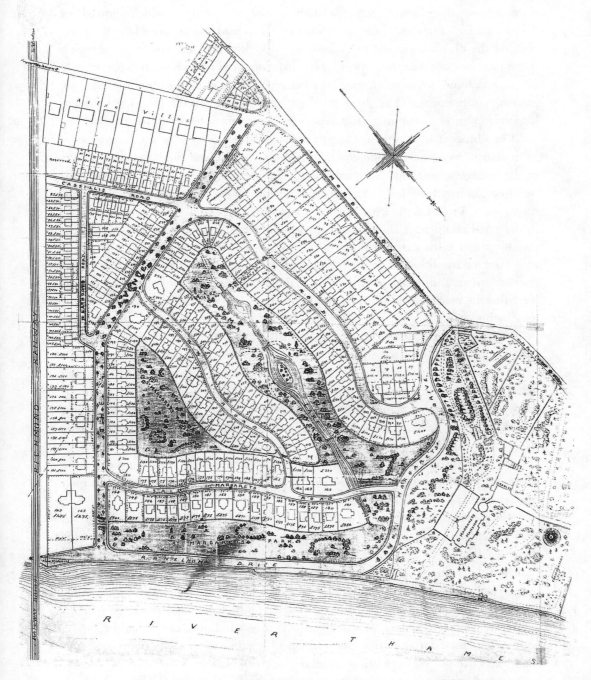

Figure 5.11. Early plat of St. Margaret's (undated; modern reproduction). This illustrates the interconnected areas of parkland and the distribution of detached and semidetached houses.

From the back doors of their houses many residents of St. Margaret's thus had access to something much more elaborate than residents of almost any other contemporary suburban development: a fully developed landscape of leisure, extending some distance, including lawns, trees, plantings, a lake, and bridges, which allowed for promenades, picturesque vistas, or sitting quietly to read and contemplate. By intertwining the pleasure ground so thoroughly with dwellings and roadways, the plan turned the focus of the estate inward, as an instrument of retirement, in a particularly unusual fashion, stressing connections between the rear of the dwelling and the interior leisure domain. The "back yard" or "garden" side of a dwelling was hardly as important again in a suburban subdivision until Radburn, begun in 1929.

On a broader scale, the St. Margaret's plan also positioned the dwelling to serve as an instrument of negotiation among the ideals of urban and rural, and the interests of the bourgeois resident. If urbanity could be identified with the Richmond railway line running from left to right across the advertising poster, or located in Richmond itself, a mile's walk across the river, and the best of rural retirement was found in the gated and private landscape of the interior pleasure grounds, then the rows of dwellings and yards that separated the roadways from the pleasure grounds served as a kind of transition zone, in part protecting the parkland from corruption or encroachment, and in part affording the resident a place for decompression in passing from the urban world into the rural. The rows of dwellings also amounted to a lengthy linear filter around the enclosed interior parkland, isolating and protecting it in its aesthetic perfection from contact with the material corruptions of the world beyond, just as it protected the residents themselves in their pursuit of retirement, leisure, and recreation from contact with the mundane activities in surrounding streets and the world beyond. In other words the dwelling was not only an apparatus in its own right that articulated certain dimensions of the bourgeois self, but it also became an intermediary, transitional apparatus for negotiating the passage of that self back and forth between the realms of *urbs* and *rus*. Still, the realm of *rus* remained most distinctly oppositional to that of *urbs*. Instead of wedding each to the other, the apparatus of the subdivision was at least as effective at demarcating each from the other.

But the more immediate raison d'être of the St. Margaret's Estate had less to do with the self-articulation of any individual resident in the domestic realm than with the establishment of a basis for interested members of the bourgeoisie to obtain the franchise. Ever since 1832, when the Reform Act extended the franchise to owners of property of a certain modest value, first Liberals and later Conservatives realized that purchase and sale of freeholds, often through building societies, could be used to extend their party's political power. By midcentury building societies had become a common method for acquiring freehold land for subdivision in suburban areas, in some cases irrespective of political agendas.[27] Such was not the case with the Conservative Land Society, founded in 1852, as suggested in its first annual report, issued in December 1853:

In respect to the increase of the franchise, it is necessary to repeat here that the Society was primarily established as a defensive measure, and they have reason to be proud that the main principle—that of co-operation and mutual assistance—will be amply proved, inasmuch as the artisan, the operative, the tradesman, medical professors, members of the legal profession, clergymen, officers of the army and navy, men of science, members of the fine arts, members of universities, and the sons of peers will be enabled through the instrumentality of the Society, to obtain the most ancient mode of suffrage in this country—the Freehold Franchise: the principal object of the foundation of the Society being the support of that constitution to which England owes its prosperity.[28]

The "co-operation and mutual assistance" to which the document alluded was not a financial scheme but instead an effort to extend the franchise to a specific range of professionals, here designated in the plural, with an uncertain degree of enthusiasm for those of lesser status—artisan, operative, and tradesman—here designated in the singular. In the event, the hoped-for range of upper bourgeoisie did not immediately locate in St. Margaret's. As the original 1854 Deed of Covenant shows, the occupations of those proposing to move to St. Margaret's and build there were more generally of the merchant and tradesman rank. Included were two bankers, a "chymist & dentist," a shoemaker, a worsted dealer, a wine merchant, two accountants, a farmer, a general agent, a gardener, an architect, six clerks, a merchant, a timber merchant, a parliamentary agent, a theatrical manager, three law stationers, a vintner, three booksellers, an engraver's representative, a butler, a furrier, a professor of music, a mining engineer, a cheese monger, two butchers, a news vendor, a fishmonger, a brush maker, a woolen draper, a schoolmaster, two plumbers, an estate agent, two barristers, an oilman, a baker, a spinster, a chemist and druggist, a solicitor, a confectioner, a broker, a civil engineer, a bricklayer, a surveyor, sixteen who were simply listed as "gentleman," and others whose occupations were unspecified.[29]

In sum, the design for St. Margaret's afforded a unique possibility for the incorporation of quasi-rural space into the overall suburban fabric of the plan. But it did so by isolating that rural space as part of a larger apparatus that, on the one hand, served to sanitize its residents of the daily economic and political burdens brought back from the city, and, on the other hand, afforded its residents the property basis necessary to have political influence. At the same time it was a masterpiece of *rus in urbe* design; in other words, the design was a complex integration of urban, rural, personal, and political interests.

The same held true, in different measures, for the design for Llewellyn Park (Figure 5.12), located in West Orange, New Jersey. As early as 1857 an article in the *Crayon* called Llewellyn Park "the first development, so far as we know, of an idea which may mark a new era in Country Life and Landscape Gardening in this country," and a new stage in the perfection of "the Landscape Gardener's Art."[30] In 1853 Llewellyn Haskell, a New York City pharmaceutical merchant who suffered from rheumatism, sought out a healthful site for a country residence. He chose a location in the Orange Mountains of New Jersey, immediately adjacent to two mineral springs that had been popular resorts in the 1820s.[31] Over the next three years the well-known architect Alexander Jackson Davis carried out architectural improvements for Haskell and also built a summer residence for himself on an adjacent site.[32] An 1856 map shows a few additional residences, plus extensive landscaping in "The Glenn" and "The Forrest" to the southwest of the Haskell and Davis residences, with curving drives, woods, streams, and ponds.[33] The next year a lithographed promotional plan (Figure 5.13) appeared, showing more areas laid out as "villa sites," a scheme for which Howard Daniels, recently returned from England, may have been partly responsible.[34] At the same time an advertisement appeared in the *Orange Journal,* announcing "Villa Sites of, from 5 to 10 Acres Each," and characterizing the community for the first time as a perfect commuter suburb. The site, within an hour of New York City via the Morris and Essex Railroad, was "selected with special reference to the wants of citizens doing business in the city, and yet wanting accessible, retired, and healthful homes in the country." The privacy of all residents would be protected "by a Lodge and gate-keeper at the entrance."[35]

MAY 12, 1860.]   THE NEW-YORK ILLUSTRATED NEWS.   5

LODGE AND ENTRANCE TO LLEWELLYN PARK, ORANGE MOUNTAIN, NEW JERSEY.

Figure 5.12. *Lodge and Entrance to Llewellyn Park, Orange Mountain, New Jersey.* From *The New-York Illustrated News,* May 12, 1860. An early view of the gate lodge at the main entrance, perhaps exaggerating the site's bucolic splendor but clearly emphasizing its significance as a natural preserve.

Thus gated and fenced in, set in a comparatively remote location, with no commerce or trade permitted within, Llewellyn Park appeared to offer an isolation of residence and family in "nature," rendering the domestic domain a distinct and special preserve. But such apparent opportunities could be afforded only in the context of conditions equally complex as at St. Margaret's, albeit unique to its own situation. Unlike St. Margaret's, which lay just across the river from Richmond, Llewellyn Park was not within walking distance of a suburban commercial center. It was intentionally removed from the city and dependent on mechanized transport for access to and from the city. Its plan and landscaping were replete with features antithetical to the city, but economically its residents (here more so than at St. Margaret's) were dependent on the fruits of capital investment or professional skills employed in the city. Every aspect of Llewellyn Park seemed to suggest harmony with nature, while any productive use of the land was prohibited, in favor of picturesquely composed "scenes" offering pastoral idylls suited for private contemplation. As at St. Margaret's, one of the principal amenities was the large portion of the landscape laid out for common use in rustic pursuits. And since Llewellyn Park was already an entirely enclosed community, these common-use areas, The Forest and The Glen, did not need to be

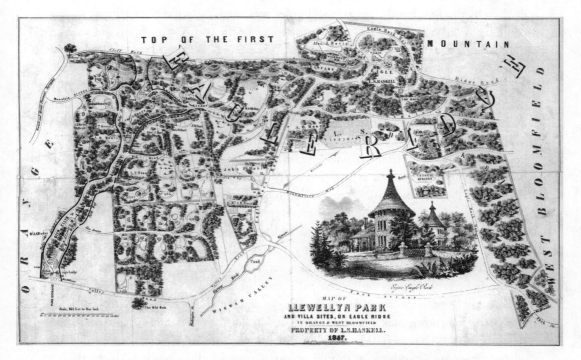

Figure 5.13. *Map of Llewellyn Park and Villa Sites, on Eagle Ridge,* promotional plan, 1857. The estate was entered from the Valley Road, via the Gate Lodge at the far lower left of the plan. The land flanking the roadway from the entrance gate up to the mountain ridge was open to all residents for their enjoyment. On the plan, it is outlined in heavy black line; at the bottom it was called "Glyn Ellyn" (also known as "The Glen"), and at the top it was called "The Forest." The large illustration of a dwelling at the lower right shows the "Eyrie," on Eagle Ridge (top right on the map), belonging to Llewellyn Haskell. Courtesy of the Metropolitan Museum of Art; all rights reserved.

walled off from road access by the houses themselves. Instead houses in Llewellyn Park could have individual private yards, in addition to the common pleasure grounds. Here as at St. Margaret's the pleasures were still those of leisure, retirement, recreation, contemplation, and tranquility, but once inside the common gate the Llewellyn Park resident would experience them well out of sight or awareness of any dwelling. In other words, land again had been transformed from a productive material resource into an aesthetic and social resource, but here any notion of its role as property, whether in possible relation to the franchise or as an instrument for the isolation of residential precincts from surrounding encroachment, had been erased in favor of the aesthetics of an idyllic preserve.[36]

But not all would-be suburbanites were drawn immediately to the same paradigms, however enticing, as those who settled in St. Margaret's or Llewellyn Park. As with any social innovation, different groups experimented with different variations to suit different circumstances, and one such case was the group who founded Evergreen Hamlet, Pennsylvania, laid out in 1851 atop a ridge and a bluff in the hills north of Pittsburgh (Figure 5.14). Here an ironic combination of a late-Jeffersonian yeoman farmer ideology together with the practical realities of commuting to jobs in a capitalist workplace resulted in a remarkable quasi-communitarian, quasi-suburban experiment. On the one hand, Evergreen Hamlet was as picturesque a settlement as any could be in the rolling hills of Pennsylvania. Due to the comparatively rugged terrain, the plan did not consist of winding, landscaped avenues, but its layout still remained thoroughly picturesque, with one-acre lots and open vistas. The six original founders, professional men and merchants with businesses in Pittsburgh, commuted daily by plank road and, eventually, by rail from nearby Bennett's Station (now Millvale). Their desires for this community were couched in part in the standard language of *rus in urbe*. They wanted "to combine, if possible, some of the benefits of country and city life; and, at the same time, avoid some of the inconveniences and disadvantages of both." At the same time a promotional description of the community clearly was pitched to "those whose business necessarily requires their daily attendance in the city."

On the other hand the founders of Evergreen Hamlet, unlike those of most other contemporary developments, sought to address more openly the contradictions of living in a bourgeois mercantile economy. Perhaps the greatest effort in this direction was the communal ownership of the home economy. According to the private constitution that established the eighty-five-acre community, the maximum sixteen families who would live there all would own the forty-acre farm, dairy, fruit orchards, gardens, and pasturage communally. Yet in practice it was hardly a communitarian enterprise: the farm was to be managed by a professional farmer, and members would individually purchase farm produce "as similar products are sold in the market." Nevertheless the founder expected that economies of scale would result in residents having more time and thus the freedom and opportunity for "cultivation and exercise of the higher and more refined taste for rural embellishment" and for "relaxation."[37] Similarly, by making the community's one-acre house lots all contiguous and connecting them

with "footways," the founders expected to afford a suitable degree of "friendly and frequent intercourse" while forestalling the sort of strife that might arise from overly
dense accommodations of the sort found in cities.[38] This community's efforts to
address such a wide range of economic and social concerns depended on an amalgamation of capitalism and socialism in an experimental suburban plan, an experiment
that eventually failed but at least facilitated an active role for the residents in the political and economic structuring of their own bourgeois aspirations.

Because the residents of Evergreen Hamlet had a unique understanding of their
political and economic situation in mid-nineteenth-century America, and since at
that time there was no single predominant mode of financing suburban development
in America, their unique suburban combination of bourgeois capitalism and socialism
was one of many experiments that might have had a future.[39] But within a quarter
century the predominant engine of development became the capitalist entrepreneur,
whether small-scale developers and builders of small houses, or large-scale developers
and builders of large mansions. Capitalist development of suburban tracts already had

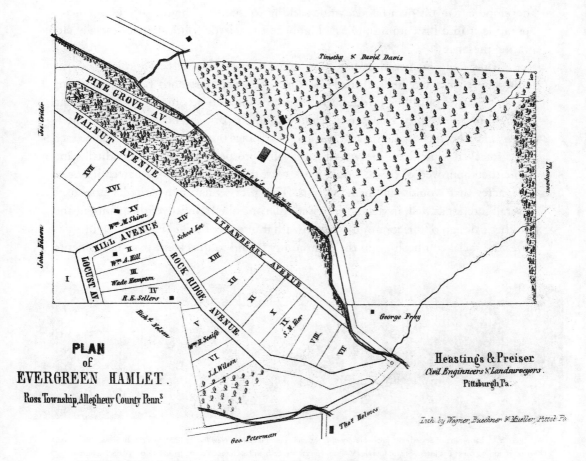

Figure 5.14. William Shinn, plan of Evergreen Hamlet. From *The Constitution of Evergreen Hamlet,* 1851.

a well-established history in England, notably including the early gated community of Victoria Park near Manchester begun by a private company of eight men in 1836.[40] In America private companies sometimes were established to develop suburban tracts for the benefit of educational institutions, as in the case of suburban Lake Forest, north of Chicago, which was established in 1856 for the purpose of founding a university.[41] And sometimes a group of entrepreneurs formed a company for the purpose of developing a suburb simply as an investment vehicle, as in the case of the eastern businessmen who commissioned the plan of Riverside, west of Chicago, from the firm of Olmsted, Vaux and Co. in 1868–69.[42]

Thus during the 1850s, and especially following the Civil War, suburbia rapidly became a terrain for the full spectrum of individual and corporate entrepreneurship. And while these entrepreneurs produced many beautiful, successful, and enduring plans, and began the inexorable demographic transformation of America into a suburban nation, most remained within well-established *rus in urbe* paradigms.[43] But rather than attend to this entire range of undertakings, the discussion here will turn to just one private entrepreneur who, like Llewellyn Haskell, kept the reins of development in his own hands, while seeking to intensify the role of *rus,* by incorporating it into his community as a highly aestheticized, politically and socially elevating presence.[44]

In 1874, almost two decades after the founding of Llewellyn Park, but only six miles away (and ten miles from New York), Stewart Hartshorn began assembling over 1,500 acres of rolling forested land that he wanted to become an "ideal suburban village" in Short Hills, New Jersey. Unlike countless British and American counterparts, Hartshorn chose not to plat his land in advance but rather to individualize each plot for every purchaser. He would meet with prospective parties individually and if he then approved of them, would work with them in arranging a parcel of one to five acres that would suit their interests. This process naturally suited Hartshorn's overall interest as well, in that he exercised full control not only over the planning and aesthetic design of the community, often with impressive results (Figure 5.15), but also over the social composition of the community.[45] And to the extent that the residents'

Figure 5.15. Panorama of Short Hills. From *History of Essex and Hudson Counties, New Jersey,* 1884, by William Shaw. The illustration captures the intentions of founder William Hartshorn to blend architecture and nature into an "ideal suburban village" according to picturesque, highly aestheticized principles.

interests and tastes all mirrored Hartshorn's, the community naturally became a site for mutual confirmation and reinforcement of those tastes.

One of Hartshorn's stated ambitions was to make Short Hills into the most artistically perfected community to be found, and perhaps due to the modus operandi just described, within a decade it had moved far in acquiring that very reputation. As the essayist for *Lippincott's Magazine* gushed in 1884, Short Hills was

> a settlement in which the very newest phase of American rural architecture is much more completely exemplified than the oldest is exemplified anywhere. . . . It is scene-painters' architecture in an opera village. . . . And you must be of an unthankful spirit if when you leave Short Hills you do not invoke blessings upon its proprietor for having afforded you so much entertainment by building you this unique and delightful suburb.[46]

In the same year another essayist, Alfred Matthews, also emphasized Hartshorn's aesthetic efforts at Short Hills, suggesting that because this was "the work of an individual rather than a company," there was a far greater opportunity to realize such a perfected solution to the "long baffling problem of how to make beautiful and healthful suburban homes." Matthews pointed to several aspects of Hartshorn's work: "the place was given the appearance of a great park," but on the other hand there was an understood individualism implicit within the whole: "No two houses in the two-score or more already erected are alike, and yet each group reveals harmony, and every house gains something from its neighbor as well as from the broad picture formed by natural surroundings." The essay then expanded on these qualities by extolling the variety of revival styles already in evidence, such as Gothic, Norman, Flemish, Colonial, and Dutch.[47] Thus individual enterprise, an array of stylistic choices, and individualized designs all had contributed to a perfect realization of individualistic expression for all. Moreover, these were contained in their nominal diversity by the unifying—if socially neutral and aesthetically elevating—frame of nature.

For all the beauty of this "new park village," it also was evident that Hartshorn's initial interview and negotiation with individual clients over lot layout and dwelling design were part of a process of turning aesthetics into a much more powerful apparatus for maintenance of bourgeois social distinction and class status. As Matthews indicated, Hartshorn was "a firm believer in the utility of beauty," and to that end he introduced what Matthews termed "a few restrictions" into the design. In particular these involved "a wide border of field and forest" around the perimeter so that there could be "no obtrusion of undesirable buildings to mar the plan of the town or of evil institutions to mar the morals of the little community and neutralize the influences of home life."[48] In other words, in Hartshorn's hands the suburb first became an instrument of bourgeois social filtration, by virtue of the process by which he admitted residents. Then it became an instrument for the articulation of the bourgeois self-as-individual in highly aestheticized terms through intense engagement with nature, not only by favoring architectural and landscaping styles that harmonized richly with each other but also by giving nature the appearance of being the apolitical principal framework for the community as a whole.

However innovative one community design, or idyllic another, the debate over the role of city and country in the life of the bourgeois individual continued to be lively throughout the nineteenth century. As suburban populations grew, the rhetoric of *rus in urbe* continued to frame not only promotional copy for individual suburbs but also philosophical and political debates about the future of English and American society. For the latter half of the nineteenth century, those debates were anchored in two principal positions, with a third arriving at the turn of the twentieth century. One position construed suburbia, having originated as a combination of *rus* plus *urbs,* to have evolved in Darwinian fashion to a higher stage on the evolutionary scale beyond country or city. The other position, more simply, found suburbia to be a place of equanimity or equilibrium in between the two. The third position, which by far has held the greatest sway since its introduction at the beginning of the twentieth century, is the Garden City ideal, according to which a "marriage" of town and country produces, in Hegelian fashion, a new civilization. To conclude the discussion of the *rus in urbe* ideal, a brief synopsis of these three positions follows.

First, as several authors took pains to note, that state of *rus in urbe* in which the best of both worlds existed was quite distinct from the separate states of *rus* and *urbs.* At stake was an understanding of *rus in urbe* as something ultimately different from either country or city, in which case it would signal an advanced state of culture and a legitimation of bourgeois endeavors. Otherwise it simply would be nothing more than a sum of its parts, hardly meriting elevated status or consideration. Moreover, if *rus in urbe* was somehow a different state, then necessarily there had to be grounds to differentiate it from city or country, but those grounds needed only to show difference, not always superiority. After all, arguments maligning the many faults of cities were not hard to come by, but as the century progressed the necessity for cities continued to appear unassailable on many grounds, not least of which was their economic importance to those who lived everywhere else. Thus the challenge often was cast in terms of finding the best possible formula for balancing city and country, or integrating them, under the given circumstances. Some partisans of suburbia readily noted that certain advantages were to be found only in towns: according to John Claudius Loudon, these included libraries, museums, theaters, concerts, assemblies, art exhibitions, and so forth.[49] Or as an essayist wrote in the *Atlantic Monthly* in 1861, cities were in effect a necessary evil. Even though "the first murderer was the first city-builder," cities also had their uses, such as encouraging democracy, agriculture, and commerce:

> As cities have been the nurses of democratic institutions and ideas, democratic nations, for very obvious reasons, tend to produce them. They are the natural fruits of a democracy. And with no people are great cities so important, or likely to be

so increasingly populous, as with a great agricultural and commercial nation like our own.[50]

For many authors, this thinking led in rather Darwinist fashion to the conclusion that suburbia was a higher state of civilization toward which Western society had been destined to evolve. As Loudon put it, suburban residences "may be considered as the ultimatum, in point of comfort and enjoyment, of the great mass of society; not only at present, but even after society has advanced to a much higher degree of civilisation, and to a comparative equalisation of knowledge, wealth, and taste."[51]

Second, the suburbs, that in-between space between city and country, might be seen as a site of equilibrium between those two poles. That is exactly what Samuel Sloan, a major midcentury American architectural practitioner and author, indicated in prefatory remarks to his design for a suburban mansion when he suggested that the "man of wealth" building this house would be in search of just such a balanced psychological state. On the one hand, such a businessman client after years of toil would be seeking a place of comparative quiet. "Yet his mind," wrote Sloan,

> from having long been accustomed to the throng and incessant activity of the city, desires not the settled repose of country life, but is inclined to choose a suburban location. Here, all the conveniences to which he has been accustomed can be readily procured; and here, undisturbed by the discord of a thousand rumbling wheels, he can hear the merry chimes that his boyhood heard—enjoying an equilibrium between the stirring influences of a whirlwind of business and the slumber-inviting calm of a rural atmosphere. He seeks not the selfish seclusion of solitude, but provides for the reception and entertainment of his friends, and the enjoyment of such social and domestic pleasures as may be compatible with his particular circumstances; and his children are provided with such means of instruction and amusement as combine to render home the most attractive spot on earth.[52]

Finally a third, more powerful paradigm arrived at the turn of the century with the publication of Ebenezer Howard's manifesto of the Garden City, *Garden Cities of To-morrow* (1902), in which he stressed neither evolutionary destiny nor personal equilibrium but rather the need for planning to take an active part in transforming a moribund civilization: "Town and country *must be married,* and out of this joyous union will spring a new hope, a new life, a new civilisation."[53] Such a notion, that only a carefully designed, vital hybrid of the two could succeed in the brave new industrial world of the twentieth century, has remained perhaps the most persistent planning ideology in Britain and America for the ensuing century. This has been evident in Britain in formal campaigns such as the Garden City and New Town movements, in their American formal counterparts such as Radburn, the Greenbelt Town Program, and 1960s new towns such as Reston, as well as in certain aspects of New Urbanist and related movements at the end of the twentieth century.[54] The Garden

City mode also has triumphed in a perverse sort of way as American mass culture has embraced many ideals consistent with Garden City philosophy such as partiality toward nature and antipathy to urban congestion, corruption, and pollution, while American politics has simultaneously undercut so many Garden City principles by balkanization of residential suburban municipalities and favoring the construction of single-family houses. Indeed by midway through the twentieth century America's version of suburbia—Sloan's onetime "equilibrium"—had evolved into an object of contention in its own right, drawing critical scorn in comparison to both city and country. From combining the best of country and city, in the eyes of some it had moved to combining the worst of both.[55]

Suburban Pastorale

The mythos of nineteenth-century suburbia was not always in accord with the realities of the residential landscape nor descriptive of the lives of the bourgeois inhabitants. Just as the twentieth-century "dream house" often lay more in the mind of the owner than in the eye of the beholder, as the next chapters will show, so nineteenth-century suburbs could be overlaid with rhetoric, imagery, and practices that evoked the pastoral, along with all the delights and privileges that might be associated with it, even if no true pastoral existed. The nineteenth-century popular press, including novels, magazines, and newspapers, frequently incorporated articles extolling the beauties and advantages of suburbia, implicitly equating the lifestyle to be expected there with ideals of Arcadian pastoral life.[56] Nevertheless in light of the discussion in chapter 3 of the pastoral ideal and the related concept of *negotium,* the ways in which these motifs were incorporated into the design and experience of nineteenth-century American suburbia frequently seem to have reduced them to little more than suggestions of spontaneous happiness.

Where there was a serious engagement with notions of pastoral and leisure, nature for obvious reasons became the apparatus of choice by which the bourgeois householder sought to implement that goal, and the suburban locale became a perfect site. Still, two different frameworks for achieving those ends presented themselves throughout the century: the aesthetic integration of the locale with nature, and performance of leisure activities within nature.

Humphry Repton, the renowned English gardener and writer on landscape, was a partisan of the first approach. Early in the century he pronounced that the domestic landscape "must studiously conceal every interference of art, however expensive, by which the natural scenery is improved; making the whole appear the production of nature only."[57] Understanding that by *art* Repton meant *artifice,* and by extension *labor,* the clear implication was that the domestic environment must appear to be a construction of "nature," and therefore wholly a matter of aesthetics.

Americans remained committed to the aestheticization of nature and the domestic environment well into the century. For many, the intrusion of any form of artifice into the appreciation of nature was cause for considerable disquietude. Frederick S.

Cozzens, for example, complained in a fictional essay of 1855 that the increasingly suburbanized land near Dobbs Ferry, New York, was being progressively ruined by the "ornate façades, cornices, and vestibules" of the houses, however nice, that people were building on lands formerly characterized by "meadows, boulders, wild shrubbery and uplifted trees." Another commentator, writing in 1843, suggested that the culprit simply was suburbia itself: "There is a suburban look and character about all the villages on the Hudson which seems out of place among such scenery. They are suburbs; in fact steam [in the form of steamboats] has destroyed the distance between them and the city."[58]

For others architecture, suitably designed and deployed, could be an asset to the overall aesthetic composition. As Nathaniel Parker Willis took a steamboat journey past the cities of the Susquehanna River, for example, he marveled at

> the distribution of white villas along the shore, on spots where Nature seemed to have arranged the ground for their reception. I saw thousands of sites where the lawns were made, the terraces defined and levelled, the groves tastefully clumped, . . . and, in everything, the labor of art seemingly all anticipated by Nature. I grew tired of exclaiming, to the friend who was beside me, "What an exquisite site for a villa! What a sweet spot for a cottage!"[59]

Unfortunately not all travelers could be so favorably impressed everywhere they went. A visitor to the "suburban villages" dotting the beautiful environs of Cincinnati in 1852 instead found: "Already the smoke covered houses begin to ascend the brows of hills, and soon we shall have the city of dwellings there, looking down upon the mighty throng of busy, restless, industrious mortals, in their shops and stores below!" But despite the expectation that so much of this landscape that was picturesque, charming, soft, gentle, and peaceful would be gone in ten years, at least in some respects it was fortunate that it would retain its "lovely distant view." The writer only hoped that lots and streets on the hills could be laid out "with more regard to space and air than has been done in the city."[60]

The subject of views and vistas was of more than aesthetic concern to Downing. He argued that vistas, properly fashioned, also could serve as instruments of appropriation of nature directly to the homeowner. A simple sweeping panorama, he wrote, "wants interest." Much preferable were specific views, vistas, or even partial views with rich foregrounds because these afforded "the home-like feeling of appropriation."[61] Not only did these offer greater interest, presumably because of richer detail, but since they remained in the immediate visual domain of the homeowner, comparatively safe from corruption by the onslaught of other dwellings in the immediate vicinity, they facilitated one of the key opportunities of suburbia, as Downing signaled here: *appropriation* of the natural environment for the private consumption of the individual bourgeois homeowner. Instead of an aestheticized, ultimately transcendent experience of property transformed into nature, such as Repton and his followers allowed, Downing here endorsed something quite different. Consistent with the capitalist-Enlightenment ideology of possessive individualism (see chapter 1), the dwelling became an instrument for the appropriation of nature (and its aesthetic value) for its bourgeois inhabitant.

The second common framework by which nineteenth-century American suburban households engaged notions of pastoral and leisure was to engage directly in corresponding activities. Commonly suburbanites turned to gardening. But because productivity was counter to ideals of leisure and pastoral, actual production of food for human consumption declined, particularly with the rise of distribution and retail systems that made it easier and cheaper for the bourgeoisie to purchase food at the market. Thus gardening increasingly was recognized as valuable for its restorative and moral benefits, rather than for any economic purpose. As Joseph Breck stated as early as 1851, gardening could serve as the businessman's antidote to the pressures and passions of the day, a focal point for family togetherness, and a natural lesson to all individuals:

> Nature, in her gay attire, unfolds a vast variety which is pleasing to the human mind, and, consequently, has a tendency to tranquillize the agitated passions, and exhilarate the man,—nerve the imagination, and render all around him delightful. Who, that has been confined to the business of the day, toiling and laboring in the "sweat of his brow," does not feel invigorated and refreshed, as he takes his walk in the cool of the evening, with the happy family group about him, and marks the progress of his fruits and flowers? . . .
>
> The moral lesson that can be obtained from flowers also forms another fine characteristic in the flower-garden; for flowers not only please the eye and gratify the passing observer, but contain a beauty in their structure, in the most minute parts and coloring, that conveys a pleasing and natural lesson to the most accurate and intelligent observer, with everything to please and nothing to offend.[62]

For similar reasons Catharine Beecher saw gardening as crucial to the education of children. Even in such an elite community as Short Hills, gardening remained a central aspect of daily life for many residents. Businessman William Ingraham Russell was one. A metals broker in New York, he recounted in a memoir that in the late 1870s he would spend as much as two to three hours each morning working in his one-acre kitchen garden, taking pleasure from his success at raising small crops.[63]

But even more than the garden, the lawn became the quintessential apparatus by which the bourgeois householder defined the home as a site of leisure. Not only was the lawn itself a nonproductive asset, it also banished sight of productive assets, such as crops, or animals grown for the household's use, to other parts of the property. Once the lawn became recognized as a formal part of dwelling and neighborhood design, and caring for the lawn fell into the category of leisure activity (Figure 5.16), having and using a lawn became a principal means by which bourgeois householders could define some of the leisure dimensions of their lives, often with quasi-pastoral overtones.[64] Broad swaths of grass and grazing sheep had afforded just those overtones to many an English country estate, particularly after the style of Capability Brown became popular in the middle of the eighteenth century. And by the early nineteenth century grass lawns had become de rigueur for American country residences. As John Haviland wrote in 1818, the portion in front of the house "may be from a quarter of an acre, or less, to six or eight acres, or more, according to the extent and situation of the ground." Beyond that some lawns might extend over a ha-ha (a sunken ditch) even farther, to as much as sixty acres.[65] One limiting factor for a lawn was simply the amount of land one could afford, but just as serious a consideration was maintenance. When sheep or a human labor force using scythes were the only ways to tend a lawn, it necessarily was expensive to maintain. But with the invention and patenting in 1830 of a lawn mower that could be propelled by a single human being (Figure 5.17),[66] the domestication of the lawn could become a reality for the suburban bourgeois household. Many nineteenth-century illustrations and advertisements suggested that the lawn mower was not restricted to a laborer's use, or that it hardly required any labor to operate. Rather, its apparent ease of use by women as well as men, all shown in proper dress, rendered it an instrument of leisure, to maintain that perfect token of leisure, the lawn. The lawn became a preferred setting for passive activities, or no activity at all. Indeed leisure sometimes could be overdone: as a satirical commentary

Figure 5.16. Trade card for Charter Oak Lawn Mower, ca. 1885. As a means of selling lawn mowers, mowing was advertised to look ever easier and more like a leisure activity. Here the choice of a young girl to do the mowing epitomized these characteristics. Courtesy of Baker Library, Harvard Business School.

and accompanying vignette in H. C. Bunner's *The Suburban Sage* (1896) made clear, even upkeep of the lawn was an activity honored more in the breach than in the doing (Figure 5.18).

Yet despite the attention given to leisured aspects of bourgeois household life, the production of food was never taken entirely for granted. The premier nineteenth-century architectural and landscape publications almost always show grounds laid out to include fruit and vegetable gardens (Figure 5.19). Eating food fresh from one's own garden was universally recommended as a distinct advantage of suburban living. One midcentury author, envisioning a commute of the sort that would have been common in New York or other East Coast cities at the time, envisioned the suburban ideal in the following terms:

> What more agreeable and healthy for a man harassed by the cares and fatigues of business, than to leave the confined and heated streets of the city, to step on board one of our splendid river boats, breathe the pure and refreshing air from off the water, get "home," eat his dinner in a cool room, with fruits and vegetables from his own garden, and then, with his family, enjoy the evening stroll in his own grounds, free from the restraint of dress and etiquette.[67]

Figure 5.17. "Budding's Machine for Cropping or Shearing the Vegetable Surface of Lawns, Grass-plots, &c.," *The Gardener's Magazine,* 1832. An illustration of the first design for a lawn mower.

Likewise for Henry Cleaveland and the Backus brothers, in *Villas and Farm Cottages* (1856), there was no question that bourgeois homeowners would raise at least some of their own food: "Such a family should produce, in part, at least, their own vegetables, poultry, eggs, and pork. In very many cases, a cow might be added . . ."[68] (Figure 5.20).

By the early twentieth century the production of food had become a matter of contention. For those who understood the pastoral suburban landscape as a heightened state of leisure, as a potential opportunity for transcendence from the realm of work and commerce to that of family and domesticity through aesthetics, the sight of labor and its products was thoroughly disruptive. In many cases developers found it profitable to add deed restrictions specifically prohibiting most productive uses of suburban yards.[69] But in other cases suburban agriculture and husbandry were seen as crucial to the welfare of American families and, by extension, the nation. Explaining "Why I Chose a Suburban Home" shortly after the turn of the twentieth century,

Figure 5.18. Vignette by C. J. Taylor on page 5 of H. C. Bunner, *The Suburban Sage,* 1896. The lawn became a setting for passive activities, or for little more than commentary on inactivity, as in this vignette accompanying a conversation between two suburbanites about the suburban "disease" of borrowing among neighbors without ever returning items borrowed.

DESIGN No. 45.

PLAN FOR LAYING OUT A LOT ONE HUNDRED AND FIFTY FEET BY TWO HUNDRED FEET.

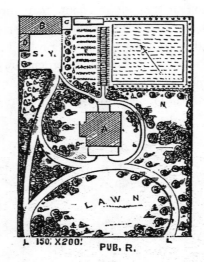

FIG. 136.

A, House.

B, Stable.

D, Henery.

C, Manure Pit.

S Y, Stable Yard.

H, Hot-beds.

G, Dwarf fruit.

N, Drying-yard.

F, Raspberries, along one side of which is a grape arbor covering the walk.

LL, Entrances.

Currant and other small fruits around outside border.

Figure 5.19. George E. Woodward, *Plan for Laying Out a Lot One Hundred and Fifty Feet by Two Hundred Feet.* Figure 136 in *Woodward's Architecture and Rural Art,* 1867–68. The plan included specific references to hot-beds and places to grow dwarf fruit, raspberries, grapes, currants, and other small fruits.

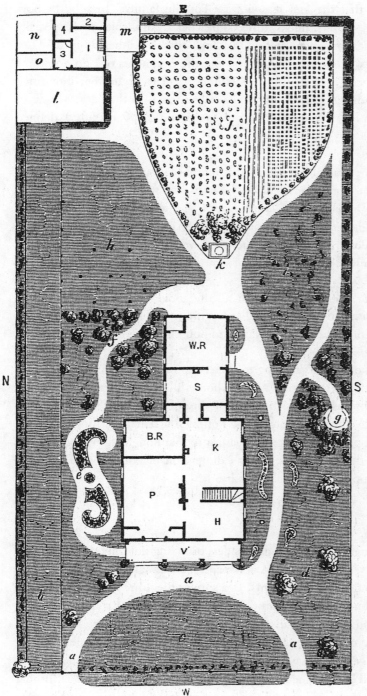

REFERENCES.

a, Walk.
b, Stable path.
c, Lawn.
d, Shrubbery.
e, Flower bed.
f, Evergreen screen.
h, Clothes yard.
i, Fruit.
j, Vegetables.
g, Summer house.
k, Well.
l, Cow yard.
m, Poultry yard.
n, Piggery.
o, Manure pit.

HOUSE.

v, Verandah.
H, Hall.
P, Parlor.
K, Kitchen.
B R, Bedroom.
s, Scullery.
W R, Wood room.

STABLE.

1, Tool room.
2, Poultry room.
3, Cow stall.
4, Feed room.

Figure 5.20. Henry W. Cleaveland, William Backus, and Samuel D. Backus, layout of a sample lot. Page 168 in *Villas and Farm Cottages,* 1856. This lot, 75 by 150 feet, includes specific references to places for growing fruit and vegetables and for raising cattle, poultry, and pigs.

one author explained that the first reason was "For the family." In suburbs boys could raise guinea pigs, rabbits, ducks, turkeys, peacocks, dogs, colts, and especially hens: "What a vast education a boy can find in a flock of these feathered bipeds! They teach him mathematics, economics, hygienics, and the rudiments of I do not know how many other sciences."[70] A decade later, some began to argue that intensified gardening and husbandry in the suburbs were instrumental to the very survival of American society. John R. McMahon, author of *Success in the Suburbs* (1917), defined that "success" as

> an independent home establishment in a fairly countrified suburb; a household that is self-supporting as to fruits, vegetables, eggs, broilers, and such-like, produced for home use and chiefly by the efforts of the family itself; an enterprise that means health and happiness; a self-helping institution that pays no cash dividends but, reckoned in terms of edibles produced and economies effected above the cost of living in the city, returns an annual profit on the investment of something like twenty-five percent.[71]

The essential factor for McMahon was that all the above benefits far outweighed what to him was a minimal investment of labor (Figure 5.21). Thus as late as 1917 there was evidently still no consensus whether yard and household environs were places of economy or leisure.

In the end, a host of reasons relating to the economics of food production, the nature of employment, and the articulation of home life vis-à-vis the modern consumer economy have brought about the impossibility of any sort of self-supporting household such as McMahon advocated. The notion still remains strong that one's own garden produce is preferable for many reasons to that bought commercially, but for much of America that produce remains a dimension of bourgeois leisure, well removed from economic or nutritional necessity.

Suburban Uncertainty

Nineteenth-century English and American readers browsing not only through books of architectural designs but also through newspapers, fashionable magazines such as *Harper's,* novels, illustrated travel accounts, and similar literature might have gotten the impression that suburbia was an unmitigated blessing for all the reasons discussed above and more. As industrial capitalism increasingly turned cities into sites of pollution, congestion, and corruption, as commuter transportation made suburbs more accessible, and as bourgeois employment and incomes made residence in the suburbs more feasible, suburban living came to represent the best possible alternative. But that did not leave the city without its continuing supporters, nor did it leave suburbia without a substantial number of dubious observers who worried that all was not shaping up as it was supposed to be. As early as 1835, for example, one British critic condemned suburbs as wanting in basic aspects of aesthetics that central cities all possessed:

In the central city . . . all looks firm, respectable, and of old established consequence. In the suburb you see nothing of this. . . . [T]here may be prettiness and even elegance, but nothing respectable or exclusive. The honours of a suburb are like those of a new mercantile gentleman—they have a quality of spick and span, which does not somehow excite veneration. The place, moreover, wants completeness and variety.[72]

Four years later Sarah Stickney Ellis worried over the damaging effects that suburban living was having on the family, particularly the fact that fathers did not have time to see their children except on Sunday.[73]

By the last decade of the century, as Gail Cunningham has well demonstrated, a number of British writers had developed strong suspicions and hostilities toward suburbia. Among other concerns, many portrayed it as a locale that threatened and limited individuality, particularly in the case of the male, who had become emasculated and feminized there. But suburbia was no better for women, encouraging them at best to follow useless pursuits such as overindulgence in interior decoration, at worst to extend themselves inappropriately into spheres traditionally dominated by men.[74] By the early years of the twentieth century, *suburban* had for some become a term of

It Is No Trouble to Plant with a Seeder

Figure 5.21. John R. McMahon, "It Is No Trouble to Plant with a Seeder." Plate facing page 208 in *Success in the Suburbs*, 1917. McMahon considered it essential to the survival of American society that suburban households be able to support themselves as fully as possible with produce from the land.

disdain and contempt. As the Edwardian critic and novelist Thomas Crosland wrote in *The Suburbans* (1905), "Whatever, in short, strikes the superior mind as being deficient in completeness, excellence, and distinction may with absolute safety be called suburban." Just as Sarah Ellis had seen in the 1830s, Crosland too found that suburbia was almost totally devoid of men except on Sundays, thus rendering it ironically "more suburban still." And when men could be found at home, they were unable to engage in any process of individual fulfillment; rather they were henpecked into a relationship between "over-woman" and "galley-slave."[75]

In America the literature generally was not as acerbic, and as one might expect there was quite an atmosphere of boosterism about the undertaking of almost every new suburban enterprise. For communities such as Llewellyn Park, Lake Forest, Riverside, and hundreds of far lesser renown, the press was full of praise for the aesthetic and economic contributions that were being added to the community and to the region. Likewise few voices of dissent were recorded with regard to specific suburbs or subdivisions. But this does not necessarily imply the conclusion, which many have drawn, that nineteenth-century suburbia was uniformly desirable and highly appreciated in its own time.

Rather, throughout the nineteenth century there were undercurrents of misgiving over suburbia, generally focusing on two areas of concern: first, that in reality suburbia had to serve a much broader range of people and maintain a greater diversity of building types than the elite bourgeois households illustrated in architectural manuals and popular magazines; and second, that suburbs did not necessarily live up to their advertised ideals. As passages cited earlier have shown, suburbs on the outskirts of major cities often contained mixed social classes, and at times they were more typically inhabited by poor people than the bourgeoisie. The author of an 1832 essay describing a walk "through the suburbs of our city" noticed these characteristics,[76] as did Alice Cary in her novel *Clovernook* (1852) in her description of suburban development around young cities along the Ohio River. On the far outskirts of such cities the scene was idyllic, with garden walks, smooth lawns, and white houses. But closer in were candle and soap factories, and droves of bleating lambs and calves heading to the slaughterhouses. She reported that smoke from chimneys had become a prominent feature of the suburban landscape, along with dense slums with multitiered porches bordering narrow alleys filled with refuse. Leaning against the porches were large groups of men smoking, quarreling, and swearing, while half-naked children played in pools of stagnant water.[77] Much the same sentiment, though cast in terms that were not quite so horrific, formed part of William Ranlett's appeal in 1856 to incorporate the professional training and aesthetic sense of an architect in the design of suburban dwellings, so that suburbs would no longer have to be a "shabby frame" to the beauty of America's cities.[78]

By midcentury a more widespread antipathy toward suburbia, particularly elite bourgeois suburbs, began to emerge in contemporary American commentary. At first it was tentative and lighthearted, but by the end of the century it had become a serious (if by no means dominant) dimension of the discourse on suburbia. In 1851, one year after Downing hit the peak of his career with the publication of *The Architecture of Country Houses,* Nathaniel Parker Willis published *Hurry-Graphs,* in which he included a critique of the elite bourgeois dwellings that populated Westchester County to the exclusion of all other types. Somewhat tongue in cheek, Willis complained that it had become "rather a defect in the general scenery" that Westchester now consisted entirely of country seats, with no housing for humble or poor people anywhere. Couching his critique coyly in the rhetoric of aesthetics, he continued, "Miles upon miles of unmitigated prosperity weary the eye," complaining that all the fine houses, large stables, gates, lawns, and other landscaping were simply "notes upon one chord."[79] A decade later another critic argued against the type of isolated living that single families encountered in suburbs on grounds that certain aspects of that lifestyle, including "hardship, absence of social excitements and public amusements, simple food, [and] freedom from moral exposure," were "decidedly opposed to health and virtue."[80]

One of the most extended American critiques of suburbia was *Suburban Sketches* (1871), in which William Dean Howells left no doubt about his harsh and uncomplimentary views of life in the suburban vicinity of Boston. Perhaps foremost was his finding that suburbia was neither *rus* nor *urbs.* From his perspective, in town you could go to the theater, in the country you could raise poultry or livestock, but in the suburbs you could just sit on the doorstep and swat mosquitoes. Meanwhile commuting was the scourge of suburbia. No matter how elegantly homes were furnished, commuter transport was unconscionably shabby. Worse, home life was governed by the need of the husband-father to turn around every night and catch the morning train, leaving little time for family, let alone relaxation or self-improvement. And finally, Howells pointedly noted that suburbia was not even an Anglo-Saxon domain, but rather consisted of different ethnic groups (he called them "races"), including Irish as well as French Canadians.[81]

By the final decade of the nineteenth century, commentators were exploring a new dimension of uncertainty about suburbia, namely its status as an in-between and indeterminate space. Instead of combining *rus* with *urbs* or otherwise synthesizing aspects of American private and public selfhood, suburbia in the eyes of some became a place of disaffection and estrangement. For Richard Harding Davis, writing in 1894, suburban New York was above all a place of incomprehensible tedium: long commutes, carrying packages to the train, fetching them from the baggage car, additional miles by carriage, boring conversations at home, and more. As an urbanite, Davis could not understand the attractions of the seemingly closed circles of suburban society.[82] The same year Henry A. Beers's *Suburban Pastoral,* much of which was set in the general vicinity of New Haven, Connecticut, portrayed suburbia in an acutely disturbing but realistic manner as a constantly moving zone of transition:

> There is one glory of the country and another glory of the town, but there is a limbo or ragged edge between which is without glory of any kind. It is not yet town—it is

no longer country. Hither are banished slaughter pens, chemical and oil works, glue factories, soap boilers, and other malodorous nuisances. Here are railroad shops and roundhouses, sand lots, German beer gardens, and tenement blocks. Land, which was lately sold by the acre, is now offered by the foot front; and no piece of real estate is quite sure whether it is part of an old field or has become a building lot. Rural lanes and turnpikes have undergone metamorphosis into "boulevards," where regulation curbstones prophesy future sidewalks, and thinly scattered lamp-posts foretell a coming population.

In Beers's book one character actually reacts positively to the experience of the changing nature of the suburban terrain. He is seen observing "the wandering horse car and empty boulevards. They were raw, but they were signs of growth—emblems of the young, hopeful, expansive American spirit. At the same time he enjoyed the pathos which attended the retreat of rural aristocracy before the advance of urban democracy." Often as not curious juxtapositions remained in this moving transition zone, such as "two or three mansions of ancient gentility stranded high and dry among squalid surroundings." Elsewhere there were populations of different races and ethnicity, including Negroes and Germans. A liquor saloon attracted a group of "'corner-boys,' ill-looking thugs." Indeed suburbia could well be a place in decline. In one of Beers's stories Doctor Putnam, taking walks in the suburbs in the 1870s, visits an "uninclosed outskirt of the town," where he is disappointed to encounter "an old-fashioned country house, now converted into a soap-boiling establishment."[83]

For others, the critique remained on the level of caricature and satire. In *Suburban Sage* (1896), H. C. Bunner satirized a number of ways that suburbia fell far short of common expectations. At the beginning of the book he pointed to the custom of neighborly borrowing of tools and other items. One might think that neighborly lending and borrowing would help establish community, but Bunner concluded the opposite: "the borrowing habit is the curse of suburban life." Tongue only partly in cheek, and understanding well enough the longstanding importance of property as a fundamental condition of bourgeois selfhood, he reasoned that the custom of borrowing "weakens a man's sense of individual ownership in property." Another disadvantage to suburbia was what he termed the "Building Craze": everyone would go to view new houses under construction, after which they would start to sketch their own plans for a house, and ultimately spend far too much money on a house that they did not want or need. Beyond this, Bunner reiterated the concern that once living in a suburb people were at the mercy of the trains (particularly their limited schedules) and servants (notably their limited training and intelligence). More solemnly, Bunner lamented that suburban residents had become "Children of the Time-Table," living a mechanized existence quite unlike the pastoral freedom that architects, subdividers, and developers so eagerly promised.[84] Much the same assessment of suburbs as antifamily appeared in a 1900 *Harper's Bazar* article that found that commuting had made the father "almost entirely a Sunday institution." The consequence was that the children often went unsupervised much of the time, and that home life inevitably was hard on women.[85]

Early in the twentieth century, the refrain continued that suburbia had not lived up to its promise of combining city and country, particularly now that its design had been taken over by developers more interested in economically efficient (and therefore rectilinear) subdivisions than in the welfare of its residents:

> It is neither city nor country, nor can it ever supply the place of either. It is not city, for it is too far from the center of things, its streets too narrow for traffic and its blocks too small, and there will be none of the privacy a city affords with houses touching yet completely separated. It can not be country with its cast-iron plan, its straight streets and its houses huddled together on mean little lots all the same size and shape, and all running the same way.[86]

As the century progressed it seemed that living in a suburb began to guarantee fewer and fewer of the amenities that many had sought when escaping the city. As one essayist wrote in 1917, the air in her suburb was not even as good as where she had lived in New York City for ten years, nor was it as quiet as it had been in her sixth-floor apartment, because cars and trucks now were passing through her suburb all day long. Still, in the last analysis, the suburb was where she wished to remain: "it is an opportunity for individualism. In a Suburb you can be as unneighborly as you wish, and yet not achieve that hard, cold, exterior of flat-dwellers. . . ."[87] But another, graver problem faced by many women who moved to suburbs during the second half of the twentieth century already had been recognized at the century's outset: the loneliness of suburban isolation. In one of the short stories included in *The Suburban Whirl* (1907), Mary Stewart Cutting wrote of the central character, Mrs. Tremley:

> no one would have dreamed that in her lonely commonplaceness she was fast locked in one of the grappling problems of life—the problem of shifting one's individuality so that it may adequately meet new and strange conditions for it.[88]

Conclusion

Even though detached villas became more and more common in the suburban landscape throughout the nineteenth century, the notion of "retirement" gradually became less attractive as a component of suburban ideology. As an American essayist wrote in 1849, the "successful statesman, professional man, merchant, trader, mechanic" initially looked to retirement as "the universal pleasure of men." Yet it actually turned out to be a disappointment for many because what "a suburban country-life" most needed was "objects of real interest, society, occupation," in other words, more of what might be called society, or community life.[89]

Suburbanites often found that community life not by a return to the density or diversity of the city, but by nurturing common interests, or reinforcing homogeneous characteristics within their own locales, while often simultaneously excluding other interests and people with different characteristics. As John Claudius Loudon recommended as early as 1838, the best choice of neighborhood for a prospective buyer would be one in which "the houses and inhabitants are all, or chiefly, of the same description and class as the house we intend to inhabit, and as ourselves." Another requisite was the opportunity for meaningful social intercourse, which for Loudon again was a limiting characteristic: the best opportunities would be found among people of comparable "education and morals," and social class, to oneself.[90]

Various means soon came into common use to ensure social homogeneity, such as leasehold covenants and deed restrictions.[91] These proliferated throughout the nineteenth century, often with lasting effects such as racial segregation that have proved difficult to undo ever since. But even by the middle of the nineteenth century commentators were well aware of the economic segregation that suburban efforts to secure homogeneity had been producing. Friedrich Engels's radical essay on the working classes in Manchester, issued in 1845, was just such a critique of the isolation of classes from one another.[92] And the same critique could be heard from within the establishment. An 1857 article in the *Economist* described the division of society into "class-colonies"—not just mutually suspicious and hostile classes but physically separated "colonies." Although the article was no less prescient of twentieth-century American gated suburbia than it was descriptive of nineteenth-century Britain, it attributed this phenomenon to a common desire among individuals to associate with their equals in taste, culture, morals, and practical interests. The author observed that as different classes had begun to go their separate ways, they achieved a greater sense of independence because they were increasingly liberated from feelings of social inequality—presumably because members of other classes were unseen and therefore unknown. And although the author was at pains to demonstrate that the classes still remained economically interdependent, his warnings concerning class separation were not destined to be persuasive in altering the course of suburban and metropolitan design.[93]

Those who proposed designs for actual suburban dwellings and their environs may not have cared to take on the question of homogeneity directly, but they were prepared to address the problem of ensuring connections and relations among the residents through aesthetic means. Among the most eloquent and explicit of these was Frank J. Scott, whose notion of a suburb as a large unitary park accorded with such prototypes as Victoria Park, Llewellyn Park, and Riverside but expanded beyond them to a much broader scale. As he put it in *The Art of Beautifying Suburban Home Grounds* (1870), suburban "neighborhoods" or "parks" should be redefined as socially and aesthetically unifying landscapes on the scale of an entire township:

> A township of land, with streets, and roads, and streams, dotted with a thousand suburban homes peeping from their groves; with school-house towers and gleaming

spires among them; with farm fields, pastures, woodlands, and bounding hills or boundless prairies stretched around;—these, altogether, form our suburban parks, which all of us may ride in, and walk in, and enjoy; and the most lavish expenditures of private wealth on private grounds can never equal their extent, beauty, or variety.

There would be lots of half an acre to five acres in size, "within easy walking distance of business."[94]

But given the unlikelihood of a nineteenth-century developer erecting a thousand homes in such a manner across an entire township, smaller-scale developments continued to be the reigning paradigm. And even though landscape design and aesthetic criteria were given elevated consideration in many communities, such as Short Hills, class considerations still remained among the principal concerns for those living there. As William Russell indicated in his autobiographical account of Short Hills, it was important to all his neighbors that they be on the same social plane, regardless of how much new or old wealth they may have accumulated: "Wealth cut no figure in that community. We all respected each other and met on the same social plane, regardless of individual means."[95] What Short Hills undertook in specific, suburbia accomplished in general: it succeeded as a site of social distinction and differentiation from the city. As Scott, with the bourgeoisie in mind, phrased it succinctly in 1870, "A *suburban* home, therefore, meets the wants of refined and cultivated people more than any other."[96]

Nevertheless as nineteenth-century designers and developers continued to artic-ulate class distinctions and spatial separations, they also maintained the importance of connecting dwellings, and the individuals inside them, with nature. Sometimes this was accomplished by dispersing the dwellings widely on lots of substantial acreage. When this was not possible, dwellings might be clustered together in one location opposite a substantial open reserve, as at Calverley Park (1827–28), the progeny of which may yet be seen in present-day sustainable communities such as Prairie Cross-ing (Grayslake, Illinois, 1992) and Jackson Meadow (Marine on St. Croix, Minnesota, 1996). Here, as in earlier examples, the course of suburban design has been to differ-entiate itself from urban and rural in much the same terms: more socially distinctive than the city, and more aware of the aesthetic and ecological characteristics of nature than rural life itself. Such were not characteristics of all nineteenth-century suburbs, nor ideals emulated by all designers. But they did serve as paradigms for many, send-ing the discussion of suburbia as a site of unique potentialities for self-distinction of individuals forward into the twentieth century.

PART III

TWENTIETH-CENTURY AMERICA: THE DREAM HOUSE IDEAL AND THE SUBURBAN LANDSCAPE

6. Nationalizing the Dream

To own one's home! Has this not been part of the democratic dream? . . . To have a good life while knowing the same good life is being enjoyed by most of the people around you. Here is a moral basis for civilization that has never before existed on so grand a scale.

    —Joseph A. Barry, "America—Body and Soul," *House Beautiful* (November 1956)

Now my pops bought the system, American dreamer
Bought a new home and a brand new Beemer
But it didn't take long for things to fall apart
Because the system that he bought ain't got no heart
From the bills for days he got blood shot eyes
The American dream was a pack of lies.

    —Kottonmouth Kings, "Suburban Life," *Scream 2* (1997)

The disparity between the two passages above is at first striking. The first is full of confidence in an American paradigm that would set civilization on an unparalleled course of virtue and prosperity. The second is an expression of the despair and injustice wreaked on one of the dream's optimistic adherents. But in a more fundamental way there are also parallels. Both recognize the political foundations of the dream, one aligning it with democracy and the other branding it an instrument of "the system." And both establish that a necessary component of the dream is to own one's own home, a place to anchor and build the good life to come.

This chapter concerns the complex set of historical processes that have been crucial to the expectations and concerns raised in the above passages. It tracks the evolution of the "American dream," a phrase that may date only to the 1930s, but that consolidates a number of critical strands in American political theory and practice, ranging from eighteenth- and nineteenth-century individualism to twentieth-century nationalist imperatives. By the 1920s the stage also was being set for the eventual amalgamation of that one idea, the "American Dream," into the apparatus that increasingly would come to represent its realization, the single-family "dream house." Early in the 1920s the goal of housing each American family in a single-family dwelling was thrust upon the nation as a goal of federal policy. Soon that goal was popularized in song and film as the "dream house" to which all aspired, and not long after the century's midpoint it became a standard in terms of which one's personal expectations and lifelong accomplishments could be measured.

Such a process could not have occurred without widespread adoption of the "dream house" ideal in retail marketing, architectural design, radio programming, and many other aspects of American culture as well. This exposure helped to raise and multiply the expectations that Americans would have of their dwellings, while at the same time identifying and expanding dimensions in which commodity culture could meet and satisfy those expectations. Today, at the beginning of the next century, in millions of daily private decisions and personal actions Americans make and remake the face of suburbia in order to realize—and improve—their own particular American dreams. This chapter is an examination of how, through the elaboration of the "dream house" as the premier instrument for realizing those dreams, architecture in the form of the dream house has managed to address and resolve challenges posed in the ongoing evolution of American culture. And so the goal of this chapter is not so much a history of the American dream or the dream house as an examination of processes by which long-standing tropes in the American ideological heritage have been transformed into material form to become a reigning paradigm of the American built environment.

The American Individualist Dream

In twenty-first-century America, "living the American dream" is a notion that pervades media and marketing campaigns of all sorts—yet despite widespread and common use of the phrase, it is seldom defined. Still, it is widely understood. A recent Time-Life volume titled *The American Dream: The 50s,* for example, never mentions the term *American Dream* beyond the title page. More than four decades ago Vance Packard's *Status Seekers* (1959) incorporated the term *American dream* more than a half dozen times in its text, but in each instance there was no further definition or clarification, as if that was unnecessary.[1] Since 1970 over twenty record albums and more than eighty songs titled "American Dream" or "American Dreams" have been issued, in genres ranging from folk and country to rock, rap, and jazz. But in these recordings there are seldom any explicit references to the particulars of what such a national dream might be. Rather, the title serves to evoke an already established notion, in relation or contrast to which the music sets its own agenda.

The origins of the term *American dream* may never be well established, but it is largely a twentieth-century construct. Before World War II the actual term appeared only infrequently, and perhaps not at all before the 1930s.[2] Generally it has been used to denote the successful pursuit of individual aspirations, often while overcoming disadvantage, prejudice, or long odds. The "America" of the dream is the Land of Promise, ranging in form from a tabula rasa to lands of plenty—offering whatever resources are required to suit the individual's circumstances. And the "dream" to be realized is a New Beginning, the opportunity to start fresh, to cast off adversity, to overcome past mistakes, to burn bridges, whether to move up the ladder or literally to build a new life. The dream promises that intensive, independent efforts to improve one's "lot in life" will be rewarded.

The roots of this notion extend back well before Horatio Alger's *Ragged Dick; or, Street Life in New York with the Bootblacks* (1866), but Alger's rags-to-riches stories, almost endlessly multiplied over thirty years in more than a hundred books that sold an estimated twenty million copies, crystallized that theme for a broad popular market. In a similar vein Russell Conwell, the founder of Temple University, delivered his lecture "Acres of Diamonds" on more than six thousand occasions between the 1870s and his death in 1925. Here he too preached the rewards of self-directed industriousness and perseverance, assuring his listeners that the opportunity for success awaited anyone and everyone who had the will to labor and the ability to make savvy decisions. "Be a man," he counseled, "be independent, and then shall the laboring man find the road ever open from poverty to wealth."[3] And for Americans from the Depression era well into the 1960s, Dale Carnegie's self-help evangelism continued the expectation that advancement necessarily awaited anyone who honed a few necessary skills and had the will to pursue success. Carnegie's *How to Win Friends and Influence People* (1936) enjoyed immediate popularity, and his success continued through the postwar period, culminating in *How to Stop Worrying and Start Living* (1948).

In addition to the expectation that hard work will be rewarded, another principal feature of the American dream has long been the belief that it is available to one and all. The roots of these expectations are traceable at least as far back as an 1861 statement by Abraham Lincoln in which he first made the promise of advancement: "there is not of necessity any such thing as the free hired laborer being fixed to that condition for life."[4] Lincoln's position in favor of universal opportunity was explicitly cast as the dream itself in a 1947 *Business Week* editorial campaign on behalf of lower taxes, which touted "the American dream as phrased by Abraham Lincoln." In Lincoln's words, according to the magazine, America was a "just and generous and prosperous system, which opens the way to all, gives hope to all, and consequent energy and progress and improvement of condition to all."[5]

From Lincoln to *Business Week* and beyond, the core of the dream always has focused on private aspirations for personal, individual advancement. Each American is correspondingly entitled to an individual, particularized version of the dream.[6] As a recent essay titled "American Dreaming" in the *New York Times Magazine* explained it, in America one has the opportunity to be "pretty much whoever you want to be." Eighty-five percent of all Americans "bear a faith in their unlimited opportunity."

They "feel they have no limits," and so even a century after Frederick Jackson Turner announced that the frontier was officially closed, "the frontier remains untapped and open for homesteading."[7]

Perhaps the most forceful expression of the dream as a thoroughly individualist enterprise appeared in a 1955 essay on "The American Dream" by William Faulkner, written as part of a larger condemnation of McCarthyite campaigns against "subversion" and communism. Casting America as a nation of, by, and for individuals, he framed its history in terms of "a new dream" that proclaimed, "There is room for you here from about the earth, for all ye individually homeless, individually oppressed, individually unindividualized." This vision, "designed to be co-eval with the birth of America itself," had unbridled individualism as its goal: to "establish a new land where man can assume that every individual man—not the mass of men but individual men—has inalienable right to individual dignity and freedom within a fabric of individual courage and honorable work and mutual responsibility."

For Faulkner, the American dream was not simply the apotheosis of economic individualism in the vein of Adam Smith and classical capitalism. It also had an explicit sociopolitical dimension, standing both as a polar antithesis to aristocracies and other old-world hierarchical orders, and, simultaneously, as an antithesis to the "will-less and docile mass" within which individuals became submerged under other sorts of oppressive regimes. Against such past and present perils, Faulkner laid out the goals of the dream in explicit terms:

> This was the American Dream: a sanctuary on the earth for individual man: a condition in which he could be free not only of the old established and closed-corporation hierarchies of arbitrary power which had oppressed him as a mass, but free of that mass into which the hierarchies of church and state had compressed and held him individually enthralled and individually impotent.[8]

Faulkner's moral and political concerns notwithstanding, Americans have far more commonly preferred to fashion the dream in terms of personal achievement and amassing wealth. The same sorts of aspirations and desires that captured the imaginations of those who read Horatio Alger, Russell Conwell, and Dale Carnegie during the first half of the twentieth century remain canonical elements of the dream at the beginning of the next. Two examples can stand for the many instances in which desires for self-advancement and riches permeate present-day culture under the banner of the American dream. One, a book titled *The American Dreams Collection,* is advertised on its Web site as "A message of hope to dreamers everywhere that it is still possible to overcome adversity and make it big in the good old U.S.A. . . . The possibilities are endless. Stories of overcoming-the-odds and rags-to-riches are accomplished everyday. We all have within us the hidden potential to build our own special dreams." Inside are profiles on historical figures such as Benjamin Franklin and Thomas Edison, as well as a "50-page goal setting section" on "Building your dreams, one-step-at-a-time."[9] The second example is a 1999 Roper Starch nationwide "American Dream survey" commissioned by Hearst Magazines that touches on the same basic features of the American dream. Without specifying exactly what the "American Dream" is, the survey found that "10% more Americans believe the American Dream is easier to obtain today than did in 1993." It also found that the top choice for "the best thing about America today" was that "people can live their lives the way they want to." However, the chief focus of the survey was money, suggesting that amassing wealth remained a key element of the dream. The survey asked, for example, how much money was necessary to be considered "rich" ($155,000 annual income), as well as whether Americans would give up some income in favor of more leisure time (only 38 percent would), and whether "a lot of money" was "one of the top ten ingredients in the good life" (63 percent agreed).[10]

But despite the currency of the term, and its continuing incorporation of individual advancement and wealth accumulation as central components, its loose definition has left it open to appropriation in other contexts. Over the past forty years hundreds of nonfiction monographs have used "American Dream" in their titles, but only a minority of them pertain to dreams of the Horatio Alger type. In addition to the expected stories of personal success on the part of entrepreneurs, immigrants, and minority individuals, the term has been appropriated as well in sociological and policy studies of economic progress and consumerism. Here the "dream" has become a metaphor for the bountiful growth of the American economy. Equally there are studies of American national history in which the "dream" is represented as the rise of nationhood and the arrival of the American political process at its present state.

By now the popularity of the term may have begun to limit its utility, as its definitional range has been stretched well beyond the limits of consistency. As Aprile Gallant has shown, the various senses in which the term *American dream* is now used already embrace a host of conflicting ideas. These include such opposites as "individualism and belonging, freedom and social responsibility, reality and aspiration,"[11] and the list could be extended much further. Thus any given number of people may be pursuing as many individual, and not necessarily consistent, dreams at any given time—a point with interesting consequences for the future of American housing in particular and suburbia in general.

Still, discussions of the "dream" in relation to dwellings and suburbia over the past century commonly do incorporate three themes that, singly or together, underlie the visions and aspirations that animate the dream. The first of these dream themes is *escape,* especially from the pressure, congestion, and corruption of urban life. Alternatively, the slow pace, open space, and bucolic splendor of suburban or country life may exercise an attractive pull. The second is the pursuit of elevated *status* or social advancement. And the last dream theme is the desire for personal achievement or *fulfillment,* sometimes cast in the form of self-realization or asserting one's individuality. While these themes do not actually define the dream with any precision or depth, they have become crucial to the evolution of twentieth-century American dwellings, suburbia, and the terms in which they are lived in and understood, a story that will be detailed in the sections that follow.

Suburban Ambitions

Well before the "American Dream" became elevated to the status of a national paradigm for the pursuit of individual aspirations, suburbia already was the terrain of choice for such pursuits. By the 1920s many had found it to be especially fertile ground for easy and rapid elevation of one's social status. As Christine Frederick wrote in 1928, "the suburb is the social climber's imagined paradise." Unfortunately, at least in Frederick's eyes, suburbia was not up to the task. "The suburban house," she wrote, is "so pathetic in its pretense of an individualism which doesn't exist. The little gingerbread attempts to achieve difference are so palpably hollow and unsuccessful."[12] But in foregrounding the "pathetic" inability of modest, look-alike dwellings that she saw invading the suburbs of her day, decrying their effacement of "individualism" and "individuality," she also pinpointed a central consideration in the minds of many people living in suburbia then and ever since: that suburbia in general was a place well suited, and perhaps even best suited, to the articulation of the individual self. At the same time, Frederick also adumbrated what has become one of the most commonplace critiques of suburbia, that the unimaginative and endless replication of any single pattern forecloses the possibility of achieving the individual distinction that so many seek.

Regardless of Frederick's worries, the climbers who moved to suburbs to pursue dreams of social elevation still depended on certain notions of suburbia that dated to medieval times. When recognized as a terrain beyond the bounds of urban convention and control, that is, sub-urbia, it became a site open to the circumvention of limits on status and self-advancement. As Vance Packard wrote three decades later, for those 1950s "status seekers" whose "dream" was to attain "superior rank," suburbia was still the place to achieve their goals.[13]

Also looking back on the 1920s, Frederick Lewis Allen assessed the increasing popularity of suburbia during this period in terms of twin desires that people had for moving there: to escape the social constraints of urban society, and to have the corresponding freedom to indulge their personal ambition. On the one hand, suburbanites wanted "to get away, by night, from the ugliness of the commercial world that supported them by day." On the other hand, they hoped "to recapture gracious ways of living that they associated with English country houses, or European estates, or the mansions of an earlier, supposedly unspoiled America"—all too evident, Allen might have continued, in the overwhelming popularity of Tudor and Colonial styles for suburban houses during this period. For the builder of a suburban house, Allen asked, "wasn't it part of his dream that he was founding an estate that would go down from generation to generation . . . ?"[14] This dream, and the quasi-Tudor house that anchored it, readily prefigured the vision of Cary Grant, pipe firmly set and shotgun at the ready, hunting dog at his side, in front of a half-timbered facade in *Mr. Blandings Builds His Dream House,* a film released in 1948 (based on the 1946 novel by Eric Hodgins) and likely well known to Allen (Figure 6.1). But as Mr. Blandings eventually realized, the terrain outside the city was neither a political nor a social tabula rasa, urban ills had their counterparts in country inconveniences, his efforts to pose as lord of the manor only made him look and feel foolish, and the costs of his efforts at social advancement far exceeded the rewards.

As the pace of suburban expansion accelerated once again in the 1950s, reasons that people moved there became much more varied, but they also tended to share an increasingly common denominator: escape. Reported in *Look* in 1967, reasons that "the typical executive" and his family moved to the suburbs included a litany of societal tensions and intrusions, the family's reaction to which could be summed up in two words: "to escape—to escape minority groups, escape taxes, escape the mental and moral restraints of the city."[15] From the viewpoint of the newly arrived suburban householder such a move may well have made considerable sense, both with respect to the alleviation of unwanted pressures, and with respect to the new horizons that

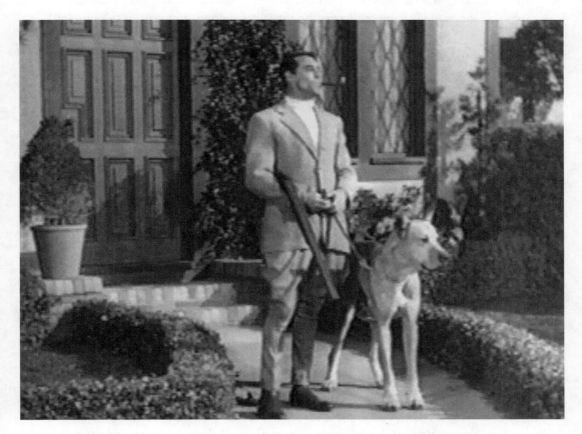

Figure 6.1. *Mr. Blandings Builds His Dream House,* RKO Radio Pictures Inc., 1948. Mr. Blandings imagined the aristocratic prestige that his half-timbered suburban house ostensibly would confer.

suburbia afforded for staking out and pursuing the American dream. But the various motives for escape detailed by *Look* also amounted to multiple abdications of personal obligation to, and engagement with, the body social. And such became the grounds on which generations of critics began to condemn suburbia as a desert of empty individualism, perilous for both the people who lived there and the larger social fabric.

As early as 1954, critic William J. Newman already had indicted suburbia as "the perfect setting for escape." He recognized that from the perspective of the individual, the American suburb promised to be the ideal apparatus for "the institutionalization of mobility." This was the mobility that on the one hand facilitated social advancement. But as Newman preferred to note, this mobility also afforded complete physical and social disconnectedness of the individual from the community. "Nowhere else but in the suburb can middle-class man achieve so perfectly the isolation he seeks from the rest of mankind—the isolation necessary to mobility. In the desert of the suburb, community life has lost whatever vestiges of meaning it ever had for Americans. . . ."[16]

Desert or no, detailed research by Newman's late-1950s contemporaries David Riesman, William H. Whyte Jr., and C. Wright Mills suggested that residents of suburbia increasingly were challenged by the contradictions inherent in the simultaneous pursuit of social ambition and escape.[17] The common finding was that suburbanites all too often achieved neither. The detached, landscaped, single-family house in one respect implied the apotheosis of individualism, but compared to its identical neighbors throughout the subdivision, it bespoke homogeneity and conformity. And as Newman, Whyte, and others pointed out, achievements of any sort were ultimately tied to the very same real world from which suburbia was the ostensible escape, thus implying no escape at all. Worse, the bureaucratic, hierarchical structure of the corporate workplace to which so many middle-class suburbanites commuted all too often undermined, even punished, independence and individualism.[18]

Such were the dilemmas explored in Sloan Wilson's timely novel *The Man in the Gray Flannel Suit* (1955; film version released 1956). One of the central tensions in the novel is the growing realization by Tom Rath, the suburban-commuter advertising executive, that he is uncomfortably situated between two very distinct variants of the dream. On the one hand there is the older dream of entrepreneurial success, here couched in terms of opportunities for Tom to rise to the top of the corporate hierarchy at the United Broadcasting Company. On the other hand there is the notion that a fine house and family in a suburb are not simply trappings of the entrepreneurial dream but rather a distinct goal in themselves—and quite possibly at odds with the conditions of career advancement.

As Tom advances in the corporate world, and as he and his wife, Betsy, move from a tract house to a much finer dwelling, Betsy remarks that "there seems to be something hanging over us, something that makes it hard to be happy," and Tom agrees. He soon realizes that his dream and hers have diverged. Hers has remained the same as it was before the war, an expectation "that he would get a job which would soon lead to the vice-presidency of J. H. Nottersby, Incorporated," and that "before long they would move into a house something like Mount Vernon." Tom realizes that not only had her dream not come true, but also that his interest in prioritizing family over work—realized by turning down a very advantageous promotion at United Broadcasting Corporation—actually subverted Betsy's dream.

Equally trenchant here is the gendering of the two different dream versions. The ostensibly feminine dream oriented toward home and family is Tom's reason for turning down corporate advancement. Betsy's dream, on the other hand, is cast in masculine terms—her hopes for Tom's elevation in wealth and prestige, toward which she constantly eggs him on. The rub, of course, is that Betsy had abandoned any possibility of advancement on her own terms, pegging all her expectations (in stereotypical 1950s wifely fashion) on her husband's anticipated success. Thus when Tom, weary of the pressures in his own life, tells Betsy, "You've had an easy life" as a homemaker, she—both robbed and insulted—explodes in anger and frustration: "*Go to hell.*"[19]

Suburbia, or more accurately the individual householder in suburbia, had become a site of contestation among spheres that increasingly were inconsistent and incompatible with each other. Far from being the promised land of self-realization and pastoral pleasure, suburbia instead focused and concentrated the conflicting demands and expectations of postwar culture into every household and onto every resident. Tom Rath comes to this realization early in *The Man in the Gray Flannel Suit*. Reflecting on the "four completely unrelated worlds" that he is part of—his personal heritage, the horrors of World War II, his work at United Broadcasting Company and the Schanenhauser Foundation, and his nuclear-family wife and children in suburbia—he despairs that there is no way to connect them. "There must be some way in which the four worlds were related, he thought." But the novel instead makes plain the incompatibility of these contradictory claims and expectations, ultimately leaving Tom to confront his shattered dream: "The trouble hadn't been only that he didn't believe in the dream any more; it was that he didn't even find it interesting or sad in its improbability."[20]

By the 1950s and 1960s, a cohort of social critics, notably including Daniel Bell, Christopher Lasch, and Richard Sennett, echoed Wilson's fictional account in at least one important respect.[21] In their condemnation of those who had bought into the suburban individualist dream, in judging suburbanites' quests for independence and self-fulfillment as nothing more than self-delusions, these critics turned responsibility for the ultimate inefficacy of many a dream back onto the dreamer. This has remained a consistent critical approach to the dream through to the present day. Andres Duany's recent book, for example, which bemoans "the Decline of the American Dream" due to sprawl, verges on an indictment of the dream for its own success.[22]

Critics notwithstanding, the goal of some sort of satisfaction of one's self has remained at the heart of the American suburban dream. Be it a radically upward change in status, or more simply an effort to establish a sense of autonomy by possessing property, such efforts are centered on the individual. Suburbia, as a quintessential terrain of privatized space, is by no coincidence the tailor-made apparatus for many forms of self-realization. As Fred Dewey has put it, suburbia promises "the potential to inhabit and create your own private fiction, individually crafted, physically enhanced, and relentlessly adhered to. . . ."[23] However, it remains an open question whether a "private fiction" can be realized on a scale as small as the private dwelling. In Tom Rath's case, as for many twentieth-century Americans, the demands of family and work, not to mention social expectations, personal aspirations, time, and material resources, comprise a far more difficult complex of elements to resolve in that private fiction.

Often the reaction to such difficulties has been a headlong pursuit of even greater isolation—through distance, barriers, or both—the better to ward off forces that could despoil the dream. Such efforts have been instrumental in the endless advance of suburban sprawl, the rising popularity of gated communities, the fashion for "cocooning," and even the rash of SUV commercials (conspicuously marketed to suburbanites) emphasizing the vehicle's capacity to isolate the driver from the stresses and pressures of the surrounding world, or to serve as an "escape" vehicle altogether.

But to blame suburbia, or suburbanites, for destroying the fabric of American society begs questions as to who are the victims and whether they should be blamed. Escape and individualism, fundamental components of the dream, have long been topoi central to American culture. They were crucial, for example, to the theology of the first Puritan settlers, and to the expansion of the Western frontier, as well as to modern suburban refugees.[24] But if one reward of an individualist dream is a measure of freedom and autonomy, then one consequence—a consequence that just as well could be laid at the feet of John Locke or Adam Smith—is that any failure is a failure of the self, not of more broadly based ideologies and practices. Unfortunately such a critique, widespread as it is, discourages examination of conditions and circumstances that propagate and reinforce the dream, a shortcoming that the next chapter is in part an effort to redress.

The most common exception to the notion that suburbia is a theater of individualist ambitions, albeit an exception that may well prove the rule, is the choice that many make to live in the suburbs "for the children." By the end of the nineteenth century it was already common for people to move there for just this reason, as H. C. Bunner noted satirically in 1896. The "suburbanite," he wrote, often would explain "that he despises suburban life; that he only takes to it for the sake of the children, and that it is merely a temporary expedient in the interests of sanitary science."[25] Six years later Howard Allen Bridgman pointed approvingly to the child-centered activities of suburban women, implying that this basis on which they came to know each other so well was far better than through the urban-oriented "conventions of society."[26] Similarly in 1907 Francis E. Clark indicated that the number one reason "Why I Chose a Suburban Home" was because of the opportunities, unavailable in the city, that the children would have for coasting, skating, canoeing, swimming, floriculture, and raising pets, rabbits, ducks, turkeys, horses, and other animals.[27] By 1928 Ethel Longworth Swift proudly noted in her "Defense of Suburbia" that she and her husband "moved to a suburb . . . because we believed that our small children would find there a more normal, healthy environment than the city was providing."[28] The same year in "Is Suburban Living a Delusion?" Christine Frederick even cited cases of couples who moved to the suburbs "for the children's sake" but who ultimately never had children.[29]

Following World War II, suburbia became a terrain increasingly dedicated to the raising and welfare of children. Phyllis McGinley wrote in 1949 that her metropolitan New York suburb "seems designed by providence and town planning for the happiness of children."[30] Harry Henderson, commenting on Levittown, Park Forest, and other large-scale postwar developments, wrote in 1953: "Children love living in these towns, the first large communities in America which have literally been built for them; everything from architecture to traffic control takes into consideration their safety, their health, and the easing of their parents' worries."[31] That same year the editors of *Fortune* found the entire culture of suburbia centered on children: "middle-class Suburbia . . . has centered its customs and conventions on the needs of children and geared its buying habits to them." In "the newer Suburbia," not only do "children set much of the pattern of life," but "their wants are the family's wants, and even their friendships are the family's friendships." Noting a higher propensity to have second and third babies among suburban families than elsewhere in metropolitan areas, *Fortune* suggested that suburbia itself may have been partly responsible for the Baby Boom: "Suburbia, in short, seems to have been an important factor in today's high birth rate."[32]

By 1956 the move to suburbia was seen as the ultimate act of deferred gratification. According to the study of one new suburb by John R. Seeley, R. Alexander Sim, and Elizabeth W. Loosley, "The peculiar twist of the American dream is that the pursuit of the goal is not for oneself alone but for one's children."[33] By extension, this statement also suggested that the suburban focus on children may well be a highly individualist pursuit, that raising children may be a dimension of individuation and self-realization that suburbia facilitates best. Still, different individuals necessarily articulate different dreams, and as the *Chicago Tribune* observed in 1957, the apparatus that suits one type of dream, no matter how popular, may be inimical to another. In a marketing assessment of Park Forest, a newly established suburb south of Chicago, the *Tribune* found a thoroughly "child-dominated community," its families so "intensely child-centered" that "the mother who cannot find self-fulfillment in child-centered activities will usually be frustrated."[34] The individualist dream, in other words, can be compromised by an apparatus explicitly laid out to serve the interests of other-minded individuals.

Often the suburban dream has been couched less in terms of children than in terms of family, fashioning the ideal as a domestic unit rather than as an individual's private dream or an individual devoting the dream to the children. Since at least

World War II, that ideal has been the nuclear family, a more discrete and distinct unit than previous generations of suburban houses accommodated. But the compactness of the nuclear family, and its isolation in a detached house, does not establish a unity or even commonality of interests among all the family members. Rather, it has been apparent that until recently suburbia generally has served as a support apparatus for the husband-father and his career. At the same time the wife-mother frequently forwent meaningful employment, remaining home either bored or maybe stultified by day after day of unrelieved parenting. The situation was apparently obvious enough to the Ford Motor Company that it based a 1957 television commercial on the need to purchase a second family car for the housewife. Informing us from the standpoint of her suburban kitchen that her husband "needs the car every day for business," she had no way to go shopping or get together with friends. Her all-too-common experience of the dream house was almost a form of purdah. "When he was gone, I was practically a prisoner in my own home."[35] The happy solution was to become a two-car family.

But outside the world of automobile commercials, the ongoing strength of patriarchy in suburbia did not go unrecognized. Also in 1957, for example, William J. Newman offered a remarkably wide-ranging critique of many patriarchal aspects of suburbia, ultimately suggesting that suburbia had been built deliberately as the apparatus necessary to realize and legitimate the dreams of the *pater familias* alone:

> It is his life, his activity, which creates the suburb and which sets the standards and activities, the goals and functions of suburban existence. . . . [T]he man has created the suburb as an expression of *his* way of thinking. But the man is in, not of, the suburb. He lives there temporarily; it is for him a sort of super-motel. . . . The suburb is only a fraction of his existence. But it is an important fraction, for it is the place where his system of values, his ultimate aims are to be realized. More than any other spot on earth, the suburb is the place where the bourgeois [man] is to make himself what he wants to be, to come to the realization of himself as embodied in his values. Here he will find himself.[36]

Inventing the Dream House: Policy and Popular Culture

For at least half a century the "American Dream" has been associated with one principal vision of its realization, signifying the dream has been achieved: the detached, single-nuclear-family house. That association has never been stronger; perhaps this is most succinctly exemplified by a recent slogan of the Federal National Mortgage Association, "We're in the American Dream Business."[37] In 2001 President George W. Bush made that rhetoric official, stating in a radio address that "homeownership lies at the heart of the American Dream," and urging all Americans "to make the American Dream a reality for more families." His own administration began doing just that through a series of initiatives in 2002, discussed in a white paper, "A Home of Your Own," issued over the president's name in June, and then in the Department of Housing and Urban Development's "Blueprint for the American Dream." The following year the Republican Congress became involved, beginning with a proposal for an "American Dream Tax Relief Act" introduced in January 2003, followed by the "American Dream Downpayment Act" introduced in March and signed into law on 16 December 2003.[38] The American dream, in the form of the dream house, is central not only to how we design our physical world and orchestrate our lives but also to public and fiscal policy.

The notion of realizing personal aspirations through dwelling design is, in its broadest sense, probably as old as housing. As seen in earlier chapters, the particularly bourgeois version of these aspirations that we have today—employing the dwelling as an apparatus by which a middle segment of the population can pursue certain social aspirations and maintain a particular family structure—has its origins in eighteenth-century England. Histories of the American "dream" and "dream house" alike often select as a departure point Thomas Jefferson's pastoral-republican vision of America as a nation of gentleman farmers. As that ideal grew increasingly central to nineteenth-century American political discourse, it was exemplified by the detached single-family home. Standing as the moral, economic, and political epitome of self-reliance, the individualized, isolated dwelling, seat of an individual land-based proprietorship, became recognized as instrumental to the moral and political welfare of the nation.

There also is a more romantic dimension to some visions of the dream house, which for many people may hold a correspondingly stronger attraction. Early in the twentieth century Canadian novelist Julia Cruikshank's book *Whirlpool Heights: The Dream-House on the Niagara River* (1915) chronicled the aspirations of a woman and her husband to erect what they called a "Dream House" on a plot of land overlooking the Whirlpool on the Canadian side of the Niagara River. Glad to have abandoned the city, "the stuffy rooms, the dirt and noise of trains and streets," the wife-narrator expresses her intoxication with the Thoreauian existence of living in the woods as they build their house:

> I feel so full of energy. Life is full of delight. I am awakened by the song of birds. The freshness of the air, the cool bath, and the stepping directly out under the blue sky makes me feel it is a joy to be alive. While E. [her husband] shaves I eat breakfast out on the edge of the bank. This is certainly the poetry of living: to fry bacon and make coffee, conscious all the time of the wondrous panorama of wooded banks, green river, and blue sky. We cook, eat, and wash dishes in the open air, in the midst of beauty.

It is this romantic connection with nature that she expects her dream house will sustain. In passages throughout the book she imagines "the ivy and purple and white clematis climbing around the little porch," while the house itself fronts "the most beautiful spot on the place." Here "a clump of sassafras-trees is magnificent, the large leaves have turned a most brilliant scarlet. I have found a sheltered spot right in the midst of them. I hold my breath for fear the beauty will disappear. There must be some great purpose behind all this beauty." An architect has been drawing up plans for the dream house, and "even if the house were commonplace the views from the windows would redeem it." But ultimately the builders' estimates for the house prove too expensive, and with great disappointment she realizes that "the Dream House will always be a dream."[39] Still, we realize that the point of the house, and of the novel, is not to build a dwelling per se but rather to utilize the house as a dream-motif that guides the narrator's two-year Walden-like endeavor to merge the glories of nature with domesticity.

The notion of the "American dream" may not have come into American parlance until the 1930s, but the notion of the "dream house" achieved broad currency a decade or two earlier. In part this was due to a transformation of the term in American popular culture, from its comparatively Thoreauian usage by Cruikshank to a term expressing more immediate emotional and material aspirations. Already in Cruikshank's time the dream house (or cottage) had come to signify a cozy retreat, destined to be a place for two lovers to start a family, often in a splendid natural environment, the perfection of which served to emphasize the intensity of the young couple's love. Such was the case with "The Dream Cottage," a song composed by Rudolf Pickthall in 1916. It describes "a quaint little cottage I found in a dream / Under the Cliff by the sea," which appears to be inaccessible to all who try. The key turns out to be love:

> For if love doesn't let you, you'll never get in,
> For it's Love who has charge of the key.[40]

Nevertheless this was not yet a place to set up housekeeping or consummate their love. Rather, the dream cottage was a metaphor for the elusive nature of love per se.

Two years later, Mary R. St. Clair's poem "My Dream House" came much closer to articulating the particulars of a dwelling. Writing in the first person, the narrator sits by the hearth, building a dream house in the gleaming flicker of the flames:

> To a castle tall
>   Or a marble hall
> My visions ne'er incline
>   For the flames all show
>   That it's long and low;
> It's a bungalow for mine.
>
>   It is spacious quite
>   And it looks just right
>   With its broad verandas twain.
>   Such a "homey" place
>   Must win the race.
>   For it's built so strong and plain.

There's a kitchen neat
    And quite complete
And room where we may dine,
    While the bedrooms four
    (We can add more)
Just make you sleep so fine.

    There's a bath or two,
        And the den would do
    For a library, you know.
        While the living room
        With its flowers in bloom
    Is the heart of the bungalow.

    This is long and wide,
        On the western side
    Is the fireplace—how it gleams
        With a rosy light!
        For the logs burn bright
As I build my house of dreams.[41]

Many aspects of the dream-house genre as it would mature in poetry and music over the next several decades already were foreshadowed here: the repeated emphasis on coziness; the emphasis on family, indicated here by the number of bedrooms and the possibility of more; the give and take between the first-person narrator and the second-person object of her affections ("you sleep," "you know"); and the expectations that "we" will be living together in this dream house someday. In other words the dream house was the consummation of the individual's hopes of fulfillment in marriage and family. Still, as examples below will show, this was hardly an exclusively feminine genre.

By the 1920s, phrases such as "house of dreams" and "dream house" were creeping into the common vocabulary of household decoration, in books like Greta Gray's *House and Home* and Ethel Davis Seal's *House of Simplicity*.[42] But the major impetus to widespread recognition and regard for these notions was a political campaign under the Harding and Coolidge administrations to make the single-family detached house the ideal of every family in America. Undertaken at least as much in response to the specter of bolshevism as in the interests of American capitalist enterprise, one goal of the campaign was to ensure that property ownership would be as widespread as possible among the American population. As Vice President Calvin Coolidge argued in "A Nation of Home-Owners" (1922), capitalism could not prevail without widespread ownership of property. Therefore it was "time to demonstrate more effectively that property is of the people," which he proposed to do—in words subsequently echoed by George W. Bush—by urging "America to become a nation of home-owners."[43]

Instrumental to this process was Herbert Hoover, who as secretary of commerce under Harding and Coolidge took an active role in orchestrating federal government support for several organizations that supported the goal of home ownership, among them the Better Homes of America Movement (which Hoover served as its president), the Architects' Small House Service Bureau, and the Home Modernizing Bureau.[44] Hoover was especially worried about the spread of bolshevism. In his best-selling tract *American Individualism* (1922) the opening line worried that "we have witnessed in this last eight years the spread of revolution over one-third of the world."[45] However, America could inoculate itself against this threat by broadening its citizens' participation in the capitalist economy, quite specifically through home ownership. As Hoover wrote in a foreword to the government-produced manual *How to Own Your Home* (1923), "The present large proportion of families that own their own homes is the foundation of a sound economic and social system and a guarantee that our society will continue to develop rationally as changing conditions demand." With a nod of approval to the expansion of suburbia—"the development of the automobile has given a great impulse to suburban life and an increasing possibility of home ownership"—he set a goal of "maintaining a high percentage of individual home owners" because they "have an interest in the advancement of a social system that permits the individual to store up the fruits of his labor."[46]

Four years later Hoover cast the growth of single-family houses, and specifically those in suburbia, as a national triumph: "The tremendous post-war expansion of suburban areas with detached houses which the development of the automobile has helped to make possible is one of the finest achievements of the present period of increasing national prosperity."[47] Coolidge went Hoover one better, suggesting that single-family home ownership was almost a patriotic duty: "No greater contribution could be made to assure the stability of the Nation, and the advancement of its ideals, than to make it a Nation of home-owning families."[48] By the end of the decade, at least one popular magazine portrayed the home as the preeminent apparatus for inculcating patriotism in the American population: "Give us a nation of homes, with each family loving and beautifying and developing its own, and there will be small need for teaching patriotism."[49]

The Better Homes in America campaign, launched in 1922 by Mrs. William Brown Meloney, editor of the ladies' magazine *The Delineator,* eventually spawned over nine thousand local Better Homes committees in as many cities and towns nationwide, hundreds of which displayed model houses each year throughout the rest of the decade. While much of the campaign's agenda concerned improvements to household efficiency, order, and cleanliness, the widespread popularity of the campaign also served to promote the ideal of home ownership per se. As Hoover observed, inculcation of the values of home ownership could not start early enough: "There can be no sounder guarantee of the progress of our nation than that in every child there should be implanted the ideal of an owned home as the center of happy family life. . . ."[50] And adult visitors' responses to some of the local exhibits expressed a remarkable hunger to be converted. In 1924 an Italian woman, visiting one of the Better Homes with her three children, reportedly remarked on viewing the kitchen: "All while no grease! No smells! We must learn to live like that!" And on parting, she waxed even more effusive: "Here's the place where they learn you how to live! This is what America means!"[51]

With the force of such a national campaign promoting single-family home ownership as a national ideal and a patriotic duty, it could only be expected that it would find expression in popular culture. Already in 1925 a model home sponsored by the Electrical Co-operative League of Denver was advertised on a billboard at the site as "A Dream Bungalow" (Figure 6.2).[52] The notion of a dream *house* was the central motif of the 1926 hit recording "Dream House" by Earle Foxe and Lynn Cowan, a popular standard for decades to come. The first line announced, "I've got a secret to tell you," and the lyrics went on to reveal:

> I have built a Dream House
> Cozy little dream house
> Happiness is there, hiding ev'rywhere.

The building of this "Dream House" clearly anticipated a wedding, and beyond that it entertained the hope of children:

> Preacher man is waiting
> Folks are congregating
> All it needs is your
> YES,

Figure 6.2. Electrical Co-Operative League of Denver, "Dream Bungalow," *Electrical World,* 4 July 1925. An early example of the commercial exploitation of the notion of the "dream house."

I'll do the rest
There's a pretty Blue Room
Cozy Bride and Groom Room
Roses 'round the door,
You will love it more
ev'ry day
. . .
Someday there may be Tea for THREE
In that little Dream House
That I've built for you.[53]

The next year another song incorporated the dream house motif, this time clearly articulated as a place in a lover's imagination where he could further his romance despite the loneliness of his "empty arms":

Last night with empty arms I pressed you,
And with a burning kiss caressed you.
Last night a million tear drops blessed you,
I hope we meet again tonight.
In my little dream house on the hill,
You're as close to me when all is still.[54]

Tom Coakley's rendition of "East of the Sun (and West of the Moon)," which topped the charts at number one in 1935, maintained a similar focus on the dream house as a locus of romantic aspirations, promising a "dream house of love" close to the sun by day and to the moon by night.[55] The popular rhythm and blues singer Jesse Belvin maintained this romantic focus into the mid-1950s. His warm and heartfelt rendition of his own song titled "Dream House" similarly was a tender promise to his loved one that he would build a dream house for them to live in.[56]

Not long after the war the dream house motif also began to be associated with nostalgia for a simpler, more wholesome life. Evoking it in song became a way of escaping from the tensions of modern life to that better place and time. Such was the sense in which Bing Crosby used the "dream house" in "Dear Hearts and Gentle People," a top-ten hit in 1950. Describing the "Dear hearts and gentle people / Who live in my home town," he characterized building a dream house as his way to get back to a place "Where your friendly neighbors smile and say 'Hello'" and "It's a pleasure and a treat to meander down the street."

They read the good book from Fri' till Monday
That's how the weekend goes
I've got a dream house I'll build there one day
With picket fence and ramblin' rose.[57]

But within only a few years the dream house motif shifted dramatically, from being an object of nostalgia to being an object of heartbreak, especially in country music.[58] "Dream House for Sale" by Joe and Rose Lee Maphis, recorded in 1953, recounted a tale of failed love, a broken heart, and an empty house for sale. A different song with the same title, Red Sovine's "Dream House for Sale," was one of the top country hits of 1964. It pulled out all the stops. Cast in the form of an advertisement in the paper, the lyrics portrayed a life of ruined dreams, now encapsulated in the forlorn emptiness of the erstwhile "dream house":

> One dream house for sale
> It's a bargain for nothing down.
> And there's no closing costs for the dreams I lost
> When the girl I loved left town.
> There's five rooms, a bath, on an acre of land
> And a nursery painted pink and blue
> A baby bed and a little white high chair
> And it's all almost brand new.
> There's a sad-eyed old dog and a picket fence
> Around a yard that's full of weeds.
> Why, just one look and it's easy to see
> A little love is all that it needs.
> The only thing wrong with this house of mine
> Is the black cloud that hangs above.
> I guess it's there to keep out the sunshine
> Since mine was a house without love.
> That's just about all there is to tell
> About a boy and his love that failed.
> Four words tell the rest of my story:
> Dream house for sale.[59]

Comparable sentiments prevailed in John Eddie's "Dream House" (1986), where again the dream was over:

> Well I still drive by
> Our little dream house
> With the three step front porch
> And the fenced in lawn
> . . .
> But the dream is gone.[60]

Likewise in Neal Coty's song "My Heart Wasn't in It," issued by country singer Ronna Reeves in 1995, instead of a hoped-for romance in prospect, the dream house marked the failure of love:

There's an empty old house
On top of a hill
Covered with branches and vines
It was a dream house
We saved up to build it
Back when he was mine
. . .
The walls are standing
But the love is gone.[61]

Long absent from genres other than country music, the dream house recently has made a tentative reappearance in folk music. In "Dream House" (jp jones, 2000) the building of the dream house still is undertaken with a loving partner ("my baby") in mind, but here it is also elevated into an act of spiritual, almost mystical, engagement. In this house built "from sacred trees," one can feel "a million years go by"; here "you wake up to life unfolding." Now united and holding hands, "we . . . turned the secrets inside out / when i built my dream house."[62]

Magazine articles and films also were instrumental in developing the motif of the dream house, particularly in envisioning how it might actually look. For an article in the February 1927 issue of *The American Magazine,* Magner White interviewed Frank L. McGuire, a "home-seller extraordinary" in Portland, Oregon. "All women have their 'dream homes,'" McGuire observed, after which he enumerated "six things women look for when buying a house." These included its environment (especially "the type of neighbors"), cleanliness, convenience of arrangement (e.g., proximity of the bathroom to the kitchen), closet space, adaptability of the house to the family's needs and furniture, and value. McGuire offered a distinctly different list of things that men looked for, including proximity to work, quality of construction, maintenance requirements, and "enhancement possibilities," that is, opportunities for "air-castle additions"—prefiguring the very sort of dream fancies that Mr. Blandings indulged in when house hunting in *Mr. Blandings Builds His Dream House.* But perhaps the most telling aspect of the masculine dream that McGuire presented was the desire for "A Retreat (for himself): . . . some nook or corner of the house that will be his—and his alone."[63] Looking back not only to the eighteenth-century ideal of the suburban dwelling as a place of "retirement" but also to the eighteenth-century recognition of the dwelling as an apparatus for differentiation of gender roles, McGuire's comments continued to advance an understanding of dwellings in terms of feminine domestic labor and masculine self-realization.

The film *Modern Times* (1936), starring Charlie Chaplin as a factory worker and Paulette Goddard as a young woman of the streets, offers a detailed image of such a dream house. Halfway through the film there is a daydream sequence in which Chaplin and Goddard are seen to be living together in a small cottage, she as the housewife to whom he returns after his day at work. Pastoral plenty is an integral part of the dwelling: while waiting for dinner, he picks an orange off the tree branch right outside the living room window. As Goddard serves dinner, Chaplin calls the cow, which stops right outside the kitchen door and spontaneously streams milk from its udder into a bowl. Meanwhile he eats grapes from vines that grow right outside the kitchen door (Figure 6.3). Still, the upshot of the movie is not yet the standard "American Dream." For in this case, although Chaplin vows that he will work to achieve this goal, he never makes it. The dream remains an unfulfilled aspiration, not yet every American's opportunity or entitlement.[64]

Selling the Dream in War and Peace

Dreams such as these necessarily remained unfulfilled during the years of World War II, but that did not stop government or private entities from harnessing the power of

Figure 6.3. *Modern Times*, Charles Chaplin Productions, 1936. During a daydream while resting on a curb in a suburban subdivision, Chaplin's character, impoverished and unemployed, imagines himself enjoying the fruits of pastoral plenty inside one of the many houses nearby: he eats ripened grapes from a vine outside the kitchen door, and a cow obligingly strolls up and gives milk directly into a pitcher.

those dreams and reinforcing them for patriotic and commercial ends. In a series of thirteen radio plays developed in 1942 by the U.S. Office of Facts and Figures to marshal public support for American allies, the opening vignette of one play, titled *To the Young,* clarifies what the war is all about from the perspective of a young soldier and his girlfriend:

> BOY: I love *you,* Betty. I guess that's one of the things this war's *about.*
>
> GIRL: About us?
>
> BOY: About *all* young people like us. About love, and gettin' hitched, and havin' a house and some kids, an' breathin' fresh air out in the suburbs like this, an'—well, about livin' an' workin' *decent,* like free people. . . .[65]

A year later General Electric seized upon this association of patriotic duty with marriage and a house in the suburbs, and amplified it in an advertisement titled "It's a Promise!" (Figure 6.4). A soldier and his girlfriend sitting together on a park bench are smiling and gazing intently down at the ground where he has used a stick to sketch a small Cape Cod–style house in the sand. "Jim's going away tomorrow," reads the copy, "and there will be long, lonely days before he comes back." But the young couple are smiling, after all, because "that little home sketched there in the sand is a symbol of hope and courage." It is also "a promise" by General Electric that the "Victory Homes of tomorrow will make up in part at least for all the sacrifices of today"— to be accomplished in no small measure through new consumer appliances, fourteen of which are arrayed across the bottom of the advertisement. These houses would "have *better living built in* . . . electrical living with new comforts, new conveniences, new economies to make every day an adventure in happiness." And just to clinch the point, the next month General Electric ran a similar ad, this time centered around the theme of making "*your* wish come true," featuring an illustration of the realization of that dream: a suburban rambler complete with attached garage, trees, yard, and white picket fence.[66]

As the war thus neared its end manufacturers keenly anticipated the postwar return of a consumer economy, and many realized that concerted efforts to broaden desire for home ownership would be key to the growth of postwar sales.[67] Not only would manufacturers of building materials prosper, but houses designed and equipped to hold an array of new appliances, from dishwashers and disposals to air conditioning and television, would mean rapid expansion of sales for those manufacturers as well. In the 1930s producers of consumer goods and building materials already had begun to promote the design and exhibition of model houses in efforts to increase their sales. In 1935 General Electric sponsored a "House for Modern Living" architectural competition that drew 2,040 entries, then helped build a nationwide series of all-electric "New American Homes" from these plans. Perhaps not to be left behind, Nash-Kelvinator built over a hundred "Kelvin Homes" in twenty-six states and used them quite effectively to leverage increased newspaper coverage of their products.[68]

Figure 6.4. General Electric Corporation advertisement, "It's a Promise!" *Life*, 10 May 1943. Well before war's end, General Electric was already presenting the array of domestic appliances that would be awaiting GIs eager to start their own families—in their own new homes.

Producers of energy and building commodities undertook parallel strategies. In 1936 the Niagara Hudson utility company surveyed its customers regarding the most desirable characteristics of a new home, and then erected a series of "Five Star Homes" in its distribution area, the five stars representing wiring, lighting, hot water, climate control, and up-to-date kitchens. In 1937 several building-materials companies, among them Johns-Manville, Reynolds, Weyerhaeuser, and the Portland Cement Association, sponsored demonstration homes that showcased the advantages of their own products. And in 1939 the gas industry managed to place forty pages of promotional material featuring all-gas homes in the May issue of *American Builder.*

The West Coast Lumbermen's Association apparently did not produce any model homes, choosing instead to echo government political initiatives of the 1920s. Their advertisements promoted the home as America's principal resource against threats both foreign and domestic:

> All agree that the home is the first line of defense against the allied forces of crime and their within-the-law agencies. . . . It is in the American home . . . that we have our real vital defense against foreign isms, subversive movements and revolutionary propaganda. . . . Let's defend America. Let's combat crime. LET'S BUILD HOMES![69]

Not long after the establishment of the Federal Housing Administration (FHA) in 1934, corporate interests soon found ways to piggyback on government campaigns to promote the ideal of private home ownership. In 1935 General Electric sponsored a weekly series of FHA radio programs titled "What Home Means to Me," on which a series of "nationally known" personalities discussed what home meant to them and others. A stated goal of the programs was to "emphasize the true significance of home." By 1940 the FHA officially recognized the confluence of business and government interests in its mission to extend home ownership to as much of the American population as possible. In the words of M. R. Massey, FHA underwriting supervisor, business and government had a joint responsibility to extend home ownership across the spectrum of American incomes: "Home ownership on an extensive scale by persons in all income brackets provides a bulwark for our whole economic structure, and the encouragement of home ownership by persons of low incomes is a direct responsibility of business and government." That year a new FHA advertising campaign specifically targeted "families in the lower-income brackets" with an array of printed materials bearing slogans such as "*Your* family can own a home like this," and featuring vignettes of small detached houses on nicely landscaped suburban plots (Figure 6.5).[70]

By early 1945, with the end of the war in view, manufacturers of building products and appliances took advantage of the opportunity to promote the dream house ideal, usually defined in terms of a detached, suburban, single-nuclear-family house,

Figure 6.5. Federal Housing Administration, promotional card, 1940. This and similar cards illustrated the suburban ideal that the government promoted to those in lower income brackets.

as an expectation to which returning GIs and their families could justifiably look forward after years of separation, privation, and loss (Figure 6.6). Many such advertising campaigns anticipated a retooling of the postwar economy to produce sufficient houses to satisfy this demand and simultaneously necessitate the purchase of countless new products. An advertisement for Kelvinator kitchen appliances, for example, employed the dream house ideal to create a market for its appliances in "your postwar kitchen." The very title of the advertisement, "We'll Live in a Kingdom All Our Own," along with the central image—father, mother, and boy—suggested the dream vision of a properly propertied nuclear family household. The copy for the advertisement, ostensibly in the form of a letter from a woman to her serviceman overseas, imitated the lyrics of a "dream house" song:

When you come home to stay . . .
We'll live in a kingdom all our own . . .
A kingdom just big enough for three . . . with a picket fence for boundary. And I can picture as plain as day, ivy climbing a garden wall and smoke curling up from a tall, white chimney . . . and a fanlight growing over our front door. The door of the house we'll build . . . after the war!

The letter concluded:

It's all a part of our lovely dream . . .
And we'll make it come true when you come home . . . when we live in a kingdom all our own.

And yet, the advertisement promised, "This is no dream." Rather, it was the realization of the nation's destiny, now secured by the war effort: "a strong, vital and growing America—where every man and every woman will have the freedom and the opportunity to make their dreams come true."[71] And those dreams, as encapsulated in vignettes at the bottom of the page, were located in the single-nuclear-family detached house furnished with Kelvinator kitchen appliances.[72]

In the years immediately after the war, the popular media frequently featured the "Dream House" as an object of aspiration, not least as cover art on popular magazines. On one *New Yorker* cover a man holds up blueprints for a house, and together with his wife and daughter, all holding hands, they stare skyward (Figure 6.7). Dreamlike, they see a vision of their house realized in the clouds. On a *Saturday Evening Post* cover the dreams of a young couple take shape in the starry night sky (Figure 6.8). Here outlined in constellation-like patterns are a ranch-style house with its accoutrements, including a pool, two cars, two pets, three children, a stereo, a television, a washer and dryer, a drill press, an air conditioner, a stereo, a television, and an assortment of other appliances.[73]

Figure 6.6. R.O.W. Wood Window Units, "Are You Weaving a Magic Carpet?" *House Beautiful,* October 1945. The castle and magic carpet imagery reinforced the notion that GIs and their wives would now be building their dream houses.

Figure 6.7. *The New Yorker,* 20 July 1946. Husband, wife, and daughter see a vision of their house realized, dreamlike, in the clouds.

Figure 6.8. *The Saturday Evening Post,* 15 August 1959. Dreams of a young couple are projected in the form of nighttime constellations, coalescing in the shape of a ranch house and associated products and appliances.

The 1948 release of *Mr. Blandings Builds His Dream House,* with its recognition that suburban aspirations sometimes entailed unexpected complexities in designing the house and selecting its furnishings, proved the perfect opportunity for corporate cross-marketing campaigns. General Electric mounted the most extensive of these campaigns, actually constructing seventy-seven model "Dream Houses" in cities across the United States. Proclaiming that "General Electric has made your *Dream House* come true!" and exhorting the public to "See the Blandings Dream Kitchen-Laundry," a nationwide advertising campaign featured General Electric's fully "automatic" kitchens, including dishwasher, disposal, range, and refrigerator, as well as other electric features such as air conditioning and television (Figure 6.9).[74] In addition to three divisions of General Electric, as many as twenty-four other manufacturers of household equipment, such as Yale hardware and Rheem hot water heaters, also ran advertising campaigns tied in with *Blandings.* Even Youngstown Kitchens, which as a supplier of products similar to General Electric's probably was blocked from a direct tie-in with the film, still managed to piggyback on all the dream-house buzz with its advertisement, "Your kitchen dream . . . so easy to own."[75]

General Electric also extended its dream-house campaign well beyond the Blandings tie-in. In a 1948 advertisement the company promoted the fully electric houses then being built in Levittown on Long Island as its own version of "dream homes" (Figure 6.10). Featuring photographs of Levittown and prominent quotations on the subject of "dream homes" attributed to William J. Levitt, the advertisement heavily promoted the electric kitchen-laundry as an essential component of such homes. In words ascribed to Levitt, "A dream home is a house the buyer and his family will want to live in a long time—a house that makes living comfortable and easygoing by taking the chores out of running a home. That goes for cottages as well as for mansions."

Into this democratized vision of the dream house, Levitt then plugged the crucial dream-enabling apparatus: "The best way to build a dream house is first to make sure it's designed for better living, *electrically!* Because an electric kitchen-laundry is the one big item that gives the homeowner all the advantages and modern conveniences that can make his home truly livable"[76]—and presumably, by extension, make his dream come true. In many respects Levitt houses themselves became the perfect postwar commodity. As reported in both *Life* and *Time,* by 1950, some Levittowners found themselves buying a new house there every year, "just as they would a new car," "as soon as the new model is on the market."[77]

By the late 1940s, then, a complex of government, media, and corporate interests had forged a dream-house ideal that would, in considerable measure, govern the production of housing and the shape of the American landscape into the next century. Nevertheless for the better part of a decade following the war, the American housing industry proved thoroughly unsuited to the task of accommodating the returning GIs' dreams. As a flurry of books, articles, government reports, and an entire issue of *Fortune* magazine made abundantly clear, the industry was woefully unprepared to

General Electric has made your Dream House come true!

Here's the Dream House Mr. Blandings built. And General Electric has helped to make it your dream of modern electrical living.

There'll be more than 60 General Electric equipped Dream Houses all over the country!

BE SURE to see the one in *your* city. It has every electrical aid for better living—from the all-electric dream kitchen and laundry to the wonderful Automatic Blankets on every bed.

All the remarkable, new General Electric Appli-

ances—plus all G-E wiring, automatic heating and air conditioning, television—everything electrical for today's best living.

This wonderful, General Electric equipped Dream House is near you! Be sure to visit it!

● Just look at this Dream Kitchen! It's complete—automatic—designed for worksaving, stepsaving and timesaving. It has everything you could possibly want in your own Dream Kitchen—from automatic "Speed Cooking" to the remarkable, new Automatic Washer.

Decorated by House & Garden

THE DREAM HOUSE has come to life right out of the delightful, new R.K.O. picture, "Mr. Blandings Builds His Dream House," co-starring Cary Grant, Myrna Loy, and Melvyn Douglas—a Selznick release.

When you see the Dream House Mr. Blandings builds, you'll have to visit the *real* house right in your own city.

Dream House will be on display in every one of the following cities. See your local papers for locations and opening dates.

General Electric will plan your Dream Kitchen—FREE!

After you've visited the Blandings's Dream House, you'll want to plan a modern General Electric Dream Kitchen of your own.

The General Electric Home Bureau will draw up your kitchen and laundry plans for you—just as *you* want them—exactly suited to your needs and your space. You can get complete plans and a beautiful color picture—*free!*

See your local General Electric retailer

He'll make all arrangements. General Electric Company, Home Bureau, Bridgeport 2, Connecticut.

PHOENIX, ARIZ.	SOUTH BEND, IND.	ALBUQUERQUE, N. MEX.	PHILADELPHIA, PA.
LITTLE ROCK, ARK.	TERRE HAUTE, IND.	ALBANY, N. Y.	PITTSBURGH, PA.
BAKERSFIELD, CAL.	DES MOINES, IA.	BUFFALO, N. Y.	PROVIDENCE, R. I.
FRESNO, CAL.	LOUISVILLE, KY.	ROCHESTER, N. Y.	CHATTANOOGA, TENN.
OAKLAND, CAL.	BALTIMORE, MD.	SYRACUSE, N. Y.	KNOXVILLE, TENN.
SACRAMENTO, CAL.	BOSTON, MASS.	TARRYTOWN, N. Y.	MEMPHIS, TENN.
SAN DIEGO, CAL.	SPRINGFIELD, MASS.	UTICA, N. Y.	NASHVILLE, TENN.
SAN FRANCISCO, CAL.	WORCESTER, MASS.	GREENSBORO, N. C.	AMARILLO, TEX.
DENVER, COLO.	DETROIT, MICH.	ROCKY MOUNT, N. C.	AUSTIN, TEX.
BRIDGEPORT, CONN.	GRAND RAPIDS, MICH.	CLEVELAND, O.	DALLAS, TEX.
HARTFORD, CONN.	ST. PAUL, MINN.	COLUMBUS, O.	FORT WORTH, TEX.
WASHINGTON, D. C.	KANSAS CITY, MO.	TOLEDO, O.	HOUSTON, TEX.
ATLANTA, GA.	ST. LOUIS, MO.	OKLAHOMA CITY, OKLA.	SALT LAKE CITY, UT.
CHICAGO, ILL.	OMAHA, NEBR.	TULSA, OKLA.	SEATTLE, WASH.
INDIANAPOLIS, IND.	TENAFLY, N. J.	PORTLAND, ORE.	SPOKANE, WASH.

GENERAL *GE* **ELECTRIC**

Figure 6.9. "General Electric has made your *Dream House* come true!" *Life*, 28 June 1948. This advertisement was part of General Electric's cross-marketing campaign with the film *Mr. Blandings Builds His Dream House,* involving seventy-seven model "Dream Houses" built in cities across the United States.

Take it from
LEVITT and Sons......

Here comes Levittown!

"Six thousand new dream homes going up in Long Island in one of the most ambitious home-building projects on record. And every one of them will be designed for better living, with G-E Appliances," says William J. Levitt, president of Levitt and Sons. Read this famous builder's comments on how electrical planning makes homes more livable—*and salable!*

"People want dream homes"

"It pays to build them," says William J. Levitt, president of the Company.

Let Mr. Levitt tell the whole story—"What do they mean by *dream* homes? Well, here is what we have discovered.

"A dream home is a house the buyer and his family will want to live in a long time—a house that makes living comfortable and easygoing by taking the chores out of running a home. That goes for cottages as well as for mansions.

"And here's one more thing that's been proved in our experience—profitably!

"The best way to build a dream house is first to make sure it's designed for better living, *electrically!* Because an electric kitchen-laundry is the one big item that gives the homeowner all the advantages and modern conveniences that can make his home truly livable.

"That's the best way to make the house salable, too!

"Make all these electrical conveniences a part of the package, included in the price.

"And it will sell *faster!* Especially when you've included

Figure 6.10. General Electric advertisement bearing the endorsement of William J. Levitt, *The Architectural Forum*, June 1948. Levitt simultaneously used the advertisement to pronounce himself the quintessential marketer of dream homes.

G-E APPLIANCES make homes more livable—and salable!

General Electric Appliances—the ones most women want most because they've proved plenty dependable."

What About Small Builders?

Whether you're building ten houses or a hundred and more, you stand to sell quicker for more profit when you include G-E conveniences.

Home builders everywhere have discovered G-E Appliances make more satisfied homeowners. They're not only dependable, efficient, but even more—economical. General Electric Appliances bring enough savings through low maintenance and running costs to actually make up for the small additional monthly payment—usually less than $2.50.

Facts like that make for a lot less talking and a lot more conviction when you're selling a prospect. So—

for your next project—plan *electrically* with General Electric and *profit more!*

Learn the G-E Home Bureau Story

Contact your G-E distributor today. Or just drop a post card to the General Electric Company, Appliance and Merchandise Department, Bridgeport 2, Conn. Let us show you how to plan homes for better living, faster selling and bigger profits, *electrically*.

(Editor's Note): *In a recent nationwide survey, 51 per cent of the men and 53 per cent of the women said General Electric makes the best electrical appliances!*

The appliances most women want most

GENERAL ⊕ ELECTRIC

adopt modern methods of prefabrication and mass production.[78] Notable exceptions such as Levittown served in many respects to prove the rule—that in pursuing their aspirations for ownership, autonomy, individuality, and the nuclear family, Americans would have to be patient, be satisfied with partial measures, or both.

But the comparative shortage of readymade "dream houses" nevertheless opened another dimension of opportunity. For those whose dreams were as yet only partially realized, who perhaps lived in less than ideal dwellings, the postwar expansion of leisure time and the proliferation of new, more inexpensive power tools facilitated the pursuit of individual aspirations through one's own sweat equity. Here the long-standing "self-help" component of the American dream (from Horatio Alger to Dale Carnegie and beyond) moved from the business world to the suburbs in the form of do-it-yourself home building and home improvement. *Time's* cover story for August 2, 1954, titled "Do-It-Yourself: The New Billion-Dollar Hobby," made it clear that no matter how standardized one's suburban house may have been to begin with, personalization and customization through expansion, renovation, and remodeling were now sweeping the country.[79]

Practicing architects, on the other hand, pursued a different sort of opportunity at the end of the war. Disdaining the standardization increasingly common in suburban house building since the 1920s, they targeted the upper end of the growing middle class by offering an array of customizable designs. George Nelson and Henry Wright, for example, issued a book just prior to the war's formal conclusion that foregrounded the "American 'Dream House'" as an instrument for articulation of middle-class individuality. In *Tomorrow's House: How to Plan Your Post-War Home,* they began by roundly condemning the reigning version of the dream house. "So standardized that we can even describe it," they complained, the dream house was nothing more than "a quaint little white cottage," with a "steep gabled roof, covered with rough, charmingly weathered shingles," "tiny dormers," "a picket fence," and other features clearly characteristic of the Cape Cod cottage.

Such a design was unsuitable for a "dream house" in at least two respects. First, as one might expect from architects advancing modernist designs, they argued that to embrace a historical type such as this was to be grossly and dishonestly out of step with the times. It was, after all, "a kind of house that was developed before we finished fighting the Indians." Their second, and more trenchant, concern was over the abdication of individuality that the Cape Cod prototype—or, for that matter, any prototype—implied. A "dream house" based on such a model is appealing, they argued, "because to the person who has lost his capacity for independent thinking and feeling it represents authority, expert opinion, tradition, and cultural solidarity with his fellows." In other words, such a house "is a perfect mirror of a society most of whose members are desperately afraid of acting like independent individuals." For Nelson and Wright, then, the crucial fulcrum of domestic design needed to be the *individuality* of the person(s) for whom it would be designed: "Individuality in houses, as in people, is a fundamental expression of something real. . . . Individuality is possible only in a modern house because no other approach to building expresses life as it is today. And without expression there can be no individuality."[80] Even the very repetition of *individuality* so many times here bespoke the understood importance of making the house an instrument of individuation.

The public evidently was little persuaded by modernist offerings such as those presented by Nelson and Wright, and some critics used this dissatisfaction as grounds on which to attack the "dream" theme in general. What mattered instead was practicality. As a catalog for a Museum of Modern Art exhibition on "Tomorrow's Small House" proclaimed, "Dream Houses may be perched on clouds and rocked in nothingness, but the quality and value of a real house is largely determined by the obtrusive reality of site and surroundings."[81] Others, unlike the MoMA curators, found ways to popularize the dream ideology. Hubbard Cobb, for example, clearly read his market well. His book *Your Dream Home: How to Build It for Less than $3500*, published first in 1950 and then reissued in 1954 and 1955, proffered designs that hewed closely to Cape Cod and Colonial prototypes. Trading on the popularity of the term *dream home,* Cobb featured it prominently in his title, even though inside the book the term barely appears at all, as if it needed no explanation. But in fact the nature of the dream actually had shifted: Cobb's commitment to architectural individuation was much reduced from what Nelson and Wright had so enthusiastically embraced. On the one hand, Cobb still seemed to be appealing to individualistic tastes by providing "Tudor," "Cotswold," "Ranch," and other stylistic variations. But on the other hand, he also counseled his readers to build whatever type they might select only on a site where similar houses were adjacent. At very least, he said, this would serve to maintain property values.[82] Such advice, which could be read as stressing the importance of conformity, was hardly new in the history of architecture, or even the history of suburbia. Still, Cobb anticipated one of the most trenchant problematics surrounding the American dream house for the rest of the century, its equivocal role as a sometime instrument of individuation, and a sometime instrument of conformity.

John Keats presented the problem of conformity in near-alarmist terms in his 1956 polemic-cum-novel *The Crack in the Picture Window* (Figure 6.11). Noting that the mass-produced housing currently spreading across suburbia was often manufactured in rows after rows of identical boxes, he warned that they would shape suburbanites into legions of identical conformists. Worse, the standardized plans of such houses would force residents into the worst of stereotyped gender roles: "the familiar box on the slab contributes toward the father's becoming a woman-bossed, inadequate, money-terrified neuter, instead of helping him to accomplish the American dream of the male: rich, handsome, famous, masterful, and the dispenser of even-handed justice."[83]

The debate surrounding mass-produced housing also developed broad political implications. Put in simplest terms, the question was whether the suburban environment that resulted from seemingly endless tracts of houses sprawling across the landscape was an apparatus of liberatory individualism or crushing conformity. More critically, the debate began to question whether the privatist-individualist dream, seemingly so democratic and empowering on the one hand, could survive in a landscape that was necessarily so beholden to mass production, standardization, and corporatization. Indeed the debate was in good measure fueled by America's intense rivalry with the USSR in the 1950s, as many feared that the uniformity of America's spreading tract development foretold a capitulation to the socialist threat from abroad.

In November 1956 *House Beautiful* mounted a suitably political response, directed toward a global audience, in an issue commemorating sixty years of publication. Titled "Report to the World on How Americans Live," this issue was "distributed, in sizable quantities, to all other countries of the world." Many of the articles had a decided cold war flavor, enlisting America's postwar housing expansion as Exhibit A in the global contest of capitalism versus communism. Appropriately enough, *House Beautiful*'s assessment of contemporary domestic architecture pegged it as the realization of the individualist dream. One article, "The Freedom to Be Enterprising," featured an elegantly rehabilitated townhouse as "the story of Mr. & Mrs. Everybody of the U.S.A. . . . the story of Opportunity Unlimited, the story of deciding how and where you want to live and work and then proceeding to do so." Juxtaposed against "before" and "after" images of the house were text blocks proclaiming that "Any direction you take—if you are good—leads you to success and self-fulfillment. That's why Americans are happy." The family who made this house their own was "merely one

THE CRACK IN THE

by JOHN KEATS
illustrated by DON KINDLER
Houghton Mifflin Company, Boston
The Riverside Press, Cambridge

PICTURE WINDOW

Figure 6.11. John Keats, title page spread of *The Crack in the Picture Window* (Boston: Houghton Mifflin Company, 1956), illustration by Don Kindler. Keats's text, amplified by Kindler's illustrations, suggested that variety and individuality were all too rapidly being replaced by bland uniformity in postwar tract-house suburbia.

more example in the long series of Horatio Alger stories that '*anybody* can make good.'"[84] The quintessential realization of the American dream, in other words, was a *House Beautiful* house, and it was a dream that anybody could realize. In the words of another article in the same issue, showcasing a house built by an immigrant couple in a Miami subdivision, "no man need be common, no life ordinary."[85] The implication here was clear: the instrument for truly distinguishing one's life was the dwelling.

Also in the November 1956 issue *House Beautiful*'s editorial director, Joseph A. Barry, contributed an article titled "America—Body and Soul" in which the dwelling assumed a central role in fashioning the spiritual life of its residents:

> The new American search for the spiritual is even greater than the increasing numbers of people newly going to church and to synagogue indicate. As God's first temples were said to have been the trees, so today His first temples might be said to be man's home among the trees—on his own plot of land, independent, individual and in harmony with the restoring rhythms of nature.
>
> That is the inner content of these homes. That is the meaning of this statistic: Today 60 per cent of our families own their homes.

Hearkening back to the time of "God's first temples," Barry not only bestowed a biblical imprimatur on the detached single-family home sitting on its private, well-landscaped plot but also in near-missionary fashion encouraged multiplication and replication of that type throughout American suburbia:

> To own one's home! Has this not been part of the democratic dream? . . . To have a good life while knowing the same good life is being enjoyed by most of the people around you. Here is a moral basis for civilization that has never before existed on so grand a scale.[86]

Thus the notion of the private dwelling as the instrument of choice for fulfilling the individual American dream had become thoroughly established by the mid-1950s. As that paradigm persisted through the next decade, dream-house design focused anew on considerations of privacy. A 1966 article in the *American Builder,* for example, listed privacy among the prominent characteristics of the American dream house. Instead of "being something to escape from," the house became a center of increasingly privatized leisure and social activities. With the addition of such features as patios, decks, pools, and barbecues, all appropriately fenced from view, occupants of the featured type of "dream house" could enjoy their "entitle[ment] to life, liberty and the pursuit of happiness *in the privacy of their own yards.*"[87]

In other respects Americans also chose more home-centered lives. Herbert Gans's 1967 study of the New Jersey Levittown detailed some of the "aspirations" (synonymous with dreams) that people brought to their new homes. Four out of the top five were specifically tied to the house itself: desires for more room and comfort, for more privacy and freedom of action (compared to the limitations of an apartment), for the opportunity to work around the house and yard, and for the chance to fulfill traditional family roles as homemaker, provider, and parent. Only one of the top five aspirations concerned activities outside the home (developing a social life and making new friends), and even those were limited to the immediate neighborhood; Gans reported that very few people were interested in "activities in the wider community."[88] In other words, the dwelling itself was the principal focus of the aspirations that motivated these new residents.

Beginning in 1973 as the American economy entered a two-decade period of decline, real incomes and home ownership rates for the middle class stagnated or, more commonly, fell. By the mid-1990s a spate of publications had begun to mourn the passing of the American dream (Figure 6.12). One report noted that "Reagan came to power largely because he promised to revive the American Dream," but things had only gotten worse: between 1980 and 1988 "home ownership has declined for the first time since 1940."[89] Or as a 1993 essay on the American dream put it, for three decades following World War II, "the American Dream of moving to the suburbs, buying a house, and even sending the kids to school was no mere election slogan." Yet as of 1993, "the ideal that once defined how we lived is gone."[90] With home ownership becoming less and less affordable, employment insecurity, and shrinking leisure time, the dream was transformed into anxiety over just staying in place.

Despite the consensus that the dream-house-in-the-suburbs version of the American dream appeared to be moribund, book and magazine publications of "Dream Houses" and "Dream Homes" actually increased in the 1980s—although, just as concentrations of wealth shifted during that period toward ever higher income groups, some of the dwellings shown often were extravagant designs affordable by only the wealthiest clients.[91] These publications, like others directed at those of much more modest means, touted custom, or customizable, dream houses as premier opportunities for articulation of individuality.[92] Nevertheless many other publications appealed to comparatively capital-poor members of the middle class who sought to advance equivalent ends through do-it-yourself sweat equity.[93]

Some of these trends converged in the mid-1990s as *Life* magazine seized an opportunity to appeal to middle-class aspirations newly reinvigorated by an improving economy. Beginning in 1994 the magazine instituted an annual offering of architect-designed (and therefore prestigious) dream houses, intended to be affordable by the middle class and adaptable to their individual tastes and interests. Robert A. M. Stern's 1994 "House for All America," for example, was "adaptable to individual styles and tastes," while also sustaining the core privatist function of providing "room for retreat." The Michael Graves design for "The 1996 Life Dream House" also was advertised as "Designed to fit your lifestyle," doing so with spaces that were less functionally prescriptive than usual. Instead of narrowly privatized rooms, there were segregated zones, where, for example, children could sprawl on the floor and watch television while adults cooked dinner or simply collapsed into a soft chair. The

Figure 6.12. "Bye-Bye, Suburban Dream," *Newsweek*, 15 May 1995. *Newsweek*'s cover story, replete with a nostalgic image of family life as it supposedly was a generation earlier, was one of many journalistic pieces during the 1990s that mourned the passing of the dream.

emphasis on individuality persisted, however, in the isolability of given zones at their inhabitants' choice. The concluding article in the series, "The 1999 Life Dream House," presented two variations of a design by Sarah Susanka, author of *The Not So Big House*. Susanka emphasized individuality again, focusing on the capacity of the dwelling to sustain intimate feelings and connections in such features as the "away room" and inglenooks throughout the house. In the words of Jean Larson, then an associate of Susanka, "Our houses aren't about gasping 'Ooooh' and 'Ahhh.' They're about a series of small things that engage you. . . . The home in our country is a part of our identity."[94]

Elsewhere in the popular media the dream home is still commonly identified as a site for the personal accumulation of an ever more lavish consumer apparatus. The Sunday newspaper insert *USA Weekend*, for example, has done so in periodic cover stories such as "The New American Dream Home" (1997) and "Dream Home 2000" (1998). Inside, text and pictures focus on the integration of "technology, design, and comfort" in the form of home theater systems, or multiple sets of audio speakers throughout the house that are simultaneously programmable to different music. The "creature comforts" in such a dream house might include "high-tech lines and cables" so that "a cook in the kitchen could plug in the counter-top computer, log onto the Internet, order groceries and get them delivered, all while stirring the soup." Likewise there might be "a system set up in the dining room so a family can videoconference Grandma in and sit down with her for a 'virtual dinner.'" Such comforts, along with other dream-home features such as personal altars and "spiritual centers," suggest a consistent and growing privatization of the dream, a technological and spatial fortification of the home against a world in which public space is perceived as dangerous (or at least challenging). As in the case of the "virtual dinner" with Grandma, the imperative to wire every room "for phone, fax, computer network, high-speed Internet, video, high-definition TV and digital satellite" suggests a growing restriction of social encounters to home media systems, and so a limitation of the "dream" itself to the range of available media equipment and content.[95]

In 2002, a cover story in *Time* made it clear that despite a sagging economy, far from being moribund, the dream house was alive and on steroids: "Volume has replaced coziness, from double-height entryways to oversize garages." Kitchens and great rooms have ballooned in size, now intersect with each other, and connect with outdoor patios: "The idea is to allow family togetherness and personal space at the same time, meaning never having to reach a consensus about what to do together."[96] In other words, Americans may at last have their cake and eat it too—a house that articulates all the right features and opportunities for family togetherness, without apparently taking the idea too seriously, and certainly never at the cost of sacrificing individualism.

In the end, the power of the dream remains at least as much a matter of aspiration as of realization. As John R. Seeley and his associates most adroitly pointed out almost half a century ago, whatever the particulars of the dream, the suburban dwelling generally "does not quite actualize these aspirations; the reality cannot faithfully mirror the dream."[97] And yet those aspirations are seldom diminished or abandoned. Rather, as the dream remains one of the principal reigning paradigms by which American society projects personal success and self-fulfillment, its force continues unabated, and the private dwelling is ever more commonly the site of choice for pursuing that dream.

7. Analyzing the Dream

Anchoring Politics

Americans have replicated the single-nuclear-family dwelling millions of times across the landscape. It has become the archetypal feature of American suburbia. And as seen in the previous chapter, it is the means of choice by which people both pursue, then represent, fulfillment of their own American dream. Still, despite widespread recognition in popular media and academic studies that the dream is embodied in the house—indeed predicated on the house—few have ventured to explore in any depth the ways in which the house is engaged, on an ideological plane, with American notions of the relation between the private self and the sociopolitical self.

In *The Dream Deferred* (1976), Samuel Kaplan offered a rich, if perhaps overstated, enumeration of expectations that the dream house encompassed. "The dream of most Americans," he wrote, is

> an attractively packaged comfortable single-family home set off from its neighbors on a well-landscaped plot in an economically, socially, and racially homogeneous community of good schools and convenient shopping. It is a dream not of a challenging, involved life-style rich in excitement, of the possibility of fantasies come true, but rather of a leisurely life-style, of privacy, health, security, status, and few conflicts. . . . [T]o the majority of Americans it is suburbia that still offers the greatest hope of that dream.[1]

In *Redesigning the American Dream* (1984) Dolores Hayden offered a more succinct account of the aspirations encompassed in the postwar single-family suburban "dream house":

It may mean a chance to surmount one's class and ethnic background. [It] . . . is
an architecture of Americanization in a nation of immigrants, and it implies . . .
a private life without urban problems such as unemployment, poverty, hunger, racial
prejudice, pollution, and violent crime.[2]

Writing in 1997, Marcia Mogelonsky noted an escalation in the expectations
embodied in single-family suburban housing. Prior to 1965, she wrote, the dream
was primarily to own a house. But since then the dream had evolved to encompass
various ways of making the house "stand out," and personalizing it by providing
extended private spaces and equipment for each resident.[3] In other words, the role of
the house was not simply to realize the basic criteria of a common dream but to individualize that dream in a way that distinguished each resident from others.

The dwelling thus has become recognized as one of the premier instruments for satisfying the expectations of selfhood in America. It does so in part by pursuing the notion
of the "American dream"—a term that just by itself bears substantial ideological baggage. For at least half a century, if not twice as long, the word *American* has denoted
the object of the undertaking as something politicized. Entering widespread use in the
period of post–World War II national pride, then shifting into cold war ideological
battles,[4] the notion of an explicitly *American* dream became an exemplification of the
superiority of capitalism and of the American democratic political system. By the late
1990s, the American dream also had been wedded to the vision of America as the redoubt of privatized prosperity, and that alliance continued into the new millennium.

The notion of a "dream" introduces a different rhetorical and ideological dimension. To cast personal aspirations as one's American *dream* implies an ongoing articulation of this nationalistic vision within the most private recesses of the mind. Elements
of a much larger political agenda thus are harnessed to private energies and incorporated into individual visions of self-fulfillment. One's dream world in this respect is
not really sacrosanct; even here the nature and function of the private individual are
very much constructs of the larger political-ideological system. As I discuss in more
detail below, the "American dream" has become a rhetorical formula that defines
how individuals are expected to contribute to that system: the political and economic
prosperity of the nation is advanced by harnessing on a mass scale an individualized
imperative for private self-fulfillment.

To understand this more fully, it is necessary to recognize that embedded in the
notion of the "American dream" there are strands of deep-seated American political
and ideological currents. Several of these strands, which pertain to property, economy,
and the relation between self and society, extend back to early Enlightenment principles of political philosophy. Nor has awareness of these ideological strands ever been
far from the consciousness of those discussing or seeking the American dream. Rather,
the term *American dream* maintains much of its rhetorical power because these
strands are so deeply anchored within.

As the American dream thus articulates ties among consciousness, the individual, and the larger political realm, it also becomes central to the understanding of dwelling in relation to community. Analyses in the previous chapters make it possible to explore three of the dream's core ideological strands further in the context of the history of the single-family bourgeois dwelling and suburbia. With origins traceable to periods from the seventeenth century onwards, these three strands may be identified as possessive individualism, which is the legal notion that property attaches to the self; pastoralism, especially as envisioned in the Arcadian paradigm of suburbia; and social isolation and fragmentation, particularly as realized in the separation of work from home, in the spatial division of gender, in the detached house itself, and in segregation by race, religion, class, and other criteria.[5]

Possessive Individualism

Since the time of John Locke's *Two Treatises of Government* (1690) and *An Essay Concerning Human Understanding* (1690), Anglo-American culture increasingly has been tied to an ideology of possessive individualism—that accumulation, ownership, and privatization of resources are natural and legal rights of private individuals.[6] A crucial element of this political and economic ideology that underpins both democracy in America and capitalism in general is the understanding that private possession of land is fundamental to economic activity, liberty, and political agency. Since these have become three key dimensions of modern identity, it has followed in Western culture and especially in America that owning property, and especially land, has become a necessary basis for articulating selfhood. And the realization of this goal, in turn, is readily cast as a vision, or dream, of the private house as an articulation of the autonomous, politically potent self.

Such was the vision of the single-family dwelling popularized in nineteenth-century architectural treatises by John Claudius Loudon in Britain, and even more so by Andrew Jackson Downing in America. As Downing wrote, a dwelling "ought to be significant of the whole private life of man—his intelligence, his feelings, and his enjoyments. . . . Hence, every thing in architecture that can suggest or be made a symbol of social or domestic virtues, adds to its beauty, and exalts its character." And, perhaps most engaging of all in designing a dwelling, "every material object" associated with a house can become "the type of the spiritual, moral, or intellectual nature of man."[7]

Calvert Vaux, the English architect who later partnered with Downing in the design of New York's Central Park, explicitly connected identity, dwelling, and property together, describing the detached dwelling as the material realization of an "independent spirit" in almost every American. Writing in 1855 in *Harper's New Monthly Magazine*, Vaux marveled at the number of new detached houses "springing up in every direction." He explained that these told a story of economic and political individualism:

> These tell their tale simply and unceremoniously: they are the natural result of the
> migratory, independent spirit pervading the industrious classes in America, and offer

interesting evidences of the genuine prosperity of the country; for they show, not only that the landlord and tenant system is disliked, but that almost every store-keeper and mechanic can contrive, even when quite young, to buy his own lot and live in his own house.[8]

The house, in other words, was an emblem of liberation from both economic and political bondage. It bespoke not only the rise of the "industrious classes" to economic self-sufficiency but also the capacity of private property ownership to liberate them from the implied tyranny of a rentier system.

From the exaltation of the private house to privatization of community space was not a distant prospect. Already in 1856 the community of Llewellyn Park, in West Orange, New Jersey, had gated its entrance, allowing only residents and guests on its private roads. Other private developments such as Tuxedo Park, New York (1886), soon followed the same pattern. Even in urban St. Louis, the first of its many "private places" was established in 1851 as an early mode of zoning, not only to restrict street traffic but also to preclude any uses other than private residences. But as a St. Louis Civic League report of 1907 complained, the privatized streets exhibited "an abundance of individualism and an absence of civic or community spirit."[9] And as the evolution of gated communities ever since has proved beyond doubt, an "abundance of individualism" is precisely the point: the privatized landscape has become the preeminent locale for the articulation of self in American society—or, some would say, *against* those aspects of American society that interfere with the privatist dream.

Nevertheless others in the early twentieth century were eager to outline additional advantages of property and home ownership. As Carol Aronovici, general secretary of the Suburban Planning Association, stated in 1914, the single-family detached house as a vehicle of private idealism could become a common focus of social reform:

> The poet, the moralist, the efficiency expert and the social reformer have made the homes the center of their speculations and the means of realizing their individual and social ideals. We are all agreed that the one family house with private garden and plenty of open space is the condition towards which we should all strive. . . .[10]

In 1921 architect Charles E. White tied property and home ownership much more keenly, and directly, to such personal qualities as status, identity, and character:

> the most responsible men and women of any town . . . are the property owners. The man who does not own his home is looked upon by others as an underling or weakling. He is regarded in the eyes of his neighbors as lacking in initiative, in the eyes of his family he is considered unfortunate, in his own mind he realizes that he has never quite achieved success.[11]

One year later the notion of property as essential to selfhood became a de facto cornerstone of public policy. In an introductory essay to a pamphlet announcing the 1922 Better Homes campaign, Vice President Calvin Coolidge wrote of "that longing which exists in every human breast to be able to say: 'This is mine.'" Yet in America it was more than a longing; it was both an institution and a right—specifically, "the right to acquire, to hold, and transmit property." Still, this would be of little good if it were a right in name only. Rather, Coolidge argued somewhat ominously, unless there were a mechanism by which all members of the society could participate in this right, it might wither away. In other words, "That which is referred to in such critical terms as capitalism cannot prevail unless it is adapted to the general requirements. Unless it be of the people it will cease to have a place under our institutions, even as slavery ceased." The mechanism he touted for preserving individualism, property, and capitalism was, naturally, extending home ownership to an even greater portion of the population: "It is time to demonstrate more effectively that property is of the people," he wrote, through "building, ornamenting, and owning of private homes by the people at large—attractive, worthy, permanent homes."[12]

A decade later, well into the Depression, President Herbert Hoover could not have been more exuberant: "To own one's own home is a physical expression of individualism, of enterprise, of independence, and of the freedom of spirit."[13] And enthusiasm for this notion grew stronger, if anything, in the popular press of the cold war era. The November 1956 issue of *House Beautiful*, titled "Report to the World on How Americans Live," was "distributed, in sizable quantities, to all other countries of the world." Among several articles focusing on the private house, such as "Everybody Can Own a House," was a key article titled "The People's Capitalism," in which the very "conception of property" was presented as "basic to our Republic" not only at its founding but in the present day. Citing the words of James Madison, the author broadened the domain of property well beyond matters of land and real estate to incorporate crucial attributes of every individual:

> A man has property in his opinions and the free communications of them. He has property of peculiar value in religious opinions. He has property very dear to him in the safety and liberty of his person. He has equal property in the free use of his faculties and free choice of the objects on which to employ them.

From the author's point of view, this also warranted a cold war sanctification of private individualism: "It is not the privacy of property (in the Marxian sense) that distinguishes capitalism; it is the property of privacy, which is finally sacred. All else is means to this end. This is the end-in-itself, and the be-all and the end-all of the good life."[14] Or as another author in this issue concluded more succinctly, the suburban house (implicitly tied to property ownership) plus individualism equaled the American dream: in America, "anybody can *do, have, be* anything!"[15]

On the other hand, the individual *without* property could well be considered less than a citizen. As Constance Perin showed in 1977, the attitudes of suburban officials toward renters often construed them as a different class or kind of people from owners, and so by extension rental residences were undesirable lesions in the urban fabric.[16] A common solution to such perceived threats has been the proliferation of common-interest developments (CIDs), planned communities controlled by what amount to private governments and often limited to single-family houses. When condominium, cooperative, or rental units are included, they are generally segregated to a discretely bounded segment of the development. *Privatopia,* Evan McKenzie's study of the explosion of CIDs across America, explores the cultural and legal presumptions underlying such developments. Tellingly, but perhaps not surprisingly, he finds that the understanding of one's freedom, individuality, and autonomy is linked far more closely with ownership of private property than with engagement in the surrounding community. Residents, in consenting to a host of restrictions on what they can do with their dwellings and even their own personal activities, are in effect conceding and subordinating their personal freedoms to a regime of "property rights" that forms the basis of their homeowners' association. In many cases, CIDs represent an elevation of property over any other form of social relation. As Carol Silverman and Stephen Barton have shown in another study, residents generally "will not participate [in the community] or will do so [only] in order to protect their property rights"—that is, their interest in the dwelling as a financial investment as well as an instrument of personal autonomy—but "not out of a recognition of community interdependence."[17]

The ongoing importance of possessive individualism in American culture is demonstrated not only by the elevation of property rights above personal rights in CIDs but also by the continuing efforts of "land rights" advocates to elevate the standing in American jurisprudence of land and other forms of property. Arguing from the presumption that rights attach to land, and that "property rights are central to the biological survival and relative prosperity of many life-forms,"[18] advocates contend that "public" uses are the exception to an otherwise absolute, natural right to devote land to whatever use its private owner may choose. In the process, they lend considerable weight to the proposition that one's personal rights (and opportunities for the pursuit of personal goals) are dependent on possession of land. Proudly arguing in favor of what Marx once condemned, the notion that property has greater rights than individuals, proponents also have raised to a new plane the contentions of Coolidge and Hoover concerning the centrality of property ownership to American culture.

My Private Arcadia

Not only is it writ, at least in tradition, that "A man's home is his castle," but in the nineteenth century that notion of home as private redoubt was expanded to incorporate the surrounding landscape (front, side, and back yards, and sometimes more) as a preserve of leisure and abundance. As nineteenth-century architectural manuals and pattern books also made clear, the very isolation of the detached house in its private grounds was instrumental to the social status and moral welfare of its inhabitants.[19]

In the twentieth century, the ideal of the dwelling as a castlelike domain for defense and preservation of the private self in many respects only strengthened. Certainly this must have been part of the rationale behind the dramatic advertising imagery produced for Shaker Country Estates, adjacent to Shaker Heights, in 1927 (Figure 7.1). Here, as the accompanying copy proclaims, "Six hundred feet up in the sunshine, with trees and gardens, winding roadways and protected homes, Shaker Village is miles away from the city's grime and turmoil, but only minutes away in actual time" via the developer's streetcar line. Each house appears to occupy its own combination of a hilltop and a pillowy cloud floating high above the city, while excerpts of English poetry by Ada Smith—"Sorely throb my feet, a-tramping city pavements (Ah, the springy sod upon an upland moor!)"—complement the English Tudor taste promoted throughout the pamphlet and the Village.[20]

In a manner that may not have been overstated, a 1999 television advertisement for a Chevrolet Blazer portrayed the degree to which castellated fortification of the sanctuary continued to be part of the ideal. The Blazer and its owner reside in a fully castellated fortress, complete with rusticated stone walls and crenellated turrets, furnished inside with suits of armor ready for battle—a battle for which the far superior force of the Blazer itself is ready. Sheltering all, however, there is also the dwelling-fortress, confidently portrayed as an instrument for the protection of the private individual in the face of the dangers and terrors of a hostile world.

The *suburban* has been perceived to have such fortresslike qualities for half a century. In 1957, for example, William J. Newman challenged growing acceptance of the 1950s suburban home as "a sort of fortress where the self can be attained."[21] But while Newman may have been critiquing the early stages of a trend, the redefinition of interior dwelling space as an insular preserve for nurturing the individual clearly had achieved widespread currency by the late 1980s, warranting corporate consultant Faith Popcorn's invention of the term *cocooning* in 1987. Turning the house into an instrument of self-centered indoor isolation, cocooning was, in Popcorn's words, a way of "insulating oneself from the harsh realities of the outside world, and building the perfect environment to reflect one's personal needs and fantasies."[22] Popcorn and a host of media commentators have chronicled the sorts of changes in home furnishings and design that accommodate such desiderata—that make, in effect, an indoor Arcadia. Sofas are designed to comfort and envelop the sitter, carpet is added to make the room softer and quieter, residents buy "personal-care" appliances such as home gymnasiums, Jacuzzis, and facial steamers, and above all they install ever more personal media apparatus such as home theaters and Internet connections. All this is undertaken in considerable measure as a deliberate "retreat from the hostile world."[23]

By the end of the century the desire to privatize the home in an ever more personal manner resulted in further shifts in home design: actual reductions in house size.[24] Designers and clients preferred instead to enhance the serenity of interior spaces, providing places for meditation, wall-sized graphics to emulate tranquil natural vistas

"Sorely throb my feet, a-tramping
city pavements (Ah, the springy
sod upon an upland moor!)"

Figure 7.1. Van Sweringen Company, illustration from advertising pamphlet for *Peaceful Shaker Village*, 1927. The imagery for the company's advertising materials for Shaker Country Estates suggested Tudor castles high in the sunshine above downtown Cleveland.

(an explicit form of indoor Arcadia), and bedroom suites that could be entirely closed off from the rest of the house.[25]

Nor has the desire for an outdoor Arcadia disappeared. It simply has been folded into the insular fortified ideal. On the one hand, yards surrounding most twentieth-century suburban dwellings have shrunk to a fraction of the size illustrated in nineteenth-century treatises. But in many cases the defensive perimeter has radically expanded. In the case of gated communities, for example, the expanse of the entire landscape serves as the fortified domain. In many suburban municipalities zoning and other regulations accomplish much the same end. As the house then becomes each family's private Arcadia-within-an-Arcadia, the outdoor landscape is appropriated as part of the apparatus of self-definition. As Edward J. Blakely and Mary Gail Snyder point out in *Fortress America,* gated communities allow a person to say "I've made it," not only by choosing the elite and exclusive terms in which one's success is recognized,[26] but also by isolating oneself from the worlds of work and commerce, in a pastoral preserve free from want. Nor are such ideals limited to gated communities. As Richard Briffault has demonstrated at considerable length, the central principle of suburban municipal government today is "to protect the home and family . . . , servicing home and family needs and insulating home and family from undesirable changes in the surrounding area."[27]

The crucial feature that distinguishes such present-day Arcadian moments, evoked through means ranging from landscaping and property restrictions (planned communities) to furniture design and media equipment ("cocooning"), is the romanticized isolation of the individual (or nuclear family unit) in a manufactured Arcadian preserve. The narcissistic aspect of this ever more inward-turning privatism has been well articulated in Fred Dewey's assessment of the American dream:

> Narcissism becomes this zeitgeist's signature, not because of new-age psychologies that stretch to the horizon like desert scrub, but because the public realm, that space of plurality and enduring interaction with the truly different, has been wiped out. Private space is regarded as the only place where anything can endure, the only thing that can secure possibility. It is the only place where the dream is safe. . . . The dream has become one of a frictionless refuge where contest and conflict cannot arise.[28]

Fragmentation and Isolation

Present-day American culture is more and more a terrain of fragmentation. Postmodernist critics discuss the death of the subject, that sense of a single, unified, essential self. Robert Fishman points out that suburbia itself, as a planning artifact, fragments the metropolis and our culture. Work, family, and leisure likewise intersect each other more intrusively (for example, soccer schedules interrupt dinner; cell phones interrupt everything). This fragmentation was evident even in 1955, as Tom Rath, the suburbanite title character in *The Man in the Gray Flannel Suit,* realized: "There were really four completely unrelated worlds in which he lived." These were the worlds of his now-dead parents, his service in World War II, his present workplace, and his family. "There must be some way in which the four worlds were related, he thought, but it was easier to think of them as entirely divorced from one another."[29]

Ironically suburbia is also a place where people hope and expect to repair their fragmented lives, trying to restore a sense of identity and protect it from further erosion. And as previous chapters have shown, suburbia is a terrain that in many respects has been purpose-built to sustain the process of individual self-realization. But many of the methods that suburbia affords for doing this simultaneously advance the process of fragmentation. Especially effective are ever-increasing emphases on *security* and *segregation*—not simply by race, but commonly by class, status, wealth, and even taste—that further advance overall processes of isolation.

Segregation in particular has long been recognized as a suitable and effective, if ultimately crude, method of sustaining the purity of such personal attributes as class, status, wealth, and so forth. Viewed another way, segregation amounts to the pursuit of *homogeneity* among a certain group of people according to a certain trait or traits. That emphasis on homogeneity, no matter how crucial it appears to safeguarding the individualist dream, frequently has been among the top complaints of suburban critics. But homogeneity also has had its outspoken supporters. In the 1830s, the very early days of building suburban subdivisions, traits such as class and status, like race, were understood to be at least as much a matter of heritage and nature as they were achieved and acquired. In 1838 John Claudius Loudon, the most prolific British architectural writer of the mid-nineteenth century, published *The Suburban Gardener, and Villa Companion,* in which he explicitly presented advantages of de facto residential segregation. Discussing the process of choosing a suburban house, he stressed the benefits of maintaining social homogeneity, counseling the prospective buyer to look for a neighborhood in which the houses and inhabitants all were of the same class. He likewise recommended choosing neighbors with closely comparable education and morals.[30] The process of segregation as Loudon envisioned it was wholly a matter of self-selection. He prescribed no formal apparatus of selection or enforcement, although deed restrictions, one of the most prevalent modes of American suburban segregation in the first half of the twentieth century, were not uncommon in Loudon's time.

Segregation by race, as well as by factors like social and economic class such as Loudon envisioned, was a part of American suburbs from the beginning. There was a separate African American sector in Lake Forest, Illinois (founded 1856), as early as 1860, for example, while a remote section of otherwise posh Coral Gables, Florida (begun 1925), was devoted to shotgun cabins and row houses for African Americans. In these cases as well as many others, like Evanston, Illinois, well-to-do suburbs needed places to house their domestic service personnel, and segregated housing areas were the natural solution at the time. Beginning in the early twentieth century, however, and accelerating with the pace of black migration to northeastern cities in the late

1920s and 1930s, suburbs and subdivisions established entirely for African Americans began to proliferate in several regions of the country. In many cases these were laid out to appeal to the lowest economic echelons by building on cheap land or in undesirable areas, such as districts east of Central Avenue in Los Angeles, or just beyond the city limits of Washington, DC. For middle- and upper-class African Americans, notably in the South, it was possible to create suburbs on a scale nearly equivalent to white developments, allowing blacks to build their own houses, often of substantial size, as long this took place on the opposite side of town from the white suburbs. One such case, well documented by Thomas Hanchett, was the Washington Heights streetcar suburb of Charlotte, North Carolina, begun in 1912. As promotional materials declared, this "beautiful Negro suburb . . . with streetcars running through it . . . has beautiful streets convenient to churches and schools. In this suburb is to be found some of the best people and some of the handsomest homes to be found in any part of Charlotte." In addition, the developer baldly declared, "Washington Heights will be for the colored race exclusively. . . . The developers propose to cause Washington Heights to be a place of tone and character."[31]

In other cases, such as Chagrin Falls Park, Ohio (1921), or the Lincoln Heights Land Company subdivision in Oakwood, Ohio (1924), parcels of land may have been as big as in white suburbs, or even bigger. Here, as Andrew Wiese has shown, there were fewer restrictions and fewer services, which afforded residents of a lower echelon the opportunity to grow food for some of their own needs, improve their premises through their own sweat equity, and otherwise subsist more cheaply. After World War II, as fewer and fewer forms of segregation remained legal, and large-scale tract housing increasingly became the only affordable means of development, from time to time developments for African Americans still were being constructed. As a cover story in *Time* reported in 1950, "In Richmond, Calif., Builder Paul Trousdale . . . has teamed up with ex-Prizefighter Joe Louis and plans to build 4,000 houses for Negroes." Richmond Heights, over fifteen miles from downtown Miami, was laid out as an African American suburb in 1949. In 1954 the first residents moved into Hamilton Park, a planned black suburb of Dallas. During the 1960s other subdivisions around northern cities, such as Hollydale, near Cincinnati, and Inkster, a Detroit suburb, although not explicitly designated for blacks, nevertheless were settled primarily by African Americans.[32]

With the rapid postwar expansion of the middle class, many African Americans chose to articulate and sustain their rising class status by expanding into nearby suburban communities that already were, or quickly would become, overwhelmingly African American. Mary Pattillo-McCoy has documented this process on the South Side of Chicago along with the ensuing emphasis that middle-class families there put on home ownership, lawn care, Christmas yard decorations, and other nominally middle-class neighborhood activities. The implicit condition for this success, nevertheless, was the persistence, even hardening, of racial segregation: African Americans' *class* aspirations and achievements were allied with their continuing isolation as a *racial* group. Sometimes the consequences of this engagement of race with class aspiration were trying. As *Newsweek* reported in 1971, black homeowners in suburban North Hempstead, New York,

> bitterly challenged a proposal to erect a group of prefabricated ranch houses that were to be rented to tenants of a largely black, public-housing project in the city. In the face of the black homeowners' organized resistance, town officials finally abandoned the plan. "People who rent houses don't keep them up," one of the Negroes who fought the proposal explained to housing expert Joseph Fried. . . . "Maybe what I'm saying would be contrary to what Dr. King would say," he added. "But this is my opinion."

Sharper, more complex portraits of the many insidious motives that bring black families to suburbia inform Gloria Naylor's dark novel *Linden Hills* (1985), a depiction of a prosperous African American suburb that turns out to be inhabited by people who, in individualistic pursuit of status and prestige, have lost any sense of ethnicity or community.[33] At the opening of the twenty-first century there are many American cities, such as Atlanta, St. Louis, and Miami, where the growing African American middle class pursues the American dream in suburbs that often are majority black. These are racially homogeneous suburbs where, in the words of political science professor William Boone, "upper-income blacks want to associate more with their own people because they feel more comfortable." Perhaps the greatest concentration of black suburbs in a single area occurs east of Washington, DC, in Prince George's County, Maryland, whose residents numbered more than 50 percent African Americans in the 1990 census. Here in subdivisions with names like Paradise Acres, Enterprise Estates, Canterbury Estates, and Battersea on the Bay, the single-nuclear-family detached house with a manicured front lawn and a big backyard nevertheless continues to remain the ideal of middle-class comfort and success, for African American families as for whites.[34]

The 2000 U.S. Census further upended the perception that suburbs were places where ethnic groups preferred to assimilate into the white population. Instead it documented a widespread shift of minorities to suburban areas, where in many cases white populations declined. In two Texas border metropolitan areas, Hispanics comprised more than 80 percent of the population by the year 2000, and in the metropolitan area of Miami more than 55 percent were Hispanic; in Honolulu Asians were almost half of the suburban population.[35] Whether by preference for nonwhite practices or by simple force of numbers, the white suburb is hardly the prevailing paradigm it has often been presumed to be.

But even if categories such as class, ethnicity, and race have been well established as intellectual constructs, what Loudon and his successor advocates of residential segregation produced as a lasting consequence was a hardening and essentialization of those very categories. For the narrower the range of characteristics in any given community, and the broader the range of those excluded, the more its residents and especially children growing up there have historically understood the world in terms of narrowly essentialized categories. Such has been the risk of twentieth-century American communities with institutionalized apparatuses of segregation. These have ranged from deed restrictions proscribing uses considered less than genteel (such as in Shaker Heights, incorporated 1911), and FHA-endorsed restrictive covenants and redlining, to single-race subdivisions (such as all-white Levittown, New York, or all-black Bunche Park, a suburb of Miami), and gated communities that cater to a very narrow range of clients (such as executives of only a certain rank, people primarily interested in golf and other leisure pursuits, or those in a very narrow income band).[36]

These three ideological strands, property, pastoralism, and fragmentation, are crucial to the "American dream." They inform the dream both in fleshing out the terms of the imagined ideal (individualized self-fulfillment) and in particularizing the apparatus (dwellings, suburbs, and so on) placed at our disposal for fulfilling that dream. The dream, in turn, is instrumental in sustaining corresponding elements of American political practice. Just as comparable tropes such as "promised land" and "manifest destiny" have focused the nation's political and cultural agenda in previous eras, so the needs-no-definition status of the "American dream" bespeaks its role as a reigning paradigm of American political and economic policy. In ways that include income-tax mortgage subsidies, massive highway construction and expansion projects, progressive reductions in capital-gains and inheritance taxes, and growing recognition of NIMBY protests and "land rights" claims, American policy abets an increasingly privatist, accumulative, and insulated vision of self-fulfillment. And the same ideological strands are again reinforced and reproduced as the dream is routinely normalized in practice, for example, through the adoption of the single-nuclear-family detached house as a standard unit by which so many planners, builders, financiers, and so on reckon. It is a standard that becomes the "norm" to which further generations become habituated as they grow up in such houses. In this respect the "dream" is more than a Hollywood fairy tale à la *Modern Times,* or a cliché for personal triumph over adverse beginnings. Rather, it stands as a powerful trope that encompasses an understanding of how the individual is constituted in the private and public realms, and articulates key aspects of the role of the modern American subject in relation to self and nation.

Identical Boxes and Identity

The single-nuclear-family detached house, particularly in its mass-produced form, has hardly escaped criticism, much of it longstanding and much of it severe. In recent decades, perhaps the quintessential critique has been Malvina Reynolds's 1962 song "Little Boxes," popularized by folk singer Pete Seeger, complaining of the lack of individuation in the standardized, geometric shapes of suburban subdivisions:

Little boxes on the hillside,
Little boxes made of ticky-tacky,
Little boxes on the hillside,
Little boxes all the same.
There's a green one and a pink one
And a blue one and a yellow one,
And they're all made out of ticky-tacky
And they all look just the same.[37]

In "Suburban Home," released by the Descendents two decades later, the tone is considerably more caustic, but the critical rationale is little altered, condemning such houses as dehumanizing:

I want to be stereotyped
I want to be classified
I want to be a clone
I want a suburban home
Suburban home
Suburban home
Suburban home
I want to be masochistic
I want to be a statistic
I want to be a clone
I want a suburban home.[38]

But while critiques of this sort seem well suited to American postwar suburbia, they were hardly new. More than two centuries prior to "Little Boxes" a similar diatribe denounced the proliferation of suburban "boxes" on the outskirts of London. The author of this "Letter on the Villas of Our Tradesmen," published in 1754 in the popular periodical *The Connoisseur,* condemned the unsophisticated, underfinanced, underlandscaped sort of "box" that people with new money but no taste were putting up along the roads out of London:

A little country box you boast,
So neat, 'tis cover'd all with dust;
And nought about it to be seen,
Except a nettle-bed, that's green;
Your Villa! rural but the name in,
So desart, it would breed a famine.
. . .
'Tis not the country, you must own;
'Tis only London out of town.[39]

In early twentieth-century America, concern focused on the extent to which methods of increasingly standardized housing production might limit or inhibit a resident's individuality or, worse, tend to mass homogenization of the population. Sinclair Lewis's *Babbitt* (1922) provided an early, and now classic, statement of the case against the production of middle-class dwellings according to standardized designs and processes. Babbitt's bedroom, for example,

> displayed a modest and pleasant color-scheme, after one of the best standard designs of the decorator who "did the interiors" for most of the speculative-builders' houses in Zenith. . . . It was a masterpiece among bedrooms, right out of Cheerful Modern Houses for Medium Incomes. Only it had nothing to do with the Babbitts, or anyone else. . . . In fact there was but one thing wrong with the Babbitt house: It was not a home.[40]

Standardization simply left no room for the homeowner's individuality. Christine Frederick's 1928 essay, "Is Suburban Living a Delusion?" engaged what already had become a major debate over the influence of industrial and commercial standardization on the future of individualism in America:

> The sad truth is that the suburb standardizes those things which a true individual doesn't want standardized, and leaves unstandardized those things he most desires standardized. . . . Standardization in the suburbs is not applied, as it should be, to the comfort of living, but to the flattening out of personal individuality.

Further prefiguring some of the most mordant 1950s critiques, Frederick also lashed out at the "mass psychology of Suburbiana," and the "social delusion" that reigned there. A prominent passage nearly anticipated Malvina Reynolds word for word:

> I suppose architects get pleasure out of the neat little toy houses on their neat little patches of lawn and their neat colonial lives, to say nothing of the neat little housewives and their neat little children—all set in neat rows, for all the world like children's blocks.[41]

Her comments were echoed in 1948 by Eric Larrabee, who couched his criticism of standardized tract housing in Levittown in terms that, in their emphasis on class divisions, carried an added political charge in the formative years of the cold war. "The community that Bill Levitt has fastened onto the Long Island soil is of the most class-stratifying sort possible," Larrabee wrote.[42] He implied not only that such a hardening of class lines would be profoundly undemocratic, but also that it would limit opportunities for pursuing an individualized American dream. These would become two of the principal grounds—class stratification and lack of individuality—on which suburban developments and tract housing would be criticized for decades to come.

Nor was such criticism reserved for individual developments such as Levittown. By the mid-1950s it was freely leveled at all of suburbia, as in this typically pessimistic appraisal by sociologist David Riesman: "there seems to me to be a tendency, though not a pronounced one, in the suburbs to lose the human differentiations which have made great cities in the past the centers of rapid intellectual and cultural advance."[43] One of the bleakest portrayals of suburbia along these lines came from Lewis Mumford in his 1961 book *The City in History:*

> a multitude of uniform, unidentifiable houses, lined up inflexibly, at uniform distances, on uniform roads, in a treeless communal waste, inhabited by people of the same class, the same income, the same age group, witnessing the same television performances, eating the same tasteless prefabricated foods, from the same freezers, conforming in every outward and inward respect to a common mold, manufactured in the central metropolis.

Similar sentiments entered mainstream journalism with Ada Louise Huxtable's comment in 1964 in the *New York Times Magazine* that Long Island had "been invaded by regimented hordes of split-levels lined up for miles in close, unlovely rows. Boxes called homes march ruthlessly across the Middle West."[44]

Early in the twenty-first century, the terminology has evolved, but the charge remains much the same: instead of being condemned for its uniformity, suburbia is indicted as a monoculture. At issue is not simply the uniformity of acre after acre of detached single-family residences but also the hardening of socioeconomic class lines and practices that tracts of uniform housing ostensibly produce.[45]

Building Identity

The presumption underlying many of these critiques—unspoken in some, openly expressed in others—is that buildings have a direct and necessary effect on those who use and inhabit them. Since the late eighteenth century, a host of empirical studies have tied specific aspects of architectural design to effects on human health and welfare, particularly with respect to housing for the poor and working classes. From studies of "fever" outbreaks in late eighteenth-century London to the reformist studies of Edwin Chadwick in Britain and Jacob Riis in America, increasing attention has been paid to building design as cause, or potential cure, for residents' diseases and other pathologies.[46] From well before the nineteenth century on into the twentieth, architecture also was accorded the capacity to function as a moral beacon and educator. As Candace Wheeler declared in 1893, "A perfectly furnished house is a crystallization of the culture, the habits, and the tastes of the family, and not only expresses but *makes* character." Dwellings did not simply represent or teach morality, they produced it.[47]

Domestic architecture, in other words, clearly had the capacity to enhance residents' health and moral welfare. And in contemplating the late nineteenth-century

growth of multiple-family housing throughout the United States, ranging from tene-
ments to high-rise apartment blocks, American critics could point to one additional
advantage of the single-family house: individuation of family and self. A 1907 article
comparing "suburban cottages versus flats" argued that the popularity of apartments
was in large part due to their capacity to serve "as a haven for tired men and jaded
women" from the congestion of city life. But this was at best a halfway measure, for
apartments still failed to provide for a crucial component of domestic life: "In fact,
flat life is not home life, for home life is strongly individuated." The article also emphasized that this had become an issue of particular concern for the "middle classes,"
who were moving to the suburbs in pursuit of "less publicity," that is, involvement in
the public sphere, and "more retreat."[48]

Two decades later the same themes somewhat improbably informed R. W. Sexton's
imposing *American Apartment Houses, Hotels, and Apartment Hotels of Today* (1929).
On the first page, Sexton declared that none of these building types "should rightfully
be classed as a home" because, while they certainly offered "convenience," "they all lack
the very fundamentals on which the home was founded." The two fundamentals, key
aspects of American domesticity that apartments could not deliver, were *privacy*
and *individuality*. Sexton went on to suggest ways in which apartment design might
approach these needs, especially through interior decoration, but ultimately recognized that "the repetition of the plan, throughout the entire building," meant that
"individuality is practically non-existent."[49]

By contrast, the single-family detached dwelling, increasingly affordable to the
American middle classes since the 1920s, represented a very different opportunity. It
appeared as the instrument of choice by which individuals could achieve the distinction and self-fulfillment that were identified with the American dream. The notion of
a dwelling as an instrument of individuation was hardly new; rather, it is perhaps
as old as civilization and extends to places across the geographic and cultural diversity
of the planet.[50] Nevertheless, for most of the history of Western feudal and capitalist
society, opportunities for individuation generally had been restricted to those with the
greatest social and financial capital, such as the aristocracy, whose mansions served to
articulate heritage, lineage, connections, and power.

However, with the maturation of capitalism, as the ever growing bourgeoisie
correspondingly adopted the suburban dwelling as a standard means of personal individuation, it increasingly appeared to commentators that this could (or should)
become a universally adopted practice, if not in fact then at least in aspiration. Such
was the opinion of American architect Bruce Price, who wrote (perhaps too glibly) of
the inclination of "every man, no matter how subordinate his position in the business
world, to assert his individuality and independence by owning a home which is the
outgrowth of his special tastes and needs." Arguably a more salient aspect of Price's
essay, moreover, was the way in which he presented this inclination: as a peculiarly
"American trait," a commitment to individualism characteristic of America as a *nation*
that "the American must inevitably show . . . in his home." And the specifically

suburban proliferation of such homes, in turn, was almost the apotheosis of American nationalism: "encircling miles about our great cities, [there] have sprung up, and are still rising, the true homes of the American of to-day."[51] America, in other words, was to become the apotheosis of individual self-distinction through housing.

Mary Pattison, a disciple of labor efficiency expert Frank W. Taylor, offered a comparable understanding of the house as an instrument of self-realization in her 1915 treatise on systematization of American households, *Principles of Domestic Engineering, or the What, Why and How of a Home.* "Each home," she wrote, "should exist around an idea standing as a vitalizing influence for self-expression, not only of each member of the family in each effort of the day, but of the family as a unit, and its individual and encouraging relation to the community." Depending in part on "the skill of the architect," the house was capable of "conveying the disposition of the family through its composition, texture, color, form and quality," as well as "showing the status of individuality and native culture" of its residents. Pattison even anthropomorphized the house, asking whether the reader had ever taken a "look at a house with the impression that it was a person?" To elucidate her point, she practically mapped the house onto the human body: "the kitchen supplies the physical man," "the library [supplies] the mental side," "the bedroom [supplies] the spiritual and psychic side," and even halls and stairs corresponded to the circulation. In sum, correspondences between dwelling and self or family were profound: "the whole house should be looked upon as expressing life. The inner, or more private part, as the mind and feeling. The house itself as the outer form, or body, and the family as the soul." Such pronouncements also fit into a broader political proposition, one that readily anticipated the future hegemony of the individualistic American dream and the private dream house. The home, Pattison argued, "gives freedom to the individual," and as such it is "the cornerstone and foundation of the nation, the cradle of the citizen, and the bulwark and stability of society." Against the institutions of public realm, which she blatantly indicted as "opposed to individualism," the house would appear to serve as defense and even antidote. As Kathleen McHugh demonstrated in a recent analysis of Pattison, the private home, which for Pattison represented "values of individuality and freedom," became "the benevolent ideological and structural other" to the entire capitalist economy.[52]

No less an authority than Emily Post, who authored *The Personality of a House: The Blue Book of Home Design and Decoration* in 1930, readily accepted the house as an instrument of individuation. "Its personality should express your personality," she wrote; "the house that does not express the individuality of its owner is like a dress shown on a wax figure." In the case of her frontispiece (Figure 7.2), for example, the hallway is graced by a rug emblazoned with the motto "Home Sweet Home," and sheep are visible grazing beyond the porch through the open door, a vista no doubt meant to indicate the owner's retired, rural, pastoral existence just as in so many eighteenth- and nineteenth-century examples. Suggesting that designing and furnishing a dwelling was comparable to painting a person's portrait, Post professed that "a decorator worthy of the name interprets the personality and character of the individual houseowner for whom he (or she) creates the setting." Or, as decorator Ben Davis wrote in 1937, a house not only *represented* the individuality of the client, it *differentiated* (that is, individualized) that client from other householders.[53]

Nor was Post's use of the term *personality* in the title of her book an incidental choice. Over the previous two decades the growing interest in self-help and self-advancement had focused on personality as a key dimension of improvement necessary for personal, social, and financial success. Books such as *Personality: How to Build It* (1916) and *Masterful Personality* (1921) emphasized the importance of differentiating oneself as "entirely original," distinct and recognizable "among a crowd." The proffered advice was often a close variation on American-dream success stories, stating that necessary resources for "self-discovery" and for social and financial success lay within the private individual: "*the power to conquer* all obstacles is inside of you." Figures such as Thomas Edison or Abraham Lincoln were held up as exemplars of success through individualistic pursuits. According to the text of *Masterful Personality*, both these men

Arthur C. Holden and Associates, Architects

THE MOTTO ON THE RUG PERFECTLY EXPRESSES THE
ATMOSPHERE OF THIS HALL

[PLATE 1]

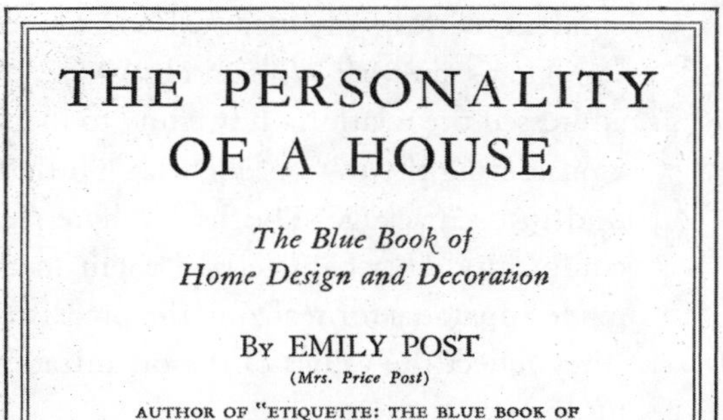

THE PERSONALITY
OF A HOUSE

*The Blue Book of
Home Design and Decoration*

By EMILY POST

(*Mrs. Price Post*)

AUTHOR OF "ETIQUETTE: THE BLUE BOOK OF
SOCIAL USAGE," ETC.

ILLUSTRATED

FUNK & WAGNALLS COMPANY

NEW YORK AND LONDON

1930

Figure 7.2. Emily Post, frontispiece and title page in *The Personality of a House* (New York: Funk & Wagnalls, 1930). The frontispiece set the keynote for the book, indicating that the design of a house might, as in this case, be crucial in facilitating its owner's retired, rural, pastoral existence.

"found themselves through self effort, through their individual, strenuous efforts to get an education, to raise themselves to the height of their conscious possibility."[54]

In contrast to Post's prewar optimistic view of the dwelling as an instrument of individuation, postwar expansion of mass-produced housing for the middle classes led critics to address the other side of the coin. The bland uniformity of much tract housing quickly became a synecdoche for all of suburbia and soon led to the rise of literary and film stereotypes portraying the crushing effects of suburban dwellings on human spirit and identity. Even before the war's formal conclusion, architects George Nelson and Henry Wright condemned the forthcoming onslaught of tract housing in just such terms. Compared to the sorts of options available to owners of architect-designed houses such as Emily Post had in mind, tract houses were utterly ineffectual: "pathetic little white boxes with dressed-up street fronts, each striving for individuality through meaningless changes in detail or color."[55] By the 1950s the terms of such critiques grew even more acerbic, epitomized in John Keats's 1956 novel *The Crack in the Picture Window*. Neatly prefiguring Malvina Reynolds's pessimistic vision, Keats condemned rows of "identical boxes spreading like gangrene" across the landscape.[56]

That same year William H. Whyte, chronicler of the "organization man," directly addressed the relation of dwelling to identity, albeit in a particularly sardonic fashion. Considering the rows of identical "little boxes" that constituted the "dormitories" of mid-1950s "package suburbs," Whyte recognized that they did not actually produce conformity. He characterized them instead as something arguably worse, a ready-made apparatus for realizing the preexisting values of those who went to live in them: "they reflect the values of the organization man. . . . They are communities made in his image."[57]

Nelson and Wright's 1945 censure of little boxes striving for individuality through color variations might apply as well to the tract of identical houses, each differing only in color, gently satirized forty-five years later in the film *Edward Scissorhands* (1990), filmed in the Carpenter's Run subdivision, built in 1998–99 in Lutz, Florida, just north of Tampa. Director Tim Burton's satire continues to the point of showing all the commuting husbands departing their houses at the same time in an orchestrated procession, a device that hearkens back to numerous 1950s critiques of lockstep suburban conformity. Yet despite the uniformity of the surroundings and the common circumstances of their lives, the filmic inhabitants of this subdivision, while hewing to stock types to exaggerate the comedic effect, differ from each other in real and substantial terms. The prediction that those who lived in identical "little boxes" would "all come out the same" here was proved patently, and disarmingly, untrue. The residents also managed to accept and understand Edward, in terms that varied from person to person, undermining stereotypical notions of suburban conformity. Nevertheless that acceptance and understanding also have overall bounds. Edward's ultimate departure from the community bespeaks the limited degree to which its residents could accommodate difference.

Set against the backdrop of identical boxlike houses, these residents' limited tolerance for difference crystallizes one of the central debates that critics of suburbia have raised concerning architecture and identity. As suggested by the lyrics and texts presented above, and as attested by countless films, photographs, and cartoons, suburban housing tracts often exhibit an unrelenting uniformity. Critics also have pointed out suburban tendencies toward demographic uniformity and social conformity. These are particularly evident in mass-produced postwar housing tracts that, by virtue of their architectural uniformity and deed and financing restrictions, appealed to very narrow economic and social strata. Coupled with the prevailing inclination of planners and developers to design suburbs for husbands who commuted elsewhere to work and housewives who stayed home to nurture the nuclear family, such physical and social conditions often meant that the residents of almost any given tract, development, or suburb were homogeneous in some substantial way. Similar in skin color, financial status, commuting habits, family size, family roles, leisure activities, political orientation, and so forth, residents of suburbs soon found themselves caricatured as nothing more than mindless clones of each other.

As observed by contemporaries ranging from musicians and Hollywood screenwriters to literary critics and sociologists, such suburban homogeneity appeared to demonstrate a connection between the built environment and how the identities of those who lived there were shaped. It is a connection that, while largely fallacious, has remained remarkably potent in the evaluation of suburbia up to the present day: that standardized housing and demographic uniformity produce a populace that is at best drearily homogeneous, or at worst made up of morbidly conformist, compliant drones. Cartoons showing the regimentation of commuters or the bewildering sameness of houses up and down the street were part of a stream of ridicule that the media regularly, and all too easily, heaped upon suburbanites.[58]

Other voices seemed more equivocal. In 1953 the editors of *Fortune* noted with some interest that suburbia was "becoming socially as well as economically more uniform," but they hardly seemed worried. Rather, they paradoxically reckoned that homogeneity might ultimately foster diversity: "The fact that almost everybody has similar ideals, standards, and incomes strengthens rather than weakens the group's hold on the individual, and the fact that those ideals may include such factors as class, racial, and religious tolerance strengthens it all the more." Neglecting to explain why such tolerance should be presumed to be present in the first place, the *Fortune* editors instead suggested how an increase in American homogeneity would pay off for their readership. The suburban market, like its population, was now becoming "bigger and more uniform: a combination made to order for the marketer who understands what Suburbia is and where it is going."[59] In other words, the more homogeneous the American dream, the better the marketer's dream of a homogeneous mass market for mass-produced consumer goods. If uniform dwellings produced uniform drones, at least that would pave the way for an economy of mass commodities.

Getting to Know Suburbia

From the immediate postwar years to the present day countless people who have lived in suburbia have not viewed themselves as hopeless victims of regimented conformity. To the contrary, many have been thoroughly optimistic about the opportunities that suburbia would afford. Such a tone is evident as early as 1945 in Helen Forrest's popular recording of "I'll Buy That Dream" (1945), which presumably spoke for many:

> We'll settle down in Dallas
> In a little plastic palace
> Oh it's not as crazy as you think.[60]

And while the stereotypical vision of suburbia as a land of endless uniformity has continued to maintain a prominent position in public discourse—particularly music and film—there has been no shortage of efforts to rebut that vision. As early as 1949 Phyllis McGinley took direct aim at charges of conformity: "There is nothing really typical about any of our friends and neighbors here [in a suburb of New York City], and therein lies my point. The true suburbanite needs to conform less than anyone else." Nor was there "some particular family whose codes must be ours. And we could not keep up with the Joneses even if we wanted to, for we know many Joneses and they are all quite different people leading the most varied lives."[61]

Even more telling were extensive interviews conducted by journalist Harry Henderson in Levittown, Park Forest, Lakewood, and other large-scale postwar developments, the results of which he published in *Harper's* in late 1953. Residents were quite aware of the criticism that tarred them and eager to set the record straight.

> One rarely hears complaints about the identical character of the houses. "You don't feel it when you live here," most people say. . . . "We're not peas in a pod. I thought it would be like that, especially because incomes are nearly the same. But it's amazing how different and varied people are, likes and dislikes, attitudes and wants. I never really knew what people were like until I came here."

The pursuit of individualism had remained alive and well. As Henderson noted, the standardized house had just shifted the focus from an exterior display of individuality to an interior one. Through interior decorating, he found, "Most people try hard to achieve 'something different.'"[62] And thanks to postwar American prosperity many residents soon tackled the identical exteriors. From the 1950s onward tract houses in Levittown and countless other suburbs underwent waves of individuation through expansion, remodeling, and redecoration. In 1958 one researcher found that

> the individuality that each family brought to Levittown continues to show through in many ways; namely, the paint on the house exterior, the maintenance and

arrangements of grounds, the design of house alterations, the home interiors, and, of course, in such personal aspects of living as clothing, cooking, selection of friends, hobbies, political and social thought, and the like.[63]

Others sought to confront directly the charge that suburbia has repressed individualism. As early as 1960 Bennett M. Berger devoted a whole chapter of his book *Working-Class Suburb* to exploding what he termed "the myth of suburbia," that is, its reputation as a place of stifling homogeneity and conformity.[64] Some 1950s developers actually marketed rows of tract houses as affording "individuality" (Figure 7.3).[65] A long history of scholarship on Levittown and other suburbs likewise reveals considerable satisfaction and pride in the diverse kinds of lives that people have lived there.[66] Even the 1997 film *Wonderland,* a quasi-documentary that endeavors to ridicule Levittowners for their idiosyncratic behavior and house furnishings, proves the point despite itself: suburbanites do lead interesting, highly individualized lives. In one scene, a man is shown in front of his house saying, "This is *my* dream come true." In other words, suburbia in the long run proved quite amenable to the many and varied ways in which its residents pursued the American dream.

Nor was a certain degree of homogeneity necessarily a bad thing. As Henderson observed, "Many also liked the idea that economically everyone is in the same class."[67] Not only did this obviate the usual tensions and jealousies between rich and poor children, as one of Henderson's interviewees reported, but it also represented a more democratic basis from which all members of the community could get an equal start in their pursuit of the dream. A marketing study of Chicago suburbs prepared by the *Chicago Tribune* in 1957 recognized that for many families the move to new postwar housing tracts offered such advantages. In many cases it was a radical reorientation of their social framework, from the vertical hierarchy of the extended patriarchal family in which most had been living, to the brave new horizontal democracy of young nuclear families, among whom no major divisions yet were established. All had comparable opportunities to succeed. In the *Tribune's* words, the move represented "a transition from the family group structure, which is somewhat hierarchical, to the neighborhood group, which is more homogeneous."[68] The postwar embrace of the "dream house" ideal went hand in hand with a wholesale rejection of the extended patriarchal family. And with the goal of individual self-realization in mind, the homogeneous community in which nobody had an entrenched claim to superiority may well have appeared to be the fairest, most democratic terrain on which to pursue the dream of "getting ahead."

Henderson's research did uncover a certain amount of conformity in the places he visited, but it was primarily within small groups rather than across the community as a whole. As one of Henderson's informants put it, "Usually you end up with five or six couples that you either have common interests with or whom you just happen to like as people." These couples then formed the basis of "our group," which because its members were self-selected on the basis of like interests, found themselves to be

AIRVIEW OF NORTHPORT COMMUNITY

INDIVIDUALITY
IS WHY THEY BUY IN

PEARSON BROS.

NORTHPORT *Community*

FLEXIBILTY is the keynote in the houses we are building in Northport Community. You can choose the features you want, many of them being included in our basic price of $12,750. A visit to our model home will prove that, as well as the high, custom-built quality of Pearson Bros. construction and craftsmanship. Special extras like brick trim, fireplaces, walkout basements, breezeways and garages can be added at little extra cost. For example, you may have a 3 bedroom rambler, with brick trim, 2 fireplaces, walkout basement, breezeway and garage, all for $15,335.00. You must see these fine houses of individuality, to appreciate how superior they are to so-called "Volume-built" houses, offered in many developments.

A
FINE
HOME
ONLY

$12,750

THE EXTRA
SPECIAL
DELUXE

$15,325

FEATURES THAT SPELL THE DIFFERENCE BETWEEN A HOUSE AND A HOME!

- Torrens Titles
- Tile Bathrooms
- Hardwood Trim
- Gliding Windows
- Colored Bath Fixtures
- Lennox Heating
- Armstrong Linoleum
- Brick Trim
- Walkout Basement
- Contour Platting

- Blacktop Streets
- Clothes Chutes
- Steel Beam Construction
- Copper Piping
- Cedar Shakes
- Fireplaces
- Breezeways—Garages
- 100 Amp. Electricity

SEE THE MODEL "HOME OF HOMES"
5649 OSSEO ROAD - - - - - OPEN TODAY 12 TO 9 P.M.
COMPLETELY FURNISHED BY CRYSTAL FURNITURE CO., 5530 WEST BROADWAY

FIFTEEN MINUTES TO SIXTH ST.

Only a fifteen minute drive from Sixth and Nicollet, and you're there. Take Highway 100 north to Highway 152. Turn north at the intersection of these two highways for ½ mile, and you're in Northport Community.

THORPE BROS.

OFFICE PHONE
AT- 2133

Exclusive Agents
• **519 MARQUETTE** •

MODEL HOME
OR 7-1181

AIRVIEW OF NORTHPORT COMMUNITY

Figure 7.3. Pearson Brothers advertisement, "Individuality Is Why They Buy in Pearson Bros. Northport Community," *Minneapolis Sunday Tribune,* 17 April 1955 (page 28C). Despite the critics of tract housing who argued that it bred conformity and worse, clearly it was marketed to the public in quite different terms, as this advertisement shows. Courtesy of The Ackerberg Group, Minneapolis, Minnesota.

very much alike "in their attitudes, values, and philosophy." While the interests that formed the basis of such groups might vary widely from one to the next, within any given group it would lead to what Henderson termed "a kind of super-conformity. For instance, if the dominant members of the group think Plymouths are the 'best buys,' then Plymouths are what they all have. Or if *they* decide women should dress up at four o'clock every afternoon, they all do that." The downside of such a tight-knit association was a resistance to criticism within the group, or a prejudice against "braininess" and "thinking too much." Such might be construed as an assertion of being "too good for the rest of us," and so, according to Henderson, "there is a premium put on a kind of amiable, thoughtless conformity." Henderson also noted a widespread propensity for establishing clubs around an almost limitless range of interests; he noted the common refrain in the communities he studied, "You name your activity and I'll bet we have a club for it here!" So while Henderson recognized a certain inclination toward conformity, at least on a small scale, he also argued that on the whole suburbs were remarkably "diversified," and that despite their often homogeneous demographics, the residents of suburbia found widespread opportunities for "self-expression" of their individual interests.[69]

Herbert Gans's study of *The Levittowners* (1967), conducted in a fashion that today would be called "participant ethnography," revealed a complexity and diversity of interests among the initial population of Levittown (later Willingboro), New Jersey, that critics of suburbia had not deemed possible. On the one hand, homogeneity was clearly a desideratum: 71 percent of those whom Gans surveyed looked forward to "having neighbors of similar age and interests" and similar income. On the other hand, he found that many residents also looked forward to meeting people with different regional, ethnic, and religious backgrounds. Gans maintained that the supposed demographic homogeneity of Levittown was "more statistical than real" since, for example, three families with the same income might well be a skilled blue-collar worker, a senior white-collar worker, and a young executive or professional. He also astutely argued that the prevailing critiques of identical dwellings were "a thinly veiled attack on the culture of working and lower middle class people, implying that mass-produced housing leads to mass-produced lives." Indeed Gans reported that Levittowners did not complain "about the similarity of their homes," but that individuality prevailed when finances permitted, as residents "made internal and external alterations in their Levitt house to reduce sameness and to place a personal stamp on their property."[70]

Other research confirmed that far from being mindless conformists, residents of suburbia maintained a keen interest in individuation, even when opportunities were limited. Ralph Bodek, the developer of Lawrence Park near Philadelphia, reported in 1958 on an extensive survey of his clientele. On the one hand, he found that "people in this kind of housing market do not object to the fact that their dwelling unit is basically the same as 1,200 others." On the other hand, there was considerable disappointment among purchasers that they would be limited in opportunities to individualize the exterior of the house on their own. His survey logged "frequent complaints from women that they could not choose the color of house that they would like."[71] Bodek unfortunately trivialized such complaints, suggesting that sufficient differentiation was possible with the choice of six standard colors that were provided.

Those who were not satisfied with Bodek's six colors had other options, however, as did residents of other developments where appearances were uniform or limited to standardized choices. As Henderson had reported earlier, residents could concentrate their interests in individuation on the interior of the house. But the consequence was that residents of standardized and mass-produced houses found that their interests in individuation were channeled more toward expression of the *private self* rather than toward engaging larger social domains such as the neighborhood or community.

Institutional entities in the broader community thus became correspondingly worried about growing recognition of the private suburban dwelling as an apparatus for defining the private self in isolation. In 1958 Reverend Andrew M. Greeley published an essay titled "The Catholic Suburbanite" in which he lamented the diminishing hold of the Catholic Church on its suburban parishioners. "Suburbia," he wrote, "represents a decisive turning point in the history of the American Church." In part this was due to a rising spirit of individualism: the suburbanite "prides himself on the fact that he is a free American and makes his own decisions." But perhaps more worrisome was the toll taken by the growing pressure on each American to define himself more in terms of "his dream house" than in terms of faith.[72]

This growing tendency to identify the self with the house soon was paralleled by efforts to articulate increasingly privatized zones and spaces within the house. Decades before "cocooning" was spotlighted by Faith Popcorn in 1987, John R. Seeley and his colleagues remarked at length on the increasing privatization of personal space in suburbia. In *Crestwood Heights* (1956), a study of a Toronto suburb, they wrote of expectations that each family member should have his or her own private space. "Privacy for each member of the family is the ideal," they wrote. "The Crestwood home, must, ideally, provide ample space for separate sleeping and working quarters for each member of the family." One Crestwood mother crystallized the point in remarking on the difference between her childhood, when "we all worked of an evening around the dining room table," and now individually "we scatter throughout the house to follow our interests."[73]

The next year, Bodek's study of Lawrence Park, near Philadelphia, confirmed the tendency toward individualist retreat. Seemingly echoing William Faulkner's essay on the American dream as a sanctuary of privacy, residents of Lawrence Park were keen to defend and reinforce their own privacy. Inside the house, they wanted a "line of demarcation" between areas for sleeping and areas for other living activities. Eschewing row houses and semidetached houses as insufficiently insulated from prying neighbors or relatives, residents viewed the amount of exterior space between single-family detached houses as affording a necessary "haven of refuge and escape." In the words of one resident, "above everything I wanted was privacy, to get away from neighbors." Bodek challenged the current mainstream thinking that suburbanites were eager to embrace picture windows and backyard patios. In the words of one resident, picture windows were definitely a disadvantage: "No privacy—house is like a fishbowl." And, Bodek concluded, "It is doubted whether most will really use the outdoor space for which they are paying—they look at it mainly as an insulating space against neighbors, a place to hang the wash, and a place for the children to play (when the latter are not nicely removed from sight in the recreation room)."[74]

The concentric zones of individuation that the detached house afforded in the 1950s—yard and exterior, interior, and private subspaces within the interior—persist in much the same form almost half a century later. Sometimes the zones and the uses to which they are put are even more highly refined. Instead of roughly demarcating parts of the house where family members can each "follow our own interests," for example, the indulgence of private pursuits is now formalized in the practice of cocooning. The most significant change to the concentric structure is perhaps the appearance of a fourth, outermost zone or ring, the precinct of the gated community. For most of their history, gated communities have restricted their residents on grounds of race, class, and income primarily to assure a degree of homogeneity and like-mindedness among neighbors. But recently, as Edward J. Blakely and Mary Gail Snyder have documented, gated communities have been explicitly designed and advertised to attract those who have, or aspire to, a certain status. What Blakely and Snyder call "Prestige Communities," for example, are marketed on the premise that they confer a certain standing, as executive, professional, rich, super-rich, and so forth.[75] Those residing in such communities can then use the apparatus of the entire community—gates, walls, landscaping, signage, and the status of other residents—to articulate that added dimension of their own identities.

Dream Casters and Nightmare Critics

The "American dream" has never been a neutral or static construct. Indeed its efficacy—its status as generally unquestioned consensus—derives from its capacity to address and adapt to changing circumstances and challenging conditions.[76] Writers and photographers, for example, have portrayed the endless anonymity of sprawl, or the placelessness of the strip, as a nightmare that robs us of our dignity and humanity. Responding to such concerns, some planners and architects have partially recast the dream itself, but often they do so in narrower terms, for example, by gating or "cocooning," which constrains the dream to be an ever more privatist enterprise.

Other changes occur well beyond the domain of architecture or design. For while the focus of the dream always has remained an individualist enterprise, and the dream is necessarily seated in the consciousness of the private individual, the actual terms in which the American dream is framed are largely provided for us through popular media and corporate marketing apparatuses.[77] Individually we do not have the opportunity to negotiate the categorical terms in which our "American dreams" are realized.

Rather, we choose from an array of options that our culture affords us, ranging from the sort of cinematic formulas seen in *Here Come the Nelsons, Leave It to Beaver, Father of the Bride,* or *The 'Burbs,* to the choices of kitchen cabinets available at Lowe's and The Home Depot. The options, of course, do not remain static, as they may be recast according to a host of related factors. Shifts in decor that enhance a sense of private, personal space, for example, are necessarily tied to an evolving array of appliances such as computers, DVD players, and large-screen televisions, among many other things.[78]

Much of the work of critiquing the dream and redefining its terms is carried on in the popular media, by writers, musicians, filmmakers, designers, and artists, who focus on the dream's current provisions and draft blueprints for its future.[79] What is striking, however, is that these critiques seldom contest the dream itself. Instead they address its particulars, the material terms in which it may be realized, ridiculing ticky-tacky boxes, for example, or endless sameness. Over the long term, the effect of such critiques may be some shift in the terms in which the dream is formulated, such as recent emphasis by New Urbanists and others on design quality and typological variety. But the power of the dream itself, as rhetorical and ideological apparatus, generally remains intact, unacknowledged, and uncontested.

The discussion that follows explores some of the ways in which assessment of the dream has proceeded since the end of World War II. Focusing in particular on critiques of the dream as it has come to be associated with the single-nuclear-family suburban house, the analysis concentrates on representations in two or three media— film and television, and music—that increasingly have dominated popular perception and understanding of the dream. In some cases these critiques have suggested ways to recast or reframe the dream, but in others, no matter how negative, the dream itself simply was reinforced.[80]

Film and Television

Beginning with the film *Mr. Blandings Builds His Dream House* (1948), continuing through such television series as *Leave It to Beaver* (1957–63), *Father Knows Best* (1954–63), and *The Jetsons* (first season, 1962–63), suburbia appeared in a highly positive light as a land of single-family houses affording nuclear families everything they needed. The upper-middle-class version of the dream was seen to be healthy and, perhaps more significant for the times, normative. The message coming into our homes over the airwaves was that our homes (at least for those of us in single-nuclear-family suburbia) were quite suitable instruments for living the dream.[81]

But Hollywood also offered darker takes on nuclear-family suburbia, beginning with *The Man in the Gray Flannel Suit* (1956)[82] and *No Down Payment* (1957). In these accounts, suburbia became a place of frustration, fear, loathing, and alienation. Only a year after the publication of *The Organization Man* (1956), Whyte's ominous study of suburban company men, the film *No Down Payment* offered a sensationalized, disturbing portrait of suburbia as unequal to the task of serving its residents' interests.[83]

Even if spiffy new subdivisions represented considerable progress over Depression and wartime housing deficiencies, they still were unable to serve the diverse needs and abilities of their individual residents, who instead succumbed to alcoholism, lust, abuse, angst, and cowardice. The individualist dream was not faulty, but the manner of its implementation was wholly inadequate.

In the next twenty to forty years, films like *Over the Edge* (1979), *SAFE* (1995), and *subUrbia* (1997) furthered this censorious critique: that the very material apparatus in which suburbia had been realized—from dwelling type to subdivision plan to strip mall—itself was at fault. Here the physical apparatus was deemed responsible for the alienation, violence, and anguish that had been visited on its inhabitants. In *Over the Edge,* for example, the short-sighted principles on which a master-planned community has been built, and the incapacity of the adults who live there to address or even recognize those shortcomings, leads inexorably to delinquency and rebellion among the community's teenagers. In *SAFE,* the material substances of which furniture, houses, and suburbia itself are built become so toxic to one resident that she has to abandon home and family for a remote site safe from all artificial contamination. In these cases the issue is not so much the dream itself, but the manner in which the material apparatus of suburbia subverts the promise. Much the same can be said of *subUrbia,* at the end of which the utter nihilism that grips the central character, Jeff, is more a realization that suburbia in its present form has killed the dream than an indictment of the dream itself.

In very recent years cinematic assessments have begun to explore ways in which the dream itself is corrupt. In films like *American Beauty* (1999) and *Crime and Punishment in Suburbia* (2000) the dream transforms inexorably into a nightmare. Here the material fabric of suburbia itself does no direct harm but instead takes on the role of enabler. It is an apparatus that can abet private urges and desires that are otherwise insufficiently checked in a culture that idealizes privatist individualism. Here the setting is more closely focused on just a single private home, and the psychological focus narrows to a single family or character. The contest boils down to this: does a single individual have the mettle necessary to make good use of all the material accoutrements of the dream, which are so abundantly present here, or will he or she descend into a nightmare of private excess?[84]

In the outcome of the contest lie profound implications for the dream. Not only is suburbia an unsuitable apparatus for its realization, but the dream itself may lead to nothing more than an existential ordeal. In *Crime and Punishment in Suburbia,* for example—a nightmare of abuse, murder, and guilt—only following the purgatory of prison does the central character get on her boyfriend's motorcycle and abandon suburbia for the open road and, perhaps, the redemptive urbanism of New York. Paralleling a growing trend in many parts of the country for dissatisfied individuals and families to return from the suburbs to the cities, Roseanne's departure for New York nevertheless still holds the urban as an untested, utopian ideal. On the other hand, her rejection of her suburban past without so much as a glance backward succinctly affirms the film's scathing judgment of suburbia as a site pathologically inimical to the sorts of social enterprise or personal growth that the city can offer.[85]

Comparable engagement with the complexities and inadequacies of the dream has likewise informed a number of recent novels. David Gates's *Jernigan* (1991), for example, displays a disappointment and disillusionment with suburbia, now seen as a place for the failed, the dysfunctional, and the incapable—those who have abandoned, or been abandoned by, their dreams. *Two Guys from Verona* (1988), by James Kaplan, is on the one hand a critique of all that is wrong with suburban possessive consumerism. But in the end it is also a revelation that the dream, so powerful when the two central characters graduated from high school in 1974, has by the end of the millennium deteriorated to the status of a memory. Or as real estate agent Frank Bascombe, the central character in Richard Ford's *Independence Day* (1995), pronounces early on, "the one gnostic truth of real estate: that people never find or buy the house they say they want. A market economy, so I've learned, is not even remotely premised on anybody getting what he wants."[86]

Still, suburbia has hardly been the exclusive locale for critiques of modern society. During the postwar period cities increasingly have been portrayed as far less amenable than suburbs to the sorts of goals embraced in the dream. Trading on demonizing visions of the city as a landscape of chaos and violence, films such as *Blade Runner* (1982) and *Grand Canyon* (1991) promulgate a vision of the city as a place where realizing the dream would be impossible.[87] Meanwhile the confidence of developers, advertisers, policy makers, and residents in the desirability of suburbia continues unabated. By encouraging the purchase of houses, furnishings, and automobiles, as well as the consumption of many other products and services, sitcoms, newscasts, and especially commercials only strengthen the hegemony of the dream itself.

Music

Some of the most caustic critiques of the dream, particularly as it has been realized in suburbia, have come from musicians. Lyrics that concern suburbia, such as "Little Boxes" (Malvina Reynolds, 1963), "Down in Suburbia" (Bob Lind, 1966), "Paper Maché" (Hal David, 1969), "Subdivision Blues" (Tom T. Hall, 1973), "Suburbanites Invade" (False Prophets, 1981), and "Subdivisions" (Neil Peart, 1982), are almost uniformly mordant. The title of William Wimsatt's 1994 hip-hop tract, *Bomb the Suburbs,* is exemplary. Nevertheless, the nature of such critiques is much the same as in film: even while casting suburbia as the antithesis of the dream, the terms in which the criticism has been cast—extolling individuality and personal expression—still serve to reinforce the legitimacy of the privatist-individualist "dream."

Neil Peart's "Subdivisions" typifies this kind of critique, as the "dreamer" is equated with the "misfit" in suburbia, in other words, the individualist whose dreams are frustrated by the uniformity and standardization of suburbia. The mass-produced landscape instead promotes consumerist satisfaction of "small desires" at the cost of abandoning one's personal "dreams":

Sprawling on the fringes of the city
In geometric order
An insulated border
In between the bright lights
And the far unlit unknown
Growing up it all seems so one-sided
Opinions all provided
The future pre-decided
Detached and subdivided
In the mass production zone
Nowhere is the dreamer
Or the misfit so alone
. . .
Some will sell their dreams for small desires
Or lose the race to rats
Get caught in ticking traps
And start to dream of somewhere
To relax their restless flight.[88]

The vast numbers of new suburban tracts expanding across America in the postwar decades became ripe territory for critique by young musicians dissatisfied with the political complacency of the era. Houses that varied little in design from one to the next, inhabited by families that seemed to be homogeneous in race, class, size, and politics, were also the very same houses in which young musicians sometimes grew up and started rock bands. Many young residents of suburbia thus experienced firsthand much of the same alienation and numbing conformity that was being censured on the screen. They were therefore ready and eager to write, and to hear, lyrics that left no doubt that manufacturing the dream as mass commodity produced results that were empty and sterile.

They were abetted in this process by media representations that increasingly pathologized suburbia en bloc. Richard Yates's novel *Revolutionary Road* (1961), for example, set in 1955, characterizes the "deadly dull homes in the suburbs" as something to be avoided out of fear of becoming "contaminated." In the words of the central character, everybody else in suburbia has come to live "in a state of total self-deception" against which he has to be continually on guard.[89] A similar state of near-paranoia energized Reverend Andrew M. Greeley, who in a 1958 lead article in the national Catholic publication *The Sign* characterized a good portion of suburbia as "a jungle of picture-windowed boxes on concrete slabs" with "poor sewage, terrible streets, overcrowded schools," and so forth. But elsewhere was no better: in more affluent suburbs "there is likely to be a high rate of bleeding ulcers, heart attacks, and nervous breakdowns."[90] Suburbia, in sum, was dangerous.

In light of such fear and loathing, suburbia became a ripe terrain for the setting of soft-core pornographic novels. Two by Dean McCoy, for example, *The Development* (1961) and *The Love Pool* (1964), proclaim the depravity of suburbia from their cover blurbs (Figures 7.4, 7.5): "A biting novel which strips bare the flimsy facade of decency concealing the unbridled sensual desires of America's sprawling Suburbia," and "the story of degenerating morals in modern suburbia—where extra-marital love is taken for granted, and loose behavior is a mark of status!"[91] One academically oriented study, Philip Slater's *Pursuit of Loneliness* (1970), condemned suburbia as a very sick locale, an exemplification of the "pathogenic forces" of privatism that had beset America.[92]

The range of pernicious consequences that musicians correspondingly tied to the suburban diaspora ranged from numbness, precipitated by social and architectural conformity, to the financial and psychic ruin precipitated by excessive consumerism. Four examples from the past thirty-five years can perhaps suggest the range that is found in dozens more. In the first, "Pleasant Valley Sunday" (Monkees, 1966), the name of the locale, as with so many subdivisions, stands in near-ironic contrast to the emptiness of the lives that are lived there:

> Another Pleasant Valley Sunday
> Charcoal burning everywhere
> Rows of houses that are all the same
> And no one seems to care
> See Mrs. Gray she's proud today because her roses are in bloom
> Mr. Green he's so serene, he's got a TV in every room
> Another Pleasant Valley Sunday
> Here in status symbol land
> Mothers complain about how hard life is
> And the kids just don't understand
> Creature comfort goals
> They only numb my soul and make it hard for me to see.[93]

Three decades later that numbness remains unabated in "Welcome to the Dollhouse" (1995), the title song of the movie of the same name. Here a band of white teenage boys sings of the loneliness and sterility of suburbia, performing all the while from the open door of their garage in a quintessentially suburban split-level house.

More caustically, in "Whiplash Liquor" (Ugly Kid Joe, 1991) the numbness of a placeless and parentless cul-de-sac is both abetted and assuaged by alcohol and music:

> Suburban white alcoholic trash
> We ain't glam and we ain't thrash
> We're victims of a society
> That fucks with me about sobriety
> . . .

At split-level Sahara Springs
every man cast covetous eyes
upon his neighbor's wife—
Every woman brazenly encouraged
these advances **THE**

DEVELOPMENT

DEAN McCOY

B414F
50c
K

A biting novel which strips bare the flimsy
facade of decency concealing the unbridled
sensual desires of America's sprawling Suburbia.

Figure 7.4. Dean McCoy, *The Development,* 1961. In soft-core pornographic novels of the 1960s, suburbia readily
became associated with depravity.

Figure 7.5. Dean McCoy, *The Love Pool*, 1964.

The weekend comes and my parents are gone
It's time to party once I mow the lawn
Havin' fun ain't that a fact
It's rock 'n' roll in the cul-de-sac![94]

The imagery becomes darker yet in "Suburban Life" (Kottonmouth Kings, 1997), as a parent's wide-eyed appetite for suburban consumerism is shown to have devastating consequences for the children of suburbia:

Now my pops bought the system, American dreamer
Bought a new home and a brand new Beemer
But it didn't take long for things to fall apart
Because the system that he bought ain't got no heart
From the bills for days he got blood shot eyes
The American dream was a pack of lies
Six months later Municipal Court
Divorce time baby, child support
I went from home cooked meals to TV dinners
No more little Steven, now it's Saint Dogg the sinner
There's no cash back cause there was no receipt
Man suburban life ain't done a dime for me.[95]

A common element of these and almost all other musical critiques of suburbia remains the complaint that suburbs, including their standardized housing and consumerist culture, repress the individuality of those who live there. The upshot is a bitter lament that no dream can be realized in suburbia, the terrain that ostensibly had been purpose-built for realizing the dream. Nevertheless throughout all these lyrics there is little occasion to doubt that the dream itself is in dispute. Rather, suburbia as realized is the wrong means for such an end; suburbia, it would seem, is not individualist enough. In fact the consistency with which rock music has critiqued suburbia over the past four decades has almost approached the same level of conformity that the music finds in suburbia's subdivisions and residents.[96] Still, underlying that critique may well be the recurring fear of architectural determinism, and thus a desire to guard against the tendency of the uniform monotonous environment to produce uniform robotic people. But the irony is that the fear of conforming may have produced exactly the uniformity of opinion that was unwanted in the first place.

Rappin' Suburbia

Over the past half century countless urban redevelopment programs and academic studies have sought to reverse both the material decay of the cities as well as the antipathy with which they have been portrayed.[97] But few musicians, despite their widespread animus toward suburbia, have engaged the city in any less negative terms.

Perhaps the most notable exception has been in hip-hop music, which offers a more complex critique of urban life. Notably popular among suburban youth as well as city dwellers,[98] hip-hop in many cases brings a trenchant critique to bear on the nexus of individualist culture and the city. On the one hand, genres such as gangsta rap foreground the verbal and physical violence that are often necessary to participate in urban life. On the other hand, in both lyric content and performance technique, rap often emphasizes the community and response of the audience, the character and tradition of specific localities, the achievement of identity through risk and difference, and an authenticity of urban experience that is unavailable in ostensibly sanitized and homogenized suburbia.[99]

For example, in the song "Who Down to Ride" (1999), Master P clearly anchors himself in a specific home-territory locale:

Nobody fuckin move, nobody get hurt
Don't make me put your face on a motherfuckin shirt
I'm from the Third Ward, where we all crack skulls. . . .[100]

Several Mobb Deep songs likewise stress the importance of connection to a specific locale, and the authenticity that such a connection engenders. For example, in "Where Ya From" (on the album *Murda Muzik,* 1999), it is not a matter of where you are, but "where you from" and whom do you "rep for":

Fuck where you at kid
Its where you from
Cause where we from niggas pack nothing but the big guns
To all my Queens Duns, Niggas who pump drugs
To all the housing projects who rep for they hood
. . .
Murda Musik my street life influenced it
Its so real bredren I wouldn't test it I rep it. . . .[101]

Another Mobb Deep song, "Murda Muzik," from the same album, stresses the connection of the group to its audience:

It's no doubt, I hold my niggaz cause they hold me too
Like if you show love for me then I'll show love for you
And if you in a situation, just be patient
Give me a minute and I'll be there with no hesitation. . . .[102]

By casting songs partially or entirely in the second person, many rappers are able to establish and strengthen the connection between rapper and audience, as well as a sense of community among those listening. Other performers invoke community in calls to collective action, as in the song provocatively titled "Kill My Landlord" (1993) by The Coup:

> Brothers and sisters we must fight this slumlord
> Overlord of the concrete jungle but I'm humble
> As I witness my opponent crumble
> Like the shack that I live in the house that I rent from him. . . .[103]

The group Public Enemy, notably hailing from suburban Long Island, achieved considerable notoriety for their explicitly political and often controversial lyrics. Their song "1 Million Bottlebags" (1991) portrays the harm that alcohol does to the community—a harm from which the white community is notably protected because the same low-grade "shit" is not available there:

> An oh lemme tell you 'bout Shorty
> . . .
> He's just a slave to the bottle and the can
> 'Cause that's his man
> The malt liquor man
> . . .
> But they don't sell the shit in the white neighborhood
> Exposin' the plan they get mad at me I understand
> They're slaves to the liquor man. . . .[104]

And while "the white neighborhood" can stand for suburbia as well as white city neighborhoods, it is hardly surprising that representations of the conventional "American dream" (nuclear-family, in the suburbs) are conspicuous by their absence in hip-hop. On the other hand, dreams of fame and "living large" are correspondingly abundant. Too $hort outlines this kind of dream in "Life Is . . . Too $hort" (1988):

> Everybody's got that same old dream
> To have big money and fancy things
> Drive a brand new Benz, keep your bank right here. . . .[105]

Thus in hip-hop the city serves as a locale for articulating identities in multiple ways, in multiple dimensions. This is no longer the stereotypical "American dream," but one of a contrasting sort that readily appeals to suburban youth bored and alienated by homogenized spaces. And this may well suggest a further question: whether the preoccupation of many suburban designers, planners, and critics with the need to fabricate *community* is overly utopist, or at least unrealistic. For if the central desiderata are a sense of identity and belonging, it is evident that these increasingly are articulated through symbolic connections and associations, not least in popular music. Peter J. Martin puts it directly: what music groups offer their audiences, "above all, is a sense of who you are and where you belong."[106] As a dimension for the formation of black identities, hip-hop in particular offers unprecedented variety and complexity, entirely unlike the managed aesthetics of so many suburban developments. As Michael Eric Dyson elaborates, the "range of musical and cultural identities" afforded by rap amounts to an "ever-expanding repertoire of created selves" ranging from griot, feminist, educator, and prophet to consumer, misogynist, criminal, and sexual athlete.[107] In sum, the diversity of identities that may be articulated through music is only with difficulty contained, much less realized, in the fixed apparatus of most contemporary built spaces.[108]

This is not to argue that music is a medium superior to architecture or built space for the production of identity or the articulation of belonging. All have crucial roles that frequently intersect. Popular music, conspicuously active for most of the twentieth century in the critique of suburbia, has been problematically limited in the scope of its assessment, still commonly replicating the worries of midcentury sociologists such as Riesman, Whyte, and Mills, rather than exploring other dimensions in which residents of suburbia anchor and differentiate identities. On the other hand, hip-hop, conspicuously inattentive to the suburban single-nuclear-family dream, has approached the problematic of identity in a manner that suggests different potentials. Acknowledging the real ways in which immediate physical, social, and economic circumstances affect identity, rappers also foreground a host of means by which those circumstances can be modified or even transcended, through active, performative means. This suggests that a comparably flexible engagement with suburbia, the dream house, and the American dream itself also may be possible; the final chapter of this book lays some of the groundwork for such an approach.

In this context the role of hip-hop cannot be taken lightly. Among the well-recognized ironies surrounding its success is its popularity among suburban youth, frequently to a degree that transforms the community planner or real-estate developer's image of suburbia substantially—with SUVs blasting tracks of the latest hits, gangsta clothing in the malls, in the schools, and on the playgrounds, and teenage behavior emulating that seen in films or music videos. The argument here is not that music is necessarily conducive to such behavior. Rather, the point is that hip-hop does speak to many of the dimensions of suburban experience today, or the dimensions in which today's suburban teenagers ache for experience (good or bad) but are restricted by physical or social means from obtaining it. Rap, its accoutrements, its sounds and its movements, provide means by which many suburban teenagers reclaim dimensions of experience that they recognize as lacking in their present lives and environments.

In their original, nineteenth-century incarnation, American suburbs were largely domestic environments that could eschew the trappings of commerce and prize their alienation from the city. By the last quarter of the twentieth century, however, circumstances had become too complex to maintain that isolation except perhaps as a nostalgic ideal. In many cases surpassing core cities in population and area, suburban municipalities took on the appearance of new urban centers. In 1991 Joel Garreau was able to describe the rapid, and recent, appearance of over two hundred "edge cities" whose characteristics no longer accorded with traditional suburban paradigms. They each featured at least 5 million square feet of leasable office space, contained at least 600,000 square feet of leasable retail space, had fewer bedrooms than jobs, were perceived by the public as "one place," and had not appeared to be like a "city" as few as thirty years previously. And as Peter Muller has shown, suburbs became centers of government bureaucracy, retail, corporate research and administration, and manufacturing and production unto themselves.[109] These functions often existed side by side with expansive domestic environments of mansionettes, tract houses, town houses, condominiums, and apartments, although the residential areas were seldom well integrated with any of the others. Often street patterns inhibited or prevented traffic from passing between residential areas and any others. Thus residents of suburbia (teenagers included) found themselves in the paradoxical situation of being at the center of where everything was happening but being engaged with very little of it, and being discouraged by the spread-out nature of suburbia from engaging any more.

Nevertheless by the end of the twentieth century the increasing density of suburbia and complexity of functions that it sustained rendered it nearly impossible to maintain most long-standing myths surrounding homogeneity in housing, or stereotypical media caricatures. The potential for growth and change in suburbia no longer rested with internal dynamics, such as local housing growth or commercial activity. Rather, it was beholden more and more to global commerce and capital, seeking to locate and adapt the best landscape for their purposes. Achieving credible and widespread diversity in housing and affording opportunities for difference and change thus have become far more complex matters than expected. In some cases, people remain quite content to adhere to given suburban lifestyle stereotypes—a position that does not receive the respect and sympathetic examination that it deserves from critics and historians. Other suburbanites, seeking change, engagement, and difference, too commonly have found a lack of ready prototypes, accommodating sites, and interested collaborators (developers, community officials, and so on) for implementing those ends in material form. Debates and proposals surrounding problems such as these are the subject of the next, and final chapter.

Conclusion: Reframing Suburbia

Dream Wars

Media representations of suburbia over the past half century have tended toward pessimism and even outright fear and loathing, warning of dire threats to self, spirit, and society. But it is also apparent that from the perspective of many suburbanites this animus is misdirected and ill informed. In suburb after suburb many people are quite happy, thank you very much, with where they live, their houses, their friends, and their communities. As Bennett M. Berger found as far back as 1966, most of the suburbanites he interviewed "harbored a view of their new suburban homes as paradise permanently gained."[1] While countless tracts of suburbia are indisputably more homogeneous, and often more conformist, than central cities, residents of suburbia do not themselves commonly complain of stifled individualism.[2]

This, in turn, poses a problem with respect to the bulk of the media critiques that I introduced earlier. For how can it be that there are films, songs, and novels saying that suburbia is not individualist enough, that it yields barren dreams, while at the same time many who live there see their individuality and dreams as far better realized, and less compromised, than they would have been elsewhere? If in fact suburbia has been delivering the American dream for so long—over half of America has moved there—then what underlies the longstanding antipathy and condescension deployed against suburbia?

As may be expected, there are many answers. I would like to sketch factors of three types—social, aesthetic, and ideological—that play into an explanation.

Social

In many cases the critics are demographically distinct from those they critique. First of all, there are class distinctions. Critics of suburbia have long spoken from the perspective of elites (often including those who have formal training in academic disciplines or the arts of film, photography, and writing). They may fear that the proliferation of mass culture may cheapen standards of elite culture. In this light it is no small irony that certain dimensions of mass culture, such as film and music, become the media by which ostensibly "elite" critiques of culture are disseminated.

Second, there are generational distinctions. Youth, chronically disaffected with their parents' world, eager to differentiate themselves from that world, may identify with cinematic characters, or compose lyrics, portraying a generational divide in terms of suburban life and landscape. And more practically speaking, the very dreams that parental generations are trying to flesh out in suburbia—dreams that involve separation from the tensions and pressures of the world at large and anchoring identity for the long term—are alien to their children, who instead seek and savor the exciting possibilities of the wider world. In other words for youth suburbia may become a suffocating terrain of social and psychic inertia. Much of the energy that informs popular music critiques of suburbia is clearly an escape from that inertial state, a state that is so readily symbolized by the stereotype of unchanging, repetitive suburban tract housing.

Aesthetic

In postwar decades the "dream" progressively became available to an increasingly democratic public, not just affluent Mr. Blandingses seeking refuge in a Connecticut village landscape, but waves of white- and blue-collar workers who could afford mass-produced houses in tract developments. The dream likewise proliferated through ever more affordable mass products and standardized materials. A consequence of such affordability was that products were designed and marketed according to increasingly reductive stereotypes. And this points to an implicit contradiction embedded in the democratization of the dream: the ideal of a personalized dream individually defined and achieved is inconsistent with its material realization in stereotyped forms and mass-produced materials.

Nor was this a new contradiction. Rather, it extended an ongoing conflict between democracy and aesthetics that has persisted in the practice of architecture and design at least since the times of William Morris. On the one hand have been those, such as Morris, who argued that the only truly viable objective for art in society is to create individually designed and handcrafted pieces for specific persons and purposes. Morris understood the making of art as a process that afforded an occasion for personal fulfillment. "The pleasure which ought to go with the making of every piece of handicraft," he wrote in 1883, includes "the self-respect which comes of a sense of usefulness."[3] And at a time when the rapid expansion of industrial production meant separation of workplace from home for increasing numbers of people, Morris argued that home was the only place where the individual could achieve the self-respect that comes from work. In an essay titled "Making the Best of It" (ca. 1879), Morris focused on decorating and furnishing the "ordinary dwelling-house." In remarks immediately preceding a discussion of the exterior, including some strictures on suburban gardening practices, Morris urged recognition "of the right of every man to have fit work to do in a beautiful home. Therein lies all that is indestructible of the pleasure of life; no man need ask for more than that, no man should be granted less."[4] Likewise only through the presence of art would "every man's house . . . be fair and decent, soothing to his mind and helpful to his work."[5] Correspondingly Morris rejected manufactured commodities and the industrial-capitalist system that produced them because they mechanized labor, and so eradicated the opportunity for deriving pleasure from both labor and its product.

Morris extended his argument in a discussion of the design and fabrication of dwellings. He extolled the "labourer's cottage built of the Cotswold limestone," fashioned in vernacular style by the village mason, according to traditional techniques. Against this ideal Morris posed the present state of London's suburbs, which he found deplorable, covered with new houses: "if there were one touch of generosity, of honest pride, of wish to please about them, I would forgive them in the lump. But there is none—not one."[6] A disciple of John Ruskin, Morris sought an architectural standard that was much the same as Ruskin's, that is, that the building embody and display, for the enrichment of all, the joy in craft and labor of those who built it. Three decades earlier, Ruskin himself may have penned the ultimate characterization of a dwelling as a material embodiment of the resident's individual life. Writing in *The Seven Lamps of Architecture* (1849), he urged that a dwelling become a monument to the individual who had it built:

> I would have, then, our ordinary dwelling-houses built to last, and built to be lovely; as rich and full of pleasantness as may be, within and without; with what degree of likeness to each other in style and manner, I will say presently, under another head; but, at all events, with such differences as might suit and express each man's character and occupation, and partly his history. This right over the house, I conceive, belongs to its first builder, and is to be respected by his children; and it would be well that blank stones should be left in places, to be inscribed with a summary of his life and of its experience, raising thus the habitation into a kind of monument. . . .[7]

Early in the twentieth century essayist Charles Keeler registered the progress of such arguments in America. Tying the house to the character of its inhabitant, he argued that "the home must suggest the life it is to encompass." And the best way to render the house "an individual expression of the life which it is to environ" would be to forgo "as far as possible all factory-made accessories" and instead for it to express "your own fondness for things that have been created as a response to your love of that which is good and simple and fit for daily companionship."[8]

On the other side of the coin have been those who welcomed the rise of industrial production because it made opportunities for individual expression available to the masses. The vast array of commodities at the disposal of the consumer, from comfortable dwellings and hygienic plumbing to a wide selection of furnishings, have provided far more affordable, and more diverse, opportunities for individuation than before mechanization. Nor would those making this argument be unaware of the obvious irony in Morris's position: although a staunch socialist, he argued for a mode of production that exceeded the capacity of most people to afford it.

Yet it was Morris's censorious view of the pernicious effects of mechanization and of suburbia as an aesthetic wasteland that persisted throughout the twentieth century. It found expression, for example, in Christine Frederick's 1928 condemnation of middle-class suburbs: "The sad truth is that the suburb standardizes those things which a true individual doesn't want standardized, and leaves unstandardized those things he most desires standardized. . . . Standardization in the suburbs is not applied, as it should be, to the comfort of living, but to the flattening out of personal individuality."[9] Prefabricated and mass-produced housing enjoyed some interest in the 1930s,[10] but large-scale mass-production techniques were not perfected until the early 1940s, during World War II. One result was a sharp rise in the production of standardized tract housing across America (Figure C.1), which for some only exacerbated the conflict between ideals of individualized aesthetic satisfaction and democratic mass opportunity. To help examine the larger framework and implications of that conflict, some understanding is necessary of the contemporary ideological debate over culture and mass production, which is discussed next.

Ideological

As this and previous chapters have shown, the history of suburbia is tied to a wide spectrum of ideological concerns, ranging from matters of self, status, and personal fulfillment to the position of the individual with respect to the larger body social and politic. Many of the debates that have grown up surrounding suburbia thus are rooted in the different sides of a broader, long-standing contest within American society. On the one hand is an idealistic vision of life as centered on opportunities for self-realization. Here one's fulfillment as an individual depends on the freedom to pursue private aspirations, a freedom that in turn is promised by the three-hundred-year heritage of Enlightenment notions of liberty, property, entrepreneurial freedom, and the right to pursue happiness. In sum, each of us has the potential to be the self-made man—even if few of us reach this ideal state.

Against this idealized, and still widely held, eighteenth-century model, is an advanced-capitalist vision of self as rendered upwardly mobile through opportunities available in an economy of commodity accumulation and consumption. Because mass-produced commodities are inexpensive and available in a wide variety of choices, elements of the "dream" become accessible to a much broader portion of the population. But although in principle such a commodity culture values choice highly, the actual dimensions of choice are limited to those that are marketed. Notions such as "self" and "happiness" are thus prone to disappear into categories of consumer products. In the end, as the marketplace becomes arbiter of "self," private aspirations and personal freedoms are correspondingly compromised. For instance, when builders and developers are asked why they consistently reproduce a certain kind of house design, they reply that they are only trying to provide the market with "what sells." Of course "what sells" means "what already has been proven to sell," a circular disincentive to experimentation, innovation, and personalization. Prospective purchasers, for whom the choice of a house may seem an opportunity to further delineate self or individuality, are in fact ill served by a market that prefers to replicate only the choices that appeal to the broadest common denominator.

The larger ideological contest—call it individualism versus commodity culture—is not a simple contest to resolve, especially because in the present day neither side can succeed without recourse to the other. For most Americans, life without some participation in the present commodity economy is inconceivable if not impossible. But that same economy still markets its products as choices through which to articulate

Figure C.1. A view of typical postwar tract housing, identical from one house to the next except for alternating reversed plans and variations in the pastel colors the exteriors were painted. Collection of Ann Forsyth.

one's individuality, couching benefits and attributes of commodities in terms of their capacity to fulfill long-standing ideals of freedom of choice and self-determination.

In many respects the suburban dwelling has become the medium of choice through which Americans pursue a material reconciliation of these two contradictory imperatives. For the most part residents are happy to pursue their lives in terms that mask such ideological fissures and contradictions. Nor do one-dimensional dream-house endorsements or critiques such as those examined so far help. In their narrow one-sidedness they often preclude analysis of the complex forces and circumstances that can make a given dwelling a highly satisfactory setting (or not) for reconciling the individualist and commodity imperatives.

One theoretical approach that can be adapted to the analysis of these contradictory imperatives was outlined in the late 1930s, in the debate between Walter Benjamin and Theodor Adorno over the relations among art, mass culture, and democracy.[11] Not only have the terms in which Benjamin and Adorno fleshed out this debate remained central to the contest between American individualism and mass culture throughout the rest of the century, but, as I propose below, they may also serve as critical tools for advancing analysis of the suburban American dream.

For his part Benjamin focused on film, a mechanically reproducible medium suited to consumption by a mass audience. Trying to assess the impact of this medium, Benjamin likened the mode by which viewers apprehend it to the manner in which people commonly apprehend architecture. What they see, whether buildings or the "content" of the film, is ordinarily something to which they are already *habituated,* so they apprehend it in an *incidental* fashion.[12] Instead of being absorbed into the work of art, as would be the case with an old-master painting, the viewer (of the film or the building) is able to understand what is happening in a comparatively free state of mind. Thus unlike the work of art that can capture the viewer for its own purposes, the mechanically produced product is available for use toward the viewer's own ends. Instead of being subsumed in the original artist's project, the viewer (or user) can tie what he or she sees to his or her own projects. In other words, despite the nature of the medium as a system of engagement with a mass audience, the individual by no means surrenders to it. Rather, individuals have considerable autonomy in pursuing their own projects, notwithstanding the claims to authority and control embodied in the filmic (or architectural) spaces that they may encounter. Such is the similar position argued more recently by Michel de Certeau: that pedestrians, far from being subject to the spatial sovereignty of city streets and buildings, instead are able to appropriate the urban topography to their own ends, without violating that topography, through a personal apparatus of "pedestrian speech acts."[13]

Against such liberatory views of the individual's relation to elements of the manufactured environment, Adorno decried the capability of mass culture to produce standardized individuals. Like Benjamin, Adorno also resorted to architecture to make his point. Writing in the early 1940s from wartime refuge in Los Angeles, he found "the new bungalows on the outskirts" of the city were "at one with the flimsy structures of world fairs in their praise of technical progress and their built-in demand to be discarded after a short while like empty food cans." In other words houses were simply disposable commodities. And because these were mass produced and standardized, Adorno (writing in collaboration with Max Horkheimer) argued that commodity culture ultimately abetted the standardization of human identity.[14] As John Keats likewise contended in his 1956 novel of suburbia, *The Crack in the Picture Window,* "the dwelling shapes the dweller. When all dwellings are the same shape, all dwellers are squeezed into the same shape." In short, cookie-cutter houses produce cookie-cutter people. Thus, "more insidious and far more dangerous than any other influence, is the housing development's destruction of individuality."[15]

Adorno and Horkheimer explained that consumers may well be presented with a vast array of "choices" for any given commodity, but the choices are not of any individual's own design.[16] Rather, to extend their argument, the individual has very little say at all in fashioning his or her material world: not only are the specific choices (for example, scents such as lemon or wintergreen) determined and synthesized by the producers, but so are the categories to which they apply (for example, air freshener, furniture polish, and so on). It is a recognized marketing strategy to provide more varieties of scent, flavor, and so on—ostensibly more consumer "choices"—primarily as a means of garnering additional shelf space, and thus more sales, for a given brand, rather than out of concern for broadening the scope of American individualism. The individual is cast as little more than "customer" or "consumer," whose role is limited to making choices from menus that afford little room for autonomy or authenticity. In effect individuality is a product of the market, in the same circular way that the array of housing features, plans, and styles from which a purchaser can select are a function of the builder's assessment of "what sells." Horkheimer and Adorno thus offered a dim assessment of claims to opportunities for individualism through mass commodities: "The effrontery of the rhetorical question, 'What do people want?' lies in the fact that it is addressed—as if to reflective individuals—to those very people who are deliberately to be deprived of this individuality."[17]

In many respects the dilemma that Benjamin and Adorno debated is a dilemma that suburbia has been attempting to resolve in the decades since. The "American dream," an individualistic ideal that coalesced in the 1930s and blossomed in the prosperity following World War II, held out the expectation of individualized self-fulfillment. And the mass-produced suburban house, made possible by building processes developed during and since the war years, became the premier means to attain that dream. In countless subdivisions, people who moved there or grew up there would have become, in Benjaminian fashion, "habitually" aware of suburbia and of what it meant and represented. Far from being standardized or homogenized by suburbia, they would see the landscape there as a tabula not-quite-rasa on which to undertake multiple and diverse acts of individuation. I call it a tabula not-quite-rasa because a true tabula rasa is a scary thing: it is the abyss of existential beginning.

In a fundamental respect what the suburban landscape provides Americans is what the landscape of any culture provides its people, a *datum* of opportunity: a set of given conditions and customs that are well recognized and observed, in other words, a knowable terrain in which needs and desires can be addressed in a practicable fashion. Through a wide variety of means, ranging from choice of house color to furnishing the yard with lawn ornaments, from turning the garage into a workshop to custom-furnishing the den, nursery, bedroom, kitchen, or basement "family room" complete with wet bar or home theater, people have been able to fashion the suburban "dream"-scape in accord with their individual goals and expectations.

Satisfaction and contentment with such pursuits, sometimes undertaken at the cost of considerable time and effort, frequently have been construed by critics as evidence of selfishness, insularity, and complacency.[18] The choices, while varied, have long been limited by the basic apparatus of the suburban dwelling: the single-family house, its yard, and the available range of mass-produced appliances and furnishings. The fact that everybody's kitchen, family room, barbecue, and so forth might look pretty much like everyone else's has been judged to be evidence of a surrender to conformity in all aspects of life. Detractors also have pointed to the accumulation and consumption of material goods—the detached house and all the "stuff" inside— as misguided efforts that ultimately would lead to a very empty manner of self-fulfillment. Paralleling such critiques of suburbia have been the arguments that Adorno and Horkheimer already had laid out in their analysis of the culture industry: that the array of goods available for ostensibly distinguishing one's individuality did little more than standardize people. Mass-produced commodities, they argued, robbed people of opportunities they otherwise might have had to define themselves as individuals.[19] Writing of popular music, but with implications for the wider realm of all goods, Adorno and Horkheimer noted that "the man with leisure has to accept what the culture manufacturers offer him."[20] The result was bleak: "The culture industry perpetually cheats its consumers of what it perpetually promises," namely the opportunity for authenticity, originality, or autonomy. Instead of seeking one's own skills and pleasures, Adorno and Horkheimer lamented that "the diner must be satisfied with the menu."[21]

But these comments actually beg a more fundamental question. Is the diner—or, more generally, the modern consumer—actually the victim here, limited in the pursuit of individuation to what the manufacturers of commodities provide, as Adorno and Horkheimer would argue? Or does the array of commodities, singly and in a host of varied combinations, afford a far greater range of possibilities for individuation, as Benjamin would argue? For the past forty-five years, critiques of suburbia overwhelmingly have hewn closer to Adorno's line than Benjamin's, not least in media representations of the sorts that I explored in previous chapters. This occurred despite a prevailing consensus in the same popular media that suburbs *can* and *ought to* function in a Benjaminian fashion as the *datum* of a privatist dream-enterprise. Confident in that expectation, countless suburbanites eagerly pursued such a dream, and documentary evidence of many sorts has affirmed suburbanites' beliefs that they have achieved the dream.[22] But since the 1950s a majority of critics have remained skeptical of such claims, arguing instead that cookie-cutter houses and mass commodities produce cookie-cutter people, along much the same lines as Adorno's contention that standardized products produce standardized identities. In effect Adorno conceded our helplessness in the face of the culture industry (nowadays subsumed into global corporate enterprise) to maintain or even know our own identity. Critics of suburbia have come to a comparable conclusion: not only do standardized products such as tract houses make standardized, homogenized people, but they even rob people of the opportunity to recognize themselves as individuals.

One of the strongest condemnations of suburbia along these lines is John Keats's polemical quasi-novel *The Crack in the Picture Window* (1956). As discussed earlier, he embraced a thoroughly determinist assessment of tract housing, arguing that identically shaped dwellings repress and destroy human individuality.[23] Alarmingly he warned that the commodified architectural menu of suburbia would conduce to even more dire consequences: "If we permit builders to continue to throw up Rolling Knolls Estates, we are going to create social and mental illness in our home towns." Citing sociologist Harold Mendelsohn, Keats continued the determinist despair over suburban planning:

> In developments, we have already seen that churches are nonexistent or too few; that parks and recreational area [sic] are most often missing. These developments are just bedrooms on the edge of town. What do you suppose will happen when the preschool children in all these places are ten years older. . . ? Of course, what the crime rate will be ten years from now when the children grow up with no place to meet or play under adult supervision is something else again.[24]

Nearly a quarter century later, the film *Over the Edge* (1979) offered a filmic realization of this prediction, ostensibly documenting the effects of master-planned communities on teenagers. Focusing on the new community of New Grenada, the film shows how its design forced youth into drugs, alcohol, vandalism, gang behavior, and a host of other dysfunctional activities.

Such determinist thinking probably was less indebted to the high-modernist era belief that architecture can reform society than to its earlier counterpart, the mid-nineteenth-century moralistic aestheticism of John Ruskin. This approach was already prefigured in the early nineteenth-century notion of "architecture parlante" as articulated by Claude-Nicolas Ledoux, who imputed to architecture the power of inculcating morality.[25] For Keats and other critics of suburbia, however, it was the inverse of this position that mattered: that architecture also had the power to expunge immorality. Yet only a few writers on suburbia have explicitly called this determinist approach into question. One of the earliest, and still most succinct, was Bennett M. Berger, writing in the introduction to the 1968 reprint of his 1960 book on working-class suburbia:

Perhaps it is because we have been too well trained to believe that there is somehow a direct relationship between the physical structure of the esthetic shape of a residential environment and the sort of values and culture it can possibly engender— so that the esthetic monotony of suburbia could house nothing but a generation of dull, monotonous people, and its cheerful poverty of architectural design could breed nothing but a race of happy robots.[26]

The dominant discourse nevertheless has remained consistent with the Adornian critique of mass culture and the sort of architectural determinism that Keats epitomized. As three more recent films demonstrate, commodity culture continues to remain linked to the decline of American society. The central character in *SAFE* (1995), for example, struggles with a near-fatal sensitivity to almost all manufactured objects. The furnishings of her suburban home have the capacity to kill her. The film *subUrbia* (1997) foregrounds many ruinous aspects of commodity culture, from the abjection of burger flipping to the way that material success irretrievably distances a successful rock star from his former friends. *Crime and Punishment in Suburbia* (2000) offers no less stringent a critique of suburban materialism, ranging from the sardonic use of an electric carving knife in murdering Fred Skolnik to love-interest Vincent's distinctly Thoreauian dwelling. His rustic bungalow suits well his outcast, spiritual character and contrasts strikingly with the Skolnik family's all-too-typical suburban mansion.

Yet these and other media critiques, portraying suburbs as insidious, pernicious, homogenizing, and commodity-bound, exist in almost paradoxical tension with the opinions that countless real suburbanites have of their own lives, confident not only that suburbia provides the opportunity to reach for the dream but also in their own success in achieving the dream.

This irony is paralleled by another: that so many critiques of commodity culture, such as "Little Boxes," *subUrbia,* and *Crime and Punishment in Suburbia,* appear in popular media that are themselves products of the culture industry. Here again an Adornian critique suggests that the consumer, the listener or the film goer, is at the mercy of Hollywood's mass product. In short, these are only vinyl or celluloid critiques. Not only do they make money for the industry, but they also afford access only to avenues of critique that are materially ineffective: after you watch the film, you go home ostensibly enlightened, perhaps entertained, but still disenfranchised. Just as SUV commercials tell mass audiences that SUVs are the way to get away from all the traffic, and thus precipitate even worse traffic, so mass-media critiques of suburbia take the viewer's money but make no real difference in the choices available.

While such an approach to the analysis of suburbia has considerable merit, I want to conclude with the suggestion that the Adornian position, for so long dominant among critics of suburbia (or at least a position to which they are sympathetic), is no longer helpful. In a society all of whose members are consumers of mass-produced commodities, it no longer stands to reason that the great portion of the population, because it must be "satisfied with the menu," must be doomed to a false individuality. To argue this is tantamount to the elitist, undemocratic position that a vast portion of the population cannot know what individuality is, that they cannot know themselves, while the critic, who uses those very same commodities, is capable of such knowledge. It may be argued, fairly, that individualism is a bankrupt ideology, and that a better understanding of the relations among members of society needs to be theorized. Such has been the focus of cultural theory for decades, and not least for Horkheimer and Adorno. My focus in this book, however, is how architecture has evolved in concert with, and in response to, the ideological framework of its times. From that perspective, my purpose is to show how the bourgeois dwelling and the suburb are instruments of an individualist ideology. Given the continuing hegemony of that ideology, it strikes me as elitist to argue that the lives of those who accept it, and who correspondingly make use of mass commodities in pursuit of an individualist dream, are unfulfilled. Rather, I would argue that in such a society, people generally act in a Benjaminian fashion, habituated to commodities, not controlled by them, and therefore able to appropriate those objects toward their own purposes. If objects are marketed with a certain brand-name value or stylistic cachet, consumers routinely use that to suit their own ends, just as Downing's readers could draw from his array of styles—Greek, rural Gothic, modern Italian, and so on—to suit their own visions of bourgeois selfhood. Correspondingly if consumers are jaded to brand names or styles, they make no use of them, which equally remains part of the process of articulating selfhood.

Codes and Community

In line with longstanding arguments underlying antipathy toward suburbia, as outlined above, there have been efforts to reform suburban design through strategies such as devising formulas for creating community or imposing design codes.

Perhaps the most frequently criticized mode of community-making commonly associated with suburbia has been "theming," a notion once applied to Disney theme parks but now seen in "village"-themed outlet and craft malls that include some housing, and increasingly found in many types of gated communities.[27] Theming of all these sorts has been condemned as inauthentic and escapist, offering little more than consumption-based simulacra that divert attention from the realities of the corporate-controlled landscape. The criticism is well justified, but it also is framed in terms that are generally too black and white, focusing primarily on the pernicious consequences of theming while failing to address reasons for its continuing popularity.

For to some degree theming, like much of suburbia, is also *constructive dreaming*. Drawing on aspirations and desires that are perhaps too restrictive or too utopian, theme parks, malls, and suburban subdivisions nevertheless share a common interest in building locales that afford safely themed—that is, well principled—homogeneity. From the ostensibly midwestern small-town "Main Street" that anchors Disneyland

(1955) and Walt Disney World (1971), to the social theming of "golf" or "executive" gated communities, to design codes that govern some New Urbanist projects, there is a common commitment to establishing and preserving a certain idealized social fabric (Figure C.2). In the case of Disney Main Streets and some of the more prominent neotraditionalist projects, the ideals are constituted in terms of myths of things that may never have existed, such as romanticized notions of nineteenth-century small towns as graced by homogeneous, harmonious "community." In other cases, it is suggested that simply building a new town to look like an old one—perhaps by distilling characteristics of "traditional architecture" from established examples—can reinstate that mythical community.[28]

Approaches such as these, notwithstanding the advantages of constructive dreaming, introduce as many dilemmas as they address. If porches and narrow lots, for example, are thought to be a means of bringing back neighborliness, that is an affirmation that design influences behavior, and so we have to start thinking of design codes as ultimately being *behavior* codes. There is no question that architecture extensively structures human behavior. Indeed the more that such processes are understood, the better that architecture can serve human needs. One might even argue that the more the user is able to understand how architecture affects human behavior, the more open and accessible architecture becomes, as the user is less susceptible to misunderstanding and manipulation. But to institute an architectural code for

Figure C.2. Kentlands, Gaithersburg, Maryland, planned in 1988 by Andres Duany and Elizabeth Plater-Zyberk. This curving drive flanked by substantial dwellings, featured in early popular and trade press accounts, established a stylistic paradigm for the community that perhaps most closely resembled Alexandria, Virginia, two centuries prior. Photograph by author.

the express purpose of channeling behavior in increasingly limited ways, however benevolent the intention, may also tend to the opposite effect, making architecture a medium of personal and social restraint, restricting both difference and change.

A second, comparable dilemma arises from the fallacious presumption that it is possible to distill essentials of "traditional" or other sorts of architecture into a form that can be replicated successfully. As Kathleen LaFrank noted in her critique of one of the first New Urbanist projects by Andres Duany and Elizabeth Plater-Zyberk, "Seaside [was] intended to be authentic, indigenous, and timeless, embodying the essential qualities of the American small town of the past."[29] To identify such essentials accurately, it is necessary to recognize that the phenomenon in question—town, community, family, whatever—remains at base a phenomenon of the past, and whatever viable qualities it possessed then were viable in reference to its own time and place. That is not to say that we could not identify those qualities and their context. But to suggest that they could be exported to a different time and place in order to clone certain admired aspects of the past would be to violate principles of both architecture and history. To bring an "authentic" past into the present as a framework for present-day life would be pointlessly anachronistic and useless.

A third dilemma arises from concerted efforts by some planners and developers to produce a readymade design for community.[30] On the one hand, this speaks to very real deficiencies in present-day American society.[31] On the other hand, efforts to establish community through architectural or legalistic means in master-planned communities and common-interest developments frequently function at odds with the interests of those whom they serve. Given the staunchly individualist, privatist character of the American dream, and the hallowed character of private property, it is acutely ironic that so many planned communities predicate their very success on legal provisions that limit property use and personal behavior. Worse, when the limitations begin to look too extreme, the proffered solution is to legislate variety: in the words of Duany, Plater-Zyberk, and Speck, "In today's suburbs and cities alike, design codes are necessary to generate the variety that we, too, hold dear."[32]

Especially troubling is the apprehension, or at least ambivalence, shown by some designers toward difference. Despite the acknowledged sameness of the suburban landscape almost everywhere, designers have long been reluctant to depart from tried and true formulas. As Michael Sorkin has lamented, "the design palette [of suburbia] is extremely limited." Explaining further, he noted that builders were "taking the same limited set of suburban typologies—single-family houses, garden apartments, small office buildings, shopping malls," and doing little more than "tweaking them." Worse, even among those who supposedly eschew such a standardized typology and palette, difference still is cast as a troublesome concern. Designer Gerald Cowart, for example, characterizing his work at Newport, South Carolina, admits an arm's-length attitude toward difference: "We are imposing a synthetic history, a time when choices were not so diverse." Likewise Duany proudly defends his reliance on specific standard models for any given location: "This way there's no possibility of error because the streets and buildings are derived from existing types that we have seen work." Or, one might well conclude, there is no possibility of difference outside a narrow approved canon. Margaret Crawford puts the matter more succinctly: "in the face of enormous fragmentation and difference, people are looking for unity and control." Thus "the whole purpose of neotraditional town planning is to deny difference."[33] And this is an approach that only backfires. For the sameness and consistency within any given project or development derive their presumptive appeal in contradistinction to the complexity and diversity of the "real" world beyond. The effort to deny difference, in other words, only succeeds insofar as its object (the "other") is recognized.

Dilemmas notwithstanding, the continuing popularity of community, tradition, and sometimes mythic themes among designers, developers, builders, and buyers begs recognition of the crucial role of those themes in informing the "dream" agenda for the American domestic landscape. In certain respects architects, planners, developers, and builders have been trying to provide a physical apparatus comparable to what *Leave It to Beaver, Life with Father,* and *Mr. Blandings Builds His Dream House* previously could only provide on celluloid: a readymade world, ready for purchase, where the buyer could simply move in and begin to live the dream as advertised. At the same time the popularity of such media representations continues, thus encouraging public investment in comparable mythic understandings of suburbia.

The 1998 film *Pleasantville* offers one of the best presentations of the ardor for a readymade implementation of myth as reality. The setting for most of the film is a 1950s-era small town that obviously bears close comparison with the fictional town of Mayfield, in which *Leave It to Beaver* was set (Figure C.3). The fact that the teenage protagonists of *Pleasantville,* siblings Bud and Mary-Sue Parker, arrive there by passing through a television set only enhances the immediacy of this myth. As a civic and domestic landscape, the town of Pleasantville is a stereotypical, paradigmatic vision of what many Americans have sought in suburbia for the past century, and its idealized vision of harmonious small-town life parrots preeminent models for suburban design today.[34]

Pleasantville also takes a critical look at the underlying conditions that lie buried in this stereotype and myth: fear of risk, aversion to change, and blind faith in conventions and conventionality. Racist antipathy toward "coloreds" is perhaps the greatest exemplification of the antipathy toward risk and change (Figure C.4), while some of the most entrenched conventions include strictly prescribed gender roles and repression of sexuality. Bud, the central character, repeatedly insists that the kind of behavior he is trying to promote—unrestrained by convention or fear—is "inside you," inside each person. The film is a lesson about the contest of individualism versus the desire to freeze the American dream in the vision of a particular myth, as well as the effect that the outcome of that contest has on community. To impose any given dream, or to freeze one in time and space, is necessarily seen as undertaking an act of enforced homogenization, which at best yields a sterile community, as rendered by limiting the screen image to black and white. Conversely, from the varied ways in which individuals blossom once they change to color, it is evident that "normal" community is predicated on and strengthened by a diverse array of individualist dreams—an array of differences (Figure C.5).

In *The Truman Show,* also released in 1998, there is a parallel critique that focuses on efforts to build frozen dreams de novo. The film concerns a megalomanic project to broadcast the entire life of title character Truman Burbank. For this purpose an entire town, called Seahaven, has been constructed under a giant dome in Hollywood to serve as the perfect environment for Truman to flourish in, and where any of five thousand hidden cameras may capture him. The actual setting chosen for filming *The Truman Show* was, significantly, the town of Seaside, Florida (1983 ff) (Figure C.6), designed by Andres Duany and Elizabeth Plater-Zyberk, who later became founding members of the Congress for the New Urbanism (CNU). Designing Seaside gave Duany and Plater-Zyberk the opportunity to develop many of the design, planning, and development principles that subsequently informed their own practice as well as to shape much of the CNU's original agenda. Significant among their principles was the notion that a well-fashioned design code would be conducive to community life and help maintain its desirability and viability, and that specific design features, such as front porches, narrower streets, and smaller lot sizes, could actively produce community, for example, by bringing neighbors together more closely and more frequently so they would be inclined to greet and chat with each other more often.[35] In the film, Truman is confronted with exactly this sort of neighborly interaction: every time he leaves the house, the same friendly neighbors greet him, always in the same way

Figure C.3. *Pleasantville,* New Line Cinema, 1998. A nostalgically perfect view of the town of Pleasantville, with a traditional milkman, picket fences, and Colonial Revival houses.

Figure C.4. *Pleasantville*. Townspeople smash the interior of the soda shop owned by Bill Johnson after colored artwork appears on the windows of his store.

Figure C.5. *Pleasantville*. Soda shop owner Bill Johnson, still a black and white character, displays his color painting of Bud's mother, Betty Parker (who has turned colored), to the sitter.

(Figure C.7). The problem is that these interactions happen so frequently and so predictably because they are all staged. Truman's neighbors are in fact cast characters who
are scripted and directed to take their places and greet him every time he steps out the
front door.

Intentionally or not, the predictable and simulated nature of these encounters
parodies the design theory and practice of Duany and Plater-Zyberk, among others,
who claim that design strategies can actively promote community.[36] Apart from the
problematic nature of nailing down what "community" is, either as a concept or as a
social nexus, there are difficult questions as to whether design codes and other rules
and regulations produce the desired ends—and, if so, whether such ends justify the
restrictive means. What Truman experiences as the genuine interest and engagement
of others in his neighborhood is only the rote participation of actors following established cues. Knowing as we do that neighbors, script, and set all are part of the same
elaborate sham world that television-show director Christof has created for Truman,
a suspicion arises that far from inducing neighborly behavior, the material apparatus
of Seahaven/Seaside is doubly suspect. Not only is all of it merely a simulacrum, but
also its viability is based on the unknowing alienation of the central character from
everyone around him. As a cinematic tale, *The Truman Show,* like *Pleasantville,* is a
paean to emancipated individualism. In the end, it is the triumph of intelligence and
independence of spirit over the comforts of safe, formulaic predictability. Nearing the

Figure C.6. *The Truman Show,* Paramount Pictures, 1998. This aerial view of "Seahaven," the setting for the movie, shows
Seaside, Florida, a New Urbanist project planned in 1983 by Andres Duany and Elizabeth Plater-Zyberk.

end of the film, Christof is asked what right he had to take over Truman's entire life, and Christof responds: "I have given Truman a chance to lead a normal life. The world, the place you live in, is the sick place. Seahaven is the way the world should be." The abundantly evident lesson is that subscribing to the way things "should be" inexorably restricts both self and community.

Such an attitude of we-know-better-than-you (or, alternatively, save-me-from-myself) points toward crucial questions about the degree to which design codes, regulations, and privatist enterprises such as master-planned communities and common-interest developments are appropriate means to the ends that Americans seek.[37] Efforts to limit the messiness and difference that ordinarily animate an open society may originate as well-intentioned efforts to refine the dream. But all too readily they become unpalatably undemocratic. Duany's defense of codes and regulations, for example—"a mob often decide[s] against its best interests"—raises serious questions. For instance, since when is the middle class a mob? Duany continues: "After being a rigorous practitioner of the public process, I have lost some confidence in it." Since the American citizenry, given the chance to make choices, "will make palpably wrong ones," Duany says he is "not the sort of planner that does what the citizens dictate."[38] This begs a crucial question: whose choice is it to define the dream and the terms of its fulfillment? And then on a more complex level: is voluntarily ceding one's

Figure C.7. *The Truman Show.* Every time Truman leaves his house, he is greeted by the same friendly waving neighbors; what he does not know is that they are cued to be there as part of the television production. The scene raises a parallel question whether design, as proposed by some New Urbanists, can successfully promote the same sort of neighborly interaction.

autonomy (for example, by membership in a CID) in the best interests of the individual citizen, or society in general, if doing so disallows difference or change? Is a dream-house theme park really the best we can do?

The American dream, for better or worse, is a project centered on the individual, and so its apparatus needs to suit the individual, not vice versa. Buying into an apparatus of fixed conventions provides access to a plane of opportunity, but if further evolution and change is precluded, it amounts as well to an acceptance of stereotype and conformity. For the individualist dream to be realized, the individual needs the opportunity to modify (or, just as important, to choose not to modify) the apparatus of self-definition. If the house is a significant element of that apparatus of self-definition then, as I suggest in the introduction, it functions in a manner consistent with Pierre Bourdieu's account of the *habitus:* the house serves to maintain a life course in accord with the individual's original dispositions when purchasing the dwelling. But the house also is (or ought to be) available to change that course should that person's dispositions change. Dispositions are those tendencies that keep us on the track of being "who we are." But for many significant and legitimate reasons ranging, for example, from physical infirmity and emotional loss to marriage, childbirth, and religious awakening, people may alter those dispositions. As Bourdieu perhaps would argue, the dwelling, like the *habitus,* is a durable apparatus for maintaining one's life course. But in neither case is change impossible, nor should it be.[39] If life circumstances occasion a change of the resident's dispositions, the dwelling needs to be considered an apparatus for sustaining those changes in ways that will again remain durable—examples might range from alterations in decor to structural additions or landscaping changes.

Yet the notion of a durable dwelling sustaining a durable dream, if taken too strictly, only begets a paradox. For unlike the dream itself, its realization—in the single-nuclear-family dwelling, in private property, in suburbia—can never be pure, safe, and sustainable over the long term.[40] Rather, as I argue below, it is by welcoming difference, negotiation, and hybridity that suburbs can best sustain their vitality while accommodating the constant evolution of individual dreams.[41]

A *Datum* of Opportunity

This and previous chapters have shown that much of the debate over suburbia has long been beholden to negative critiques of two widely held visions of selfhood in America. On the one hand is the notion that personal fulfillment is tied to the pursuit of private aspirations, defined and set autonomously. A crucial difficulty with this view is its disregard for engagement with, or responsibilities to, the larger body social. On the other hand is the promise held out by advanced capitalism that fulfillment is a function of commodity accumulation and consumption. Here society at large is recognized as instrumental to formation of the self, but only insofar as society is a means of commodity production and distribution.

These two notions, centering on individualism and commodities, frequently have been condemned as responsible for the banality of suburbia, and worse. But while there are many suitable grounds on which to critique both, it is important not to mistake the material product (suburbia and suburban life) for certain conditions in which it is produced. For in many respects suburbia has become the apparatus of choice through which Americans not only acknowledge the inescapable presence of these aspects of the modern world but also attempt to negotiate a practical, material resolution of these and many other circumstances and conditions. Understanding such efforts—to fashion one's material circumstances as instruments for dealing with complex ideological, social, and economic possibilities—is crucial to developing a less facile, more critical approach to suburbia.

One major obstacle to such an understanding is the unproblematic way in which the commodified single-nuclear-family detached suburban house has long been imagined (and marketed) as automatically realizing the American dream. This vision and the expectations to which it gives rise unfortunately disregard the crucial role of the house, and the domestic life it supports, in the very processes of negotiation in which residents are constantly engaged. The simplistic notion of a "dream" house as a ready-to-move-in commodity package not only masks the larger ideological contests that are in play. It also denies the complexities of domestic life. Unrecognized are the challenges, conflicts, frustrations, indeed, the inconsistencies and contradictions that are integral to the complex terrains that suburban residents continually negotiate as part of their everyday lives. Or, to put it another way, the purchase of a "dream house" cannot automatically bestow a resolution of the wants, desires, conflicts, and inconsistencies in any resident's life.[42] Of course it can, and should, satisfy many expectations and desires. But contrary to much promotional imagery and literature, it cannot freeze a moment or an ideal in time. In reality, especially in the global information culture of the twenty-first century, the bloom is soon off the rose. Material, social, political, and economic contexts are never static, expectations are constantly being revised, and the "dream house," like a real dream, lasts only momentarily.

A more effective approach is to recognize suburbia as a social terrain in continuous process of production, a material artifact in which and by which people negotiate—person by person, household by household, locality by locality—the resources and skills that they can marshal, the opportunities that their lives present, and the various dreams and aspirations that they may choose to pursue.[43] To approach suburbia in such a fashion is to recognize that, like everything in life, it is a messy artifact, always incomplete and full of inconsistencies. Seen as a terrain of *negotiation,* suburbia is a complex mosaic of places where people do their best to work out responses to the conflicting claims and opportunities that our culture, like most any other, presents. Residents of suburbia are, to varying degrees, quite aware of themselves as struggling to address the complex material and existential demands of individualism and of an advanced capitalist economy. Still, their daily decisions and activities ordinarily are not undertaken as comprehensive solutions to such larger ideological conflicts. Rather, their daily activities generally are framed and conducted in terms of interests that are more immediate, yet hardly less complex or serious. Accordingly it becomes reductive to essentialize suburbia as a bankrupt terrain of selfish isolation, or condemn it because of the pernicious presence of the commodity economy, or both. Instead, recognizing the agency and legitimate interests of suburbia's residents, suburbia itself is more clearly seen as a material basis from which people undertake an ongoing struggle: to choose from, pursue, and coordinate the host of conflicting, often semi-understood imperatives, claims, and desires that they encounter on a daily basis. Not incidentally, suburbia also has become the terrain of choice for a growing number of photographers exploring ambiguities and multiplicities of meaning in contemporary life. Dating from Bill Owens's path-breaking work in the 1970s, the expanding corpus of photography now includes work by Lewis Baltz, Gregory Crewdson, Joe Deal, Todd Hido, Jeff Wall, and Bob Thall, among many others. Similarly in fiction, the work of writers such as Richard Ford, David Gates, A. M. Homes, James Kaplan, and Gloria Naylor focuses on suburbia as the locale in which the sometimes harsh complexities of modern life can be explored to best advantage.

This is not meant to temper criticism of the now-global economy of property accumulation and commodity consumption or the many ways in which it affects and pervades our lives and environment. America is a markedly privatist culture, and it is inordinately invested in commodities. In too many respects suburbia indulges those tendencies, with particularly unfortunate ecological consequences. But while suburbia is a very common target of blame, it is by no means the sole culprit. Individualism and commodification pervade cities, rural areas, and many other aspects of American culture. My goal is to shift the discussion to a plane that recognizes the legitimacy and agency of those who live in suburbia, taking account of the goals that in all seriousness they are pursuing, and critically appraising the context in which those goals are shaped.

It may be futile, then, to represent suburbia itself as the problem. Rather, the suburban landscape, its dwellings, its furnishings, and not least its conventions are best regarded as a *datum*—a base-plane of understood circumstances—that people have voluntarily, even eagerly, taken on as they moved to suburbia. Once arrived at, this base-plane also functions as a *datum of opportunity:* a site from which people then are able to engage, in various possible ways, in processes of social formation, individuation, and self-realization. To arrive in suburbia, in other words, is to establish a point of reference—certain baseline conventions, conditions, and opportunities. Then, in countless decisions on how to select from, assemble, shape, and reconfigure the resources at hand, people undertake a process of constantly maintaining—or modifying—their material circumstances and life practices to keep them aligned with their own history, their current social milieus, their expectations, and their dreams.[44]

People have done so across suburbia: examples range from the wide variety of ways in which once-maligned identical "boxes" have been individualized in places such as Levittown (Figures C.8–C.11), to the extraordinary diversity of colors, patterns,

Figure C.8. Remodeled house, Levittown, Hempstead, New York. As families outgrew their original standardized Cape Cod dwellings, they added on to their homes in ways that suited their changing needs and the evolving stylistic vocabularies of their times. Photograph by author.

Figure C.9. Remodeled house, Levittown, Hempstead, New York. Photograph by author.

Figure C.10. Remodeled house, Levittown, Hempstead, New York. Photograph by author.

Figure C.11. Remodeled house, Levittown, Hempstead, New York. Photograph by author.

additions, fences, and yard art that residents have added to smaller, plainer tract houses in certain African American suburbs (as, for example, Miami suburbs such as Bunche Park and Goulds, Figures C.12–C.14). Other means of individuation are evident in ways that yards and interior spaces are used, in choices of furnishings, and in the countless varieties of lifestyle practices that Americans enjoy.

Increasingly these modes of individuation have been realized by means of mass-produced commodities—the profusely abundant resources of modern culture that people now habitually appropriate, modify, and combine in efforts to negotiate the demands and desires of modern life.[45] As Daniel Miller argues, consumption itself has long been integral to processes of personal distinction, including individuation. People appropriate objects—including industrially manufactured products—in order to "utilize them in the creation of their own image." Commodities play a similar role in positioning the self in relation to others: "the relation between [the chosen] object and others provid[es] a dimension through which the particular social position of the intended individual is experienced."[46] Be it a house designed according to a Down-ing pattern or a Benjaminian commodity, the object is chosen to define the self in the social nexus. In other words, consumption is integral to processes of personal defini-tion, social cohesion, and individual differentiation. To condemn consumption, then, as mindless capitulation to corporate marketing interests—and likewise to condemn suburbanites as dupes or tools of such interests—is to deny the very real purposes that consumption necessarily serves in a modern, industrialized society. Consumption of course is not an unmixed blessing. As with other dimensions of social behavior, it can have pernicious consequences for the environment, one's health, and family and social relations. But that should not mask the fact that consumption also affords a crucial dimension for sustaining normative social practices, as well as for articulating degrees of individuation and dissent in contradistinction to prevailing conventions.

To approach suburbia in this fashion allows each resident, family, dwelling, yard, neighborhood—each component of the suburban landscape—to be cast as part of a continually evolving matrix of multiple narratives. Every suburbanite—every person—is accorded the agency to articulate and negotiate multiple dimensions of association and of difference within the complex fabric of modern life. Instead of seeing subur-bia as an apparatus of selfish isolation, or of subjugation to the hegemony of corpo-rate interests, this approach affords a more complex critique. For example, the often standardized, repetitive fabric of suburbia—endless ticky-tacky boxes and the like—became in the eyes of many critics a suffocating apparatus of stultification or confor-mity. But a more open approach recognizes the complementary experience of many people who have moved and lived there. Among other things, the uniformity of the landscape may serve as a recognizable *datum* of achievement. To move there is to arrive at a plane where certain standards and conventions are taken for granted. And sub-urbia is a plane of opportunity from which processes of self-articulation and individ-uation can proceed. As the *Chicago Tribune* study titled *The New Consumer* clarified in 1957, young families moving to new suburbs embraced the "new homogeneity"

Figure C.12. House and yard, Bunche Park, Florida. Extensive use of yard art differentiates and individualizes the dwelling with respect to its neighbors but does not conflict with the neighborhood scale and typology. Photograph by author.

Figure C.13. Remodeled house, Goulds, Florida. Use of the patterned facade hybridizes the dwelling stylistically yet remains consistent with the surrounding vernacular. Photograph by author.

there as a way of breaking away from hierarchical family structures and making new friends on a more egalitarian plane.[47]

Suburbia has not been a deterministic apparatus that has standardized, homogenized, or commodified all who have lived there. Nor, for that matter, can "design codes" or "rules and regulations" that govern so many common-interest developments actually produce the sort of exemplary "community" that architects, planners, developers, and publicists propose, or that residents may expect. Rather, it is necessary to acknowledge, despite many critics, that residents have long experienced suburbia neither as a conformist cookie-cutter environment nor as a dream-utopia. Instead, suburbia has been understood as a terrain in which to fashion and negotiate the elements of their own, often quite distinct, individual dreams, which in turn are constantly evolving responses to the facts, demands, and opportunities of their own circumstances.

The future of suburbia cannot be secured by imposing what amount to stereotypical "solutions" such as design codes, behavior codes, and other regulatory apparatuses that are currently popular in common-interest developments (CIDs) and planned-unit developments (PUDs), and championed by some leading New Urbanist practitioners. Residents do need to be assured a secure *datum,* or point of departure. But no matter

Figure C.14. Remodeled house, Goulds, Florida. Use of initials and a heart on the facade and a highly patterned mailbox contribute to the individualization of the dwelling without removing it from the surrounding general syntax.

how much residents' interests converge at the time when they arrive at a particular locale, over time their individual interests will diverge, and should be expected to do so.[48] Everybody's narrative differs. To insist that narratives conform is to deny difference; the greater the degree of regulation, the smaller the opportunity for the play of narrative to articulate personal growth and change. Instead of fighting the tendency of personal narratives to diverge, suburbia can better serve its residents' interests by affording opportunities for individual distinction and social differentiation. To do so requires at least partially unthinking the three ideological imperatives of the American dream outlined in the previous chapter, namely possessive individualism, pastoralism, and social fragmentation. They need to be reevaluated and recast in order to allow for, and even promote, production of difference, opportunity for negotiation, and landscapes of hybridity.

Difference

Current practices valorizing private land ownership and "property values" well above other considerations, currently the standard among many planners, developers, CIDs, and PUDs,[49] yield little more than the broadest common denominator of design. Because property values generally are beholden to a narrow set of accepted market criteria, and because the investment value of a dwelling so frequently trumps other considerations, the individuality that possessive individualism ostensibly promises ironically succumbs to market conformity. Not only does this produce a sameness everywhere, but it also inordinately limits the dimensions in which change may be introduced or evolve. If difference truly is the goal, a more effective approach is to develop mechanisms by which dwellings and subdivisions can be instruments of distinction and differentiation. This is by no means a call for the eradication of all sameness. Sameness is one necessary dimension in which connections and bonds of community are established. Nor is it a call for the introduction of manufactured variety or ersatz artifacts of "difference." Rather, the desideratum is a new sensitivity to the ways in which residents historically and presently distinguish and differentiate themselves. The first step is to recognize dimensions in which distinction and difference are produced, and the techniques by which they are effected. My purpose at present is not to provide a comprehensive catalog of such dimensions and techniques, which would extend into a wide array of ethnographic, historical, stylistic, formal, technological, and other dimensions. If undertaken, however, such an inquiry might (for starters) point to ways in which the more personal rooms of the house are furnished, such as the den, study, or bedroom, or the ways in which people of different gender, ethnic, and age cohorts tend to furnish them, or the trade-offs between front- and rear-facing picture windows, or the ways in which any of these elements afford family members sites for distinguishing themselves (displaying ribbons, keepsakes, trophies, and so on) with respect to the family and the rest of the community, or how landscaping and gardening distinguish these householders from their neighbors and make them part of the neighborhood, and how the design of the house itself does the same, through such aspects as scale, style, color, window and door orientation, and so forth. Many of these could seem commonplace at the start, but the cumulative under-standing of the dimensions in which and techniques by which difference already is produced, in their fullest extent and depth, can establish broader and firmer founda-tions for the production of difference in future design.

Negotiation

The romanticized isolation of the individual (or nuclear family unit) in a manufac-tured Arcadian preserve is an increasingly untenable fiction. The suburban dwelling has long been at the intersection of multiple environmental, aesthetic, and social con-cerns, ranging from sustainability and neighborhood design to the facilitation of everyday family activities (such as children's play groups, youth sports leagues, garage rock bands, book clubs, garden clubs, Tupperware parties, bridge clubs, church activ-ities). Even if such concerns were not a factor, the fact remains that as prices rise and land becomes scarcer, homes are built closer together. The individual is no longer isolable in even a pretense of a private Arcadia. But to recognize this does not deny the ongoing expectation of personal individuation, nor does it reject the desire to pursue success in terms (such as status, leisure, wealth) that an Arcadia may have suggested. Rather, it acknowledges that individuation and success necessarily are processes that occur within a social context; they are articulated through an ongoing relation to the community apparatus. To engage an understanding of suburbia, there-fore, is to recognize the physical and social fabric of suburbia as work in progress, by which people individually and collectively participate in, and negotiate with, the larger environmental, aesthetic, and social nexus. No longer is the fiction tenable that suburbia is an isolable or timeless preserve, even with respect to efforts by some devel-opers and designers to protect landscapes or establish conservation areas. Residents and landscape alike, along with everything that sustains them, still will be negotiat-ing the forces of history and change.

Hybridity

Ingrained presumptions that suburbia is first and foremost a site of private individu-ation inexorably have led to the expectation that protecting this process is a chief obligation of planning, design, and even municipal government.[50] Suburbia remains host to an abundance of self-centered practices, although in and of themselves these are not the problem. Individuation per se is not a bad thing. More troublesome is the presumption that individuating practices alone may be read as paradigms of how best to approach the understanding and design of suburbia. In other words, one might presume that since suburbia is a terrain dominated by an ideology of individ-ualism, individualism is therefore the best answer to questions concerning suburbia, on scales ranging from the household to nationwide. But presuming so fallaciously prioritizes the concerns of individuals over regional, neighborhood, and community interests—fallaciously because doing so inordinately fragments the very social nexuses that sustain the practice of individuation. Individuation can only survive within the context of greater social frameworks.

From the point of view of a householder, the dwelling, its plan, its style, its furnishings, and the commodities enjoyed there in everyday life are all tied in complex ways to different, sometimes divergent, systems of meaning on scales ranging from local to global, with many in between. By means ranging from house type and style to such things as picture windows, patios, lawns, room layout, furniture, decorations, knickknacks, meals, music, media viewing, leisure and recreation activities, friendships, and community participation, residents do distinguish themselves as distinct individuals, despite the sometimes uniform character of the products chosen, and have done so for some time.[51] In so doing, they necessarily embrace some systems of meaning and belief (the furniture or music that they choose may be like their neighbors'), contravene others (some choices imply rejection of alternate choices), or even do both simultaneously (some choices synthesize multiple possibilities). With respect to housing choices in a given suburb, residents do this working within a larger set of local or regional conventions that articulate the basic framework of that locale in particular, and suburbia in general, as a *datum*.[52] This process of selecting and rejecting elements from a common vocabulary, all assembled within a common syntax, the residential suburb, is of course now a centuries-old process; in this respect little distinguishes people of Downing's era from our own. The purpose of the following paragraphs is to do something further with this analysis by examining suburbia as a culture of hybridity and exploring the advantages of doing so.

To date the discussion of hybridity in academic discourse has been concentrated on the production of hybrid identity and on hybrid place, with little attention paid to the intersection of the two.[53] But theoreticians of space, ranging from early phenomenologists to poststructuralists to the present, have argued the critical importance of place to the production of personal identity.[54] This argument suggests not only an ongoing gap in the study of hybridity but also an opportunity to focus on the single-family bourgeois dwelling, given its longstanding history as an intersection of identity and place. I want to argue that individual dwellings as principal components of suburbia are, like suburbia in general, far from the monotonous monocultural constructs that they are often said to be, that instead they may be examined as complex hybrid cultures that sustain rich hybrid identities.

Before proceeding further with the question of hybridity in human culture, it may be helpful to differentiate this kind of hybridity from the occurrence of hybrid organic species. The latter, whether it is a combination of two breeds or species, incorporates some characteristics of both and eliminates others. As anthropologist Mayfair Mei-hui Yang has put it, an organic hybrid generally incorporates "a smooth and unproblematic blending of traits and does not encapsulate the contested and agonistic features of the process of combination."[55] In contrast cultural hybridity is far from being such a simple product. Not only does it fail to select and/or eliminate characteristics according to classical Mendelian patterns, but the characteristics that are present may well embody a host of contradictions and differences, either internal to the self or with respect to the family or greater social milieu. These contradictions and differences are not always at odds with each other—perhaps that would be tantamount to schizophrenia—but humans are far from wholly consistent all the time, and the notion of cultural hybridity offers an opportunity to understand the notion that self, society, and place each may exist as a complex entity without losing its integrity.

One especially fruitful approach to understanding cultural hybridity is through an examination of Russian critic Mikhail Bakhtin's approach to linguistic hybridity. In his examination of the rhetorical effectiveness of several passages in the English comic novel, specifically Dickens's *Little Dorritt,* Bakhtin argued that in each case the success of the passage was due to the ability of the person speaking to shift from one voice to a second, in order to have a certain effect on another character. Bakhtin called this presence of two distinct voices, one everyday and one ceremonious in this instance, "a typical double-accented, double-styled *hybrid construction.*" Or to put it another way, the ability of a single person to adopt as part of a single utterance two different modes of parlance, each of which had a distinctly different effect on the audience, made for a hybrid communication. Bakhtin stressed that all this occurred within a single syntax, was voiced by a single speaker, and was divided by no internal boundary. Nevertheless in all that singularity the speaker managed to convey two meanings. Those two meanings in turn were grounded in two different semantic and belief systems: thus speaking in the "everyday" voice would engage the audience in one fashion, with a full complement of conventions and expectations, while speaking in the "ceremonious" voice would engage the audience quite differently. Bakhtin elaborated:

> What we are calling a hybrid construction is an utterance that belongs, by its grammatical (syntactic) and compositional markers, to a single speaker, but that actually contains mixed within it two utterances, two speech manners, two styles, two "languages," two semantic and axiological belief systems. We repeat, there is no formal—compositional and syntactic—boundary between these utterances, styles, languages, belief systems; the division of voices and languages takes place within the limits of a single syntactic whole, often within the limits of a simple sentence. It frequently happens that even one and the same word will belong simultaneously to two languages, two belief systems that intersect in a hybrid construction—and, consequently, the word has two contradictory meanings, two accents.[56]

There is nothing that limits the application of Bakhtin's approach just to literary discourse. If one regards a syntax as the grammar or organizing system of any aspect of human practice, and thinks of utterances as the mode of enacting that practice, then this approach to hybridity may be translated to a broad range of human endeavor. In the case of architecture, a given type (such as house or school), having its own well-established syntax, could support a rich variety of voices within a given room, building, or complex (the degrees to which a room is closed off from other rooms but open to the outdoors might be two such voices). Indeed architecture and planning, because they are physically present in our daily lives, and because they require money and effort to change, are notably among the most stable of any syntaxes in a given culture. Yet in a Bakhtinian fashion they also afford an opportunity to render diverse voices palpably present in a single hybrid unit. Bakhtin in fact was keen to stress the capacity of a linguistic hybrid to embed difference:

> What is hybridization? It is a mixture of two social languages within the limits of a single utterance, an encounter, within the arena of an utterance, between two different linguistic consciousnesses, separated from one another by an epoch, by social differentiation or by some other factor.[57]

If the linguistic is taken as a representative instance of a much wider possible range of cultural hybrids, the present-day single-family suburban house appears to be an exemplary case. Because of its long history as an instrument for definition of the bourgeois self and family, because of the range of ideological considerations that are embedded in dwelling design, because of the standardized spatial typologies (ranch houses, living rooms, fireplaces) that have evolved to address those considerations, and not least because in some cases suburbia appears to have been laid out in precisely the cookie-cutter fashion its critics have charged, the commonalities of a single syntax all are readily evident. And still the variety of lives that people pursue, far from what the cookie-cutter critics have predicted, is evident to all who live there. Wider understanding of that variety, and the hybrid means by which it is articulated, can provide an ongoing basis for affording more of the difference and diversity that some residents may want and need for their lives to grow.

As indicated earlier, some authors have written of hybrid identity or hybrid place. In the context of suburbia a Bakhtinian approach facilitates exploring the intersection of the two, as part of an effort to retheorize the landscape of suburbia. Part of what makes this an attractive possibility is the appearance in much of suburbia of a single syntax across a single-family residential terrain: clearly not a nationwide, panhistorical syntax (which does not exist in literature either), but at least local or regional syntaxes, reasonably stable over the period of one to several decades.[58]

The first stage in analyzing suburban hybridity amounts to a reminder of what some may have found difficult to accept: that hybridity is already there, that even in cookie-cutter houses cheek by jowl, difference is alive and well. As numerous researchers have noted and countless residents would be happy to explain, look-alike housing did not produce sameness or other modes of pathology.[59] Rather, as a *datum* of opportunity, it was a common syntax in and on which they could embroider their own levels of meaning, where they could differentiate themselves as much as they pleased, or not. The examples of the Levittown communities are a famous case in point. Starting out as a few common building types, fabricated from standardized mass-produced materials, there was barely anything to differentiate them except color. This did not stop people from leading individualized lives there, as Herbert Gans found in *The Levittowners* (1967), a study of the New Jersey Levittown. The various tactics by which they differentiated themselves—perhaps different household furnishings, a different circle of friends, joining a book club—all amounted to a form of Bakhtinian hybridization. Then as the population began to outgrow their original homes, they often chose to add on to them, as in examples found in the original Long Island Levittown (Figures C.8–C.11), quite literally turning them into hybrids, all the while staying within the standard syntax, using stock components and current styles.

The next stage is to ask how hybridization may be introduced now or in the future: how it may be facilitated and with what sorts of consequences. In his essay "The Enacted Environment of East Los Angeles," James T. Rojas has provided a glimpse of how hybridity occurs in one locale, the suburban district of East Los Angeles largely inhabited by Mexicans and Mexican-Americans.[60] He demonstrates that the given built fabric of this area, much of which is small bungalows with fenced front yards, is thoroughly and constantly embroidered by multiple ongoing activities (vendors, musicians, and so on), decorations (murals, graffiti, and so on), props (signboards, tables, chairs, and so on), and especially yard art, which affords residents a wide range of opportunity for personal expression. In all of these respects, which some Anglo architects and planners might reprove as "messy" or worse, a common syntax is available in which all may participate for their own ends, or as a means of engaging the community, or both. The syntax varies in important ways from other types of suburbs. Codes, covenants, and regulations do not limit the vitality of the streets, vendors are a prominent outdoor presence instead of being confined to shops, front yards become outdoor living rooms, places of welcome and conversation. A looser syntax, it predictably affords the culture more opportunity to enact (Rojas's term) a wide range of economic activities, territorial claims, social concerns, and personal identities.

Hybridization of a similar sort continues to occur in many houses in African American suburbs of Miami (Figures C.12–C.14). Here the syntax remains largely the same as that of Anglo suburbs, but the mode of decorating facades and yards appeals to a different semantic register than is found in most Anglo suburbs. Abundant yard art, the display of initials and a heart in bas-relief on one facade, and the patterning of another facade in faux (red) stonework in a manner that appears ambiguously giraffelike all speak of the diverse personal interests of the owners. These two facades speak far more of the owners than most Anglo suburban houses, because Anglo owners would tend to be afraid of harming property values by making such individualized alterations to the facade. Or putting it another way, they would prefer to identify with the house on the exterior as a property investment and choose other (hybrid) means and dimensions in which to pursue individualization.

Changes and alterations such as those discussed above, in Levittown, East Los Angeles, and some Miami suburbs, may beg the question of aesthetics, a frequent concern in the design and critique of suburban neighborhoods, tracts, subdivisions, and municipalities. Aesthetic critiques range from the complaint that too many look-alike houses create a boring uniformity, to the objection that houses designed or modified without regard to some standards and conventions of design create visual chaos and perhaps even disrupt community. But just as homeowners who have bought uniform tract houses and those living in stringently regulated master-planned communities have not regarded them as oppressive of their own senses of taste and beauty, those who make individualized alterations do not see their houses as sore thumbs or affronts to the neighborhood's spatial cohesion. Rather, a given house with its sometimes idiosyncratic improvements not only suits the family's practical needs but, because it is the product of the owners' endeavors, becomes an extension of the residents' aesthetic conventions. In some respects this simply follows Downing's formula: the dwelling is an expression of the values of those who live within, although instead of the stock stylistic vocabulary that Downing provided there is now a very different stock vocabulary available in decorating magazines, home improvement books and television programs, and vast stores full of home improvement tools and materials. On the one hand this vocabulary is notably democratic, because it is largely geared to stock sizes and shapes that anyone competent with the right tools can install, with simple stylistic variations added as mere veneers. On the other hand this vocabulary may bespeak all the most critical aesthetic problems of suburbia today, since style is reduced to a mere veneer, and choices as to what alterations are made are determined on a house-by-house basis with little if any regard to the context of neighbors, streetscape, neighborhood, and the larger community. The fact is that in any dwelling, whether it is a tract house or it is individually architect-designed or homeowner-remodeled, aesthetics do play a role, but they do so to varying degrees and in different dimensions. In some cases aesthetic concerns are minimally present at the outset, as in Levittown and other tract developments, but as residents have become agents of their own interests through remodeling, aesthetics are introduced according to the training and concerns of whichever residents are remodeling. In fact such remodeling long has been recognized as a positive attribute of so-called vernacular architecture; on the contrary the taste of middle-class suburban Americans presently is suspect. In practice, suburbanites in diverse circumstances do allow concerns such as property values, individual comforts, frugality, or personal expression to trump more commonly accepted principles of aesthetics. And in some of those cases, certain aesthetic approaches and considerations actually may enhance the outcome, in a manner that, for example, may further increase property values, for little extra cost, while enhancing neighborhood livability. But for a long time a similar dilemma obtained in the evaluation of vernacular building, which because it made the best of local circumstances and materials came to be seen as devoid of any pretension to the sort of aesthetic value that high style claimed. And while it is not the purpose of this book to outline a bourgeois suburban aesthetics, it becomes necessary to acknowledge that the poor adherence of suburbia to current elite aesthetic paradigms does not justify a judgment that suburbia is devoid of aesthetic interest, possibility, or engagement by its residents. Patterned stucco, fencing, dormers, and all manner of other alterations and improvements do articulate aesthetic engagement on terms that suburbia's residents patently find significant and expressive. In many respects that significance and expression are more directly engaged with the present circumstances of suburbia and its residents' lives than other modes of aesthetic expression, however coherent they may appear, may allow.

In sum, the critical perspective on present and future suburbia that I am suggesting here stresses the need to produce distinction and difference, and recognition that suburbia and its residents must intelligently negotiate the forces of history and change rather than stave them off. As an apparatus for approaching these tasks, I have explored the Bakhtinian theory of hybridity with a view to recognizing hybridity that already pervades suburbia and to exploring the further incorporation of hybridity in the design, planning, and study of suburbia. However hybridization occurs, it becomes part of the encounter between society at large, the physical environment, and the evolving needs, interests, and aspirations of the people who live there. As I have shown earlier, many householders across suburbia already lead hybrid lives every day, across a broad range of ethnicities, incomes, social classes, and other demographic criteria. Understanding better the frameworks in which this happens has been my goal in the preceding discussion, which in turn may help in affording constructive approaches to design and planning of the built environment.

Coda: Looking Ahead

Among the more consequential advantages of greater hybridity in the design of new housing—especially the single-family house in suburbia—one might look forward to an integration of scales from the personal to the regional in a better fashion than has generally been done in the past, thereby increasing access, adaptability, and perhaps even community. Doing so might also introduce greater efficiencies in the production of housing, transportation, and other aspects of infrastructure. In broad terms, hybridity at a given site would involve the overlay and intersection of elements of a heterogeneous character (for example, different geographic scales, different historical origins, different land uses, different occupations, different cultures, different relations of indoor space to nature, different family structures). The task of design would be to situate those different elements in the common syntax, to afford them recognition through aesthetic and symbolic techniques, and to incorporate those elements into the physical fabric and lived experience of those who reside, work, shop, play, visit, and travel there. In addition, a hybrid approach could afford opportunities for alternative (nontraditional, nonconforming) ways of designing space on any given scale (domestic, neighborhood, municipality, region), integrated into the common syntax. Likewise it could explore alternative ways of altering existing structures and spaces, or challenging conventional ways of building them.

Among the consequences of a hybrid approach may well be heightened awareness of a much broader range of social, cultural, economic, and political interests than most typical suburban environments offer today—rendering more visible not only lines of authority and control in a given culture, but also avenues of accountability and access, and dimensions of affinity and interest. This is possible because hybridity embraces multiple scales ranging from the personal to the regional, and it more readily allows multiple forms of cultural expression to intersect. Since the dreams that any one person pursues often are multivalent, and not necessarily consistent, hybridity is as important to people individually as it is to communities collectively. Finally, not least important, hybridity provides a sense of place and belonging for diverse identities, without diminishing or excluding others.

Preceding chapters also have shown that planners, architects, and designers still need to be mindful of the legacy of conventions built into American housing, especially the popularity of the single-nuclear-family detached suburban dwelling. Many of these remain part of many Americans' everyday expectations, and the home-buying public is not loudly demanding reform. Rather, many of the ideological principles and premises embedded in this mode of housing can be traced back to the seventeenth, eighteenth, and nineteenth centuries, as previous chapters have shown. Among those that will not be dislodged quickly are the following:

self: the dwelling is understood as a principal instrument for self-realization.

property: private property is a fundamental condition of selfhood, and of the encompassing political and economic systems.

identity: the dwelling serves as an apparatus for the articulation of identity and belonging.

privacy: opportunity for privacy is central to the articulation of identity.

pastoral: the pastoral ideal is a part of the mythic imagery of suburbia.

family unit: the principal paradigm of American housing remains the detached single-nuclear-family dwelling, which reciprocally defines the family, although other combinations and alternatives are appearing.

home-as-castle: despite, or perhaps because of, the increased complexity of relations between individuals and corporate, institutional, national, and global entities, the dwelling remains almost exclusively centered on the individual and the family, and its perimeter increasingly serves as a defense against all other forces.

Because Americans remain so fundamentally committed to these conventions and expectations, it is unrealistic to expect that they can or should be changed through design alone, hybrid or otherwise. Rather, design at least needs to acknowledge these conventions, whether it be acceptance of them or a considered approach to alternatives. And when change does occur, it needs to be in tandem with shifts (leading-edge or otherwise) in ideological, political, and economic practices.

Framing the matter in a different way, the conventions and expectations listed above are situated in the personal consciousnesses of countless people constantly building and buying dwellings across the American built landscape. And in each person's consciousness these conventions and expectations result in dispositions to act in certain ways regarding housing decisions. Quite simply this amounts in each case to a Bourdieuian habitus.[1] In his or her own consciousness each person manages a vast nexus of personal concerns, at any given time deployed across multiple scales, ranging from one's selfhood to family, neighborhood, municipality, region, nation, and the entire globe. But there are other interests deployed along other axes: occupation, race, gender, class, religion, age, income, power, form of government, status, health, love, personal political orientation, leisure, and ecology, to name some. And as previous chapters have detailed, some of these interests are explicitly designed into the single-family detached dwelling, while others are only implicitly there (such as government mortgage subsidies or the lasting effects of now-outlawed redlining).

Simply replicating the same housing stock may, in all likelihood, be conducive to replication of much the same habitus. Bourdieuian theory recognizes that housing is not determinist but also generally finds that some shift in ambient conditions (social, political, economic, and so on) is the basis for a change in habitus.[2] Constraining the habitus by replicating an inflexible housing stock can only limit the degree to which people can evolve in their own terms as individuals and families. How, then, can a more hybrid mode of design be of use in modern American housing? From a Bourdieuian perspective, the answer is simple: hybridity allows for sufficient flexibility within a common syntax so that ongoing changes in ambient conditions (new career, blended family, new hobbies, spiritual awakening) can be incorporated in design. That evolving design, in turn, can support ongoing changes in the resident's habitus.

This also bears on a complementary aspect of hybrid design: by incorporating complex dimensions of the culture, it may enhance the agency of inhabitants to engage and even alter aspects of their situation with respect to the culture. Instead of gates and walls, for example, streets leading directly to commercial areas and transit stops give residents a stake in the operation, liveliness, and longevity of these functional components of their neighborhoods. Likewise vistas from houses and yards to parks and back again, allowing parents to monitor their children at play, and children to feel reassured that they are seen, may give residents a stake in the physical infrastructure of their local amenities. Such factors give residents a greater involvement in and opportunity to build the social capital of their community, what Robert Putnam describes as the "features of social organization, such as networks, norms, and trust, that facilitate coordination for mutual benefit."[3] The crucial factor for the present discussion is to recognize the built environment as an apparatus for implementing and enacting social capital, no longer simply as an instrument for representing and fashioning the self. Moreover there is a snowballing effect: the more the built environment is recognized as such an apparatus, the greater the opportunity for it to generate even more social capital.

But if hybridity in design can help facilitate more diverse *habituses,* it is not yet commonly evident in the American suburban *habitation.* Dwelling design still faces considerable challenges, not least the introduction of greater hybridity but also the design of better technology to foster difference and to sustain diversity. This is not necessarily an argument in favor of multifamily housing, greater density, or any of the other alternatives that already are a growing part of the suburban landscape. But it is an argument to address, by way of conclusion, three specific matters that can lead to a more hybrid manner of design: first, designing dwellings to afford better opportunities for progressive change over time; second, instead of the current trend toward closing off and bounding (gating) suburbia, developing ways to build more effective connections; and third, affording opportunities for different identities and practices that we may call "suburban counterpublics."

Affording Change over Time

Suburbia has long been condemned for its cookie-cutter homogeneity, and wrongly so. In recent decades neotraditional movements in design and planning have expended considerable effort toward restoring a heritage that may never have been there. The fact is that a great portion of suburbia today is solidly nontraditional, even compared to one or two decades ago. People are transforming the nature of suburbia ever more rapidly, in ways that photographers such as Bill Owens began to depict three decades ago and Gregory Crewdson has presented more recently, ways that demographers are constantly assessing from census data, and ways that others have yet to discover.[4] Shifting demographic trends are among the easiest to summarize: in the decade 1990–2000, for example, minorities represented most of the suburban population growth. In some cities, such as Honolulu, Los Angeles/Long Beach, San Francisco, and Miami, white populations declined more sharply in the suburbs than in the cities. And in areas such as El Paso, Albuquerque, and Bakersfield, the concentration of minorities became higher in the suburbs than in the cities.[5] Nationwide, the number of households consisting of married couples with children, or nuclear families, declined from 40 percent in 1970 to just 24 percent in 2000. At the same time other changes in household living arrangements, such as single-parent families, singles living alone, and unmarried heterosexual, gay, and lesbian couples, have become more pronounced.[6] As many individual designers know, the opportunities for design to address these varied needs are enormous.

Yet the housing industry largely continues to design, build, and market a highly limited range of "model" homes, often with a further selection of specific option "packages" for the interior, and limited varieties of stylistic veneer for the exterior. The result is not only a neighborhood where uniformity outweighs difference but also diminished opportunity for further change. Departures from the model or the norm are preordained to appear wrong. Perhaps the biggest problem is that the "consumer" is perennially presented with the idea that the model is the place to start, a notion left over from the days of Loudon and Downing. In an insidious fashion the standard detached dwelling also serves as a formula on which to pattern one's living, rather than suggesting that hybridization according to one's own objectives is the goal to pursue. In Benjaminian fashion, as further elaborated by Daniel Miller (see the conclusion, this volume), people do make use of standard consumer products to articulate complex selves inside their homes, but the basic shell, room types, and room layout remain largely formulaic. In a society elsewhere beset by a nearly bewildering array of consumer choices, the housing industry has not kept up. Its typology remains nearly ossified, whether for reasons of cost, lack of marketing innovation, fear of compromising property values, or all of these concerns and more.

Processes of standardization came to American housing production by the 1920s, as shown in chapter 7, and mass production arrived during World War II. Still, the idea of using standardized production processes to make elements that are closer to modules, rather than models, has never caught on. If designed to accept such components from the beginning, a given house could be reconfigurable to suit a new family situation or changing cultural practices. Instead, a neighborhood of "starter homes" or another of "executive mansions" remains just that. Within many tracts or developments, houses remain unalterable beyond certain limits, dictated by such factors as lot size, property values, and the size and configuration of rooms within the original house plan.[7] As long as the housing stock stays healthy and its first generation or two of inhabitants is satisfied, this is probably a sufficient outcome. But eventually the housing stock may age to a point where it has outlived its usefulness, as it has in many now declining postwar tract suburbs. Had residents been able to modify it progressively, it could serve a continuously regenerating and diversifying population. Instead, upkeep may seem pointless, or the house may be marketable only to those who lack sufficient capital for major improvements. In the end, older suburbs may face much the same fate as inner cities, with long-time residents choosing to move out, declining property values, and loss of vital neighborhoods.[8] Any number of political, economic, and other factors are responsible for a given suburb's decline, but a flexible means to accommodate progressive change clearly gives residents a better chance to address and engage those factors.

Therefore the goal is neither to delineate specific new dwelling types, nor to "reprogram" the old types, but to build in ways to accommodate progressive change. An approach to at least one part of this problem involves finding ways to allow the stock of American single-family dwellings to better accommodate potential minority homeowners. In 2002, in an address in front of a minority audience at the St. Paul AME Church in metropolitan Atlanta, President George W. Bush declared his support for somewhat the reverse of such an approach, that is, helping minority homeowners afford existing single-family dwellings, which he referred to repeatedly as the realization of the American dream:

> I do believe in the American Dream. I believe there is such a thing as the American Dream. And I believe those of us who have been given positions of responsibility must do everything we can to spotlight the dream and to make sure the dream shines in all neighborhoods, all throughout our country. Owning a home is a part of that dream, it just is. Right here in America if you own your own home, you're realizing the American Dream. . . .
>
> Three quarters of white America owns their homes. Less than 50 percent of African Americans are part of the homeownership in America. And less than 50

percent of the Hispanics who live here in this country own their home. And that has got to change for the good of the country. It just does.[9]

The Bush administration's remedy for this problem became the American Dream Downpayment Fund, providing funds to assist low-income home buyers with a down payment on a house. But in addition to offering money to a limited number of recipients, can design help? Instead of subsidizing the purchase of more units built according to the usual models, built according to the usual standards of "what sells" to white America, can design and technology provide truly adaptable, expandable, variable systems of housing that could better suit the divergent needs of the complex mosaic of American citizens today? Is it possible to find building systems that are flexible enough in size, use, intelligibility, and cost that they can better accommodate varied uses, traditional and not, with structural and aesthetic integrity? One answer may be suggested by putting the question somewhat paradoxically in this form: how can standardization be used for purposes of difference? If ways can be found to prepare off-the-shelf building materials in customized packages suitable for a large proportion of improvement and expansion projects, the result will be substantially enhanced opportunities for realizing personal dreams. If indeed difference is a fact and a goal that American society should embrace ever more seriously, there remains an immense unmet need to provide spatial conventions and built forms that afford distinction—a positive degree of difference between people—and do so without making for exclusion.[10]

Un-bounding and Weaving

Since the 1980s the degree of bounding in the American domestic landscape and the variety of ways in which it has been pursued have intensified dramatically. These various kinds of bounding include gated communities, restrictive zoning, CIDs, neighborhood and municipal NIMBYism, and "cocooning" within houses, not to mention police and security systems at all levels. All of these amount to institutionalized responses to specific needs, each no doubt with some justification. Zoning, a practice now over a century old, also was just such a response. Originally it served as a relatively large-scale tool to separate functions such as residence and manufacturing at a time when residents were otherwise defenseless against expanding industries. In so doing, zoning rules followed the ideological principles of their times, but once set in place they only ossified that ideology—they afforded no flexibility for change over time. Zoning thus generally incorporates no mechanism for negative feedback, as Avi Friedman has shown. Not only does zoning consequently institutionalize mistakes, but it also neglects the dynamic possibilities of the culture.[11] The same is true of current bounding apparatuses such as CIDs and gated communities. Even on the scale of individual dwellings, many design conventions can be as counterproductive as zoning. As Renee Chow has shown, for example, conceptualizing the house as a self-enclosed shell or volume only leads to "fragmented, unintelligible, and largely underused landscapes that constitute a significant proportion of today's residential environment."[12]

Such multiple degrees of isolation tend to eliminate possibilities instead of augmenting them. The American people are being offered fewer opportunities rather than more. Instead of barricades and suspicion, residents of suburbia still do seek, and say they find, connections and community. And it is well known that community and security both are strengthened by greater interaction with others. The challenge is to exchange bounds for nexus. In some respects this is already happening: with the rise of Internet communications people can be part of many diverse communities without ever leaving home—in fact, without respect to the dwelling at all.[13] But given that human consciousness also is embodied, the task is to connect that body to the wider nexus of neighborly, community, and social interests. As framed by Jaime Salazar, the question is whether the house need serve as a "limit between our bodies and our environment," or whether, if intelligently designed, it may become more "'pervious' to action," "easier . . . to interact with by the inhabitant."[14] Chow proposes rethinking the dwelling and the surrounding landscape in terms of a fabric, engaging the threads of the surrounding landscape as part of its own warp and weft.[15] Building on this notion, it may be necessary to consider ways of weaving major and minor threads of the various scales of modern American life in and out of a given dwelling, and then affording residents ways to add, subtract, magnify, and otherwise alter these as their own lives change. Instead of the stylistic theme packages that come in many developers' portfolios—an effort to make a simple one-to-one connection between dwelling and identity that dates to Downing—and instead of the effort by some New Urbanists to capture "timeless" characteristics of a region or a lifestyle, which then are applied to an entire sector of a community, the challenge is to design houses with better options for a more open manner of configuration that can be more inviting to the presence of change (perhaps like a new narrative, perhaps like additional embroidery) in one's immediate neighborhood and community at large, and likewise more flexible in their capacity to intersect broader complexes of human and environmental relations.

Suburban Counterpublics

In a seminal essay in 1992, Nancy Fraser contested not only the notion that there was such a thing as a single "public sphere," but that the different "publics" who constitute an entire society engage on equal footings or with a common agenda. Rather, she introduced the notion of "subaltern counterpublics," subordinated social groups in stratified societies who often exist in contestation with dominant publics, and who at other times necessarily withdraw altogether from the political arena. Among Fraser's many arguments, one stands out as especially pertinent here, her discussion of the process by which social identities are formed. Public spheres—plural spaces inhabited by plural publics—are "arenas for the formation and enactment of social identities." The crucial point is that identity is not simply an individual matter, but it is a social construct, necessarily articulated (at least partly) in the public sphere. Moreover, in any given culture there are multiple social identities engaging in different public spheres. Thus even in so-called egalitarian societies—ostensibly "homogeneous" suburbs could be substituted in this line of reasoning—there are actually many different interests at play at once. In the end, whatever the surface appearance, there are actually many "social groups with diverse values, identities, and cultural styles."[16]

More recently Margaret Crawford has brought Fraser's notion of counterpublics to the discussion of cities, suggesting that the urban landscape may well be understood as a set of discursive sites where (to markedly varying degrees) multiple publics are able to pursue and contest their different interests and identities.[17] For both Fraser and Crawford, the principal advantage gained by their theoretical exploration of counterpublics appears to be an appreciation of their contestatory role: once identified as such, counterpublics have enhanced standing and capacities in their engagements with city and state. This analysis is fundamentally sound, but there is also no reason to expect that counterpublics always need to function in a contestatory manner (nor do I believe Fraser and Crawford argue this).[18] Rather, the examination of counterpublics also exposes something broader, parallel to what I argued in the conclusion: that the cultural landscape (built, discursive, and especially lived) is a hybrid domain in which multiple groups vie for recognition but may or may not speak directly to each others' interests at any given time. Because many dimensions are overlaid at once—geography, architecture, history, occupation, gender, religion, family, and so on—different publics may in fact be true *counter*publics but nevertheless exist without confrontation. Nor are counterpublics necessarily mutually exclusive of one another. One may critique or subvert another, as well as the dominant public, while all live within the larger whole. At the same time, evidence of overt contestation may at best be ambiguous.[19]

Perhaps an apposite example here is gay suburbia. During the last half of the twentieth century the heteronormative ideal of suburbia was embodied in the single-nuclear-family house. Others need not have applied, or so it appeared. Yet gay or lesbian individuals and couples did move in, sometimes among sympathetic neighbors, sometimes in a highly closeted manner, and fashioned a suburban counterpublic. In most places it was minimally visible, but the ostensible homogeneity of suburbia was belied by the presence of these residents, not to mention other nonconformist publics. And while those residents may have lived in dwellings that looked like all the others—one common syntax—the landscape was becoming more hybrid as those residents brought their beliefs and feelings, their ties to other institutions, their friends, and their activities with them.

As the example makes clear, counterpublics are hardly limited to the urban realm. But an even more pointed example is the manner in which suburban youth have embraced one of the most successful modes of counterpublic-ity, hip-hop. Rap music allows the collective performance of social identity of a subaltern group (be it urban blacks or suburban kids) through a variety of means ranging from call-and-response lyrics to particular styles of clothing.[20] Hip-hop also allows a single individual to articulate dimensions of identity by similar means, such as clothing or playing a recording—alone, in a car, at a party, and so forth—means that can change over time, according to location or with respect to the company one keeps. In this respect, as with Little League teams, church groups, skateboarders, and almost every other aspect of suburban life, hip-hop becomes another dimension (or "voice") in a hybrid culture. In instances where residents are annoyed by a single vehicle playing a recording (and its message) at high volume through an enhanced audio system, the hybrid quality and contestatory function are both more than evident. Where teenagers listen quietly through ear buds, the contestatory role is far more subtle (especially if parents worry about what is being played). But because hip-hop offers a medium through which one subgroup of residents (generally teenage boys) can coalesce as a suburban counter-public, it also necessarily hybridizes suburbia. It introduces difference and embeds it in a landscape that generally is apprehensible according to a common syntax. By and large those who participate in this culture are well behaved and well tolerated, but they are nevertheless recognized as a different presence, and that is the point: just as with fans of high school football, dance clubs, seniors' associations, and so forth, they have articulated their position as a suburban counterpublic.

For architecture, planning, and design, the challenge may be understood in similar terms. First is to articulate better the different semantic modes by which our current built environment (syntax) already sustains diverse identities and counterpublics. Then, by refining these modes and seeking others, the goal is to afford possibilities for greater hybridization: more diverse identities and more counterpublics, capable of necessary and desirable change over time with more flexible design, providing a strengthened physical and social fabric through an open spatial syntax that is amenable to many ways of reading, and many ways of living.

Notes

Prologue

1. Nicholas Cooper, *Houses of the Gentry, 1480–1680* (New Haven: Yale University Press, 1999).

Introduction

1. Martin Heidegger, "Building Dwelling Thinking," in *Poetry, Language, Thought,* trans. Albert Hofstadter (1951; New York: Harper & Row, 1975), 147. In Bachelard's words: "But over and beyond our memories, the house we were born in is physically inscribed in us. It is a group of organic habits. . . . In short, the house we were born in has engraved within us the hierarchy of the various functions of inhabiting. We are the diagram of the functions of inhabiting that particular house. . . ." Gaston Bachelard, *The Poetics of Space,* trans. Maria Jolas (Boston: Beacon Press, 1994), 14–15.

2. Christopher Alexander, *The Production of Houses* (New York: Oxford University Press, 1985), 166–67.

3. Jean Larson, quoted in Jenny Allen and Melissa Stanton, "The 1999 Life Dream House," *Life,* May 1999, 132.

4. For example, Mary Wollstonecraft, *A Vindication of the Rights of Woman: With Strictures on Political and Moral Subjects,* 2nd ed. (London: J. Johnson, 1792).

5. See Andrew Elfenbein, *Romantic Genius: The Prehistory of a Homosexual Role* (New York: Columbia University Press, 1999), 67; for a history of individualism over a longer span, see Robert N. Bellah et al., *Habits of the Heart: Individualism and Commitment in American Life* (Berkeley: University of California Press, 1996).

6. The biological and psychological investigation of the role of space in human cognition I leave to others. See, for example, George Lakoff, *Women, Fire, and Dangerous Things: What Categories Reveal about the Mind* (Chicago: University of Chicago Press, 1987); Mark Johnson, *The Body in the Mind* (Chicago: University of Chicago Press, 1987); and Maurice Halbwachs, *The Collective Memory* (1950; New York: Harper & Row, 1980).

7. The thrust of this argument derives from Michel Foucault, *Discipline and Punish: The Birth of the Prison,* trans. Alan Sheridan (New York: Vintage, 1979).

8. See, for example, James C. Scott, *Domination and the Arts of Resistance: Hidden Transcripts* (New Haven, CT: Yale University Press, 1990); and Allen Feldman, *Formations of Violence: The Narrative of the Body and Political Terror in Northern Ireland* (Chicago: University of Chicago Press, 1991).

9. Antonio Gramsci, *Selections from the Prison Notebooks,* ed. and trans. Quinton Hoare and Geoffrey Nowell Smith (New York: International Publishers, 1971); Louis Althusser, *Lenin and Philosophy and Other Essays,* trans. Ben Brewster (New York: Monthly Review Press, 1971); Foucault, *Discipline and Punish.*

10. Kevin Lynch, *The Image of the City* (Cambridge, MA: Technology Press, 1960); David Canter and Terence Lee, eds., *Psychology of the Built Environment* (London: The Architectural Press, 1974); J. Douglas Porteous, *Environment and Behavior: Planning and Everyday Urban Life* (Reading, MA: Addison-Wesley, 1977); Amos Rapoport, *The Meaning of the Built Environment: A Nonverbal Communication Approach* (Beverly Hills, CA: Sage, 1982); Omer Akin, *Psychology of Architectural Design* (London: Pion, 1986).

11. Leon Battista Alberti, *The Architecture of Leon Battista Alberti in Ten Books,* ed. James Leoni (London: Thomas Edlin, 1739), 1:[iii], [vi]–[vii].

12. The classic study of architectural metaphors for the mind is Frances A. Yates, *The Art of Memory* (Chicago: University of Chicago Press, 1966).

13. See, for example, Oliver Impey and Arthur MacGregor, eds., *The Origins of Museums: The Cabinet of Curiosities in Sixteenth- and Seventeenth-Century Europe* (Oxford: Clarendon Press, 1985); and Eilean Hooper-Greenhill, *Museums and the Shaping of Knowledge* (London: Routledge, 1992).

14. John Locke, *An Essay Concerning Human Understanding,* ed. Peter H. Nidditch (Oxford: Clarendon Press, 1975), bk. 1, chap. 2, sec. 15, 55; bk. 2, chap. 11, sec. 17, 163.

15. Émile Durkheim and Marcel Mauss, *Primitive Classification,* trans. and ed. Rodney Needham (1903; Chicago: University of Chicago Press, 1963); see also Émile Durkheim, *The Elementary Forms of Religious Life,* trans. Karen E. Fields (1912; New York: Free Press, 1995).

16. Bourdieu's first substantial discussion of this appeared in his *Outline of a Theory of Practice,* trans. Richard Nice (Cambridge: Cambridge University Press, 1977). Bourdieu later revised his work and issued *The Logic of Practice,* trans. Richard Nice (1980; Stanford, CA: Stanford University Press, 1990). More recently see Pierre Bourdieu, "Habitus," in *Habitus: A Sense of Place,* ed. Jean Hillier and Emma Rooksby (Aldershot, UK: Ashgate, 2002), 27–34; and Pierre Bourdieu, *Images d'Algérie. Une Affinité élective,* ed. Franz Schultheis and Christine Frisinghelli (Arles: Actes Sud/Sinbad/Camera Austria, 2003).

17. Murray J. Edelman, "Space and the Social Order," *Journal of Architectural Education* 32, no. 2 (November 1978): 2–7; Thomas A. Markus, *Buildings and Power: Freedom and Control in the Origin of Modern Building Types* (London: Routledge, 1993).

18. Bourdieu defined the habitus as "systems of durable, transposable dispositions, structured structures predisposed to function as structuring structures, that is, as principles which generate and organize practices and representations" (*The Logic of Practice,* 53).

19. Bourdieu, "Habitus," 27–34.

20. Perhaps most crucial and convincing is his discussion of an example of domestic architecture, the "The Kabyle House," relegated in *Logic* to the appendix, where Bourdieu deprecated this essay as overly structuralist. Nevertheless the detailed exploration of the manner in which social meanings and relations are sustained through spatial apparatus is exemplary; a comparable analysis would be equally possible and successful for dwellings in other societies, not least our own.

21. Bourdieu, *The Logic of Practice,* 76.

22. Bourdieu, *Outline of a Theory of Practice,* 90–91.

23. Bourdieu, *The Logic of Practice,* 71.

24. Further, see Erving Goffman, *The Presentation of Self in Everyday Life* (Garden City, NJ: Doubleday, 1959); Edelman, "Space and the Social Order," 2–7; Paul L. Knox, "Symbolism, Styles and Settings: The Built Environment and the Imperatives of Urbanized Capitalism," *Architecture & Comportement* 2 (1984): 107–22.

25. Bourdieu, *Outline of a Theory of Practice,* 95. Bourdieu also asks us to consider in this light the Marxian argument that "property appropriates its owner, embodying itself in the form of a structure generating practices perfectly conforming with its logic and its demands" (*The Logic of Practice,* 57).

26. Pierre Bourdieu, *Distinction,* trans. Richard Nice (Cambridge, MA: Harvard University Press, 1984).

27. See Thomas A. Markus, *Buildings and Power: Freedom and Control in the Origin of Modern Building Types* (London: Routledge, 1993), who in following the approach of Bill Hillier and Julienne Hanson, *The Social Logic of Space* (Cambridge: Cambridge University Press, 1984) extends the analysis to other building types. As with Foucault, the emphasis remains more on the articulation of relative position within a closed system than on articulation of identity per se.

28. Foucault, *Discipline and Punish;* Markus, *Buildings and Power.*

29. Michel de Certeau, *The Practice of Everyday Life,* trans. Steven Rendall (Berkeley: University of California Press, 1984), 96, 97, 100.

30. Alexis de Tocqueville noted, with some concern, the rising interest in the consumption of commodities in America early in the nineteenth century. *Democracy in America,* trans. Henry Reeve (New York: J. & H. G. Langley, 1840), 171.

31. Walter Benjamin, "The Work of Art in the Age of Mechanical Reproduction," in *Illuminations,* ed. Hannah Arendt, trans. Harry Zohn (New York: Schocken, 1969), 240. I take up Benjamin's argument at greater length in the conclusion to this volume.

32. Benjamin's argument thus lies in distinct contrast to Bourdieu's chronologically later examination of the "habitus"—which went a long way toward explaining the structures of a subject's consciousness but afforded far less insight into means by which spatial apparatuses might be employed in altering that subjectivity.

33. Daniel Miller, *Material Culture and Mass Consumption* (Oxford: Basil Blackwell, 1987), 147, 175, 190; see also 196–97 and passim.

34. As always, a change of conditions or circumstances (having children, promotion, different life stages, etc.) affords the possibility, but not ordinarily the necessity, to make different choices.

1. Locating the Self in Space

1. John Locke, *An Essay Concerning Humane Understanding* (London: Thomas Basset, 1690); and John Locke, *Two Treatises of Government* (London: Awnsham Churchill, 1690).

2. Alexander Pope, *An Essay on Man* (London: Lawton Gilliver, 1734), 19.

3. Of course to promulgate the notion that one is sovereign over one's being does not make it so, even if people are persuaded to believe that it is so. See, for example, Louis Althusser's discussion of this point in *Lenin and Philosophy,* trans. Ben Brewster (New York: Monthly Review Press, 1971), 170–77, in which he argues that the very category of subjectivity (by which we identify ourselves as "subjects," i.e., selves) is little more than

the mechanism by which state ideology locates the position and roles in which individual beings are constituted in society.

4. John Locke, *An Essay Concerning Human Understanding,* ed. Peter H. Nidditch (Oxford: Clarendon Press, 1975), bk. 2, chap. 27, sec. 9, 335. See also 342 and 345.

5. Locke, *An Essay Concerning Human Understanding,* bk. 2, chap. 27, sec. 17, 341. In a concluding remark on how the term "person" should be applied in legal ("forensick") parlance, Locke further relied on this notion of "self," using it to stress two qualities in particular: autonomy and agency (346). In both these respects the person, who was "capable of a Law"—as opposed to being granted personhood by the law—implicitly had existence prior to law and society.

6. Nor did Locke leave the selection of those terms up to the individual. As the next section will make clear, Locke established ownership of *property* as one of the apparent conditions of selfhood.

7. The point is that these attributes were not just arbitrary traits but were defining properties of selfhood per se. *Characteristic* thus is used in a double sense. To have such attributes is characteristic of selfhood; the specific attributes are characteristic of a specific self. On eighteenth-century architects' efforts to incorporate character in design, see John Archer, "Character in English Architectural Design," *Eighteenth-Century Studies* 12, no. 3 (Spring 1979): 339–71.

8. These are discussed in John Archer, *The Literature of British Domestic Architecture, 1715–1842* (Cambridge, MA: MIT Press, 1985), 77–87.

9. Although I rely frequently on the terms *bourgeois* and *bourgeoisie* throughout this book, it is a tenuous proposition to suggest that the rise of a particular type of dwelling (e.g., the "bourgeois villa") is fully mappable onto, and reciprocal with, the rise of a particular class (the bourgeoisie, or the middle class). In addition to the fact that both the social class and the architectural type are subject to a range of varying definitions, one of the principal difficulties with such a presumption is the fact that both were evolving in response to a complex nexus of shifting conditions. To expect that a social class would coalesce in response to the very same circumstances around which an architectural type evolved, at just the same time, is to fashion too perfect an account of history. Nevertheless it is fully apparent that the evolution of the ascendant bourgeoisie and of the compact villa that I discuss in the next chapter followed courses that in many respects were coincident and contingent. Put another way, the compact villa became an instrument by which the bourgeoisie could seize some opportunities and bridge some contradictions that arose in the evolution of Enlightenment ideology, jurisprudence, politics, economics, and society. For a rich social history of the middle class, see Peter Earle, *The Making of the English Middle Class: Business, Society and Family in London 1660–1730* (Berkeley: University of California Press, 1989). See also Paul Langford, *A Polite and Commercial People: England 1727–1783* (Oxford: Oxford University Press, 1989).

10. See Archer, *The Literature of British Domestic Architecture,* 59–71, 87–103.

11. Thomas Rawlins, *Familiar Architecture* (N. loc.: The Author, 1768), ii. *Familiar Architecture* was reissued in 1789 and again in 1795.

12. Rawlins, *Familiar Architecture,* iv. Not incidentally, statements such as Rawlins's are wholly consistent with the notion crystallized within a decade by Adam Smith, that the private individual was the basic unit of nature and society, and that private individuals exist in competition with each other, striving to maximize their own gain. This explicitly positions the individual as prior to (and in opposition to) the collectivity. The villa-as-realization-of-the-self is, in many respects, part and parcel of this ideology.

13. Many bourgeois villas, such as those discussed in the next chapter, serve as excellent instances of what Henri Lefebvre termed a "representational space," that is, "space as directly *lived* through its associated images and symbols. . . . This is the . . . space which the imagination seeks to change and appropriate. It overlays physical space, making symbolic use of its objects." To Lefebvre's argument that imagination here seeks to orchestrate the terms in which space is understood and lived, I would add that by shaping space through design and daily practice, the human being seeks to answer and accommodate the challenges posed by imagination (and ideology). Henri Lefebvre, *The Production of Space,* trans. Donald Nicholson-Smith (Oxford: Blackwell, 1991), 39.

14. The basis of Locke's differentiation of private from public lay in positing only two kinds of relations through which people could articulate attachments to each other and to space: family and property. Neither of these relations required prior social institutions; indeed, since both types of relations were anchored only in *individuals,* they were ontologically anterior to society and the public realm. Locke of course proceeded to articulate a strong and complex role for social and political institutions, but the grounds on which he articulated human existence, consciousness, and rights all were predicated on the autonomous *private* individual.

15. John Locke, *Two Treatises of Government,* ed. Peter Laslett, student ed. (Cambridge: Cambridge University Press, 1988), Second Treatise, sec. 32–35, 290–92.

16. Locke, *Two Treatises of Government,* Second Treatise, sec. 35, 292.

17. Locke's principal concern was to demonstrate the contingency of liberty on property rights—see Locke, *Two Treatises of Government,* Second Treatise, sec. 87, 323—but the further implications for private consumption were no less consequential.

18. Locke, *Two Treatises of Government,* Second Treatise, sec. 27, 287.

19. Peter Laslett, introduction to *Two Treatises of Government, a Critical Edition* by John Locke, ed. Peter Laslett (Cambridge: Cambridge University Press, 1967), 103.

20. David Hume, *A Treatise of Human Nature,* ed. L. A. Selby-Bigge, 2nd ed., rev. P. H. Nidditch (Oxford: Clarendon Press, 1978), 505–6, 310.

21. Even earlier Bishop George Berkeley had articulated a related understanding of the process of vision and representation in terms of property. As Jacques Lacan described it: "This is the irreducible method of Bishop Berkeley, about whose subjective method much might be said—including something that may have eluded you in passing, namely this *belong to me* aspect of representations, so reminiscent of property." Jacques Lacan, *The Four Fundamental Concepts of Psycho-Analysis,* ed. Jacques-Alain Miller, trans. Alan Sheridan (New York: W. W. Norton, 1981), 81.

22. Laslett, introduction to *Two Treatises of Government, a Critical Edition,* 103–5.

23. See, for example, Stephen Switzer, *Ichnographia Rustica* (London: D. Browne et al., 1718), 3:217–18: Enclosing one's land would increase fertility, permit lasting capital improvements, increase yields, provide employment for the poor, sustain a growing population, diminish the opportunity for damage, e.g., by stray cattle, and increase the owner's profits.

24. There was an implicit corresponding shift in human cognition of land from being *domain* that was charged and controlled by human and divine power and authority to being *territory* demarcated by abstract and universal systems.

25. *Oxford English Dictionary,* s.v. "propriety."

26. Of course, in the actuality of Locke's own time—as distinct from the putative state of existence before the institution of society—such a notion broke down very quickly, as in the case of farmhands who labored everywhere on land that would never be theirs.

John Barrell has shown how the incongruity of such labor-without-right-of-property was so troublesome during the eighteenth century that landscape painting was regularly sanitized of its presence. John Barrell, *The Dark Side of the Landscape* (Cambridge: Cambridge University Press, 1980). Nevertheless Locke established much of the underpinning of what has since come to be called the theory of "possessive individualism," a guiding principle of Enlightenment social relations. See C. B. Macpherson, *The Political Theory of Possessive Individualism* (Oxford: Oxford University Press, 1962).

27. Tom Williamson and Liz Bellamy, *Property and Landscape: A Social History of Land Ownership and the English Countryside* (London: George Philip, 1987), 116.

28. On suburbs as oppositional sites to the city, see "Colonial Suburbs in South Asia, 1700–1850, and the Spaces of Modernity," in *Visions of Suburbia*, ed. Roger Silverstone (London: Routledge, 1996), 26–54.

29. For a useful overview, see Williamson and Bellamy, *Property and Landscape*. For greater depth, see Joan Thirsk, ed., *The Agrarian History of England and Wales: Volume V, 1640–1750. II. Agrarian Change* (Cambridge: Cambridge University Press, 1985).

30. Such material terms included the privatization of the garden, family, and leisure: all became contextual resources that the resident (ordinarily the adult male) could readily appropriate as material components of self and identity. The dwelling also functioned oppositionally: the self of the bourgeois villa was constructed as "other" than such non-personal interests as economy, agriculture, urbanity, and sometimes even class, thus further articulating the isolated autonomy of the self.

31. For example, as Jean Bethke Elshtain remarks succinctly, "Filmer's world is one chain." *Public Man, Private Woman*, 2nd ed. (Princeton, NJ: Princeton University Press, 1993), 104.

32. Locke, *An Essay Concerning Human Understanding*, bk. 2, chap. 13, sec. 14, 173; bk. 2, chap. 13, sec. 3, 167 note.

33. Locke, *An Essay Concerning Human Understanding*, bk. 2, chap. 27, sec. 9, 335.

34. Locke's predecessors in fashioning the terms of this mind-body split included Descartes and Galileo. Since the eighteenth century a considerable body of social thought has focused on undoing or repairing the consequences of the ensuing detachment of individuals from social and spatial structure. Late nineteenth-century Marxism and early twentieth-century phenomenology, opposites though they were, were among the earliest serious attempts to restore the lost connections. Architectural thinking has played a leading role in such efforts, particularly among phenomenologists, postmodernists, and deconstructionists. That architecture is engaged in the forefront of twentieth-century social critique further signals the need to examine the ways in which architecture was both engaged and instrumental in rendering the challenges originally posed by Lockean thought.

35. On the role of geometric proportion in English architectural theory, see Rudolf Wittkower, "English Literature on Architecture," in *Palladio and Palladianism* (New York: George Braziller, 1974), 114–32. Note that while a geometric articulation of space may have been more conducive to democratic and autonomous notions of self, it was yet quite far from providing for the articulation of *difference* among selves.

36. Alexander Pope, *A Miscellany on Taste. By Mr. Pope, &c. Viz. I. Of Taste in Architecture. An Epistle to the Earl of Burlington* (London: G. Lawton et al., 1732), 21–22.

37. Elshtain, *Public Man, Private Woman*, 116. See also 118–19.

38. Again see Wittkower, "English Literature on Architecture."

39. Alan Macfarlane, *The Origins of English Individualism* (Oxford: Basil Blackwell, 1978), traces individualism to a much earlier period than the eighteenth century. My point here is to signal the eighteenth-century appearance of cultures of "sentiment" and

"sensibility" in many dimensions—the Gothic novel, the aesthetic of the sublime in paint-ing, the multiplying range of revival styles in architecture—all of which afforded new dimensions for exploring personal affect and expression. And the home became the site for engaging in such pursuits, by no means the least of which was architectural self-expression.

40. As an apparatus dedicated to knowledge and learning, the cabinet had commonly been as much a piece of furniture as a room. The "secret house" was notably located dis-tinctly apart from the main dwelling. On cabinets, see Eilean Hooper-Greenhill, *Museums and the Shaping of Knowledge* (London: Routledge, 1992); on secret houses, see Paula Henderson, "Sir Francis Bacon's Water Gardens at Gorhambury," *Garden History* 20, no. 2 (Autumn 1992): 116–31; and Paula Henderson, "Secret Houses and Garden Lodges: The Queen's House, Greenwich, in Context," *Apollo* 146, no. 425 (July 1997): 29–35.

41. Considerable scholarly attention has been paid to Castell. See Helen H. Tanzer, *The Villas of Pliny the Younger* (New York: Columbia University Press, 1924); Eileen Harris and Nicholas Savage, *British Architectural Books and Writers, 1556–1785* (Cambridge: Cam-bridge University Press, 1990); and Pierre de la Ruffinière Du Prey, *The Villas of Pliny from Antiquity to Posterity* (Chicago: University of Chicago Press, 1994).

42. Robert Castell, *The Villas of the Ancients Illustrated* (London: The Author, 1728), 22–24, 105–6.

43. Roger Chartier, ed., *A History of Private Life III: Passions of the Renaissance,* trans. Arthur Goldhammer (Cambridge, MA: Harvard University Press, 1989); Annik Pardailhé-Galabrun, *The Birth of Intimacy: Privacy and Domestic Life in Early Modern Paris,* trans. Jocelyn Phelps (Philadelphia: University of Pennsylvania Press, 1991).

44. Jürgen Habermas, *The Structural Transformation of the Public Sphere,* trans. Thomas Burger (1962; Cambridge, MA: MIT Press, 1991), 46. The conflation of "private" with "family" also figures prominently in Habermas's discussion.

45. Karl Marx, "Economic and Philosophic Manuscripts of 1844," in *Collected Works,* by Karl Marx and Friedrich Engels (New York: International Publishers, 1975), 274.

46. John Dixon Hunt, *Andrew Marvell: His Life and Writings* (Ithaca, NY: Cornell University Press, 1978), 80–112; Malcolm Kelsall, *The Great Good Place: The Country House and English Literature* (New York: Columbia University Press, 1993), 49–58.

47. Stephen Switzer, *The Practical Husbandman and Planter* 1, no. 1 (April 1733): lxiv.

48. *Oxford English Dictionary,* s.v. "gentleman."

49. The complex pressures bearing on the term *gentleman* during this transitional period are evidenced in its exceptionally fluid definition; within two years of the appear-ance of the *Gentleman's Magazine* the prominent horticulturist Stephen Switzer employed the term in a manner that included dukes, earls, lords, and esquires, i.e., both nobility and gentry. *Practical Husbandman and Planter* 1, no. 1 (1733): lxiv.

50. See, for example, John Archer, "Rus in Urbe: Classical Ideals of Country and City in British Town Planning," in Harry C. Payne, ed., *Studies in Eighteenth-Century Culture* 12 (1983): 159–86.

51. Daniel Defoe, *The Compleat English Gentleman,* ed. Karl D. Bülbring (London: David Nutt, 1890), 257, 267, 240. Defoe composed the essay between 1728 and 1729, but it was not published until 1890.

52. Defoe, *The Compleat English Gentleman,* 263–64.

53. Locke, *Two Treatises of Government,* First Treatise, sec. 48, 174.

54. Brathwait framed patriarchal relations explicitly in terms of the household: "As every mans house is his Castle, so is his *family* a private Common-wealth, wherein if due government be not observed, nothing but confusion is to be expected." Richard Brathwait, *The English Gentleman* (London: Robert Bostock, 1630), 155.

55. See, for example, Locke, *Two Treatises of Government*, Second Treatise, secs. 71, 77, 170, 173. For extended discussion of Locke's positions, see Gordon Schochet, *Patriarchalism in Political Thought* (New York: Basic Books, 1975). Also on patriarchy, see Gerda Lerner, *The Creation of Patriarchy* (New York: Oxford University Press, 1986); on household patriarchy before Locke, see Susan Dwyer Amussen, *An Ordered Society* (Oxford: Blackwell, 1988), chap. 2.

56. Schochet, *Patriarchalism in Political Thought*, 248–49.

57. The presumption in seventeenth-century manners literature was that household organization was an extension of civil society, and vice versa. As Gordon Schochet stated: "It was only as a member of a family that one acquired any meaning or status in society, for it was *through* the family that an individual came into contact with the outside world" (*Patriarchalism in Political Thought*, 65).

58. Still, in articulating his rationale for the family realm Locke made it clear that parental authority was exercised in fulfillment of a *social* role:

> The *Power*, then, *that Parents have* over their Children, arises from that Duty which is incumbent on them, to take care of their Off-spring, during the imperfect state of Childhood. . . .
>
> Nay, this *power* so little belongs to the *Father* by any peculiar right of Nature, but only as he is Guardian of his Children, that when he quits his Care of them, he loses his Power over them, which goes along with their Nourishment and Education, to which it is inseparably annexed, and it belongs as much to the *Foster-Father* of an exposed Child, as to the Natural Father of another. . . .
>
> It is but a help to the weakness and imperfection of their Nonage, a Discipline necessary to their education.

The family, and therefore necessarily the dwelling, thus became the locale where such "Duty," "Care," "Nourishment," "Education," and "Discipline" would be exercised: a site for the production not simply of citizens but of self-reliant individuals, who on arriving at the age of majority, according to Locke, have "attained to a state of Freedom," which brings with it the privilege of participation in the public sphere. Locke, *Two Treatises of Government*, Second Treatise, secs. 58, 65, 59, 306, 310, 307.

59. Elshtain, *Public Man, Private Woman*, 103.

60. Locke, *Two Treatises of Government*, First Treatise, sec. 47, 174.

61. Geoffrey Beard, *The Compleat Gentleman: Five Centuries of Aristocratic Life* (New York: Rizzoli, 1993), 13.

2. Villa Suburbana, Terra Suburbana

1. Some recent writers have suggested that Palladio invented the suburban villa. Robert A. M. Stern, for example, writes that "Palladio was the first to give lithic expression to the most important new social fact of the modern era, the emergence of the middle class." "The Postmodern Continuum," in *Critical Architecture and Contemporary Culture*, ed. William J. Lillyman et al. (New York: Oxford University Press, 1994), 49. Witold Rybczynski offers much the same assessment in *The Perfect House* (New York: Scribner, 2002). But their assessments are debatable given that Palladio's villas often were working farm establishments and that the notion of "middle class" may well be inappropriate for sixteenth-century Italy. I have chosen to trace the compact bourgeois villa in England along other lines because the authors and designers who evolved this new type, while not unaware of Palladio, did so while engaged with economic, social, and ideological concerns immediate to the eighteenth century, as I will discuss later.

2. This is not the place to review the burgeoning literature in cultural anthropology. But see Paul Oliver, *Dwellings: The House across the World* (Oxford: Phaidon, 1987); and Amos Rapoport, *House Form and Culture* (Englewood Cliffs, NJ: Prentice-Hall, 1969).

3. Leon Battista Alberti, *The Architecture of Leon Battista Alberti in Ten Books,* ed. James Leoni (London: Thomas Edlin, 1739), vol. 1, fol. 94^r; vol. 2, fol. 79^r–79^v.

4. Andrea Palladio, *The Four Books of Architecture,* trans. Isaac Ware (London: R. Ware, 1738), bk. 2, chap. 12, 46. I have used the Ware translation here and elsewhere because it would have been familiar to eighteenth-century English readers.

5. James Ackerman points out that the most renowned of Palladio's villas, the Rotonda, "had no agricultural function—it was built purely for pleasure," but also notes that the Rotonda nevertheless differed substantially from its English progeny such as Chiswick House in that the English proprietor "was not immersed in agriculture, preferring in the design of buildings and gardens to hide the evidence of crops, herds . . . , labor and other reminders of his economic underpinnings." James S. Ackerman, *The Villa: Form and Ideology of Country Houses* (Princeton, NJ: Princeton University Press, 1990), 106, 157.

6. Stephen Switzer, *Ichnographia Rustica: Or, the Nobleman, Gentleman, and Gardener's Recreation* (London: D. Browne et al., 1718), 3:iii.

7. The seeds of Switzer's approach possibly may be found in English Renaissance writing: Stephen Greenblatt has explored the process of self-fashioning in Renaissance England, primarily in terms of writing, albeit this was subject to considerable discipline from "family, state, and religious institutions." Stephen Greenblatt, *Renaissance Self-Fashioning from More to Shakespeare* (Chicago: University of Chicago Press, 1980), 1–2.

8. Anthony Ashley Cooper, 3rd Earl of Shaftesbury, *Characteristicks of Men, Manners, Opinions, Times* (n.p., 1711), 3:30; 2:366. The inspiring power is variously the divine Genius and the primary, central quality of any individual object or place, the "genius loci."

9. Switzer, *Ichnographia Rustica,* 3:iii–v.

10. The title page of Morris's *Essay upon Harmony* (London: T. Cooper, 1739) prominently featured an extract from Shaftesbury's *Characteristicks.* Morris's book *An Essay in Defence of Ancient Architecture* (London: D. Browne et al., 1728) was the first book to be illustrated exclusively with designs for compact villas.

11. John Archer, *The Literature of British Domestic Architecture, 1715–1842* (Cambridge, MA: MIT Press, 1985), 62.

12. A much broader discussion of the notion of "retirement" appears in chapter 3.

13. Robert Morris, *Lectures on Architecture* (London: J. Brindley, 1734–36), 2:169.

14. Morris, *Lectures on Architecture,* 2:171–75.

15. Morris, *Lectures on Architecture,* 1:74, 81, 101–2.

16. Contemplative activity in such a setting "fills us with noble Ideas of the Power which such Proportions have on the Mind." Morris, *Lectures on Architecture,* 1:101.

17. Sir John Summerson, "The Classical Country House in 18th-Century England," *Journal of the Royal Society of Arts* 107, no. 5036 (July 1959): 539–87. On page 571 he noted that by the *end* of the eighteenth century the villa, as an architectural *type,* had taken on a "small, compact character." He also noted that the villa had become a predominantly "middle-class type of house" and generally "suburban" as well. While continuing to embrace Summerson's valuable work, my approach differs in that I am not primarily tracing the history of a building *type* such as the villa. Rather, I am exploring ways in which architecture evolved, starting at an earlier time, to address a broad range of cultural concerns.

18. James Gibbs, *A Book of Architecture* (London: n. pub., 1759), plate 40. For more on Gibbs's work at Sudbrook and for the Duke of Argyll, see Terry Friedman, *James Gibbs*

(New Haven: Yale University Press, 1984), 133–37; for other "villas" possibly by Gibbs, see ibid., 140, 142, 144, 315, 316, 345. Gibbs dedicated his entire treatise to Argyll, and the illustration of Sudbrook is fourth among thirty plates of residential designs, suggesting the considerable significance of this commission.

19. Friedman, *James Gibbs,* 135. The manuscript cited here is possibly by Gibbs, certainly of his time.

20. The room was adorned with military trophies, according to the Gibbs manuscript at Sir John Soane's Museum.

21. On activities, plans, etc., see Mark Girouard, *Life in the English Country House* (New Haven: Yale University Press, 1978), chap. 7.

22. Gibbs, *A Book of Architecture,* plates 59 and 60. The alternative design appears in plate 62. For further discussion, see Friedman, *James Gibbs,* 137–38.

23. The literature on Burlington, Chiswick, and their central role in the Palladian revival is voluminous. A recent thorough historical account on which I have relied is Richard Hewlings, *Chiswick House and Gardens,* 2nd ed. (London: English Heritage, 1991). In the present paragraph and those that follow I have also drawn from Malcolm Kelsall, *The Great Good Place: The Country House and English Literature* (New York: Columbia University Press, 1993); John Harris, *The Design of the English Country House* (London: Trefoil Books, 1985); and Kerry Downes, "Chiswick Villa," *Architectural Review* 164, no. 980 (October 1978): 225–36.

24. Downes, "Chiswick Villa," 226.

25. In addition to the very early examples discussed here, a number of others may be mentioned as harbingers of the bourgeois compact villa genre. The following, all by Colen Campbell, appear in volume 3 of *Vitruvius Britannicus* (London: The Author, 1725), and several are quite diminutive, although none was explicitly called a "villa" by Campbell in the text: Mereworth (plates 35–38), Stourhead (plates 41–43), Newby (plate 46), Ebberston (plate 47), Pembroke (plate 48), and Goodwood (plates 51–54). Newby was the first compact villa designed with the facade incorporating a 1—3—1 window grouping and a temple portico (see Lindsay Boynton, "Newby Park, Yorkshire," in *The Country Seat,* ed. Howard Colvin and John Harris [London: Allen Lane, 1970], 99). Giles Worsley suggests that Campbell was perhaps responsible for the introduction of this type, although Worsley also was careful to indicate that the dwellings Campbell produced were neither suburban resorts nor Palladian-style farms. Giles Worsley, *Classical Architecture in Britain* (New Haven, CT: Yale University Press, 1995), 106–13. Other premier examples of compact villas mentioned by Worsley, some of which were suburban retreats, include Marble Hill, Twickenham, White Lodge, Richmond (which was more properly a hunting lodge than a dwelling), Westcombe House, Blackheath, Waverley Abbey, Surrey, Hackney House, Middlesex, Combe Bank, Kent, Whitton Place, Middlesex, South Dalton Hall, Yorkshire, and Rokeby Park, Yorkshire, all designed or executed before the end of the 1730s. For Marble Hill House, illustrated in the third volume of Colen Campbell, *Vitruvius Britannicus* (1725), plate 93, see Marie P. G. Draper, *Marble Hill House* (London: Greater London Council, 1970). The White Lodge is illustrated in the fourth volume of Thomas Badeslade and John Rocque, *Vitruvius Britannicus* (London: John Wilcox, George Fosler, and Henry Chappelle, 1739), plates 1–4; see "The Duke of York's New Home," *Country Life* 53 (21 April 1923): 526–27; and Howard Colvin et al. *The History of the King's Works, Volume V: 1660–1782* (London: HMSO, 1976), 230–33. South Dalton, illustrated in the fourth volume of *Vitruvius Britannicus* (1739), plates 90–91, is discussed in W. A. Eden, "South Dalton, Yorkshire," in *The Country Seat,* ed. Colvin and Harris, 117–20. Another early example of the standard formula for a compact villa, though

considerably closer to the urban center, was Lord Herbert's house in Whitehall, illustrated in the third volume of *Vitruvius Britannicus* (1725), plate 48; see Montagu H. Cox and G. Topham Forrest, *Survey of London XIII: The Parish of St. Margaret, Westminster—Part II* (London: London County Council, 1930), 167–75. Finally, two other comparatively diminutive dwellings appeared in the first volume of *Vitruvius Britannicus* (1715), Wilbury House, Wiltshire, plates 51–52; and Orleans House, Twickenham, plates 77–78, in the general vicinity of which modern suburbia was just then beginning to coalesce.

26. Marcus Binney, *Sir Robert Taylor* (London: George Allen & Unwin, 1984), 40, 49.

27. A generation after Taylor, James Gandon produced comparable domestic designs in Ireland. However, Gandon's circulation pattern was much more static than many of his British predecessors: in his villas the rooms were all dead ends, offering a notably heightened sense of privacy. See Edward McParland, *James Gandon* (London: A. Zwemmer, 1985), 130, 138.

28. The design may date from before 1753: Maurice Craig, *The Volunteer Earl: Being the Life and Times of James Caulfield First Earl of Charlemont* (London: Cresset Press, 1948), 82–83. On the building recession, see Worsley, *Classical Architecture in Britain*, 223–26.

29. Though loosely indebted to Palladio's Villa Rotonda, a comparatively compact villa that is symmetrical about two axes, the design for the Casino at Marino is still several removes from the Vicenzan prototype. For example, where the Rotonda is open, Marino is closed; where the Rotonda is a hierarchically arranged array of multiple elements, Marino appears to be a single, four-porticoed cella.

30. John Cornforth, "The Casino at Marino, Dublin—I," *Country Life* 182, no. 5 (4 February 1988): 73.

31. Craig, *The Volunteer Earl*, 123–24.

32. Redmill and Bristow conclude that "Charlemont's original intention was to live in the Casino as a learned bachelor, surrounded by peace and his collection of art treasures." John Redmill and Ian C. Bristow, "The Casino at Marino, Dublin," Association for Studies in the Conservation of Historic Buildings, *Transactions* 9 (1984): 32. But Charlemont eventually married, and it seems that once completed, despite the original design, the house was destined primarily for use as a party house. Nevertheless the house is not scaled to grand entertainment. It holds only six to eight persons comfortably in any given room, and access to the upper floor is difficult.

33. This is not a discussion of intentionality. Given the existing documentation, there is no way to know now what intentions were on the minds of Chambers and Caulfield as this structure was designed and built. Pursuing such a question may be futile since motivations and desires often remain hidden or confused, particularly when dealing with new challenges and opportunities. Instead, I am offering a discussion of *instrumentality:* given the context in which this building was built, and given the dimensions and degrees in which its design departed from contextual norms, my purpose here is to explore ways in which those departures may be seen as dialectical responses to changed conditions. By their very nature, efforts to contend with new conditions are eccentric, and it is in part by analyzing certain eccentricities of design (i.e., *innovations*) that I seek to understand responses to such conditions.

34. Ackerman, *The Villa*, 9.

35. Roger North, *Of Building*, ed. Howard Colvin and John Newman (Oxford: Clarendon Press, 1981), 62.

36. The unabridged text of the passage is as follows: "a *Villa*, or little House of Pleasure and Retreat, where Gentlemen and Citizens betake themselves in the Summer for

their private Diversion, there to pass an Evening or two, or perhaps a Week, in the Conversation of a Friend or two, in some neat little House amidst a Vineyard or Garden, sequestered from the Noise of a City, and the Embarras and Destraction of Business, or perhaps the anxious and servile Attendance of a Court." Timothy Nourse, "Essay of a Country House," in *Campania Foelix* (London: T. Bennet, 1700), 297. On Nourse's wider significance and influence, see Maren-Sofie Røstvig, *The Happy Man,* 2nd ed. (Oslo: Norwegian Universities Press, 1962–71), 2:33ff.

37. Henry Aldrich, *The Elements of Civil Architecture* (Oxford: D. Prince et al., 1789), 59.

38. Robert Castell, *The Villas of the Ancients Illustrated,* 128 pp. ed. (London: The Author, 1728), preface. Harris and Savage indicate that Castell's efforts here were intended as prefatory to producing an English edition of Vitruvius. Eileen Harris and Nicholas Savage, *British Architectural Books and Writers, 1556–1785* (Cambridge: Cambridge University Press, 1990), 150. On the one hand it is worth emphasizing that from many possibilities Castell chose to investigate a particular class of *dwelling*. On the other hand, Castell's expectation that his research would yield universal rules for such dwellings hardly suggests that his principal concern was an expansion of opportunities for individualistic expression. Still, Pliny himself perhaps contributed to Castell's optimistic search for rules. As Métraux has noted, Pliny was far stronger on rhetoric than on anything suggesting the economic and material process of actually building a villa. Guy Métraux, "Villa rustica alimentaria et annonaria," in *The Roman Villa: Villa Urbana,* ed Alfred Frazer (Philadelphia: The University Museum, University of Pennsylvania, 1998), 1–3. Also on Pliny, see Ackerman, *The Villa;* Lise Bek, *Towards Paradise on Earth* (Odense: Odense University Press, 1980); Kelsall, *The Great Good Place;* Pierre de la Ruffinière du Prey, *The Villas of Pliny* (Chicago: University of Chicago Press, 1994).

39. Castell, *The Villas of the Ancients Illustrated,* 19–20. Castell referred to Pliny's description in Book 9, Letter 40, of his wintertime daily routine at his Laurentine villa, ". . . employing a considerable part of the night in study, either before sunrise or after sunset. . . ." *The Epistles of Pliny,* trans. William Melmoth, ed. Clifford H. Moore (Boston: Bibliophile Society, 1925), 3:101.

40. Castell, *The Villas of the Ancients Illustrated,* 2n, 55.

41. Castell, *The Villas of the Ancients Illustrated,* 2n, 9n, 50–51, 55, 77, 96, 124–25. As Castell noted (50–51), Pliny "was obliged to buy all his provisions" in neighboring settlements.

42. In the second paragraph of his preface, Castell wrote glowingly of Varro as a seminal writer, praising him over many others for having "discours'd more fully than any of them on those Parts of the *Villa* that were design'd as well for the Pleasures of a retir'd Life as the Conveniencies and Profits of Agriculture."

43. Castell, *The Villas of the Ancients Illustrated,* 2.

44. Castell, *The Villas of the Ancients Illustrated,* 2, 9, 15, 13, 111; see also 10, 24, 25, 38, 39, 40, 51, 82, 83, 85, 86, 87, 96.

45. Leon Battista Alberti, *The Architecture of Leon Battista Alberti in Ten Books,* trans. James Leoni (London: Thomas Edlin, 1726). My citations are to the second edition (London: Thomas Edlin, 1739).

46. Alberti, *The Architecture of Leon Battista Alberti,* 1:94^r. Mark Wigley, "Untitled: The Housing of Gender," in *Sexuality and Space,* ed. Beatriz Colomina (New York: Princeton Architectural Press, 1992), 332, 317–89 passim.

47. Alberti, *The Architecture of Leon Battista Alberti,* vol. 2, fol. 79^r–79^v. Alberti distinguished between only two types of "Ville," those "designed for Gentlemen, . . . perhaps

for pleasure," and those designed for "Husbandmen, . . . invented for use" (1:95ᵛ). This represents a shift from the tripartite typology indicated by Columella and Pliny—according to which a villa was an estate with three distinct parts for production, storage, and leisure—to a dual typology according to which a villa was either part of a productive farmstead, or it was a suburban retreat.

48. Switzer, *Ichnographia Rustica;* citations are to the second edition (London: J. and J. Fox et al., 1742). For villa as agricultural establishment, see 3:91 and appendix:10; for manor or estate, see 3:xiii and 3:87; for seat, see 3:iii and 3:77.

49. *Practical Husbandman and Planter* 1, no. 3 (June 1733): 1, 3. For Alberti's bipartite typology, see note 47 above. Alberti, unlike Switzer, did not see the pleasure villa as part of a larger establishment; in that sense Switzer remained closer to Pliny.

50. John Woolfe and James Gandon, *Vitruvius Britannicus* (N.loc.: n.p., 1767–71), 4:9, 5:3.

51. Samuel Richardson, *The History of Sir Charles Grandison,* ed. Jocelyn Harris (London: Oxford University Press, 1972), 3:273.

52. Thomas Overton, *Original Designs of Temples* (London: The Author, 1766), plates 35–42, 45–47. This book was also issued in 1766 and reissued in 1774, as *The Temple Builder's Most Useful Companion.*

53. Isaac Ware, *A Complete Body of Architecture* (London: T. Osborne and J. Shipton, 1756), preface, 293, 405. At an apparently earlier date Henry Aldrich, Dean of Christ Church, Oxford, had developed a more elaborate typology of houses according to occupation. But although Aldrich died in 1710, the treatise in which he elaborated this typology was not published until 1789. There he differentiated among housing types appropriate for men of ordinary fortune, money lenders, lawyers, merchants, men in office, and noblemen. Henry Aldrich, *The Elements of Civil Architecture* (Oxford: D. Prince et al., 1789), 45.

54. "The Cit's Country Box," *The Connoisseur* 4, no. 135 (26 August 1756), 6th ed. (Oxford: J. Rivington et al., 1774): 233–38. William Cowper took up the censure of suburban "boxes" in his poem "Retirement," published in 1782: "Suburban villas, highwayside retreats, / That dread th'encroachment of our growing streets, / Tight boxes, neatly sash'd, and in a blaze / With all a July sun's collected rays, . . ." *The Complete Poetical Works* (London: Oxford University Press, 1907), 119, lines 481–84. For the twentieth-century continuation of this theme see chapter 7, the section "Identical Boxes and Identity."

55. "To the Printer, &c.," *London Magazine* 36 (November 1767): 547–48. In a similar satirical vein, see "Mr. Wright's Description of His Villa at Byer's Green," *Gentleman's Magazine* 63 (1793): 213–16; this is reprinted in Du Prey, *The Villas of Pliny,* 319–22.

56. For the course of British architectural publication during this period, see Archer, *The Literature of British Domestic Architecture;* and Harris and Savage, *British Architectural Books and Writers, 1556–1785.*

57. Farmhouses might be combined with or substituted for cottages. Both were associated with labor on the land; thus their absence or relegation to low position. The lack of attention to town houses, at least in published treatises, testifies to the ongoing persistence of "country" ideology, which stressed the importance of land ownership as a basis for social status and political power.

58. Often this correspondence was articulated in terms of architectural "decorum" or "character." On the latter, see John Archer, "Character in English Architectural Design," *Eighteenth-Century Studies* 12, no. 3 (Spring 1979): 339–71.

59. Morris, *Lectures on Architecture,* 80–81. Compare Ware's remarks in *A Complete Body of Architecture,* 293. For Aldrich's typology, see note 53 above.

60. Archer, *The Literature of British Domestic Architecture;* also chapter 5, this volume.

61. See, for example, Robert Fishman, *Bourgeois Utopias* (New York: Basic Books, 1987), 6–7.

62. John Twyning, *London Dispossessed* (New York: St. Martin's Press, 1997), 57, 72.

63. W. C. Hazlitt, ed., *Inedited Tracts* (London: Roxburghe Library, 1868), 78. This is a reprint of *The English Courtier* (London: Richard Jones, 1586), 1st ed., 1579. Also in a suburban locale there is the dual advantage of *company* when you want it and *solitude* ("when you lust to tarry alone") when you want it (81).

64. John Norden, *Speculum Britanniae* (London: n.p., 1593), 12.

65. Thomas Fuller, *The History of the Worthies of England,* ed. P. Austin Nuttall (London: Thomas Tegg, 1840), 2:311. The original edition was published in London for Thomas Williams in 1662.

66. Henry Cockeram, *The English Dictionarie* (London: Nathaniel Butter, 1623), unpaginated.

67. Defoe's opinion of Hackney, albeit in fashionable Middlesex, was less enthusiastic: "This town is so remarkable for the retreat of wealthy citizens, that there is at this time near a hundred coaches kept in it; tho' I will not join with a certain satyrical author, who said of Hackney, that there were more coaches than Christians in it." Daniel Defoe, *A Tour through England and Wales* (London: J. M. Dent & Sons, 1928), 1:168, 2:2. In larger terms, Isaac Kramnick aptly characterizes Defoe's *Tour* as describing "the economic and social leadership of the nobility and gentry being replaced by the rising wealth and prominence of the middle class." Isaac Kramnick, *Bolingbroke and His Circle* (Cambridge, MA: Harvard University Press, 1968), 197.

68. Defoe, *A Tour,* 1:160, 161.

69. John Cloake, *Richmond Past* (London: Historical Publications, 1991), 8, 21, 22, 25, 26.

70. Barbara Denny, *Notting Hill and Holland Park Past* (London: Historical Publications, 1993), 9.

71. Nicholas Cooper, *Houses of the Gentry* (New Haven: Yale University Press, 1999), 131, 133, 136; Denny, *Notting Hill and Holland Park Past,* 15; Barbara Denny and Carolyn Starren, *Kensington Past* (London: Historical Publications, 1998), 7, 13, 15, 27.

72. Cooper, *Houses of the Gentry,* 128, 131–41.

73. Gillian Clegg, *Chiswick Past* (London: Historical Publications, 1995), 6, 35–36; Andrew Saint et al., *London Suburbs* (London: Merrell Holberton, 1999), 208.

74. Malcolm Kelsall proposed that Pope's villa was "the first major instance of the suburbanisation of the country house in England" in *The Great Good Place,* 78. In light of matters taken up in chapter 1, there is no small irony that Pope, defender of the Great Chain of Being, turned to such privatist opportunities for self-definition as his suburban house and grotto.

75. Friedman, *James Gibbs,* 140.

76. Friedman, *James Gibbs,* 139–40.

77. See chapter 1, the section on "Recasting Privacy."

78. Indeed, to refer to his garden as "landscape" in the modern sense would be anachronistic; the understanding of natural environment in this modern sense of an "object of regard" became current only about midcentury. On Pope's garden, see Maynard Mack, *The Garden and the City* (Toronto: University of Toronto Press, 1969).

79. Susan Reynolds, ed., *A History of the County of Middlesex* (London: Oxford University Press, 1962), 3:141.

80. "The Wish," *The Student, or, The Oxford, and Cambridge Monthly Miscellany* 2 (1751): 397.

81. Jael Henrietta Mendez Pye, *A Short Account, of the Principal Seats and Gardens, in and about Twickenham* (London: n.p., 1760). Quotations are from the final edition, *A Peep into the Principal Seats and Gardens in and about Twickenham* (London: J. Bew, 1775), 52.

82. See the explicit comparison to Twickenham in Peter Martin, "'Long and Assiduous Endeavours': Gardening in Early Eighteenth-Century Virginia," *Eighteenth-Century Life* n.s. 8:2 (January 1983): 107–16. Also see Elizabeth McLean, "Town and Country Gardens in Eighteenth-Century Philadelphia," in the same issue, 136–47. Around London, in addition to suburbs mentioned in the text above, Clapham became especially popular after the opening of bridges across the Thames at Westminster in 1750 and Blackfriars in 1769.

83. The reason was stated often enough, however. See chapter 3, the section on "Dimensions of Retirement."

84. E. P. Thompson, *Whigs and Hunters* (New York: Pantheon, 1975), 263–64.

3. The Apparatus of Selfhood

1. Henry Wotton, *The Elements of Architectvre* (London: John Bill, 1624), 82.

2. This is not to ignore the long history of the notion of privacy that antedates the eighteenth century, which is far too complex to introduce here. Suffice it to say, I am arguing that along with the introduction of architectural techniques for emphasizing and increasing privacy early in the eighteenth century also came a shift in the definition of privacy. To sketch the shift in brief terms, the sense of the word *private* changed from "personal" or "pertaining to the person" to "alone, with all others excluded." Thus prior to the eighteenth century the hierarchical staging of privacy (as a sequence of rooms with ever more restricted access) was a means of rendering in material terms the social distinctions accorded to the person (as a social being) of the resident and the visitor. The eighteenth-century notion of spatial privacy—exclusion of all others from a domain dedicated exclusively to oneself—was by contrast accorded on the grounds of the ontological autonomy of the self.

3. Alice T. Friedman, *House and Household in Elizabethan England* (Chicago: University of Chicago Press, 1989), 90–96.

4. Nicholas Cooper, *Houses of the Gentry* (New Haven, CT: Yale University Press, 1999), 128–54.

5. Leon Battista Alberti, *The Architecture of Leon Battista Alberti in Ten Books,* ed. James Leoni (London: Thomas Edlin, 1739), vol. 1, fol. 98^v.

6. Orest Ranum, "The Refuges of Intimacy," in *A History of Private Life III: Passions of the Renaissance,* ed. Roger Chartier, trans. Arthur Goldhammer (Cambridge, MA: Harvard University Press, 1989), 208–10.

7. Samuel Rolleston [also attributed to Benjamin Buckler], *A Philosophical Dialogue Concerning Decency. To Which Is Added a Critical and Historical Dissertation on Places of Retirement for Necessary Occasions* (London: James Fletcher; J. and J. Rivington, 1751), 3, 4. Mark Girouard has noted that places called privy chambers existed since the Middle Ages. Mark Girouard, *Life in the English Country House* (New Haven, CT: Yale University Press), 57.

8. According to Norbert Elias, in Erasmus's time (at least on the Continent) it was commonplace to meet someone in the act of urinating or defecating. Norbert Elias, *The Civilizing Process: The History of Manners,* trans. Edmund Jephcott (New York: Urizen Books, 1978), 135.

9. Robert Morris, *Lectures on Architecture* (London: J. Brindley, 1734–36), 166.

10. My argument here runs counter to that proposed by Girouard in *Life in the English Country House,* that changes in the plan and use of eighteenth-century dwellings were consequences of what he termed an increasingly public, democratic character of English society (130, 205–6). My argument is that the design of eighteenth-century dwellings tended instead to differentiate the private self in multiple ways *from* the public domain.

11. Maurice Howard, *The Early Tudor Country House* (London: George Philip, 1987), 83–87.

12. Oliver Hill and John Cornforth, *English Country Houses: Caroline* (London: Country Life, 1966), 90–96; Girouard, *Life in the English Country House,* 123, 138. Girouard notes that back stairs had existed in France since the sixteenth century, and that they could be found in England beginning in the seventeenth.

13. For example, James Gibbs, *A Book of Architecture* (London: n.p., 1728), plates 43, 44, 52, 66; Morris, *Lectures on Architecture,* 125; Abraham Swan, *A Collection of Designs* (London: The Author, 1757), plate 2.

14. Gibbs, *A Book of Architecture,* plate 52.

15. On the chambermaid's work, see *Domestic Management, or the Art of Conducting a Family; with Instructions to Servants in General. Addressed to Young Housekeepers* (London: H. D. Symonds, [n.d.]), 50ff. Her responsibilities included the chamber pot, water, fire, curtains, bedding, towels, sashes, candlesticks, bed-warming, and general tidying.

16. In and of itself the motif of dual staircases, symmetrically placed, was not new. They appeared, for example, in designs for Palladio's Villas Saraceno and Poiana; from here the motif was imported into designs such as William Benson's plan for Wilbury House (1715). The distinctive aspect of Morris's design is the need to pass from the central hall through to the other side of an additional room to reach either staircase.

17. Marcus Binney, *Sir Robert Taylor* (London: George Allen & Unwin, 1984), 39–40.

18. James Leoni, *Some Designs Both Publick and Private* (London: Thomas Edlin, 1726), fol. 1ᵛ. Another example of separate staircases dedicated to individual bedchambers can be found at Chiswick House, erected ca. 1727–29.

19. Richard Pococke, *The Travels through England,* ed. James Joel Cartwright (Westminster: Camden Society, 1888), 1:63.

20. Swan, *A Collection of Designs in Architecture,* 1:2.

21. Howard, *The Early Tudor Country House,* 88–93.

22. "Explanation of the Design," ca. 1700. 1 sheet MS, The Getty Center for the History of Art and the Humanities, Special Collections, 850700*. Vanbrugh's remarks were prepared to accompany a design (now lost) that he had prepared for a Mr. Hedworth. Overall Vanbrugh recommended corridors because they conduced to privacy, quiet, and safety in the case of fire.

23. Gibbs, *A Book of Architecture,* plates 41, 44; on Kirkleatham, see Terry Friedman, *James Gibbs* (New Haven, CT: Yale University Press, 1984), 296. Gibbs frequently highlighted privacy. The text accompanying plate 52 in *A Book of Architecture* advertises that the upstairs "Lodging Rooms . . . are all made private by a common Passage between the Stairs," while that for plate 56 mentions that "there are seven small Lodging Rooms, all private." Similarly, see Morris, *Lectures on Architecture,* 125; William Halfpenny, *Six New Designs for Convenient Farm-Houses* (London: Robert Sayer, 1751), and *Useful Architecture* (London: Robert Sayer, 1752), passim; Swan, *A Collection of Designs,* plate 2; and Thomas Rawlins, *Familiar Architecture* (N. loc.: The Author, 1768), plates 11, 16.

24. Where a full suite of rooms was required, Ware recommended connecting them

in addition by "passages from behind," that is, a subsidiary corridor system. Isaac Ware, *A Complete Body of Architecture* (London: T. Osborne and J. Shipton, 1756), 328.

25. [John Payne], *Twelve Designs of Country-Houses* (Dublin: The Author, 1757), 12.

26. For an analysis of the ways in which room suites and corridors articulate systems of power and control, see Thomas A. Markus, *Buildings and Power: Freedom and Control in the Origin of Modern Building Types* (London: Routledge, 1993).

27. Computations for Whitton are based on measurements taken from the original drawings in the Yale Center for British Art, B1977.14.1142 and B1977.14.1144. Computations for Mr. Prescot's House are based on measurements taken from the original drawings at the Getty Research Institute, 850939**.

28. Robert Castell, *The Villas of the Ancients Illustrated* (London: The Author, 1728), 123; Morris, *Lectures on Architecture*, 89.

29. Sir Roger Pratt, "Certain Short Notes Concerning Architecture" (1660), in *The Architecture of Sir Roger Pratt*, ed. R. T. Gunther (Oxford: Oxford University Press, 1928), 27.

30. Sir Roger Pratt, "Certain Heads to Be Largely Treated of Concerning the Undertaking of Any Building," in Gunther, *The Architecture of Sir Roger Pratt*, 64.

31. Mrs. Lybbe Powis, *Diaries*, quoted in Binney, *Sir Robert Taylor*, 41. For additional eighteenth-century commentary on servant spaces, see Ware, *A Complete Body of Architecture*, 413, for differentiation of servants' spaces and locations according to their function and rank; and, for example, William Halfpenny in *A New and Compleat System of Architecture* (London: John Brindley, 1749), passim, for the precise specification of servants' spaces in various designs.

32. The view of Coptfold was drawn by Thomas Malton in 1792; see Binney, *Sir Robert Taylor*, plate 32. Barlaston, Staffordshire, (1756–57) likewise had a basement and a subbasement, although the basement was not entirely underground; see Binney, *Sir Robert Taylor*, 42, 45.

33. Samuel Richardson, *The History of Sir Charles Grandison*, ed. Jocelyn Harris (London: Oxford University Press, 1972), 3:284.

34. Giles Worsley, *Classical Architecture in Britain* (New Haven, CT: Yale University Press, 1995), 284. On Hagley, also see Girouard, *Life in the English Country House*, 201–2.

35. Arthur Oswald, "Ragley Hall, Warwickshire—I," *Country Life* 123 (1 May 1958): 938–41; Girouard, *Life in the English Country House*, 135; Peter Leach, "Ragley Hall Reconsidered," *Archaeological Journal* 136 (1979): 265–68; Sebastiano Serlio, *The Third Booke* [*of Architecture*] (London: Robert Peake, 1611), fol. 71ᵛ.

36. Leach, "Ragley Hall Reconsidered," 267.

37. Sir John Summerson explicitly indicated that the design owed much to the Chiswick villa. *Architecture in Britain 1530 to 1830* (Baltimore: Penguin, 1969), 201.

38. Richardson, *The History of Sir Charles Grandison*, 3:274, 278, 272.

39. Richardson, *The History of Sir Charles Grandison*, 3:290.

40. Richardson, *The History of Sir Charles Grandison*, 3:269. The term *companionate marriage* is from Lawrence Stone, *The Family, Sex, and Marriage in England, 1500–1800* (New York: Harper & Row, 1977), chap. 8.

41. A listing of all books containing designs for domestic architecture published before 1842 can be found in John Archer, *The Literature of British Domestic Architecture, 1715–1842* (Cambridge, MA: MIT Press, 1985). I have based the present analysis on examination of designs for dwellings in books from this list published before 1770. Also on British architectural literature, see Eileen Harris and Nicholas Savage, *British Architectural Books and Writers, 1556–1785* (Cambridge: Cambridge University Press, 1990).

42. Robert Morris, *An Essay in Defence of Ancient Architecture* (London: D. Browne et al., 1728), 93. Morris, *Lectures on Architecture*, 146.

43. Diversification and specialization of furniture types and consumer goods in the period 1700–1720 helped make this possible. See Charles Saumarez Smith, *Eighteenth-Century Decoration: Design and the Domestic Interior in England* (New York: Harry N. Abrams, 1993), 49–50.

44. Richard Leppert, *Music and Image* (Cambridge: Cambridge University Press, 1988), 122–23. I am also indebted to Richard Leppert for extended helpful discussions on this point.

45. G. J. Barker-Benfield, *The Culture of Sensibility* (Chicago: University of Chicago Press, 1992), 257, 276.

46. Cooper, *Houses of the Gentry 1480–1680*, 293. Girouard, *Life in the English Country House*, 104, 203. Girouard cites a "dining chamber" at Donington Park as early as 1634.

47. The history of the codification of specific uses for individual rooms is particularly well detailed in John Fowler and John Cornforth, *English Decoration in the Eighteenth Century* (London: Barrie & Jenkins, 1974), and Cooper, *Houses of the Gentry 1480–1680*. I have especially relied on Fowler and Cornforth for this paragraph.

48. Quoted in Christopher Hussey, *English Country Houses: Early Georgian 1715–1760* (London: Country Life, 1955), 196.

49. Robert and James Adam, *The Works in Architecture* [1773–79], ed. Robert Oresko (London: Academy Editions, 1975), 48–49.

50. Also see Girouard, *Life in the English Country House*, 40.

51. In 1660 Sir Roger Pratt specified that each bedchamber must "have a closet, and a servant's lodging with chimney both which will easily be made by dividing the breadth of one end of the room into two such parts as shall be convenient and to the servant's room a pair of back stairs ought to be adjoining, which ought fitly to serve for all of that kind at that end of the building, and should be very private and near a backyard." Somewhat incongruously he insisted that the back stairs be "very private" in order that the servant could remain as invisible as possible, yet the fact that the servant lived adjacent to the master (or mistress) clearly undermined any privacy to be enjoyed in the bedchamber. Pratt, "Certain Short Notes Concerning Architecture," 27. Elsewhere Pratt again specified that each principal bedchamber (for the man and for his wife) should have its own closet as well as a servant's bedchamber with access to a back stair. Pratt, "Certain Heads to Be Largely Treated," 64. Concerning their design for the Earl of Derby's House in Grosvenor Square, Robert and James Adam wrote: "By means of an intersol over the closet and powdering-room, we have introduced a servant's sleeping-room adjoining to this apartment; and a private stair gives convenient access and communication to both stories." *The Works in Architecture*, 59.

52. The compact villas of Sir Robert Taylor are exemplary. The principal floor generally has only a hall, saloon, dining room, and library; bedrooms are almost always upstairs, and suites of rooms are not found. Binney, *Sir Robert Taylor*, 39–40.

53. Girouard states that the term *dressing room* seems to have appeared in the second half of the seventeenth century, and suggests that it was an English invention, the product of English couples sleeping in the same room but dressing separately. Sometimes the man's dressing room would have been on the ground floor and doubled as a study. The dressing room also would have served as a private sitting room, and it could be larger than the bedroom. Girouard, *Life in the English Country House*, 150, 206.

54. "Sometimes have I lent her my dressing-room for their love-meetings." Richardson, *The History of Sir Charles Grandison*, 2:275, 3:473.

55. Ware, *A Complete Body of Architecture*, 432.

56. Frequently the words were interchangeable. Girouard, *Life in the English Country House*, 129.

57. Girouard, *Life in the English Country House*, 56.

58. Francis Bacon, *Gesta Grayorum*, ed. Desmond Bland (Liverpool: Liverpool University Press, 1968), 47–48; Eilean Hooper-Greenhill, *Museums and the Shaping of Knowledge* (London: Routledge, 1992), 78.

59. Peter Thornton, *Authentic Decor: The Domestic Interior 1620–1920* (New York: Viking, 1984), 25, 52. Dan Cruickshank and Neil Burton, *Life in the Georgian City* (London: Viking, 1990), 58. Richardson, *The History of Sir Charles Grandison*, 1:441. Nevertheless the closet did not necessarily have to be located in the "private" realm of the dwelling. Sir Charles introduced Harriet Grandison to her new closet—located, notably, adjacent to the drawing room and apparently no longer near the bedroom—in much the same terms: "Your Oratory, your Library, my Love, when you shall have furnished it, as you desired you might, by your chosen collection from Northamptonshire" (ibid., 3:270).

60. Elias, *The Civilizing Process*, 138–42.

61. Note in this regard an eighteenth-century manual on domestic service that placed considerable emphasis on keeping the door to any room closed, presumably to assure privacy: *Domestic Management, or the Art of Conducting a Family; with Instructions to Servants in General* (London: H. D. Symonds, [n.d.]), 16–18.

62. Halfpenny, *A New and Compleat System of Architecture*, plates 34, 35. This book went through one French and four English editions between 1749 and 1772. Although Halfpenny was a provincial surveyor and carpenter, the corpus of his published work includes eighteen titles, some running to several editions, which are therefore representative of many aspects of architectural thinking and practice during this period. This, together with the nature of his executed work (church buildings, a barracks, and a few modest residences), suggests that he was no less well attuned to the tastes and aspirations of the bourgeois ranks of society than the authors of more prestigious treatises.

63. Access to each room is restricted. It is afforded by a single narrow passage, which apparently can be entered only through a doorway underneath the landing of an enclosed staircase—the principal staircase (for the master's room) or the service staircase (for the mistress's room). It is notable that there is no bedchamber suite on the principal, or "parlour," floor in the central bloc of the house. The two stories above are designated "chamber" and "attick" stories.

64. Cooper, *Houses of the Gentry*, 300.

65. Donald W. Rude, ed., *A Critical Edition of Sir Thomas Elyot's The Boke Named the Governour* (New York: Garland, 1992), 50.

66. Cooper, *Houses of the Gentry*, 300. The terms *study* and *library* remained interchangeable until the mid-eighteenth century.

67. A reproduction may be found in Thornton, *Authentic Decor*, 77.

68. Girouard, *Life in the English Country House*, 169, 174.

69. Girouard, *Life in the English Country House*, 179, 180.

70. Thornton, *Authentic Decor*, 150. Rosamond Bayne-Powell, *Housekeeping in the Eighteenth Century* (London: John Murray, 1956), 38.

71. Morris, *Lectures on Architecture*, 89.

72. Joyce Godber, *The Marchioness Grey of Wrest Park* (Bedford: Bedfordshire Historical Record Society, 1968), 30.

73. Ware, *A Complete Body of Architecture*, 324, 348, plate 37. The practice of placing a study or library in the east, or using it in the morning, was not original to England or

the eighteenth century. Much the same advice can be found, for example, in the second chapter of Book II of Palladio.

74. William Halfpenny, John Halfpenny, Robert Morris, and T. Lightoler, *The Modern Builder's Assistant* (London: James Rivington et al., 1757). See, for example, no. 6 and no. 9.

75. Rawlins, *Familiar Architecture.* Studies: plates 4, 12, 14, 15, 17, 21, 23, 24, 25, 27, 28, 29, 34, 38, 40. Libraries: plates 19, 30, 32, 33; in plate 19, the library is proposed as part of a separate wing. For his bourgeois clientele, Rawlins only provided four designs with libraries—a room of more substantial size than a study—and one of these was equivocally called a "Library or Study." Unlike his contemporaries, Rawlins did not seem to endorse the notion of a library as a place of gathering, since he generally located them away from the principal areas of social intercourse—among the bedrooms on a chamber floor or in a more distant part of the principal floor. Three of Rawlins's four libraries are at the most remote end of a wing. For other examples of published designs for comparatively small dwellings in which libraries are marked, see Colen Campbell, *Vitruvius Britannicus* (London: The Author, 1715), 1: plates 19, 53; and Halfpenny, Halfpenny, Morris, and Lightoler, *The Modern Builder's Assistant,* plate 28, design 7. In the two designs in *Vitruvius Britannicus,* both unexecuted and both by Campbell, the "Library" is the only room in the entire design that is explicitly labeled according to its function, although dashed lines outlining beds also make the bedchambers apparent.

76. John Crunden, *Convenient and Ornamental Architecture* (London: The Author, 1767), plates 42 and 52/53.

77. On the increasing tendency to use the library as a place for socializing, see Girouard, *Life in the English Country House,* 234.

78. Girouard offers a graphic illustration of the place of the library in the division between private and public zones in his discussion of Hagley Hall (1753–59), where the library is incorporated into the private or family quarters at the east end of the house. See *Life in the English Country House,* 201–2.

79. Richardson, *The History of Sir Charles Grandison,* 2:64. The study is described in more detail later (3:271); it also includes glass cases "stored with well-chosen books in all sciences," additional "instruments of all sorts, for geographical, astronomical; and other scientific observations." The pictures include some "of the best masters of the Italian and Flemish schools." There are also "two rich cabinets of medals, gems, and other curiosities."

80. The library could also be an instrument for the articulation and solidification of class status. In Grandison Hall Sir Charles also keeps a library (in this case contained in a piece of furniture located in the housekeeper's room) of improving literature for the servants. It is divided into "three classes: One of books of *divinity* and *morality:* Another for *housewifry:* A third of *history,* true adventures, voyages, and innocent amusement." Likewise "the gardener had a little house in the garden, in which he had his own books." Richardson, *The History of Sir Charles Grandison,* 3:286.

81. Halfpenny, *A New and Compleat System of Architecture,* plates 44, 45.

82. The customary broad planar facade of a dwelling had its semantic uses: it ascribed unity and homogeneity to what ordinarily would have been a quite stratified, quite gendered household; and by its size and scale it could signify the status, wealth, prestige, or other qualities of the family or its members. The multiple segments of which Halfpenny's facade is composed could render the latter qualities only poorly, and unity or homogeneity not at all.

83. The design appears to compartmentalize human activity into discrete geometric domains. In later examples, particularly in France, these domains literally were "spheres"

of human conduct, for there were curved designs. The designs of Boullée and Ledoux in France are perhaps better known, but cylindrical designs are not unusual in England in the late eighteenth and early nineteenth century: see especially the work of John Plaw. For obvious reasons, however, regular right-angled figures were far easier to build, and designs for spherical structures remained scarce.

84. Emil Kaufmann, *Architecture in the Age of Reason* (Cambridge, MA: Harvard University Press, 1955), 3–31. Archer, *The Literature of British Domestic Architecture*, 41. Rudolf Wittkower, *Architectural Principles in the Age of Humanism* (New York: Random House, 1965), part 4.

85. The design by Rawlins appears on plate 38. His discussion on p. 28 noted that Ware (*A Complete Body of Architecture*, 303) and Ephraim Chambers (*Cyclopaedia: Or, an Universal Dictionary* [London: James and John Knapton et al., 1728]) had "utterly Rejected" the triangle as "incapable of any tolerable Division within, except into other Triangles"—although Rawlins made an attempt in this design to "make some regular Distribution of it," largely by using leftover angular spaces as closets and staircases. One could infer from the text that the reason he adopted the triangle was not infatuation with geometry nor with mathematical balance of spaces, but rather that the site afforded not four, not two, but "three Vistos." Unlike the Halfpenny design, the geometric nature of the plan was not continued in the facade; it was a standard Palladian facade, seven openings wide, with a rusticated basement, and fronted by a tetrastyle engaged portico, all of which was flanked by round turrets at the two sides. For another geometric design, see William Newton's draught for a villa for Daniel Giles at Twickenham in the RIBA Drawings Collection, London.

86. See the section "A Site for Self-Creation" in chapter 2, this volume.

87. Presumably Morris and Shortess would have included architecture itself among those arts. Just as Stephen Switzer had earlier suggested that the owner's active engagement in the planning ("distribution") of a villa would enhance its character as a personal "Creation," Morris encouraged the study of architecture in "Retirements," that is, places such as Shortess's "museum." Stephen Switzer, *Ichnographia Rustica: Or, the Nobleman, Gentleman, and Gardener's Recreation* (London: J. and J. Fox et al., 1742), 3:iii. Robert Morris, *The Architectural Remembrancer* (London: The Author, 1751), v–vi.

88. *Oxford English Dictionary*, s.v. "Museum." Hooper-Greenhill, *Museums and the Shaping of Knowledge*, as well as the anchor of much of her thinking, Michel Foucault, *The Order of Things* (London: Tavistock, 1970).

89. Jefferson, no stranger to France, may have been following a pattern of domestic arrangement at least as common in France as in England. On châteaux and large urban houses in sixteenth-century France with studies adjacent to the master's bedroom, see Ranum, "The Refuges of Intimacy," 227. What distinguished Jefferson's house was the union of those two otherwise differentiated spaces in the body of the proprietor.

90. John Locke, *Two Treatises of Government*, ed. Peter Laslett, student ed. (Cambridge: Cambridge University Press, 1988), First Treatise, sec. 48, 174.

91. Household space had long been gendered, and historically that gendering occurred in different ways. See, for example, Alice T. Friedman, *House and Household in Elizabethan England: Wollaton Hall and the Willoughby Family* (Chicago: University of Chicago Press, 1989). The point here concerns a shift in practices of gendering space in response to changing notions of self and identity. Exterior spaces (gardens, landscapes, etc.) commonly were gendered as well, and while that is beyond the scope of this chapter, it is addressed to some degree in parts 2 and 3. Also see John Archer, "Landscape and Identity: Baby Talk at the Leasowes, 1760," *Cultural Critique* 51 (Spring 2002): 143–85.

92. Of course there were examples of women who employed their dwellings in such a "masculine" fashion, among them the Countess of Suffolk at Marble Hill House.

93. Crunden, *Convenient and Ornamental Architecture*, plates 42 and 52/53. Although Crunden was not among the ranks of major Georgian architects, his work endured lasting popularity, presumably among the bourgeoisie who could afford to purchase it. It went through eight editions and reissues between 1767 and 1815.

94. Halfpenny, *A New and Compleat System of Architecture*, plates 34, 35.

95. The exact use of these rooms remains unclear. In the central bloc of the house there is no designated bedchamber suite on the principal, or "parlour," floor. The two stories above are designated "chamber" and "attick" stories. One may conjecture that the chamber floor would have included a bedchamber to be shared by the master and mistress. Rooms "Q" and "R" thus would have been available to serve as a private library or study for each.

96. Instances of designs providing for ostensibly equivalent "his and her" spaces do reappear in Anglo-American nineteenth- and twentieth-century domestic architecture, notably in Victorian country houses and modernist dwellings. But despite such instances, the overt separation of genders has remained the exception. In the case of Halfpenny's design, the rigorous balance and perfection of his solution suggest an optimistic effort to introduce, in idealizing terms, a balanced division between genders that was quite foreign to current social practice but which offered opportunities for rearticulating domestic practice according to new paradigms. Unfortunately the abstractness of Halfpenny's balance and rigor, like the abstractness of Enlightenment epistemology in general, was less than suitable to the pragmatic demands of everyday life.

97. Recent theoretical discussion of these sorts of fine-grained spatial practices includes Michel de Certeau, *The Practice of Everyday Life* (Berkeley: University of California Press, 1984); David Harvey, *The Condition of Postmodernity: An Enquiry into the Origins of Cultural Change* (New York: Blackwell, 1989); Henri Lefebvre, *The Production of Space,* trans. Donald Nicholson-Smith (Oxford: Blackwell, 1991).

98. See, for example, the remarks of Robert and James Adam on the differences between French and English eating rooms. The French used them only for eating per se, while the English, after dinner, reserved them for male conversation about politics and other matters. Thus the style of decoration was, at least in part, determined by the desire not to have materials that would retain smells. By contrast the withdrawing room was "for the ladies to retire to" after dinner, as well as "for the reception of company before dinner." Robert and James Adam, *The Works in Architecture*, 48–49. See also Cruickshank and Burton, *Life in the Georgian City,* 40–43, 70.

99. In 1792 Mary Wollstonecraft pointed very succinctly to the tension between women's individuality and their other roles and responsibilities in a wider social context: "Connected with man as daughters, wives, and mothers, their moral character may be estimated by their manner of fulfilling those simple duties; but the end, the grand end of their exertions should be to unfold their own faculties. . . ." *A Vindication of the Rights of Woman* (London: J. Johnson, 1792), 48. On the dwelling as the site for the articulation of manliness from the mid-eighteenth century onwards, see Philip Carter, *Men and the Emergence of Polite Society: Britain, 1660–1800* (Harlow: Longman, 2001), 98–99. Research shows that at least in some cases the house plan itself was articulated to define gender and other categories. At Newby Hall, for example, a household inventory of 1794 indicates that interiors literally were divided along spatial axes in order to articulate social divisions in different dimensions. The inventory shows that as of two years earlier at least three such spatial axes prevailed: (1) the north/south axis was the line of family/public separation on

the first floor, with Mrs. Weddell's private apartments on the north side and several guest bedchambers on the south side; (2) the upstairs/downstairs plane defined separate zones of privacy and gathering, with bedchambers upstairs and the Great Hall, Great Dining Room, Gallery, Drawing Room, Library, and the like on the ground floor; and (3) a more complex balance prevailed between male and female spaces on the ground floor, with the center of the house shared by the neutral Great Hall and the female Drawing Room, serving almost as a pivot point on either side of which were balanced the male spaces—to the north, Mr. Weddell's Dressing Room and the Library, and to the south (albeit disproportionately heavy) the Dining Room and Gallery. Jill Low, "Newby Hall: Two Late Eighteenth-Century Inventories," *Furniture History* 22 (1986): 137–43.

100. *Oxford English Dictionary*, s.v. "Retire," I.1.a. and I.1.e., and "Retirement," 1.a, 2.a, 2.b, and 3.a. Maren-Sofie Røstvig, *The Happy Man: Studies in the Metamorphoses of a Classical Ideal*, 2nd ed. (Oslo: Norwegian Universities Press, 1962–71). Throughout the period under discussion here, *retirement* largely lacked its modern connotation of a stage of life that follows the termination of one's active employment in the workforce. In the *Oxford English Dictionary*, s.v. "Retire," the modern sense of the word as a practice of withdrawing from an office or occupation and living on a pension appears to have evolved beginning in the second half of the seventeenth century. The first mention in the *OED* of professionals retiring upon an annuity per se, referring to surgeons, is dated 1806.

101. In Andrew Marvell's famous poem "Upon Appleton House" the garden was arranged in figures emblematic of General Fairfax's military career, not as images of a rarified or perfected Nature that transcends mundane affairs. James Fenton has suggested that a "classical" definition of gardening would be "that activity with which I busy myself when I am not fighting (or otherwise serving the state)." Here gardening sounds identical to the classical notion of retirement. Malcolm Kelsall, *The Great Good Place: The Country House and English Literature* (New York: Columbia University Press, 1993). James Fenton, "War in the Garden," *New York Review of Books*, 24 June 1993, 23–26.

102. In many respects the opposition that many proponents of retirement embraced, that of town versus country, could more accurately be characterized in terms of society versus self.

103. Stephen Switzer, who advocated inclusion of productive farmland in the landscape of retirement, nevertheless saw its presence as conducive not to thoughts of production and wealth, but rather to an elevation of private consciousness: "'Tis in the quiet Enjoyment of Rural Delights, . . . 'Tis there [that] Reason, Judgment, and Hands are so busily employed, as to leave no room for any vain or trifling Thoughts to interrupt their sweet Retirement: And 'tis from the Admiration of these that the Soul is elevated to unlimited Heights above. . . ." Switzer, *Ichnographia Rustica*, 1:v.

104. Morris, *An Essay in Defence of Ancient Architecture*, 75; plate facing p. 85.

105. "Letter on the Villas of Our Tradesmen," *The Connoisseur* 1, no. 33 (17 September 1754), 6th ed. (Oxford: J. Rivington et al., 1774): 255–62. Also see "The Cit's Country Box," *The Connoisseur* 4, no. 135 (26 August 1756), 6th ed. (Oxford: J. Rivington et al., 1774), 233–38, discussed in chapter 2, this volume, in the section on "Reconceiving a Type." Another excerpt, also relevant here, follows: "Some three or four mile out of town, / (An hour's ride will bring you down,) / He fixes on his choice abode, / Not half a furlong from the road: / And so convenient does it lay, / The stages pass it ev'ry day: / And then so snug, so mighty pretty, / To have an house so near the city!"

106. Especially for the existential, see again Røstvig, *The Happy Man*.

107. Michel de Montaigne, *Essayes*, trans. John Florio (London: J. M. Dent, 1910), 1:254.

108. Paula Henderson, "Secret Houses and Garden Lodges: The Queen's House, Greenwich, in Context," *Apollo* 146, no. 425 (July 1997): 29–35.

109. *The Spectator* no. 15 (1711), in Alexander Chalmers, ed., *The British Essayists* (London: J. Johnson et al., 1808), 6:72.

110. *The Gentleman's Library, Containing Rules for Conduct in All Parts of Life* (London: W. Mears, 1715), 390, 399.

111. *The Gentleman's Library,* 391–92, 409–10.

112. *Grotesque Architecture, or, Rural Amusement* (London: Henry Webley, 1767); also 1790, (n.d.), 1802, and 1815.

113. Timothy Nourse, "Essay of a Country House," in *Campania Foelix. Or, a Discourse of the Benefits and Improvements of Husbandry* (London: T. Bennet, 1700), 297.

114. Pope's cave at Twickenham, discussed in the section "Terra Suburbana" of the previous chapter, was another example of such a privatized space.

115. Gibbs, *A Book of Architecture,* plate 55. On Gibbs's work for Prior, see Friedman, *James Gibbs,* 140–44, 299–300. Prior died in 1721, precluding execution of the design.

116. Great Britain, Historical Manuscripts Commission, *Calendar of the Manuscripts of the Marquis of Bath Preserved at Longleat. Wiltshire. Vol. III. (Prior Papers.)* (Hereford: HMSO, 1908), 1:504.

117. Matthew Prior, *The Literary Works,* ed. H. Bunker Wright and Monroe K. Spears, 2nd ed. (Oxford: Clarendon Press, 1971), 1:189.

118. See, for example, Peter Longueville, *The Hermit; or, the Unparalled Sufferings and Surprising Adventures of Mr. Philip Quarll* (Westminster: J. Cluer and A. Campbell for T. Warner, 1727); "On the Queen's Grotto," *Gentleman's Magazine* 3 (1733): 41; "To the Rev. Mr. R—— on His Hermitage," *Gentleman's Magazine* 17 (1747): 391; and Abraham de la Pryme, "A Poem on the Said Hermit," *Gentleman's Magazine* 17 (1747): 23–24.

119. A succinct discussion of the difference between "negotium" and "otium" may be found in James S. Ackerman, *The Villa* (Princeton, NJ: Princeton University Press, 1990), 37.

120. Opposition of country and city was a favorite theme in eighteenth-century literature, and it has been discussed at such length that it need not be reviewed here. See especially Raymond Williams, *The Country and the City* (New York: Oxford University Press, 1973). The purpose of the present discussion is to understand the role that the villa played in this dialectic.

121. Chapters 4, 7, and the conclusion explore subsequent efforts to establish greater connections between architecture and morality.

122. Ambrose Philips, *The Poems of Ambrose Philips,* ed. M. G. Segar (New York: Russell & Russell, 1969), 3.

123. Philips, *The Poems of Ambrose Philips,* 3. See too the contemporary poem "The Happiness of Retirement," which declared that "The Mind its pleasurable Good pursues" best when far from "the licentious Court." In contrast, "True Good" is to be found "within," "Resulting from the Pleasures of the Mind," a pursuit best undertaken in "Retreats" and "Rural Seats." *The Happiness of Retirement* (London: J. Oswald, 1733), 8, 21.

124. Morris, *Lectures on Architecture,* 88. However, as the discussion in chapter 2, this volume, indicated, Morris's interest lay more in pursuit of neoplatonism than in Philips's poetics.

125. Morris, *Lectures on Architecture,* 169–72.

126. A concatenation of binaries converges in the practice of "retirement": city/country; otium/negotium; labor/leisure; georgic/pastoral.

127. Among the many proponents of unfettered genius as a necessary component of

aesthetic quality was a major figure in eighteenth-century British aesthetics, Sir Joshua Reynolds. See his *Discourses on Art,* ed. Robert R. Wark, 2nd ed. (New Haven: Yale University Press, 1997).

128. Morris, *Lectures on Architecture,* 88, 80, 103, 102. The neoplatonic character of Morris's polemic is discussed in chapter 2, this volume. Morris's emphasis on achieving a transcendental experience has been consistently undervalued in British architectural history, as the focus remains instead on the parade of historicist revival styles and borrowings from classical and Renaissance examples—all of which interested Morris little. Morris's emphasis on proportion and transcendence, however, is thoroughly consistent with the insistence in Renaissance design on geometrical rigor, though by the early decades of the eighteenth century his interest in geometry and proportion may have had more to do with the Enlightenment challenge to anchor the autonomous self in some system of rigor and abstract certainty. Nor has Morris's interest in transcendence been sufficiently examined in connection with the Burkean sublime. Morris's position is frequently underestimated because of his ostensibly retrogressive orientation toward Shaftesbury and the Cambridge Neoplatonists, as well as his insistence on an often impractical ideal-perfectionism. Nevertheless the "awful Contemplations" that Morris proposed were close to the kind of transcendental expansion that Burke identified as part of the sublime. The second, expanded edition of Edmund Burke's *Philosophical Enquiry into the Origin of Our Ideas of the Sublime and Beautiful* appeared in 1759, notably the same year in which the first volume of Morris's *Lectures* was reprinted in a second edition.

129. Locke, *Two Treatises of Government,* Second Treatise, sec. 6, 271.

130. Switzer, *Ichnographia Rustica,* 3:9, 2:201–2. In other portions of his text, however, Switzer was hardly an advocate of landscaping that afforded intimate engagement with untouched Nature. In discussing woods and groves, for example (2:211–24), Switzer clearly regarded them as opportunities for geometrically patterned paths and proportioned layouts, not for contemplation, reverie, or expressive feeling.

131. Ware, *A Complete Body of Architecture,* 134.

132. William and John Halfpenny, *Rural Architecture in the Gothick Taste* (London: Robert Sayer, 1752), 7, plates 11 and 12.

133. Ware, *A Complete Body of Architecture,* 96.

134. Rawlins, *Familiar Architecture,* i, ii, plates 24 and 28, and passim.

135. This shift toward understanding farmland as capital in need of active economic management was, of course, simultaneously a reason for and a product of the legal and epistemological shift toward the understanding of *land* as *property.* See Tom Williamson and Liz Bellamy, *Property and Landscape: A Social History of Land Ownership and the English Countryside* (London: George Philip, 1987); and Joan Thirsk, ed., *The Agrarian History of England and Wales: Volume V, 1640–1750. II. Agrarian Change* (Cambridge: Cambridge University Press, 1985).

136. Switzer, *Ichnographia Rustica,* 3:vi, 1:280, 3:217–18. For a brief discussion of enclosure, see chapter 1, this volume.

137. Morris, *Lectures on Architecture,* 1:85–88.

138. A cautionary note is necessary in this broad discussion of pastoral. Although Horace was held up as an exemplar by many, an even more complex shift was under way. Horatian pastoral, for example, his Second Epode, often referred to ploughing *paternal* fields. English enclosure was a shift from patriarchal forms of land tenure to capitalist employment of tenants, or erasure of labor from the landscape.

139. The literature on pastoral is extensive. For representative studies, see James E. Congleton, *Theories of Pastoral Poetry in England, 1684–1798* (New York: Haskell House,

1968); Annabel Patterson, *Pastoral and Ideology: Virgil to Valéry* (Berkeley: University of California Press, 1987); Renato Poggioli, *The Oaten Flute: Essays on Pastoral Poetry and the Pastoral Ideal* (Cambridge, MA: Harvard University Press, 1975); Roger Sales, *English Literature in History, 1780–1830: Pastoral and Politics* (New York: St. Martin's Press, 1983); John Barrell, *The Dark Side of the Landscape: The Rural Poor in English Painting 1730–1840* (Cambridge: Cambridge University Press, 1980); David Solkin, *Richard Wilson: The Landscape of Reaction* (London: Tate Gallery, 1982); Harriet Ritvo et al., *An English Arcadia: Landscape and Architecture in Britain and America* (San Marino, CA: Henry E. Huntington Library and Art Gallery, 1992). Also see Røstvig, *The Happy Man.*

140. For the notion of "a spontaneously happy community" and specific insights into country-house poems and "Dawley Farm," I am indebted to the wide-ranging and incisive discussion in Kelsall, *The Great Good Place,* esp. 12–16, 32–37, 44–47, 60–66.

141. Nourse, *Campania Foelix,* 5, 297, 339–40.

142. Quoted in Kelsall, *The Great Good Place,* 80.

143. "Dawley FARM," *Fog's Weekly Journal,* 26 June 1731, 2. The phrase "St. J——— in his sweet Recess" refers to Henry Saint John, Lord Bolingbroke, in his retirement at Dawley Farm.

144. As a member of the nobility, Bolingbroke's interests would not necessarily have been congruent with those of the bourgeoisie. Still, his contributions were paradigmatic; as Isaac Kramnick has shown, Bolingbroke was "the appropriate political philosopher" for much of the lesser landowning gentry who saw their landholdings threatened during this period. Isaac Kramnick, *Bolingbroke and His Circle* (Cambridge, MA: Harvard University Press, 1968), 60.

145. Edward Walford, *Village London* (London: Cassell, 1883), 1:201. Further on Dawley, see B. T. White, *The History of Dawley* (Uxbridge: Hayes & Harlington Local History Society, 2001).

146. Addison's definition of *Georgic* (1697): "A *Georgic* therefore is some part of the science of husbandry put into a pleasing dress, and set off with all the Beauties and Embellishments of Poetry." Joseph Addison, *The Miscellaneous Works,* ed. A. C. Guthkelch (London: G. Bell and Sons, 1914), 4.

147. As Barrell demonstrated in *The Dark Side of the Landscape,* eighteenth-century English artists commonly endeavored to devise a harmonious blend of pastoral and georgic, suggesting that each was requisite to the other.

148. Thus the incentive, for example, to hide stables and farm buildings from the view of the main house, and to disguise farm buildings about some estates as ruined castles, priories, and the like.

149. *Guardian* no. 23 (7 April 1713). John Barrell, *The Birth of Pandora* (Philadelphia: University of Pennsylvania Press, 1992), 46–47.

150. William Cowper also considered retirement to be a contradictory state, but on a different basis. In his poem "Retirement," composed in 1781 and published in 1782, he noted that the practice of retirement had become a bourgeois practice, engaged in by statesmen, lawyers, merchants, and tradesmen. In addition to being an escape from the corruption, vanity, and greed of cities, and offering traces of Edenic settings, retirement also afforded access to a kind of transcendent understanding. But highwayside suburban villas, tight boxes two miles from town, did not offer any such opportunity. Instead, people inside were imprisoned like bees and wasps. As such, retirement was hardly as easy or as simple as its proponents made it sound. Nor was it "pastoral" in the sense of putting a horse out to pasture. Rather, Cowper found that the benefits and the complexities of retirement were thoroughly misunderstood by the vast majority of the bourgeoisie who

professed to practice it. William Cowper, *The Complete Poetical Works* (London: Oxford University Press, 1907), 109 line 5, 110–11, 119–20, 122.

151. See especially W. Watts, *The Seats of the Nobility and Gentry, in a Collection of the Most Interesting & Picturesque Views, Engraved by W. Watts. From Drawings by the Most Eminent Artists. With Descriptions of Each View* (Chelsea: W. Watts, 1779); and William Angus, *The Seats of the Nobility and Gentry, in Great Britain and Wales in a Collection of Select Views, Engraved by W. Angus. From Pictures and Drawings by the Most Eminent Artists. With Descriptions of Each View* (Islington: W. Angus, 1787).

152. Parallel shifts are visible in the composition of conversation pieces, for example, comparing the periods 1720–40 to 1740–50; see Saumarez Smith, *Eighteenth-Century Decoration*, 70–71, 123. Comparable shifts are visible in landscape garden design as well; see Archer, "Landscape and Identity," 143–85.

4. Republican Pastoral

1. John Archer, *The Literature of British Domestic Architecture* (Cambridge, MA: MIT Press, 1985), 28–32.

2. For suburban sites in England, see chapter 5, this volume, and the opening pages of John Archer, "Country and City in the American Romantic Suburb," *Journal of the Society of Architectural Historians* 42, no. 2 (May 1983).

3. Given my approach here, examining the production of housing, and given the larger framework of this book, this chapter makes only minimal use of accounts of those who actually lived in the houses about which I write. Accounts of this sort are presented in excellent fashion in Margaret Marsh, *Suburban Lives* (New Brunswick, NJ: Rutgers University Press, 1990); Mary P. Ryan, *Cradle of the Middle Class* (New York: Cambridge University Press, 1981); and Mary Corbin Sies, "The Domestic Mission of the Privileged American Suburban Homemaker, 1877–1917: A Reassessment," in *Making the American Home,* ed. Marilyn Ferris Motz and Pat Browne (Bowling Green, OH: Bowling Green State University Popular Press, 1988), 193–210. Also, the themes of domesticity and individualism have been taken up from a different perspective than my own by Gillian Brown in *Domestic Individualism: Imagining Self in Nineteenth-Century America* (Berkeley: University of California Press, 1990).

4. E. Anthony Rotundo, *American Manhood* (New York: BasicBooks, 1993), 6, 20.

5. Note, for example, the ironically undemocratic formulation of equality in Samuel R. Wells's *How to Behave: A Pocket Manual of Republican Etiquette* (New York: Fowler & Wells, 1856), 124: "True republicanism requires that every man shall have an equal chance—that every man shall be free to become as unequal as he can."

6. Henry Clay, "In Defence of the American System," *The Life and Speeches of Henry Clay,* ed. Daniel Mallory (Hartford, CT: Silas Andrus & Son, 1853), 2:31.

7. David Leverenz, *Manhood and the American Renaissance* (Ithaca, NY: Cornell University Press, 1989), 78; and Michael Kimmel, *Manhood in America* (New York: Free Press, 1996), 28.

8. These citations come from Kimmel, *Manhood in America,* 26. Also see Samuel Smiles, *Self-Help* (London: John Murray, 1859), which shortly became very popular in both England and America. As Kimmel also notes (p. 369), these are *self-improvement* books, a genre quite distinct from later genre of *upward-mobility* books associated with Horatio Alger and the American dream, which I discuss in the next chapter. That the ideal of the self-made *man* led to considerable tension within the family is evident throughout the literature of the period. For example, a series of articles written for *Godey's*

Lady's Book in 1855 on "Model Husbands" concluded that a husband's "denial of self" might do much not only to help his wife but also to strengthen the marriage and family as a whole. T. S. Arthur, "Model Husbands," *Godey's Lady's Book* 50 (January 1855): 37–40; 50 (February 1855): 110–12; 50 (March 1855): 206–8. "Denial of self" appears on p. 112.

9. The quoted phrase is from Michael Kimmel, who argues that much of the nineteenth century was devoted to this sort of regressive effort. Kimmel does not address the subject of architecture, however. Michael S. Kimmel, "Masculinity as Homophobia," in *Theorizing Masculinities,* ed. Harry Brod and Michael Kaufman (Thousand Oaks, CA: Sage, 1994), 124.

10. Kenneth H. Wayne, *Building the Young Man* (Chicago: A. C. McClurg, 1912), 20.

11. Bruce Price, "The Suburban House," *Scribner's Magazine* 8, no. 1 (July 1890): 19.

12. Tocqueville made this observation during a visit in 1835. It appears in *Journeys to England and Ireland,* trans. George Lawrence and K. P. Mayer, ed. J. P. Mayer (London: Faber and Faber, 1958), 88. In the original, the word is *individualité.*

13. Mill is referenced by Asa Briggs in "The Language of 'Class' in Early Nineteenth-Century England," in *Essays in Labour History in Memory of G. D. H. Cole,* ed. Asa Briggs and John Saville (London: Macmillan, 1960), 55. In a lengthy exegesis of a "System of Individualism" another author, William Maccall, declared that "the grandest attribute of every man is his Individuality," and that "England will begin that new civilization which is founded on and emanates from the system of Individualism." *The Elements of Individualism* (London: J. Chapman, 1847), 34, 248. Further on the subject of individualism, see the excellent studies by Koenraad W. Swart, "'Individualism' in the Mid-Nineteenth Century (1826–1860)," *Journal of the History of Ideas* 23 (1962): 77–90; and Steven Lukes, *Individualism* (Oxford: Blackwell, 1973).

14. Tocqueville, *Journeys to England and Ireland,* 88.

15. Alexis de Tocqueville, *Democracy in America,* trans. Henry Reeve (New York: J. & H. G. Langley, 1840), 104. Some authors applied both the terms *individualism* and *individuality* to American culture in a positive way. Nevertheless, to the English-language reader, Tocqueville's choice of *individualism* to describe America (versus *individuality* to describe England) was significant. Tocqueville used *individuality* in reference to England because of its connotations of liberty and equality. It also connoted the primacy of self under the laissez-faire capitalist system and therefore was associated with the economic and social benefits that resulted from such a system. But from his French perspective, Tocqueville understood *individualism* as a pejorative term, carrying with it connotations of the excesses of the French Revolution (inspired in part by individualist Enlightenment authors), the atomization of society that was presumed to occur in a democracy, and the rapacious evils of capitalism. Even today there remains a fundamental conflict between the individual and society. Robert N. Bellah et al. noted in *Habits of the Heart: Individualism and Commitment in American Life* (Berkeley: University of California Press, 1985) that Americans believe that "the individual is prior to society, which comes into existence only through the voluntary contract of individuals trying to maximize their own self-interest" (143).

The use of the term *individualism* in Tocqueville's treatise was the first in a foreign account of American culture. But the word appeared simultaneously in America in an article titled "The Course of Civilization" in *United States Magazine and Democratic Review* 6 (1839): 208–17. Here it was used to extol the moral and social progress of America under capitalism: "The course of civilization is the progress of man from a state of savage individualism to that of an individualism more elevated, moral, and refined" (209). The author of this article did not share all of Tocqueville's animadversions on individualism per se but nevertheless shared his optimism for the young republic, particularly to the degree that it was overcoming the "savage" aspects of individualism. Further see Lukes, *Individualism,* 26–27; and Yehoshua Arieli, *Individualism and Nationalism in American Ideology* (Cambridge, MA: Harvard University Press, 1964), 191–94.

16. Tocqueville, *Democracy in America,* 104–6. Still, Tocqueville remarked that on many occasions enlightened self-interest did motivate Americans to cooperate with and assist each other (130–31).

17. These conclusions are drawn from Arieli, *Individualism and Nationalism in American Ideology,* 263–75.

18. On Emerson, see also John William Ward, *Red, White, and Blue: Men, Books, and Ideas in American Culture* (New York: Oxford University Press, 1969), 235–36.

19. Andrew Jackson Downing, *The Architecture of Country Houses* (New York: D. Appleton & Company, 1850), 262. In this passage Downing actually used the term *individuality* rather than *individualism;* but since Downing clearly used it in the sense in which Tocqueville applied *individualism* to America, I have maintained the term *individualism* in my own text.

20. Zephaniah Baker, *The Cottage Builder's Manual* (Worcester, MA: Z. Baker & Co., 1856), 10, 26.

21. In some respects it may be possible to distinguish between "country" and "suburban," but it is clear that with increasing frequency through the century country designs were appropriated for suburbia. Moreover the terms often overlapped so much that no significant distinction is justified. For example, in "Mistakes of the Suburbans," *Cambridge Chronicle,* 9 September 1854, 2, the discussion proceeded in terms of "those who have moved from the city to the country," engaged in "rural pursuits," and so on, but by the end of the article it was clear that the "country" was terrain that the suburban commuter would reach by a ten- to twenty-mile daily train ride. Downing made the equivalence clear in an 1848 essay titled "Hints to Rural Improvers," in which he commented not only on the transformation of the landscape afforded by the railroads but also on the role of the suburban cottage in achieving the American ideal of retirement: "Hundreds and thousands, formerly obliged to live in the crowded streets of cities, now find themselves able to enjoy a country cottage, several miles distant,—the old notions of time and space being half annihilated; and these suburban cottages enable the busy citizen to breathe freely, and keep alive his love for nature, till the time shall come when he shall have wrung out of the nervous land of commerce enough means to enable him to realize his ideal of the 'retired life' of an American landed proprietor." Andrew Jackson Downing, *Rural Essays,* ed. George William Curtis (New York: Leavitt & Allen, 1857), 111.

22. The essay originally appeared in *Horticulturist* 4, no. 12 (June 1850): 537–41, and is reprinted in Downing, *Rural Essays,* 236–43.

23. [Josiah Gilbert Holland], *Titcomb's Letters to Young People,* 40th ed. (New York: Charles Scribner & Co., 1867 [copyrighted 1858]), 231–32. "Why Is a Suburb? By a Woman Who Lives in One," *Countryside Magazine and Suburban Life* 24 (July 1917): 370.

24. Robert E. Shalhope, "Toward a Republican Synthesis," *William and Mary Quarterly* 3rd ser. 29 (1972): 57.

25. As Robert Shalhope has discussed at some length, one of the central concerns of republicanism was finding a means to assure the proper functioning of the state under a democratic system (rather than having it imposed by a monarchy). To the extent that this required pursuit of the "common good," it would be done by a citizenry with what amounted to a common value system, which in the nineteenth century was to be *privately* cultivated as "virtue" or "character." See, among others, Shalhope, "Toward a Republican

Synthesis," 70, 72; Shalhope, "Republicanism and Early American Historiography," *William and Mary Quarterly* 3rd ser. 39, no. 2 (April 1982): 341, 344, 348–49; and Linda Kerber, "The Republican Ideology of the Revolutionary Generation," *American Quarterly* 37, no. 4 (Autumn 1985): 474–95.

26. By the middle of the nineteenth century the processes by which one might obtain property afforded considerable confusion when it came to understanding virtue. Consider the implications of the following passage from a popular nineteenth-century advice manual to young men: "True republicanism requires that every man shall have an equal chance—that every man shall be free to become as unequal as he can." Wells, *How to Behave*, 124.

27. Shalhope, "Toward a Republican Synthesis," 58–59. See too Caroline Robbins, *The Eighteenth-Century Commonwealthman* (Cambridge, MA: Harvard University Press, 1961).

28. See the section below headed "Style."

29. James Cunningham, *Designs for Farm Cottagers and Steadings* (Edinburgh and London: William Blackwood & Sons, [1842]), 1:9.

30. Downing, *Rural Essays*, 210, 212, 116–17.

31. John Bullock, *The American Cottage Builder* (New York: Stringer & Townsend, 1854), 222, 223. As discussed above, at note 21, the term *rural* often encompassed suburban houses.

32. Henry W. Cleaveland, William Backus, and Samuel D. Backus, *Villas and Farm Cottages* (New York: D. Appleton and Company, 1856), 2, 44.

33. John J. Thomas, *Illustrated Annual Register of Rural Affairs, for 1864–5–6* (Albany: Luther Tucker & Son, 1873), 130. See too the remarks by Palliser, Palliser, & Co., indicating home was a site that sustained virtue for a lifetime: "Let us have permanent homes . . . where the manly virtues may grow strong and flourish, and which our children will ever remember in after years with pride." *Palliser's American Architecture* (New York: J. S. Ogilvie, 1888), Design 22.

34. Louisa C. Tuthill, *History of Architecture* (Philadelphia: Lindsay and Blakiston, 1848), 322–25, 327. Tuthill's transcription of Dwight is imperfect and abridged; the original can be found in Timothy Dwight, *Travels in New-England and New-York* (London: William Baynes and Son, 1823), 2:316–17.

35. E. C. Gardner, *Homes and All about Them* (Boston: James R. Osgood and Company, 1885), 220.

36. John Claudius Loudon, *An Encyclopaedia of Cottage, Farm, and Villa Architecture,* new ed. (London: Longman, Orme, Brown, Green, & Longmans, 1839), 5; Andrew Jackson Downing, *Cottage Residences,* ed. George E. Harney (New York: John Wiley and Son, 1873), 2.

37. Downing, *Cottage Residences*, 4, 13.

38. Loudon, *An Encyclopaedia*, 773–74.

39. John Haviland, *The Builders' Assistant* (Philadelphia: John Bioren, John Haviland, and Hugh Bridport, 1818), 36. The reverse position also was possible. At midcentury Samuel Sloan argued that the crowning feature of a landscape ought to be "the habitation of man." Samuel Sloan, *The Model Architect* (Philadelphia: E. S. Jones & Co., 1852), 1:26.

40. Samuel Burrage Reed, *House-Plans for Everybody* (New York: Orange Judd Company, 1898), 92.

41. Downing, *Cottage Residences*, 22–23, 115, 140.

42. "Rural Architecture," *Cultivator* 4, no. 3 (March 1847): 74.

43. Downing, *The Architecture of Country Houses*, 40.

44. Downing, *The Architecture of Country Houses,* 139.

45. Lewis F. Allen, *Rural Architecture. Being a Complete Description of Farm Houses, Cottages, and Out Buildings* (New York: Orange Judd, 1852), xii, 189.

46. Downing, *The Architecture of Country Houses,* 257, 258.

47. Loudon, *An Encyclopaedia of Cottage, Farm, and Villa Architecture,* 763.

48. Downing, *The Architecture of Country Houses,* 262. For brief discussion of Ruskin, see John Archer, "Character in English Architectural Design," *Eighteenth-Century Studies* 12, no. 3 (Spring 1979): 370–71.

49. Archer, "Character in English Architectural Design," 339–71.

50. Pierre Bourdieu, *Distinction,* trans. Richard Nice (Cambridge, MA: Harvard University Press, 1984).

51. Claude-Nicolas Ledoux, *L'Architecture considérée sous le rapport de l'art, des moeurs et de la législation* (Paris: L'auteur, 1804), 1:12. The translation is my own of the passage, "plonge dans la barbarie les peuples ingrats ou insouciants qui négligent ses faveurs." On moral instruction: "Le caractère des monuments, comme leur nature, sert à la propagation et à l'épuration des moeurs" (1:3). Since the mid-nineteenth century these ideas have earned Ledoux the reputation as the first acknowledged theorist of "architecture parlante." See "Études d'architecture en france," *Le magasin pittoresque* 20 (1852): 388.

52. Andrew Jackson Downing, *A Treatise on the Theory and Practice of Landscape Gardening,* 8th ed. (New York: Orange Judd & Company, 1859), 318.

53. Downing, *The Architecture of Country Houses,* 22. Also see 23, 25; and Downing, *Rural Essays,* 207–8, 220; Downing, *Treatise,* 356.

54. Downing, *The Architecture of Country Houses,* 321.

55. Downing, *The Architecture of Country Houses,* 285–86.

56. James Thomson, *Retreats* (London: J. Taylor, 1827), 17, 21, 19.

57. Peter Frederick Robinson, *Designs for Ornamental Villas,* 3rd ed. (London: Henry G. Bohn, 1836), 15.

58. Tuthill, *History of Architecture,* 299.

59. James H. Hammond, *The Farmer's and Mechanic's Practical Architect* (Boston: John P. Jewett, 1858), 41–42.

60. Fredrika Bremer, *The Homes of the New World: Impressions of America,* trans. Mary Howitt (New York: Harper & Brothers, 1853–54), 1:405.

61. Orson Squire Fowler, *A Home for All* (New York: Fowlers and Wells, 1854), 10–12.

62. Henry Ward Beecher, "Building a House," *Star Papers* (New York: J. C. Derby, 1855), 285–92.

63. Samuel Sloan, *Sloan's Homestead Architecture* (Philadelphia: J. B. Lippincott & Co., 1861), 138.

64. Cleaveland, Backus, and Backus, *Villas and Farm Cottages,* 66.

65. H. Hudson Holly, "Modern Dwellings," *Harper's New Monthly Magazine* 52, no. 312 (May 1876): 859–60.

66. Charles A. Rich, "Suburban Residence Built of Brick," *Brickbuilder* 7, no. 7 (July 1898): 157.

67. Reed, *House-Plans for Everybody,* 10.

68. Gustav Stickley, *Craftsman Homes* (New York: Craftsman Publishing Company, 1909), 194, 197.

69. Robert Dunn, "Sketches of Cottages," in *Report of the Committee of the Cottage Improvement Society, for North Northumberland, for 1842* (London: Whittaker and Co., [1842]), 7–11. On agricultural improvement, see Joan Thirsk, ed., *The Agrarian History of England and Wales V, 1640–1750: II. Agrarian Change* (Cambridge: Cambridge University

Press, 1985); and G. E. Mingay, ed, *The Agrarian History of England and Wales VI, 1750–1850* (Cambridge: Cambridge University Press, 1989). For Owen, see, for example, his *Report to the County of Lanark* (Glasgow: Wardlaw & Cunninghame, 1821), which contains his prospectus for "Establishing an Institution on Mr. Owen's System in the Middle Ward of the County of Lanark."

70. Clarence Cook, *The House Beautiful* (New York: Charles Scribner's Sons, 1881), 49, 188, 198.

71. Katherine Grier, *Culture and Comfort: People, Parlors, and Upholstery 1850–1930* (Rochester, NY: Strong Museum, 1988), 1 and passim; John Conron, *American Picturesque* (University Park: Pennsylvania State University Press, 2000), chap. 10. A number of designs in Sloan's *Model Architect,* including those for an Ornamental Villa, a Norman Villa, an Oriental Villa, two Italian Villas, a Wayside Cottage, a Mansion, a Villa, a Parsonage, and a Model Cottage, incorporate a library and/or office on the main floor. More often than not they also have an immediate or adjacent separate entrance. See Sloan, *The Model Architect,* 1: plates 36, 40, 74, 84; 2: plates 8, 11, 20, 31, 57, 86.

72. Catharine Beecher, *A Treatise on Domestic Economy* (Boston: Marsh, Capen, Lyon, and Webb, 1841), 13.

73. Beecher, *A Treatise on Domestic Economy,* 286; Colleen McDannell, *The Christian Home in Victorian America* (Bloomington: Indiana University Press, 1986).

74. Mrs. L. G. Abell, *Woman in Her Various Relations* (New York: R. T. Young, 1853), 74–75.

75. Catharine Beecher, *The American Woman's Home* (New York: J. B. Ford and Company, 1869), 24–25.

76. Beecher, *The American Woman's Home,* 191–96, 84.

77. Adam Sweeting, *Reading Houses and Building Books* (Hanover, NH: University Press of New England, 1996), 106.

78. Marsh, *Suburban Lives,* 29–30, 85; Mary Corbin Sies, "The City Transformed: Nature, Technology, and the Suburban Ideal, 1877–1917," *Journal of Urban History* 14, no. 1 (November 1987): 98; Mary Corbin Sies, "'God's Very Kingdom on the Earth': The Design Program for the American Suburban Home, 1877–1917," in *Modern Architecture in America,* ed. Richard Guy Wilson and Sidney K. Robinson (Ames: Iowa State University Press, 1991), 16–22.

79. The term and the underlying notion are from Robert L. Griswold, *Fatherhood in America* (New York: BasicBooks, 1993), 13.

80. Lydia Sigourney, *Letters to Young Ladies,* 2nd ed. (Hartford, CT: William Watson, 1835), 178–79, 36, 30. Also see Sarah Stickney Ellis, *The Women of England* (London: Fisher, Son, & Co., [1839]), 22, 46; and Abell, *Woman in Her Various Relations,* 303.

81. Rotundo, *American Manhood,* 18. Rotundo, however, remains wedded to the notion of "separate spheres," 22–23.

82. The literature is vast, but representative scholarship would include Nancy Armstrong, *Desire and Domestic Fiction* (New York: Oxford University Press, 1987); Leonore Davidoff and Catherine Hall, *Family Fortunes* (London: Hutchinson, 1987); Cathy N. Davidson and Jessamy Hatcher, eds., *No More Separate Spheres!* (Durham, NC: Duke University Press, 2002); Linda K. Kerber, "Separate Spheres, Female Worlds, Woman's Place: The Rhetoric of Women's History," *Journal of American History* 75, no. 1 (June 1988): 9–39; Marsh, *Suburban Lives;* Carole Shammas, "The Domestic Environment in Early Modern England and America," *Journal of Social History* 14, no. 1 (Fall 1980): 3–24; Lawrence Stone, *The Family, Sex, and Marriage in England, 1500–1800* (New York: Harper & Row, 1977). For analysis of Renaissance precedents, see Mark Wigley, "Untitled: The

Housing of Gender," in *Sexuality and Space,* ed. Beatriz Colomina (Princeton, NJ: Princeton Architectural Press, 1992), 327–89.

83. Catherine Hall, "Gender Divisions and Class Formation in the Birmingham Middle Class, 1780–1850," in *People's History and Socialist Theory,* ed. Raphael Samuel (London: Routledge and Kegan Paul, 1981), 174.

84. Dror Wahrman, "'Middle-Class' Domesticity Goes Public," *Journal of British Studies* 32, no. 4 (October 1993): 396–432; and *Imagining the Middle Class* (Cambridge: Cambridge University Press, 1995), chap. 11. Among other things, Wahrman found that characteristics that Davidson and Hall used to identify the middle class also were present simultaneously in elites and the working population, and that by 1832 the chief organizing category of identity among those concerned was "middle-class," not "male" or "female."

85. Kerber, "Separate Spheres," 88; Davidson and Hatcher, eds., *No More Separate Spheres!*

86. This is by no means to downplay the importance of understanding how real people actually lived in, and experienced, their houses and communities; to do so adds an entire new dimension to the story. This manner of research has its own challenges and rewards; see, for example, the fine discussion by Mary Corbin Sies, "Toward a Performance Theory of the Suburban Ideal, 1877–1917," in *Perspectives in Vernacular Architecture IV,* ed. Thomas Carter and Bernard L. Herman (Columbia: University of Missouri Press, 1991), 197–240. For a spatial approach to the manner in which people experience dwellings, see the excellent work by Renee Y. Chow, *Suburban Space: The Fabric of Dwelling* (Berkeley: University of California Press, 2002).

5. Suburbanizing the Self

1. Robert Fishman, *Bourgeois Utopias* (New York: Basic Books, 1987); John Archer, "Country and City in the American Romantic Suburb," *Journal of the Society of Architectural Historians* 42, no. 2 (May 1983): 139–56.

2. By the early twentieth century, American suburbia embraced a wide spectrum of classes and ethnic groups. See James Borchert, "Residential City Suburbs: The Emergence of a New Suburban Type, 1880–1930," *Journal of Urban History* 22, no. 3 (March 1996): 283–307; Richard Harris, "Chicago's Other Suburbs," *Geographical Review* 84 (1994): 394–410; Richard Harris, *Unplanned Suburbs: Toronto's American Tragedy: 1900 to 1950* (Baltimore: Johns Hopkins University Press, 1996); Richard Harris and Robert Lewis, "Constructing a Fault(y) Zone: Misrepresentations of American Cities and Suburbs, 1900–1950," *Annals of the Association of American Geographers* 88, no. 4 (1998): 622–39; Becky M. Nicolaides, *My Blue Heaven: Life and Politics in the Working-Class Suburbs of Los Angeles, 1920–1965* (Chicago: University of Chicago Press, 2002); Becky M. Nicolaides, "'Where the Working Man Is Welcomed': Working-Class Suburbs in Los Angeles, 1900–1940," *Pacific Historical Review* 68, no. 4 (November 1999): 517–59; Fred W. Viehe, "Black Gold Suburbs: The Influence of the Extractive Industry on the Suburbanization of Los Angeles, 1890–1930," *Journal of Urban History* 8 (1981): 3–26; Andrew Wiese, "The Other Suburbanites: African American Suburbanization in the North before 1950," *Journal of American History* 85, no. 4 (March 1999): 1495–1524; Andrew Wiese, "Places of Our Own: Suburban Black Towns before 1960," *Journal of Urban History* 19, no. 3 (May 1993): 30–54. Most recently see the counterpoint between Mary Corbin Sies and Andrew Wiese: Mary Corbin Sies, "North American Suburbs, 1880–1950: Cultural and Social Reconsiderations," *Journal of Urban History* 27, no. 3 (March 2001): 313–47; Andrew Wiese,

"Stubborn Diversity: A Commentary on Middle-Class Influence in Working-Class Suburbs, 1900–1940," *Journal of Urban History* 27, no. 3 (March 2001): 348–55; Mary Corbin Sies, "Moving Beyond Scholarly Orthodoxies in North American Suburban History," *Journal of Urban History* 27, no. 3 (March 2001): 356–62.

3. Kenneth Jackson, *Crabgrass Frontier* (New York: Oxford University Press, 1985), 27. Dolores Hayden, *Building American Suburbia* (New York: Pantheon, 2003); her book became available too late for consideration in preparation of this book. Moreau de St. Méry reported in his journal of the mid-1790s: "The trip from New York to Brooklyn is now made by steamboats. . . ." The crossing "takes eight minutes. Brooklyn has about one hundred houses, most of them only one story high. . . . Just south of Brooklyn [i.e., these hundred houses] and overlooking the river is a small chain of hills, on which are the country houses of many wealthy New Yorkers. Its proximity to New York leads New Yorkers to rent the houses and send their families there during the hot season. The men go to New York in the morning, and return to Brooklyn after the Stock Exchange closes." Moreau de St. Méry, *Moreau de St. Méry's American Journey [1793–1798]*, trans. and ed. Kenneth Roberts and Anna M. Roberts (Garden City, NY: Doubleday, 1947), 168, 170.

4. William Strickland, *Journal of a Tour in the United States of America, 1794–1795*, ed. J. E. Strickland (New York: New-York Historical Society, 1971), 213. For an assessment of Boston's mid-eighteenth-century suburbs, see Carl Bridenbaugh, *Cities in Revolt* (New York: Capricorn Books, 1964), 25. "A Glance at the Suburbs," *Rural Repository* 8, no. 20 (25 February 1832): 156.

5. Alice Cary, *Clovernook,* new ed. (New York: A. C. Armstrong & Son, 1884), 20, 56, 58. "Random Notes on Horticulture," *Horticulturist* 3, no. 5 (November 1848): 222–23.

6. See, for example, the "Plan of a Suburban Garden" facing the first page of the *Horticulturist* 3, no. 8 (February 1849).

7. William Bailey Lang, *Views, with Ground Plans, of the Highland Cottages at Roxbury* (Boston: L. H. Bridgham and H. E. Felch, 1845), introduction.

8. S. B. Gookins, "Hints on the Formation of Rural Taste," *Horticulturist* 3, no. 10 (April 1849): 470. As chapter 6 shows, the two eventually were equated in the twentieth century.

9. *Horticulturist* 3, no. 11 (May 1849): 521–22, and illus.; *Ballou's Pictorial* 8, no. 24 (16 June 1855): 376–77.

10. William Ranlett, *The City Architect* (New York: De Witt & Davenport, 1856), 12.

11. "Rural Enjoyment," *American Monthly Magazine* 1, no. 6 (1 August 1833): 397.

12. "Landscape Gardening and Rural Architecture in America," *United States Magazine and Democratic Review* 16, no. 82 (April 1845): 356.

13. George Jaques, "The Morale of Rural Life," *Horticulturist* 3, no. 8 (February 1849): 372–74.

14. "Editor's Easy Chair," *Harper's New Monthly Magazine* 7, no. 37 (June 1853): 129–30.

15. Andrew Jackson Downing, *The Architecture of Country Houses* (New York: D. Appleton & Company, 1850), 268–69.

16. Designers closely connected with American parks and suburbs were among the early visitors to such English examples as Regent's Park, Prince's Park in Liverpool, and Birkenhead Park in Birkenhead. See Archer, "Country and City in the American Romantic Suburb," 139–56.

17. C. Lennart Carlson, *The First Magazine: A History of the Gentleman's Magazine* (Providence, RI: Brown University, 1938).

18. [James Stuart], *Critical Observations on the Buildings and Improvements of London* (London: J. Dodsley, 1771), 9.

19. Thomas H. Shepherd and James Elmes, *Metropolitan Improvements; or, London in the Nineteenth Century* (London: Jones and Co., 1827), 12.

20. John Britton and W. H. Leeds in *Illustrations of the Public Buildings of London* by John Britton and Augustus Pugin (London: J. Taylor, 1828), 2:231.

21. S. Y. Griffith, *Griffith's New Historical Description of Cheltenham*, 2nd ed. (London: Longman, Rees, Orme, Brown, and Green, 1826), xi. See also xiii. Only minimal portions of Pittville had been built at the time that Griffith wrote, but he did single out one particular residence, which bordered on the part of Pittville closest to the proposed new Pump Room, to describe as "a perfect 'rus in urbe.'" Griffith, *Griffith's New Historical Description of Cheltenham*, 2:47.

22. Paul Amsinck, *Tunbridge Wells, and Its Neighbourhood* (London: William Miller, 1810), 17.

23. A. B. Granville, *The Spas of England* (London: Henry Colburn, 1841), 2:622–23; John Britton, *Descriptive Sketches of Tunbridge Wells and the Calverley Estate* (London: The Author, 1832), vii; William Gaspey, *Brackett's Descriptive Illustrated Hand Guide to Tunbridge Wells* (London: W. Brackett, 1863), 23.

24. Elsewhere around the globe by the early nineteenth century colonial suburbs already existed in a clearly *contrapositional* relationship with the central city, each playing a distinct counterpart to the other. See John Archer, "Colonial Suburbs in South Asia, 1700–1850, and the Spaces of Modernity," in *Visions of Suburbia*, ed. Roger Silverstone (London: Routledge, 1997), 1–25.

25. This is not to suggest that the designers of either site were explicitly concerned with articulating some form of *rus in urbe*. Rather, I proceed with the understanding that by midcentury this notion was sufficiently widespread and longstanding that it was implicit in the design of any such site. Andrew Jackson Downing, America's most prolific writer on architecture before midcentury, visited Europe at midcentury, and his remarks on Regent's Park are telling: he admired the private villas in the center of the park for being "the perfection of a residence in town, viz., a country-house in the midst of a great park," a perfect *rus in urbe*. Andrew Jackson Downing, *Rural Essays*, ed. George William Curtis (New York: Leavitt & Allen, 1857), 547–57. His remarks originally appeared in *Horticulturist* 6, no. 6 (June 1851): 281–86. Downing's tone, however, suggested disapproval of the undemocratic way in which the Regent's Park villas were reserved for "certain favored nobles." Two years earlier William H. Ranlett, who agreed with Downing on many points, noted with some resignation that "a suburban residence combines, to some extent, the advantages and pleasures of city, and country, life, but does not contain those of either to the full." *The Architect* (New York: Dewit & Davenport, 1849), 1:19. In a vein similar to Downing, Frederick Law Olmsted wrote in 1871 that suburbs are communities of "detached dwellings with sylvan surroundings yet supplied with a considerable share of urban convenience." Staten Island Improvement Commission, *Report of a Preliminary Scheme of Improvements* (1871), in *Landscape into Cityscape*, ed. Albert Fein (Ithaca, NY: Cornell University Press, 1968), 180. Or see the following statement: "The village of Hyde Park constitutes one of the oldest and best known, as it is one of the most easily accessible, suburbs of Chicago. It combines to a degree only rivaled by Evanston the delights of *rus in urbe*. . . ." Everett Chamberlin, *Chicago and Its Suburbs* (Chicago: T. A. Hungerford & Co., 1874), 352. Finally, there is Edward Everett Hale's well-meant but assuredly hyperbolic statement in "Fairmount Park," *Old and New* 3, no. 1 (January 1871): 124: "William Penn intended Philadelphia to be an example of *rus in urbe* of the purest kind."

26. The detailed presentation of St. Margaret's and Llewellyn Park is not meant to suggest that the style of suburban development that they represent was preeminent, either in a quantitative or in a paradigmatic sense. Throughout the century the most common form of development on both sides of the Atlantic would have been the standard rectilinear subdivision, done in a manner to maximize the developer's profit. Typical British builders' manuals illustrating the process include *The Builder's Practical Director* (Leipzig: A. H. Payne, [1855–58]), in which see plates 23 and 45, and Fowler Maitland, *Building Estates: A Rudimentary Treatise* (London: Crosby Lockwood and Co., 1883). The latter, ironically, expresses some regret at the early onslaught of sprawl, as witnessed by those who "see their favourite pleasure-resorts one by one lose their charms, and the enjoyment of country walks become more and more difficult to obtain" (2–3). In America at the same time that Llewellyn Park was being laid out, others were already complaining of the pernicious effects of suburban lots laid out on rectangular grids. In 1856 one writer took on the proposal of a putative "Improver" who wanted to lay out "single lots, twenty feet by one hundred; double lots, just twice that size. In the alleys you see here on the plan, the plots are fifteen by sixty. It cuts up beautifully!" Here it was clear that the beauty was in the "much greater profit" that such a plan afforded. As a counterproposal the writer almost seemed to offer a recipe for Llewellyn Park itself: "make a properly curved drive through the place, which shall approach in its gentle sweeps every acre or half-acre of the *park!* Yes, a park, for the residence of reasonable human beings, who have enough of city when they are obliged to go to it for shopping. Let every plot be in itself a rural home, so contrived that its owner can pluck his own fruit, keep his own pony phæton, if he pleases, and look out of his own windows without seeing brick houses." "Parks versus Villages," *Horticulturist* n.s. 6 (April 1856): 153–55. For typical rectilinear suburban subdivisions see, for example, those described for Englewood in Chamberlin, *Chicago and Its Suburbs,* 401.

27. Alan C. B. Urwin, *Twicknam Parke* (Hounslow: Thomasons, Ltd., 1965), 116–17. Among other reasons, the failure of Chartism in 1848 rendered partisan purposes less urgent.

28. *Times* [London], 16 March 1857, p. 7, col. 4.

29. "Deed of Covenant as to the Occupation of Plots of Ground in the St. Margarets Estate," 31 August 1854, Certified Copy by Calvert Smith & Co., 5–7.

30. "Landscape-Gardening," *Crayon* 4, no. 8 (August 1857): 248.

31. Little is known of Haskell's personal history. On his "rheumatic complaint," see David Lawrence Pierson, *History of the Oranges* (New York: Lewis Historical Publishing Co., 1922), 2:306. The two most authoritative studies of Llewellyn Park are Jane Davies, "Llewellyn Park in West Orange, New Jersey," *Antiques* 107, no. 1 (January 1975): 142–58; and Richard Guy Wilson, "Idealism and the Origin of the First American Suburb: Llewellyn Park, New Jersey," *American Art Journal* 9, no. 4 (October 1979): 79–90.

The springs, known variously as Chalybeate Springs, Condit's Spring, and Orange Springs, were discovered and developed beginning in 1820, and the resorts flourished until the mid-1830s. In 1823 a newspaper article described the site in terms portentous of Llewellyn Park, noting it was frequented by those "who seek relaxation from business and the turmoil of a city residence" (*Centinel of Freedom* 27, no. 48 [12 August 1823]: 3). Additional articles and advertisements appear in issues of the *Centinel* dated 15 August, 29 August, and 19 September 1820; 18 March, 8 May, and 12 June 1821. See also Joseph Warren Greene Jr., "Orange Springs a Century Ago," in New Jersey Historical Society, *Proceedings* n.s. 15 (July 1930): 361–71; Pierson, *History of the Oranges,* 2:255–58; Harry B. Weiss and Howard R. Kemble, *They Took to the Waters* (Trenton, NJ: Past Times Press,

1962), 115–19; and Henry Whittemore, *The Founders and Builders of the Oranges* (Newark, NJ: L. J. Hardham, 1896), 305–9.

32. Davies, "Llewellyn Park in West Orange, New Jersey," 143; Wilson, "Idealism and the Origin of the First American Suburb," 80–81. Some have suggested that between 1853 and 1856 or 1857 Haskell conducted a communitarian experiment in utopian Perfectionism here: see *Pageant in Honor of . . . Llewellyn S. Haskell* (N. loc.: n.p., 1916), 8; Christopher Tunnard, "The Romantic Suburb in America," *Magazine of Art* 40, no. 5 (May 1947): 184–87; and Wilson, "Idealism and the Origin of the First American Suburb." Nevertheless sound evidence of Haskell's commitment to Perfectionism is scanty, and Perfectionist sentiments of other residents are not well documented.

33. Thomas Hughes's Map of the Town of Orange, 1856, includes an inset titled "Map of Eagle-Ridge Property of L. S. Haskell 1856." There is a copy of the map in the collection of the New Jersey Historical Society. It is unclear who was responsible for landscaping The Glen and The Forest. Davies found no evidence of such work among Davis's records, and attributed the design to Haskell, as did the author of an article on "Landscape-Gardening" in *Crayon* 4, no. 8 (August 1857): 248. These portions of Llewellyn Park are illustrated in Henry Winthrop Sargent's supplement to Downing's *Treatise on the Theory and Practice of Landscape Gardening*, 8th ed. (New York: Orange Judd & Company, 1859), figures 105 and 106.

34. Daniels had returned by February 1856: see "Howard Daniels, Esq.," *Horticulturist*, n.s. 6, no. 2 (February 1856): 98. Contrary to this hypothesis, a newspaper article of 1860 attributed this "plan for constructing a park, which should make the locality a desirable residence for business men of New-York" to Haskell. See "Llewellyn Park at Orange, N.J.," *World* 1, no. 74 (8 September 1860): 3. Nevertheless the article dated the "plan" to spring 1856, which still would permit time for Daniels to have made a contribution.

35. *Orange Journal*, 3, no. 47 (16 May 1857): 3. The advertisement appeared regularly, with minor changes, through 28 November 1863. The article on "Landscape-Gardening" in the *Crayon*, 248, highlighted three aspects of the design: the picturesque layout, the division of the estate into lots of one to ten acres, and the privacy of the estate. Further discussion of its suburban characteristics appears in the *Orange Journal* for 6 June 1857 and 26 March 1859. Sargent, in his supplement to Downing, enumerated several "advantages" of this "social park" designed for "merchants or professional men, who seek a refuge from . . . the city." *A Treatise on the Theory and Practice of Landscape Gardening*, 571, 567. In February 1857 Haskell placed the most picturesque portion of the landscape under community control by conveying his title to the area then known as Llewellyn Park (i.e., The Forest and The Glen, now known as The Ramble) to three trustees; the area was to be reserved for the use of all persons buying land in the community: *Pageant in Honor of . . . Llewellyn S. Haskell*, 6–7; and Davies, "Llewellyn Park in West Orange, New Jersey," 143. I am grateful to Lawrence Wilkinson of Llewellyn Park, Ingrid Meyer of the West Orange Public Library, and Elinor Hancock for assistance with my research at Llewellyn Park.

36. The extension of this principle to twentieth-century suburbia is examined with considerable sophistication by Nancy G. Duncan and James S. Duncan in "Deep Suburban Irony: The Perils of Democracy in Westchester County, New York," in *Visions of Suburbia*, ed. Roger Silverstone (New York: Routledge, 1997), 161–79.

37. [William Shinn], *The Constitution of Evergreen Hamlet* (Pittsburgh?: n.p., 1851?), 6, 3. The community never achieved its full complement of sixteen families and was dissolved in 1866; Charles C. Arensberg, "Evergreen Hamlet," *Western Pennsylvania Historical*

Magazine 38 (1955): 123. I am grateful to Susan Grieve of Evergreen Hamlet for sharing with me her knowledge and historical documentation of the community.

38. [Shinn], *The Constitution of Evergreen Hamlet,* 2. On railroad connections, see Charles C. Arensberg, "Evergreen Hamlet," *Western Pennsylvania Historical Magazine* 38 (1955): 130. Shinn also noted the "health, comfort, and happiness" of a country location. But unlike "the usual isolated plan of country residences," this community would have "the benefits of convenient neighborhood, and social intercourse," which were of particular advantage in "the education of children" and in preventing loneliness (ibid., 1–2). Also see William M. Shinn, *Home and Education: An Address Delivered at the Opening of the School House, at Evergreen Hamlet* (Pittsburgh: W. S. Haven, 1856), in which Shinn offered an extended listing of specific advantages of this location over a residence either in the country or in the city. Advantages over life in the country included "society of our own selection," "a market at our own doors," and facilities for providing gas and water. Advantages over city life included "perfect freedom from anxiety about the health and morals of our children," fresh food, beautiful scenery, and freedom from the prying eyes and meddlesome curiosity of "'next door neighbors'" (30–31).

39. Françoise Choay, *The Modern City: Planning in the Nineteenth Century,* trans. Marguerite Hugo and George R. Collins (New York: Braziller, 1969), offers a brief account of Fourierist-inspired socialist planning. Charles Nordhoff, *The Communistic Societies of the United States* (New York: Harper & Brothers, 1875), offers a rich account of the vast number of nineteenth-century American settlements with socialist-utopian ideals.

40. In 1836 a private company of six merchants, one landowner, and an architect set out to develop this private suburb specifically as an exclusive residential enclave. The middle-class character of the enterprise is readily apparent in that most of the founders were closely connected with middle-class political causes, and the Anti-Corn-Law League in particular. Many of the early residents were associated with the same causes. By 1845 the homogeneous social character of the community was apparent as well: the thirty-nine houses then built were inhabited by eleven manufacturers, twenty-four merchants, and four professionals, typically self-made men, most of them principal figures in modest business enterprises.

41. In 1856 the Presbyterian churches of Chicago formed the Lake Forest Association, which purchased 2,300 acres at this site with the goal of establishing a university and other institutions of higher learning (eventually realized in the 1870s). The 1,300 acres east of the already extant railroad line were subdivided into lots according to a plan by Almerin Hotchkiss. Half were given to shareholders in the association, and the other half were sold to raise funds for the various educational institutions. By 1874, Everett Chamberlin could boast, "Lake Forest boasts of more elegant private residences than almost any other suburb." *Chicago and Its Suburbs,* 396–97. On Lake Forest, see *Articles of the Lake Forest Association* (Chicago, 1856); A. H. G., "Lake Forest the Beautiful Suburb of Chicago," *House and Garden* 5, no. 6 (June 1904): 264–75; American Communities Company, *Lake Forest. Art and History Edition* (Chicago, 1916); Edward Arpee, *The History of Lake Forest Academy* (Chicago: R. F. Seymour, 1944) (including a useful reconstruction of the plan of Lake Forest as of 1868); Edward Arpee, *Lake Forest Illinois* (Lake Forest: Rotary Club of Lake Forest, 1963); Michael H. Ebner, *Creating Chicago's North Shore: A Suburban History* (Chicago: University of Chicago Press, 1988); Franz Schulze, Rosemary Cowler, and Arthur H. Miller, *30 Miles North: A History of Lake Forest College, Its Town, and Its City of Chicago* (Chicago: University of Chicago Press, 2000).

42. Riverside was well publicized in its own time and has received much critical

attention ever since, but it was not unique. In 1874 nearby Clarendon Hills appeared much the same: "There probably never was a section of land (640 acres) made in better shape for a suburban town. . . ." "The gentle swells, the steeper hills—some of them extending to a height of two hundred feet above the lake level—and the beautiful valleys. . . ." The portion south of the railroad was bought in 1867; the portion to the north was bought in 1868. "Immediately after that, the entire tract was laid out in park form, with curved streets, and here and there small public grounds, and a large public park on the north line. Streets were nicely graded and planted with trees, and the idea of the enthusiastic originator seemed a simple consequence, or circumstance, to almost any one who had the pleasure of riding over the finely made streets, with the beautiful curves and undulations, and the lovely lawns, already made, and sloping gracefully to the streets, on almost every acre of it." "Aside from the 640 acres, which is all laid out in lots from fifty to one hundred feet front, large provision has been made for parties who want ten-acre blocks, more or less." Chamberlin, *Chicago and Its Suburbs,* 421–22.

With Riverside, the model of a "park" was abandoned: the *Preliminary Report* by Olmsted, Vaux, & Co., recommended against designing the suburb to appear as a single large park. "The landscape character of a park, or of any ground to which that term is applied with strict propriety, is that of an idealized, broad stretch of pasture," they wrote. In visual terms, this was inconsistent with a suburb: "the essential qualification of a park is *range,* and to the emphasizing of the idea of range in a park, buildings and all artificial constructions should be subordinated." This was unacceptable for a suburb, which after all functioned primarily as a site of human residence, so Olmsted and Vaux proposed instead that "the essential qualification of a suburb is domesticity"; everything else should be subordinated "to the idea of habitation." As the *Report* put it, two criteria were necessary for success in suburban design: "first, that of the domiciliation of men by families, each family being well provided for in regard to its domestic in-door and out-door private life; second, that of the harmonious association and co-operation of men in a community." Olmsted, Vaux, & Co., *Preliminary Report upon the Proposed Suburban Village at Riverside, near Chicago* (New York: Sutton, Bowne & Co., 1868), 26–27.

43. Fishman, *Bourgeois Utopias;* Archer, "Country and City in the American Romantic Suburb," 139–56.

44. There is room to explore the degree to which elites establish the terms and influence the course of any cultural practice, but it is clear that the role of elites in nineteenth-century American suburbia was substantial. Also on this point see Mary Corbin Sies, "The City Transformed: Nature, Technology, and the Suburban Ideal, 1877–1917," *Journal of Urban History* 14, no. 1 (November 1987): 81–111.

45. Van Reintjes, "Stewart Hartshorn," in *Sticks, Shingles, and Stones: The History and Architecture of Stewart Hartshorn's Ideal Community at Short Hills, New Jersey* (Millburn, NJ: Millburn-Short Hills Historical Society, 1980), 2. Celeste Penney, "Historical Perspective," ibid., 3–4. Also see Sies, "The City Transformed," 81–111.

46. "Some Suburbs of New York," *Lippincott's Magazine* n.s. 8, no. 1 (July 1884): 21, 23. See also "An American Park," *American Architect and Building News* 16, no. 446 (12 July 1884): 15–16.

47. Alfred Matthews, "Short Hills," in *History of Essex and Hudson Counties, New Jersey,* comp. William H. Shaw (Philadelphia: Everts & Peck, 1884), 709–10.

48. Matthews, "Short Hills," 711.

49. John Claudius Loudon, *The Suburban Gardener, and Villa Companion* (London: Longman, Orme, Brown, Green, and Longmans, 1838), 10.

50. Thus "cities, and the immediate neighborhood of cities, are rapidly becoming the

chosen residences of the enterprising, successful, and intelligent." "Cities and Parks," *Atlantic Monthly* 7, no. 42 (April 1861): 418–19.

51. Loudon, *The Suburban Gardener, and Villa Companion*, 10.

52. Samuel Sloan, *City and Suburban Architecture* (Philadelphia: J. B. Lippincott, 1859), 84.

53. Ebenezer Howard, *Garden Cities of Tomorrow* (London: Swan Sonnenschein & Co., 1902), 18, italics in original. This analysis of Howard is based on the introduction to Scott Donaldson's essay, "City and Country: Marriage Proposals," *American Quarterly* 20, no. 3 (Fall 1968): 547.

54. The literature is predictably vast. A suitable and recent entry point is Kermit C. Parsons and David Schuyler, eds., *From Garden City to Green City* (Baltimore: The Johns Hopkins University Press, 2002).

55. Peter Blake, *God's Own Junkyard* (New York: Holt, Rinehart, and Winston, 1964), 17–22. Donaldson, "City and Country," 563.

56. Downing's description of suburban Brookline, Massachusetts, put the case in explicit terms: "The whole of this neighborhood of Brookline is a kind of landscape garden, and there is nothing in America, of the sort, so inexpressibly charming as the lanes which lead from one cottage, or villa, to another. No animals are allowed to run at large, and the open gates, with tempting vistas and glimpses under the pendent boughs, give it quite an Arcadian air of rural freedom and enjoyment." Downing, *A Treatise on the Theory and Practice of Landscape Gardening*, 40. In a collection of essays published in 1849 that ran to seven editions in as many years, Nathaniel Parker Willis addressed an urban bourgeois readership ("you who have had no experience of country life"), telling them of fulfilling his own ideals ("in my out-of-doors life, I am approaching a degree nearer to Arcadian perfectibility"), which he nevertheless had to abandon and return to the city. Nathaniel Parker Willis, *Rural Letters* (Auburn, NY: Alden, Beardsley & Co., 1854), 179, 21, 207.

57. Humphry Repton, *An Enquiry into the Changes of Taste in Landscape Gardening* (London: J. Taylor, 1806), 34. This was part of the much larger course of the picturesque in English landscape gardening, a topic too large to sketch here. A useful introduction is David Watkin, *The English Vision* (New York: Harper & Row, 1982).

58. [Frederick S. Cozzens], "Living in the Country," *Putnam's Monthly* 6, no. 32 (September 1855): 299. "The Catskill Mountains," *New Mirror* 1, no. 23 (9 September 1843): 353.

59. Willis, *Rural Letters*, 133. On page 317 Willis deplores the despoliation of landscapes by the use of red ochre, a cheaper pigment than white lead, to paint farm houses.

60. "The Environs of Cincinnati," *Western Horticultural Review* 2, no. 9 (June 1852): 399–400.

61. Andrew Jackson Downing, *Hints to Persons about Building in the Country* (New York: John Wiley, 1859), iv.

62. Joseph Breck, *The Flower-Garden; or, Breck's Book of Flowers* (Boston: John P. Jewett, 1851), 14–15.

63. Catharine Beecher, *The American Woman's Home* (New York: J. B. Ford and Company, 1869), 41. William Ingraham Russell, *The Romance and Tragedy of a Widely Known Business Man of New York*, 3rd ed. (Baltimore: William I. Russell, 1913), 67. For more on Russell and Short Hills, see Mary Corbin Sies, "The Domestic Mission of the Privileged American Suburban Homemaker, 1877–1917: A Reassessment," in *Making the American Home*, ed. Marilyn Ferris Motz and Pat Browne (Bowling Green, OH: Bowling Green State University Popular Press, 1988), 197–98. See too the more satirical account of

the pleasures of suburban gardening offered a decade earlier in Robert Barry Coffin, *Out of Town* (New York: Hurd and Houghton, 1866), 162–63.

64. Virginia Scott Jenkins, *The Lawn: A History of an American Obsession* (Washington, DC: Smithsonian Institution Press, 1994); Georges Teyssot, ed., *The American Lawn* (New York: Princeton Architectural Press, 1999).

65. John Haviland, *The Builders' Assistant* (Philadelphia: John Bioren, 1818), 41.

66. "Budding's Machine for Cropping or Shearing the Vegetable Surface of Lawns, Grass-plots, &c." *Gardener's Magazine* 8, no. 36 (February 1832): 34–36. The text mentions that the mower had been patented and was seen in use in Regent's Park.

67. James C. Sidney, *American Cottage and Villa Architecture* (New York: Appleton & Co., 1850), 4.

68. Henry W. Cleaveland, William Backus, and Samuel D. Backus, *Villas and Farm Cottages* (New York: D. Appleton and Company, 1856), 13.

69. Helen Monchow, *The Use of Deed Restrictions in Subdivision Development* (Chicago: Institute for Research in Land Economics and Public Utilities, 1928). As one commentator eventually put it, suburbia simply was closer to God: "Some men can see God in bricks and mortar, in artificial parks, and fountains that can be turned on and off with a stop-cock; but most men can see Him more clearly in hill and valley and running brook." Francis E. Clark, "Why I Chose a Suburban Home," *Suburban Life* 4, no. 4 (April 1907): 189.

70. Clark, "Why I Chose a Suburban Home," 188.

71. John R. McMahon, *Success in the Suburbs* (New York: G. P. Putnam's Sons, 1917), x–xi.

72. "Suburbs," *Chambers' Edinburgh Journal* no. 200 (28 November 1835): 345.

73. Sarah Stickney Ellis, *The Women of England* (London: Fisher, Son, & Co., [1839]), 77.

74. Gail Cunningham, "The Riddle of Suburbia: Suburban Fictions at the *fin de siècle*," chap. 3 in *Expanding Suburbia: Reviewing Suburban Narratives,* ed. Roger Webster (New York: Bergham Books, 2000). My discussion of English sources, except for *Chambers's Edinburgh Journal* and Crosland, derives from Cunningham's account.

75. Thomas William Hodgson Crosland, *The Suburbans* (London: J. Long, 1905), 7, 20–21, 76.

76. "A Glance at the Suburbs," *Rural Repository* 8, no. 20 (25 February 1832): 156.

77. Cary, *Clovernook,* 20, 24, 56, 58.

78. "The suburbs of our cities are, generally, like a shabby frame to a fine picture." Ranlett, *The City Architect,* 12.

79. Nathaniel Parker Willis, *Hurry-Graphs* (New York: Charles Scribner, 1851), 129–33.

80. "Cities and Parks," *Atlantic Monthly* 7, no. 42 (April 1861): 420.

81. William Dean Howells, *Suburban Sketches* (New York: Hurd and Houghton, 1871), 90, 112, 86, 63–72.

82. Richard Harding Davis, "Our Suburban Friends," *Harper's New Monthly Magazine* 89, no. 579 (June 1894): 156–57.

83. Henry A. Beers, *A Suburban Pastoral* (New York: Henry Holt and Company, 1894), 5–6, 7, 21–22, 28, 243.

84. Bunner also observed that trains were class-segregated according to departure time: office-boys earliest, senior executives latest. Nor was it possible to take a stroll after work or before dinner or the theater, because the suburbanite always was racing for the train. Henry Cuyler Bunner, *The Suburban Sage* (New York: Keppler & Schwarzmann, 1896), 6, 37–42, 58–63, 52, 55, 92–96, 146–48.

85. "Rapid Transit and Home Life," *Harper's Bazar* 33, no. 48 (1 December 1900): 2003.

86. H. A. Caparn, "Parallelogram Park—Suburban Life by the Square Mile," *Craftsman* 10, no. 6 (September 1906): 767–74.

87. "Why Is a Suburb? By a Woman Who Lives in One," *Countryside Magazine and Suburban Life* 24 (July 1917): 370.

88. Mary Stewart Cutting, *The Suburban Whirl* (New York: The McClure Company, 1907), 189–90.

89. "On the Mistakes of Citizens in Country Life," *Horticulturist* 3, no. 7 (January 1849): 305–9.

90. Loudon, *The Suburban Gardener, and Villa Companion*, 32–34.

91. T. R. Slater, "Family, Society and the Ornamental Villa on the Fringes of English Country Towns," *Journal of Historical Geography* 4, no. 2 (April 1978): 134; Monchow, *The Use of Deed Restrictions*.

92. Friedrich Engels, *The Condition of the Working Class in England*, trans. W. O. Henderson and W. H. Chaloner (Stanford, CA: Stanford University Press, 1968).

93. "Class-Localities and Local Self-Government," *Economist* (20 June 1857): 669–71. See too William Ellery Channing's pronouncement in 1841 that in most large cities, both English and American, the population was becoming separated into "two nations." *A Discourse on the Life and Character of the Rev. Joseph Tuckerman, D.D.* (Boston: W. Crosby & Co., 1841), 7.

94. Frank J. Scott, *The Art of Beautifying Suburban Home Grounds* (New York: D. Appleton & Co., 1870), 27, 29.

95. Russell, *The Romance and Tragedy*, 83.

96. Scott, *The Art of Beautifying Suburban Home Grounds*, 31.

6. Nationalizing the Dream

1. *The American Dream: The 50s* (Alexandria, VA: Time-Life Books, 1998); Vance Packard, *The Status Seekers* (New York: David McKay, 1959).

2. See Merle Curti, "The American Exploration of Dreams and Dreamers," *Journal of the History of Ideas* 27 (July–September 1966): 391; Warren I. Susman, *Culture as History* (New York: Pantheon, 1984), 154, 302–3. For a very different perspective on this notion see Cal Jillson, *Pursuing the American Dream: Opportunity and Exclusion over Four Centuries* (Lawrence: University of Kansas Press, 2004).

3. "Acres of Diamonds," http://www.temple.edu/about/temples_founder/acres_text.html, 22 July 2003.

4. Eli Chinoy, *Automobile Workers and the American Dream*, 2nd ed. (Urbana: University of Illinois Press, 1992), 4.

5. James H. McGraw Jr., "Your Chances of Getting Ahead," *Business Week*, 7 June 1947.

6. This was the case at least as early as the 1940s, as is evident from the language that *Life* used to characterize one individual's "own particular dream and how it has come true." "U.S. Success Story 1938–1946: Auto Dealer Romy Hammes," *Life* 21, no. 13 (23 September 1946): 29.

7. Richard Powers, "American Dreaming," *New York Times Magazine*, 7 May 2000, 67.

8. William Faulkner, "On Privacy: The American Dream: What Happened to It." *Harper's Magazine* 211, no. 1262 (July 1955): 34, 33.

9. American Dreams: The Web's Resource on the American Dream, http://www.usdreams.com, February–March 2001.

10. Roper Starch Poll, "New Nationwide Survey on 'American Dream' at Millennium Reveals Surprising Ambivalence about Work and Technology," http://www.roper.com/news/content/news169.htm, 9 March 2001.

11. Aprile Gallant, "An American's Dreams," in *Love and the American Dream: The Art of Robert Indiana* (Portland, ME: Portland Museum of Art, 1999), 30.

12. Christine Frederick, "Is Suburban Living a Delusion?" *Outlook* 148, no. 8 (22 February 1928): 290–91, 313.

13. Packard, *The Status Seekers.*

14. Frederick Lewis Allen, "The Big Change in Suburbia: Part I," *Harper's Magazine* 208, no. 1249 (June 1954): 24–25.

15. William Hedgepeth, "Apostle to the Affluent," *Look* 31, no. 10 (16 May 1967): 41.

16. William J. Newman, "Americans in Subtopia," *Dissent* 43 (Summer 1957): 261, 256–57.

17. As Elizabeth Long observed, "the period when the American Dream seemed closest to fulfillment was, paradoxically, the first time when the limits and contradictions of that dream became widely apparent." *The American Dream and the Popular Novel* (Boston: Routledge & Kegan Paul, 1985), 1. For a highly pertinent study of Riesman, Whyte, and Mills, see her chap. 6, "The Social Critics."

18. Newman, "Americans in Subtopia," 264. William H. Whyte, *The Organization Man* (New York: Simon and Schuster, 1956).

19. Sloan Wilson, *The Man in the Gray Flannel Suit* (New York: Simon and Schuster, 1955), 143, 191, 71 (egging him on), 207. For a comparable version of this career-versus-self story produced for the stage in 1958, see Albert Beich and William H. Wright, *The Man in the Dog Suit* (New York: Dramatists Play Service, 1959).

20. Wilson, *The Man in the Gray Flannel Suit,* 26, 192.

21. On the contribution of Bell, Lasch, and Sennett to this debate, see Long, *The American Dream and the Popular Novel,* 165 ff.

22. Andres Duany et al., *Suburban Nation: The Rise of Sprawl and the Decline of the American Dream* (New York: North Point Press, 2000). In 1995 *Newsweek* likewise bemoaned the proliferation of "suburban slums" in an article titled "Bye-Bye, Suburban Dream," 15 May 1995, 40–54.

23. Fred Dewey, "Cyburbanism as a Way of Life," in *Architecture of Fear,* ed. Nan Ellin (New York: Princeton Architectural Press, 1997), 262–63.

24. A sampling of the vast literature on this subject includes Perry Miller, *Errand into the Wilderness* (Cambridge, MA: Harvard University Press, 1956); Peter N. Carroll, *Puritanism and the Wilderness: The Intellectual Significance of the New England Frontier 1629–1700* (New York: Columbia University Press, 1969); Charles M. Segal and David C. Stineback, *Puritans, Indians, and Manifest Destiny* (New York: Putnam, 1977); Roderick Nash, *Wilderness and the American Mind,* 3rd ed. (New Haven, CT: Yale University Press, 1982); Robert N. Bellah et al., *Habits of the Heart: Individualism and Commitment in American Life* (Berkeley: University of California Press, 1996); and Robert D. Putnam, *Bowling Alone: The Collapse and Revival of American Community* (New York: Simon & Schuster, 2000).

25. H. C. Bunner, *The Suburban Sage* (New York: Keppler & Schwarzmann, 1896), 146.

26. Howard Allen Bridgman, "The Suburbanite," *Independent* 54, no. 2784 (10 April 1902): 863.

27. Francis E. Clark, "Why I Chose a Suburban Home," *Suburban Life* 4, no. 4 (April 1907): 188. Clark went on to note that raising farm animals was educational: it taught "mathematics, economics, hygienics, and the rudiments of I do not know how many other sciences." A contributor to *The Craftsman* wrote in 1910 that suburban living "offers a growing opportunity for growing children to have plenty of fresh air and open country to grow up in, and to carry into later life the memory of a home instead of a flat." "Park Hill," *Craftsman* 17, no. 5 (February 1910): 576. The *Craftsman* was a major voice in favor of suburban living as an alternative to urban life and industrial work.

28. Ethel Longworth Swift, "In Defense of Suburbia," *Outlook* 148, no. 14 (4 April 1928): 543. See as well Caroline Bartlett Crane's discussion of the prizewinning home in the 1924 Better Homes in America competition, in which the very first line of the text is, "Here is a house built around a mother and her baby." *Everyman's House* (Garden City: Doubleday, 1925), 1.

29. Frederick, "Is Suburban Living a Delusion?" 290–91.

30. Phyllis McGinley, "Suburbia, of Thee I Sing," *Harper's Magazine* 199, no. 1195 (December 1949): 80.

31. Harry Henderson, "Rugged American Collectivism: The Mass-Produced Suburbs Part II," *Harper's Magazine* 207, no. 1243 (December 1953): 83.

32. "The Lush New Suburban Market," *Fortune,* November 1953, 128, 131.

33. John R. Seeley, R. Alexander Sim, and Elizabeth W. Loosley, *Crestwood Heights* (New York: Basic Books, 1956), 7. "Crestwood Heights" was actually a pseudonym for a suburb of Toronto, but as the quoted passage suggests, the authors had difficulty discerning differences between the "American dream" and the "North American Dream"—terms they used almost interchangeably. Likewise they had difficulty differentiating between the ways such dreams were realized in Canada and in the United States (3–12).

34. *The New Consumer* (Chicago: Chicago Tribune, 1957), 19, 16.

35. "Two Ford Freedom," Ford Motor Company, 1957. Worries about the deteriorating role of women in modern America persisted for decades, even intensified; see Hans Sebald, *Momism: The Silent Disease of America* (Chicago: Nelson-Hall, 1976).

36. Newman, "Americans in Subtopia," 260.

37. Credit line used on National Public Radio, 2000–2001. Or see the 1999–2001 advertising campaign by the BNY [Bank of New York] Mortgage Company, which included a poster showing eight detached single-family houses and three single-family town houses bearing the slogan "Every Dream House Deserves a Dream Mortgage." (Another version of the poster showed just ten houses.) The terms *dream* and *dream house* are ubiquitous in the real-estate industry. One company, currently operating in Atlanta, Scottsdale, and Las Vegas, annually presents a group of newly completed custom-designed higher-end homes under the trademarked name "Street of Dreams®." And as Constance Perin made clear in 1977, in the real-estate context the term *American dream* is commonly synonymous with the single-family detached house; *Everything in Its Place* (Princeton, NJ: Princeton University Press, 1977), 10, 64, 90.

38. "Radio address by President Bush to the Nation," 9 June 2001, http://www.whitehouse.gov/news/releases/2001/06/print/20010608-7.html, 8 July 2003; George W. Bush, "A Home of Your Own," June 2002 (PDF file), http://www.whitehouse.gov/infocus/homeownership/homeownership-policy-book-whole.pdf, 4 July 2003; Department of Housing and Urban Development, "Blueprint for the American Dream" (PDF file), http://www.hud.gov/news/releasedocs/blueprint.pdf, 4 July 2003; 108th Congress, H.R. 311, http://thomas.loc.gov, 4 July 2003; 108th Congress, H.R. 1276, http://thomas.loc.gov, 4 July 2003.

39. Julia Cruikshank, *Whirlpool Heights: The Dream-House on the Niagara River* (London: George Allen & Unwin, 1915), 7, 77, 115, 117, 171–72, 215, 254.

40. Rudolf Pickthall (lyrics) and Fred W. Sparrow (music), "The Dream-Cottage" (New York: Boosey & Co., 1916).

41. Mary R. St. Clair, "My Dream House," *Bungalow Magazine* 7, no. 1 (January 1918): 17. For an earlier, less specific example of dream-house reverie in bungalow literature, see "Hearth-Fires," *Representative California Homes* (Los Angeles: E. W. Stilwell & Co., 1916), 5.

42. Greta Gray, *House and Home* (Philadelphia: J. B. Lippincott, 1923), 233; Ethel Davis Seal, *The House of Simplicity* (New York: The Century Co., 1926), 36.

43. Calvin Coolidge, "A Nation of Home-Owners," *Delineator*, October 1922, 17. A year later President Harding was quoted as tying "the soundness of our social system and stability of our country" to "individual home-ownership." "Better Homes in America," *Delineator*, June 1923, 2.

44. Hoover's efforts are superbly documented in Janet Hutchison, "Building for Babbitt: The State and the Suburban Home Ideal," *Journal of Policy History* 9, no. 2 (1997): 184–210. Further on the role of government in the 1920s and 1930s, see John Peebles Dean, *Home Ownership: Is It Sound?* (New York: Harper & Brothers, 1945), chap. 4. See also Janet Hutchison, "The Cure for Domestic Neglect: Better Homes in America, 1922–1935," in *Perspectives in Vernacular Architecture II,* ed. Camille Wells (Columbia: University of Missouri Press, 1986), 168–78.

45. Herbert Hoover, *American Individualism* (Garden City, NY: Doubleday, 1922), 1; see also 18, 36.

46. Herbert Hoover, foreword to John M. Gries and James S. Taylor, *How to Own Your Home* (Washington, DC: Government Printing Office, 1923), v.

47. Herbert Hoover, "Home Building and Home Ownership: Their National Significance," *Child Welfare Magazine* 21, no. 8 (April 1927): 357.

48. Coolidge was quoted in an article touting the importance of "propaganda" efforts to advance the building industry: "Better Homes Week: A Force for Good Construction," *Building Age and National Builder,* May 1925, 103.

49. "Patriotism," *American Home* 2, no. 4 (July 1929): 463.

50. Hoover, "Home Building and Home Ownership," 358.

51. Blanche Brace, "Good Homes—The Right of All Citizens," *Delineator,* January 1925, 53.

52. "Third Electrical Home Draws 7,028 People," *Electrical World* 86, no. 1 (4 July 1925): 23.

53. "Dream House," lyrics by Earle Fox, melody by Lynn Cowan (San Francisco: Sherman, Clay & Co., 1926).

54. "In My Little Dream House on the Hill," by Sam Lewis and Joe Young ([New York]: Waterson, Berlin & Snyder Co., 1927). In 1928 a popular recording group, The California Ramblers, issued another, entirely instrumental recording titled "Dream House."

55. "East of the Sun (and West of the Moon)," lyrics by Brooks Bowman (Anne-Rachel Music Corporation, c/o Warner/Chappell Music Inc., Los Angeles).

56. "Dream House" was written and composed by Jesse Belvin and Joseph Bihari (Joe Josea). It was reissued in 1991 on the compact disc *Goodnight, My Love,* ACE CDCHD336.

57. "Dear Hearts and Gentle People," words by Bob Hilliard, music by Sammy Fain (Better Half Music and Edwin H. Morris and Co., 1949).

58. The association of heartbreak with dwellings other than a "dream house" per se

has a longer history. Lyricist Larry Conley, for example, began the chorus of "A Cottage for Sale" (1930) with the line "Our little dream castle with ev'ry dream gone." Written about the time that Conley's first marriage was breaking up, the song laments a departed love in terms of all the hopes that a couple had placed on their lawn, garden, and the cottage itself. "A Cottage for Sale," lyrics by Larry Conley, music by Willard Robison (New York: De Sylva, Brown and Henderson, 1930).

59. "Dream House for Sale," by Wayne P. Walker (1962). Note the beginning of an as yet small countercurrent, with the song "Dream House" (1987, lyrics by Chandler Travis) performed by the new-wave rock group the Incredible Casuals. It is a typical mid-1980s song of teenage alienation that nevertheless focuses on a hopeful outcome, cast in terms of building a dream house as the culmination of romance between two people.

60. "Dream House," words and music by John Eddie, from the composer's Web site: http://www.lostamericanthrillshow.com/lyrics/ldream.html, 15 November 2003.

61. "My Heart Wasn't in It," by Neal Coty (Murrah Music Corporation [BMI], 1995).

62. "Dream House," by jp jones (Vision Industry Publishing [ASCAP], 2000).

63. Magner White, "Six Things Women Look for When Buying a House," *American Magazine,* February 1927, 42–43, 137, 140, 142. The notion of designating a room as the male householder's private retreat extends back to the eighteenth-century "study" and to the Elizabethan "cabinet," although the latter, limited to aristocratic households, could be for man or woman. The proliferation of the "den" in postwar suburban housing—still a predominantly male space, unlike the more unisex spaces afforded by "cocooning" since the late 1980s—was gently satirized in the play *The Man in the Dog Suit* (New York: Dramatists Play Service, 1959). Oliver, contemplating with some dread the loss of his individuality entailed by the gray-suit dress code of his new position at the bank, is offered the possibility of moving to a house with a den, "A room of your own that you can go into," presumably a place where he could restore that lost sense of identity (43).

64. The film *Roman Scandals* (1933), starring Eddie Cantor, features a similarly fantastic, but more collective approach to the problem of Depression homelessness. In the song "When We Build a Little Home," Cantor exhorts those who have just been dispossessed of their homes by a project for a new jail to establish their new residence together in the street. Suggesting that "Every single little dream / Is a shingle or a rafter," Cantor promises that "We're sure of getting by" simply "on happiness alone." "When We Build a Little Home," from the film *Roman Scandals,* music by Al Dubin, Alfred Newman, and Harry Warren (Samuel Goldwyn Company, 1933).

The Chaplin daydream is echoed half a century later in the film *Little Shop of Horrors* (1986, based on the 1982 Broadway musical). In the semiparodic number "Somewhere That's Green" Audrey dreams of herself and her lover Seymour, inhabitants of Skid Row, as the happy owners of a suburban cottage, literally taken from the pages of *Better Homes and Gardens,* complete with lawn, dog, children, trellises, grill, appliances, frozen dinners in front of the television, and a Tupperware party.

65. Sherman H. Dryer, *Radio in Wartime* (New York: Greenberg, 1942), 282–83. As Norman Corwin, the writer-producer of this series explained, "The duty and responsibility of American radio is to explain to the people . . . what we stand to lose by defeat and gain by victory" (297).

66. Advertisements, *Life* 14, no. 19 (10 May 1943): 19; *Life* 14, no. 26 (28 June 1943): 49. Italics and ellipsis in originals.

67. Dean, *Home Ownership,* chap. 3; John Morton Blum, *V Was for Victory* (New York: Harcourt Brace Jovanovich, 1976), 100–101; Adam Rome, *The Bulldozer in the Countryside* (Cambridge: Cambridge University Press, 2001), 32–35.

68. "A House for Modern Living," *Architectural Forum* 62, no. 4 (April 1935): 275–398; "Buyers Approve All-Electric Houses," *American Builder* 59, no. 5 (May 1937): 77; Dean, *Home Ownership*, 30; David E. Nye, *Electrifying America* (Cambridge, MA: MIT Press, 1990), 358–59; "New American," *General Electric Review* 38, no. 10 (October 1935): 490.

A decade earlier General Electric had developed a series of advertising campaigns that promoted the wiring of existing homes and equipping them with new electrical products. These mid-1920s campaigns (and their accompanying brochures) had titles such as *Make Your House a Home, Home of a Hundred Comforts* (1925), and *Building an Electrical Consciousness*. Nye, *Electrifying America*, 268–70. As early as 1925 model electric homes were opened to the public in Canton, Illinois, and Denver. "Twenty-Five Hundred Visit Home in Week," *Electrical World* 85, no. 16 (18 April 1925): 829; "Third Electrical Home Draws 7,028 People," *Electrical World* 86, no. 1 (4 July 1925): 23.

69. Dean, *Home Ownership*, 32–33; West Coast Lumbermen's Association, "The Small Home's Social Values," *Lumber & Building Material Dealer* 7, no. 8 (August 1938): 1.

70. Radio Section, Federal Housing Administration, "Radio News of Better Housing," FHA form 163 (Washington, DC: Federal Housing Administration, n.d.); Dean, *Home Ownership*, 31–33, 36, 38, 51, 54; "Publicizing the Model House," *Architectural Forum* 67, no. 6 (December 1937): 522–25; "A New Small-Home Ownership Program," *Insured Mortgage Portfolio* 4, no. 8 (February 1940): 3–4, 21.

71. Nash-Kelvinator Corporation, "We'll Live in a Kingdom All Our Own," *Life* 18, no. 4 (22 January 1945): inside front cover; ellipses in original.

72. In 1946 General Electric issued a sixty-four-page brochure titled *Planning Your Home for Better Living . . . Electrically*, again to stimulate demand for its products. The brochure did not include the phrase "dream house," but it came close: "We have prepared a room-by-room tour of your electric home of the future—to open your eyes to a new and better kind of living. And, at the end of this tour, you will have acquired the information you need for planning and obtaining the wonders you have been dreaming about for your home" (5).

73. *New Yorker*, 20 July 1946; *Saturday Evening Post*, 15 August 1959. Also see the following additional *Saturday Evening Post* covers: a backyard barbecue in the rain (28 July 1951); two cars bumping each other while backing out of their respective driveways (4 August 1956); a view across multiple suburban backyards (18 May 1957); a gathering of neighbors for a backyard barbecue (13 September 1958); a family being shown the interior of a new split-level home (28 September 1957); and fixing a go-cart in a suburban driveway (18 October 1958).

74. "77 Dream Houses," *Banking* 41, no. 1 (July 1948): 66, 112; advertisement, *Life* 24, no. 26 (28 June 1948): 78; advertisement, *Architectural Forum* 89, no. 1 (July 1948): 43; advertisement, *Saturday Evening Post* 220, no. 52 (26 June 1948): 55. Also see Catherine Jurca, "Hollywood, the Dream House Factory," *Cinema Journal* 37, no. 4 (Summer 1998): 29–30. Blandings houses originally were intended for one hundred cities: see "Mrs. Blandings' Dream Kitchen," *General Electric Review* 51, no. 6 (June 1948): 54.

75. For the three General Electric divisions and twenty-four other manufacturers, see the Selznick Collection at the Harry Ransom Humanities Research Center, University of Texas at Austin, Box 3824, Folder 6, and Box 3829, Folder 1. For Yale, see *Saturday Evening Post* 220, no. 52 (26 June 1948): 74; and 221, no. 4 (24 July 1948): 70. For Rheem, see *Life* 24, no. 24 (14 June 1948): 125. For Youngstown Kitchens, see *Saturday Evening Post* 221, no. 2 (10 July 1948): 13. A substantial portion of the *House & Garden* issue for June 1948 was devoted to Blandings-related articles, including a Blandings game board and rooms

decorated specifically for the Blandings house. Advertisers in this issue with special Blandings tie-ins included Cortley curtains, Kimsul insulation, Lightolier lighting, Rheem hot
water heaters, and Sure-Fit slipcovers.

76. Advertisement, *Architectural Forum* 88, no. 6 (June 1948): 138–39.

77. "Levitt Adds 1950 Model to His Line," *Life* 28, no. 21 (22 May 1950): 141; "Up
from the Potato Fields," *Time* 56, no. 1 (3 July 1950): 69. As Brian Horrigan has shown,
hopes of commodifying the house as something "you would buy [like] a package of cereal
or face powder" had been raised by the housing prefabrication industry in the mid-1930s,
but they were never realized; "The Home of Tomorrow, 1927–1945," in *Imagining Tomorrow,* ed. Joseph J. Corn (Cambridge, MA: MIT Press, 1986), 150.

78. See, for example, Charles Abrams, *The Future of Housing* (New York: Harper,
1946); "The Promise of the Shortage" (special issue), *Fortune* 33, no. 4 (April 1946). For a
detailed overview, see Rome, *The Bulldozer in the Countryside,* 32–35.

79. Two years earlier *Business Week* similarly had declared, "This is the age of do-it-
yourself." "The New Do-It-Yourself Market," *Business Week* 1189 (14 June 1952): 60. More
generally, see Carolyn M. Goldstein, *Do It Yourself: Home Improvement in Twentieth-
Century America* (New York: Princeton Architectural Press, 1998).

80. George Nelson and Henry Wright, *Tomorrow's House: How to Plan Your Post-War
Home Now* (New York: Simon and Schuster, 1945), 4–7.

81. *Tomorrow's Small House* (New York: Museum of Modern Art, 1945), 8. I am
indebted to Timothy Mennel for this reference.

82. Hubbard Cobb, *Your Dream Home: How to Build It for Less Than $3500* (New
York: Wm. H. Wise, 1950).

83. John Keats, *The Crack in the Picture Window* (Boston: Houghton Mifflin, 1956),
181. In support of his argument Keats cited Robert Woods Kennedy's book *The House and
the Art of Its Design* (New York: Reinhold, 1953). But Keats's conclusion was hardly consistent with Kennedy's argument, which instead focused on the opportunities that domestic design provided for broadening both male and female gender roles. Still, Keats echoed
abundant anxiety at the time over the rise of a "new matriarchy." See, for example,
Andrew M. Greeley, *The Church and the Suburbs* (New York: Sheed & Ward, 1959), 84.
But this only raised the same fears that critics of suburbia had raised in the latter half of
the nineteenth century. See the discussion in chapter 5, this volume, in the section on
"Suburban Uncertainty."

84. Frances Heard, "The Freedom to Be Enterprising," *House Beautiful* 98, no. 11
(November 1956): 249–50, 247, 307.

85. "No Man Need Be Common, No Life Need Be Ordinary," *House Beautiful* 98,
no. 11 (November 1956): 220.

86. Joseph A. Barry, "America—Body and Soul," *House Beautiful* 98, no. 11 (November 1956): 242, 272.

87. "America's Dream House Is Illegal," *American Builder* 99, no. 9 (September 1966):
60–61, italics in original. Note as well the parallel rise in interest in the legal right to privacy; see William L. Prosser, "Privacy," *California Law Review* 48, no. 3 (August 1960):
383–423.

88. Herbert J. Gans, *The Levittowners* (New York: Pantheon, 1967), 37–41.

89. The quotations are from George J. Church, "Are You Better Off?" *Time,* 10 October 1988, 28–30. Earlier, see Lance Morrow, "Downsizing an American Dream," *Time,* 5
October 1981, 95–96. See also Marc Levinson, "Living on the Edge," *Newsweek,* 4 November 1991, 22–25; Katherine S. Newman, *Declining Fortunes: The Withering of the American
Dream* (New York: BasicBooks, 1993); Wallace C. Peterson, *Silent Depression: The Fate of*

the American Dream (New York: W. W. Norton, 1994); Jolie Solomon, "Are You Anxious? You're Not Alone," *Newsweek,* 30 January 1995, 42B; John Cassidy, "American Dream Dept.: Who Killed the Middle Class?" *New Yorker,* 16 October 1995, 113–24.

90. Cassidy, "American Dream Dept.,"114, 113. Newman concurred on the passing of the dream in *Declining Fortunes,* esp. 3, 29–30.

91. See, for example, *The New Previews' Dream House Catalog: A Guide to the World's Finest Real Estate* (New York: Harmony Books, 1980).

92. See, for example, Charles J. Daniels, *Dream House—Custom House: The Adventure of Planning and Building a Custom Home* (New York: Collier, 1989). A number of Web sites, such as DesignsPlus.com, offer dwelling designs with an individually customizable set of features, albeit they must be selected from an array of standardized elements (e.g., style, square footage, number of bedrooms, etc.). Marcia Mogelonsky suggests a shift occurred between the 1960s and 1990s: formerly the dream was just to own a house, but now the dream is having the opportunity to personalize it and make it stand out. "Reconfiguring the American Dream (House)," *American Demographics* 19, no. 1 (January 1997): 30 ff.

93. See, for example, Scot Thomas Runyan, *How to Build Your Dream Home Today and Start without Cash or Credit* (Bainbridge Island, WA: Innovative Opportunity Enterprises, 1984); and Jerold L. Axelrod, *Dream Homes: 66 Plans to Make Your Dreams Come True* (Blue Ridge Summit, PA: Tab Books, 1987); and dozens of other publications offering readymade plans.

94. Stephen Petranek and Jennifer Allen, "A House for All America," *Life,* June 1994, 82 ff; Jenny Allen, "The 1996 Life Dream House," *Life,* May 1996, 112; Jenny Allen and Melissa Stanton, "The 1999 Life Dream House," *Life,* May 1999, 132.

95. "The New American Dream Home," *USA Weekend,* 1–3 August 1997, cover story; all quotations are from "Dream Home 2000," *USA Weekend,* 3–5 April 1998, cover story. See too the front-page story in *USA Today* announcing that the "American Dream Is Back," 7 April 1998, 1A.

96. Bill Saporito, "Inside the New American Home," *Time,* 14 October 2002, 67.

97. Seeley, Sim, and Loosley, *Crestwood Heights,* 12.

7. Analyzing the Dream

1. Samuel Kaplan, *The Dream Deferred: People, Politics, and Planning in Suburbia* (New York: Seabury Press, 1976), 1–2.

2. Dolores Hayden, *Redesigning the American Dream* (New York: Norton, 1984), 18. For a rich elaboration of foundations and precedents for the present dream, see Mary Corbin Sies, "The City Transformed: Nature, Technology, and the Suburban Ideal, 1877–1917," *Journal of Urban History* 14, no. 1 (November 1987): 81–111. For other accounts of the components of the dream, see Gwendolyn Wright, *Building the Dream* (Cambridge, MA: MIT Press, 1981); Barbara M. Kelly, *Expanding the American Dream* (Albany: State University of New York Press, 1993); Wallace C. Peterson, *Silent Depression* (New York: Norton, 1994), 20–21; and George J. Church, "Are You Better Off?" *Time,* 10 October 1988, 28. A certain teleology of the dream as suburban is built into Robert A. M. Stern et al., *Pride of Place: Building the American Dream* (Boston: Houghton Mifflin, 1986); and Andres Duany, Elizabeth Plater-Zyberk, and Jeff Speck, *Suburban Nation: The Rise of Sprawl and the Decline of the American Dream* (New York: North Point Press, 2000).

3. Marcia Mogelonsky, "Reconfiguring the American Dream (House)," *American Demographics* 19, no. 1 (January 1997): 30.

4. Elaine Tyler May, *Homeward Bound: American Families in the Cold War Era* (New York: Basic Books, 1988). See as well the November 1956 issue of *House Beautiful,* discussed below.

5. As broadcast through a variety of American media over the past half century. I am not suggesting that all three components are necessarily present in equal measure in every dream; rather, these are strands around which common and prominent versions of the dream have been woven. Nor am I trying to characterize the reasons for which people actually move to suburbia (see the brief historical summary in Kaplan, *The Dream Deferred,* 207–8), or the material expectations of any given group of suburban residents.

6. The history of possessive individualism is traced in depth in C. B. Macpherson, *The Political Theory of Possessive Individualism* (Oxford: Oxford University Press, 1962). For extended discussion of individualism in American society, see Robert N. Bellah et al., *Habits of the Heart: Individualism and Commitment in American Life* (Berkeley: University of California Press, 1985). Also relevant is George Lipsitz, *The Possessive Investment in Whiteness* (Philadelphia: Temple University Press, 1998).

7. Andrew Jackson Downing, *The Architecture of Country Houses* (New York: D. Appleton & Co., 1850), 22–23.

8. Calvert Vaux, "Hints for Country House Builders," *Harper's New Monthly Magazine* 66, no. 11 (November 1855): 763.

9. *A Year of Civil Effort,* Annual Report of the Civic League of St. Louis, 1907, 22; cited in Charles C. Savage, *Architecture of the Private Streets of St. Louis* (Columbia: University of Missouri Press, 1987), 3. Also see David T. Beito and Bruce Smith, "The Formation of Urban Infrastructure through Nongovernmental Planning: The Private Places of St. Louis, 1869–1920," *Journal of Urban History* 16, no. 3 (May 1990): 263–303.

10. Carol Aronovici, "Housing and the Housing Problem," *Annals of the American Academy of Political and Social Science* 51 (January 1914): 3.

11. Charles E. White Jr., *Successful Houses and How to Build Them* (New York: Macmillan, 1921), 1.

12. Calvin Coolidge, "Better Homes," in *Better Homes in America: Plan Book for Demonstration Week* (New York: The Delineator, 1922), 5. The irony seems to have escaped Coolidge that there would be a need to shore up capitalism in circumstances that he otherwise paralleled to slavery.

13. Herbert Hoover, "Address of President Hoover," in John M. Gries and James Ford, ed., *Housing Objectives and Programs* (Washington, DC: The President's Conference on Home Building and Home Ownership, 1932), 2.

14. T. V. Smith, "The People's Capitalism," *House Beautiful* 98, no. 11 (November 1956): 317, 316–17.

15. Wolfgang Langewiesche, "The Builder House: What Kind of House Is It?" *House Beautiful* 98, no. 11 (November 1956): 230–32.

16. Constance Perin, *Everything in Its Place* (Princeton, NJ: Princeton University Press, 1977), 40–42, 56, and passim.

17. Evan McKenzie, *Privatopia: Homeowner Associations and the Rise of Residential Private Government* (New Haven, CT: Yale University Press, 1994), 25 (of which the previous sentence is a close paraphrase), 140. See also Richard Louv, *America II* (Los Angeles: Jeremy P. Tarcher, 1983). Carol J. Silverman and Stephen E. Barton, "Common Interest Communities and the American Dream," Working Paper No. 463 (Berkeley: Institute of Urban and Regional Development, University of California, 1987), 17.

18. Bruce Yandle, ed., *Land Rights: The 1990s' Property Rights Rebellion* (Lanham, MD: Rowman & Littlefield, 1995), xii–xiii. Phrases such as "individual owners of property

rights" (xii) imply that rights attach to land and perhaps other real property. More recently on property rights, see Eric T. Freyfogle, *The Land We Share: Private Property and the Common Good* (Washington, DC: Island Press, 2003).

19. Frank J. Scott, *The Art of Beautifying Suburban Home Grounds* (New York: D. Appleton & Co., 1870), 9–31. Downing, *The Architecture of Country Houses*, xix–xx and passim. David P. Handlin, *The American Home: Architecture and Society, 1815–1915* (Boston: Little, Brown and Company, 1979), 12–26. Through the nineteenth century it was commonplace even for elite suburban residences to have kitchen gardens and larger expanses of row crops on their grounds. See, for example, William Ingraham Russell, *The Romance and Tragedy of a Widely Known Business Man of New York,* 3rd ed. (Baltimore: William I. Russell, 1913), 66–67. But to have household grounds in other than ornamental cultivation eventually became too easily associated with labor rather than leisure, an unseemly terrain of production rather than aesthetic display. Twentieth-century deed restrictions for upscale suburban developments commonly proscribed raising crops or livestock, while in working-class suburbs the ability to raise one's own provisions remained part of the economic resources and personal freedom that residents valued once they arrived outside of the city.

20. The image is part of an advertising pamphlet titled *Peaceful Shaker Village* issued by the Van Sweringen Company in 1927. The advertising copy went on to say that "in England there are towns like Shaker Village—with the same calm quiet, the same parks and well-kept lawns and distinctive homes," and pointed out that there was no longer any need to journey to England to enjoy such amenities. There is also perhaps more than a passing affinity here between this development and J. M. Richards's classic paean to the Bedford Park model of suburbanity, *The Castles on the Ground* (London: Architectural Press, 1946). For information on the Van Sweringen pamphlet, I am grateful to Kristen Pool, the archivist/local history librarian at the Shaker Heights Public Library.

21. William J. Newman, "Americans in Subtopia," *Dissent* 43 (Summer 1957): 257. This is Newman's deprecatory, and overstated, distillation of the characterization of suburban dwellings by Seeley et al., in *Crestwood Heights* (New York: Basic Books, 1956). Nevertheless the notion of the home as "a retreat from the perils of the world outside" was already current in the early 1950s; "The New Do-It-Yourself Market," *Business Week* 1189 (14 June 1952): 61.

22. Quoted in Beth Ann Krier, "The Essence of Cocooning," *Los Angeles Times,* 7 August 1987. The practice of cocooning was picked up by the popular press in early 1987, for example, by George Will, "The Consumer Is Running Out of Steam," *Washington Post,* 9 April 1987.

23. Larry Gordon, "Suburbia's Dream House Goes Casual," *Los Angeles Times,* 24 June 1995, A1. Gordon notes two parallel shifts in the articulation of interior domestic space. Some areas became open to greater family interaction; for example, activities such as meal preparation, television watching, and homework all could be done in the same location. But there was a complementary trend toward greater privatization in master bedroom suites, with their own deep bathtubs, separate showers, Jacuzzis, private sitting areas, and even mini-kitchens—providing isolation for the parents not only from the world at large but also from family. In the following decade designers developed elaborate kitchen products and housewares to satisfy cocooners' desires to stay at home. Lynn Underwood, "New Housewares Aimed at Keeping Cocooning Consumers Happy," *Star Tribune,* 26 January 2003, E1, E8.

24. See the rapid success of Sarah Susanka's twin volumes, *The Not So Big House* (Newtown, CT: Taunton Press, 1998); and *Creating the Not So Big House: Insights and Ideas for the New American Home* (Newtown, CT: Taunton Press, 2000).

25. Sheryl Weinstein, "For the 2000s, More Cocooning Predicted," *Star Tribune,* 4 January 2000; Connie Koenenn, "Wall-Size Murals Allow Serious 'Cocooners' to See the Big Picture," *Los Angeles Times,* 4 May 2000; Helen K. Marshall, "Suite Retreat," *Chicago Sun-Times,* 19 November 2000.

26. Edward J. Blakely and Mary Gail Snyder, *Fortress America: Gated Communities in the United States* (Washington, DC: Brookings Institution, 1997).

27. Richard Briffault, "Our Localism: Part II—Localism and Legal Theory," *Columbia Law Review* 90 (March 1990): 382, 444, and passim.

28. Fred Dewey, "Cyburbanism as a Way of Life," in *Architecture of Fear,* ed. Nan Ellin (New York: Princeton Architectural Press, 1997), 262–63.

29. Sloan Wilson, *The Man in the Gray Flannel Suit* (New York: Simon and Schuster, 1955), 26.

30. John Claudius Loudon, *The Suburban Gardener, and Villa Companion* (London: The Author, 1838), 32. William Ingraham Russell described his awareness of such concerns in his move to the new suburb of Short Hills, New Jersey, in 1879. Most of the residents were "about my age, and with the exception of the owner of the Park, of moderate means. . . . We all respected each other and met on the same social plane, regardless of individual means." *The Romance and Tragedy of a Widely Known Business Man of New York,* 83.

31. The standard reference on African American suburbanization is Andrew Wiese, *Places of Their Own: African American Suburbanization in the Twentieth Century* (Chicago: University of Chicago Press, 2004). I am grateful to Andrew Wiese for his generous help in discussions and on field trips. The information regarding Lake Forest is from Franz Schulze, Rosemary Cowler, and Arthur H. Miller, *30 Miles North: A History of Lake Forest College, Its Town, and Its City of Chicago* (Chicago: University of Chicago Press, 2000), 19. For the information on Evanston I am indebted to Ronald Karr. On wholly African American towns from the 1870s to the 1960s, see Harold M. Rose, "The All-Negro Town: Its Evolution and Function," *Geographical Review* 55, no. 3 (July 1965): 362–81. For discussion of Washington Heights, see Thomas W. Hanchett, *Sorting Out the New South City* (Chapel Hill: University of North Carolina Press, 1998), 140–41.

32. Andrew Wiese, "Places of Our Own: Suburban Black Towns before 1960," *Journal of Urban History* 19, no. 3 (May 1993): 30–54; Wiese, "The Other Suburbanites: African American Suburbanization in the North before 1950," *Journal of American History* 85, no. 4 (March 1999): 1495–1524; and Wiese, *Places of Their Own.* On Richmond, see "Up from the Potato Fields," *Time,* 3 July 1950, 68. On African American subdivisions and suburbs of the 1960s, see Harold X. Connolly, "Black Movement into the Suburbs," *Urban Affairs Quarterly* 9, no. 1 (September 1973): 91–111; Reynolds Farley, "The Changing Distribution of Negroes within Metropolitan Areas: The Emergence of Black Suburbs," *American Journal of Sociology* 75, no. 4 (January 1970): 512–29; and Rose, "The All-Negro Town." On Hamilton Park, see William H. Wilson, *Hamilton Park: A Planned Black Community in Dallas* (Baltimore: The Johns Hopkins University Press, 1998).

33. Mary Pattillo-McCoy, *Black Picket Fences* (Chicago: University of Chicago Press, 1999), 41 and passim. Harry Waters, "The Battle of the Suburbs," *Newsweek,* 15 November 1971, 64. Gloria Naylor, *Linden Hills* (New York: Ticknor & Fields, 1985). The literature on *Linden Hills* is extensive; for a short analysis of *Linden Hills* and commentary on certain other topics raised in this chapter, see Robert Beuka, *SuburbiaNation: Reading Suburban Landscape in Twentieth-Century American Fiction and Film* (New York: Palgrave Macmillan, 2004).

34. Ron French, "Atlanta: Black-White Gap Shrinks," *Detroit News,* 28 January 2002,

http://mumford1.dyndns.org/cen2000/othersay/detroitnews/Stories/Atlanta%20Black-white%20gap%20shrinks%20-%2001-28-02.pdf, 15 October 2003; Boone is quoted on p. 3. On Prince George's County, see David J. Dent, "The New Black Suburbs," *New York Times Magazine,* 14 June 1992, 18–25. On black suburbs in this and other metropolitan areas, see Paul Caine, "Black Suburbs Lose Out on Home Investment," *Chicago Reporter,* September 1993; Philip L. Clay, "The Process of Black Suburbanization," *Urban Affairs Quarterly* 14, no. 4 (June 1979): 405–24; Connolly, "Black Movement into the Suburbs"; Farley, "The Changing Distribution of Negroes within Metropolitan Areas"; William P. O'Hare and William H. Frey, "Booming, Suburban, and Black," *American Demographics,* September 1992, 30–38; and Wiese, *Places of Their Own,* 269–81.

35. William H. Frey, *Melting Pot Suburbs: A Census 2000 Study of Suburban Diversity* (Washington, DC: Brookings Institution, Center on Urban & Metropolitan Policy, 2001), 5, 11, 14. See too Wei Li, "Building Ethnoburbia: The Emergence and Manifestation of the Chinese Ethnoburb in Los Angeles' San Gabriel Valley," *Journal of Asian American Studies* 2, no. 1 (1999): 1–28.

36. On these various types of gated communities, see Blakely and Snyder, *Fortress America.*

37. From the song "Little Boxes," words and music by Malvina Reynolds (Schroder Music Co., 1962).

38. "Suburban Home," by Tony Lombardo (Cesstone Music [BMI], 1982).

39. "Letter on the Villas of Our Tradesmen," *The Connoisseur* 1, no. 33 (17 September 1754). Also see, two years later, similarly satirical remarks in "The Cit's Country Box," *The Connoisseur* 4, no. 135 (26 August 1756).

40. Sinclair Lewis, *Babbitt* (New York: Harcourt, Brace, 1922), 14–15. See also 5, 91–92. For a rewarding discussion of this and other novels, see Catherine Jurca, *White Diaspora: The Suburb and the Twentieth-Century American Novel* (Princeton, NJ: Princeton University Press, 2001).

41. Christine Frederick, "Is Suburban Living a Delusion?" *Outlook* 148, no. 8 (22 February 1928): 290–91. More generally, see Jurca, *White Diaspora,* chap. 2, and Margaret Marsh, *Suburban Lives* (New Brunswick, NJ: Rutgers University Press, 1990), 149.

Despite Frederick's distaste for standardization, and Sinclair Lewis's before her, a significant portion of the literature on the subject was favorable. Mary Pattison's *Principles of Domestic Engineering* (New York: Trow Press, 1915) was a comprehensive effort to bring the benefits of Frank Gilbreth's time and motion studies and Frank W. Taylor's studies of labor efficiency to the home. Pattison included an entire chapter (17) on "Standardization" in which she argued that "standardization of the home" would "produce the best citizens and the happiest folk generally" (163). And J. George Frederick argued that standardization and individuality could evolve in tandem. "Standardization—Bane or Blessing?" *Outlook* 145, no. 2 (12 January 1927): 50–51.

Nevertheless as early as 1929 an editorial in *American Home* foreshadowed the common complaints after World War II about the standardization of housing production, deploring "the rows of houses of one design going up all over the country." "Better Small Homes," *American Home* 3, no. 1 (October 1929): 3. Also see Caroline Crane's concern over the application of "mass production" to housing in *Everyman's House* (Garden City, NY: Doubleday, 1925), 209–10.

Other commentators seemed to suggest that while suburbs were internally homogeneous, each established a certain individuality vis-à-vis cities and other suburbs. In a study of suburban weekly newspapers Margaret V. Cossé stated that "among large cities there is very little to differentiate them one from another," while "each suburban community exists as an individual social unit in which the residents are akin," each possessing its own "community individuality." *Suburban Weekly* (New York: Columbia University Press, 1928), 8–9. Also see the campaign undertaken by the *Cincinnati Enquirer* to "personalize" various Cincinnati suburbs in the eyes of its advertisers, describing "the type of woman characteristic of that suburb" in a few paragraphs of text and an accompanying drawing. For Mrs. Oakley, for example, her "Living room, dining room, kitchen—each looks like a picture from 'House and Garden,'" while Mrs. Fernbank "might have stepped from a page in Vogue." Mrs. Fort Mitchell was personified by a specific house style: "A Dutch Colonial, set in a landscaped lawn." Advertisements in *Printer's Ink* 135, no. 6 (6 May 1926): 66–67; and 135, no. 12 (17 June 1926): 74–75; and *Advertising and Selling Fortnightly* 5, no. 12 (7 October 1925): 43. The series in *Advertising and Selling Fortnightly* ran from October 1925 through April 1926.

42. Eric Larrabee, "The Six Thousand Houses That Levitt Built," *Harper's Magazine* 197, no. 1180 (September 1948): 88.

43. David Riesman, "The Suburban Dislocation," *Annals of the American Academy of Political and Social Science* 314 (November 1957): 134.

44. Lewis Mumford, *The City in History* (New York: Harcourt, Brace & World, 1961), 486; Ada Louise Huxtable, "'Clusters' instead of 'Slurbs,'" *New York Times Magazine,* 9 February 1964, 37.

45. Among recent critiques continuing this line of argument, see Kian Tajbakhsh, *The Promise of the City* (Berkeley: University of California Press, 2001), 181.

46. William F. Bynum, "Hospital, Disease and Community: The London Fever Hospital, 1801–1850," in *Healing and History: Essays for George Rosen,* ed. Charles E. Rosenberg (New York: Science History Publications, 1979), 97–115; William F. Bynum, "Cullen and the Study of Fevers in Britain, 1760–1820," in *Theories of Fever from Antiquity to the Enlightenment,* ed. William F. Bynum and Vivian Nutton (London: Wellcome Institute for the History of Medicine, 1981), 135–47; William F. Bynum, "Ideology and Health Care in Britain: Chadwick to Beveridge," *History and Philosophy of the Life Sciences* 10: Supplement (1988): 75–87; John V. Pickstone, "Dearth, Dirt and Fever Epidemics: Rewriting the History of British 'Public Health,' 1780–1850," in *Epidemics and Ideas: Essays on the Historical Perception of Pestilence,* ed. Terence Ranger and Paul Slack (Cambridge: Cambridge University Press, 1992), 125–48. An excellent analysis of Riis's work is found in Keith Gandal, *The Virtues of the Vicious: Jacob Riis, Stephen Crane and the Spectacle of the Slum* (New York: Oxford University Press, 1997).

47. Candace Wheeler, "The Philosophy of Beauty Applied to House Interiors," in *Household Art,* ed. Candace Wheeler (New York: Harper & Brothers, 1893), 14, italics in original. More generally, see David Watkin, *Morality and Architecture* (Oxford: Oxford University Press, 1977). Some understood the relationship between the dwelling and owner as a recursive process. See, for example, C. R. Henderson, writing in the vein of William Morris's socialist aesthetics: "We make our houses and they turn upon us the image of our own taste and permanently fix it in our very nature. Our works and our surroundings corrupt or refine our souls. The dwelling, the walls, the windows, the roof, the furniture, the pictures, the ornaments, the dress, the fence or hedge—all act constantly upon the imagination and determine its contents." *The Social Spirit in America* (Meadville, PA: Flood and Vincent, 1897), 37.

48. "Suburban Cottages versus Flats," *Independent* 62, no. 3040 (7 March 1907): 748.

49. R. W. Sexton, *American Apartment Houses, Hotels, and Apartment Hotels of Today* (New York: Architectural Book Publishing Company, 1929), 1, 8.

50. Paul Oliver, *Dwellings: The House across the World* (Oxford: Phaidon, 1987).

51. Bruce Price, "The Suburban House," *Scribner's Magazine* 8, no. 1 (July 1890): 19.

52. Pattison, *Principles of Domestic Engineering*, 31, 198, 199, 200, 32–33. For an insightful discussion of Pattison's position, see Kathleen Anne McHugh, *American Domesticity: From How-to Manual to Hollywood Melodrama* (New York: Oxford University Press, 1999), 73; also see 62. Pattison was not alone in her thinking. For example, see the writing of her contemporary Agnes Foster, in her chapter on "Creating Personality in Bedrooms," referring to the woman of the household: "It is usually her dream to make it an expression of herself." In *Inside the House of Good Taste,* ed. Richardson Wright (New York: McBride, Nast & Co., 1915), 97. Likewise note Elsie de Wolfe's statement that "it is the personality of the mistress that the home expresses. Men are forever guests in our homes, no matter how much happiness they may find there." In *The House in Good Taste* (New York: The Century Co., 1913), 5.

53. Emily Post, *The Personality of a House: The Blue Book of Home Design and Decoration* (New York: Funk & Wagnalls, 1930), 3, 274. Ben Davis, "Individuality as the Decorator Sees It," *California Arts & Architecture,* March 1937, 19. Davis concurred with Post that designing a room was like painting a portrait (40). Post echoed Pattison in anthropomorphizing parts of the house: "windows are the smiles of the house," and the front door should be "like a beautiful hand held out in welcome" (7).

54. Orison Swett Marden, *Masterful Personality* (New York: Thomas Y. Crowell, 1921), 97 (see also 22–23), 11. Henri Laurent, *Personality: How to Build It,* trans. Richard Duffy (New York: Funk & Wagnalls), 185 (italics in original), 191. More generally, see Warren I. Susman, *Culture as History* (New York: Pantheon, 1984), chap. 14.

55. George Nelson and Henry Wright, *Tomorrow's House: How to Plan Your Post-War Home Now* (New York: Simon and Schuster, 1945), 2.

56. John Keats, *The Crack in the Picture Window* (Boston: Houghton Mifflin, 1956), xi.

57. William H. Whyte, *The Organization Man* (New York: Simon and Schuster, 1956), 273, 267. Although Whyte's book often is cited as evidence of the robotic conformity of suburbanites, it is to his credit that he actually portrayed them as making use of a considerable degree of freedom to pursue diverse interests and activities.

58. Developers were equally exposed to criticism. In a play produced in 1958, the developer George Stoddard, a rather dislikable person, is satirized by another character who remarks on one of his tract developments: "What we like about Willow Wood is that the houses are all small and pretty much alike. George felt there would be less jealousy that way—makes for a happier neighborhood." Albert Beich and William H. Wright, *The Man in the Dog Suit* (New York: Dramatists Play Service, 1959), 27. Nor was this simply a fictional construct. As Constance Perin has shown, suburban developers and lenders commonly act on the presumption that homogeneity affords "a lower probability of conflict. . . : conflict will generally be avoided by not mixing income groups, housing types, tenure forms, or land-use activities." *Everything in Its Place*, 83–86.

59. "The Lush New Suburban Market," *Fortune,* November 1953, 131.

60. "I'll Buy That Dream," lyrics by Herbert Magidson, music by Allie Wrubel (Edwin H. Morris & Co., 1945).

61. Phyllis McGinley, "Suburbia, of Thee I Sing," *Harper's Magazine* 199, no. 1195 (December 1949): 79–80.

62. Harry Henderson, "The Mass-Produced Suburbs: I. How People Live in America's Newest Towns," *Harper's Magazine* 207, no. 1242 (November 1953): 26.

63. Only a decade after Levittown was founded, Harold Wattel found that "a great deal of individual living is taking place." He noted considerable activity among residents in adding "unique features" to their houses due in part to growing family size. Wattel cited

the addition of attic dormers, extra bedrooms, garages, dining rooms, dens, expanded living rooms, cellars, and porches. Harold L. Wattel, "Levittown: A Suburban Community," in *The Suburban Community,* ed. William M. Dobriner (New York: G. P. Putnam's Sons, 1958), 297, 301, 300.

64. Bennett M. Berger, *Working-Class Suburb: A Study of Auto Workers in Suburbia,* 3rd printing (Berkeley: University of California Press, 1960), chap. 1. See too his "Suburbia and the American Dream," *Public Interest* 1 (1966): 83, 85, 86. In fact the common caricatures and stereotypes of suburbia have themselves come to function as a homogenizing myth. And critiques of suburbia, to the extent that they simply attack the stereotypes, are at best only critiques of the myth and not of real places and houses. Also see the article by Thomas Ktsanes and Leonard Reissman challenging the common presumptions that suburbia was homogeneous, middle class, and conformist: "Suburbia—New Homes for Old Values," *Social Problems* 7, no. 3 (Winter 1959–60): 187–95.

65. "Individuality Is Why They Buy in Pearson Bros. Northport Community," *Minneapolis Sunday Tribune,* 17 April 1955, 28C.

66. See, for example, Wattel, "Levittown," 287–313; Kelly, *Expanding the American Dream;* Lizabeth Cohen, "A Middle-Class Utopia? The Suburban Home in the 1950s," in *Making Choices,* ed. Janice Tauer Wass (Springfield: Illinois State Museum, 1995), 62, 64; the series of articles written by Geoffrey Mohan for *Newsday* in 1997 and now available at www.lihistory.com; and Rosalyn Baxandall and Elizabeth Ewen, *Picture Windows* (New York: Basic Books, 2000).

67. Henderson, "The Mass-Produced Suburbs," 30. Henderson's remarks would have found support in the standard planning literature of the previous generation. See, for example, Thomas Adams, *The Design of Residential Areas* (Cambridge, MA: Harvard University Press, 1934), 161: "It has to be recognized that most people desire to live in places where they can associate with neighbors who have earnings and standards of education similar to their own. This attitude exists on the part of the average-income and the low-income groups as well as on the part of the highest-income groups. There exist also corresponding groupings on racial grounds. Thus, there arises the need for establishing zones for types of houses that will accord with economic and social requirements. Homogeneity is promoted and maintained either by zoning regulations or private restrictions on property, or both."

68. *The New Consumer* (Chicago: Chicago Tribune, 1957), 3.

69. Harry Henderson, "Rugged American Collectivism: The Mass-Produced Suburbs Part II," *Harper's Magazine* 207, no. 1243 (December 1953): 80–81, 86.

70. Herbert J. Gans, *The Levittowners* (New York: Pantheon, 1967), 38, 167, 166, 171, 172. Gans discussed the matter of conformity at greater length on pp. 174–81.

71. Ralph Bodek, *How and Why People Buy Houses: A Study of Subconscious Home Buying Motives* (Philadelphia: Municipal Publications, 1958), 53.

72. Reverend Andrew M. Greeley, "The Catholic Suburbanite," *Sign,* February 1958, 30–32. Also see Greeley's subsequent book, *The Church and the Suburbs* (New York: Sheed & Ward, 1959).

73. Seeley et al., *Crestwood Heights,* 56.

74. Bodek, *How and Why People Buy Houses,* 24, 31–32, 46–47, 49–50. But others saw the backyard as a site of enhanced privacy. In the mid-1950s the Community Builders' Council of the Urban Land Institute was chaired by Hugh Potter, one of those who in the 1920s developed River Oaks as Houston's premier suburb. The 1954 edition of the Council's *Community Builders Handbook* (Washington, DC: Urban Land Institute, 1954) noted the shift from front porches—popular in prewar decades for sitting and socializing—"to

the rear or garden side of the house where they are better related to pleasant living and afford a much greater degree of privacy." Drawing a contrast between the "public front yard" and the "private rear out-door living yard," and the consequent opportunities for "much more enjoyable indoor-outdoor living" (104), the *Handbook* clearly saw the rear yard as a privacy enhancement, especially when combined with "the increased use of high walls, fences, and landscape treatment" (102). Still, the *Handbook* inexplicably came to the summary conclusion that "it is not contemplated that many of the features of privacy and climate control can as yet be incorporated to any great degree into lower cost developments" (102). Two years later *House Beautiful,* noting the increase in street traffic precipitated by the growing reliance on automobiles in suburbia, remarked on the tendency to surround gardens with "fences, shrub hedges, masonry walls, earth mounds, and other such visual barriers between our yards and the street." This afforded an opportunity for living spaces to extend outward from the house into the garden. As Marion Gough wrote in the same issue, the newest American housing was characterized by "outdoor terraces and patios, as liveable and lived in as inside rooms." But as *House Beautiful* also noted, this entailed a diminished connection with the broader community: "Privacy for the garden is rapidly becoming a must," for it is here that people enjoy "many of the pleasures formerly provided by the community." "How Our Cars Have Changed Our Gardens," *House Beautiful* 98, no. 11 (November 1956): 257; Marion Gough, "How to Visit the Future," *House Beautiful* 98, no. 11 (November 1956): 336.

75. Blakely and Snyder, *Fortress America,* chap. 4.

76. Technology, for example, has remained central to the dream, although the particular types of technology have changed over time, resulting in modest variations to the dream itself. In a 1956 Frigidaire "Design for Dreaming" film advertisement, kitchen technology was shown liberating the housewife from all tasks except choosing the meal and serving it. Half a century later the technology is still there, but many cooks are now engaged with cooking almost as an engineering process—affording the personal satisfaction of perfected achievement, versus the 1956 satisfaction derived from private leisure.

77. The ongoing prominence of the notion of an "American Dream" in American culture has been due in considerable measure to its propagation in the media. See Roland Marchand, *Advertising the American Dream: Making Way for Modernity, 1920–1940* (Berkeley: University of California Press, 1985), 24: 1920s and 1930s advertising techniques "brought a modern cast to the American Dream by subtly refining the terms of its fulfillment."

78. Krier, "The Essence of Cocooning"; Weinstein, "For the 2000s, More Cocooning Predicted"; Marshall, "Suite Retreat."

79. This is not to minimize the role of academic discourse. It recognizes, however, the much wider exposure and impact of the popular media.

80. Here it is possible to provide only a brief mention of photographers' contributions, which deserve discussion at much greater length. In addition to those who have offered powerful critiques of the impact of suburbia on the landscape—Peter Blake, Chris Faust, Alex McLean—there are those who have portrayed the complex social and ideological space of suburbia in which the aspirations, pride, compromises, and failures of those who live, work, and invest there are articulated and negotiated; see especially the work of Bill Owens, Robert Adams, Bob Thall, Jeff Wall, Gregory Crewdson, and Todd Hido, among others. Robert Adams, *Denver: A Photographic Survey of the Metropolitan Area* (Boulder: Colorado Associated University Press, 1977); Robert Adams, *What We Bought: The New World. Scenes from the Denver Metropolitan Area 1970–1974* (Hannover: Stiftung Neidersachsen, 1995); Peter Blake, *God's Own Junkyard: The Planned Deterioration of America's Landscape* (New York: Holt Rinehart and Winston, 1964); Alex S. MacLean and Bill

McKibben, *Look at the Land: Aerial Reflections on America* (New York: Rizzoli, 1993); Frank Martin and Chris Faust, *The Cities of Our Time* (forthcoming); Bill Owens, *Suburbia* (San Francisco: Straight Arrow Books, 1973); Bob Thall, *The New American Village* (Baltimore: Johns Hopkins University Press, 1999); Thierry de Duve, Arielle Pelenc, Boris Groys, and Jean-François Chevrier, *Jeff Wall,* 2nd ed. (New York: Phaidon, 2002); Gregory Crewdson, *Twilight* (New York: Harry N. Abrams, 2002); Todd Hido, *House Hunting* (Tucson, AZ: Nazraeli Press, 2001).

81. In the 1950s, the television (and later the color television) was one of the accoutrements of wealth and status for individuals as well as the family unit; as such it served as one of the premier milestones along the path to the dream.

As Stephanie Coontz points out, the "traditional" family of the 1950s was in fact a new phenomenon: "For the first time in more than one hundred years, the age for marriage and motherhood fell, fertility increased, divorce rates declined, and women's degree of educational parity with men dropped sharply." *The Way We Never Were* (New York: Basic Books, 1992), 25.

82. The negative portrayal of the city here was preceded, notably, by Lewis Mumford's 1939 cinematic paean to greenbelt suburbs, *The City.*

83. The film was based on John McPartland's novel of the same year, *No Down Payment* (New York: Simon and Schuster, 1957). Rick Moody offered a comparably dark view of the pathology of suburban living in the novel *The Ice Storm* (Boston: Little, Brown, 1994), which also was made into a film (1997).

84. Michael Haas's assessment of *Crime and Punishment in Suburbia* as portraying the abyss of narcissism speaks equally well of other suburban films such as *American Beauty.* "Narcissistic individualism," he writes, "is the obvious source of the poisonous alienation" experienced by the characters in the film. Michael Haas, "PFS Film Review: *Crime and Punishment in Suburbia,*" www.geocities.com/~polfilms/crimepunishment. html.

85. *The Family Man,* released in 2000, is a rare counterstatement that perhaps bespeaks an emerging trend toward a positive assessment of suburbia in film. The central character, Jack Campbell, rejects a life of success and affluence in Manhattan for a vision of life in suburbia, where he has a wife, two children, a minivan, and a career as a tire salesman. He wins back Kate, his college sweetheart, by encouraging her to abandon her own successful professional career in Paris, in the course of which he blurts out, "We have a house in Jersey!" and describes the nuclear family that he sees himself and Kate raising there.

86. Richard Ford, *Independence Day* (New York: Vintage, 1996), 41. Bascombe's clients the Markhams in fact are moving out of their Vermont "dream house" to move to New Jersey (42).

87. Stephen Macek, "Urban Nightmares: The Moral Panic over the Post-Industrial City in American Culture and Media" (Ph.D. diss., University of Minnesota, 2001).

88. "Subdivisions," by Neal Peart (Core Music Publishing [SOCAN], 1982). Neil Peart and the group Rush that performed "Subdivisions" are from Canada, not the United States. But their perspective on the "dream" is legitimate to no lesser degree than Canadian suburbs incorporate United States ("American") paradigms.

89. Richard Yates, *Revolutionary Road* (Boston: Little, Brown, 1961), 21, 65.

90. Andrew M. Greeley, "Suburbia: A New Way of Life," *Sign* 37, no. 6 (January 1958): 12.

91. Dean McCoy, *The Development* (New York: Universal Publishing and Distributing Corporation, 1961), front cover. Dean McCoy, *The Love Pool* (New York: Universal Publishing and Distributing Corporation, 1964), front cover.

92. Philip E. Slater, *The Pursuit of Loneliness: American Culture at the Breaking Point* (Boston: Beacon Press, 1970), 74, 7–9, 12.

93. "Pleasant Valley Sunday," words and music by Gerry Goffin and Carole King (Screen Gems—EMI Music, 1967).

94. "Whiplash Liquor," by K. Eichstadt, R. Lahr, and W. Crane (Sloppy Slouch Music [ASCAP], 1991).

95. "Suburban Life," by Kottonmouth Kings. As performed on the music video included with the DVD release of the film *Scream 2*, 2001.

In recent years the musical critique of suburbia also has recognized the fact that much of actual suburbia is far grittier than the clean and orderly, if overly uniform, depictions seen in the likes of "Subdivisions" or "Pleasant Valley Sunday." See, for example, the dystopic portrayal of suburbia by the punk rock band Less than Jake in their 2000 release, "Suburban Myth":

> So let's hit the streets tonight
> And I'll show you where I lost my job
> And where I got chased by the cops
> We'll jump the fence at 13th and 10th
> To see where we played our first show
> I told you so
> I told you everybody loses sight of
> All the how it's been and never was
> So let's hit the streets tonight
> And I'll show you where I drank on the job
> And hung out in that parking lot
> Left at the light there's park 16th on the right
> And that's the place that we called home
> I told you so
> That place you'll never get a chance to know
> And all the people through the years you could've known
> It makes me wonder what you're seeing is almost "home."

"Suburban Myth," by Less than Jake (Gainesville, FL: Sarcastic Sugar Music [ASCAP], 2000).

96. Additional examples of musical critiques include "Hey Suburbia," released on several albums from 1987 through 2000 by the Chicago punk group Screeching Weasel, and the album *Suburban Teenage Wasteland Blues* (1996) by the Southern California punk rock group Strung Out.

97. Some academic studies also chronicled the rise of urban alternatives to the suburban dream, such as the conversion of city lofts to residential spaces as part of a "larger modern quest for authenticity"—a reaction against the failure of suburbia to realize the dream. Such lofts had "an identity that comes from years of continuous use, and an individuality that creates a sense of 'place.'" Sharon Zukin, *Loft Living: Culture and Capital in Urban Change* (New Brunswick, NJ: Rutgers University Press, 1989), 67–68. As Zukin demonstrates by her use of the terms *authenticity* and *individuality*, parts of the individualist dream remained fully intact; they were simply migrating from increasingly hostile suburbia to the city to find more fertile ground.

98. Conventional wisdom has it that 70 percent of rap music purchases are made by white suburban teenagers, although estimates of this sort are difficult to verify. See Adam Krims, *Rap Music and the Poetics of Identity* (Cambridge: Cambridge University Press, 2000), 4–5.

99. Michael Eric Dyson, *Reflecting Black: African-American Cultural Criticism* (Minneapolis: University of Minnesota Press, 1993); Tricia Rose, *Black Noise: Rap Music and Black Culture in Contemporary America* (Hanover, NH: Wesleyan University Press, 1994); Murray Forman, *The 'Hood Comes First: Race, Space, and Place in Rap and Hip-Hop* (Middletown, CT: Wesleyan University Press, 2002).

100. "Who Down to Ride," written by Master P. (Los Angeles: Big P Music [BMI], 1997).

101. "Where Ya From?" by P. Smith, T. Jones, K. Muchita, and A. Johnson (Beverly Hills, CA: Loud Records LLC, 1999).

102. "Murda Music," by K. Muchita and A. Johnson (Beverly Hills, CA: Loud Records LLC, 1999).

103. "Kill My Landlord," by The Coup (Wild Pitch Records, 1999).

104. "1 Million Bottlebags," by Carlton Ridenhour, Stuart Robertz, Gary G-Wiz, and Cerwin Depper (Burlington, VT: Del America Songs, 1991).

105. "Life Is . . . Too $hort," by Too $hort (Beverly Hills, CA: Zomba Recording Corporation, 1988).

106. Peter J. Martin, *Sounds and Society: Themes in the Sociology of Music* (Manchester: Manchester University Press, 1995), 275.

107. Dyson, *Reflecting Black,* 276.

108. It could be argued that no given space should be expected to support any more diversity than any given genre of music, or perhaps any given song. But built space is unlike music in that it is comparatively permanent, immovable, and confining. And so to the degree that any given space narrows or precludes diversity, it renders other choices inaccessible; with music, one need only change the station or download another song track. My interest is not that spaces become all things to all people—that is both impossible and undesirable, since defined spaces are necessary apparatuses for the particularization of self and society. But overambitious efforts to define and produce community through spatial and legal means—examples range from CIDs to artificial "town square" projects—may result instead in narrow, sterile homogeneity.

109. Joel Garreau, *Edge City: Life on the New Frontier* (New York: Doubleday, 1991), 4, 6–7; Peter O. Muller, "The Suburban Transformation of the Globalizing American City," *Annals of the American Academy of Political and Social Science* 551 (May 1997): 44–58. Also see Robert Fishman, "America's New City: Megalopolis Unbound," *Wilson Quarterly* 14 (1990): 25–46. Previous chapters have shown that nineteenth-century suburbs often incorporated many industrial plants, not to mention the pollution they produced. In the early twentieth century the introduction of trucking made the dispersal of industry to suburban locations even more attractive for many plant owners, since here labor and land costs were lower, and less congestion meant that supplies and products could be transported more efficiently. See Kenneth Jackson, *Crabgrass Frontier* (New York: Oxford University Press, 1985), 183–84.

Conclusion

1. Bennett M. Berger, "Suburbia and the American Dream," *Public Interest* 1 (1966): 81. As early as 1958 studies began to document the positive experience of suburbia; see William M. Dobriner, *The Suburban Community* (New York: Putnam, 1958); Herbert J. Gans, *The Levittowners: Ways of Life and Politics in a New Suburban Community* (New York: Pantheon, 1967); and Scott Donaldson, *The Suburban Myth* (New York: Columbia University Press, 1969). For a 1953 study by Harry Henderson, see chapter 7, this volume, the section "Getting to Know Suburbia."

2. The argument could be made that suburban residents are content with the limited range of (standardized, mass-produced) choices available to them because their horizons are not broad enough to understand the degree to which standardization and commodification suppress individuality. But there is also merit to the counterargument that in an individualistic culture it should be the individual, not the critic, who assesses the parameters of one's individuality.

3. He went on: "As to the hope of creation, the hope of producing some worthy or even excellent work which without you, the craftsman, would not have existed at all, a thing which needs you and can have no substitute for you in the making of it—can we any of us fail to understand the pleasure of this?" William Morris, "Art under Plutocracy" (1883), in *On Art and Socialism* (London: John Lehmann, 1947), 139–40.

4. William Morris, *The Collected Works* (London: Longmans Green, 1914), 22:86–87. Morris's ideal is counterposed to precisely the sort of situation in which Tom Rath would find himself in *The Man in the Gray Flannel Suit:* home and work irreparably separated from each other.

5. William Morris, *Stories in Prose, Stories in Verse, Shorter Poems, Lectures and Essays,* ed. G. D. H. Cole (London: Nonesuch Press, 1946), 515. Morris folded this hope into his own version of a dream-dwelling: "so in no private dwelling will there be any signs of waste, pomp, or insolence, and every man will have his share of the *best.* It is a dream, you may say . . . ; true, it is a dream; but dreams have before now come about of things so good and necessary to us, that we scarcely think of them more than of the daylight . . ." (516).

6. William Morris, "The Prospects of Architecture in Civilization" (1881), in *On Art and Socialism* (London: John Lehmann, 1947), 252–54.

7. John Ruskin, *Works,* ed. E. T. Cook and Alexander Wedderburn (London: G. Allan, 1903), 8:228–29.

8. Charles Keeler, *The Simple Home* (San Francisco: Paul Elder & Co., 1904), 3, 36–37.

9. Christine Frederick, "Is Suburban Living a Delusion?" *Outlook* 148, no. 8 (22 February 1928): 290. More generally on the migration of Ruskin's and Morris's views to America, see Eileen Boris, *Art and Labor: Ruskin, Morris, and the Craftsman Ideal in America* (Philadelphia: Temple University Press, 1986).

10. The prospects for prefabricated housing are discussed in Archibald MacLeish, *Housing America: By the Editors of "Fortune"* (New York: Harcourt, Brace, 1932). See also Albert Bruce and Harold Sandbank, *A History of Prefabrication* (New York: John B. Pierce Foundation, 1943).

11. Walter Benjamin, "The Work of Art in the Age of Mechanical Reproduction" (1936), in *Illuminations,* ed. Hannah Arendt, trans. Harry Zohn (New York: Schocken, 1969); Theodor Adorno, "On the Fetish Character in Music and the Regression of Listening" (1938), in *Adorno: The Culture Industry* (London: Routledge, 1991), 29–60.

12. Benjamin, "The Work of Art," 240.

13. Michel de Certeau, *The Practice of Everyday Life,* trans. Steven Rendall (Berkeley: University of California Press, 1984), 97. See too de Certeau's argument that an individual may transform the constraining order (of public housing, for example) into difference. The inhabitant "creates for himself a space in which he can find *ways of using* the constraining order of the place or of the language. Without leaving the place where he has no choice but to live and which lays down its law for him, he establishes within it a degree of *plurality* and creativity. By an art of being in between, he draws unexpected results from his situation" (30).

14. Max Horkheimer and Theodor W. Adorno, *Dialectic of Enlightenment,* trans. John Cumming (New York: Continuum, 1997), 120, 124, 127.

15. John Keats, *The Crack in the Picture Window* (Boston: Houghton Mifflin, 1956), 61, 193. For similar determinist sentiments, see pp. 43, 50, 181.

16. Horkheimer and Adorno, *Dialectic of Enlightenment*, 123, 136.

17. Horkheimer and Adorno, *Dialectic of Enlightenment*, 144–45.

18. For example, see David Riesman's pessimistic assessment in 1958: "And here is where the suburbanites' immense liking for Ike is portentous: it expresses the wish of so many of the college seniors mentioned above that civics and the Community Chest replace politics; it expresses the hope, built into the very structure of credit and the additive-extrapolative style of thought, that nothing serious will occur, that everything will go on as before." David Riesman, "The Suburban Sadness," in *The Suburban Community*, ed. William M. Dobriner (New York: Putnam, 1958), 400. Of course a critical analysis of the dream itself might well conclude that insularity and complacency are exactly what the dream is best able to produce: by focusing on private fulfillment rather than social engagement, the dream encourages individuals to pursue isolated strategies of self-satisfaction.

19. The culture industry "robs the individual of his function. Its prime service to the customer is to do his schematizing for him." Horkheimer and Adorno, *Dialectic of Enlightenment*, 124.

20. Horkheimer and Adorno, *Dialectic of Enlightenment*, 124. The basic thrust of this analysis readily extends to all mass-produced commodities, not least to dwellings, cars, kitchen appliances, bedroom furnishings, etc.

21. Horkheimer and Adorno, *Dialectic of Enlightenment*, 139.

22. I refer to the example of the film *Wonderland*, mentioned in chapter 7, showing a man in front of his house declaring, "This is my dream come true," and to the body of scholarship, discussed earlier, documenting the satisfaction of suburban residents (Bennett M. Berger, *Working-Class Suburb: A Study of Auto Workers in Suburbia* [Berkeley: University of California Press, 1960]; Berger, "Suburbia and the American Dream"; Harold L. Wattel, "Levittown: A Suburban Community," in *The Suburban Community*, ed. William M. Dobriner [New York: G. P. Putnam's Sons, 1958], 287–313; Barbara M. Kelly, *Expanding the American Dream* [Albany: State University of New York Press, 1993]; the series of articles written by Geoffrey Mohan for *Newsday* in 1997 and now available at www.lihistory.com; and Rosalyn Baxandall and Elizabeth Ewen, *Picture Windows* [New York: Basic Books, 2000]).

23. Keats, *The Crack in the Picture Window*, 43, 50, 61, 181, 193.

24. Keats, *The Crack in the Picture Window*, 189, 147–48.

25. Claude-Nicolas Ledoux, *L'architecture considérée sous le rapport de l'art, des moeurs et de la législation* (Paris: H. L. Perronneau, 1804). See chapter 4, this volume, the section headed "Style."

26. Bennett M. Berger, *Working-Class Suburb* (Berkeley: University of California Press, 1969), xxi. Also see Gans, *The Levittowners*, xvi.

27. On theming, see Michael Sorkin, *Variations on a Theme Park: The New American City and the End of Public Space* (New York: Hill and Wang, 1992); Mark Gottdiener, *The Theming of America: Dreams, Media Fantasies, and Themed Environments*, 2nd ed. (Boulder, CO: Westview Press, 2001).

28. For "traditional architecture," see Andres Duany, "New Urbanism Bites Back," *Preservation*, January/February 2000, 8; Andres Duany, Elizabeth Plater-Zyberk, and Jeff Speck, *Suburban Nation: The Rise of Sprawl and the Decline of the American Dream* (New York: North Point Press, 2000). For excellent critiques, see Karen Till, "Neotraditional Towns and Urban Villages," *Environment and Planning D: Society and Space* 11 (1993):

709–32; David Hamer, "Learning from the Past," *Planning Perspectives* 15 (2000): 113. Till's discussion of the invented and ambiguous nature of "tradition" as used among neo-traditionalists is particularly compelling. For a lengthy list of New Urbanism's disappointments, see Alex Krieger, "Arguing the 'Against' Position," in *The Seaside Debates*, ed. Todd W. Bressi (New York: Rizzoli, 2002), 51–52. For a critique of the practice of inventing a "tradition" when there is no tradition there, see Wende Vyborney Feller, "Urban Impostures: How Two Neighborhoods Reframed Suburban Sprawl as a New Urbanist Paradise without Changing a Thing," in *Suburban Sprawl: Culture, Theory, and Politics,* ed. Matthew J. Lindstrom and Hugh Bartling (Lanham, MD: Rowman & Littlefield, 2003), 50 and passim.

Ironically there may be less "new" about the New Urbanism than its proponents suggest. As early as 1902 Howard Allen Bridgman wrote in terms just as nostalgic, just as enamored of porches as those used a century later, calling for improvements to "the wholesomeness of suburban life" through "a renaissance of the old, beautiful neighborhood life that characterized this nation before the rush to the cities began. The piazza of the next house looks inviting, and the temptation is to loiter there a few moments for a friendly chat." "The Suburbanite," *The Independent* 54, no. 2784 (10 April 1902): 863.

I should emphasize that in this and subsequent references to New Urbanism I purposely concentrate on certain principal founding figures (Duany, Plater-Zyberk, and other framers of the *Charter of the New Urbanism*) and some of the best-known work done in the New Urbanist vein (Seaside, Kentlands, Celebration). This is for two reasons. First, the salient positions that these people have articulated and the examples set by their work have established much of what the general population understands as "New Urbanism" today. Second, from these points of departure the larger body of New Urbanist adherents has since taken off in many different directions. While the variety of new work produced under this banner has resulted in much that is advantageous, there also is much that is facile and pedestrian. My concern is not so much that interlopers may be hijacking New Urbanism; rather, it is that it has become such a diffuse body of work that to critique it sensibly is nearly impossible. Thus for the purposes of my discussion, which is to advance a new and different line of critique, I have chosen to remain close to a narrow understanding of New Urbanism.

29. LaFrank accurately portrays the design vocabulary at Seaside as the product of a highly problematic process of "abstracting and idealizing vernacular architecture." Kathleen LaFrank, "Seaside, Florida," in *Shaping Communities: Perspectives in Vernacular Architecture, VI,* ed. Carter L. Hudgins and Elizabeth Collins Crowley (Knoxville: University of Tennessee Press, 1997), 111, 119. See also Hamer, "Learning from the Past," 118.

30. Evan McKenzie puts it succinctly: "a CID is a prefabricated framework for civil society in search of a population." *Privatopia: Homeowner Associations and the Rise of Residential Private Government* (New Haven, CT: Yale University Press, 1994), 145.

31. As Bettina Drew optimistically notes, New Urbanism promises "a reassertion of government or civic power." *Crossing the Expendable Landscape* (St. Paul, MN: Graywolf Press, 1998), 195.

32. Andres Duany, Elizabeth Plater-Zyberk, and Jeff Speck, "Suburban Planning," *New Yorker,* 8 May 2000, 8.

33. Sorkin's words appear in "Cities and Suburbs," *Harvard Magazine* 102, no. 4 (January–February 2000): 64. Cowart is quoted in Heidi Landecker, "Is New Urbanism Good for America?" *Architecture* 85, no. 4 (April 1996): 71. Duany is quoted in James W. Shields, "The Building as Village," *Reflections* 6 (Spring 1989): 63. Margaret Crawford is quoted by Landecker in "Is New Urbanism Good for America?" 70.

34. This ideal dates back at least to Alexander Jackson Downing's prescription for an ideal "rural village," originally presented in the *Horticulturist* 4, no. 12 (June 1850): 537–41; and reprinted in A. J. Downing, *Rural Essays*, ed. George William Curtis (New York: G. P. Putnam, 1857), 236–43. See chapter 4, this volume, the section headed "Individualism."

35. For example, the CNU charter states that "the economic health and harmonious evolution of neighborhoods, districts, and corridors can be improved through graphic urban design codes that serve as predictable guides for change." Similarly, "within neighborhoods, a broad range of housing types and price levels can bring people of diverse ages, races, and incomes into daily interaction, strengthening the personal and civic bonds essential to an authentic community." http://cnu.org/aboutcnu/index.cfm, 23 July 2003. In defending New Urbanism, Emily Talen argues that "none of the principles" in the CNU *Charter* is "explicitly related to community, except in terms of the inclusion of some descriptive statements," a position that appears debatable in light of the two principles just quoted. Part of Talen's concern is that for too long critics of New Urbanism have maligned it on grounds that may be unfair, i.e., that it was promoted as a tool for producing community. Still, the defensive nature of her argument may only prove the critics' point: that whatever the intentions of the founding New Urbanists, their instruments and methods in many cases were oversold and then underperformed. Perhaps more to the point, if New Urbanism cannot successfully address the problem of community, then a serious matter awaits consideration. See Emily Talen, "The Social Goals of New Urbanism," *Housing Policy Debate* 13, no. 1 (2002): 165–88; the quotation is from p. 171. For a critique of New Urbanists' engagement with "community," see David Harvey, "The New Urbanism and the Communitarian Trap," *Harvard Design Magazine,* Winter/Spring 1997, 68–69. Harvey worries that the kind of "community" that New Urbanists propose may be so uniform that it would stifle the kind of growth and change necessary for a flourishing society. Also see Robert Shibley, "The Complete New Urbanism and the Partial Practices of Placemaking," *Utopian Studies* 9, no. 1 (1998): 80–102.

36. See, for example, Andres Duany, Elizabeth Plater-Zyberk, and Chester E. Chellman, "New Town Ordinances and Codes," *Architectural Design* 59, no. 5–6 (1989): 71–75; Alex Krieger, ed., *Andres Duany and Elizabeth Plater-Zyberk: Towns and Town-Making Principles* (New York: Rizzoli, 1991); Andres Duany and Elizabeth Plater-Zyberk, "The Second Coming of the American Small Town," *Wilson Quarterly,* Winter 1992, 19–50. There are certainly design strategies that are more and less friendly to community. The question remains to what degree design can produce community, which is what some New Urbanists sometimes come close to claiming.

37. The difficulty in realizing the intended results through an apparatus of planning and codes is evident in practice. See, for example, the discussions of Kentlands and Celebration in Alex Marshall, "Suburb in Disguise," *Metropolis,* July/August 1996, 70–71, 100–103; Tom Martinson, *American Dreamscape* (New York: Carroll & Graf, 2000), 113; Andrew Ross, *The Celebration Chronicles* (New York: Ballantine, 1999); and Douglas Frantz and Catherine Collins, *Celebration, U.S.A.: Living in Disney's Brave New Town* (New York: Henry Holt and Company, 1999). Nor are such difficulties new or unusual. The "Homeowners Guide" by which Levitt and Sons instituted a set of standards regulating home appearance and upkeep in their Pennsylvania Levittown succumbed to residents' own preferences within a few years. See C. Maurice Kimmel, "Revisiting Levittown, Pennsylvania: Transformations within America's First Planned Suburban Community," Spring Conference, New England Sociological Association (28 April 2001), 10.

38. Andres Duany, Ron Shiffman, and Susana Torre, "The New Urbanism, the Newer

and the Old," *Places* 9, no. 2 (Summer 1994): 91–92. The other two panelists whose remarks appear in this article took exception to Duany's antidemocratic position.

39. For Bourdieu's emphatic statement of this point, see Pierre Bourdieu, "Habitus," in *Habitus: A Sense of Place,* ed. Jean Hillier and Emma Rooksby (Aldershot, UK: Ashgate, 2002), 27–34.

40. There is a second paradox here: since the dream quite rightly allows the choice *not* to modify, and a CID affords that choice, one might argue that CIDs are a perfect dream machine. As Evan McKenzie argues, however, there is no guarantee that a particular CID will afford any particular individual's dream in perpetuity, nor does the homeowner-association form of government allow for the eventuality that people do change their minds and feelings over time. One might argue that people should be able to continue to live their dreams without necessarily being forced to move. McKenzie, *Privatopia.*

41. Peter Calthorpe's approach to design incorporates some of the flexibility and openness to diversity that I am suggesting. He advocates "infill and redevelopment that creates a greater range of housing and services in the area," and adding jobs, facilities, and varying housing types in order "to balance the neighborhood and create more choice—in housing and in commuting patterns." Peter Calthorpe and William Fulton, *The Regional City* (Washington, DC: Island Press, 2001), 205.

42. Inconsistencies, for example, are already integral to the material and social fabric of suburbia, as they are to life in any other type of locale. In suburbia, lawns are contrived to portray an environment of leisure and pastoral plenitude, but in fact they entail considerable costs of labor and environmental degradation. Families of a given racial or ethnic heritage may move to a "white-bread" suburb to satisfy certain needs and aspirations, but in the eyes of relatives or others of the same race or ethnicity they may be seen as traitors to their heritage. The fact is that people continue to live such contradictions, constantly negotiating their lives and circumstances as working compromises between their expectations and available resources.

43. For an understanding of space as social product, I rely on Henri Lefebvre, *The Production of Space,* trans. Donald Nicholson-Smith (Oxford: Blackwell, 1991). For space as the site of complex negotiation, see Doreen Massey, *Space, Place, and Gender* (Minneapolis: University of Minnesota Press, 1994), 1–16, 167–73. For a rewarding discussion of locality that is complementary to, if not congruent with, Massey's discussion of place and locality, see Arjun Appadurai, *Modernity at Large* (Minneapolis: University of Minnesota Press, 1996), chap. 9.

44. My thinking here derives from Pierre Bourdieu's discussion of the complex tension between habitus and agency in any given culture: *The Logic of Practice,* trans. Richard Nice (Stanford: Stanford University Press, 1990).

45. Mary Douglas and Baron Isherwood argue the importance of consumption and consumer goods in the process of self-identification: *The World of Goods* (New York: Basic Books, 1979), 65. See also Richard Ohmann, *Selling Culture* (London: Verso, 1996), 172–73.

46. Daniel Miller, *Material Culture and Mass Consumption* (Oxford: Basil Blackwell, 1987), 147, 175, 190; see also 196–97 and passim.

47. *The New Consumer* (Chicago: Chicago Tribune, 1957), 3.

48. As Constance Perin shows, the apparent uniformity of many a suburban landscape may only be a matter of residents having similar incomes; in countless other respects they may already differ from each other along multiple axes. On the other hand, in many cases suburban conventions and practices discourage difference, not least with respect to conditions that may affect property values. *Belonging in America* (Madison: University of Wisconsin Press, 1988), 104, passim.

49. McKenzie, *Privatopia*.

50. Richard Briffault, "Our Localism: Part II—Localism and Legal Theory," *Columbia Law Review* 90 (March 1990): 382, 444, and passim.

51. See note 1.

52. I admit to being intentionally vague about any possibility here for a definition of what a suburb is. The experience of living in a suburb is historically and culturally specific: what it was in the nineteenth century is not what it is today, nor is the experience of European suburbs like that of Australian suburbs, which is unlike that of American suburbs. Even within America there are regional differences: those of Phoenix are unlike those of Boston or New York. Efforts at defining *suburb* often become mirrors of the methodology of the researcher, whether demographer, planner, historian, or something else. For my own part, I remember countless hours spent among a group of seasoned professionals drawn from various disciplines trying to come up with a suitable definition of "first-ring" suburbs, a seemingly simple problem, but even that was intractable. Instead, I would emphasize that suburbs evolve as sets of recognized *conventions,* along with which—or against which—people conduct their lives.

53. See, for example, Homi K. Bhabha, *The Location of Culture* (London: Routledge, 1994); Néstor Garcia Canclini, *Hybrid Cultures,* trans. Christopher L. Chiappari and Silvia L. López (Minneapolis: University of Minnesota Press, 1995); Robert J. C. Young, *Colonial Desire: Hybridity in Theory, Culture and Race* (London: Routledge, 1995); Avtar Brah and Annie E. Coombes, ed., *Hybridity and Its Discontents: Politics, Science, Culture* (London: Routledge, 2000). But see also Nezar AlSayyad, ed., *Hybrid Urbanism: On the Identity Discourse and the Built Environment* (Westport, CT: Praeger, 2001).

54. For a recent succinct discussion of this issue, see Massey, *Space, Place, and Gender,* 1–16.

55. Mayfair Mei-hui Yang, "Putting Global Capitalism in Its Place: Economic Hybridity, Bataille, and Ritual Expenditure," *Current Anthropology* 41, no. 4 (August–October 2000): 477–95. I am indebted to Yang's article for her lucid approach to hybridity and Bakhtin, which I parallel here; Yang in turn was partly indebted to Young, *Colonial Desire,* 20–23.

56. Mikhail Mikhailovich Bakhtin, *The Dialogic Imagination,* trans. Caryl Emerson and Michael Holquist (Austin: University of Texas Press, 1981), 304 (emphasis in original), 304–5.

57. Bakhtin, *The Dialogic Imagination,* 358.

58. In my discussion of hybridity I focus specifically on the suburbia of single-family dwellings since that is consistent with the focus of the rest of this book. But my argument should be understood as applying equally to the intersection of hybrid place and hybrid identity in other forms of dwelling or, for that matter, any form of inhabited structure. In the past several decades suburbia has evolved to become considerably more than residential terrain, and so I would argue that the syntax of suburbia has evolved as part of that process to encompass a broader range of what might be equivalent to Bakhtin's "semantic" elements: the office park, the commercial (light industry) park, the "lifestyle village," the gated community, and so forth.

59. See note 1.

60. James T. Rojas, "The Enacted Environment of East Los Angeles," *Places* 8, no. 3 (Spring 1993): 42–53. See too Margaret Crawford, "Blurring the Boundaries: Public Space and Private Life," in *Everyday Urbanism,* ed. John Chase, Margaret Crawford, and John Kaliski (New York: Monacelli Press, 1999), 22–35.

Coda

1. On Bourdieu, see the introduction, this volume, the section titled "Constituting Identity."

2. Pierre Bourdieu, "Habitus," in *Habitus: A Sense of Place,* ed. Jean Hillier and Emma Rooksby (Aldershot, UK: Ashgate, 2002), 29.

3. Robert D. Putnam, "The Prosperous Community: Social Capital and Public Life," *American Prospect* 4, no. 13 (21 March 1993), http://www.prospect.org/print-friendly/print/V4/13/putnam-r.html, 15 March 2004. The notion of social capital dates at least to the late 1980s, when James Coleman published "Social Capital in the Creation of Human Capital," *American Journal of Sociology* 94: Supplement (1988): S95–S120. More recently, see Robert D. Putnam, *Bowling Alone: The Collapse and Revival of American Community* (New York: Simon & Schuster, 2000); and Nan Lin, *Social Capital: A Theory of Social Structure and Action* (Cambridge: Cambridge University Press, 2001).

4. Bill Owens, *Suburbia* (San Francisco: Straight Arrow Press, 1973); Gregory Crewdson, "Dream House," *New York Times Magazine,* 10 November 2002, 39.

5. William H. Frey, "Melting Pot Suburbs: A Census 2000 Study of Suburban Diversity" (Washington, DC: Brookings Institution, 2001).

6. Jason Fields and Lynne M. Casper, *America's Families and Living Arrangements: March 2000,* Current Population Reports, P20-537 (Washington, DC: U.S. Census Bureau, 2001).

7. In some postwar tract suburbs, such as Levittown, New York, expansions and improvements have been an ongoing phenomenon, keeping much of the housing stock in line with surrounding communities. Part of the reason for the success of Levittown is its location in the already densely populated New York metropolitan area. Compared to other metropolitan regions, property values are high, and new housing is being built much farther away from the city center; both of these factors increase the incentive for families to stay put. Elsewhere, in lower-density metropolitan areas, it has been easier for first- and second-generation families to sell off their aging suburban housing stock. The expanding stock of new housing in nearby communities and their comparative proximity to the metropolitan center are attractive to these buyers; this also tends to depress property values of older houses, making it financially unwise to do large-scale improvements. My argument here is that if customized packages of off-the-shelf materials could be made continuously available for incremental improvements, as I suggest below, more of the housing stock could evolve and improve rather than be left to decline.

8. Myron Orfield, *Metropolitics: A Regional Agenda for Community and Stability* (Washington, DC: Brookings Institution Press, 1997).

9. "Remarks by the President on Homeownership," St. Paul AME Church, Atlanta, Georgia, 17 June 2002, http://www.whitehouse.gov/news/releases/2002/06/print/20020617-2.html, 8 July 2003. Also see George W. Bush, "A Home of Your Own," June 2002 (PDF file), http://www.whitehouse.gov/infocus/homeownership/homeownership-policy-book-whole.pdf, 4 July 2003; Department of Housing and Urban Development, "Blueprint for the American Dream" (PDF file), http://www.hud.gov/news/releasedocs/blueprint.pdf, 4 July 2003.

10. One promising approach to the question of producing difference from standardization is offered by Manuel Gausa, "Kit-Hauses—Kinder Houses," in *Single-Family Housing: The Private Domain,* ed. Jaime Salazar and Manuel Gausa (Basel: Birkhäuser, 1999), 143–48. The notion of distinction without exclusion is derived from Iris Marion

Young, *Justice and the Politics of Difference* (Princeton, NJ: Princeton University Press, 1990), 238.

11. Building codes, while entirely necessary, have similarly restrictive aspects. Avi Friedman, *Planning the New Suburbia* (Vancouver: UBC Press, 2002), 17–19.

12. Renee Y. Chow, *Suburban Space: The Fabric of Dwelling* (Berkeley: University of California Press, 2002), 34–35. Chow nevertheless does not dismiss advantages of the detached dwelling, which include light and air from all sides, access at ground level direct to the street, and autonomy to build, maintain, remodel, buy, or sell (27).

13. Fred Dewey, "Cyburbanism as a Way of Life," in *Architecture of Fear*, ed. Nan Ellin (New York: Princeton Architectural Press, 1997), 261–79. One could readily read the situation Dewey describes with a positive spin. See too Keith Hampton and Barry Wellman, "Neighboring in Netville: How the Internet Supports Community and Social Capital in a Wired Suburb," *City & Community* 2, no. 4 (December 2003): 277–311.

14. Jaime Salazar, "The House as an Artefact," in *Single-Family Housing: The Private Domain*, ed. Jaime Salazar and Manuel Gausa (Basel: Birkhäuser, 1999), 93, 92.

15. Chow, *Suburban Space*.

16. Nancy Fraser, "Rethinking the Public Sphere: A Contribution to the Critique of Actually Existing Democracy," in *The Phantom Public Sphere*, ed. Bruce Robbins (Minneapolis: University of Minnesota Press, 1993), 1–32, especially 13–18; quotations are from p. 16.

17. Margaret Crawford, "Blurring the Boundaries: Public Space and Private Life," in *Everyday Urbanism*, ed. John Chase, Margaret Crawford, and John Kaliski (New York: Monacelli Press, 1999), 24–25.

18. Also see Michael Warner, "Publics and Counterpublics," *Public Culture* 14, no. 1 (Winter 2002): 49–90. Warner discusses the degree to which counterpublics must retain some degree of being "counter" but is more expansive than Fraser or Crawford.

19. The process of articulating "counterpublics" bears close comparison with Michel de Certeau's discussion of the varied processes through which places may be appropriated by, or as, "local authorities"—processes such as "pedestrian speech acts" and "walking rhetorics." Michel de Certeau, *The Practice of Everyday Life*, trans. Steven Rendall (Berkeley: University of California Press), 106, 97, 100. The process of walking through the city, particularly as a group (or a mob), creates its own gravity, its own rules, its own manner of writing and reading space.

20. The booklets inside CD jewel cases for rap music are often filled more with offers for clothing and other products than with lyrics, biographies, or other information about the music and its performers. One might argue that this is "just marketing," but it also speaks to the suburban teenage consumer who is eager to identify with the image and the discursive position of the group.

Permissions

Every effort was made to obtain permission to reproduce material used in this book. If any proper acknowledgment has not been made, we encourage copyright holders to notify us.

"A Cottage for Sale," lyrics by Larry Conley, music by Willard Robison. Copyright 1930, De Sylva, Brown and Henderson, Inc., New York.

"Dear Hearts and Gentle People," words by Bob Hilliard, music by Sammy Fain. Copyright 1949 by Better Half Music and Edwin H. Morris and Co.; copyright renewed. All rights reserved. International copyright secured.

"Dream House," words and music by John Eddie. From the composer's Web site, http://www.lostamericanthrillshow.com/lyrics/dream.html. Accessed 15 November 2003.

"Dream House," lyrics by Earle Fox, melody by Lynn Cowan. Copyright 1926, Sherman, Clay & Company, San Francisco.

"Dream House," by jp jones. Copyright 2000 jp jones. Vision Industry Publishing (ASCAP).

"Dream House for Sale," by Wayne P. Walker. Copyright 1962, Universal-Cedarwood Publishing on behalf of Cedarwood Publishing (BMI). All rights reserved. Used by permission.

Index

Abell, Mrs. L. G., 198
Ackerman, James S., 68, 383n5
Adam, James, 125–26, 396n98
Adam, Robert, 125–26, 396n98
Adams, Thomas, 430n67
Addison, Joseph, 150
Adorno, Theodor, 13, 336–41
aesthetics, xix, 8; a basis of personal fulfillment, 332; in the critique of suburbia, 241, 362–63; effect of, on residents, 198, 340; and landscape, 28, 72, 91, 158, 167, 217, 230; need for new paradigms in suburbia, 258, 362–65, 370; in nineteenth-century dwelling design, 185, 198; in nineteenth-century English architectural theory, 332–34, 339; in nineteenth-century suburban design, 173, 207–8, 217–20, 224, 226–28, 230–32, 235, 238, 240–41, 244–45; in twentieth-century cultural criticism, 336–37
African American suburbs, 242, 300–302, 354, 362, 369–70
agriculture: and pastoralism, 161–63; and suburbia, 208, 235; and the villa, 23, 46, 68–70
Alberti, Leon Battista, 5–6, 46, 51, 72–73, 95, 386n47

Albuquerque, NM, 368
Aldrich, Henry, 69, 387n53
Alexander, Christopher, 3
Alger, Horatio, xix, 251–53, 285
Allen, Frederick Lewis, 254–55
Allen, Lewis F., 188
American Beauty, 319
American Builder, 285
American dream: advanced by George W. Bush, 369–70; and African Americans, 302; anchor of identity and fulfillment, 313, 332, 337; and children, 259; and the dream house, xv, xvii, xix, 250, 418n37, 423n92; in film and television, 318–20; genesis of the notion, xix, 249–54, 282–83, 286, 292, 295, 303, 317, 418n33; an individualist undertaking, 305, 308, 349; limited in suburbia, 343–44; in literary fiction, 320–24; in music, 250, 318, 320–22, 325–28; politicized, 292–93, 305, 308; a privatist undertaking, 299; realized through home ownership, 260–61, 285, 288, 291–92, 307, 337, 350; and sprawl, 257; and suburbia (*see under* suburb)
American Dream Downpayment Act, 261
American Dream Downpayment Fund, 370

447

John Archer is an architectural historian and professor in the Department of Cultural Studies and Comparative Literature at the University of Minnesota. His research interests have taken him to five continents, and he has published on the history of colonial cities and suburbs, English landscape, British architecture, and English and American suburbs. His book *The Literature of British Domestic Architecture, 1715–1842* is a standard reference. His current work concerns opportunities for difference and hybridity in present-day built environments, especially suburban areas, and the implications of widespread importation of American-style suburbs to less-developed areas of the world.